D1610979

Windows® 2000
TCP/IP
Black Book

Ian McLean

President and CEO *Keith Weiskamp*	**Windows® 2000 TCP/IP Black Book**

Limits of Liability and Disclaimer of Warranty

The author and publisher of this book have used their best efforts in preparing the book and the programs contained in it. These efforts include the development, research, and testing of the theories and programs to determine their effectiveness. The author and publisher make no warranty of any kind, expressed or implied, with regard to these programs or the documentation contained in this book.

The author and publisher shall not be liable in the event of incidental or consequential damages in connection with, or arising out of, the furnishing, performance, or use of the programs, associated instructions, and/or claims of productivity gains.

Trademarks

Trademarked names appear throughout this book. Rather than list the names and entities that own the trademarks or insert a trademark symbol with each mention of the trademarked name, the publisher states that it is using the names for editorial purposes only and to the benefit of the trademark owner, with no intention of infringing upon that trademark.

President and CEO
Keith Weiskamp

Publisher
Steve Sayre

Acquisitions Editor
Charlotte Carpentier

Development Editor
Michelle Stroup

Marketing Specialist
Tracy Schofield

Project Editors
Lynette Cox
Dan Young

Technical Reviewer
George Aslanishvili

Production Coordinator
Laura Wellander

Cover Designer
Jody Winkler

Layout Designer
April Nielsen

CD-ROM Developer
Michelle McConnell

The Coriolis Group, LLC
14455 N. Hayden Road
Suite 220
Scottsdale, Arizona 85260

(480) 483-0192
FAX (480) 483-0193
www.coriolis.com

Library of Congress Cataloging-in-Publication Data

McLean, Ian, 1946-
    Windows 2000 TCP/IP black book / by Ian McLean
       p. cm.
    Includes index.
    ISBN 1-57610-687-X
    1. TCP/IP (Computer network protocol)   2. Microsoft Windows (Computer file)   I. Title.
TK5105.585 .M395   2000
004.6'2--dc21   00-060258
                                                   CIP

Printed in the United States of America
10 9 8 7 6 5 4 3 2 1

The Coriolis Group, LLC • 14455 North Hayden Road, Suite 220 • Scottsdale, Arizona 85260

Dear Reader:

Coriolis Technology Press was founded to create a very elite group of books: the ones you keep closest to your machine. Sure, everyone would like to have the Library of Congress at arm's reach, but in the real world, you have to choose the books you rely on every day *very* carefully.

To win a place for our books on that coveted shelf beside your PC, we guarantee several important qualities in every book we publish. These qualities are:

- *Technical accuracy*—It's no good if it doesn't work. Every Coriolis Technology Press book is reviewed by technical experts in the topic field, and is sent through several editing and proofreading passes in order to create the piece of work you now hold in your hands.

- *Innovative editorial design*—We've put years of research and refinement into the ways we present information in our books. Our books' editorial approach is uniquely designed to reflect the way people learn new technologies and search for solutions to technology problems.

- *Practical focus*—We put only pertinent information into our books and avoid any fluff. Every fact included between these two covers must serve the mission of the book as a whole.

- *Accessibility*—The information in a book is worthless unless you can find it quickly when you need it. We put a lot of effort into our indexes, and heavily cross-reference our chapters, to make it easy for you to move right to the information you need.

Here at The Coriolis Group we have been publishing and packaging books, technical journals, and training materials since 1989. We're programmers and authors ourselves, and we take an ongoing active role in defining what we publish and how we publish it. We have put a lot of thought into our books; please write to us at **ctp@coriolis.com** and let us know what you think. We hope that you're happy with the book in your hands, and that in the future, when you reach for software development and networking information, you'll turn to one of our books first.

Keith Weiskamp
President and CEO

Jeff Duntemann
VP and Editorial Director

To Rocky—In memoriam.

About the Author

I've been around computers for a long, long time. I met my first such beast in 1958 at the age of eleven, and subsequently became one of the first microprocessor programmers (that was in 1969—tempus fugit). I've had a bit of experience with networks, and, for my sins, am a Microsoft Certified Database Administrator. Systems Engineer plus Internet, and Trainer. I first came across the concept of the World Wide Web in the mid-1980s. I was researching methods of delivering distance learning and found out about some work being done by some real bright people at Berkley. I don't think even they visualized what it was all leading to!

Anyway, I got hooked, learned about TCP, IP, FTP, Telnet, and the rest of the gang, and built a Unix network. Happy days.

Currently, I run my own consulting company. That's OK—my mother thinks I've a real job. This is my thirteenth book—unlucky for some unfortunate rain forest. I also edited a technical magazine for fifteen years and have written more articles and academic papers than I'd care to admit to.

I'm married to a lovely Irish lass—that she chose me when she had plenty to choose from is still a source of amazement and joy to me. That she's put up with me through thirteen books and twenty-six years is just plain incredible. I have two wonderful children, both adults now and doing far better than their old Dad ever will.

Acknowledgments

Writing a book is a team effort, and this one owes much to the outstanding people with whom I worked at The Coriolis Group. Stephanie Wall, my acquisitions editor, gave me a whole heap of encouragement and support, especially in the difficult first stages. Stephanie left the project to further her career and passed me into the safe hands of Michelle Stroup. Michelle was my very first contact at The Coriolis Group, and it was great to work with her again.

Paulette Miley, my copy editor, spotted all sorts of inconsistencies that I'd missed, corrected my English, explained the corrections (which was of enormous assistance) and maintained a style sheet that contributed greatly to the quality of the book. The mainstay of this entire project was Lynette Cox, my project editor, a true professional who guided and encouraged me through the days when I *knew* I was never going to get the thing finished! Lynette left the project near its end to get married and complete her Doctorate, but passed me on to another true professional, Dan Young, the project editor on my previous book. I enjoyed working with Dan again, very much indeed.

Special thanks are due to Laura Wellander, Jody Winkler, April Nielsen, and Tracy Schofield for their instrumental work behind the scenes.

I also owe a great deal to George Aslanishvili, my technical editor. George's comments were always pertinent and perceptive, and his suggestions added much of value to the book. George researched and passed on information on numerous occasions and generally gave me assistance well beyond the call of duty.

There are few creatures more anti-social than an author in mid-book. I would have got nowhere without the support of my beautiful wife, Anne, and my son and daughter, Drew and Bryony. They've all been through it before, and will go through it all again, and still they love me. I'm a lucky guy.

—*Ian McLean*

Contents at a Glance

Table of Contents

Chapter 20
Internet Protocol Version 6 711

Introduction

The TCP/IP (Transmission Control Protocol/Internet Protocol) suite is what makes the World Wide Web work. It's widely used in intranets and contains components that service email and newsgroups, but mainly TCP/IP is the Internet protocol suite, the "nuts and bolts" of the Internet. I'm not sure "nuts and bolts" is the best analogy. The phrase suggests something static and rigid, and the Internet is anything but. Vast, sprawling, sometimes chaotic, disorderly, raucous, and even dangerous, the "Net" nevertheless ranks (arguably) with the internal combustion engine and advanced medical technology as one of the major advances of the twentieth century. It's certainly the most significant communications development in the last two decades.

The pace of change has been incredible. Even as an electronics engineer who's used to today's miracle becoming tomorrow's garbage, I've found the rate of Internet development and uptake breathtaking. Not only is everyone I know "on the Net," most have their own Web site. As the Internet develops, so does TCP/IP, the engine that drives it (now, there's a better metaphor). The protocol suite now has components that handle real-time video and audio. The new Internet Protocol version 6 (IPv6) provides a huge increase (dare I say a quantum leap) in address space. The old, faithful protocols such as TCP have been upgraded, and new features have been added. The Microsoft Windows 2000 TCP/IP enhancements represent a significant upgrade and, together with TCP/IP basics, provide the topic for this book.

Who This Book Is For

This book is for network professionals, or for those aspiring to that title. Today's networking professional (even in a Netware or Apple Macintosh environment) needs to know about TCP/IP. I cover TCP/IP basics, so you can use this book even if you've no TCP/IP experience. Ideally, however, you'll know something about TCP/IP and realize that you need to know a lot more. If you can configure a host with an IP address and subnet mask, but aren't sure exactly what happens if you change the subnet mask value, then this book is for you.

The book contains in-depth theory for the network designer, consultant, engineer, or academic who wants to know exactly how the protocols work. The structure of the book, with its "Immediate Solutions" sections, also makes it ideal for the network troubleshooter or support engineer who wants to learn the facts, carry out the procedures, and solve the problems—fast. Finally, the book covers the significant Windows 2000 abstraction layers and Network Application Interfaces and describes the facilities and routines provided with the Windows 2000 drivers development kit (DDK) and the Windows platform software development kit (SDK). It therefore provides useful reference material for device driver, transport driver, and applications developers.

How This Book Is Organized

The book is structured so that it starts at the lower TCP/IP layers and works its way up. This progress is, however, more of a meander than a march. I think it's better to look at features in context rather than in strict numerical order, so I'll be taking the odd detour. On the way, I'll take a fresh look at some old friends from the 1980s: IP, TCP, File Transfer Protocol (FTP), Telnet, and so on. I'll also investigate some of the new kids on the block, such as Internet Protocol Security (IPSec), Real-time Transport Protocol (RTP), Real-time Streaming Protocol (RTSP) and, of course, IPv6.

It's traditional to start with an overview chapter, and I see no reason to break with tradition. Chapter 1 takes a broad-brush approach, introducing the topics that will be described in detail later in the book, and the terms and acronyms that you'll come across time and time again. The purpose of the chapter is to provide an overview, familiarize you with the concepts, and let you decide which topics are of particular interest to you. I've also included a brief history of TCP/IP and the development of the Internet, which I believe to be valuable in putting the whole thing in context. Controversially, I've dated the Internet from 1985, following the specification of the hierarchical domain namespace and the implementation of the Domain Name System. Some consider that the Internet truly started with the development of the first browser in 1990. I reckon I was using the Internet before then!

Chapter 2 covers the low-level, abstraction layer that implements version 5 of the Network Driver Interface Specification (NDIS5). The NDIS5 library, or *wrapper*, contains routines that link Network Interface Card (NIC) drivers to the NIC hardware and to the protocol stack. This enables a single NIC to use multiple protocols and to use them in a specified order. NDIS5 also provides Plug and Play (PnP) facilities and lets you configure computer power states. The chapter describes how to download and use the DDK.

The Address Resolution Protocol (ARP) resolves IP addresses (that humans can understand) to hardware Media Access Control (MAC) addresses (that computers can understand). Chapter 3 describes ARP, but to describe a protocol you need to look at its structure. Microsoft's Network Monitor is a good tool for this purpose and is therefore covered in Chapter 3.

Chapter 4 describes IP (or, more correctly, IPv4). Because the function of IP is to route packets through an internetwork, the protocols that generate route tables—Routing Internet Protocol (RIP) versions 1 and 2 and the Open Shortest Path First (OSPF) protocol—are also described. The chapter provides design considerations that can help you decide whether static routing, RIP, or OSPF is the appropriate choice. Chapter 5 is about another aspect of IP. In my many years of teaching the subject, it's what I was asked about most—Subnetting and Supernetting. Many papers and books have covered this subject, but I make no apology for tackling it again. It's important, it's not easy, but I think I've provided as straightforward an explanation as is possible.

Two protocols provide support to IP at the Internet Layer, and these are covered in Chapter 6. Internet Control Management Protocol (ICMP) is a maintenance protocol used to build and maintain route tables, perform router discovery, adjust flow control to prevent link or router saturation, and diagnose problems. IP has no messaging facilities, and ICMP is sometimes described as the "voice" of IP. Internet Group Management Protocol (IGMP) version 2 provides full support for IP multicasting. Multicasting—sending data to a group of computers identified by a single IP address—is becoming increasingly significant on the Internet, particularly for the transmission of real-time traffic.

Chapter 7 introduces Internet Protocol Security (IPSec), which provides a method, invisible to the user, of securing all network traffic against both outsiders and malicious insiders. Although Internet traffic can be secured using such protocols as Secure Sockets Layer version 3 (SSL3), these protocols can be used only by applications (such as browsers) that understand them, and they protect only against external attacks. IPSec is a recently developed, evolving protocol that's optional in IPv4 networks, but compulsory in IPv6.

TCP, arguably, the most significant transport protocol in the TCP/IP suite, is responsible for establishing a connection between the sender and receiver and transmitting data reliably over a network. Chapter 8 covers the basic operation of the protocol and the many enhancements provided in Windows 2000. Transmission problems are described, together with the algorithms that can solve them.

Chapter 9 describes the other major transport protocol, User Datagram Protocol (UDP). UDP provides a best-effort, unreliable, connectionless service and is used where the overhead of creating a TCP connection isn't justified (for example, email) or where the time taken to establish a connection is unacceptable (for example, real-time video). Because UDP can't guarantee bandwidth, a separate Quality of Service (QoS) methodology is required, particularly for real-time traffic that has high bandwidth requirements. The chapter therefore covers the various QoS levels and mechanisms, as well as bandwidth reservation using Resource Reservation Protocol (RSVP). Finally, the chapter describes the real-time multimedia protocols, such as RTP and RTSP, that operate over UDP.

The application layer protocols interact with application programs and actually let you do things, as you'll discover in Chapter 10. File Transfer Protocol (FTP) and Hypertext Transport Protocol (HTTP) are used to implement FTP and Web sites, respectively. Email applications make use of Trivial File Transport Protocol (TFTP), Simple Mail Transport Protocol (SMTP), and Post Office Protocol version 3 (POP3). Newsgroups are implemented through Network News Transport Protocol (NNTP). In addition to their use in applications, some of these protocols (such as FTP) offer command-line tools that can be used to transfer data across a network directly. The Telnet protocol and its terminal emulation features are covered in the chapter, as is the use of Secure HTTP (HTTPS) to secure a Web site.

Chapter 11 covers Kerberos 5, the Windows 2000 default authentication protocol. The chapter describes how mutual authentication is achieved using a shared secret protocol and discusses shared keys, session keys, key distribution centers, Kerberos tickets, the ticket granting service, and cross-domain authentication.

Microsoft's Internet Information Service version 5 (IIS5) is a comprehensive tool that lets you set up Web sites, FTP sites, and newsgroups and can be integrated with BackOffice products, such as Exchange and SQL. Chapter 12 investigates the many features provided by IIS5, such as host header names, HHTP keep-alives, virtual directories, and so on. The chapter covers Internet security and user authentication and describes how to configure the various types of sites. IIS5 offers a number of new features, such as the WebDAV extension of the Hypertext Transport Protocol version 1.1 (HTTP 1.1) that's used to set up collaboration projects. These new features are described in the chapter.

Chapter 13 covers Dynamic Host Configuration Protocol (DHCP) and the dynamic configuration of IP addresses, subnet masks, default gateways, Windows Internet Name Service (WINS) server addresses, Domain Name System (DNS) server addresses, and a wide range of options. The chapter describes how DHCP works, the operation of BOOTP relay agents, how DHCP unicast and multicast scopes are allocated, and how scopes can be combined for administrative purposes. DHCP forms an integral part of the Dynamic DNS (DDNS) system, and DHCP/DNS interaction is covered. The chapter describes the Windows 2000 enhancements, methods of providing failover protection, and DHCP deployment.

DNS resolves host names to IP addresses and is the most widely used name resolution in the world. Chapter 14 covers the concept of hierarchical domain namespace, which was one of the major factors in the creation of the World Wide

Web. The various types of DNS records are described, as is DNS database replication and how Fully Qualified Domain Names (FQDNs) can be resolved over the Internet. The static DNS database is no longer adequate in modern networking environments, and the chapter looks at how the dynamic WINS database can be integrated with DNS in mixed environments. The Windows 2000 enhancements, particularly Active Directory integration and Dynamic DNS, are described in detail.

Chapter 15 describes WINS, which provides a dynamic, centralized database that holds Network Basic Input/Output System (NetBIOS) names mapped to their corresponding IP addresses. The chapter covers NetBIOS names, the various methods of resolving these names to IP addresses, and the order in which these methods are attempted. The use of WINS proxies to enable WINS services to be offered to non WINS-aware hosts is described, as is WINS database replication. The chapter covers Windows 2000 WINS enhancement, such as partner autodiscovery, manual tombstoning, and so on.

Windows 2000 offers an integrated Routing and Remote Access Service (RRAS). However, routing was covered in Chapter 4, so Chapter 16 concentrates on the Remote Access Service (RAS). The various RAS configurations are described, as are the RAS encapsulation and authentication protocols and encryption methods. RAS can be implemented either using Dial-in networking or through Virtual Private Networks, and both methods are described. The chapter covers tunneling in some detail and describes the Point-to-Point Tunneling Protocol (PPTP) and Layer 2 Tunneling Protocol, together with the use of Microsoft Point-to-Point Encryption (MPPE) and IPSec. The use of Remote Authentication Dial-in User Service (RADIUS) clients and the Internet Authentication Service (IAS) RADIUS server to provide access control and accounting services is also described.

Chapter 17 covers the Transport Driver Interface, which is the high-level abstraction layer between the protocol stack and the application layer. Arguably, I should have covered this topic after the transport layer protocols, but it seemed more appropriate to keep all the protocols and services together. The TDI provides a single common interface to which all transport drivers make procedure calls, and enables several protocols to be used by (or bound to) high-level services, such as file and printer sharing. This chapter revisits the DDK, this time to investigate the facilities provided for transport driver designers.

Windows 2000 applications use two major Network Application Interfaces, NetBIOS and Windows Sockets (Winsock). NetBIOS is supported for backward compatibility, and Chapter 18 therefore concentrates mainly on Winsock, particularly on Winsock version 2 (Winsock2). The chapter describes the various parameters, routines, and extensions provided by this interface and how the Windows platform SDK can be downloaded and used to take advantage of these features. The SDK offers a wide range of application development aids and debugging tools. The use of these tools is described in the Immediate Solutions section of the chapter.

Many tools are available for troubleshooting networks, possibly because networks have many troubles. Chapter 19 describes the wide variety of tools provided Windows 2000 for network management and troubleshooting. It covers Simple Network Management Protocol, Event Viewer, the Performance Logs and Alerts Tool, System Monitor, Network Monitor, and the various command-line tools. This is a highly practical chapter that's of particular relevance to network support personnel.

Finally, the book looks at the protocol that will take the Internet into the new (well, almost new) millennium. IPv6 is still under development, but there's plenty of activity on the 6bone (the IPv6 portion of the Internet). Chapter 20 investigates IPv6 addresses, address notation, and address types and covers Neighbor Discovery and Address Autoconfiguration. IPv6 supports unicast, multicast, and anycast (but not broadcast), and the alternatives to broadcast-based protocols (such as ARP) are described, as is the link between hardware (48-bit and 64-bit) addresses and IPv6 addresses. The chapter covers IPv6 to IPv4 configuration and the use of the IPv6 tools provided with the Microsoft technology preview version of IPv6.

Three appendices cover all the Registry parameters that you'll ever want to know about, and the fourth describes the powerful and useful Network Shell utility. There's a comprehensive glossary and index, so you can find the information you want quickly and easily.

How to Use This Book

This book can be read through from start to finish and will provide a sound knowledge of TCP/IP. However, you may feel it's more appropriate to skip around, finding examples and procedures that will help with current tasks or with any problems you may encounter. The book is a reference resource. Please use it in the way best suited to your needs and experience.

No book on TCP/IP is totally comprehensive. Big though this one is, I find I have as much material again that I couldn't put in. Throughout the book, I've recommended additional sources of information, such as Request for Comments documents. I think I've covered everything that's important, but if I've missed out your favorite topic, I can only apologize. I would welcome any comments and constructive criticism. My email address is **ianm@cableinet.co.uk**. Please include the book title in your email message.

Chapter 1

Overview

In Depth

A History of TCP/IP

Transmission Control Protocol/Internet Protocol (TCP/IP) is a suite of protocols, tools, and services more correctly (but less commonly) known as the *Internet Protocol Suite*. TCP/IP has become a term in common use, rather than an abbreviation, and nowadays the full name is seldom used. It's the protocol of the Internet and of large routed intranets, and TCP/IP implementations exist for all modern hardware.

To understand what TCP/IP is and why it has become the protocol of choice for so many network implementations, it's worthwhile to look at how it developed. The history of TCP/IP is closely linked with the development of the Internet.

In the 1960s, the U.S. Department of Defense became concerned with the vulnerability of its mainframe computer network to nuclear attack. The Defense Communications Agency began to look into ways of improving security, and the Advanced Research Projects Agency (ARPA), created in 1968, was funded to develop a high-speed packet-switching communications network. In 1970, this network, now known as ARPAnet, began using the Network Control Protocol (NCP). In 1972, the U.S. Defense Advanced Research Projects Agency (DARPA) replaced ARPA and in the following year the first Telnet (terminal emulation) specification was submitted as a Request for Comment (RFC) document, RFC 318. In the following year, the File Transfer Protocol (FTP) was specified in RFC 454.

ARPAnet had many successes and was an innovator in introducing a layered architecture almost a decade before the ISO OSI (International Standards Organization Open Systems Interconnection) seven-layer model was specified. However, the first generation protocols were expensive, slow, and prone to crash. In 1974, Vinton Cerf and Robert Kahn proposed a new set of core protocols, and TCP was specified in detail. In 1981, IP was specified in RFC 791.

TCP/IP was chosen for internetworking, rather than the Xerox Networking System (XNS) protocol stack, which was the other major protocol stack available at that time, for the following reasons:

- TCP/IP utilizes a defined routing hierarchy that allows large internetworks to be managed in a structured way.
- TCP/IP addresses are centrally administered.

The Department of Defense granted permission to universities that were government contractors, such as the University of California at Berkeley, to use TCP/IP. Version 4.2 of Berkley Software Distribution (BSD) Unix, released in September 1983, was the first to include TCP/IP protocols in the generic operating system, and this was eventually carried over into commercial versions of Unix. Sun Microsystems published their Open Network Computing (ONC) standards, better known as the Network Filing System (NFS). NFS is designed to utilize the TCP/IP stack, although it uses User Datagram Protocol (UDP) rather than TCP as its transport protocol.

With ARPAnet up and running and using TCP/IP, and with higher education getting into the act, it wasn't long before other institutions started using the network and sharing information. The introduction of the Domain Name System (DNS) in 1984 and the concept of domain namespace paved the way for a truly worldwide system (or World Wide Web). The Department of Defense retained MILnet, a TCP/IP network developed in parallel with ARPAnet, for its own use. ARPAnet migrated into the public domain and became the Internet, and the TCP/IP protocol suite gained worldwide acceptance. Figure 1.1 shows the significant stages in the development of TCP/IP and the Internet.

Microsoft's NT Implementation

In the early 1990s, Microsoft started a project to create a TCP/IP stack and services that would improve the scalability of its networks. Microsoft introduced a completely rewritten TCP/IP stack in its NT3.5 release. The stack is a high-performance, portable, 32-bit implementation of the industry-standard TCP/IP protocol, and it has evolved with each version of NT to include new features and services designed to enhance performance and reliability.

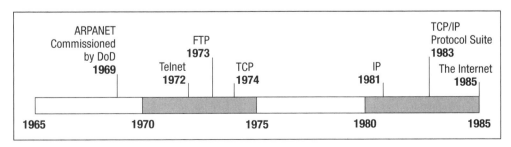

Figure 1.1   TCP/IP timeline.

Microsoft's stated goal for its enhanced TCP/IP was that it should meet the following criteria:

- Standards-compliant
- Interoperable
- Portable
- Scalable
- High-performance
- Versatile
- Self-tuning
- Easy to administer
- Adaptable

Microsoft has introduced a considerable number of enhancements, including additional protocols, services, utilities, and tools to the original TCP/IP suite. These will be described in detail throughout the book, but it's appropriate to summarize them in this overview chapter.

Dead Gateway Detection

TCP/IP is normally set up with a default gateway IP address specified. This address identifies the multihomed device (or router) that enables routing from the local subnet to remote subnets on an intranet or to the Internet. Dead gateway detection allows TCP to detect a failure of the default gateway and to adjust the IP route table so that another gateway is used. The Microsoft TCP/IP stack uses the triggered reselection method described in RFC 816, with slight modifications based on customer experiences and feedback. Dead gateway detection was introduced in Windows NT4 service pack 4, and is also implemented in Windows 98. It is enabled by default in Windows 2000.

TCP Fast Retransmit

When TCP is transmitting a data stream across a network, it splits the data into segments and gives each segment a sequence number, so that the data can be reassembled in the correct order at the target host. If the target detects a number that's out of sequence and if the packet that has the expected sequence number isn't subsequently received within a predefined time period, then all of the data held in that segment group (or *TCP Window*) must be retransmitted. When a receiving host that supports TCP Fast Retransmit receives data that has a sequence number beyond the current expected one, it assumes that one or more segments were dropped and immediately sends an acknowledgment signal, or ACK, with the ACK number set to the sequence number that it was expecting.

The receiver continues to do this for each additional incoming TCP segment that contains data subsequent to the missing data in the incoming stream. Thus, the sender receives a stream of ACKs that contain the same sequence number, and that sequence number is earlier than the current sequence number being sent. From this information the sender can infer that a segment (or more) is missing. A sender that supports the TCP Fast Retransmit algorithm will immediately retransmit the segment that the receiver is expecting. This can improve performance significantly in a network environment where data loss is a problem.

TCP Fast Retransmit was introduced in Windows NT4 service pack 4, and is also implemented in Windows 98 and later versions of Windows 95. It is enabled by default in Windows 2000.

Selective Acknowledgment

Selective Acknowledgment (SACK) conveys extended acknowledgment information from the receiver to the sender over an established TCP connection. SACK is especially important for connections that use large TCP window sizes. Prior to SACK, a receiver could acknowledge only the latest sequence number of contiguous received data. When SACK is enabled, the receiver continues to use the ACK number to acknowledge the latest sequence number, but it can also acknowledge other blocks of received data individually. SACK, defined in RFC 2018, is implemented in Windows 98 and later versions of Windows 95. It is enabled by default in Windows 2000.

Large TCP Windows

Window size determines the maximum number of packets that can be sent without waiting for positive acknowledgment. Large TCP Windows can improve TCP/IP performance when large amounts of data are in transit between the sender and receiver. Typically, the maximum window size is fixed when a connection is established and is limited to 64K. With Large-Windows support, however, you can recalculate and scale the window size dynamically. With this option, more data packets are in transit on the network at one time, which increases throughput. The disadvantage is that, when a network is prone to losing data, larger amounts of data may have to be retransmitted.

Large-Windows support is also implemented in Windows 98 and later versions of Windows 95. It is disabled by default in Windows 2000.

Internet Protocol Version 6

Traditional IP, IPv4, uses 32 bits (or four octets) to define an IP address. Typically, IP addresses are written in dotted decimal notation (for example, 194.23.184.110). Unfortunately, almost all of these addresses are now allocated. IPv6 uses 128 bits, or 16 octets, to define addresses, making a very large number of such addresses available. An IPv6 address is normally written in hexadecimal format (for example, 4A65:61C4:7A33:4389:012F:3489:AA2F:2342).

Dynamic DNS

DNS converts Fully Qualified Domain Names (such as **www.coriolis.com**) to IP addresses, using either a local DNS server or a hierarchy of servers in the domain namespace. Conventional DNS uses static databases. If, for example, an IP address assignment is altered, the administrator is required to change the DNS zone file manually. This worked when TCP/IP was configured manually and there were relatively few changes in IP addressing. With the advent of Dynamic Host Configuration Protocol (DHCP), which dynamically and automatically assigns IP numbers, static DNS was no longer adequate.

Microsoft addressed this problem in Windows NT4 by integrating DNS with the Windows Internet Name Service (WINS), which maintains a dynamic database of NetBIOS names and associated IP addresses. This reduced manual reconfiguration considerably, but it wasn't a total solution because it relied on NetBIOS and host names being the same and worked only for those hosts that were WINS-enabled.

Dynamic DNS (DDNS) implements the dynamic update capability, as defined in RFC 2136. DDNS is introduced in Windows 2000 and is enabled by default.

Media Sense Support

Media Sense Support is included in version 5 of the Network Driver Interface Specification (NDIS5). It enables the Network Interface Card (NIC) to notify media connect and media disconnect events to the protocol stack. Windows 2000 TCP/IP utilizes these notifications to assist in automatic configuration.

In previous Windows implementations, if a computer was moved to another subnet without being rebooted or was taken off the network altogether, the protocol stack received no indication of the event. Thus, the configuration parameters became out of date, or *stale*. Media Sense Support allows the protocol stack to react to events and invalidate stale parameters. If a computer that is running Windows 2000 is unplugged from the network, TCP/IP will invalidate the associated parameters after a damping period (currently 20 seconds).

Media Sense Support is introduced in Windows 2000 and, provided the NIC supports it, is enabled by default.

Wake-on-LAN Power Management

NDIS5 power management policy is no-network-activity based. All participating network components must agree to a power-down request before the NIC can be switched to a lower power state. If there are any active sessions or open files over the network, the power-down request can be refused.

The computer can also be awakened from a lower power state. The following can cause a wakeup signal:

- Detection of a change in the network, such as a cable reconnection
- Receipt of a network wakeup frame
- Receipt of a magic packet

Magic Packets

A *magic packet* is a specific frame that's sent to a node, or station, on the network. If a PC capable of receiving this frame goes to sleep, it will enable magic packet mode in its network controller. When the network controller receives a magic packet frame, it will alert the system to wake up. A magic packet can take a number of formats, depending on the network technology employed, but the wakeup sequence is typically the station's MAC address repeated 16 times, preceded by a synchronization stream of 6 bytes of FFh.

Wake-on-LAN Power Management is introduced in Windows 2000 and is enabled by default.

Network Address Translation

A Network Address Translation (NAT) server is used to protect a corporate intranet by converting internal intranet IP addresses (typically private-class addresses) to legal Internet IP addresses at a firewall or other NAT device. Microsoft Proxy Server is an example of a NAT device. In the Windows 2000 TCP/IP stack (and in Windows 98), NAT is integrated with the operating system and doesn't require a separate server. NAT is enabled by default in Windows 2000.

Kerberos v5

There's nothing new about Kerberos. The Kerberos v5 shared-secrets protocol is an industry standard, providing a high level of security and overcoming most of the weaknesses of NT LAN Manager (NTLM), which was used in previous versions of Windows NT. Kerberos is the default security protocol in Windows 2000, although NTLM is also supported for backward compatibility.

Internet Protocol Security

Internet Protocol Security (IPSec) is a low-level security protocol that exists below the transport level and provides network-level data protection that's invisible to the user. Protocols such as Secure Sockets Layer version3/Transport Layer Security (SSL3/TLS) are used to protect sensitive data, but these protocols can be used only by applications that understand them (such as browsers). IPSec, specified by the Internet Engineering Task Force (IETF), provides security for all TCP/IP communications on both sides of an organization's firewall. IPSec provides data integrity, confidentiality, and authentication, and it extends encryption support to Virtual Private Networks (VPNs).

Windows 2000 includes an implementation of IPSec. IPSec is a new protocol, still under development, and future Windows 2000 releases are likely to incorporate additional features. IPSec is enabled by default.

NOTE: *For details of the latest Internet Engineering Task Force (IETF) IPSec drafts, access **www.itef.org/html.charters/ipsec-charter.html**.*

Point-to-Point Tunneling Protocol

Point-to-Point Tunneling Protocol (PPTP) is used to create a tunnel through a public network, thus implementing a secure VPN. PPTP is based on Point-to-Point Protocol (PPP) and allows IP, IPX (Internetwork Packet Exchange), or NetBEUI (Network Basic Input/Output System Enhanced User Interface) traffic to be encrypted, encapsulated in an IP header, and sent across an IP network, such as the Internet. PPTP is a layer 2 (data-link layer) protocol and was introduced in Windows NT 4. It is also implemented in Windows 98 and later versions of Windows 95. PPTP is enabled by default in Windows 2000.

Layer 2 Tunneling Protocol

Like PPTP, Layer 2 Tunneling Protocol (L2TP) is a data-link layer protocol based on PPP and is used in the implementation of VPNs. L2TP encapsulates PPP frames to be sent over IP, X.25, Frame Relay, or Asynchronous Transfer Mode (ATM) networks. It can be used as a tunneling protocol over the Internet, and it can also be used directly over various WAN media (such as Frame Relay) without an IP transport layer. The protocol uses UDP for tunnel maintenance and to send L2TP-encapsulated PPP frames as the tunneled data. The payloads of encapsulated PPP frames can be encrypted, compressed, or both. L2TP is introduced in Windows 2000 and is enabled by default.

NOTE: *PPTP is documented in the draft RFC "Point-to-Point Tunneling Protocol" (pptp-draft-ietf-ppext-pptp-02.txt). L2TP is documented in the draft RFC "Layer 2 Tunneling Protocol L2TP" (draft-ietf-pppext-l2tp-09.txt).*

IP Helper Application Programming Interface

The IP helper Application Programming Interface (API) solves a problem associated with the Address Resolution Protocol (ARP), which resolves IP addresses to

Media Access Control (MAC) addresses. ARP queues only one outbound IP datagram for a specified destination address while that IP address is being resolved to a MAC address. If a UDP-based application sends multiple IP datagrams to a single destination address without any pauses between them, some datagrams may be dropped. An application can compensate for this by calling the IP helper API (iphlpapi.dll) routine **SendArp( )** to establish an ARP cache entry before sending the stream of packets.

The IP helper API was introduced in Windows NT4 and is also implemented in Windows 98. It is enabled by default in Windows 2000.

Windows Sockets Version 2 API

Access to the TCP/IP protocol stack is normally via either the Transport Driver Interface (TDI) or the NDIS interface. The Windows Sockets version 2 (Winsock2) API also provides direct access to the protocol stack for supported applications. An application creates a socket by specifying the IP address of the host, the type of service (TCP for connection-based or UDP for connectionless), and the number of the protocol port the application is using. An application can create a socket and use it to send connectionless traffic to a remote application. Alternatively, a socket created by one application can connect to a socket created by another application, and data can be sent reliably over this connection.

Support for Winsock2 is implemented in Windows 98 and in the OSR-2 release of Windows 95. It is enabled by default in Windows 2000.

Generic Quality-of-Service API

The Generic Quality-of-Service (GQoS) API is an extension to the Winsock programming interface. It includes interfaces and system components that provide applications with a method of reserving network bandwidth between client and server. Windows 2000 automatically maps GQoS requests to QoS mechanisms, such as Resource Reservation Protocol (RSVP), Differentiated Services (DiffServ), 802.1p, or ATM QoS.

RSVP is defined later in this section. DiffServ is a layer 3 (network layer) QoS mechanism. It defines 6 bits in the IP header that determine how the IP packet is prioritized. DiffServ traffic can be prioritized into 64 possible classes, known as *Per Hop Behaviors* (PHBs). 802.1p is a layer 2 (data-link layer) QoS mechanism that defines how devices, such as Ethernet switches, should prioritize traffic. Integrated Services over ATM (ISATM) is a QoS mechanism that automatically maps GQoS requests to ATM QoS on IP over ATM networks. The GQoS API is implemented in Windows 98 and is enabled by default in Windows 2000.

Packet Scheduler

The Packet Scheduler is one of the system components involved in QoS and RSVP. It maintains separate queues for each classification of traffic and includes a Conformance Analyzer, Shaper, and Packet Sequencer. The Shaper manages flows into the packet queues at an agreed rate. The Sequencer feeds packets to the network interface in the order of priority from the queues that it manages. Traffic that has no QoS specification goes into the best-effort queue, which is lowest in priority.

The Packet Scheduler is introduced in Windows 2000 and is disabled by default.

Resource Reservation Protocol

RSVP is a layer 3 signaling protocol used to reserve bandwidth for individual flows on a network. It's what is known as a *per-flow* QoS mechanism, because it sets up a reservation for each traffic flow. RSVP is implemented in Windows 98 and is enabled by default in Windows 2000.

Integrated Services over Low Bit Rate

Integrated Services over Low Bit Rate (ISSLOW) is a QoS mechanism that improves latency for prioritized traffic on slow WAN links. ISSLOW is implemented in Windows 98 and is enabled by default in Windows 2000.

Router Discovery

Router discovery provides an additional method of configuring and detecting default gateways. Rather than using DHCP or manually configuring default gateways, hosts can discover routers on their subnet dynamically. If the primary router fails or if the network administrator changes router preferences, hosts can switch to a backup router automatically. Internet Router Discovery Protocol (IRDP) is implemented as part of Internet Control Message Protocol (ICMP). It was introduced in Windows NT with NT4 service pack 5, and is also implemented in Windows 98 and later versions of Windows 95. It is enabled by default in Windows 2000.

Offload-TCP

To improve reliability, TCP uses a checksum on both the headers and the data in each TCP segment. NDIS5 provides support for task offloading, and Offload-TCP takes advantage of this by allowing the NIC to perform the TCP checksum calculations, provided that the NIC driver offers support for this function. Offloading the checksum calculations to hardware can result in performance improvements, particularly in very high throughput environments. Offload-TCP is introduced in Windows 2000 and is enabled by default.

Offload-IPSec

When IPSec is used to encrypt data, network performance generally drops because of the encryption processing overhead. One method of reducing the impact of this overhead is to offload the processing onto a hardware device. Because NDIS5 supports task offloading, encryption hardware can be included on an NIC. Offload-IPSec is introduced in Windows 2000 and is enabled by default.

Automatic Private IP Addressing

The Automatic Private IP Addressing (APIPA) feature can be used to configure TCP/IP with an IP address in the reserved range from 169.254.0.1 through 169.254.255.254 and a subnet mask of 255.255.0.0. There's no automatic configuration of a default gateway, DNS server, or WINS server. APIPA is designed for networks that consist of a single network segment and aren't connected to the Internet.

Plug and Play

The main impact that Plug and Play support has on protocol stacks is that network interfaces can come and go at any time. The Windows 2000 TCP/IP stack and related components have been adapted to support Plug and Play.

Plug and Play has the following capabilities and features:

- Dynamic recognition of installed hardware. This includes initial system installation, recognition of static hardware changes that may occur between boots, and response to runtime hardware events, such as dock, undock, and insertion or removal of cards.

- Streamlined hardware configuration, including dynamic hardware activation, resource arbitration, device driver loading, and drive mounting.

- Support for particular buses and other hardware standards that facilitate automatic and dynamic recognition of hardware and streamlined hardware configuration. Supported standards include Plug and Play Industry Standard Architecture (ISA), Peripheral Component Interconnect (PCI) bus architecture, the Personal Computer Memory Card International Association (PCMCIA) standard, PC Card/CardBus, Universal Serial Bus (USB), and IEEE 1394 (the Institute of Electrical and Electronic Engineers Firewire standard).

- A Plug and Play infrastructure to facilitate the design of new device drivers. This includes device information (INF) interfaces, APIs, kernel-mode notifications, and executive interfaces.

- Mechanisms that allow user applications to discover changes in the hardware environment so that they can take appropriate action.

There was some Plug and Play support in Windows 95, but a full implementation wasn't introduced until Windows 98. Windows NT4 offered no Plug and Play facilities. Windows 2000 is the first Microsoft Network Operating System (NOS) to provide this support. Support for Plug and Play is enabled by default.

The Windows 2000 TCP/IP Implementation

The continuing development of the TCP/IP protocol suite since the days of ARPAnet, coupled with the new features implemented by Microsoft, results in the TCP/IP implementation provided by the Windows 2000 operating system—Windows 2000 enhanced TCP/IP. This overview chapter summarizes the enhanced TCP/IP features, which will be described in depth in subsequent chapters.

The Windows 2000 TCP/IP suite is designed to facilitate integration with large-scale corporate, government, and public networks and to operate over those networks in a secure manner.

NOTE: There will inevitably be some duplication between the previous section, which describes facilities, services, and extensions to the TCP/IP protocol suite that Microsoft has developed, and this section, which describes Microsoft enhanced TCP/IP as it currently exists. The duplication is deliberate. The aim of this section is to provide an overview of the current protocol suite, without the necessity of referring back to previous material.

Core Protocols

The following list of protocols is not exclusive; additional subprotocols are covered in subsequent chapters in this book. There are still more protocols that can be installed for interworking with foreign networks or with BackOffice products. Only the core protocols of the TCP/IP stack are covered in this overview chapter.

Internet Protocol

IP controls packet sorting and delivery. Each incoming or outgoing packet, or *IP datagram*, includes the source IP address of the sender and the destination IP address of the intended recipient. The IP addresses in a datagram remain the same throughout a packet's journey across an internetwork. IP is responsible for routing. Datagrams are passed to IP from UDP and TCP and from the NIC. IP examines the destination address on each datagram, compares it to a route table, and decides what action to take. Routes and route tables can be set up statically or dynamically using either Routing Internet Protocol (RIP) or Open Shortest Path First (OSPF). ICMP (see below) provides routing facilities for IP. Windows 2000 supports both IPv4 and IPv6. Currently Windows 2000 TCP/IP is configured for IPv4 by default.

Internet Control Message Protocol

ICMP provides maintenance and routing facilities for IP. ICMP messages are encapsulated within IP datagrams and can be routed throughout an internetwork. The protocol builds and maintains route tables, performs router discovery, assists in Path Maximum Transmission Unit (PMTU) discovery, adjusts flow control to prevent link or router saturation, and provides diagnostic tools, such as ping and tracert (described later in this section).

Internet Group Management Protocol

IGMP provides support for IP multicasting. Windows 2000 supports IGMP v2, which provides full support for IP multicasting, as described in RFC 1112 and RFC 2236. IP multicasting is the transmission of an IP datagram to a *host group*, that is, a number of hosts identified by a single IP destination address.

Address Resolution Protocol

ARP resolves IP addresses to Media Access Control (MAC) addresses used by network hardware devices, such as NICs. A MAC address identifies a device within its own physical network, using a 6-byte (48-bit) number programmed into the device's Read-Only Memory (ROM). MAC addresses are typically displayed in hexadecimal notation (for example, 00-CF-62-E5-82-3B).

Transmission Control Protocol

TCP provides a reliable, connection-based, byte-stream service to applications. It is used for logon, file and print sharing, replication between Domain Controllers (DCs), transfer of browse lists, and other common functions. It can be used only for one-to-one communications where the start and endpoints are defined and the transmission route is established by a handshake protocol.

User Datagram Protocol

UDP provides a connectionless, unreliable transport service and is generally used for one-to-many communications that use broadcast or multicast IP datagrams. Because delivery of UDP datagrams is not guaranteed, applications that use UDP must supply their own reliability mechanisms. UDP can be used for logon, browsing, and name resolution.

Services

Windows 2000 enhanced TCP/IP provides a large number of services, the more significant of which are described briefly in this overview chapter. Detailed descriptions of Windows 2000 services will be given in subsequent chapters.

Dynamic Host Configuration Protocol

DHCP automatically assigns IP addresses to DHCP-enabled hosts. It assigns IP addresses from one or more scopes and handles IP number leasing and renewal.

Exclusion ranges can be defined for non–DHCP-enabled hosts, and static assignments can be made to specific MAC addresses. DHCP can also specify the IP address of the default gateway(s) and primary and secondary WINS servers.

Windows Internet Name Service

WINS resolves NetBIOS names to IP addresses. It provides a dynamic database, in which each client registers its NetBIOS name and IP addresses on power-up or if either is changed. A WINS server can span multiple domains.

Domain Name System

DNS resolves Fully Qualified Domain Names (FQDNs) to IP addresses (and vice versa). A local DNS server can perform this function on its own subnet, or the concept of a hierarchical domain namespace can be used to resolve FQDNs over the Internet.

Dynamic Domain Name System

DDNS provides a dynamic DNS database. Traditionally, DNS uses a static database, which is a disadvantage when IP addresses are allocated dynamically (for example, by DHCP). DDNS uses the concept of a dynamic database and enables dynamic updates to resolve this problem.

Dial-up

Dial-up enables remote access through telephone lines, using either PPP or Serial Line Internet Protocol (SLIP). SLIP is slower and less secure than PPP and is included to provide compatibility with non-Microsoft networks.

Point-to-Point Tunneling Protocol

PPTP allows IP, IPX, or NetBEUI traffic to be encrypted, encapsulated in an IP header, and sent across an IP network.

Layer 2 Tunneling Protocol

L2TP encapsulates PPP frames to be sent over IP, X.25, Frame Relay, or ATM networks.

TCP/IP Network Printing Support

TCP/IP network printing support provides the facility to accept print jobs from non-Microsoft TCP/IP hosts (such as Unix clients). The Line Printer Daemon (LPD), installed on a Windows 2000 print server, responds to Line Printer Remote (LPR) and Line Printer Queue (LPQ) requests from the client.

Simple Network Management Protocol

Originally developed to monitor routers and bridges, SNMP can also monitor computers, gateways, hubs, and terminal servers. The Microsoft SNMP service is SNMP Agent software that allows Microsoft Windows 2000 and NT-based computers to be monitored and to send alerts to management systems.

Network Basic Input/Output System

NetBIOS defines a software interface and a naming convention. The Windows 2000 implementation of NetBIOS over TCP/IP, *netbt.sys*, is a kernel-mode component that supports the TDI. While services such as the Workstation and Server service use the TDI directly, traditional NetBIOS applications have their calls mapped to TDI calls by the NetBIOS system driver.

Windows Sockets Version 2

Winsock2 provides direct access to the protocol stack for supported applications. An application creates a socket by specifying the IP address of the host, the type of service (TCP or UDP), and the number of the protocol port the application is using.

Remote Procedure Call Support

RPC support allows an application on a client to call a function on a server. During an RPC, data is sent and received, and External Data Representation (XDR) functions are provided so that data is represented on the network in a standard fashion and is readable at both ends.

Network Dynamic Data Exchange

NetDDE uses NetBIOS APIs to communicate with underlying network components and thus maintains a link between client and server applications.

Wide Area Network Browsing

Internet Explorer version 5 is included in the default installation and is an integral component of active desktop as well as a fully featured WAN browser.

Microsoft Internet Information Server

IIS v5 is installed by default. It provides a fully featured Internet information service, which can host sites for Hypertext Transport Protocol (HTTP), FTP, and Network News Transfer Protocol (NNTP). Virtual directories allow the contents of a large site to be spread across multiple machines, and host headers enable you to implement multiple Uniform Resource Locators (URLs) on the same server.

Server Software for Simple Network Protocols

The facilities provided include character generator, daytime, discard, echo, and quote of the day.

Management and Diagnostic Tools

Windows 2000 extended TCP/IP provides a full set of management and diagnostic tools, including the following:

- *Arp*—Used to view and modify the ARP cache.
- *Hostname*—Returns the host name of a computer.

- *Ipconfig*—Determines a host's MAC address, IP address, default gateway address, WINS server address, and subnet mask. Ipconfig can be used to release and renew a dynamically allocated IP configuration.

- *Lpq*—Queries the print job list of an LPD print server.

- *Nbtstat*—Returns NetBIOS over TCP/IP information, for example the names that applications (such as the server and redirector) have registered locally on the system. Nbtstat can also display session statistics and display the NetBIOS name cache, purge it, and reload it from the lmhosts file. A new feature in Windows 2000 enables nbtstat to re-register all names with the name server.

- *Netstat*—Displays protocol statistics and current TCP/IP connections. Netstat can display all connections or the route table and any active connections. The tool can also be used to display Ethernet statistics.

- *Ping*—Verifies IP-level reachability. The ping command can be used to send an ICMP echo request to a target name or IP address. Ping was originally an acronym for Packet Internet Groper, but is now a computer term in its own right.

- *Route*—Used to view or modify the route table. **Route print** displays a list of known current routes. **Route add** adds routes to the table. **Route delete** removes routes from the table.

- *Nslookup*—Used for troubleshooting DNS problems, such as host name resolution. It shows the host name and IP address of the DNS server that's configured for the local system, followed by a command prompt. If, for example, you want to use DNS to look up the IP address of a host, type the host name and press Enter. The debug mode of this command provides a useful troubleshooting feature. You invoke this mode by typing **set debug** or, for even greater detail, **set d2**. In debug mode, nslookup lists the steps being taken to complete its commands.

- *Tracert*—Uses the IP Time-to-Live (TTL) field and ICMP error messages to determine the route from one host to another through a network.

Connectivity Utilities

Windows 2000 provides the following connectivity utilities:

- *Finger*—Used to obtain information about a user currently logged onto a remote host.

- *Ftp*—Uses FTP to copy files from and to a remote computer. FTP uses TCP to create a guaranteed first-class connection; it provides a common interface to a wide variety of file storage methods and directory structures.

- *Rcp*—Uses the Remote Copy Protocol (RCP) to copy files from one computer to another. One or both computers can be remote. You can copy multiple files, and even entire directories, by using wildcards. The main function of this utility is to copy files between Windows 2000 and Unix computers.

- *Rexec*—Runs a process on a remote computer. This utility is often used for remote debugging.

- *Rsh (remote shell)*—Runs commands on a remote Unix host.

- *Telnet*—Provides terminal emulation services to a TCP/IP host that is running Telnet server software.

- *Tftp*—Uses Trivial File Transport Protocol (TFTP) to send information to and get information from a remote host. TFTP uses UDP to provide connection-less, best-effort information transfer. It's used by Microsoft Exchange and other email packages.

Standard Features

Windows 2000 supports many standard TCP/IP features, the more significant of which are summarized in this overview chapter. TCP/IP features are discussed in more detail throughout the book.

Logical and Physical Multihoming

A computer that's configured with more than one IP address is referred to as a *multihomed* system. Multihoming is supported in three ways:

- Multiple IP addresses per NIC

- Multiple NICs per physical network

- Multiple networks and media types, including Ethernet 802.3, Subnetwork Access Protocol (SNAP), Fiber Distributed Data Interface (FDDI), Token Ring (802.5), and ATM

NOTE: *NetBIOS over TCP/IP (NetBT) binds to only one IP address per interface card. When a NetBIOS name registration is sent out, the IP address that's listed first in the user interface is registered.*

Internet Group Management Protocol Version 2

As discussed under Core Protocols in this section, IGMP v2 provides support for IP multicasting, which is the transmission of a datagram to a host group defined by a single IP address. Host group addresses are from the class D range, 224.0.0.1 to 239.255.255.254.

Duplicate IP Address Detection

When the TCP/IP stack on a host is first initialized, ARP requests are broadcast for the IP addresses of that host. If another host replies to any of these ARPs, this indicates that the IP address is already in use. When this happens, the host still boots, but with IP on the offending address disabled. An error message is displayed at the host that's defending the address, but its interface continues to operate.

Multiple Default Gateways

Multiple gateways can be specified, with differing metric values, either manually or through DHCP. Hosts can also discover routers on their subnet dynamically, using IRDP.

Dead Gateway Detection

Dead gateway detection allows TCP to detect a failure of the default gateway and to adjust the IP routing table so that another gateway is used.

Automatic Path Maximum Transmission Unit Discovery

PMTU discovery is implemented through TCP. When a connection is established, the two hosts involved exchange their TCP Maximum Segment Size (MSS) values. The smaller of these two values is used for the connection. Historically, the MSS for a host has been the MTU at the link layer minus 40 bytes for the IP and TCP headers. However, Windows 2000 support for additional TCP options has increased the typical TCP+IP header to 52 or more bytes.

Internet Protocol Security

IPSec implements network-level data protection that's invisible to the user. It provides security for all TCP/IP communications on both sides of a firewall, data integrity, confidentiality, and authentication. In addition, IPSec extends encryption support to VPNs.

Quality-of-Service

Windows 2000 supports several QoS mechanisms, such as RSVP, DiffServ, 802.1p, and ATM QoS.

Internet Protocol over Asynchronous Transfer Mode

Windows 2000 supports IP over ATM or, more accurately, a Logical IP Subnet (LIS) over an ATM network. An LIS is a set of IP hosts that can communicate directly with each other, rather than through an IP router. Because an ATM network is nonbroadcast, ARP broadcasts can't be used. Instead, a dedicated ARP server provides IP-to-ATM address resolution.

Virtual Private Networks

A VPN provides a tunnel through a public network, such as the Internet, to enable remote hosts to communicate in a secure fashion. Windows 2000 supports both PPTP, which can be used in an IP network, and L2TP, which can be used in IP, X.25, Frame Relay, or ATM networks.

TCP/IP Performance

Windows 2000 TCP/IP is self-tuning. It can adapt to most network conditions and can provide the best throughput and reliability possible on a per-connection basis. To quote Microsoft, "attempts at manual tuning are often counter-productive." That having been said, an experienced network engineer could tune performance still further, but only after extensive data analysis.

Performance is enhanced by protocol stack tuning, with increased default window sizes. TCP scalable window size can also be employed, although this option is disabled by default. SACK conveys extended acknowledgment information from the receiver to the sender and is especially important for connections that use large TCP window sizes. TCP Fast Retransmit can improve performance significantly in a network environment where data loss is a problem. The algorithms for calculating Round Trip Time (RTT) and Retransmission Timeout (RTO) have been amended and improved. In short, Windows 2000 TCP/IP is designed to be scalable and tunable to any network size and, in particular, offers improved performance in networks that have large numbers of connections.

The TCP/IP Architectural Model

TCP/IP was developed well before the ISO OSI seven-layer model was specified and fits rather more neatly into its own four-layer model. Figure 1.2 shows how the TCP/IP four-layer model maps to the ISO OSI specification. All protocols in the TCP/IP protocol suite are located in the top three layers of this model.

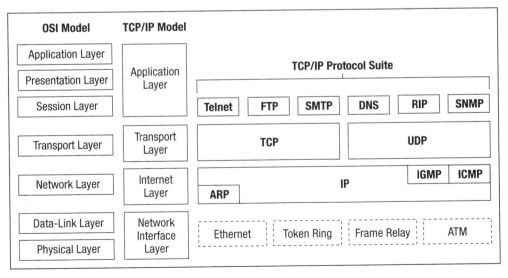

Figure 1.2   The TCP/IP architectural model.

The Application Layer

This layer defines the TCP/IP application protocols and provides interfaces between host application programs and transport layer services. The application layer contains application protocols and services, such as HTTP, Telnet, FTP, TFTP, SNMP, DNS, SMTP, and X Windows.

The Transport Layer

This layer provides communication sessions between host computers. It defines the level of service (first-class or best-effort) and the status of the connection (connection-based or connectionless) used when transporting data. It contains such protocols as UDP and TCP.

The Internet Layer

In this layer, data is packaged into IP datagrams. These contain source and destination address information that is used to transmit the data between hosts and across networks. IP routing is implemented at this layer. It contains such protocols as IP, ICMP, IGMP, and ARP.

The Network Interface Layer

This layer specifies the physical details of how data is sent through a network. It defines the electrical specification of how hardware devices transmit data bits across such network media as coaxial cable, optical fiber, or twisted-pair copper wire. The layer implements Ethernet, Token Ring, FDDI, X.25, frame relay, RS-232, and similar standards.

Supported RFCs

TCP/IP standards are published in a series of RFCs. These documents are an evolving series of reports, proposals for protocols, and protocol standards. They describe the internal workings of TCP/IP and the Internet.

Not all RFCs specify standards. Individuals voluntarily write and submit draft proposals to the IETF and other working groups. Submitted drafts are reviewed and then assigned a status. If a draft passes this initial review stage, it is circulated to the larger Internet community for a period of further comment and review and assigned an RFC number.

If changes are made to the proposed specification, revised or updated drafts are circulated, using a new RFC number. Thus, the higher the RFC number the more recent the document.

An RFC can be assigned one of five status levels, as shown in Table 1.1.

Table 1.1   RFC status levels.

Status	Description
Standard protocol	An official standard Internet protocol.
Draft standard protocol	Under active consideration to become a standard protocol.
Proposed standard protocol	May in the future become a standard protocol.
Experimental protocol	Designed for experimental purposes and not intended for operational use.
Informational protocol	Developed by another standards organization.
Historic protocol	Superceded by other protocols.

Obtaining an RFC

You can obtain RFCs by accessing **www.rfc-editor.org**. This site provides facilities for RFC search and retrieval and provides information on how to submit an RFC. It also has a frequently asked questions section and a catchall "Other Information" section. A list of RFCs can be obtained by accessing **ftp://ftp.isi.edu/in-notes/rfc-index.txt**. If you know the number of a specific RFC, you can access it through **ftp://ftp.isi.edu/in-notes/rfc*xxxx*.txt**, where *xxxx* is the RFC number.

If the above sites aren't available, you can access any one of the following FTP sites:

- **nis.nsf.net**
- **wuarchive.wustl.edu**
- **src.doc.ic.ac.uk**
- **ds.internic.net**
- **nic.ddn.mil**

RFCs Supported by Windows 2000 TCP/IP

Table 1.2 lists the RFCs supported by Windows 2000 TCP/IP. It's usual to list RFCs in numerical order, but I find it more convenient to have a list in alphabetical title order and have therefore used that order here.

Table 1.2   Supported RFCs.

Title	RFC Number
Address Resolution Protocol (ARP)	826
Architecture for IP Address Allocation with CIDR	1518
Character Generator Protocol (CHARGEN)	864

(continued)

21

Table 1.2   Supported RFCs (continued).

Title	RFC Number
Clarifications and Extensions for the Bootstrap Protocol	1542
Classless Inter-Domain Routing (CIDR): An Address Assignment and Aggregation Strategy	1519
Compressing TCP/IP Headers for Low-Speed Serial Links	1144
Daytime Protocol (DAYTIME)	867
DHCP Options and BOOTP Vendor Extensions	2132
Discard Protocol (DISCARD)	863
Domain Name System (DNS)	1034, 1035
Dynamic Host Configuration Protocol	2131
Dynamic Updates in the Domain Name System (DNS UPDATE)	2136
Echo Protocol (ECHO)	862
ESP DES-CBC Transform	1829
ESP Triple DES-CBC Transform	1851
Fault Isolation and Recovery	816
File Transfer Protocol (FTP)	959
HMAC: Keyed Hashing for Message Authentication	2104
HMAC-MD5 IP Authentication with Replay Prevention	2085
Host Requirements (communications and applications)	1122, 1123
ICMP Router Discovery Messages	1256
IEEE 802.5 MIB using SMIv2	1748
IEEE 802.5 Station Source Routing MIB using SMIv2	1749
Internet Control Message Protocol (ICMP)	792
Internet Group Management Protocol (IGMP)	1112
Internet Group Management Protocol, Version 2	2236
Internet Protocol (IP)	791
Internet Standard Subnetting Procedure	950
Interoperation between DHCP and BOOTP	1534
IP Authentication Header (AH)	1826
IP Authentication using Keyed MD5	1828
IP Authentication using Keyed SHA	1852
IP Broadcast Datagrams (broadcasting with subnets)	919, 922

(continued)

*Table 1.2 **Supported RFCs** (continued).*

Title	RFC Number
IP Encapsulating Security Payload (ESP)	1827
IP over ARCNET	1201
IP over Ethernet	894
IP over FDDI	1188
Line Printer Daemon Protocol	1179
NetBIOS Service Protocols	1001, 1002
Path MTU Discovery	1191
Point-to-Point Protocol (PPP)	1661
PPP Challenge Handshake Authentication Protocol (CHAP)	1994
PPP in HDLC-like Framing	1662
PPP Internet Protocol Control Protocol (IPCP)	1332
PPP Internetwork Packet Exchange Control Protocol (IPXCP)	1552
Quote of the Day Protocol (QUOTE)	865
Requirements for IP Version 4 Routers	1812
Resource Reservation Protocol (RSVP), Version 1 Functional Specification	2205
Security Architecture for the Internet Protocol	1825
Simple Network Management Protocol (SNMP)	1157
Standard for the Transmission of IP Datagrams over IEEE 802 Networks	1042
TCP Extensions for High Performance	1323
TCP Selective Acknowledgment Options	2018
Telnet Protocol (Telnet)	854
Transmission Control Protocol (TCP)	793
Transmission of IP over Serial Lines (IP-SLIP)	1055
Trivial File Transfer Protocol (TFTP)	783
User Datagram Protocol (UDP)	768

Immediate Solutions

Configuring TCP/IP

TCP/IP configuration is normally specified during Windows 2000 installation. You may, however, want to reconfigure TCP/IP if, for example, you want a host that was previously configured statically to use DHCP address allocation (or vice versa). You may also want to specify more than one IP address for the NIC (if, for example, you're setting up several FTP sites), to specify DNS or WINS servers, or to enable IP filtering.

Configuring TCP/IP for a Local Area Connection

To configure TCP/IP for a local machine or Local Area Network (LAN) connection, proceed as follows:

1. Log on as an administrator.

2. Access Start|Settings|Network and Dial-up Connections and click Local Area Connection.

3. Click Properties and select Internet Protocol (TCP/IP).

4. Click Properties. The Internet Protocol (TCP/IP) Properties dialog box appears.

5. If appropriate, you can select the options of obtaining an IP address and DNS server address automatically. Alternatively, you can specify an IP address, subnet mask, default gateway, and preferred and alternate DNS servers, as shown in Figure 1.3.

6. Click Advanced. On the IP Setting tab you can bind additional IP addresses to the NIC and specify additional default gateways, as shown in Figure 1.4. The Interface metric setting determines the order in which gateways are accessed.

7. Select the DNS tab. This enables you to specify DNS server addresses in order of use, as shown in Figure 1.5. DNS suffixes will be discussed in Chapter 14.

8. Select the WINS tab, which enables you to specify one or more WINS server addresses, as shown in Figure 1.6. This dialog box also allows you to enable or disable lmhosts lookup, to import the lmhosts file, and to disable NetBIOS over TCP/IP (NetBT).

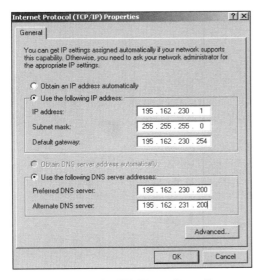

Figure 1.3   Static TCP/IP configuration.

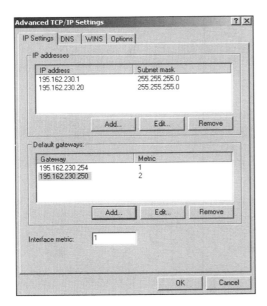

Figure 1.4   Advanced IP settings.

1. Overview

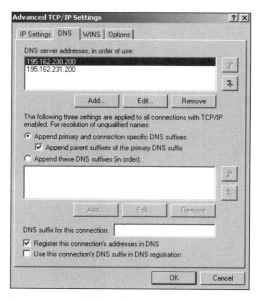

Figure 1.5   DNS settings.

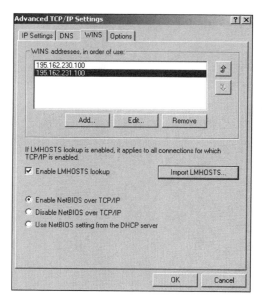

Figure 1.6   WINS settings.

9. Select the Options tab. This enables you to set IPSec and TCP/IP filtering properties.

10. Access the IP Security Properties dialog box, as shown in Figure 1.7. This enables you to set the level of IP security or to disable it altogether. IPSec is discussed in Chapter 7.

11. Close the IP Security Properties dialog box, then access the TCP/IP Filtering dialog box. This enables you to restrict traffic by TCP port, UDP port, or protocol. Figure 1.8 shows TCP traffic being restricted to FTP (ports 20 and 21) and HTTP (port 80). TCP and UDP ports are discussed in Chapter 8 and Chapter 9. Unless you're already familiar with ports and have a specific requirement to restrict traffic, don't change the TCP/IP filtering settings right now.

12. Close all dialog boxes by clicking OK on each. Reboot your computer if prompted to do so.

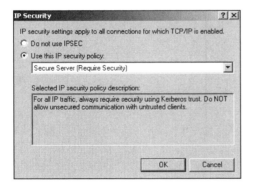

Figure 1.7   Setting the IP Security level.

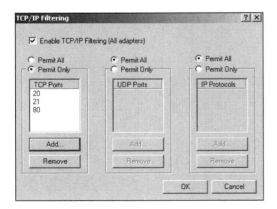

Figure 1.8   Restricting TCP port traffic.

1. Overview

Configuring TCP/IP for Non-Local Area Connections

Configuring connections other than the LAN connection (for example, a VPN connection) is similar to but not the same as configuring the LAN connection. The next procedure highlights the differences and skips over the steps that are the same as the last procedure.

To configure TCP/IP for a connection that's not a local area connection, proceed as follows:

1. Log on as an administrator.

2. Access Start|Settings|Network and Dial-up Connections and right-click the connection you want to configure.

3. From the pop-up menu, select Properties.

4. On the Networking tab, select Internet Protocol (TCP/IP) and click Properties.

5. The Internet Protocol (TCP/IP) Properties dialog box enables you to input an IP address (but not a subnet mask or default gateway) and to specify a preferred and an alternate DNS server. Alternatively, these addresses can be supplied automatically.

6. Click Advanced. In the General tab, you can specify whether or not you want data that can't be sent on the local network to be forwarded to the dial-up network, as shown in Figure 1.9.

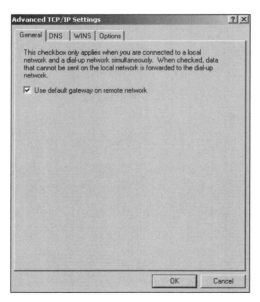

Figure 1.9   Using the default gateway on a remote network.

7. The DNS and WINS tabs are identical to those in the previous procedure (refer to Figures 1.5 and 1.6). Access the Options tab. Only the IPSec settings are available under this tab, because TCP/IP filtering can be set only for a local area connection.

8. Make any configuration changes you require, and exit from all the dialog boxes by clicking OK on each. If prompted to do so, reboot the computer.

Configuring TCP/IP Automatically

Windows 2000 uses either DHCP or APIPA to automate TCP/IP configuration. By default, the computer first tries to contact a DHCP server on the network and dynamically obtain a configuration for each installed network connection. If a DHCP server is reached and a configuration is successfully leased, then the process is complete. Otherwise, the computer uses APIPA to automatically configure TCP/IP. When APIPA is used, an IP address is allocated from the range 169.254.0.1 through 169.254.255.254. This address is used until a DHCP server is located. The subnet mask is set to 255.255.0.0.

APIPA is designed for networks that consist of a single network segment and aren't connected to the Internet. It does not, therefore, specify a default gateway, DNS server, or WINS server.

NOTE: *The Internet Assigned Numbers Authority (IANA) reserves the range of IP addresses used for APIPA (169.254.0.1 through 169.254.255.254). IP addresses within this range aren't used on the Internet.*

To configure TCP/IP for automatic configuration, proceed as follows:

1. Log on as an administrator.

2. Access Start|Settings|Network and Dial-up Connections and right-click the connection you want to configure.

3. From the pop-up menu, select Properties.

4. On the General tab (for a local area connection) or the Networking tab (for all other connections), select Internet Protocol (TCP/IP), and click Properties.

5. Click Obtain an IP address automatically.

6. Click Obtain DNS server address automatically.

7. Click OK.

8. Click OK to close the Connection Properties dialog box.

TIP: *You can display the network connection status on the taskbar by selecting a connection, right-clicking it, clicking Properties, and checking the Show icon in taskbar when connected checkbox.*

Displaying the TCP/IP Configuration

You can display a computer's local area TCP/IP configuration, in addition to NIC details and MAC address, by using the ipconfig tool. The procedure is as follows:

1. Access Start|Programs|Accessories and select Command Prompt.

2. Enter **ipconfig /all**, as shown in Figure 1.10.

TIP: *If you're obtaining your TCP/IP configuration automatically, then* ipconfig /release *releases your current configuration and* ipconfig /renew *obtains a new one. You would carry out these procedures if, for example, the address scope were changed on the DHCP server or if DHCP were introduced in a network that formerly used APIPA.*

```
Command Prompt                                                        _ |□| ×|
Microsoft Windows 2000 [Version 5.00.2183]
(C) Copyright 1985-1999 Microsoft Corp.

E:\>ipconfig /all

Windows 2000 IP Configuration

        Host Name . . . . . . . . . . . : W2000S
        Primary DNS Suffix  . . . . . . : coriolis.com
        Node Type . . . . . . . . . . . : Hybrid
        IP Routing Enabled. . . . . . . : Yes
        WINS Proxy Enabled. . . . . . . : No
        DNS Suffix Search List. . . . . : coriolis.com

Ethernet adapter Local Area Connection:

        Connection-specific DNS Suffix  . :
        Description . . . . . . . . . . : Intel(R) PRO/100B PCI Adapter (TX)
        Physical Address. . . . . . . . : 00-A0-C9-D6-B6-8F
        DHCP Enabled. . . . . . . . . . : No
        IP Address. . . . . . . . . . . : 195.162.230.20
        Subnet Mask . . . . . . . . . . : 255.255.255.0
        IP Address. . . . . . . . . . . : 195.162.230.1
        Subnet Mask . . . . . . . . . . : 255.255.255.0
        Default Gateway . . . . . . . . : 195.162.230.254
        DNS Servers . . . . . . . . . . : 195.168.230.200
                                          195.168.231.200
        Primary WINS Server . . . . . . : 195.162.230.100
        Secondary WINS Server . . . . . : 195.162.231.100

E:\>
```

Figure 1.10   Displaying the TCP/IP configuration.

Installing TCP/IP Services

TCP/IP services are installed using the Windows Components Wizard. This procedure installs DHCP and WINS. Note that a server running either service should be configured with a static IP address.

TIP: *Some services require the computer to be rebooted after they are installed and you exit from the Wizard. If, therefore, you are installing several services, install them all at the same time and then configure them. This avoids multiple reboots.*

To install DHCP and WINS, proceed as follows:

1. Log on as an administrator.

2. Start the Windows Components Wizard. This can be done in two ways:

   • Access Start|Settings|Control Panel and double-click the Add/Remove Programs icon. Click Add/Remove Windows Components.

   • Insert the Windows 2000 Server CD-ROM. On the splash screen, click Install Add-On Components.

3. In the Components box of the Windows Components Wizard, select Networking Services. Click Details.

4. Check Dynamic Host Configuration Protocol (DHCP).

5. Check Windows Internet Name Service (WINS).

6. Click OK. Click Next.

7. If you're installing from a network share, type the full path to the Windows 2000 distribution files when prompted, and click Continue. (If the Windows 2000 Server CD-ROM is inserted in your machine, installation will proceed automatically.)

8. Click Finish.

WARNING!   You're not prompted to reboot the computer after installing WINS or DHCP, and both services appear to be running and ready for configuration directly after installation. However, the Microsoft online documentation for both services states that the server software "can be used after restarting the system". I haven't encountered any problems through not rebooting at this point, but you may consider it safer to do so.

Configuring a DHCP Scope

There are a large number of DHCP options that can be set, and DHCP is discussed in detail in Chapter 13. This procedure introduces you to the DHCP configuration tool and sets up a simple DHCP scope for use in a small LAN intranet.

To configure a DHCP scope, proceed as follows:

1. Log on to the DHCP server as an administrator.

2. Access Start|Programs|Administative Tools and select DHCP.

3. If the server is unauthorized (indicated by a red down-arrow), then right-click the server icon and select Authorize. The authorization process can take some time. Check the authorization status by pressing F5. A green up-arrow indicates that the process is complete.

4. Click the server icon. In the Action pull-down menu, select New Scope.

5. The New Scope Wizard appears. Click Next.

6. Type a name and description for the new scope. Figure 1.11 shows my choice for this exercise, but you may want to use something more relevant to your organization.

7. Set up the scope range and enter the subnet mask, as shown in Figure 1.12. The subnet mask can be set up either by specifying the number of network bits in the Length box or by typing in the dotted decimal value. Note that altering the Length box automatically alters the number in the Subnet mask box, but if you type a number into the Subnet mask box it won't alter the value in the Length box unless you click on that box.

8. Click Next. If you want to, you can exclude one or more addresses within the DHCP scope from being leased, as shown in Figure 1.13.

9. Click Next. Set the lease duration. A DHCP client will attempt to renew its lease halfway through the lease period, seven-eighths of the way through the lease period, and each time it reboots. The default of eight days is a suitable value for most purposes.

10. Click Next. If you want to, you can set up a scope now and apply the values later. Usually, however, the default of configuring the options now is chosen.

11. Click Next. You can now specify routers that are used by the DHCP clients. However, because the purpose of this exercise is to set up a simple scope for a small, nonrouted LAN intranet, no entries should be made on this page.

12. Click Next. DHCP clients can be supplied automatically with the IP addresses of one or more DNS servers and with a parent domain name. This information is entered into the DHCP server, as shown in Figure 1.14.

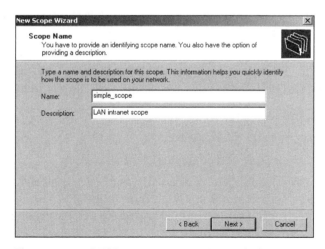

Figure 1.11   DHCP scope name and description.

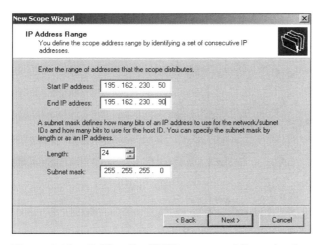

Figure 1.12   Setting the DHCP scope and the subnet mask.

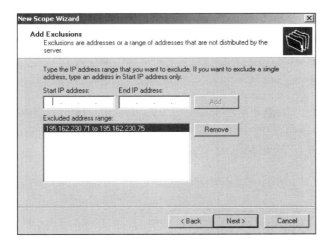

Figure 1.13   Excluding addresses within the DHCP scope.

TIP: *If a DNS server has already been configured, then clicking Resolve will automatically generate the IP number information for the dialog box shown in Figure 1.14.*

13. Click Next. One or more WINS servers may be specified.

14. Click Next. You can choose whether to activate the scope now or later.

15. Click Next. Click Finish. A red down-arrow indicates an inactive scope. If the scope node has no arrow displayed, then the scope is activated.

16. Close the DHCP console.

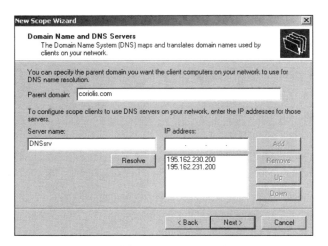

Figure 1.14   Specifying DNS server information.

Viewing and Administering the WINS Database

WINS uses a dynamic database and typically requires very little configuration. Unlike a DHCP server, a newly installed WINS server is started by default. You can start, stop, pause, and resume the WINS service by selecting the WINS server icon and accessing the Action pull-down menu. You can also pause, start, or stop the service from a command prompt using the following commands:

- **net start wins**
- **net stop wins**
- **net pause wins**

The WINS database can be viewed using the following procedure:

1. Log on to the WINS server as an administrator.
2. Access Start|Programs|Administration Tools and select WINS.
3. Expand the WINS server icon and select Active Registrations.
4. In the Action pull-down menu, select Find by Owner.
5. In the Find by Owner dialog box, specify All Owners and click Find Now. You should obtain a list similar to that shown in Figure 1.15.
6. On the Action pull-down menu, select Find by Name.
7. In the Find by Name dialog box, enter the name of the computer you wish to find. You need only enter sufficient characters to uniquely identify the computer. You should obtain a list similar to that shown in Figure 1.16.
8. Close the WINS console.

Record Name	Type	IP Address	State	Owner	Vers...	Expiration
--__MSB...	[01h] Other	195.162.230.50	Active	195.162.230.1	1	2/7/2000
CORIOLIS	[1Bh] Domain Ma...	195.162.230.1	Active	195.162.230.1	9	2/7/2000
ADMIN	[03h] Messenger	195.162.230.1	Active	195.162.230.1	6	2/7/2000
ADMINIS...	[03h] Messenger	195.162.230.50	Active	195.162.230.1	E	2/7/2000
CORIOLIS	[00h] Workgroup	195.162.230.1	Active	195.162.230.1	B	2/7/2000
CORIOLIS	[1Ch] Domain Co...	195.162.230.1	Active	195.162.230.1	A	2/7/2000
CORIOLIS	[1Eh] Normal Gro...	195.162.230.1	Active	195.162.230.1	8	2/3/2000
INet~Ser...	[1Ch] Domain Co...	195.162.230.1	Active	195.162.230.1	7	2/7/2000
IS~W20...	[00h] WorkStation	195.162.230.1	Active	195.162.230.1	5	2/7/2000
SERVER10	[20h] File Server	195.162.230.2	Active	195.162.230.1	C	2/7/2000
W2000S	[00h] WorkStation	195.162.230.1	Active	195.162.230.1	4	2/7/2000
W2000S	[03h] Messenger	195.162.230.1	Active	195.162.230.1	2	2/7/2000

Figure 1.15   The WINS database.

Active Registrations   Items found by name: 3

Record Name	Type	IP Address	State	Owner	Version	Expiration
W2000S	[00h] WorkStation	195.162.230.1	Active	195.162.230.1	4	2/3/2000
W2000S	[03h] Messenger	195.162.230.1	Active	195.162.230.1	2	2/3/2000
W2000S	[20h] File Server	195.162.230.1	Active	195.162.230.1	3	2/3/2000

Figure 1.16   The WINS database filtered by computer name.

Configuring and Administering DNS

DNS is required for Active Directory and is installed by default on a Windows 2000 Domain Controller (DC). The next procedure adds an address (A) record to the DNS database. The various types of DNS records are discussed in Chapter 14.

To add a record to the DNS database:

1. Log on to the DNS server (normally a DC) as an administrator.

2. Access Start|Programs|Administrative Tools and select DNS.

3. Expand *server-name*. Expand Forward Lookup Zones.

4. Select the primary zone (usually identified by domain name; for example, coriolis.com).

5. On the Action pull-down menu, select New Host.

6. Supply a computer name and IP address. If you check the Create associated pointer (PTR) record box, then you also create a reverse lookup record. This means that DNS can resolve the IP address to the computer name as well as vice versa. Figure 1.17 shows a new host being specified.

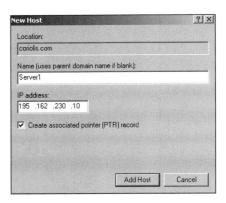

Figure 1.17   Specifying a new host.

7. Click Add Host. Click OK.

8. If required, you can add more records in the same way. Click Done when all the host records have been added.

9. Exit from the DNS console.

Enabling DNS to Use WINS Resolution

The limitations of the static DNS database can be addressed either by enabling DNS for WINS resolution or by enabling dynamic updates. The following procedure describes the first of these methods:

1. Log on to the DNS server as an administrator.

2. Access Start|Programs|Administrative Tools and select DNS.

3. Expand *server-name*. Expand Forward Lookup Zones.

4. Select the primary zone (usually identified by domain name; for example, coriolis.com).

5. On the Action pull-down menu, select Properties.

6. Select the WINS tab.

7. Check the Use WINS forward lookup checkbox.

8. Add the IP address of the WINS server you want to use for WINS forward lookup. If your network uses primary and secondary WINS servers, enter the primary first.

9. If you are replicating with DNS servers that don't recognize WINS (for example, Unix servers), check the Do not replicate this record checkbox. Figure 1.18 shows WINS forward lookup being enabled.

10. Clicking Advanced enables you to alter the cache and lookup time-out values. These are discussed in Chapter 15. Don't alter them at this point. Click Cancel to close the Advanced dialog box.

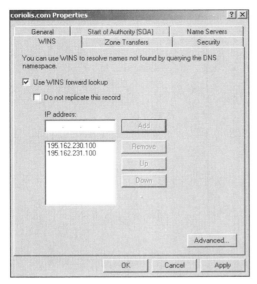

Figure 1.18   Enabling WINS forward lookup.

11. Click OK to close the Properties dialog box.

12. Close the WINS console.

Configuring DNS to Allow Dynamic Updates

As an alternative to using WINS resolution, Windows 2000 enables DNS to be set up to allow dynamic updates. This feature can be implemented only for a primary zone or for a zone that's Active Directory-integrated.

DNS is configured to allow dynamic updates as follows:

1. Log on to the DNS server as an administrator.

2. Access Start|Programs|Administrative Tools and select DNS.

3. Expand *server-name.* Expand Forward Lookup Zones.

4. Select the zone you want to configure.

5. On the Action pull-down menu, select Properties.

6. On the General property tab, verify that the zone type is either Primary or Active Directory-integrated.

7. In the Allow dynamic updates drop-down menu, select Yes. Figure 1.19 shows dynamic updates being enabled.

8. Click OK. Close the DNS console.

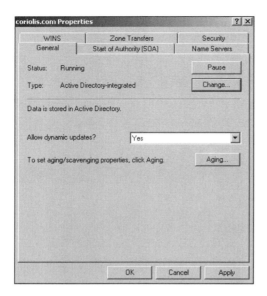

Figure 1.19   Enabling dynamic updates.

Configuring a Dial-in Host

Where a remote host is using the Routing and Remote Access Service (RRAS) to log onto a domain, it can obtain its TCP/IP configuration in the same way as any other host—by DHCP, by APIPA, or manually. However, network administrators will usually allocate a range of IP addresses, known as a *static IP pool*, specifically for such clients. The RRAS server will then allocate an IP address from this pool to the dial-in host. No special configuration is required on the host—it's set up to obtain its TCP/IP parameters automatically in the same way as any other client. However, the RRAS server needs to be set up to allocate IP addresses.

The procedure to specify a static address pool on an RRAS server is as follows:

1. Log on to the RRAS server as an administrator.
2. Access Start|Programs|Administrative Tools and select Routing and Remote Access.
3. Click on the server name. In the Action pull-down menu, select Properties.
4. On the IP tab, select the Static address pool radio button.
5. Click Add.
6. Type in a start address and either an end address or the number of addresses in the range. Click OK.

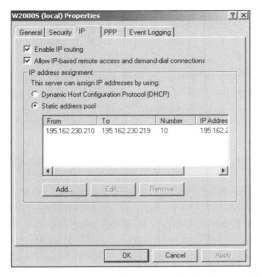

Figure 1.20   Specifying a static address pool.

7. The Properties dialog box should look similar to Figure 1.20. The RRAS
    server will configure a dial-in host with an IP address from the static pool
    and a subnet mask calculated to ensure that all the dial-in hosts and the
    RRAS server are in the same subnet.

8. Click OK. Close the Routing and Remote Access console.

Chapter 2

The Network Driver Interface Specification

In Depth

The Network Driver Interface Specification (NDIS) is a document developed by Microsoft and 3Com. Windows device driver interfaces written to this specification enable a single Network Interface Card (NIC) to bind to multiple network protocols across the *NDIS interface*. A library of device driver interfaces, known as the *NDIS wrapper*, enables any type of NIC for any supported medium to bind to any or all of the networking protocols (TCP/IP, NWLink, or NetBEUI) installed in the machine. The order in which an NIC uses these protocols, called the *binding order*, can be altered, and an NIC can also be allocated more than one IP number.

Prior to NDIS, compatibility issues between various networking implementations made it difficult to accomplish some basic networking functions (for example, implementing two protocols on the same NIC). The traditional solution was to use two drivers, but when one of the drivers took control of the board, it tended to interrupt or corrupt the operation of the other. What was needed was a single driver that could control the adapter and could be shared by the two protocols. In May 1988, the NDIS document was released to address this need.

The NDIS Interface

The NDIS interface includes a protocol manager that accepts requests from the network driver (at the transport layer) and passes these requests to the NIC (at the data-link layer). Thus, multiple NDIS-conforming network drivers can coexist. Also, if a computer is multihomed and contains multiple NICs, the NDIS interface can route traffic to the correct card.

NDIS provides access to the network services at the data-link layer. Software developers who need to employ their own network protocol implementations can program to the specification, and use NDIS-compliant drivers provided by network hardware vendors. This frees the protocol developer from having to write separate programs for every type of network interface card. It also solves compatibility problems on machines that have multiple protocols. All network software components that are compliant with NDIS definitions are drivers. These drivers can be classified into two types:

• Protocol drivers

• Media Access Control (MAC) drivers

Figure 2.1 shows the architectural concept of the NDIS interface and wrapper.

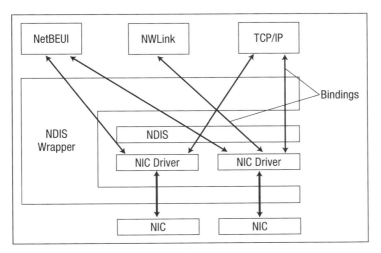

Figure 2.1   NDIS architecture.

NDIS Releases

NDIS releases built on rather than superceded previous specifications; NDIS4 and NDIS4.1 contain all the features of NDIS3.1 plus their own additional features, and NDIS5, in turn, extends NDIS4. To obtain the full specification for NDIS5, we therefore also need to look at NDIS3.1, NDIS4, and NDIS4.1.

NDIS3.1

NDIS3.1 supports basic services that allow a protocol module to send packets over a network device and allow that same module to be notified of incoming packets received by a network device.

NDIS4

NDIS4 adds several new features to NDIS3.1. These are listed below.

Out-of-Band Data Support

In out-of-band signaling, an extra signal is transmitted alongside the information signal to monitor and control the transmission. It uses a separate channel of the Local Area Network (LAN) and allows network management devices to access LAN devices even when the LAN itself is not functioning, thus providing an additional layer of resilience. Out-of-band data support is required for Broadcast PC.

NOTE: *Broadcast PC enables a computer to import and process multimedia streams from a variety of sources, including cable, Direct Broadcast Satellite (DBS), and Digital Video Disk (DVD). Devices that support Broadcast PC should be compliant with Microsoft's PC 99 video and broadcast requirements, available from* **www.microsoft.com**.

Wireless Wide Area Network Media Extension

Wireless media can use infrared or ultrasound transmission. For wide area networks, however, microwave wireless transmission at very high frequency is used as the communication method. It is typically used in satellite communication.

High-Speed Packet Send and Receive

The facility of sending data over high-speed media, such as Asynchronous Transfer Mode (ATM), gives a significant performance increase.

Fast IrDA Media Extension

The Infrared Data Association (IrDA) is a group of device manufacturers that publish a standard for transmitting data via infrared light waves. IrDA wireless transmission could, typically, be implemented between a laptop computer and a printer in the same room, where there is a clear line of sight between them.

Media Sense

Media sense enables the NIC to notify media connect and media disconnect events to the protocol stack. Windows 2000 TCP/IP utilizes these notifications to assist in automatic configuration. In previous Windows implementations, if a computer was moved to another subnet without being rebooted or was taken off the network altogether, the protocol stack received no indication of the event. Thus, the configuration parameters became out of date, or *stale*. Media sense support allows the protocol stack to react to events and invalidate stale parameters. If a computer running Windows 2000 is unplugged from the network, TCP/IP will invalidate the associated parameters after a damping period (currently 20 seconds).

All Local Packet Filter

The All Local Packet Filter prevents Network Monitor from monopolizing the CPU. Network Monitor is discussed in detail in Chapter 3.

NOTE: *NDIS communicates with network hardware by the use of miniport drivers. The hardware accesses the NDIS interface by making a miniport driver function call, and it receives and transmits information by the same method. Details about miniport drivers and function calls are contained in the Windows 2000 Driver Development Kit (DDK), which is discussed later in this chapter.*

NDIS4.1

NDIS4.1 (also known as CoNDIS) accommodates raw access to connection-oriented media. It was released to facilitate the development and testing of ATM miniport drivers.

NDIS5

NDIS5 adds considerable functionality. Becase NDIS5 functionality is the main topic of this chapter, it's discussed in detail in the next section. The new features are therefore listed here for later discussion:

- Power management
- Plug and Play (PnP) support
- Support for Windows Management Instrumentation (WMI)
- Support for a single device information (INF) format
- Deserialized miniport
- Task offload mechanisms
- Broadcast media extension
- Connection-oriented NDIS
- Support for Quality of Service (QoS)
- Intermediate driver support

NDIS5 Functionality

NDIS5 adds a considerable number of new features to NDIS3.1, NDIS4, and NDIS4.1. Microsoft lists the goals for these new features as follows:

- Increasing ease of use and reducing Total Cost of Ownership (TCO)
- Improving performance
- Enabling new media types, services, and applications
- Improving flexibility in the driver architecture

WARNING! Most of the new features in NDIS5 are accessible only by using the miniport driver model and are not supported for full MAC drivers or older miniport drivers.

The NDIS5 interface allows multiple protocol drivers of different types to bind to a single NIC driver and allows a single protocol to bind to multiple NIC drivers. NDIS5-compliant drivers are available for a wide variety of NICs from many vendors. The NDIS5 document describes the multiplexing mechanism used to accomplish this. Bindings can be viewed or changed from the Windows Network Connections user interface, as described in the Immediate Solutions section of this chapter.

Windows 2000 TCP/IP provides support for the following media:

- Ethernet
- 802.3 Subnetwork Access Protocol (SNAP)
- Fiber Distributed Data Interface (FDDI)
- Token Ring (802.5)
- ATM
- ARCNET
- Switched virtual circuit Wide Area Network (WAN) media, such as Integrated Services Digital Network (ISDN), X.25, and dial-up or dedicated asynchronous lines (note that some ATM adapters support LAN emulation and appear to the protocol stack as a media type, such as Ethernet)

NOTE: *LAN emulation provides transparent support for legacy protocols and provides mechanisms for more efficient resolution of specific legacy protocol addresses, such as IP addresses, to their native address formats.*

Power Management

Power management takes a system-wide, integrated approach to the use and conservation of power. Computer systems that include hardware and software support for power management have the following advantages:

- *Minimal startup and shutdown delays*—The system can sleep in a low-power state, from which it can resume operation without a complete reboot.

- *Greater overall power efficiency and battery life*—Power is applied to devices only when they are delivering services to the user. If a device is not in use, it can be powered off and powered up on demand.

- *Quieter operation*—Hardware and software can manage electrical current load and thermal load, resulting in computers that are nearly inaudible when sleeping.

Power management works on two levels, one applying to individual devices and the other to the system as a whole. If all drivers in the system support power management, the power manager (part of the operating system [OS] kernel) can manage power consumption on a system-wide basis, utilizing not only the fully on and fully off states, but also various intermediate system sleep states. Legacy drivers written before the OS supported power management continue to work as they did previously. However, systems that include legacy drivers can't enter any of the intermediate system sleep states, but operate only in the fully on or fully off state.

Device power management applies to individual devices. A driver that supports power management can turn its device on or off as needed. Devices that have the hardware capability can enter intermediate device power state. The presence of legacy drivers in the system doesn't affect the ability of newer drivers to manage power for their devices.

NDIS power management is required for network power management and network wakeup. The NDIS5 implementation is based on the network device class power management reference specification, which defines the behavior of network devices as it relates to power management and, specifically, to the network device class power management reference specification defined for the OnNow architecture initiative. The purpose of this initiative is to eliminate startup and shutdown delays, to reduce power consumption by powering down idle devices, and to allow a computer to "sleep" when idle and "wake up" quickly when requested.

The OnNow specification defines four device power states, shown in Table 2.1.

TIP: *The network device class power management reference specification is available at* **www.microsoft.com/hwdev/onnow/**.

Table 2.1   Device power states, as defined by OnNow.

State	Description
D3 power state	Power may have been fully removed from the device. The device context is saved by hardware when in this state. Any device driver associated with the device must reinitialize or restore the device to full-on operation when exiting from the D3 power state to the D0 power state. In the D3 power state, the total restore time for the device is at its highest because it may be necessary to reinitialize the device completely.
D2 power state	Power consumption is equal to or greater than the D3 state. Power usage is reduced to the minimum level at which device state restoration is still possible. The device context may be preserved or lost, depending on class-specific definitions. The device driver function in this state is also according to class-specific definitions. The time required to restore the device from the D2 state to the D0 state is equal to or greater than resumption time from the D1 state. Actual response times are according to class-specific definitions.
D1 power state	Power consumption is equal to or greater than the D2 state, but less than the D0 state. The device context may be preserved or lost, depending on class-specific definitions. The device drivers' function in this state is according to class-specific definitions. The time required to restore the device from the D1 state to the D0 state is less than resumption from D2 (whenever possible). Minimizing the delay in restoring the device is a higher priority than power consumption in this state. Actual response times are according to class-specific definitions.
D0 power state	This is assumed to be the highest level of power consumption. The device is completely active and responsive. The driver is functioning normally.

2. The Network Driver Interface Specification

NDIS specifies that network adapters can power down when either the user or the system requests a power level change. For example, the system may request a power level change based on keyboard or mouse inactivity, or the user may want to put the computer into sleep mode. Disconnecting the network cable can also initiate a power-down request, provided that the NIC supports this functionality. In this case, because the disconnect could be the result of temporary wiring changes on the network rather than the disconnection of a cable from the network device itself, the system waits a configurable time period before powering down the NIC.

NDIS power management policy is *no network activity*-based. This means that all the relevant network components must agree to the request before the NIC can be powered down. If there are any active sessions or open files over the network, the power-down request can be refused by any or all of the components involved.

The computer can also be awakened from a lower power state. A wakeup signal can be caused by:

- Detection of a change in the network link state (for example, cable reconnect)
- Receipt of a network wakeup frame
- Receipt of a magic packet (see Chapter 1)

When a miniport driver is initialized, NDIS queries the miniport capabilities to determine if it supports magic packet, pattern match, or link change wakeups and, also, to determine the lowest required power state for each wakeup method. The network protocols then query the miniport capabilities. The protocol sets the wakeup policy at runtime, using Object Identifiers (OIDs), such as **Enable Wakeup**, **Set Packet Pattern**, and **Remove Packet Pattern**.

NOTE: *Details about OIDs are available from the Windows 2000 DDK, which is discussed later in this chapter.*

Windows 2000 TCP/IP registers the following packet patterns at miniport initialization:

- Directed IP packet
- ARP broadcast for a station's IP address
- NetBIOS over TCP/IP broadcast for a station's assigned computer name

Power management and Plug and Play (PnP) are the major features of Windows 2000 from the driver writer's point of view. (See the section, "Plug and Play.") Nearly every system component that interfaces to drivers has been modified to interact with the Windows 2000 PnP manager and power manager. The NDIS5 library encapsulates support for PnP and power management for all network drivers that communicate with or through NDIS, including NIC miniports, intermediate NDIS drivers, and NDIS protocols—as do the system-supplied video port drivers for video miniports and display drivers.

If possible, Windows 2000 drivers should support both PnP and power management. Although Windows 2000 continues to support legacy drivers, driver support for PnP and power management increases the potential market for peripheral device(s).

Plug and Play

PnP hardware and PnP software support enable a computer to recognize and adapt to hardware configuration changes with little or no intervention by the user. A user can add devices to and remove devices from a computer without manual reconfiguration and without detailed knowledge of computer hardware. With PnP a user can, for example, dock a portable computer and use the docking station keyboard, mouse, and monitor without a manual configuration change.

Windows 2000 PnP is modeled on Windows 95 PnP support as far as the NDIS implementation is concerned. To the user, it looks like Windows 98 PnP support (which is also based on the Windows 95 model), but this is a function of the PnP library rather than of NDIS. PnP support is transparent to the miniport drivers. When a PnP network interface is identified, a miniport is installed, loaded, and bound. If the network interface is removed, the miniport is unbound, shut down, and unloaded. The main impact that PnP support has on the protocol stack is that network interfaces can come and go at any time.

PnP has the following capabilities and features:

- Dynamic recognition of installed hardware. This includes initial system installation, recognition of any static hardware changes that occur between boots, and response to runtime hardware events, such as dock, undock, and insertion or removal of cards.

- Streamlined hardware configuration, including dynamic hardware activation, resource arbitration, device driver loading, and drive mounting.

- Support for streamlined hardware configuration and for particular buses and other hardware standards that facilitate automatic and dynamic recognition of hardware. Supported standards include PnP Industry Standard Architecture (ISA), Peripheral Component Interconnect (PCI) bus architecture, the Personal Computer Memory Card International Association (PCMCIA) standard, PC Card/CardBus, Universal Serial Bus (USB), and IEEE 1394 (the Institute of Electrical and Electronic Engineers Firewire standard).

- A PnP infrastructure to facilitate the design of new device drivers. This includes INF interfaces, Application Programming Interfaces (APIs), kernel-mode notifications, and executive interfaces.

- Mechanisms that allow user applications to discover changes in the hardware environment so that they can take appropriate action.

Figure 2.2 shows the software components that support PnP.

TIP: *If you currently write device drivers or plan to do so, you should be aware that only* **DriverEntry()** *should be "init." All other miniport initialization code should be "page", because it might be used after system initialization. Use the standard registry keywords defined in the Windows 2000 DDK.*

The PnP Manager

The PnP manager is divided into two parts: the kernel-mode PnP manager and the user-mode PnP manager. The kernel-mode PnP manager interacts with the OS to configure, manage, and maintain devices. The user-mode PnP manager interacts with user-mode setup components to configure and install devices. The user-mode PnP manager also registers applications for notification of device changes and notifies an application when a device event occurs.

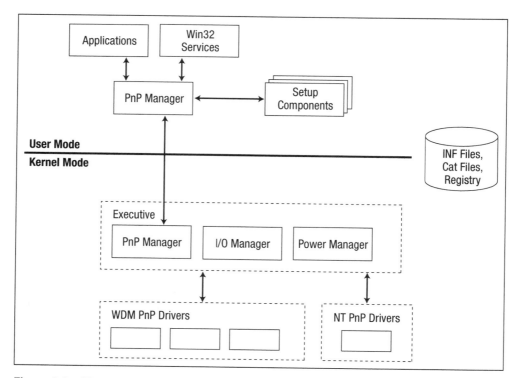

Figure 2.2   Plug and Play components.

PnP drivers support physical, logical, and virtual devices on a machine. A Windows Driver Model (WDM) driver supports devices on both Windows 2000 and Windows 98 systems. WDM PnP drivers communicate with the PnP Manager and other kernel components through APIs and Input/Output Request Packets (IRPs). The Windows 2000 DDK gives a complete description of those APIs and IRPs. Note that a Windows 2000 machine might have some PnP drivers that don't support WDM.

TIP: *If you're designing or installing drivers, ensure that they support PnP and power management. If a driver doesn't support PnP and power management, it constrains the PnP and power management support of the system as a whole.*

Support for PnP

Devices that don't have PnP hardware support can still have some PnP functionality if PnP drivers support them. For example, an Industry Standard Architecture (ISA) sound card can be manually installed and then treated as a PnP device by the appropriate PnP driver. On the other hand, if the driver doesn't support PnP, the hardware will have no PnP functionality, whether it's PnP-enabled or not.

Legacy drivers written before the OS supported PnP will continue to work as they did before, with no PnP capability. If you purchase PnP-enabled hardware devices, they should come with PnP drivers. All new drivers should support PnP.

Windows Management Instrumentation

Windows Management Instrumentation (WMI) provides control of NDIS miniports and their associated adapters that is compatible with Web-Based Enterprise Management (WBEM).This enables applications to perform the following functions:

- Enumerate device classes, devices per class, and properties per device.

- Query and set properties per device.

- Register for event notification on applicable properties (WMI properties translate to NDIS OIDs).

At initialization, NDIS queries the miniport drivers for device-specific properties. Legacy miniport drivers will fail the query, thus indicating no device-specific properties. NDIS registers these properties with WMI. The properties include the standard properties for all miniport drivers (defined as NDIS DDK mandatory OIDs), and any device-specific properties provided by the miniport driver.

WMI is a kernel-mode service used by drivers to make measurement and instrumentation data available to user-mode applications. A driver can use WMI mechanisms to publish information, permit configuration of its device, and supply notifications and logging of events. A driver that supports WMI has the following advantages:

- *It can make driver-defined data and events accessible to user-mode applications.* Any application that's a WMI client can access this data. On initialization, the driver registers its Globally Unique Identifiers (GUIDs) with WMI, which then adds the driver's data blocks to the Common Information Model Object Manager (CIMOM) database, making the driver's blocks accessible to WMI client applications. When a WMI client accesses a given data block, the WMI kernel component sends a query request to the driver for its data. The format of the driver-defined data is transparent to WMI, which simply passes the data to the user-mode client.

- *It can define read/write items that WMI clients can set.* When a WMI client user sets the value of a read/write item, the WMI kernel component sends a set request that has the new value to the driver. This enables user-mode applications to configure a device through a standard interface, rather than through a custom control-panel application.

- *It can notify user-mode applications of driver-defined events without requiring the application to poll or to send IRPs.* Within the driver, certain blocks are defined as *event blocks*. These define the events that the driver can send. When a WMI client user requests notification of an event, the WMI kernel component sends an enable-event request to the driver. After an event is enabled, the driver sends the event block to WMI whenever the event occurs, until WMI sends a disable-event request. WMI routes the event block to all users that have requested notification of the event.

- *It reduces driver overhead by collecting and sending only requested data to a single destination.* After a driver registers its data and event blocks, it needs to provide data and events only when users request them. The driver can stop accumulating data after WMI sends a disable-collection request and can stop sending the event after WMI sends a disable-event request.

- *It documents data and event blocks implicitly, with descriptive class names and optional descriptions.* WMI clients can access the driver-defined class names and optional descriptions of all data and event blocks and can display them to users, making data and event blocks self-documenting.

The Windows 2000 DDK gives details of how to build and test drivers that support WMI. Downloading and using the DDK is discussed in the Immediate Solutions section of this chapter.

Support for Single INF Format

An INF file is a text file that contains all the necessary information about the devices and files to be installed—for example, driver images, registry information, and version information. All NDIS5 drivers must have an INF file to be used by the setup components. NDIS5 INF files don't contain installation scripts. The installation procedures are part of a Win32 installer application, such as the New Device wizard and the Add/Remove Hardware wizard, with each INF file acting as a resource.

The NDIS5 common INF format is based on the Windows 95 format, with extensions. Because Windows 2000 uses drivers and Windows 95 uses Virtual Device Drivers (VxDs), the format has been extended in a nonintrusive manner to allow the INF to install a service on Windows 2000. NDIS5 supports a single INF format. To understand what this involves, it's necessary to look at the differences between Windows 95 and Windows NT4 INFs.

Windows NT4 network INFs are interpreted. This enables an INF language with sophisticated constructs—such as definable variables and IF and GOTO commands. The interpreter for the INF files is the class installer. Windows NT4 INFs are flexible but complex and can be difficult to support and debug. Also, they have complex binding definitions. They can, however, be extended by calling Dynamic Link Library files (DLLs).

Windows 95 INFs are declarative. They define and list information that the system-level class installer will use. This makes them simpler but less flexible than interpreted INFs. They are easier to support and debug and have simple binding definitions.

In Windows NT4, the network components don't use the Windows 95 INF format. As a result, Windows NT4 network INFs are different from other INFs, and it's impossible to have compatible INFs between the two OSs. For this reason, network driver developers need to write separate INFs for Windows 95 and Windows NT4.

NDIS5 provides enhanced extensibility for INFs using COM interfaces to DLLs and uses the same binding definitions as Windows 95. Thus, NDIS5 INFs should be backward compatible with both Windows 95 and NT4, assuming that these operating systems support the appropriate device. New Windows 2000 (and Windows 98) format INF files must be written to accommodate all network drivers, including NDIS drivers, transport drivers, network file/print providers, and other peripherals.

Existing network INF files created for Windows 95 or Windows NT4 (or earlier) won't work under Windows 2000. This is also the case where a card, protocol, or service is already installed and running under Windows NT4 or Windows 9x, and then the OS is upgraded to Windows 2000. If the card, protocol, or service doesn't have a new-style INF file written for Windows 2000, it will stop working after the upgrade.

NOTE: *Details of the structure of INFs, as well as sample code, can be found in the Windows 2000 DDK.*

Deserialized Miniport

A deserialized miniport provides a significant performance gain over a standard miniport, which can't execute any functions simultaneously, and over the Windows NT4 full-duplex miniport, which can execute only simultaneous send and receive (and imposes restrictions on even this limited functionality). If an NIC can run in deserialized mode in a Symmetrical Multiprocessor (SMP) computer, then communications can be deserialized between NDIS5 and the NIC's miniport driver, resulting in the simultaneous execution of any type of functions.

At initialization time, the miniport driver indicates that it supports deserialized operations. NDIS5 then offloads the synchronization and queue management to the miniport driver.

NOTE: *Full-duplex is still supported for NICs that don't support deserialized communication. Full-duplex allows a miniport driver to send and receive information simultaneously to both the OS and the MAC layer on an SMP computer.*

Task Offload Mechanisms

Provided the NIC supports this functionality, considerable performance gains can result from offloading processor-intensive operations to hardware. By using query OIDs, a protocol can request the miniport's *task offload capabilities mask*. NDIS5 sets this mask and predefines the tasks that can be offloaded. The protocol then specifies the tasks it wants to offload to the miniport. Additional task-specific OIDs may be required for task parameter negotiation. At runtime, the protocol delegates task processing to the miniport driver and to the network card. NDIS5 supports the task offload mechanisms described here.

TCP/IP Checksum Calculation

TCP/IP queries the miniport capabilities and specifies the checksum calculations to be offloaded. These include Add (Send) and Verify (Receive) for TCP, UDP, and IP checksums. When sending, TCP/IP passes packets to the miniport with a flag bit set to request the checksum calculation. In the verify operation, the miniport passes the packet with a flag bit set if the checksum failed.

Fast Packet Forwarding

Fast packet forwarding (or fast forward path) occurs when either multiport or single-port network adapters, such as 802.3, FastEthernet, or FDDI, are used with Windows 2000 routing code to forward packets from one port to another on the same or a similar card without passing the packet to the host processor.

On initialization, the routing protocol queries the miniport's capability and requests fast packet forwarding. At runtime, the network adapters monitor and record which ports are used for which routes. If the route is known on packet receipt, the network card forwards the packet directly to the other port. If the route changes, the routing protocol instructs the miniport (using an OID) to flush known routes.

Internet Protocol Security Encryption

When IPSec is used to encrypt data, network performance drops because of the encryption processing overhead. IPSec queries the miniport to determine whether the appropriate encryption hardware is implemented on the NIC. IPSec then requests this function, and IPSec encryption is implemented by the NIC rather than by the host processor.

Broadcast Media Extension

NDIS5 includes an extension that supports high-speed unidirectional broadcast media, such as Direct TV, PrimeStar, or Intercast. The extension includes new OIDs and definitions for the following:

- Receiver tuning
- Multiple media stream negotiation and fast (zero copy) data streaming to user mode
- Support for UDP/IP multicast packets via a Microsoft-provided Local Area Multicomputer (LAM) emulation driver that implements a full implementation of the Message-Passing Interface (MPI)

The broadcast media extension also accommodates broadcast services for Windows (Broadcast PC).

Connection-Oriented NDIS

NDIS4 supported network interface card driver development and deployment of connectionless network media, such as Ethernet, Token Ring, ArcNet, and FDDI. NDIS5 extends this interface to provide efficient support for connection-oriented media, such as ATM—including ATM/ADSL (Asymmetric Digital Subscriber Line) and ATM/cable modem—ISDN, and data-transfer media that support QoS. The new architecture also enables support for streaming of multimedia data.

NDIS5 defines interfaces between connection-oriented client protocol drivers, usually at the bottom of a transport stack, and standalone call-management protocols, such as the system-supplied call manager for ATM networks. It also defines the interfaces between all standalone connection-oriented call managers and the underlying miniports that control connection-oriented NICs. The following sets of standard driver functions are defined:

- Functions common to both connection-oriented clients and standalone call managers
- Functions specific to connection-oriented clients
- Functions specific to connection-oriented call managers
- Functions specific to connection-oriented NIC drivers

TIP: *For detailed information about connection-oriented driver functions, search for ProtocolCoXxx, ProtoclClXxx, ProtocolCmXxx, and MiniportCoXxx in the Windows 2000 DDK documentation.*

NDIS5 provides sets of functions that enable connection-oriented NDIS drivers to communicate with each other. It also provides support for integrated Miniport Call Managers (MCMs) that control NICs with on-board connection-oriented pro-tocol-signaling capabilities. A miniport that controls such an NIC provides sup-port to NDIS5 client protocols, both as a connection-oriented NDIS miniport and as a connection-oriented call manager.

Support for QoS

Typically, when a network segment becomes congested, the hub-and-switch workload results in the delay (latency) of packets, or in packet loss. If QoS is supported, however, a packet that has a higher priority receives preferential treat-ment and is serviced before a packet that has a lower priority. For example, 802.1p packet priority is implemented by an extension to the standard MAC header in network packets. This extension includes a 3-bit value that hubs and switches use to establish packet priority in shared-media 802 networks. Operating system components that are QoS-aware provide 802.1p priority information to miniport drivers. The NDIS packet structure that describes each transferred packet is used to send priority information. QoS-aware components derive this priority informa-tion by mapping service types to 802.1p priority values.

Unless a host computer has negotiated QoS with the network, it will mark trans-mitted packets with a "best effort" 802.1p priority value. If the host computer has a packet scheduler installed, however, it uses the appropriate QoS-signaling com-ponents to negotiate with the network for higher 802.1p priority values. The packet scheduler then passes the appropriate priority values in NDIS packets to the miniport driver.

The originator of a call on a Switched Virtual Connection (SVC) can specify QoS parameters for the call. Depending on the signaling protocol being used, a call manager, or MCM, that sets up an outgoing or incoming call, can negotiate the QoS with a network entity, such as a network switch or a remote client. A connec-tion-oriented client can request a change of QoS on an active Virtual Connection

(VC) for an outgoing or an incoming call—assuming that the signaling protocol supports this functionality. A remote client can also make such a request. In this case, a call manager, or MCM driver, indicates the remote client's incoming request to change the QoS.

Virtual Connections

The concept of virtual connections is important in understanding QoS negotiation. On a local system, a VC is an endpoint (or association) between a client, call manager, or MCM and a miniport that can host a single call. On a network, a VC refers to a connection between two communicating endpoints, such as two connection-oriented clients. Several VCs can be active on an NIC at the same time, allowing the NIC to service calls simultaneously. Each connection can be to different endpoints on different computers.

VCs on a network vary in the type of service that they provide to clients. For example, a VC can provide unidirectional or bidirectional service. QoS parameters for each direction can guarantee specific performance thresholds, such as bandwidth and latency.

A VC on a network can be an SVC or a Permanent VC (PVC). An SVC is created as needed for a particular call. A PVC is created manually and will eventually be deleted by an operator using a configuration utility. The QoS for a PVC is configured by the operator and isn't negotiable over the network.

In NDIS5, a VC consists of resources allocated by a miniport to maintain state information about a connection on a network. These resources include memory buffers, events, and data structures. The miniport is requested to create a context for a VC by a connection-oriented client for an outgoing call or by a call manager for an incoming call.

Before a created VC can be used for data transmission, it must be activated by a call manager, or MCM. To activate a VC, a miniport or MCM sets up resources for the VC and communicates with its NIC as necessary to prepare the NIC to receive or transmit data on the VC. When terminating (or *tearing down*) a call, the call manager or MCM deactivates the VC used for the call. After a call is torn down, the creator of the VC can either initiate the deletion of the VC or use the VC for another call.

Intermediate Driver Support

NDIS5 provides intermediate driver support. Intermediate drivers are required for Broadcast PC, virtual LANs, LAN emulation over ATM, and satellite broadcast television.

A class driver is an intermediate driver that provides a simplified interface between the OS and a hardware-specific driver. NDIS5 includes a class driver for kernel streaming, stream.sys, that separates the driver writer from most of the complexities of writing a full cross-platform WDM driver.

Most classes of device, such as video capture devices and external sound devices, are supported by a streaming class driver. The exception is internal sound cards, for which Microsoft provides a separate architecture.

Windows 2000 class and filter drivers for peripheral storage devices provide an interface between intermediate or high-level drivers and system-supplied port drivers. Input/output (I/O) requests from a user application, or kernel component, reach storage class drivers through Windows 2000 I/O system services and one or more intermediate or high-level drivers, such as a file system driver. Storage class drivers translate standard IRPs into IRPs that have system-defined Small Computer System Interface (SCSI) Request Blocks (SRBs) containing SCSI-2 Command Descriptor Blocks (CDBs), before passing each IRP on to a lower-level driver. A storage port driver translates SRBs from class drivers into bus-specific commands, which it then sends to the I/O bus driver, possibly via one or more filter drivers.

Additional NDIS5 Features

Although this section covers the significant features of NDIS5, it's not possible (or desirable) to cover every single feature here. Additional features include support for IEEE 1394, support for protocol rebind when the network interface card media type changes, and mechanisms to provide direct media access for kernel mode streaming. A full description of all NDIS5 features is included in the Windows 2000 DDK documentation, together with details of how to implement these features in driver routines.

Data-Link Layer Functionality

NDIS drivers work at the level of the Open Systems Interconnection (OSI) data-link layer. It's the responsibility of this layer to send frames from the network layer to the physical layer. The data-link layer also receives raw data from the physical layer and packages it into data frames. Figure 2.3 shows a simple data frame. Destination and source identify the receiving and sending computers (or, more accurately, NICs), usually by MAC address. The control data is used for frame type, routing, and segmentation information. The Cyclic Redundancy Check (CRC) is used for data verification and error correction. The data-link layer is responsible for providing the error-free transfer of frames across the physical layer. When the network layer receives data from the data-link layer, it will assume that this data is error-free.

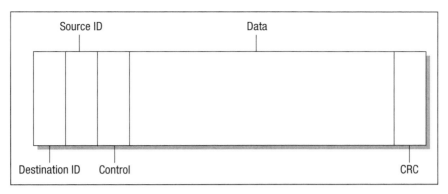

Figure 2.3   A simple data frame.

Data-link layer functionality is implemented by NIC hardware, by the card driver, and by the low-level protocol stack driver. The NIC hardware/driver combination filters are based on the destination MAC address of each frame. Normally, the hardware filters out all incoming frames, except those that contain one of the following destination addresses:

• The MAC address of the host's NIC

• The all-ones broadcast address (FF-FF-FF-FF-FF-FF)

• Multicast addresses in which a protocol driver on the host has registered interest

Because the first filtering decision is made by the hardware, the NIC discards any frames that don't meet the filter criteria—without requiring any CPU processing. All frames (including broadcasts) that pass the hardware filter are passed up to the NIC driver through a hardware interrupt. The NIC driver brings the frame into system memory from the interface card. Then the frame is *indicated* (passed up) to the appropriate bound transport drivers. Frames are passed up to all bound transport drivers in the order in which they are bound. Any frames that pass through the initial hardware filter require CPU processing.

TIP: *The full (or Systems Management Server) version of Network Monitor, as well as Network Monitor Agent, put NICs into **promiscuous mode** by default. This inhibits the initial hardware filtering so that every frame the host detects on the network is indicated. In this way, Network Monitor can capture all the traffic on a subnet, but at considerable cost in CPU processing time. NDIS provides the All Local Packet Filter to ensure that Network Monitor doesn't gain exclusive use of the CPU.*

As a packet traverses a network or series of networks, the source MAC address is always that of the NIC that placed it on the network media, and the destination MAC address is that of the NIC that will pull it off the media. In a routed network, therefore, the source and destination MAC addresses change with each hop through a router.

The Maximum Transmission Unit (MTU)

Each media type has a maximum frame size, or MTU, that must not be exceeded. The data-link layer is responsible for discovering this MTU and reporting it to the protocols. The protocol stack can query NDIS drivers to obtain the local MTU. Upper layer protocols, such as TCP, use MTU information to optimize packet sizes automatically for each media. TCP Path Maximum Transmission Unit (PMTU) discovery is discussed in Chapter 8.

If an NIC driver uses LAN emulation mode, it may report a higher MTU than expected for the media type that's emulated. For example, an ATM driver may emulate Ethernet, but report an ATM MTU of 9,180 bytes. Windows 2000 accepts and uses the MTU size reported by the adapter, even when it's larger than expected for the media type reported.

Sometimes the MTU reported to the protocol stack is less than what would be expected for a given media type. For instance, use of the 802.1p standard reduces the reported MTU size by 4 bytes because of size increases in the data-link layer headers.

Immediate Solutions

Installing Network Protocols

The Windows 2000 default installation installs TCP/IP as the local area connection protocol. If you want to use other protocols and to optimize the binding order, you must first install those protocols.

To install additional network protocols:

1. Log on as an administrator.
2. Access Start|Settings|Network and Dial-up Connections, right-click Local Area Connection, and select Properties.
3. Click Install.
4. Select Protocol and click Add.
5. Select the protocol you want to install. If you're installing from the Windows 2000 CD-ROM, you can click OK. If you're installing from a network share or other source (such as a floppy disk), click Browse, specify the path to the installation files, and click OK.
6. Depending on the protocol you've installed, you may be prompted to reboot the computer. If you want to install additional protocols, click No at this stage and repeat the procedure. After you've installed all the protocols you need, reboot the machine.

WARNING! A newly installed protocol will be placed at the top of the bindings list for both NICs and services. This is not usually what is wanted—so always check and reconfigure your binding order after installing a network protocol.

Configuring Bindings

Bindings between protocols and NICs (and also between protocols and services) can be enabled or disabled, and the binding order can be changed. If, for example, most of the traffic on your subnet is local, with very few packets being sent to the router for onward transmission, you may want NetBEUI to be used as a first-choice protocol, rather than TCP/IP. If most of the clients on your subnet are Netware hosts running the Internetwork Packet Exchange/Sequenced Packet Exchange (IPX/SPX) protocol, then you may want to move NWLink up the binding order on your servers.

WARNING!   Changing the binding order can improve performance dramatically. Selecting the incorrect binding order can, therefore, cause an equally dramatic performance drop. Take care when reconfiguring TCP/IP bindings; always carry out a traffic analysis, using Network Monitor, first.

To configure TCP/IP bindings, proceed as follows:

1. Log on as an administrator.

2. Access Start|Settings, right-click Network and Dial-up Connections, and select Open.

3. Select the connection you want to configure.

4. On the Advanced pull-down menu, select Advanced Settings.

5. Select a protocol bound to an adapter or service and use the up or down arrow to change its binding order. Un-checking the checkbox to the left of the protocol will disable the binding. Figure 2.4 shows the Advanced Settings dialog box.

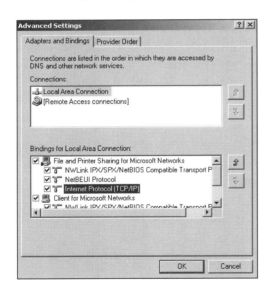

Figure 2.4   Configuring bindings.

Configuring Power Saving

The power saving properties for a particular device can be configured in the device driver. However, for general system devices such as the monitor, hard disk, and so on, user configuration is possible through the control panel.

To configure power saving from the control panel, proceed as follows:

1. Access Start|Settings and select Control Panel.

2. Open the Power Options Properties dialog box.

3. A list of the power schemes available can be accessed in the Power schemes drop-down list, shown in Figure 2.5. The Always On selection is used mainly for servers, although some organizations use it for all PCs. Select Always On and note the default settings.

4. Access the Turn off hard disks drop-down list, shown in Figure 2.6. If you're configuring a server, you'll probably keep this setting at Never, because access times could otherwise become unacceptable.

5. Similar options are available in the Turn off monitor drop-down list. If you're configuring a server, you'll probably want to turn off the monitor (assuming one is connected).

6. Select the Advanced tab. Checking the checkbox will display the Power Management icon on the taskbar. This is useful if you change the power settings frequently.

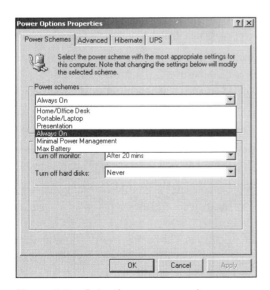

Figure 2.5   Selecting a power scheme.

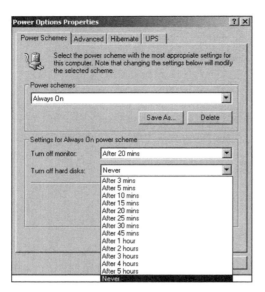

Figure 2.6   The Turn off hard disks options.

7. Select the Hibernate tab. Note that enabling hibernation requires a significant amount of free disk space, typically 128MB. Hibernation isn't normally
enabled on a server.

8. Select the UPS (Uninterruptible Power Supply) tab. You can select and/or
configure a UPS from this dialog box.

9. On the Power Schemes tab, select and apply all of the schemes in turn and
note the default settings. The setting options are the same as for Always On.

10. Set up the computer's power management to your requirements. Click Save
as, and specify a name for your power scheme. This name should be
available in the Power scheme drop-down list as soon as you've saved it.

Using the Windows 2000 Driver Development Kit

The amount of user configuration of NDIS5 settings possible through administrative tools and the CP is limited. The remainder of this chapter is therefore of
interest only if you currently write or intend to write miniport drivers. This is not,
nor does it purport to be, a book on C++ coding. There are many excellent publi-
cations on that topic. The remainder of this chapter, therefore, will cover the
installation of the DDK, using predefined macros to build drivers, using the driver
verifier tool, and using debugging tools, such as breakpoints.

The purpose of the procedures in this section is to outline the tools and facilities available in the DDK and discuss the methodology provided to generate driver source code. It is neither practical nor desirable to attempt in-depth treatment of these topics here. Detailed documentation can be downloaded with the DDK, in addition to sample code.

TIP: *Unless you're already an experienced C++ programmer and have driver development experience, the best way to start is with the sample programs supplied with the DDK. Study the way these programs are built, use the driver verifier tool, and implement breakpoints.*

Installing the Driver Development Kit

To develop and debug miniport drivers, you'll need at least two machines: one as the driver-development PC and the second as a driver-testing machine. If you intend to write drivers that support deserialized miniport operation, your driver-testing machine needs to be an SMP PC. It should have the Windows 2000 OS installed and should have at least 128MB RAM. (Although Microsoft claims that you can use a 64MB PC, I really wouldn't recommend it.)

The driver-development PC requires the following:

- Windows 2000.

TIP: *It's possible to develop Windows 2000 drivers on a Windows NT4 or Windows 98 machine and test them on a Windows 2000 system. This is not, however, a wholly satisfactory development strategy. In some circumstances, such as when you're carrying out kernel debugging on a driver that's under development, two Windows 2000 machines are necessary.*

- Microsoft Visual C++ v 5 or later (preferably later). You'll need the Professional or Enterprise edition. The Academic and Standard editions are not supported.

- The latest Visual C++ service pack for the version you're using.

- A CD-ROM drive or Internet access.

- At least 128MB of RAM. Again, Microsoft specifies a 64MB minimum. My development PC has 256MB and sometimes struggles.

- 1GB free hard disk space. You can install the DDK on 200MB, but you'll need 750MB if you intend to compile all the samples. Then, of course, you'll need some space for your own routines.

TIP: *Ensure that all the devices on both PCs are fully compatible with Windows 2000. Check your PC specification against the hardware compatibility list, available at **www.microsoft.com/hcl**.*

You require administrator rights for the installation. You also need a clean PC that doesn't already have a previous version of the DDK installed (if so, uninstall it).

> **WARNING!   Do not install the Windows 2000 DDK over previous Windows 2000 DDKs or over DDKs for other OSs.**

To install the Windows 2000 DDK:

1. If you have the CD-ROM from the Microsoft Developers Network (MSDN&trade), run setup.exe from the CD-ROM. Otherwise, access the Microsoft Driver Development Kit Web site at **www.microsoft.com/ddk** and download and run X86DDK.exe (for x86 systems). The file is 42MB and takes some time to download.

Resources for Developers

MSDN&trade, the Microsoft Developers Network, is accessed at **http://msdn.microsoft.com**. It provides tools and information to assist software development. This information includes downloads for service packs or patches for Microsoft development tools; platform SDK releases; access to user groups, chats, and event information; and the MSDN online library.

The Microsoft Driver Development Kit Web site at **www.microsoft.com/ddk** provides resources for driver development, including the latest version of the Windows 2000 DDK for download, the latest DDK documentation, news about DDK developments, a feedback form, a Frequently Asked Questions (FAQ) page, and extended release notes.

2. Click Next.

3. Read and accept the license conditions.

4. Choose the components you want to install. Unless you're an experienced driver programmer, I recommend that you install all of them.

5. Decide whether you want a free-build or debugging environment. Initially, you will almost certainly require the latter. The environments are as follows:

   - *Free build*—The end-user version of the operating system. The system and drivers are built with full optimization, and debugging is disabled. A free build system and driver is smaller, faster and uses less memory than checked build. Free build is sometimes known as *retail build*.

   - *Checked build*—Used when testing and debugging drivers. Checked build contains error checking, argument verification, and debugging information that's not available in free build. A checked system or driver can help isolate and track down problems that can cause unpredictable behavior, memory leaks, or improper device configuration. Checked build consumes more memory and disk space than free build, and system and driver performance is slower.

6. From Programs|Development Kits|Windows 2000 DDK, select either a free or checked console window.

7. From the console command prompt, run setenv.bat. Note that this will close all Windows programs. Also, the batch file won't run unless Visual C++ is installed.

8. From the console command prompt, enter **build -cZ**. This compiles and links all drivers in the source tree of the current directory. Note that any directory in which you run **build -cZ** must contain a file called *sources*. If this file doesn't exist in the directory, then the directory doesn't contain any driver source files.

TIP: *You can verify your installation by running **build -cZ** from the \destination\src subdirectory. This builds a complete set of installed drivers. The process can take about 30 minutes.*

Building Drivers

The DDK provides a set of macros that are recognized by the build utility. These are split into sources file macros, which specify the components for a build product or products, and dirs file macros, which enable the build utility to create an entire source tree from several sources files in directories that are subdirectories of the dirs file subdirectory. In addition, a set of build environment variables is provided. Sample code is available from the DDK.

The format for macro definitions is:

```
MACRONAME=Value
```

where *Value* is a text string. For example:

```
TARGETNAME=mylibrary
```

To specify the components for a build product:

1. Create a directory tree. Source directories should be subdirectories of a source code tree, the root of which will contain the dirs file.

2. In each source directory, create a file called sources. A text editor can be used to create this file, and the file shouldn't have a file type extension.

3. Place your source code in the sources file. The macros available are shown in Table 2.2.

4. Reference environmental variables as required using the syntax $(*VariableName*). The available environmental variables are shown in Table 2.3.

5. Create a dirs file in the root directory of the source code tree. Like the sources file, this file can be created using a text editor and shouldn't have a file type extension. The macros shown in Table 2.4 can be defined in the dirs file.

6. Run the build utility. If, for example, directory1 and directory2 were specified in the OPTIONAL_DIRS macro, then the command is **build -cZ directory1 directory2**.

Table 2.2   Macros used in the sources file.

Macro	Function
TARGETNAME	Specifies the name of the library being built.
TARGETPATH	Specifies the name of the destination directory for all build products (EXE, DLL, LIB files, and so on). Build creates platform-specific subdirectories under this directory. Note that build always creates an \obj subdirectory (\objfre or \onbjchk) under the directory that contains the sources file.
TARGETPATHLIB	Specifies a file path and destination directory for import libraries created by the build operation. If the file path isn't specified, import libraries are placed in the same subdirectory as other build product files.
TARGETTYPE	Specifies the type of product being built. This is typically LIBRARY or DYNLINK (for DLLs).
TARGETEXT	Specifies the file name extension for DLLs (for example, CPL). The default file name extension for DLLs is DLL.
TARGETLIBS	Specifies the set of import libraries with which your driver must be linked.
INCLUDES	Contains a list of paths to be searched for header files during compilation. Build also searches for header files in a default list of directories. The paths specified by INCLUDES are searched before the default paths.
SOURCES	Contains a list of source file names with extensions. These files must reside in the directory in which the sources file resides. Source files that contain a main function are listed using UMAPPL or UMTEST rather than SOURCES.
UMTYPE	Specifies the type of product being built. The choices are Win32 (user mode), kernel mode, and Win32 console.
UMAPPL	Contains a list of source files that contain a main function. If you use UMAPPL, build will automatically create executable files.

(continued)

Table 2.2   Macros used in the sources file (continued).

Macro	Function
UMTEST	Contains a list of source files that contain a main function. If you use UMTEST, you must identify the files you want built by listing them in the build command line.
UMAPPLEXT	Specifies the file name extension for executable files (for example, COM). The default file name extension for executable files is EXE.
UMLIBS	Contains a list of path names of libraries to be linked to the files specified by UMTESTor UMAPPL. The library specified by SOURCES should be included here. The path names must be absolute.
NTPROFILEINPUT	Enables you to use a file that lists the order in which the linker should access functions. This file should be in the same directory as the sources file and should be named *TargetName*.prf, where *TargetName* is the file name specified by the TARGETNAME macro. NTPROFILEINPUT is set to one (binary) if the PRF file is to be used.
DLLORDER	Enables you to specify a file that lists the order in which the linker should access functions. The macro must be set to the name of the file that contains the order list. You can use this macro instead of NTPROFILEINPUT.
386_WARNING_LEVEL	Specifies the compiler warning level.

Table 2.3   Environmental variables.

Environmental Variable	Function
BASEDIR	Contains the base of the build product's source tree (i.e., the directory that contains the dirs file).
BUILD_ALT_DIR	Appends specified characters to the \obj subdirectory name. The free and checked build environments use this variable to create the \objfre and \objchk subdirectories.
BUILD_DEFAULT	Contains a list of default parameters to pass to the build utility.
BUILD_DEFAULT_TARGETS	Contains a list of default target switches.
BUILD_MAKE_PROGRAM	Contains the name of the make utility used by build. This variable must take the value "nmake.exe".
CRT_INC_PATH	Contains the path to a directory that contains Windows 2000 header files.
CRT_LIB_PATH	Contains the path to a directory that contains Microsoft-supplied C import libraries.
DDK_INC_PATH	Contains the path to a directory that contains DDK-specific, Microsoft-supplied header files.

(continued)

Table 2.3 Environmental variables (continued).

Environmental Variable	Function
DDK_LIB_PATH	Contains the path to a directory that contains DDK-specific, Microsoft-supplied C import libraries.
DDK_LIB_DEST	Contains the path to the destination directory for a DDK-specific import library that's a build product.
OAK_INC_PATH	Contains the path to a directory that contains Microsoft-supplied header files.
SDK_LIB_DEST	Contains the path to the destination directory for an import library that's a build product.
SDK_LIB_PATH	Contains the path to a directory that contains Microsoft-supplied C import libraries.
WDM_INC_PATH	Contains the path to a directory that contains Microsoft-supplied, WDM-specific header files.
C_DEFINES	Defines switches that are passed to compilers.
O	Identifies the subdirectory into which build product files will be placed.
NTDEBUG	Set to "ntsd" in the checked environment. This causes the compiler to create symbolic debugging information.
BUILD_OPTIONS	Can be initialized by the user. This variable contains a list of optional subdirectories that should be scanned during a build operation. These are the subdirectories identified by the OPTIONAL_DIRS macro in the dirs file.

Table 2.4 Macros used in the dirs file.

Macro	Description
DIRS	Contains a list of subdirectories to be built by default.
OPTIONAL_DIRS	Contains a list of subdirectories to be built only if specified in the build command.

Verifying Drivers

The driver verifier will check that a driver unloads properly and releases any memory it has used (i.e., it's not "leaky"). It will check memory overruns, reveal paging violations, test the driver's response to a low-memory condition, and monitor I/O handling. The verifier.exe utility can be used from the command line using command-line switches, but it's more convenient to use the Driver Verifier Manager Graphical User Interface (GUI) provided.

To use the Driver Verifier Manager to verify a driver, proceed as follows:

1. Start the Driver Verifier Manager from the Start|Programs|Development Kits|Windows 2000 DDK menu or run verifier.exe from a command line with no switches specified. The verifier.exe file is located in the Ntddk\tools subdirectory.

NOTE: *This file won't run, nor will the Driver Verifier Manager appear on the appropriate menu, unless the DDK has been fully installed and the build environment set up (refer to the previous procedure).*

---

2. The Driver Status tab appears by default. This lists the drivers that are loaded and are being verified and indicates which driver verifier options are active. The Global flags section shows which driver verifier options are enabled. The Verified drivers section lists all drivers that driver verifier has been instructed to verify and their current verification status. Refresh rate for this screen can be set using the radio buttons. Selecting Manual disables automatic updates. The Refresh Now button causes the Status column to be refreshed immediately. Figure 2.7 shows the Driver Status tab.

3. Select the Global Counters tab. This screen displays statistics that monitor the driver verifier's actions. The Allocations counters monitor memory pool use by standard kernel-mode drivers. Figure 2.8 shows the Global Counters tab.

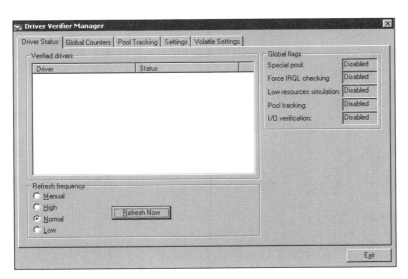

Figure 2.7   Driver status verification.

2. The Network Driver Interface Specification

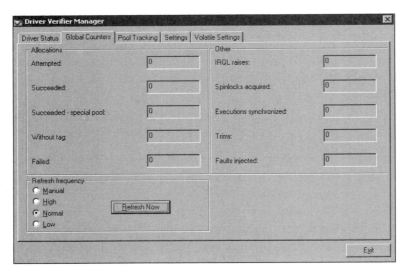

Figure 2.8   Global counters used by the driver verifier.

4. Select the Pool Tracking tab. This screen displays information on paged and nonpaged memory pool allocations. The Individual counters section displays statistics for one driver at a time, specified in the drop-down list at the top of this section. In the Global counter section, the Not tracked allocations counter displays the number of untracked allocations from all the drivers currently being verified. Figure 2.9 shows the Pool Tracking tab.

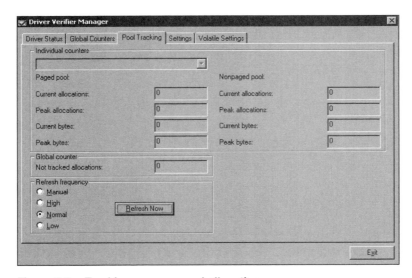

Figure 2.9   Tracking memory pool allocation.

5. Select the Settings tab. This screen enables you to select the drivers to be verified. You can set the verification type and the level of I/O verification. Right-clicking on a driver lets you control verification from a pop-up menu. The Verify these additional drivers after next reboot window lets you enter the names of drivers not currently loaded on the system. If Verify all drivers is selected, driver verifier will verify all drivers after reboot. When this option button is selected, the list of drivers and the Verify and Don't Verify buttons are grayed-out. The Preferred Settings button is a quick way to turn on the most commonly used options. When settings are made using this screen, click Apply, exit from the Driver Verifier Manager, and reboot the computer. The changed settings won't take effect until after a reboot. Figure 2.10 shows the Settings tab.

6. Select the Volatile Settings tab. This screen enables you to make alterations to the driver verifier settings immediately (rather than after a reboot). Special pool, Force IRQL checking, and Low resources simulation can be enabled or disabled for all the drivers being verified. The new settings take effect immediately when the Apply button is clicked. Figure 2.11 shows the Volatile Settings tab.

7. Make the changes you require on all the screens described and close the Driver Verifier Manager. Reboot if necessary.

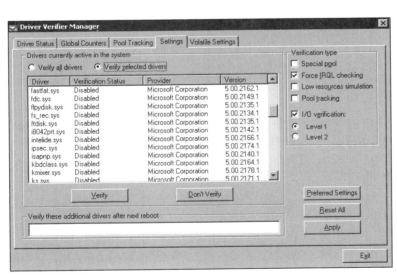

Figure 2.10   Selecting the drivers to be verified and setting the verification type and level.

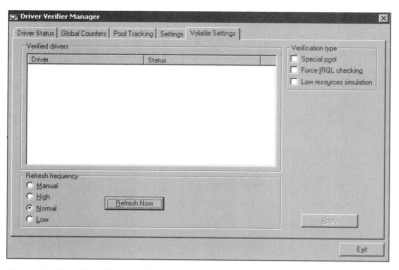

Figure 2.11   Volatile settings.

Debugging Drivers

Newly written drivers (or any other type of program) seldom work the first time. The Windows 2000 DDK provides extensive debugging facilities, including routines such as OutputDebugString and DebugBreak for user-mode drivers and DbgPrint, KdPrint, DbgBreakPoint, DgbBreakPointWithStatus, KdBreakPoint, KdBreakPointWithStatus, ASSERT, and ASSERTMSG for kernel mode drivers. These routines can be inserted into source code for debugging purposes. Syntax details and samples are available from the DDK.

There is, however, a more user-friendly tool available—the Windows Debugger (WinDbg). This procedure looks at the facilities available from this GUI. To access and use the Windows debugger, proceed as follows:

1. Access Start|Programs|Development Kits|Windows 2000 DDK|Debugging Tools and select WinDbg. The Windows Debugger GUI appears, as shown in Figure 2.12.

2. The File menu enables you to open a source file, an executable file, or a crash dump. You can also manage your workspace from this menu.

3. In the Edit menu, select Breakpoints. The Breakpoint drop-down list offers the breakpoint options available, as shown in Figure 2.13. Make the selection you require, and click OK.

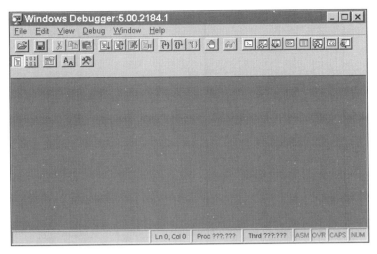

Figure 2.12   The Windows Debugger.

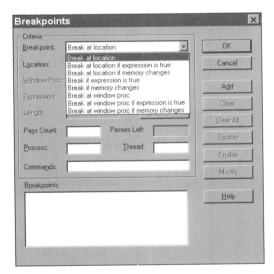

Figure 2.13   Selecting a breakpoint option.

4. In the View menu you have a choice of view items, such as registers, memory, and call stack. Figure 2.14 shows the memory view options available.

5. In the Debug menu you can start or stop debugging, step into a routine or step over a breakpoint, enable or disable source mode (disabling source mode starts the disassembler), and set exceptions, as shown in Figure 2.15.

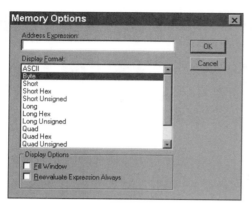

Figure 2.14   The memory view display format options.

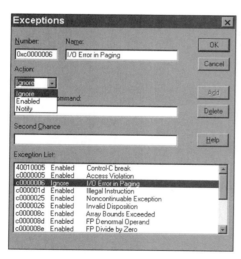

Figure 2.15   Setting exceptions.

6. The tool also has a number of buttons that provide shortcuts to menu items. The Options button, for example, provides the same functionality as View|Options. Explore all the tabs on this dialog box. Figure 2.16 (for example) shows the Debugger tab.

As stated previously, the purpose of describing the DDK-related procedures in this chapter is to explore the facilities available for generating, verifying, and debugging driver programs. A full treatment of how to write C++ source code and use all the DDK facilities would take a book at least as big as this one. Fortunately, extensive documentation is available with the DDK (if you choose to download it), as are sample programs.

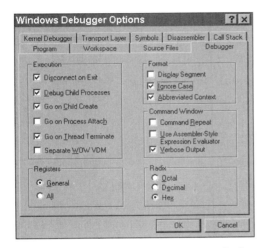

Figure 2.16   The Windows Debugger Options dialog box.

Chapter 3

Address Resolution Protocol

In Depth

Address Resolution Protocol (ARP) is a required TCP/IP standard, defined in Request for Comments document RFC 826. This RFC is well worth reading, not only for its technical details, but also for the light it sheds on Internet development. In 1982, the author was already talking about the "ARPA Internet community" and referring to the Department of Defense (DOD) protocol as the "Internet" protocol.

This chapter discusses how ARP works, the use of the ARP cache, ARP packet structure, and the arp utility. Because Network Monitor is used in the Immediate Solutions section of the chapter, I've taken the opportunity to discuss the tool in some detail here. Network Monitor will be used in most chapters of this book, and I want to introduce it at an early stage. I must, however, emphasize that Network Monitor is a general tool that can capture and display frames generated by a wide range of protocols. It is not specific to ARP.

How ARP Works

ARP resolves Internet Protocol (IP) addresses, used by TCP/IP-based software, to Media Access Control (MAC) addresses, used by network hardware, such as Ethernet. The protocol performs IP address to MAC address resolution for outgoing packets. As each outgoing IP datagram is encapsulated in a frame, source and destination MAC addresses must be added. ARP determines the destination MAC address for each frame.

When ARP receives a request to resolve an IP address—for example, during a ping operation—it first checks to ascertain whether it has recently resolved that address or whether it has a permanent record of the IP address/MAC address pair for the protocol address requested. This information is held in a memory store that's called the *ARP cache*. If it can't resolve the IP address from cache, ARP broadcasts a request that contains the source IP and MAC addresses and the target IP address.

When the ARP request is answered, the responding PC and the original ARP requester record each other's IP address and MAC addresses in the ARP cache.

Hardware Addressing

Hardware built for use on Local Area Networks (LANs) must contain a unique address that's programmed into the device's Read-Only Memory (ROM) by the manufacturer. For Ethernet and Token Ring LAN hardware, this address is known as a Media Access Control (MAC) address. Some types of Wide Area Network (WAN) media also use MAC addresses—for example, some Asynchronous Transfer Mode (ATM) adapters support LAN emulation and appear to the protocol stack as a LAN media type, such as Ethernet.

Each MAC address identifies the device within its own physical network with a 48-bit (6-byte) number that's programmed into ROM on each physical hardware device, such as a network adapter. MAC addresses are typically displayed in hexadecimal format (for example, 00-00-E8-5A-E3-B0).

The Institute of Electrical and Electronics Engineers (IEEE) oversees the authorization and registration of MAC addresses. Currently, the IEEE registers and assigns unique numbers for the first 3 bytes of the MAC address to individual manufacturers. Each manufacturer then assigns the last 3 bytes to individual network adapters.

The ARP Cache

The ARP cache is a table held in memory that stores IP address/MAC address pairs. Whenever a source computer resolves a target IP address using an ARP request broadcast, the address pair for the target computer is stored in the source computer's cache. Similarly, when a target computer responds to an ARP request with an ARP reply, the address pair of the source computer is stored in the target computer's cache. Cache entries generated automatically by ARP operation are called *dynamic entries*. They remain in the cache for a specified Time to Live (TTL) and, if not accessed during that time, are then discarded.

Address pairs for frequently accessed targets, such as gateways, can be entered manually. Manually entered address pairs are called *static entries*; they persist in cache until Windows 2000 is rebooted or until they're manually deleted.

If a computer is multihomed—that is, it has more than one Network Interface Card (NIC)—then there's a separate ARP cache for each interface.

The ARP cache can be viewed, deleted, or amended using the Arp command-line utility. This utility is discussed in the Immediate Solutions section of this chapter.

ARP Cache Aging

Windows 2000 adjusts the size of the ARP cache automatically. If a new dynamic entry isn't used by an outgoing datagram for two minutes, it's removed from the ARP cache. If an entry is referenced again before it's removed, its TTL is increased by another two minutes. Thus, a frequently referenced entry can increase its TTL up to a maximum of 10 minutes. Any dynamic entry whose TTL expires is removed from the cache. Manually added static entries remain in the cache until they're manually removed or until Windows 2000 is re-initialized. The Immediate Solutions section of this chapter gives details of how to add and delete static entries. The Registry parameter, *ArpCacheLife*, enables you to alter the default TTL for dynamic entries. This parameter is described in Appendix A.

Resolving Local Addresses

The following example shows how ARP resolves an IP address to a MAC address for hosts on the same local network. A **ping** command has been issued on Host A, specifying an IP address. Internet Control Message Protocol (ICMP), which implements commands such as **ping**, instructs ARP to resolve this IP address.

ARP checks the cache on Host A. If the IP address isn't resolved in cache, then an ARP request is broadcast to all the hosts on the subnet—supplying the source IP and MAC addresses and requesting a MAC address that corresponds with the IP address specified. Because the ARP frame is a broadcast, all hosts on the subnet will process it. However, hosts that don't have the corresponding IP address (such as Host B) will reject it. Host C recognizes the IP address as its own and stores the IP address/MAC address pair for Host A in its cache. This process is illustrated in Figure 3.1.

Host C sends an ARP reply message that contains its MAC address directly back to Host A. When Host A receives this message, it updates its ARP cache with Host

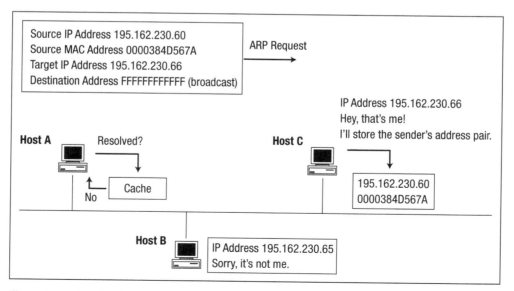

Figure 3.1   The ARP request.

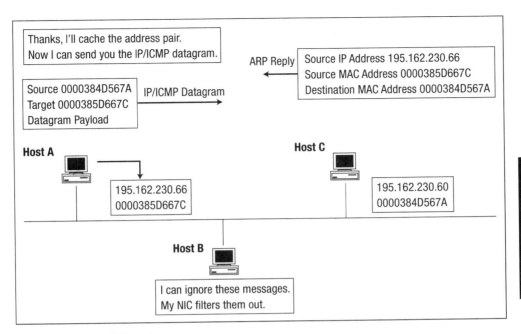

Figure 3.2   The ARP reply.

C's address pair. Host A can now send the ICMP ping datagram (or any IP datagram) directly to Host C. This process is illustrated in Figure 3.2.

Resolving Remote Addresses

When the target address of an IP datagram is on a remote subnet, ARP will resolve the IP address to the MAC address of the NIC in the gateway or router that's on the source host's local interface.

The following example shows how ARP resolves IP addresses when the source and target hosts are on different physical networks that are connected by a common gateway. As before, ARP first checks its cache on the source host (Host A). If the IP address can't be resolved from cache, an ARP request is broadcast. ARP doesn't know that the target host is remote—routing is an IP function, not an ARP function. The ARP request to resolve a remote IP address is therefore exactly the same as the ARP request to resolve a local address.

All the ordinary hosts on the local subnet reject the request because none of them has a matching IP address. The Gateway, however, checks its routing table and determines that it can access the subnet for the remote host. It then caches the IP address/MAC address pair for Host A in its cache for Host A's local interface and sends back an ARP reply that specifies the MAC address of the Gateway NIC that accesses that interface. On Host A, ARP caches that MAC address with the IP address it's resolving. As far as ARP on Host A is concerned, it has done its job.

Thus, Host A resolves a remote IP address to the MAC address of its default gateway.

At this stage, ARP on the Gateway takes over the task of IP address resolution. First, it checks its cache for the target host's interface. If it can't resolve the target host's IP from cache, it broadcasts an ARP request to the target host's subnet, supplying the IP address and MAC address of the gateway NIC that accesses the target host's interface.

In the example illustrated in Figure 3.3, Host B recognizes its own IP address, caches the IP address and MAC address of the gateway NIC that accesses its local interface, and returns its MAC address in an ARP reply frame directed to its default gateway. On the Gateway, ARP caches host B's MAC address along with the IP address it's resolving, and the process is complete. The address pairs in the ARP caches shown in Figure 3.3 are the result of a successful resolution.

Thus, when Host A sends an IP datagram to Host B's IP address, it actually sends it to its default gateway—specifying its own MAC address as the source and the MAC address of the Gateway NIC that accesses its interface as the target. At the Gateway, the source and destination information is stripped from the datagram. It is replaced by a source MAC address that corresponds to the Gateway NIC that accesses the target host's interface and a target MAC address that identifies the target host. This process is illustrated in Figure 3.4.

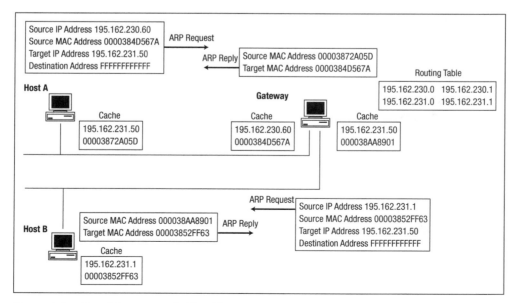

Figure 3.3   Resolving a remote IP address.

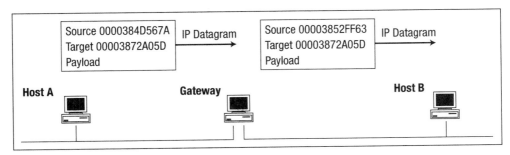

Figure 3.4   Sending an IP datagram to a remote host.

Where there are several hops between the source and target hosts, the IP address resolution and IP datagram transmission processes are passed from gateway to gateway (or router) until the payload eventually reaches its destination.

The ARP Frame Structure

Network Monitor is used in the Immediate Solutions section to capture and view ARP frames. The ARP frame is split into a number of fields, as follows:

- *Destination address*—For an ARP request, this is FFFFFFFFFFFF, the broadcast address. For an ARP reply, it's the MAC address of the host that broadcast the ARP request. In either case, the field length is 6 bytes for token ring or Ethernet.

- *Source address*—For an ARP request, this is the MAC address of the host that broadcast the request. For an ARP reply, it's the MAC address of the responding host. In either case, the field length is 6 bytes for token ring or Ethernet.

- *Frame type*—This identifies the frame as an ARP frame. If Ethernet is the transmission medium, the Ethernet frame type (or *Ethernet Type*) is 0806 hex. The field is 2 bytes long.

- *Hardware type*—This identifies the hardware being used. For example, 10Mb Ethernet is identified as 0001. The field is 2 bytes long.

- *Protocol type*—Although ARP can be used with protocols other than IP, this field normally contains the value 0080 hex, which identifies the protocol as IP. The field is 2 bytes long.

- *Hardware address length*—For Ethernet and Token Ring, this is 04. The field is 1 byte long.

- *Protocol address length*—For standard IP (IPv4), this is 06. For IPv6, it's 10 hex. The field is 1 byte long.

- *Operation code*—For an ARP request, this is 0001. For an ARP reply, it's 0002. The field is 2 bytes long.

- *Sender's hardware address*—For an ARP request, this is the MAC address of the host that broadcast the request. For an ARP reply, it's the MAC address of the responding host. For local IP address resolution, the sender's hardware address in an ARP reply is the MAC address that corresponds to the IP address to be resolved. For remote IP address resolution, it's the MAC address of the requesting host's default gateway. In either case, the field length is 6 bytes for Token Ring or Ethernet.

- *Sender's protocol address*—For an ARP request, this is the IP address of the host that broadcast the request. For an ARP reply, it's the IP address of the responding host. For local resolution, this is the IP address to be resolved. For remote resolution, it's the IP address of the requesting host's default gateway. In the latter case, ARP on the requesting host won't cache this address, but will instead store the IP address whose resolution it requested, along with the hardware address of its default gateway, as an address pair. This field is 4 bytes long for standard IP.

- *Target's hardware address*—For an ARP request, this is 000000000000, because the MAC address for the target is unresolved at this stage. For an ARP reply, it's the MAC address of the host that broadcast the ARP request. The field length is 6 bytes for Token Ring or Ethernet.

- *Target's protocol address*—For an ARP request, this is the IP address to be resolved. For an ARP reply, it's the IP address of the host that broadcast the ARP request. The field is 4 bytes long for standard IP.

- *Frame padding*—The ARP reply frame is padded with 18 bytes of 00.

For Ethernet or Token Ring media and for standard IP, the length of an ARP request frame is 42 bytes. For an ARP reply frame, it's 60 bytes. Figure 3.5 shows a typical ARP request, broken down into fields.

Destination address	FFFFFFFFFFFF
Source address	00A0C9D6B68F
Frame type	0686
Hardware type	0001
Protocol type	0800
Hardware address length	06
Protocol address length	04
Operation code	0001
Sender's hardware address	00A0C9D6B68F
Sender's protocol address	C3A2E601
Target's hardware address	000000000000
Target's protocol address	C3A2E632

Figure 3.5   An ARP request frame.

The IP Helper Application Programming Interface

The IP helper Application Programming Interface (API) solves a problem associated with ARP. ARP queues only one outbound IP datagram for a specified destination address while that IP address is being resolved to a MAC address. If a User Datagram Protocol (UDP)-based application sends multiple IP datagrams to a single destination address without any pauses between them, some datagrams may be dropped. An application can compensate for this by calling the IP helper API (iphlpapi.dll) routine SendArp() to establish an ARP cache entry, before sending the stream of packets.

NOTE: *Refer to knowledge base article Q193059 (on Technet) or to the Windows 2000 platform Software Development Kit (SDK) documentation for detailed information about the IP helper API.*

Network Monitor

Network Monitor is a Graphical User Interface (GUI) tool provided with all versions of Windows 2000 Server. Its function, as its name suggests, is to monitor traffic on a network. The standard version of Network Monitor supplied with the Server software enables you to monitor all incoming and outgoing traffic to and from the server on which it's running. A full version of Network Monitor, supplied with Microsoft System Management Server (SMS), enables you to monitor all network traffic on your server's subnet.

In order to do this, the full version of Network Monitor disables the hardware filters on your server's NIC, so that the server processes every frame on the network. This is known as putting the NIC into *promiscuous mode*, which results in the server's suffering a significant performance hit. The full version of Network Monitor is a very powerful tool, but it should be used sparingly. In the Immediate Solutions section of this chapter, the operation of Network Monitor is discussed in detail. The standard version of Network Monitor is sufficient for all the procedures described in this chapter.

The Network Monitor Capture Window

The Network Monitor capture window is shown in Figure 3.6. This is the first window to appear when the tool is enabled. The capture window is used to analyze overall network performance and to start, stop, and save network captures; it is also used to set view and capture filters and capture triggers. All of these techniques are discussed in Immediate Solutions.

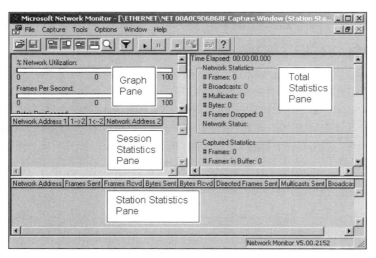

Figure 3.6   The Network Monitor capture window.

The capture window is divided into four areas, or *panes*. These can be toggled on or off by clicking on the toggle buttons. Table 3.1 lists the main function of each pane.

The Network Monitor Capture Summary Window

When data has been captured or if a capture file is loaded, details of the captured frames can be viewed using the Network Monitor capture summary window (Figure 3.7). Viewing network frames is discussed extensively in Immediate Solutions.

Table 3.1   Network Monitor capture window panes.

Pane	Function
Graph	Displays current network activity (assuming that data is being captured). This activity is displayed as a set of bar charts, indicating network utilization, frames per second, bytes per second, broadcasts per second, and multicasts per second.
Session statistics	Summarizes the traffic between two hosts and indicates which host is initiating broadcasts or multicasts.
Total statistics	Displays statistics for all captured traffic, statistics for the frames captured, per-second utilization statistics, and network adapter card statistics.
Station statistics	Summarizes the total number of frames initiated by a host, the number of frames and bytes sent and received, and the number of broadcast and multicast frames initiated.

The capture summary window is divided into three panes. From top to bottom, these are:

- The summary pane
- The detail (or decode) pane
- The hex pane

As with the capture window, these can be toggled on or off by clicking on the toggle buttons. Table 3.2 lists the main function of each pane.

The summary pane contains nine columns that can be sorted, moved, or resized. The contents of these columns are described in Table 3.3.

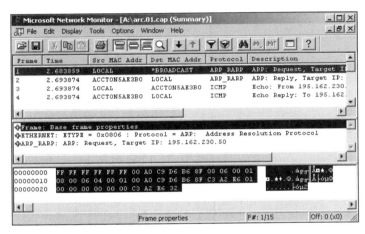

Figure 3.7   The Network Monitor capture summary window.

Table 3.2   Network Monitor capture summary window.

Pane	Function
Summary	Lists all frames included in the current view of the captured data. When a frame is highlighted in the summary pane, its contents are displayed in the detail and hex panes.
Detail	Displays the protocol information of the frame currently highlighted in the summary pane. If a frame contains several protocol layers, the outermost layer is displayed first. Frame contents can be displayed by clicking on the plus sign to the left of a protocol, double-clicking it, or highlighting it and pressing Enter.
Hex	Displays the content of the selected frame in both hex and ASCII (American Standard Code for Information Interchange) formats. If information is highlighted in the detail frame, the corresponding hex and ASCII data appears highlighted in the hex frame.

Table 3.3   Network Monitor summary pane columns.

Column	Contents
Frame	Displays the frame number. Frames are numbered in order of capture.
Time	Displays the frame's capture time. It can be configured to display either the time of day that the frame was captured or the time elapsed since the start of capture.
Source MAC address	Displays the hardware address of the host that sent the frame.
Destination MAC address	Displays the hardware address of the target host.
Protocol	Displays the protocol used to transmit the frame.
Description	Summarizes the frame's contents. Summary information can include details of the protocols used in a frame.
Source other address	Displays a source address other than the MAC address. Depending on the frame, this could be (for example) an IP address or an Internetwork Packet Exchange (IPX) address.
Destination other address	Displays a destination address other than the MAC address. As with the source other address, this could be an IP address or an IPX address.
Type other address	Specifies the type of addresses displayed in the previous two columns; for example, IP or IPX.

Immediate Solutions

Using the Arp Utility

To use the Arp command-line utility to view and modify the ARP cache, proceed as follows:

1. From Start|Programs|Accessories, select Command Prompt.

2. Enter **arp**. When entered with no arguments, the utility lists the command syntax (as does **arp /?**). Figure 3.8 shows the syntax screen.

3. Enter **arp –a**. This displays the current ARP cache, as shown in Figure 3.9.

4. If you have a multihomed PC, you can use the interface addresses to display the ARP cache for each interface. The syntax for this command is **arp –a –N** *ip_address*, as shown in Figure 3.10.

3. Address Resolution Protocol

```
Command Prompt                                                    _ □ ×
E:\>arp

Displays and modifies the IP-to-Physical address translation tables used by
address resolution protocol (ARP).

ARP -s inet_addr eth_addr [if_addr]
ARP -d inet_addr [if_addr]
ARP -a [inet_addr] [-N if_addr]

  -a              Displays current ARP entries by interrogating the current
                  protocol data.  If inet_addr is specified, the IP and Physical
                  addresses for only the specified computer are displayed.  If
                  more than one network interface uses ARP, entries for each ARP
                  table are displayed.
  -g              Same as -a.
  inet_addr       Specifies an internet address.
  -N if_addr      Displays the ARP entries for the network interface specified
                  by if_addr.
  -d              Deletes the host specified by inet_addr. inet_addr may be
                  wildcarded with * to delete all hosts.
  -s              Adds the host and associates the Internet address inet_addr
                  with the Physical address eth_addr.  The Physical address is
                  given as 6 hexadecimal bytes separated by hyphens. The entry
                  is permanent.
  eth_addr        Specifies a physical address.
  if_addr         If present, this specifies the Internet address of the
                  interface whose address translation table should be modified.
                  If not present, the first applicable interface will be used.
Example:
  > arp -s 157.55.85.212   00-aa-00-62-c6-09  .... Adds a static entry.
  > arp -a                                    .... Displays the arp table.

E:\>_
```

Figure 3.8   The **arp** command syntax.

```
Command Prompt                                        _ □ ×
E:\>arp -a

Interface: 195.162.230.1 on Interface 0x2
  Internet Address       Physical Address      Type
  195.162.230.50         00-00-e8-5a-e3-b0     dynamic
```

Figure 3.9   The ARP cache.

Figure 3.10   Displaying the ARP cache for a specified interface.

5. The command **arp –d *ip_address*** will delete an individual cache entry. Use **arp –d** without arguments to delete all cache entries, as shown in Figure 3.11.

6. The **ping** command uses ARP broadcasts to resolve an IP number to a MAC address. Once resolved, the mapping is placed in the ARP cache as a dynamic entry. Ping a PC on your local subnet, then display the ARP cache. Figure 3.12 shows this procedure.

7. If you have a routed network, ping a remote host. The resulting ARP cache entry will contain the IP address of the remote host paired with the MAC address of your gateway PC—not with the MAC address of the remote host. If you don't have access to a routed intranet, ping a remote host on the Internet (for example, 207.46.130.45). The **ping** command may time out, but your ARP cache will still store the remote Internet address paired with the MAC address of your gateway.

Figure 3.11   Deleting the ARP cache.

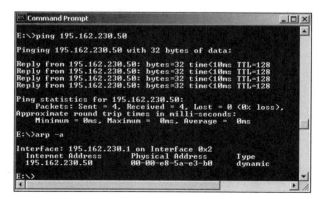

Figure 3.12   The **ping** command adds an entry to the ARP cache.

8. Frequently accessed machines on your subnet, such as the default gateway, should be placed in the ARP cache as static entries. Use the command **arp –s *IP_Address MAC_address*** to add a static entry, as shown in Figure 3.13.

9. Wait for 10 minutes, then list the ARP cache entries. The dynamic entries are removed after their TTLs have expired. The static entry will remain until Windows 2000 is rebooted. Static entries can, however, be removed using the **arp –d** command.

TIP: *To make static ARP cache entries persistent, add **arp –s** commands to a batch file that runs at system startup.*

Related solution:	See page:
Using the Command-Line Tools	709

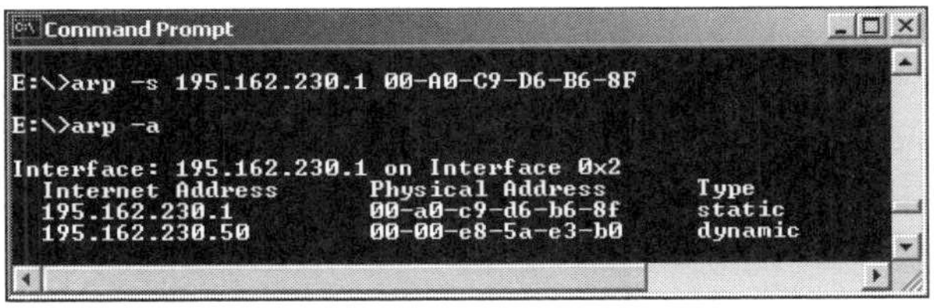

Figure 3.13   Adding a static entry.

Installing Network Monitor

The version of Network Monitor that comes with the Windows 2000 Server operating systems is normally installed by default. The full version, supplied with SMS, enables you to look at all packets on your subnet, whereas the standard version enables you to look only at packets received or sent by the server on which it's installed. Both versions of Network Monitor can run only on a server.

The standard version of Network Monitor is adequate for all the procedures described in the remainder of this chapter. If you want to, you can use the full version—the procedures will be the same, except that the full version will be accessed directly from Start|Programs rather than from Start|Programs|Administration Tools.

Network Monitor is normally installed with Windows 2000 Server. If it is not, or if it has been de-installed, the following procedure is required to install it:

1. Access Start|Settings and select Control Panel.

2. Open the Add/Remove Programs dialog box.

3. Select Add/Remove Windows Components.

4. In the Windows Components Wizard, select Management and Monitoring Tools. Click Details.

5. Check the Network Monitor Tools checkbox. Click OK.

6. If you are prompted for additional files, insert your Windows 2000 Server CD-ROM or type a path to the location of the files on the network.

NOTE: *Installing Network Monitor tools automatically installs the Network Monitor driver.*

Capturing and Displaying Network Traffic

This procedure uses Network Monitor to capture and display network traffic. In the procedure, we look at methods of displaying the traffic that's of interest and setting up capture filters so that only that traffic is captured. Specifically, the procedure looks at capturing and displaying ARP frames.

To capture and display network traffic, proceed as follows:

1. Access Start|Programs|Administration Tools and select Network Monitor.

2. If this is the first time Network Monitor has been accessed, you'll be prompted to select a network. In this case, expand Local Computer and select the network where the value of the Dial-up Connection Blob (Binary Large Object) tab is FALSE, as shown in Figure 3.14. This ensures you're monitoring your local connection. Click OK.

3. The Network Monitor capture window (refer to Figure 3.6) appears. On the Capture menu, click Start.

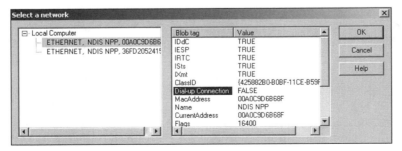

Figure 3.14   Setting Network Monitor to monitor a local connection.

4. From Start|Programs|Accessories, select Command Prompt.

5. Ping a computer on your local subnet.

6. On the Network Monitor Capture menu, click Stop and View. The Network Monitor capture summary window appears (refer to Figure 3.7).

NOTE: *This capture file is provided as arc_01.cap on the CD-ROM that accompanies this book.*

---

7. On the Display menu, click Colors. Select ARP_RARP, choose a foreground color (for example, red), and click OK. All ARP frames are then displayed in that color.

TIP: *If you didn't capture any ARP frames, then the MAC address was supplied from your ARP cache. In this case, clear the cache using **arp –d** and repeat the procedure.*

---

8. Double-click on the ARP request frame. Your screen should look similar to Figure 3.15.

9. Using the control buttons, toggle off the summary and hex panes and expand the detail pane, as shown in Figure 3.16. This pane shows the contents of the Ethernet broadcast (Destination address: FFFFFFFFFFFF, Source address: the server's MAC address) and the contents of the ARP request. At this stage, the target's MAC address is not yet determined and is recorded as all zeros.

10. Collapse the detail pane tree and toggle the hex pane back on. This gives you details of frame contents right down to the bit level, as shown in Figure 3.17. You can identify, for example, the source and destination addresses in the Ethernet frame.

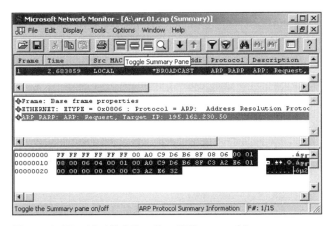

Figure 3.15 Highlighting the ARP request frame.

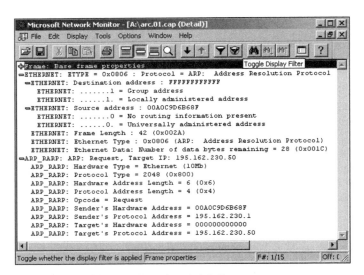

Figure 3.16   Ethernet broadcast details.

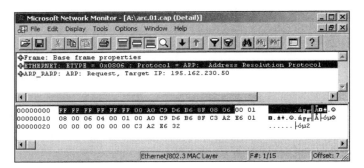

Figure 3.17   The hex and ASCII contents of the Ethernet broadcast.

TIP: *Don't ignore the hex frame, and particularly the ASCII representation to the right. This often contains information about messages sent, file names, and so on.*

---

11. Toggle the summary pane back on and investigate the contents of the ARP reply. The target's hardware address is resolved in this frame.

12. Save your capture by clicking Save As in the File menu and specifying a file name. By default, the capture is saved as a CAP file. If you start a new capture or attempt to exit Network Monitor without saving your capture, you will be prompted to save it.

Filtering the Network Monitor Display by Protocol

Only a small number of frames were captured in the last procedure. If you had captured a large number, possibly over an extended period, then color highlighting might not be an adequate method of selecting the frames that are of interest to you. In this case, you can specify a *display filter*, so that only frames that meet specific criteria are displayed. This next procedure uses the capture you carried out previously—or the sample capture file, arc01.cap, on the CD-ROM—to demonstrate this technique.

To design a display filter, proceed as follows:

1. Access Start|Programs|Administration Tools and select Network Monitor.
2. From the File menu, open the capture file you created in the previous procedure (or arc01.cap).
3. On the Display menu, click Filter.
4. In the Display Filter dialog box, click Expression and select the Protocols tab.
5. Click Disable All.
6. In the Disabled Protocols box, select ARP_RARP.
7. Click Enable.
8. Click OK. Click OK to close the Display Filter dialog box. Network Monitor will now display only ARP frames.

NOTE: Disabling a protocol doesn't always result in that protocol's frames not appearing in Network Monitor capture screens. A protocol that contains subprotocols—for example, the Service Message Block (SMB) protocol—will still be displayed if its subprotocols remain enabled.

9. If you want to display all the frames except ARP frames at this point, access the Display Filter dialog box, select the ARP_RARP protocol in the decision tree, and click NOT, then click OK. To return to the previous filter, double-click the NOT box beside the protocol until it displays AND.

Filtering the Network Monitor Display by Protocol Property

You can refine the protocol filter still further by filtering by specific protocol properties, such as source protocol address, source MAC address and so on. The procedure to do this is as follows:

1. If you have just carried out the previous procedure, then you can go directly to Step 2 in this one. Otherwise, perform Steps 1 to 9 of the previous procedure ("Filtering the Network Monitor Display by Protocol").
2. On the Network Monitor capture summary screen (refer to Figure 3.7), select Filter from the Display menu.
3. In the Display Filter dialog box, click Expression.

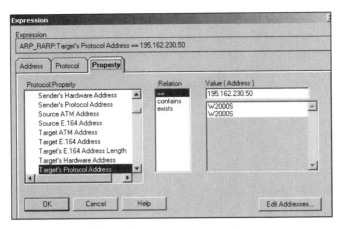

Figure 3.18   Filtering by protocol property.

4. Select the Property tab. Set the condition that the target's protocol address is equal to the IP address of the local host that you pinged earlier, as shown in Figure 3.18.

5. Click OK. Click OK to exit the Display Filter dialog box. Network Monitor will now display only the ARP request frame, because the ARP reply frame's target IP address isn't the address specified. If you had pinged several hosts, only the ARP reply frame for that host whose target address you specified would be displayed.

6. On the Display menu, select Filter. Highlight the filter condition that you created, as shown in Figure 3.19. In the Delete section, click Line. Click OK. The capture summary screen will now display all captured frames.

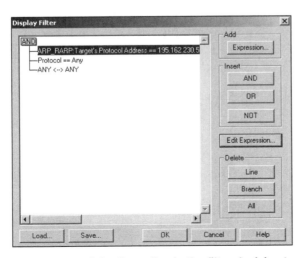

Figure 3.19   Selecting a line in the filter decision tree.

Filtering the Network Monitor Display by Address

The two previous procedures filtered the Network Monitor display by protocol and by protocol property. Sometimes, however, you want to see all the traffic between the server and one particular host on the network, whatever protocols are used, and you want to filter out traffic to and from other hosts. The procedure to set up such a filter is as follows:

1. Access Start|Programs|Accessories and select Command Prompt.

2. Enter **arp –d** to clear the ARP cache.

3. Enter **arp –a** to ensure the cache is empty. If it isn't, repeat Step 2.

4. Access Start|Programs|Administrative Tools and select Network Monitor. (If Network Monitor's already started, then close and re-open it.)

5. On the Capture menu, click Start.

6. Ping two local hosts on your subnet from your server.

7. Ping your server from the same two local hosts.

8. On the Network Monitor Capture menu, click Stop and View.

9. On the File menu, click Save As and save your capture file.

TIP: *If you prefer, you can load capture file arc_02.cap from the CD-ROM supplied with this book.*

10. On the Display menu, click Filter.

11. In the Display Filter dialog box, click Expression.

12. In the Expression dialog box, select the Address tab, and click Edit Addresses.

13. Click Add. Add the IP address of one of the hosts that you pinged, as shown in Figure 3.20. Click OK. Click Close.

14. Select two-way traffic where Station 1 is specified by the local (hardware) address of your server and Station 2 by the host IP address that you've just added. Figure 3.21 demonstrates this selection. Click OK. Click OK to close the Display Filter dialog box.

Figure 3.20   Specifying an address for filtering.

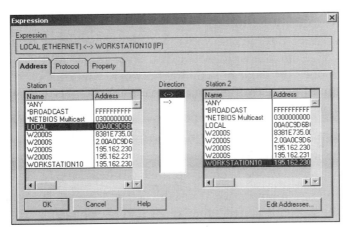

Figure 3.21   Selecting an address pair.

15. Check that the frames displayed contain only traffic between your server and the selected host.

16. On the Display menu, click Filter. Highlight and delete the line you've just added to the decision tree.

17. Repeat the filter setup to display the broadcast traffic that your server puts on your subnet. Select the local (hardware) address for Station 1, the single arrow, and the broadcast address for Station 2. Check that only broadcast frames are displayed.

Modifying the Display Filter Decision Tree

The display filter decision tree is a very powerful and flexible tool. If you're familiar with Boolean logic, you can set up some very sophisticated filter criteria using this tool. The only way to learn this technique is by practice. The next procedure demonstrates how you go about changing the tree. What decisions you make when doing so will be determined by your individual requirements.

To modify the display filter decision tree structure, proceed as follows:

1. Open Network Monitor and load one of the capture files that you created (or a capture file from the CD-ROM).

2. On the Display menu, click Filter. This accesses the display filter decision tree.

3. To add a logical operator, select the line to which you want the operator to apply. Click AND to find frames that satisfy all expressions in the branch; click OR to find frames that satisfy one or more of the expressions in the branch; click NOT to exclude frames that satisfy the expressions in the branch.

4. To change a logical operator, double-click it until the operator you want appears.

5. To modify an expression, select it and click Edit Expression.

6. To add an expression to a branch, select the line below which you want to insert the new expression, then click Expression. The expression can then be defined on the Protocol, Property, or Address tab of the Expression dialog box, as described in the previous procedures.

7. To delete a single expression or logical operator, select the line and click Line in the Delete group.

8. To delete a branch, select the top branch that you want to delete and click Branch in the Delete group. Confirm that you want to delete the branch and all the branches underneath it.

9. To clear the decision tree, click All in the Delete group. Confirm that you want to clear the decision tree contents.

Implementing a Capture Filter

In the previous procedures, Network Monitor was used to capture all incoming and outgoing frames on a server. Display filters were then set up to display subsets of this total capture, as defined by the filter criteria.

An alternate technique is to set up a capture filter, so that only those frames in which you're interested are captured. In other words, the filter is applied before the capture, rather than afterward. This has the advantage that a busy server on a busy network takes a smaller performance hit, because fewer frames are captured; and the capture files are smaller. It has the disadvantage that a total capture can sometimes catch unexpected frames that indicate network problems, where a filtered capture will miss such frames.

To implement a capture filter, proceed as follows:

1. Start Network Monitor. On the Capture menu, click Filter. The Capture Filter information box gives an excellent explanation of the difference between Network Monitor supplied with Windows 2000 Server and the full version. Read this carefully, then click OK to close the box.

2. To filter by protocol, select the SAP/ETYPE line in the capture filter decision tree, and click Edit. The dialog box is similar, but not identical, to the display filter Protocol tab. Disable all protocols and then enable ARP. Click OK.

3. Click OK to close the Capture Filter dialog box.

4. On the Capture menu, click Start.

5. Open the Command Prompt.

6. Enter **arp –d** to clear the ARP cache.

7. Enter **arp –a** to check that the cache is empty.

8. Ping one or more local hosts on your subnet.

9. On the Network Monitor Capture menu, click Stop and View.

10. Check that only ARP frames have been captured. (You may also see a STATS entry that tells you the number of frames captured).

11. Close the capture summary screen.

12. On the Capture menu, click Filter.

13. Highlight the SAP/ETYPE line on the capture filter decision tree. Click Edit. Enable all protocols. Click OK to return to the Capture Filter dialog box.

14. Highlight Address Pairs and click Address. Setting up an address-pair capture filter is almost identical to setting up an address-pair display filter, except that incoming, outgoing, or two-way traffic can be specified.

15. Click Edit Addresses.

16. Click Add. Add the IP address of one of the hosts on your subnet (refer to Figure 3.20). Click OK. Click Close.

17. Select two-way traffic where Station 1 is specified by the local (hardware) address of your server and Station 2 by the host IP address that you've just added (refer to Figure 3.21). Click OK. Click OK to close the Capture Filter dialog box.

18. Start a capture. In the command prompt, clear the ARP cache. Then, from your server, ping both the host whose IP address you specified in the address-pair filter and another local host. Ping your server from both these hosts.

19. Stop the capture and view the frames. You should have captured only the traffic between the host you specified and your server.

20. Close the capture summary screen.

21. On the Capture menu, select Filter.

22. In the capture filter decision tree, delete the line under Address Pairs. This removes the address-pair filter condition that you set up previously.

23. You can also specify a capture filter using pattern matching. Select the Pattern Match line on the capture filter decision tree, and click Pattern.

24. In the Pattern Match dialog box (Figure 3.22), you can set a pattern, or data string, in either hex or ASCII. Typically, you want to find a string in the frame data. You can therefore specify an offset of a specified number of hexadecimal bytes, either from the start of the frame or from the end of the topology header.

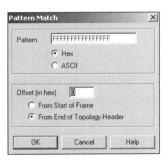

Figure 3.22 **Specifying a pattern match.**

NOTE: *A topology header is a section of a frame that identifies the network type. It includes information such as the source and destination address of the frame, but doesn't include information from the frame's data field.*

---

25. Set a pattern, such as FFFFFFFFFFFFFFFF (hex), as shown in Figure 3.22, and click OK. Click OK to close the Capture Filter dialog box.

26. As before, start a capture, clear the ARP cache, and ping one or more local hosts on your network.

27. Stop the capture and display the data. Check that all the captured frames contain the specified data string.

NOTE: *ASCII pattern matching can be useful if you want to capture frames that contain a message, computer name, or username, and these are sent across the network in plain text.*

Setting a Capture Trigger

Network Monitor can be set so that it takes a predefined action if it captures a frame that meets specified criteria. For example, a frame that contains a particular pattern could cause Network Monitor to stop the capture, sound a warning, or start an executable program. The pattern has to occur at the start of a frame, unless an offset is specified. A capture trigger can also be set so that it gives a warning or stops a capture when the capture buffer (memory that Network Monitor has set aside to hold captured frames) is nearly full.

To set a capture trigger, proceed as follows

1. Open Network Monitor.

2. On the Capture menu, click Trigger. The Capture Trigger dialog box is shown in Figure 3.23.

3. Specify the trigger condition. Table 3.4 shows the effect of each of the available selections.

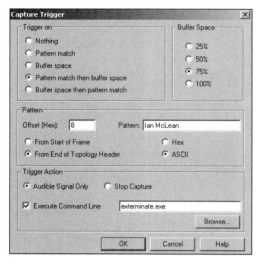

Figure 3.23   The Capture Trigger dialog box.

Table 3.4   Capture trigger conditions.

Selected Condition	Action
Nothing	Turns off trigger actions during data capture.
Pattern match	Engages the trigger if a pattern match occurs.
Buffer space	Engages the trigger when a capture fills a specified percentage of the capture buffer.
Pattern match then buffer space	After a pattern match occurs, the buffer space is monitored. The trigger is engaged when both specified conditions exist.
Buffer space then pattern match	After a capture has filled a specified percentage of the capture buffer, a pattern match is sought. The trigger is engaged when both specified conditions exist.

4. If one of the pattern-matching options is chosen, specify the pattern (in hex or ASCII). If required, you can specify the offset as a number of hexadecimal bytes, either from the start of the frame or from the end of the topology header.

5. Specify the action that Network Monitor should take if the trigger is engaged.

6. Test the trigger action in a simulated situation.

Chapter 4

Internet Protocol

(continued)

In Depth

This chapter discusses Internet Protocol (IP) as it's currently implemented on the Internet, in other words, IP version 4 (IPv4). Throughout the chapter and throughout this book, IP is taken to mean IPv4. IP is responsible for packet sorting and delivery. Each incoming or outgoing IP packet is referred to as a *datagram*. IP creates a datagram by encapsulating the *payload* with the source IP address of the sender and the destination IP address of the intended recipient. Unlike the Media Access Control (MAC) addresses (refer to Chapter 3), the IP addresses in a datagram remain the same throughout a packet's journey across a network.

The IP Datagram

The IP datagram typically contains another protocol packet as its payload. The network monitor capture in Figure 4.1 shows an Internet Control Message Protocol (ICMP) ping message encapsulated with an IP header. This capture is contained in arc02.cap, which is provided on the CD-ROM.

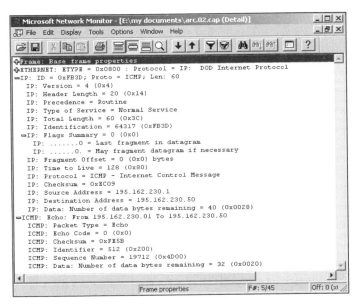

Figure 4.1   An IP datagram.

The IP header can be broken down into a number of fields, as follows:

- *Version*—Indicates the IP version. This field is 4 bits long and contains either 4 or 6.

- *Header Length*—Indicates the number of 32-bit (4-byte) words in the IP header. This field is 4 bits long and contains a value of 0x5 (20 bytes) or greater. Optionally, IP can extend the header length 4 bits at a time. If an IP option doesn't use all 32 bits of a word, the remaining bits are padded with zeros, so that the IP header length is always a multiple of 32 bits.

- *Precedence and Type of Service*—Indicates the Quality of Service (QoS) settings. This field is 8 bits long and contains information about precedence, delay, throughput, and reliability characteristics. QoS is described in detail in Chapter 10.

- *Total Length*—Indicates the total length of the IP datagram (header plus payload). This field is 16 bits long and contains the number of 32-bit words in the datagram.

- *Identification*—Identifies the specific IP datagram. This field is 16 bits long. If the IP datagram is fragmented during routing, the information in this field is used for reassembly at the destination.

- *Flag Summary*—Contains the fragmentation flags. This field is 3 bits long, but currently only two of these are used. The least significant bit indicates whether this is the final fragment in the datagram (or whether there are more to follow). The second least significant bit indicates whether or not the datagram can be fragmented.

- *Fragment Offset*—Indicates the position of the fragment relative to the original IP payload. This field is 13 bits long.

NOTE: *Fragmentation is described in detail in Chapter 8.*

- *Time to Live*—Indicates the time in seconds that a datagram will remain on the network before being discarded. Each time a datagram goes through a router, the Time to Live (TTL) is decremented by at least one second. Because a router typically forwards the IP diagram in less than a second, the TTL setting effectively becomes a hop count. The field is 8 bits long.

- *Protocol*—Indicates the protocol that gave the payload to IP to send. This field is 8 bits long. The information in this field is used by the higher-level layers in the destination host to process the payload. ICMP, for example, is indicated by a value of 1 in this field.

- *Checksum*—Used to check the integrity of the IP header only, and is therefore sometimes referred to as the *Header Checksum*. The payload may include its own checksum. This field is 16 bits long. Because the TTL is altered at each hop, the checksum is recalculated each time the datagram passes through a router.

- *Source Address*—Contains the IP source address. This field is 32 bits long for IPv4 (128 bits for IPv6).

- *Destination Address*—Contains the IP destination address. This field is 32 bits long for IPv4 (128 bits for IPv6).

- *Options and Padding*—Specifies IP options. If it exists, this field is 32 bits or a multiple of 32 bits long. A padding value of zero is used to ensure the entire header length is a multiple of 32 bits.

The length and structure of the payload that follows the header depends on its protocol and the information being transmitted. Like the header, however, it will always be padded so that it contains a multiple of 32 bits.

Figure 4.2 shows the hex and ASCII code associated with the IP datagram in Figure 4.1. Because not all fields in the header are a multiple of 4 bits, some of this information requires conversion to binary to interpret it. Examining the ASCII code tells you the message that's sent during a ping operation. Although this information isn't confidential, many IP payloads are. The ease with which this IP payload was captured demonstrates the need for message encryption.

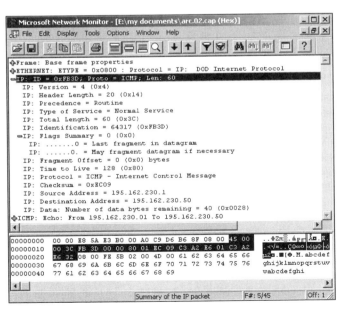

Figure 4.2   Hex and ASCII contents of an IP datagram.

Routing

By default, Windows 2000 systems don't behave as routers and don't forward IP datagrams between interfaces. If, however, a Windows 2000 server is multihomed, with two Network Interface Cards (NICs), and if the Routing and Remote Access Service (RRAS) is installed, then the server can be configured to provide full multiprotocol routing services.

Datagrams typically are sent to IP from the User Datagram Protocol (UDP) and the Transport Control Protocol (TCP) above (for outgoing packets) and from the NICs below (for incoming packets). IP examines the destination address on each datagram, compares it to a locally maintained routing table, and decides what action to take. These are the three possibilities:

- The datagram is passed to a protocol layer above IP on the local host.
- The datagram is forwarded using one of the locally attached NICs.
- The datagram is discarded.

Every computer that runs TCP/IP makes routing decisions that are determined by the IP routing table A routing table maintains four different types of routes, listed in the order that they are searched for a match:

- Host (a route to a single, specific IP address)
- Subnet (a route to a subnet)
- Network (a route to an entire network)
- Default (used when there is no other match)

Figure 4.3 displays the routing table for a multihomed host that has two NICs, which have been configured with IP addresses 195.162.230.1 and 195.162.231.1. It contains the following entries:

- The first entry is the default route to the active default gateway.
- The second entry is the default route for the first NIC. Because the PC is multihomed and is its own gateway, the second entry is the same as the first.
- The third entry is the default route for the second NIC.
- The fourth entry is for the loopback address.
- The fifth entry is for the network 195.162.230.0, on which the first NIC resides.
- The sixth entry is a host route for the local host on the first network. It specifies that a datagram bound for the local host is looped back internally and specifies the loopback address 127.0.0.1.
- The seventh entry is for the network broadcast address for the first network.
- The eighth entry is for the network 195.162.231.0, on which the second NIC resides.

Figure 4.3   A multihomed routing table.

- The ninth entry is a host route for the local host on the second network. It specifies that a datagram bound for the local host is looped back internally and specifies the loopback address 127.0.0.1.

- The tenth entry is for the network broadcast address for the first network.

- The eleventh entry is for IP multicasting, which is described later in this chapter.

- The twelfth entry is for the limited broadcast (all ones) address.

- The currently active default gateway is also listed. This is useful when multiple default gateways are configured.

Suppose that, on this host, a datagram is sent to 195.162.230.50. The routing table is first scanned for a host route, which isn't found, and then for a network route (195.162.230.0), which is found. The packet is sent via the local interface 195.162.230.1. The datagram could, for example, have been transmitted from the source host 195.162.231.60, in which case the router will receive it on gateway 195.162.231.1 and will transmit it on network 195.162.230.0, via gateway 195.162.230.1, to destination host 195.162.230.50. Figure 4.4 illustrates this process.

The IP routing table places information in columns. The significance of each column is as follows:

- *Destination*—The destination host, subnet address, network address, or default route. The destination for a default route is 0.0.0.0.

- *Netmask*—Used in conjunction with the destination to determine when a route is used. For example, a host route has a mask of 255.255.255.255, which means that only an exact match is accepted. A default route has a mask of 0.0.0.0, which means that any destination can use this route. A netmask, when written in binary, consists of a group of ones followed by a group of zeros. A one is significant (must match), and a zero is insignificant (does not need to match).

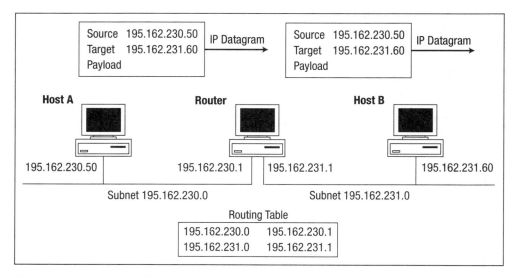

Figure 4.4   Routing an IP datagram.

NOTE: *A netmask in a routing table operates in a manner similar to a subnet mask, although its function isn't quite the same. Subnet masks are described in detail in Chapter 5.*

- *Gateway*—The IP address of the next router where a packet needs to be sent. On a Local Area Network (LAN) link (such as Ethernet or Token Ring), the gateway must be directly reachable from the router using the interface indicated in the Interface column.

- *Interface*—Indicates the interface that is to be used to reach the next router.

- *Metric*—Indicates the relative cost of using the route to reach the destination. A typical metric is hops, or the number of routers to cross to reach the destination. If there are multiple routes that have the same destination, the route that has the lowest metric is the best route. If there is a choice of default gateways, the computer will use the one that has the lowest metric unless it appears to be inactive, in which case dead gateway detection may trigger a switch to the next lowest metric default gateway in the list.

NOTE: *Dynamic Host Configuration Protocol (DHCP) servers provide a base metric and a list of default gateways. If a DHCP server provides a base of 10 and a list of three default gateways, the gateways will be configured with metrics of 10, 11, and 12, respectively. A DHCP-provided base isn't applied to statically configured default gateways.*

NOTE: *The terms "route table" and "routing table" are interchangeable. I prefer the former, but have used "routing table" in this chapter because the term appears in a dialog box accessed in the Immediate Solutions section.*

Routers and Gateways

The terms *router*, *gateway*, and *gateway machine* are often used as if they were equivalent. In a multihomed device, a gateway is the IP address of the NIC that resides on a particular subnet. A multihomed device that's capable of routing from one subnet to another using a routing table is called a router. Routers can be hardware devices, with little functionality other than routing. Alternatively, routing may be set up on a multihomed PC running the Windows 2000 RRAS. In this case, the RRAS server is a router and may also be referred to as a gateway machine.

Multiple Routers

The example illustrated in Figure 4.4 is the simplest possible routed network—two networks connected by a single router. In practice, a routed internetwork will have multiple routers. Figure 4.5 illustrates this.

In this situation, if the simple default routing tables are used, datagrams from Host A can be routed to Host B via Router 1. Similarly, datagrams from Host C

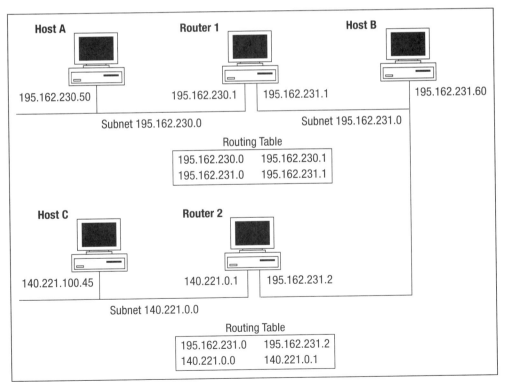

Figure 4.5   Multiple routers.

can be routed to Host B via router 2. Host B can send datagrams to Hosts A and C. However, Router 1 has no knowledge of Host C's network (140.221.0.0), and Router 2 has no knowledge of Host A's network (195.162.230.0). Datagrams can't, therefore, be routed between Hosts A and C.

Two methods are used to implement routing between Hosts A and C:

- The administrator can add static routes.

- A routing protocol, such as Routing Internet Protocol (RIP) or Open Shortest Path First (OSPF), can be implemented. Routing protocols cause routers to *advertise* their routing tables, so that Router 1 has access to Router 2's routing table in order to download details of routes of which it's not already aware. Similarly, Router 2 would download routing information from Router 1.

TIP: *When the routing topology contains direct router-to-router links, a network identity must be specified for the router-to-router connection, even though there are no hosts on the router-to-router network (other than the routers themselves). This is the normal topology for backbone routers on a large internetwork. Imagine Figure 4.5 without Host B.*

Static routing, RIP, and OSPF are described in the next three sections of this chapter.

Static Routing

A static routed IP environment is best suited to a small, single-path, static IP internetwork. All of the routing information is stored in a static routing table on each router. It's the administrator's responsibility to ensure that each router has the appropriate routes in its routing table, so that traffic can be exchanged between any two endpoints on the internetwork.

Static routing doesn't scale to larger internetworks. To deploy static routing successfully, your internetwork should meet the following criteria:

- No more than 10 networks.

- Only a single path for packets to travel between any two endpoints on the internetwork.

- The topology of the internetwork won't change over time.

Normally, small businesses and branch offices use static routing. In the latter case, a single default route at the branch office router ensures that all traffic not destined for a computer on the branch office network is routed to the main office. This avoids the overhead of running a routing protocol over a low-bandwidth Wide Area Network (WAN) link between the branch and the main office. The main office routers typically use a routing protocol for external (and possibly internal) routing.

Static routing has no fault tolerance. If a router or link goes down, static routers don't sense the fault and inform other routers, and the single path topology prevents messages from being sent by alternative routes. For a small organization, however, routers and links don't normally fail often enough to justify deploying a multipath topology and a routing protocol.

If a new network is added to or removed from a statically routed internetwork, routes to the new network must be added or removed manually. If a new router is added, it must be configured with all the network routes.

Static Routing Design Issues

A number of issues need to be taken into account in designing a static network.

Peripheral Routers

A peripheral router is a router attached to multiple networks, only one of which has a neighboring router. Peripheral routers should be configured with a default route that points to the neighboring router.

Routing Loops

Do not configure two neighboring routers with default routes that point to each other. Because a default route passes all traffic that's not on a directly connected network to the configured router, two routers that have default routes pointing to each other may produce routing loops for traffic that has an unreachable destination.

Demand-Dial

Two methods exist for configuring static routes for Demand-Dial interfaces:

- Configure a default route.
- Use auto-static routes.

NOTE: *The term Dial on Demand Routing (DDR) is sometimes used for such interfaces. Microsoft documentation, however, refers to Demand-Dial interfaces.*

A default route is configured on the branch office router that uses the demand-dial Remote Access Service (RAS) interface. The advantage of this method is that a single route needs to be added only once. The disadvantage is that any traffic that's not on the branch office network causes the branch office router to call the main office—including traffic for unreachable destinations.

Auto-static routes are static routes that are automatically added to the routing table for a router after routes are requested across a demand-dial connection by using the RIPv2 routing protocol (refer to the next section of this chapter). The advantage of auto-static routes is that unreachable destinations don't cause the router to call the main office. The disadvantage is that they must be periodically updated to reflect the networks that are reachable at the main office. If a new network is added to the main office and the branch office hasn't performed an auto-static update, all destinations on the new main office network are unreachable from the branch office.

Security

To prevent the intentional or unintentional modification of static routes on routers, place the routers in a locked room so that users can't access them. Also, assign administrator rights only to those users who will be running RRAS.

RIP

RIP is designed for exchanging routing information within a small to medium internetwork. It is simple to configure and deploy, but doesn't scale to large or very large internetworks. The maximum hop count used by RIP routers is 15; networks that are 16 hops or more away are considered unreachable.

As internetworks grow larger in size, periodic announcements by each RIP router can cause excessive traffic. Because RIP is a distance vector routing protocol, each routing table has a complete list of all network identities (IDs) and of every possible way of reaching each ID. Routing tables that are generated using RIP can be very large. This can lead to multiple RIP packets and a large volume of network traffic.

When the network topology changes or when a router goes down, it may take several minutes before the RIP routers reconfigure themselves to the new topology. This is known as the *slow convergence problem*. While the internetwork reconfigures itself, routing loops may form that result in lost or undeliverable data.

Initially, the routing table for each router includes only the networks that are physically connected. A RIP router periodically sends announcements that contain its routing table entries to inform other local RIP routers of the networks it can reach. RIP version 1 uses IP broadcast packets for its announcements; RIP version 2 uses either multicast or broadcast packets. Windows 2000 supports both RIPv1 (for backward compatibility) and RIPv2. RIPv2 supports multicast announcements and simple password authentication and provides more flexibility in the use of Variable Length Subnet Masks (VLSM) and Classless Interdomain Routing (CIDR) environments. VLSM and CIDR are described in detail in Chapter 5.

RIP routers can communicate routing information through triggered updates. Triggered updates occur when the internetwork topology changes, and updated routing information is sent that reflects those changes. With triggered updates, the update is sent immediately rather than waiting for the next periodic announcement.

The Windows 2000 implementation of RIP has the following features:

- Selection of which RIP version to run on each interface for both incoming and outgoing packets.
- Split-horizon, poison-reverse, and triggered-update algorithms. These are used to avoid routing loops and speed up recovery when topology changes occur.
- Route filters for choosing which networks to announce or accept.
- Peer filters for choosing which router's announcements are accepted.
- Configurable announcement and route aging timers.
- Simple password authentication support.
- The ability to disable subnet summarization.

Implementation of these features is described in the Immediate Solutions section of this chapter. For detailed information about the operation of RIP for IP, see the Windows 2000 resource kit, downloadable from **www.microsoft.com** and available on Technet.

WARNING! *If you are using multiple IP routing protocols, configure only a single routing protocol per interface.*

A RIP-routed environment is best suited to a small to medium, multipath, dynamic IP internetwork. To deploy RIP successfully, your internetwork should meet the following criteria:

- Between 10 and 50 networks.
- Multiple paths for packets to travel between any two endpoints on the internetwork.
- The topology of the internetwork changes over time because networks are added and removed, and links occasionally go down and come back up.

Medium-sized businesses, large branch offices, or satellite offices that have multiple subnets normally use RIP.

RIP Implementation Issues

A number of issues should be taken into account when implementing RIP.

Internetwork Diameter

The *diameter* of an internetwork is a measure of its size in terms of hops or other metrics. The maximum diameter of RIP internetworks is 15 routers. However, the Windows 2000 router considers all non-RIP learned routes to be at a fixed hop count of two. Static routes, even static routes for directly connected networks, are considered non-RIP learned routes.

When a Windows 2000 RIP router advertises its directly connected networks, it advertises them at a hop count of 2 even though there is only one physical router to cross. Therefore, a RIP-based internetwork that uses Windows 2000 RIP routers has a maximum physical diameter of 14 routers. The maximum can be less than 14 routers if there is a mixture of static and RIP-supplied routes throughout the internetwork.

Defining RIP Metrics

RIP uses the hop count as a metric to determine the best route. This can lead to undesired routing behavior. Suppose, for example, two sites were connected together by using a T1 link, with a lower-speed satellite link as a backup. RIP would treat both links as having the same metric, and the router would be free to select either of them, even though one is slower.

To prevent the satellite link from being chosen in this example, you would assign a custom cost (such as 2) to the satellite interface. If the T1 link goes down, then the satellite link is chosen as the next best route.

If, however, you use custom costs to indicate link speed, delay, or reliability factors, you must ensure that the accumulated cost (hop count) between any two endpoints on the internetwork doesn't exceed 15.

Mixed RIPv1 and RIPv2 Environments

If there are routers in your internetwork that don't support RIPv2, you can use a mixed environment. However, RIPv1 doesn't support CIDR or VLSM implementations. You may, therefore, experience routing problems because CIDR and VLSM are supported in one part of your internetwork but not in another.

If an internetwork is using a mixture of RIPv1 and RIPv2 routers, you must configure the Windows 2000 router interfaces to advertise using either RIPv1 or RIPv2 broadcasts (or multicasts) and to accept either RIPv1 or RIPv2 announcements.

Password Authentication

If you use RIPv2 simple password authentication, you must configure all of the RIPv2 interfaces on the same network with the same case-sensitive password. You can use the same password for all the networks of your internetwork, or you can have a different password for each network.

Demand-Dial Links

To perform auto-static updates across demand-dial links, each demand-dial interface must be configured to advertise using RIPv2 multicast announcements and to accept such announcements. Otherwise, the RIP request for routes sent by the requesting router won't be answered by the router on the other side of the demand-dial link.

Using RIP over Frame Relay

Because RIP is a broadcast- and multicast-based protocol, a special configuration is required for RIP operation over nonbroadcast technologies, such as Frame Relay. This configuration depends on how the Frame Relay virtual circuits appear as network interfaces on computers running Windows 2000. Either the Frame Relay adapter appears as a single adapter for all the virtual circuits (single adapter model), or each virtual circuit appears as a separate adapter with its own network ID (multiple adapter model).

Single Adapter Model

With the single adapter model, also known as the Non-Broadcast Multiple Access (NBMA) model, the Frame Relay service provider's network, or Frame Relay *cloud*, is treated as an IP network, and its endpoints are assigned IP addresses. To ensure that RIP traffic is received by all of the appropriate endpoints on the cloud, configure the Frame Relay interface to unicast its RIP announcements to all of these endpoints. Configuring RIP unicast neighbors, described in the Immediate Solutions section of this chapter, implements this functionality.

In a spoke and hub Frame Relay topology, the Frame Relay interface for the hub router must have split-horizon processing disabled. Otherwise, the spoke routers never receive each other's routes. The Immediate Solutions section of this chapter describes how to enable split-horizon processing.

Multiple Adapter Model

In the multiple adapter model, each Frame Relay virtual circuit appears as a point-to-point link with its own network ID, and all endpoints are assigned IP addresses. Because each virtual circuit is its own point-to-point connection, you can either broadcast or multicast RIP announcements. Broadcasting assumes that both endpoints are on the same IP network.

TIP: *Using RIP over other nonbroadcast technologies, such as X.25 and Asynchronous Transfer Mode (ATM), follows the same principles as using RIP over Frame Relay.*

RIP Security

As with static routing security, routers should be kept locked away, and rights should be given only to those who must have them. RIP security can be enhanced through the use of RIPv2 authentication, peer security, route filters, and neighbors.

RIPv2 Authentication

RIPv2 router interfaces may be configured to use simple password authentication, so that received RIP announcements that don't match the password are discarded. The purpose of this is to prevent the corruption of RIP routes by an unauthorized RIP router. Although Microsoft lists RIP authentication as a security feature, its main purpose is identification. The password is sent in plain text, and any user who has a network sniffer, such as Network Monitor, can capture the announcements.

> **WARNING!   Security that you think is providing a safeguard when it isn't is worse than no security at all.**

Peer Security

You can specify, by IP address, a list of routers from which RIP announcements are accepted. RIP announcements from unauthorized RIP routers will then be discarded. Adding peer filters is described in the Immediate Solutions section of this chapter.

Route Filters

Route filters can be configured on each RIP interface so that the only routes considered for addition to the routing table are those that reflect reachable network IDs. Adding route filters is described in the Immediate Solutions section of this chapter.

Neighbors

Normally, RIP either broadcasts or multicasts announcements. To prevent RIP traffic from being received by any node except neighboring RIP routers, the Windows 2000 router can unicast RIP announcements. Configuring RIP unicast neighbors ensures that RIP announcements are directed to neighboring RIP routers. Configuring unicast neighbors is described in the Immediate Solutions section of this chapter.

Silent RIP

Windows 2000 Professional provides a RIPv1 silent component, called the RIP Listener, that's installed as an optional networking component. A silent RIP host processes received RIP announcements, but doesn't broadcast RIP advertisements. The RIP announcements are used to build the routing table for the host.

Silent RIP is also used in Unix environments. If there are silent RIP hosts on a network, you must determine which version of RIP they support. If they support only RIPv1, you must use RIPv1 on the network.

WARNING! *If you configure RIP routers to unicast to neighboring RIP routers, the ability of silent RIP hosts to receive RIP traffic is impaired. In this case, you need either to add the silent RIP hosts as neighbors or to configure the Windows 2000 router to broadcast or multicast in addition to unicasting to RIP neighbors.*

OSPF

OSPF is designed for exchanging routing information within a large or very large internetwork. It requires little network overhead, even in very large internetworks. Planning and configuring OSPF is, however, complex, and it's more difficult than RIP to administer. OSPF uses the Shortest Path First (SPF) algorithm to compute routes in the routing table. This algorithm computes the shortest (least cost) path between the router and all the networks of the internetwork, and SPF-calculated routes are always loop-free.

Unlike RIP routers, OSPF routers don't exchange routing table entries. Instead, they maintain a map, or *link state database*, of the internetwork that's updated after any change to the network topology. The link state database is synchronized across all the OSPF routers and is used to compute the routes in the routing table.

Neighboring OSPF routers form an *adjacency*, which is a logical relationship between routers used to synchronize the link state database. Changes to internetwork topology are flooded across the entire internetwork to ensure that the link state database on each router is synchronized and accurate at all times. When a router receives changes to the link state database, its routing table is recalculated.

As the size of the link state database increases, so do memory requirements and route computation times. To address this scaling problem, OSPF divides the internetwork into *areas* (collections of contiguous networks) that are connected to each other through a backbone area. Each router keeps a link state database only for those areas that are connected to it. Area Border Routers (ABRs) connect the backbone area to other areas. An OSPF internetwork is illustrated in Figure 4.6.

TIP: *If you're using multiple IP routing protocols, configure only one routing protocol per interface.*

Hello and Dead Intervals

An OSPF router announces its presence on an interface by means of a periodic *hello package*. This identifies the router and, if so configured, contains a plaintext password. The *hello interval* is the number of seconds between transmissions of hello packets. The *dead interval* is the number of seconds before a silent remote

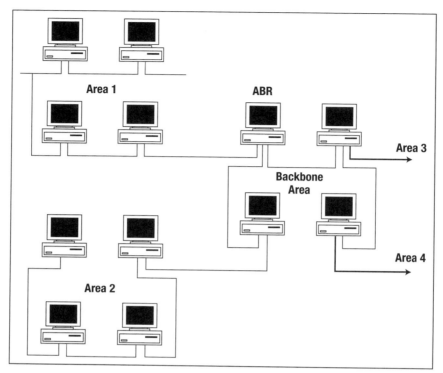

Figure 4.6   An OSPF internetwork.

router—that is, a router that isn't transmitting hello packets—is declared to be down. The dead interval is a multiple (typically either four or six) of the hello interval.

Virtual Links

Normally, ABRs have a physical connection to the backbone area. If this is impossible or impractical, you can use a virtual link to connect the ABR to the backbone.

A virtual link is a logical point-to-point connection to an ABR that's physically connected to the backbone from an ABR that isn't. The area that is physically connected to the backbone is known as the *transit area*. To create a virtual link, both routers, called virtual link neighbors, are configured with the transit area, the router ID of the virtual link neighbor, matching hello and dead intervals, and a matching password. Refer to the Immediate Solutions section of this chapter to set up virtual links.

OSPF Deployment Criteria

Properly deployed, an OSPF environment automatically updates routes when networks are added and removed from the internetwork. Each router needs to be configured so that OSPF-based route advertisements are propagated to OSPF routers. An OSPF-routed environment is best suited to a large to very large, multipath, dynamic internetwork. To deploy OSPF successfully, your internetwork should meet the following criteria:

• More than 50 networks.

• Multiple paths for packets to travel between any two endpoints on the internetwork.

• The topology of the internetwork changes over time because networks are added and removed, and links occasionally go down and come back up.

Worldwide corporate or institutional internetworks, owned by multinational organizations, or large, geographically widespread national institutions, such as major universities, typically use OSPF.

WARNING! Windows 2000 routers don't support the use of OSPF in a demand-dial configuration that uses nonpermanent, dial-up links.

OSPF Design Considerations

A number of design issues must be taken into consideration before you implement OSPF. Firstly, you need to choose the design level. The three levels of OSPF design are:

• Autonomous system design

• Area design

• Network design

Autonomous System Design

When you design an OSPF autonomous system, Microsoft recommends the following guidelines:

• Divide the OSPF system into areas that can be summarized.

• Subdivide your IP address space into a network/area/subnet/host hierarchy whenever possible.

• Make the backbone area a single, high-bandwidth network.

• Create stub areas whenever possible. An area can be configured as a stub when there's only one exit point from the area (or when the choice of exit point need not be made on a per-external-destination basis). In Figure 4.6, for example, area 2 could be a stub area.

• Avoid virtual links if possible.

4. Internet Protocol

Area Design

When you design each OSPF area, the following guidelines are recommended:

- Ensure that all areas are assigned network IDs that can be expressed as a small number of summary routes. This means that, whenever possible, the IDs of networks within an area should be contiguous, so that they can be *supernetted* into a few (preferably one) network ID. Supernetting is described in Chapter 5.

- If an area can be summarized with a single route, make the area ID the single route being advertised.

- Ensure that multiple ABRs for the same area are summarizing the same routes.

- Ensure that there are no *back doors* between areas. A back door exists when one ABR can send traffic to another without crossing the backbone area.

- Restrict each area to less than 100 networks.

Network Design

When you design a network, the following guidelines are recommended:

- Assign router priorities so that the least busy routers are the designated router and backup designated router. A designated router compiles, synchronizes, and advertises the network link state and is adjacent to all the other routers on its network. The backup designated router also maintains an adjacency to all the routers on its network and can take over the functions of the designated router if the latter goes down.

- Set link costs to reflect bit rate, delay, or reliability characteristics.

- Assign a password.

OSPF over Frame Relay

How OSPF is configured for Frame Relay depends on how the Frame Relay virtual circuits appear as network interfaces on computers that are running Windows 2000. Either the Frame Relay adapter appears as a single adapter for all the virtual circuits (single adapter model), or each virtual circuit appears as a separate adapter (multiple adapter model).

Single Adapter Model

With the single adapter, or NBMA, model, the Frame Relay cloud is treated as an IP network, and its endpoints are assigned IP addresses. To ensure that OSPF traffic is received by all of the appropriate endpoints on the cloud, configure the Frame Relay interface to unicast its OSPF announcements to all of these endpoints. For a Windows 2000 router, this is done by designating the interface as an NBMA network and adding OSPF neighbors. Adding OSPF neighbors is described in the Immediate Solutions section of this chapter.

In a spoke and hub Frame Relay topology, the Frame Relay interface for the hub router must have a router priority set to one or greater, and the Frame Relay interfaces for the spoke routers must have a router priority set to zero. Otherwise, the hub router can't become the designated router, and adjacencies can't form across the Frame Relay network.

Multiple Adapter Model

In the multiple adapter model, each Frame Relay virtual circuit appears as a point-to-point link with its own network ID, and all endpoints are assigned IP addresses. Because each virtual circuit is its own point-to-point connection, you can configure the interface for the point-to-point network type.

TIP: *Using OSPF over other NBMA technologies, such as X.25 and ATM, follows the same principles as using OSPF over Frame Relay.*

External Routes

The OSPF routers in an organization define an Autonomous System (AS), and by default only OSPF routes that correspond to directly connected network segments are propagated within the AS. An external route is any route that isn't within the AS. External routes can come from many sources, including the following:

- Other routing protocols such, as RIP

- Static routes

- Routes set on the router through Simple Network Management Protocol (SNMP)—refer to Chapter 19

External routes are propagated throughout the AS through one or more Autonomous System Boundary Routers (ASBRs). An ASBR advertises external routes within the OSPF AS. If, for example, you want to advertise the static routes of a Windows 2000 router, you should enable that router as an ASBR.

External Route Filters

By default, OSPF routers acting as ASBRs import and advertise all external routes, and it may be necessary to filter out some of these routes. External routes can be filtered on the ASBR using the following criteria:

- *External route source*—ASBR is configured to accept or ignore the routes specified by external sources.

- *Individual route*—ASBR is configured to accept or discard specific routes by specifying one or more destination/network mask pairs.

WARNING! *You can use external route filters to filter routes only from non-OSPF sources. You can't filter OSPF routes within the OSPF AS.*

OSPF Security

As with static routing security, routers should be kept locked away, and rights should be given only to those who must have them. OSPF security can be enhanced through the use of external route filters (see previous section) and OSPF authentication.

OSPF Authentication

OSPF interfaces on a Windows 2000 router are configured to send a password hello message (that is, a hello message containing a simple password). This password—the default is "12345678"—helps prevent the corruption of OSPF data from an unauthorized router on a network and is sent in plain text. OSPF authentication is for identification rather than security, although Microsoft lists it as a security feature. Plain text passwords can be captured and displayed using a network sniffer, such as Network Monitor.

Event Logging

Windows 2000 RRAS logs errors in the system event log. You can use this information to troubleshoot the routing processes.

Four levels of logging are available:

- Log errors only.
- Log errors and warnings (default).
- Log all information (verbose).
- Disable event logging.

Logging consumes system resources, and verbose logging information can be complex and very detailed. The verbose setting should, therefore, be used sparingly. After an event has been logged or the problem has been identified, you should reset logging to its default value (log errors and warnings).

TIP: *Logging may be set up by expanding* server-name/*IP Routing in the RRAS snap-in; right-clicking General, RIP, or OSPF; and selecting Properties.*

Duplicate IP Address Detection

In addition to routing, IP implements duplicate address detection. When the stack is first initialized, gratuitous Address Resolution Protocol (ARP) requests are broadcast for the IP addresses of the local host. The number of these requests is controlled by the **ArpRetryCount** registry parameter, which defaults to 3.

If another host replies to any of these ARP requests, the IP address is already in use. When this happens, the Windows 2000 computer (the *offending* computer) still boots, but its IP address is disabled. If the *defending* computer is a Windows 2000 (or Windows NT*x*) computer, a system log entry is generated, and an error message displayed, on that computer. Its interface, however, continues to operate. To repair possible damage to ARP caches on other computers, the offending computer rebroadcasts another ARP request, this time impersonating the defending computer by using its MAC address as the source address in the request. This corrects the mapping for the address in the ARP caches of the other computers.

A DHCP-enabled client informs the DHCP server when an IP address conflict is detected and requests a new address. The DHCP server then flags the conflicting address as bad. This is known as DHCP *decline support*.

Multihoming

A computer that's configured with more than one IP address is referred to as *multihomed*. Multihoming is supported in three different ways:

- Multiple IP addresses per NIC
- Multiple NICs, one per physical network
- Multiple networks and media types

NOTE: *There are limitations to configuring multiple IP addresses per NIC. This is not a method of setting up a router—each separate network requires its own configured NIC. Also, NetBIOS over TCP/IP (NetBT) binds to only one IP address per interface card. This registration occurs over the IP address that is listed first in the User Interface (UI). Multiple IP addresses per NIC are configured if (for example) you're setting up multiple File Transfer Protocol (FTP) sites on a Web server.*

An IP datagram sent from a multihomed host is placed on the interface that has the best apparent route to the destination. The datagram can, therefore, contain the source IP address of one interface in the multihomed host, yet be placed on the media by a different interface. When a computer is multihomed with NICs attached to *disjoint* networks (networks that are separate from and unaware of each other), routing problems can arise. It may be necessary to set up static routes to remote networks in this situation.

TIP: *A RAS-connected network and a local connection, attached to separate NICs on the same computer, would be disjoint networks.*

The best practice when configuring a computer that's multihomed on two disjoint networks is to set the default gateway on the main or largest network. Then, either add static routes or use a routing protocol to provide connectivity to the hosts on the smaller network. Do not configure a different default gateway on each side—this can result in loss of connectivity.

IP Multicasting

Multicasting uses the IP address range 224.0.0.0 to 239.255.255.255, known as Class D addresses. Address classes are described in detail in Chapter 5. At this point, it's sufficient to know that there are three "standard" address classes—A, B, and C—that are used (for example) in DHCP scopes. Classes D and E are used for multicasting and experimental purposes, respectively. In TCP/IP networks, you must first configure each host with its own IP address, taken from one of the standard address classes, before you can configure it to support and use a multicast IP address.

A group of TCP/IP host computers shares the use of a multicast IP address. When the destination address for a datagram is a multicast address, the datagram is forwarded to all members of a *multicast group*, which is a set of hosts identified by the address. The membership of a multicast group is dynamic, and individual hosts can join or leave the group at any time.

Membership and use of multicast groups are unrestricted, group membership can be any size, and hosts can be members of many multicast groups. You can reserve multicast group addresses permanently, or you can assign them temporarily and use them as needed. If you want to reserve a permanent group IP address for Internet use, you must register it with the Internet Assigned Numbers Authority (IANA).

Internet Group Management Protocol (IGMP), described in Chapter 6, is used to manage IP multicasting.

Multicast Scopes

Multicast scopes are supported through the use of Multicast Address Dynamic Client Allocation Protocol (MADCAP), which defines how MADCAP servers can provide IP addresses dynamically to MADCAP clients. Typically, a MADCAP client might also be a Multicast Server (MCS) that manages the shared or group use of the allocated multicast IP address and streams data traffic to members that share the use of the specified group address. Once an MCS is configured and is allocated a group IP address, multicast clients that have registered their membership with the MCS can receive streams sent to this address. The MCS also manages the multicast group list, updating its membership and status so that all current members receive multicast traffic.

Multicast Scope Ranges

The Internet Engineering Task Force (IETF) Multicast Allocation (malloc) working group recommends two methods of determining the IP address ranges to use for multicast scopes on a MADCAP server. These are:

- *Administrative scoping*—Employed when specifying multicast IP addresses on a private intranet. The recommended range is 239.192.0.0/14 (that is, network 239.192.0.0, with a subnet mask of 255.252.0.0). This range is known as the IPv4 organization local scope and is intended for use by an organization setting multicast scopes privately for its own internal or organizational use. The range provides 262,144 (2^{18}) group addresses.

TIP: *For more information, refer to RFC 2365, which can be obtained at* **www.rfc-editor.org**.

- *Global scoping*—Employed when specifying multicast group IP addresses in a public network address space, particularly the Internet. The 233.0.0.0 range of the Class D address space is the recommended global scope range. When this range is used, a network registry, such as the IANA, allocates and reserves the first 8 bits of the range (233). The next 16 bits are based on a previously assigned AS number. This number is recorded with the IANA registry for your region. (Refer to Table 4.1 for details of how to obtain this number.) The last 8 bits in the address are for local use. A subnet mask of 255.255.255.0 (/24) should be applied. This provides 255 multicast group addresses for use on the Internet.

TIP: *For more information on global scoping, refer to the draft "Static Allocation in 233/8" at the IETF Web site,* **www.ietf.org**. *For more information on AS numbering, refer to RFC 1930, available at* **www.rfc-editor.org**.

MADCAP and DHCP

The Windows 2000 DHCP Server service supports both the DHCP and MADCAP protocols. These protocols function independently of each other. Multicast scopes don't support the use of DHCP options and can be configured with a finite lifetime.

Table 4.1   Obtaining an AS number.

Location	Details
United States	Access **www.arin.net/intro.html**
The Americas, Caribbean, and Africa	Email **hostmaster@arin.net**
Europe	Email **ncc@ripe.net**
The Asia-Pacific region	Email **admin@apnic.net**

IP over ATM

Windows 2000 supports IP over ATM (IP/ATM) or, more precisely, a *Logical IP Subnet* (LIS) over an ATM network. A LIS is a set of IP hosts that can communicate directly with each other. Two hosts that belong to different LISs can communicate only through an IP router that's a member of both subnets.

ATM Address Resolution

Because an ATM network is nonbroadcast, ARP broadcasts can't be used for address resolution. An ATM ARP server is, therefore, needed to provide IP-to-ATM address resolution. For multicast operation, a Multicast Address Resolution Server (MARS) is also required. IP/ATM network components can reside on a server or an ATM switch.

One of the stations in a LIS is set up as an ARP server, and each ARP client on the LIS is configured with this station's ATM address. When an ARP client initializes, it makes an ATM connection to the ARP server and sends a packet to the server that contains the client's IP and ATM addresses. The ARP server builds a table of IP address/ATM address mappings. When a client sends an IP packet to another client (whose IP address is known), it queries the ARP server for the ATM address of its target. When it receives a reply that contains the required ATM address, the client establishes a direct ATM connection to the target.

Clients close inactive ATM connections, including the connections to the server. By default, clients refresh their IP and ATM address information with the server every 15 minutes, and the server purges an entry that isn't refreshed after 20 minutes.

TIP: *The operation of an IP/ATM network is defined in RFC 1577 and RFC 2255.*

Multihoming and ATM Support

A multihomed IP host can be reached at more than one IP address and may or may not possess multiple physical network interfaces. With IP over ATM, you can configure multiple logical or virtual network interfaces on a single ATM adapter. The IP layer sees these as multiple ARP interfaces, even if they're all created on the same physical adapter.

Each virtual interface is part of a separate IP/ATM LIS, and its ARP client entity can (potentially) connect to a different ARP server. Using this concept, it's possible to build a router for an IP/ATM network that operates on multiple virtual interfaces, all configured on the same ATM link. The TCP/IP stack supports the existence of more than one ARP module. ARP for Ethernet and Token Ring is built into the tcpip.sys driver. ARP support for ATM is provided in separate drivers (atmarpc.sys and atmarps.sys), which are located between IP and the Network Driver Interface Specification (NDIS) interface.

IP/ATM Broadcasting and Multicasting

A broadcast or multicast is used to establish point-to-multipoint connections between the requesting client and multiple end stations on the network. The process of broadcasting and multicasting on IP/ATM can follow two different methods:

- *Direct point-to-multipoint connection*—If a client needs to send an IP packet to a broadcast or multicast IP address, it sends a request to the MARS to resolve the IP address to a list of end stations. The MARS sends a group of addresses to the client, allowing it to set up a point-to-multipoint connection.

- *Point-to-multipoint connection through a multicast server*—The Windows ATM ARP/MARS has an integrated multicast server, which registers one or more multicast groups with the MARS and receives a list of members in each multicast group from it. The MARS updates the multicast server when clients join or leave a multicast group. When a client makes a multicast or broadcast request to the MARS, the MARS returns the address of the multicast server. The client contacts the multicast server, which creates a point-to-multipoint connection with the multicast group. The multicast server copies and distributes the packets sent by the client that initiated the point-to-multipoint call to end stations on the multicast list.

Immediate Solutions

Deploying Static Routing

If static routing is appropriate for your IP internetwork, it should be deployed as follows:

1. Draw a map of the topology of your IP internetwork that shows the separate networks and the placement of routers and TCP/IP hosts.

2. Assign a unique IP network ID for each network.

3. Assign IP addresses to each router interface. It's common practice (but not mandatory) to assign the first IP addresses of a given IP network to router interfaces. For example, for an IP network ID of 195.162.230.0 with the default subnet mask 255.255.255.0 (sometimes written 195.162.230.0/24), the router interface is assigned the IP address 195.162.230.1.

4. Compile a list of routes to be added to the routing table for that router. Each route consists of a destination ID, a subnet mask, a gateway IP address, a metric, and the interface to be used to reach the network. In the example illustrated in Figure 4.5, the route to be added to Router 1 is defined in Table 4.2.

TIP: *The interface number (2 is a local area connection) is used by the **route add** command. This is optional—if no interface number is specified, the **route** utility will find the best interface.*

---

5. Add static routes by one of two methods:
   • The **route** command
   • The Routing and Remote Access MMC snap-in

6. Use the **ping** and **tracert** commands to test the routing paths. These commands are described in detail in Chapter 19.

Related solutions:	*Found on page:*
Configuring TCP/IP	24
Using the Command-Line Tools	709

Table 4.2   Route details.

Parameter	Value
Destination ID	140.221.0.0
Subnet Mask	255.255.0.0
Gateway	195.162.231.2
Metric	2
Interface	195.162.231.1 (2)

Adding a Static Route Using the **Route** Command

The **route** command can be used from the command prompt to add or delete routing table entries and to display the routing table. Figure 4.7 gives the syntax of this command. If static routes need to be persistent—that is, they are retained on initialization—the **-p** switch should be used. The following command sets up the additional route on Router 1 (see Figure 4.5) that's specified in Table 4.2.

```
route -p add 140.221.0.0 MASK 255.255.0.0 195.162.231.2 METRIC 2 IF 2
```

TIP: *Persistent routes are stored in the HKEY_LOCAL_MACHINE\SYSTEM Registry hive, under the subkey \CurrentControlSet\Services\Tcpip\Parameters\PersistentRoutes.*

Adding a Static Route Using the RRAS Snap-In

A static route can also be added using the RRAS snap-in. To add a route by this method, proceed as follows:

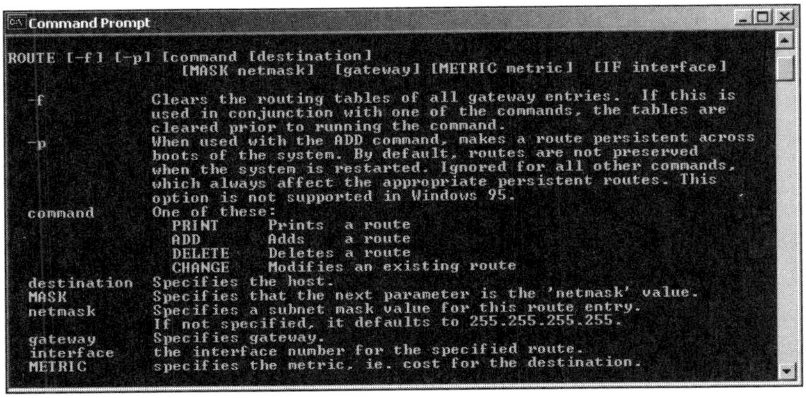

Figure 4.7   The **route** command syntax.

1. Open Routing and Remote Access in the Start|Programs|Administrative Tools menu.

2. Expand *server name*|IP Routing and right-click Static Routes.

3. Select New Static Route.

4. In the Interface drop-down list, select Local Area Connection.

5. Type the route details in the boxes provided.

6. Click OK and exit from the MMC snap-in.

Viewing a Routing Table

A routing table can be viewed by entering the **route print** command from the Command Console. Alternately, the RRAS snap-in can be used. To view a routing table using the RRAS snap-in, proceed as follows:

1. Open Routing and Remote Access in the Start|Programs|Administrative Tools menu.

2. Expand *server name*|IP Routing and right-click Static Routes.

3. Select Show IP routing table.

Deploying RIP

If dynamic routing using RIP is appropriate for your IP internetwork, it can be deployed as follows:

1. Design your internetwork and specify network IDs and gateway IP addresses, as described in the "Deploying Static Routing" immediate solution.

2. On a per-interface basis, decide whether router interfaces will be configured for RIPv1 or RIPv2. If an interface is configured for RIP v2, decide whether the RIPv2 announcements will be broadcast or multicast.

3. Add the RIPv2 routing protocol and configure the appropriate interfaces for RIPv1 or RIPv2 for each Windows 2000 router.

4. When your configuration is complete, allow a few minutes for the routers to update each other's routing tables and then test the internetwork.

Adding the RIPv2 Routing Protocol

All the RIP procedures in the following sections assume that the RIPv2 protocol is installed, that the RRAS service is enabled, and that you're logged on as an administrator. To add the RIPv2 protocol, proceed as follows:

1. In the Start|Programs|Administrative Tools menu, select Routing and Remote Access.

2. Expand *server-name*|IP Routing and right-click General.

3. Select New Routing Protocol.

4. In the Select Routing Protocol dialog box, highlight RIPv2 for Internet Protocol and then click OK.

5. Exit from the MMC snap-in.

Adding a RIP Interface

To use RIP on an interface, you must add the interface to the RIP IP routing interface list. To do this, proceed as follows:

1. Open Routing and Remote Access in the Start|Programs|Administrative Tools menu.

2. Expand *server name*|IP Routing and right-click RIP.

3. Click New Interface and select the interface you want to configure.

4. Click OK and exit from the MMC snap-in.

Configuring RIP

RIPv1 requires little configuration, but has limited functionality. If you select RIPv2 on an interface, you have access to the additional features that this protocol provides. The next set of procedures configures RIP features. This configuration is implemented in the Properties dialog box for the interface you wish to configure. The first procedure, to access this box, is therefore used by all the following procedures in this section.

Accessing the Interface Properties Dialog Box

To access the Interface Properties dialog box, proceed as follows:

1. Open Routing and Remote Access in the Start|Programs|Administrative Tools menu.

2. Expand *server-name*|IP Routing and select RIP.

3. In the details pane, right-click the interface you want to configure and select Properties.

Figure 4.8 displays the Properties dialog box for the Local Area Connection interface.

4. Internet Protocol

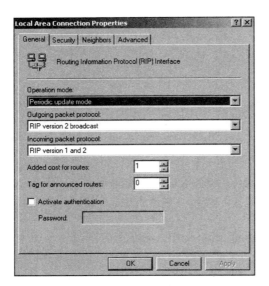

Figure 4.8   The Local Area Connection Properties dialog box.

Configuring a RIP Interface

To configure a RIP interface, proceed as follows:

1. Access the Interface Properties dialog box.

2. On the General tab, in Outgoing packet protocol, do one of the following:

   - Select RIP version 1 broadcast.

   - If there are RIPv1 routers on the same network as this interface, select RIP version 2 broadcast.

   - If there are only RIPv2 routers on the same network as this interface or if the interface is a demand-dial interface, select RIP version 2 multicast.

3. On the General tab, in Incoming packet protocol, do one of the following:

   - Select RIP version 1 broadcast.

   - If you want to use RIPv2 and there are RIPv1 routers on the same network as this interface, select RIP version 1 and 2.

   - If there are only RIP version 2 routers on the same network as this interface or if the interface is a demand-dial interface, select RIP version 2 only.

   - If you don't want to receive information from other routers on the internetwork, select Ignore incoming packets.

4. Click OK and exit from the MMC snap-in.

Configuring Authentication

Password authentication can be configured for RIPv2 only. All RIPv2 routers on a network must use matching passwords. To configure authentication, proceed as follows:

1. Access the Interface Properties dialog box.

2. On the General tab, check the Activate authentication checkbox and then type a password in the Password box.

3. Click OK and exit from the MMC snap-in.

Enabling Auto-Static Routes

Auto-static routes are added when a router requests RIP to update routing information for a specific interface. To enable this feature, proceed as follows:

1. Access the Interface Properties dialog box.

2. On the General tab, in Operation mode, check the Auto-static update mode checkbox.

3. Click OK and exit from the MMC snap-in.

Adding Route Filters

Route filters can be specified for both incoming and outgoing routes. To add a route filter, proceed as follows:

1. Access the Interface Properties dialog box.

2. On the Security tab, in Action, do one of the following:

   - If you want filters to be applied to incoming announcement packets, select For incoming routes.

   - If you want filters to be applied to outgoing announcement packets, select For outgoing routes.

3. In the Range from and To boxes, type the initial and final IP addresses of the route filter range, respectively.

4. Click Add and then do one of the following:

   - To process all routes, check Accept all routes (for incoming routes) or Announce all routes (for outgoing routes).

   - To process only routes in the ranges listed, check Accept all routes in the ranges listed or Announce all routes in the ranges listed.

   - To discard all routes in the ranges listed, click Ignore all routes in the ranges listed or Do not announce all routes in the ranges listed.

5. Click OK and exit from the MMC snap-in.

4. Internet Protocol

Adding Peer Filters

The peer filter settings you select apply to all the peer routers and can't be set per router. The process of adding peer filters is the same as that for adding route filters, except that For incoming routes must be selected in the Action drop-down list.

To add peer filters, proceed as follows:

1. Access the Interface Properties dialog box.

2. On the Security tab, select For incoming routes in the Action drop-down list, type the IP address of the router whose announcements you want to filter into the Router IP address box, and then click Add.

3. For the routers listed, do one of the following:

   • To process all announcements from all routers, click Accept announcements from all routers.

   • To process announcements only from the listed routers, click Accept announcements from listed routers only.

   • To discard all announcements from the listed routers, click Ignore announcements from listed routers.

4. Click OK and exit from the MMC snap-in.

Setting Timers for Periodic Update

Unless you've configured them as auto-static, RIP-generated routing table entries are dynamic, and you can set timer values for expiry and removal. The same dialog box allows you to set the interval between periodic route announcements. To set the RIP timers, proceed as follows:

1. Access the Interface Properties dialog box.

2. On the Advanced tab, type the appropriate times into the Periodic announcement interval (seconds), Time before routes expire (seconds), and Time before route is removed (seconds) boxes.

3. Click OK and exit from the MMC snap-in.

Enabling Split-Horizon Processing

Split-horizon processing prevents routes from being advertised in the same direction that they were learned. This helps prevent routing loops. To set split-horizon processing, proceed as follows:

1. Access the Interface Properties dialog box.

2. On the Advanced tab, check the Enable split-horizon processing checkbox.

3. Click OK and exit from the MMC snap-in.

Enabling Poison-Reverse Processing

Poison-reverse processing advertises all network identities. However, those learned in the same direction that they are advertised are given a hop count of 16, indicating that the network is unavailable. This improves RIP convergence performance. To enable poison-reverse processing, proceed as follows:

1. Access the Interface Properties dialog box.
2. On the Advanced tab, check the Enable poison-reverse processing checkbox.
3. Click OK and exit from the MMC snap-in.

TIP: The Advanced tab of the Interface Properties dialog box can also be used to enable triggered updates, send cleanup updates when stopping, include default routes and/or host routes in send announcements, and process default routes and/or host routes in received announcements.

Adding Unicast Neighbors

Unicast Neighbors are neighboring routers to which traffic can be forwarded without using broadcast or multicast packets. To specify a neighboring router as a unicast neighbor, proceed as follows:

1. Access the Interface Properties dialog box.
2. On the Neighbors tab, in the IP address box, type the IP address of the unicast neighbor.
3. Click Add.
4. For the neighbors listed, select an option. This option is applied to all of the unicast neighbors. The choices are as follows:
   - Use broadcast or multicast only. This disables the use of unicast neighbor routers. If this option is selected, the IP address box is grayed out.
   - Use neighbors in addition to broadcast or multicast.
   - Use neighbors instead of broadcast or multicast.
5. Click OK and exit from the MMC snap-in.

Testing the RIP Configuration

Each time you configure RIP, you should test the RIP configuration. The recommended procedure is to set up and test a simple RIP configuration and, when you've tested this thoroughly, set up the more advanced options as described in the previous procedures. To test the RIP configuration, proceed as follows:

1. View the RIP neighbors to ensure that a router is receiving RIP announcements from all of its adjacent RIP routers.

2. View the routing table for each router and verify that all of the routes that should be learned from RIP are present. The procedures to view routing tables are described earlier in this chapter.

3. Test the routes using the **ping** and **tracert** commands. These commands are described in detail in Chapter 19.

Related solution:	Found on page:
Using the Command-Line Tools	709

Viewing RIP Neighbors

To view RIP neighbors, proceed as follows:

1. Open Routing and Remote Access in the Start|Programs|Administrative Tools menu.

2. Expand *server-name*|IP Routing, right-click RIP, and select Show neighbors.

Enabling Silent RIP

If silent RIP is enabled, your computer can learn other routes on the network by listening to RIPv1 (not RIPv2) messages and then updating the routing table. This service can be useful when, for example, a Windows 2000 Professional workstation is operating as a remote access client over a dial-up connection. Before you can enable silent RIP, the RIP Listening network component must be installed.

To enable silent RIP, proceed as follows:

1. Access the Interface Properties dialog box.

2. On the General tab, in Outgoing packet protocol, click Silent RIP.

3. Click OK and exit from the MMC snap-in.

Adding the OSPF Routing Protocol

All the OSPF procedures in the following sections assume that the OSPF protocol is installed, that the RRAS service is enabled, and that you're logged on as an administrator. To add the OSPF protocol, proceed as follows:

1. In the Start|Programs|Administrative Tools menu, select Routing and Remote Access.

2. Expand *server-name*|IP Routing and right-click General.

3. Select New Routing Protocol.

4. In the Select Routing Protocol dialog box, select Open Shortest Path First (OSPF), then click OK.

5. Exit from the MMC snap-in.

Configuring OSPF

OSPF requires configuration of both global and interface settings. Global settings are configured using the OSPF Properties dialog box. Interface settings are configured using the OSPF Interface Properties dialog box. Both of these dialog boxes are accessed through the RRAS snap-in.

Configuring OSPF Global Settings

Four procedures are involved in configuring OSPF global settings:

• Creating an OSPF area

• Specifying ranges for an OSPF area

• Configuring an ASBR

• Adding a virtual interface

Accessing the OSPF Properties dialog box is common to all these procedures and is, therefore, described first.

Accessing the OSPF Properties Dialog Box

To access the OSPF Properties dialog box, proceed as follows:

1. In the Start|Programs|Administrative Tools menu, select Routing and Remote Access.

2. Expand *server-name*|IP Routing and right-click OSPF.

3. Select Properties.

The OSPF Properties dialog box is displayed in Figure 4.9.

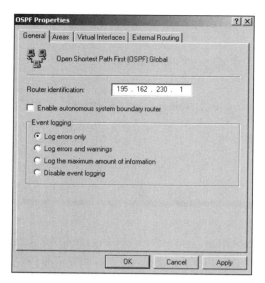

Figure 4.9   The OSPF Properties dialog box.

Creating an OSPF Area

In this procedure you can add an area, configure it as a stub, and enable the plain text password. You can't configure the backbone area (area ID 0.0.0.0) as a stub area, nor can you configure virtual links through stub areas. To create an OSPF area, proceed as follows:

1. Access the OSPF Properties dialog box.
2. On the Areas tab, click Add.
3. On the General tab, in Area ID, type the dotted decimal number that identifies the area.
4. To use a plain text password, verify that the Enable plaintext password checkbox is selected.
5. To mark the area as a stub, select the Stub area checkbox.
6. Specify the stub metric.
7. To import routes of other areas into the stub area, select the Import summary advertisements checkbox.
8. Click OK to close the OSPF Area Configuration dialog box.
9. Click OK and exit from the MMC snap-in.

Specifying Ranges for an OSPF Area

To specify OSPF area ranges, proceed as follows:

1. Access the OSPF Properties dialog box.

2. On the Areas tab, click Add.

3. On the Ranges tab, in Destination, type the IP network ID for the range.

4. In Network mask, type the network mask for the range and then click Add.

5. To delete a range, click the range you want to delete and then click Remove.

6. Click OK to close the OSPF Area Configuration dialog box.

7. Click OK and exit from the MMC snap-in.

Configuring an ASBR

To configure an ASBR, proceed as follows:

1. Access the OSPF Properties dialog box.

2. On the General tab, select Enable autonomous system boundary router.

3. To configure external route sources, do the following:

    • On the External Routing tab, click either Accept routes from all route sources except those selected or Ignore routes from all route sources except those selected.

    • Select or clear the appropriate checkboxes next to the route sources.

4. To configure external route filters, do the following:

    • On the External Routing tab, click Route Filters.

    • In Destination and Network mask, specify the route you want to filter, then click Add.

5. Repeat the preceding step for all the routes you want to filter.

6. Click either Ignore listed routes or Accept listed routes, depending on the appropriate filtering action, then click OK.

7. Click OK and exit from the MMC snap-in.

Adding a Virtual Interface

A virtual interface must be added and configured for each virtual link neighbor, and the hello interval, dead interval, and password must be the same for all virtual link neighbors. To add and configure a virtual interface, proceed as follows:

1. Access the OSPF Properties dialog box.

2. On the Virtual Interfaces tab, click Add.

3. In Transit area ID, click the transit area over which you're connecting the virtual link.

4. In Virtual neighbor router ID, type the OSPF ID of the router at the other endpoint of the virtual link.

4. Internet Protocol

5. Set the transit delay.

6. Set the retransmit interval.

7. Set the hello interval.

8. Set the dead interval. The virtual interface dead interval should be a multiple (typically six) of the hello interval.

9. If the backbone area is configured to have a password, type a password in the Plaintext password box.

10. Click OK to close the Virtual Interface Configuration dialog box.

11. Click OK and exit from the MMC snap-in.

Configuring OSPF Interface Settings

Four procedures are involved in configuring OSPF interface settings:

- Adding an interface to OSPF
- Configuring the OSPF interface
- Configuring hello and dead intervals
- Adding an OSPF neighbor

In addition, this set of procedures describes how to access the OSPF Interface Properties dialog box and how to verify that OSPF is enabled on an interface.

Adding an Interface to OSPF

To add an interface to OSPF, proceed as follows:

1. In the Start|Programs|Administrative Tools menu, select Routing and Remote Access.

2. Expand *server-name*|IP Routing and right-click OSPF.

3. Select New Interface.

4. In Interfaces, select the interface you want to add and then click OK.

5. Exit from the MMC snap-in.

Accessing the OSPF Interface Properties Dialog Box

The OSPF Interface Properties dialog box will be used in the rest of the procedures in this section. To access this dialog box, proceed as follows:

1. In the Start|Programs|Administrative Tools menu, select Routing and Remote Access.

2. Expand *server-name*|IP Routing and select OSPF.

3. In the details pane, right-click the OSPF interface you want to configure and then click Properties.

The OSPF Interface Properties dialog box for the local area connection is displayed in Figure 4.10.

Verifying That OSPF Is Enabled

To verify that OSPF is enabled for an interface, proceed as follows:

1. Access the OSPF Interface Properties dialog box.

2. On the General tab, verify that the Enable OSPF for this address checkbox is checked.

3. Click OK and exit from the MMC snap-in.

Configuring an OSPF Interface

This procedure configures an OSP interface for a specified IP address. If the interface has multiple IP addresses, the General tab will display an IP Address box. In this case, you need to configure OSPF settings for each IP address on the interface.

To configure an OSPF interface, proceed as follows:

1. Access the OSPF Interface Properties dialog box.

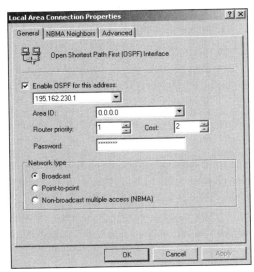

Figure 4.10   The OSPF Local Area Connection Properties dialog box.

2. On the General tab, check the Enable OSPF for this address checkbox.

3. In Area ID, click the ID of the area to which the interface belongs.

4. In Router priority, set the priority of the router over the interface. A router priority of zero specifies that the router can't become an OSPF-designated router.

5. In Cost, set the cost of sending a packet over the interface. A larger cost means the interface won't be used as much as interfaces that have a lower cost.

6. If the area to which the interface belongs is enabled for passwords, type a password in the Password box. All interfaces in the same area that are on the same network must use identical passwords. However, interfaces in the same area that are on different networks can have different passwords.

7. Under Network type, select the OSPF network interface type.

8. Click OK and exit from the RRAS snap-in.

Configuring the Hello and Dead Intervals

The hello and dead intervals must be the same for all routers attached to a common network, and the interface dead interval should be a multiple (typically four) of the hello interval. To configure hello and dead intervals, proceed as follows:

1. Access the OSPF Interface Properties dialog box.

2. On the Advanced tab, set the hello interval in the Hello interval (seconds) box.

3. Set the dead interval in the Dead interval (seconds) box.

4. Click OK and exit from the RRAS snap-in.

TIP: *The Advanced tab can also be used to set the transit delay, the retransmit interval, the poll interval, and the size of the Maximum Transmission Unit (MTU) for the interface.*

Adding an OSPF Neighbor

All the routers that are attached to the nonbroadcast network should be added as OSPF neighbors. The priority that's set during this procedure determines the neighbor's eligibility to become a designated router. When an interface to a nonbroadcast network is detected, the router sends hello packets only to those neighbors eligible to become designated routers until the identity of the designated router is discovered.

To add an OSPF neighbor, proceed as follows:

1. Access the OSPF Interface Properties dialog box.

2. On the NBMA Neighbors tab, in Neighbor IP address, type the IP interface address (not the router ID) of the router you want to add as an OSPF neighbor. This router must be attached to the nonbroadcast network.

3. In Router priority, set the priority for the neighbor and then click Add.

4. Click OK and exit from the RRAS snap-in.

Testing the OSPF Configuration

Once you have configured OSPF and after each configuration change, the OSPF configuration should be tested. To test OSPF configuration for a router, proceed as follows:

1. View the OSPF neighbors to ensure that a router is receiving OSPF announcements from all of its adjacent OSPF routers.

2. View the routing table for each router and verify that all of the routes that should be learned from OSPF are present. The procedures to view routing tables are described earlier in this chapter.

3. Test the routes using the **ping** and **tracert** commands. These commands are described in detail in Chapter 19.

Related solution:	Found on page:
Using the Command-Line Tools	709

Viewing OSPF Neighbors

To view OSPF neighbors, proceed as follows:

1. In the Start|Programs|Administrative Tools menu, select Routing and Remote Access.

2. Expand *server-name*|IP Routing and right-click OSPF.

3. Click Show Neighbors.

4. Click OK and exit from the RRAS snap-in.

Using Network Shell Routing Commands

In addition to the facilities provided by the RRAS snap-in, IP routing can be configured and tested from the command prompt using the Network Shell (**netsh**) routing commands. For example, the following command enables IP routing on the local area connection:

```
netsh routing ip set interface name="local area connection" state=enable
```

OSPF and RIP can be configured using **netsh**. For example, the first of the following two commands sets an OSPF nonstub area, with password authentication, that imports summary advertisements. The second adds a RIP filter for a server that can be configured as a peer.

```
netsh routing ip ospf set area 195.162.321.0 auth=password stubarea=no
sumadv=yes
```

```
netsh routing ip rip add peerfilter server=195.162.231.1
```

Network Shell routing commands configure and display static, RIP, and OSPF routing settings and can also be used to configure settings for IGMP, DHCP, the Domain Name Service (DNS), the Windows Internet Name Service (WINS), and the Network Address Translation (NAT) service. Network Shell can also be used to configure demand-dial interfaces and the remote access service (RAS). In addition, there are Network Shell commands to configure Internetwork Packet Exchange (IPX) and Network Basic Input/Output System Extended User Interface (NetBEUI) settings, but these are outside the scope of this book. The Network Shell commands relevant to TCP/IP are listed in Appendix D.

Installing the ATM ARP/MARS Service

The ATM ARP/MARS service supports IP-to-ATM address resolution for ATM network hosts active on the same logical IP subnet as the Windows 2000 server on which it's installed. Configure only one ATM ARP/MARS for each virtual LAN on your network. If you have multiple ARP servers on the same network segment and your ARP client is configured with the addresses for these servers, the ARP caches could become out of synchronization, and parts of the network could become unreachable.

The ATM ARP/MARS service includes a preconfigured default list of IP address ranges for which broadcast and multicast forwarding are provided by the service. This default is known as *hubbed mode* operation.

If the IP address range list is empty, the ATM ARP/MARS service defaults to *non hubbed mode* operation. In this mode, the service won't perform forwarding for multicast group clients.

WARNING! **This procedure, and the next one, will not work unless you have an ATM network adapter installed on your computer.**

To install the ATM ARP/MARS service, proceed as follows:

1. On the Start|Settings menu, select Network and Dial-up Connections.
2. Click the ATM connection that corresponds to the ATM network adapter installed on the computer.
3. On the File pull-down menu, click Properties and select Install.
4. In Select Network Component Type, in the list of network component types, click Protocol and then click Add.
5. In Select Network Protocol, in the list of network protocols, click ATM ARP/MARS Service and then click OK.
6. The ATM ARP/MARS service is installed with the Windows 2000 default configuration.

TIP: *By default, Windows 2000 uses the predetermined address 47007900010200000000000000000A03E00000200 for simple configuration. This is a Network Service Access Point (NSAP) address selected to simplify configuration and enhance interoperability of ATM ARP/MARS service with other Windows 2000 computers running ATM services.*

Configuring an Advanced TCP/IP-over-ATM Connection

For ATM ARP or MARS server lists, you can either use the Windows 2000 default address or add entries for other computers and switches on your network. If you add multiple addresses to the ARP or MARS server address lists, the ATM ARP client tries the first address on the list; if it fails to connect using that address, it tries each address in turn, in the order that it appears on the list.

1. On the Start|Settings menu, select Network and Dial-up Connections.
2. Click the ATM connection that corresponds to the ATM network adapter installed on the computer.
3. On the File pull-down menu, click Properties.
4. Select the checkbox for Internet Protocol (TCP/IP) from the list of network components and then click Properties.

4. Internet Protocol

5. In Internet Protocol (TCP/IP) Properties, specify an IP address for use with this ATM connection. (By default, the TCP/IP connection uses a DHCP server to obtain an IP address.)

6. In Internet Protocol (TCP/IP) Properties, click Advanced.

7. Select the ATM ARP Client tab.

8. If you want TCP/IP to be used only over Permanent Virtual Circuits (PVCs) configured using the ATM Call Manager, select PVC only.

9. For ARP Server Address List, use Add, Edit, and Remove to update the address entry for the ATM ARP server on your network. When additional server addresses are added, use the up and down arrow buttons to reorder the list.

10. Use Add, Edit, and Remove to update the MARS address list with entries for any ATM MARS server on your network. After adding new server addresses, use the up and down arrow buttons to reorder the list.

11. Configure other advanced TCP/IP properties that this ATM connection will use, such as multiple IP addresses, DNS servers, or WINS servers, and then click OK.

12. If required, specify a static IP address for use with this ATM connection. You can also specify the default, which is to use a DHCP server to obtain an IP address.

TIP: *Windows ATM ARP clients are preconfigured with the ARP/MARS addresses of Windows ATM services. In most cases advanced client configuration is not required.*

---

4. Internet Protocol

Chapter 5

Internet Protocol Addressing

In Depth

This chapter describes how Internet Protocol (IP) addresses and subnet masks work together to identify both a particular *host* on a network—where a host could be a computer, a router gateway, or a device such as a network printer—and the network itself. IP version 4 (IPv4) functionality is described because IPv4 is the version currently used on the Internet and on IP intranets. IP version 6 (IPv6) is described in Chapter 20.

IP Addresses

In IPv4, an IP address is a 32-bit binary number that's used to uniquely identify a host and its network. No two hosts on a network can have the same IP address. IP addresses may be written in binary (for example, 11000011101000101110011000000001), but this is cumbersome. They may also be written in hexadecimal (for example, C3A2CB01). This is shorter, but still difficult to remember. They could, of course, be converted directly to decimal (3,282,225,921 in the example given), but this format is almost as hard to remember as the hexadecimal. It is also considerably less useful, because the value of each of the 4 bytes in the 32-bit number is important and not readily calculable from the decimal value.

Normal practice, therefore, is to split an IP address into 4 bytes, or *octets*, and then calculate the decimal value for each octet. A full stop, or dot, separates the octets, hence the term *dotted decimal notation*. The dotted decimal value for the example given is 195.162.230.1. There was nothing of particular significance about this notation when it was chosen. It was simply a compromise between readability and usability.

Dotted decimal format is used to enter and display IP addresses in a wide range of Graphical User Interfaces (GUIs), but always remember that an IP address (and, for that matter, a subnet mask, which we'll be discussing later in this chapter) is simply a 32-bit binary value. Figure 5.1 illustrates the relationship between the binary, hexadecimal, and dotted decimal formats.

Classful IP Addresses

A 32-bit binary number gives a total range of 4,294,967,296 addresses (not all of which can be used). When the IP address space was specified, these addresses were divided into groups, or *classes*. Although this seems an obvious thing to do

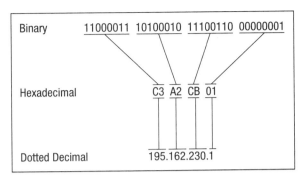

Figure 5.1   IP address formats.

with more than four billion addresses, it was, in retrospect, probably a mistake. However, the address classes are still widely used. The initial binary bits in the address define the address classes, as shown in Table 5.1. First octet values of 0, 127, and 255 are not permitted.

For example, 195.162.230.1 is a Class C address.

Class A Networks

In a Class A network, the network identity is defined by the value of the first octet, or 8 bits. Class A networks are, therefore, sometimes referred to as /8 networks. Because the range of values for the first octet of a Class A address is, by definition, 1 to 126, there are 126 unique Class A networks. The remaining 24 bits in the address identify the host. Host identities can't be all ones or all zeros, so the maximum number of hosts on any Class A network is 2^{24}-2, or 16,777,214.

The Class A address block contains 2^{31} individual addresses (including the reserved first octet values of 0 and 127), and the IPv4 address space contains a maximum of 2^{32} addresses. The Class A address space is, therefore, 50% of the total IPv4 address space.

All IP addresses must be unique in their own internetwork. If, however, two internetworks have no knowledge of each other and could never appear on the

Table 5.1   IP address classes.

Class	Initial Bits	First Octet Value
A	01	1 to 126
B	10	128 to 191
C	110	192 to 223
D	1110	224 to 239
E	1111	240 to 254

same route, then the same IP address could appear on both. Thus, an intranet that's never directly routed to the Internet can use whatever address range its administrator chooses, provided all internal addresses are unique. Typically, the Class A network 10.0.0.0 is used for internal intranet addressing. If hosts on a 10.0.0.0 network are to access the Internet, then a Network Address Translation (NAT) service must be implemented.

Class B Networks

In a Class B network, the network identity is defined by the value of the first two octets, or 16 bits. Class B networks are, therefore, sometimes referred to as /16 networks. The first 2 bits identify the network as a Class B, which leaves 14 bits to specify unique network identities. Thus, 2^{14}, or 16,384, Class B networks can be defined, each with as many as 2^{16}-2, or 65,534, hosts. The Class B address block contains 2^{30} (1,073,741,824) addresses and represents 25% of the total IPv4 address space.

Class C Networks

In a Class C network, the network identity is defined by the value of the first three octets, or 24 bits. Class C networks are, therefore, sometimes referred to as /24 networks. The first 3 bits identify the network as a Class C, which leaves 21 bits to specify unique network identities. Thus, 2^{21}, or 2,097,152, Class C networks can be defined, each with up to $(2^8$-2), or 254, hosts. The Class C address block contains 2^{29} (536,870,912) addresses and represents 12.5% of the total IPv4 address space.

Classes D and E

Class D networks are used for multicasting, where a single network address identifies a group of hosts. Multicasting was introduced in Chapter 4 and will be discussed further in Chapter 6. Class E networks are reserved for experimental purposes. The Class D block represents 6.25% of the total IPv4 address space, and the Class E block represents a slightly smaller proportion, because 255 isn't used as a first-octet value.

The Subnet Mask

The subnet mask, like the IP address, is a 32-bit binary number, but it has a very specific format. It must consist of a group of ones followed by a group of zeros—for example, 11111111111111110000000000000000. Subnet masks are, typically, written either in dotted decimal format (255.255.0.0) or in *slash* format, where the value after the slash represents the number of ones (/16).

Slash vs. Dotted Decimal Format

Dotted decimal format has been described as the "old fashioned" way of specifying subnet masks for a number of years, but it's still, arguably, the most commonly used. It's neater to specify a network as 195.162.230.0/24, rather than 195.162.230.0, subnet mask 255.255.255.0, but the latter format maps more closely to the information that you need to type into IP configuration dialog boxes. NT4 doesn't use the slash format (unless I missed it somewhere), and Windows 2000 doesn't use it in all dialogs. The dotted decimal format is often used in subnetting calculations, whereas Classless Interdomain Routing (CIDR) and supernetting can use the abbreviated notation to advantage. The best advice is to be familiar with both conventions.

The function of a subnet mask is to identify what part of the IP address defines the network, and what part defines the host. The ones specify that the equivalent bits in the IP address are network bits, and the zeros specify the host bits. In traditional classful addressing, the initial address bits define the address class, which in turn defines the host and network ranges. Thus, when IP addresses and classful addressing were introduced, subnet masks weren't implemented.

However, analysis of the initial bits of an address is tedious, and subnet masks simplify the process. A binary AND operation causes the zeros in the subnet mask to mask the host part of the IP address, leaving only the bits that identify the network, or the *network prefix*. Class A addresses (/8 addresses) have a default /8 subnet mask (225.0.0.0). Classes B and C have default subnet masks of /16 (255.255.0.0) and /24 (255.255.255.0), respectively.

Originally, subnet masks were introduced to facilitate network address calculation. However, it wasn't long before they were being used for another purpose—to split Class A, B, and C networks into smaller sections, employing a technique known as *subnetting*.

Subnetting

In 1985, RFC 950 defined a standard procedure to support subnetting, which was introduced because a local administrator who needed a second network had to request another network number, even though there were still host addresses available (often a large number of host addresses) on the originally allocated network.

Subnetting adds an additional level of hierarchy to the IP addressing structure. Instead of the classful two-level hierarchy, subnetting supports a three-level hierarchy. It divides the standard classful host-number field into two parts—the subnet-number and the host-number on that subnet.

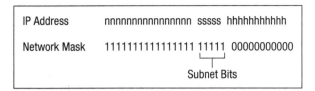

Figure 5.2   Allocating subnet bits.

In essence, subnetting takes bits from the host address and allocates these bits to the network address instead, thus subdividing the network. Figure 5.2 shows a Class B (/16) network, in which five *subnet bits* have been taken from the host address allocation and added to the network address allocation, thus giving more networks with less hosts on each.

Because a subnet mask assigns a binary one to a network address bit and a binary zero to a host address bit, the subnet bits in the subnet masks take binary one values. By default, for a Class B network the subnet mask is 255.255.0.0 (/16), but it becomes 255.255.248.0 (/21) when 5 bits are allocated for subnetting.

This is best illustrated using a specific example. Suppose you have the Class B network 131.11.0.0. Then, in binary form, any address on this network is:

```
10000011 00001011 hhhhhhhh hhhhhhhh
```

where "h" denotes a host address bit.

To subdivide the network, we keep the network ID the same, but use some bits (in this example, 5 bits) from the host identity (ID) to form a subnet ID, as follows:

```
IP Address      10000011 00001011 ssssshhh hhhhhhhh
Subnet mask     11111111 11111111 11111000 00000000
```

where "s" denotes a subnet mask bit.

If two hosts are on the same network segment, or *subnet*, they must have the same network ID and the same subnet ID. If they are on different subnets, then they have identical network IDs, but different subnet IDs. For example, the IP addresses:

```
IP Address 1    10000011 00001011 10010011 00100000 (131.11.147.64)
IP Address 2    10000011 00001011 10010100 00110000 (131.11.148.96)
Subnet mask     11111111 11111111 11111000 00000000 (255.255.248.0)
```

are on the same subnet. However, the IP addresses:

```
IP Address 3    10000011 00001011 10011011 00100000 (131.11.153.64)
IP Address 2    10000011 00001011 10010101 00110000 (131.11.149.96)
Subnet mask     11111111 11111111 11111000 00000000 (255.255.248.0)
```

are on different subnets. In other words, for two addresses to be on the same subnet, the bits that correspond to binary ones in the subnet mask must be identical for both addresses.

Calculating the Number of Subnets and Hosts

Given a network ID and a subnet mask, how many subnets can we form, and how many hosts can reside on each subnet?

Let's take the example of 3 subnet bits. In IP addresses, these bits can take the values:

```
000
001
010
011
100
101
110
111
```

However, subnet bits in an IP address can't be all ones or all zeros, so the values 000 and 111 are excluded. Thus, there are six possible values for the subnet bits.

In general, there are 2^x-2 possible subnets, where x represents the number of subnet bits. In the example we considered earlier, there are 5 subnet bits, so there are 2^5-2 (i.e., 30) subnets.

TIP: *Some modern routers accept all ones in the subnet bits. If you have an intranet using only routers that have this facility, you can increase the number of subnets. If, however, your routers are exchanging routing table information with other, older routers or with routers on the Internet, then the all-ones setting shouldn't be used.*

Again using the example we considered earlier, if we take 5 bits from the range of host addresses, this leaves 11 bits for host addresses. A host address can't be all ones or all zeros, so a maximum of 2^{11}-2 (i.e., 2,046) hosts can reside on each subnet. If, on the other hand, we allocated only 3 subnet bits, we would have 13 bits remaining for host addresses, giving 2^{13}-2 (i.e., 8,190) hosts IDs on each of our six subnets.

NOTE: *The example illustrated is a subnetted Class B network. Exactly the same principles can be applied to Class A and Class C networks. Procedures for carrying out these calculations are given in the Immediate Solutions section of this chapter.*

Calculating the Range of IP Addresses for a Subnet

After we've calculated the number of subnets and number of hosts per subnet for an IP address/subnet mask pair, the next step is to work out the range of IP addresses for each subnet. To illustrate this technique, we'll use the example we considered before, a network ID of 131.11.0.0 with a subnet mask of 255.255.248.0 (sometimes written 131.11.0.0/21).

We apply three rules:

• The subnet mask bits can't all be zero.

• The host ID bits can't all be zero.

• The host ID bits can't all be one.

Thus, the first subnet value that we can use is 00001, the first host ID that we can specify is 00000000001, and the last ID host that we can specify is 11111111110. For the first subnet, this gives the values:

```
Network ID        10000011 00001011 00000000 00000000 (131.11.0.0)
Subnet mask       11111111 11111111 11111000 00000000 (255.255.248.0)
First IP address  10000011 00001011 00001000 00000001 (131.11.8.1)
Last IP address   10000011 00001011 00001111 11111110 (131.11.15.254)
```

Thus, in the example given, the IP address range for the first subnet is 131.11.8.1 to 131.11.15.254. Applying the same calculation to the second subnet gives a range of 131.11.16.1 to 131.11.23.254. For any network ID/subnet mask pair, the same technique can be applied, and a table of subnet ranges similar to Table 5.2 can be derived.

Table 5.2   Subnet address ranges for network 131.11.0.0/21.

Subnet	Address Range
1	131.11.8.1 to 131.11.15.254
2	131.11.16.1 to 131.11.23.254
3	131.11.24.1 to 131.11.31.254
-	- - - - - - - - - - - - - - - - - - - -
-	- - - - - - - - - - - - - - - - - - - -
30	131.11.240.1 to 131.11.247.254

In this section, we've derived the number of subnets, number of hosts per subnet, and address ranges for each subnet from first principles using binary arithmetic. It's necessary to do this in order to understand how a network is subnetted and how the numbers are calculated. However, it would be tedious in the extreme to do the full binary calculation every time you want to subnet. In the Immediate Solutions section of this chapter, we'll see how to build a subnet table that will ease the burden of calculation and enable us to calculate the optimum subnetting structure, given the requirements for the number of subnets and number of hosts per subnet.

> **WARNING!** *No matter how proficient you get at using a subnet table, always ensure you can work out subnetting from first principles and understand how the numbers are derived. Shortcuts are great when everything goes right.*

Variable Length Subnet Masks

There is sometimes confusion between subnetting and Variable Length Subnet Masks (VLSM). This is understandable—the core of the subnetting technique consists of altering the length of the subnet mask. However, when you subnet a network, you split it into segments that are all the same size. A single subnet mask, albeit not the default subnet mask, is applied to the whole network.

In 1987, RFC 1009 specified how a network could use more than one subnet mask to implement segments of different lengths. VLSM allows more than one subnet mask to be assigned to a network, so the extended network prefixes of different network segments have different lengths.

Unfortunately, some routing protocols, such as Routing Internet Protocol version 1 (RIPv1), require subnet masks to be uniform across the entire network prefix. RIPv1 allows only a single subnet mask to be used within each network number, because it doesn't provide subnet mask information as part of its routing table update messages.

However, more flexible routing protocols, such as RIPv2 and Open Shortest Path First (OSPF), allow VLSM. There are several advantages in assigning multiple subnet masks to a given IP network number:

- They permit more efficient use of an organization's assigned IP address space.
- They permit *route aggregation*, which can significantly reduce the amount of routing information within an organization's routing domain.

Efficient Use of Assigned IP Address Space

One of the major problems with the earlier limitation of supporting only a single subnet mask across a given network prefix was that, once the mask was selected, it locked the organization into a fixed number of equally sized subnets. Taking the example we worked out earlier in this chapter, the 131.11.0.0/21 network provided 30 subnets, each with as many as 2,046 hosts. But let's imagine that the Class B subnet has been allocated to an organization that has two major facilities, each requiring approximately 5,000 IP addresses. The organization also has 25 branch offices, each requiring at most 200, and often considerably fewer, IP addresses.

Both of the major facilities would need at least three subnets and would probably be allocated four. This represents a major, and possibly unnecessary, investment in routers. There may be other reasons for segmenting an 8,000-user network (such as the reduction of broadcast traffic), but the network designer should be given the option of specifying the most efficient segmentation, rather than being forced to use 2,000-host segments.

What is much more of a problem, however, is that each of the 200-user branch offices is required to use 2,000-host subnets. This represents a serious waste of IP address space. In fact, with eight subnets already allocated to the major facilities, the organization doesn't have enough subnets left to allocate one to each branch office. It therefore either requires a second network, even though it's using far fewer IP addresses than the 65,000 that its Class B network (theoretically) provides, or else it has to implement a /22 subnet mask (62 subnets). The latter solution would result in even more routers at the major facilities and a twofold increase in advertised routes.

NOTE: *I haven't gone through the binary mathematics to justify the figures that I'm quoting in this example. This is quite deliberate. If you don't see where the figures come from, work them out using the technique outlined in the previous section ("Subnetting") in this chapter.*

The VLSM solution is to specify six /19 subnets, each with a capacity of 2^{13}-2 (i.e., 8,190) host addresses. Two of these can be allocated to the major facilities, and a third can be further partitioned using a /24 subnet mask—giving 30 sub-subnets, each with 254 users. The organization still has three /19 subnets, or half its allocated address space, remaining for future expansion. Figure 5.3 illustrates this subnetting strategy.

Route Aggregation

VLSM works by dividing a network into subnets that are the largest size required (the *backbone* subnets) and then further subdividing these large subnets as required. This *recursive* division allows address space to be reassembled and

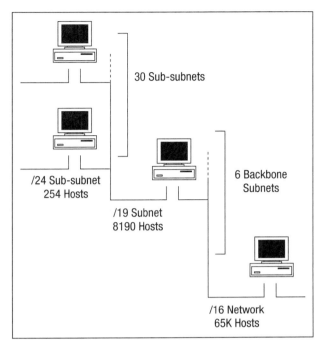

30 Sub-subnets

/24 Sub-subnet
254 Hosts

/19 Subnet
8190 Hosts

6 Backbone
Subnets

/16 Network
65K Hosts

Figure 5.3   Using VLSM to implement efficient network segmentation.

aggregated, which in turn reduces the amount of routing information at the top level and allows the detailed structure of routing information for one subnet group to be hidden from routers in another subnet group.

> **NOTE:**   *This discussion assumes that subnetting is the only technique used. In practice, a Network Address Translation (NAT) server could be used, both to reduce the number of routes an organization advertises on the Internet and to protect the organization's internal IP addresses.*

For example, in the subnetting example discussed earlier in this chapter, all 30 of the /21 subnets would be advertised, both internally and externally, by the organization's routing tables. If, however, the VLSM solution is applied, as shown in Figure 5.4, then Router A advertises only the one routing table network entry (131.11.0.0/16) to the Internet. Router B aggregates all the /24 subnets into a single /19 subnet identity, which it advertises on the organization's backbone. This results in smaller routing tables and less routing advertisement traffic.

The Longest Match Algorithm

Routers implement a consistent forwarding algorithm based on the *longest match* algorithm. If VLSM is used, larger subnets (with smaller network prefixes) are further divided to form smaller sub-subnets (with larger network prefixes). The

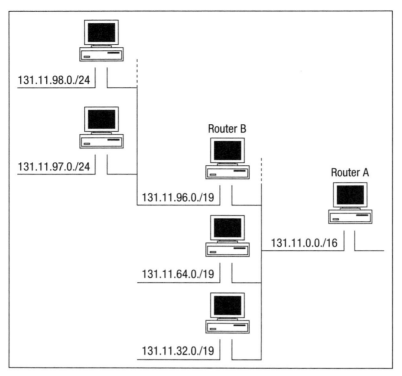

Figure 5.4   Route aggregation using VLSM.

sub-subnets are said to be *more specific*, because a longer network prefix more closely defines the location of a host on the network.

For example, in Figure 5.5, the network route to host 131.11.97.5 could be specified as 131.11.0.0/16, 131.11.96.0/19, or 131.11.97.0/24. Because the more specific segments are subnets of the less specific segments, the host is on all three routes.

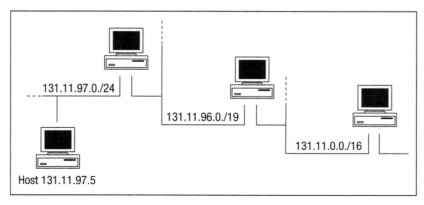

Figure 5.5   The longest match algorithm.

Using the longest match algorithm, a forwarding router will route to the most specific subnet, which is 131.11.97.0/24. This means that host 131.11.97.5 must be installed on the 131.11.97.0/24 subnet. If, by error, this host were connected to the 131.11.96.0/19 backbone, it could never be reached.

Deploying VLSM

Deploying the hierarchical subnetting scheme provided by VLSM requires careful planning. You need to work your way down through the address plan until you get to the bottom level, where you must make sure that the smallest, or *leaf*, subnets are large enough to support the required number of hosts. If VLSM is deployed using a logical hierarchical structure—so the address plan reflects the structure, or *topology*, of the network—then the addresses from each subnet can be aggregated into a single address block that keeps the backbone routing tables from becoming too large.

There are three requirements for the successful deployment of VLSM.

- Routing protocols must carry extended network prefix information with each route advertisement. Protocols such as RIPv2 and OSPF have this functionality.

- Routers must implement the longest match algorithm.

- Addresses must be assigned so that they have topological significance, thus enabling route aggregation.

Classless Interdomain Routing

Classless Interdomain Routing (CIDR), described in RFCs 1518 and 1519, removes the concept of class from IP address assignment and management. Instead of predefined classes (A, B, and C), CIDR allocations are defined by a starting address and a range. The range (in effect, the subnet mask) defines the network part of the address.

This allows more efficient use of available space. For example, an Internet Service Provider (ISP) might allocate 151.26.2.128/25 to a client. The client can then use the IP addresses 151.26.2.129 to 151.26.2.254. Historically, an organization with (say) 10,000 employees asked for (and received) a full Class B network that contained more than 65,000 IP addresses. Along with other factors discussed later in this chapter, this has resulted in the near-exhaustion of the IPv4 address space. CIDR allows flexible allocation of address numbers more commensurate with an organization's needs.

RFC 1917 requests that the Internet community return unused address allocations to the Internet Assigned Numbers Authority (IANA) for redistribution. These allocations include unused network numbers, addresses for networks that will never be connected to the Internet for security reasons, and allocations from sites that are using only a small percentage of their address space. As these IP addresses are reclaimed, they will be reallocated using classless CIDR techniques. Unfortunately, many organizations that have unused addresses don't want to return them, because they are viewed as an asset.

Deploying CIDR

CIDR and VLSM both allow a part of the IP address space to be divided into smaller pieces. The difference is that, with VLSM, the segmentation is performed on the address space previously assigned to an organization and is invisible to the Internet. CIDR, on the other hand, permits the allocation of an address block by an Internet Registry to a high-level ISP, which will allocate segments to a mid-level ISP. This ISP will further segment its allocation to provide an address block to a low-level ISP, which will then allocate addresses to a private organization.

Because of the similarities between the two techniques, the prerequisites for successful CIDR deployment are the same as for VLSM, namely:

- Routing protocols must carry extended network prefix information with each route advertisement. Such protocols as RIPv2 and OSPF have this functionality.

- Routers must implement the longest match algorithm.

- Addresses must be assigned so that they have topological significance, thus enabling route aggregation.

In addition, routers and the installed operating system (OS) must support CIDR. In effect, subnet masks of any length must be supported. Some legacy systems insist on classful default subnet masks, while others accept masks that are longer than the default (allowing subnetting and VLSM), but won't accept masks that are shorter (preventing full implementation of CIDR). Windows 2000 TCP/IP includes support for zeros and ones subnets, as described in RFC1878, and enables full CIDR implementation.

Supernetting

Had CIDR been implemented from the very start of the Internet, we probably wouldn't be facing the IP address space problems that we have now. However, when CIDR was introduced, a large installed base of classful systems already existed. Therefore, the initial use that was made of CIDR was to concatenate pieces of the Class C space, using *supernetting.*

Supernetting can be used to consolidate several Class C networks into one logical internetwork. The technique isn't necessarily confined to Class C addresses; Class A and B networks can also be supernetted. However, Class B supernetting is rarely required, and it's most unlikely that you'll ever be called on to supernet Class A networks. This discussion, therefore, concentrates on Class C.

The network addresses that are to be combined using supernetting must share the same high-order bits. This implies they must be contiguous—you couldn't, for example, combine 172.168.5.0 and 210.23.56.0. In supernetting, the subnet mask is shortened to take bits from the network part of the address and allocate them instead to the host part. This is best illustrated by an example.

Let's suppose your organization has been allocated two Class C networks, 195.162.230.0/24 and 195.162.321.0/24. For convenience, and to save the cost of a router, you want to concatenate these networks, giving you a single network that has 510 usable addresses. The solution in this case is to shorten the subnet mask by 1 bit, so that the CIDR definition of your network becomes 195.162.230.0/23. Lets see what this looks like in binary:

```
First network ID    11000011 10100010 11100100 00000000 (195.162.228.0)
Second network ID   11000011 10100010 11100101 00000000 (195.162.229.0)
Subnet mask         11111111 11111111 11111110 00000000 (255.255.254.0 [/23])
```

The network bits, identified by the subnet mask, are identical. Thus, the condition for a cohesive network is satisfied, and the 510-host network 195.162.228.0/23 is defined, with the IP address range 195.162.228.1 to 195.162.229.254. Within this range, both 195.162.228.255 and 195.162.229.0 are valid, usable IP addresses. (I must confess to a personal reluctance to use them, but that's probably due to old age!)

A similar binary calculation should convince you that 195.162.228.0/22 combines four Class C networks, giving a 1,022-host network that has the address range 195.162.228.1 to 195.162.231.254. Similarly, 195.162.228.0/21 combines eight Class C networks, giving a 2,046-host network that has the address range 195.162.228.1 to 195.162.235.254.

Supernetting Boundary Restriction

If you thought the subnetting example described above was just a bit too easy to be true, or at least to be universally applicable, you were right. The value in the third octet was chosen carefully to make it work. Let's consider what happens if, instead of 195.162.228.0/24 and 195.162.229.0/24, the organization in question had been allocated 195.162.229.0/24 and 195.162.130.0/24. If we attempt to apply a /23 subnet, we get the following result:

```
First network ID    11000011 10100010 11100101 00000000 (195.162.229.0)
Second network ID   11000011 10100010 11100110 00000000 (195.162.230.0)
Subnet mask         11111111 11111111 11111110 00000000 (255.255.254.0 [/23])
```

In this case, the network bits defined by the /23 subnet mask aren't identical, and the condition for a cohesive network is violated. 195.162.229.0/23 is therefore not a valid network specification.

In general, if you want to combine two Class C networks using supernetting, then the networks must be contiguous, and the value in the third octet of the first network must be divisible by two. If you want to combine four Class C networks, then the networks must be contiguous, and the value in the third octet of the first network must be divisible by four—and so on. Similarly, if you want to combine two Class B networks, then the networks must be contiguous, and the value in the second octet of the first network must be divisible by two.

Address Allocation for Private Intranets

RFC 1918 requests that organizations make use of the private intranet address space for hosts that require IP connectivity within their enterprise networks, but don't require external connections to the Internet using the specified internal IP addresses. The IANA has reserved the following address blocks for private intranets:

- 10.0.0.0/8 (10.0.0.1 to 10.255.255.254)
- 172.16.0.0/12 (172.16.0.1 to 172.32.255.254)
- 192.168.0.0/16 (192.168.0.1 to 192.168.255.254)

Any organization that elects to use addresses from these reserved blocks can do so without contacting the IANA or an Internet Registry. Because these addresses are never routed on to the Internet, this address space can be used simultaneously by many different organizations. Of course, there's nothing to prevent an organization from using any address system it chooses on its own intranet, provided there's no possibility of these internal addresses being routed to the Internet. The advantage of the reserved blocks is that they'll be rejected automatically by any Internet router and will therefore never route to the Internet by accident.

This addressing scheme (or any other private intranet addressing scheme) requires that an organization uses a NAT server for Internet access. However, the use of the private address space and a NAT server make it easier for clients to change their ISP without the need to alter their IP addresses. Also, within a large organization, only a proportion (sometimes a small proportion) of employees needs to access the Internet at any one time. Thus, although every host in the organization has its own IP address from the private allocation, a smaller number of global Internet addresses needs to be specified, reducing the demand on the IPv4 address space.

IPv4 Address Space Exhaustion

The problem of the current scarcity and imminent exhaustion of the IPv4 address space has been mentioned throughout this chapter. There are lessons to be learned from IPv4 address allocation, which will, hopefully, prevent the future waste of scarce resources (if such lessons are ever learned).

First, any resource is finite and valuable. In the early days of the Internet, with only a few military and educational networks in existence, more than four billion Internet addresses must have seemed an almost infinite, ultimately future-proof, resource. As a result of this and, also, as a result of the inflexibility of classful addressing, IP networks were allocated based on demand rather than need. An organization that had a couple thousand employees didn't want the hassle of implementing (say) 10 Class C networks (particularly in the days before supernetting), and therefore asked for, and got, a full Class B network. Entire /8 networks, such as 0.0.0.0, 127.0.0.0 and 255.0.0.0, are unusable because of the way the default, loopback, and broadcast functions are implemented.

NOTE: *The address space 64.0.0.0/2 remains unallocated at the time of writing. Refer to RFC 1817 for details.*

Subnetting gave more flexibility in internal network allocation, but (arguably) made matters worse as far as address wastage is concerned. Subnetting can be very wasteful. Let's take the example of a Class B network (say 154.12.0.0) with a /19 subnet mask. This gives 3 subnet bits or, in theory, eight subnets. However, as we've seen earlier, two of these subnets (all ones and all zeros) can't be used. Therefore, the first usable address on the network is 154.12.32.1, and the last usable address is 154.12.223.254. In other words, a quarter of the total Class B network address pool (more than 16,000 addresses) can't be used. If 2 subnet bits are used (a /18 subnet mask), half the Class B address pool becomes unusable.

There are a number of initiatives to win back and reallocate Internet address space. As mentioned previously in this chapter, the IANA are requesting the voluntary return of unused address space for re-allocation through CIDR. Other groups, such as the Internet Engineering Task Force (IETF) working group Procedures for Internet/Enterprise Renumbering (PIER), are looking at issues such as address ownership versus address leasing. The PIER group is also charged with the task of developing a renumbering strategy.

Ultimately, however, the IPv4 address space will run out. The Internet won't stop working—there's simply too much invested in e-commerce to allow that to happen. Nor will IPv4 disappear. There will, instead, be interfacing between IPv4 address space and IPv6 address space.

IPv6 addresses are 128-bit binary numbers. The theoretical size of the IPv6 address space is 2^{128}. Stating this number in decimal form would be meaningless, because it's too large to comprehend.

I'm told that IPv6 address space is an almost infinite resource that could never become exhausted. I'm told that IPv6 is totally future-proof. I'm told that there are some lessons that the human race never seems to learn. I believe only one of these statements.

Immediate Solutions

Building a Subnet Chart

Subnetting calculations can all be done from first principles, using binary arithmetic. The calculations aren't particularly difficult, but they are tedious and time consuming. Many networking professionals prefer to generate a subnet chart, which they can then use as a reference and save both the time and effort involved in repeating the same, or similar, calculations again and again.

WARNING! You will notice that I said "generate" the chart, not "memorize." If you learn how to generate the chart and know the principles behind its construction, then a few minutes of work will produce a calculation aid that you know is correct. If you try to memorize it, you'll have difficulty remembering, and your network designs won't work.

Working Out the Subnet Mask

In subnetting, all calculations stem from the number of subnet bits. Normally, there's a maximum of 8 subnet bits. There can be more—a Class B network could, for example, be split into 510 subnets, each with 126 hosts—but this level of subdivision is unusual. The subnet bits can't all be one or all zero. Therefore, there can't be only 1 subnet bit. The range of subnet bits for practical purposes is therefore 2 to 8.

To work out the subnet mask for a given number of subnet bits, proceed as follows:

1. Determine whether the network is Class A, B, or C.
2. Take the default subnet mask (/8, /16, or /24, respectively) and add the number of subnet bits. Thus, a Class B (/16) network that has 3 subnet bits has a /19 subnet mask.
3. To calculate the subnet mask in dotted decimal notation, take the first zero octet of the default subnet mask. For Class B (255.255.0.0), this is the third octet.
4. Convert the most significant bits of the octet to ones to match the subnet mask bits. That is, if there are 3 subnet mask bits, convert the first 3 bits of the octet to ones.

5. Calculate the decimal value of the octet, given that 10000000 binary equals 128, 01000000 binary equals 64, and so on.

6. From these calculations, generate Table 5.3.

TIP: *Most people find it easier to start from the bottom of this table and work up.*

Calculating the Number of Subnets

The number of subnets can be calculated directly from the number of subnet bits. All you need to remember here is to subtract 2, because the bits can be all ones or all zeros. To calculate the number of subnets, proceed as follows:

1. Calculate 2^x, where x represents the number of subnet bits (2^2=4, 2^3=8, 2^4=16, and so on).

2. Subtract 2 from each of these numbers.

3. Append the results to Table 5.3 to generate Table 5.4.

Table 5.3   Working out the subnet mask.

Subnet Bits	Mask
2	192
3	224
4	240
5	248
6	252
7	254
8	255

Table 5.4   Appending the number of subnets.

Subnet Bits	Mask	Subnets
2	192	2
3	224	6
4	240	14
5	248	30
6	252	62
7	254	126
8	255	254

Calculating the Increment

The *increment* is a value that's used to calculate the range of addresses in each subnet. It represents the difference, or *jump*, within the appropriate octet (second for Class A, third for Class B, fourth for Class C) between the start addresses for each subnet. In the example we worked out from first principles in the In Depth section of this chapter, the subnetted Class B network 131.11.0.0/21 (5 subnet bits), the first address in the first subnet was 131.11.8.1, and the first address in the second subnet was 131.11.16.1. The increment is, therefore, 8.

If the same network is subnetted with 3 subnet bits (/19), then the first address in the first subnet is 131.11.64.1, the first address in the second subnet is 131.11.128.1, and the increment is, therefore, 64.

This is a fairly complex and time-consuming binary calculation. Fortunately, there's a very simple method of calculating the increment:

1. Take the previously calculated octet value for the subnet mask.

2. Subtract this value from 256.

3. Append the increment values to Table 5.4 to generate Table 5.5.

Calculating the Number of Hosts per Subnet

The calculation of the number of hosts per subnet is straightforward, even in binary. To calculate the number of hosts, proceed as follows:

1. Take the number of bits allocated to host IDs by default (24 for Class A, 16 for Class B, 8 for Class C).

2. Subtract the number of subnet bits to obtain a value y.

3. Calculate 2^y for each row in the table.

4. Subtract 2 from each value (because a host address can't be all ones or all zeros).

Table 5.5 Appending the increment values.

Subnet Bits	Mask	Subnets	Increment
2	192	2	64
3	224	6	32
4	240	14	16
5	248	30	8
6	252	62	4
7	254	126	2
8	255	254	1

Table 5.6   The subnet chart.

Subnet Bits	Mask	Subnets	Increment	Class A Hosts	Class B Hosts	Class C Hosts
2	192	2	64	4M	16K	62
3	224	6	32	2M	8K	30
4	240	14	16	1M	4K	14
5	248	30	8	500K	2K	6
6	252	62	4	250K	1K	2
7	254	126	2	130K	510	—
8	255	254	1	65K	254	—

5. Append the resulting host numbers to Table 5.5 to obtain the subnet chart shown in Table 5.6. Normally, there's no need to calculate host numbers above 510 accurately; therefore, approximations are used.

TIP: *It's unlikely that you'd work out every number-of-hosts value from scratch. Once you've worked out one, or at most one from each class, the pattern is fairly obvious (add 2, double, subtract 2). I start with the Class B, 8 subnet bits number. Because Class B with 8 subnet bits has the same subnet mask as a default Class C, I know it has 254 hosts. I can usually work out the rest from there.*

Subnetting a Class A Network

Large organizations sometimes use Class A networks (particularly 10.0.0.0) in company intranets. You may, therefore, be called on to subnet a Class A, although it's unlikely to be a global Internet network.

NOTE: *The function of this procedure is to describe a technique, rather than to reflect a real-life situation. In practice, even the largest organization is likely to utilize only a part of the 10.0.0.0/8 address space and will use VLSM to further segment its backbone subnets. When you're familiar with the technique, you can apply it to any IP network, including a subnet, that requires additional segmentation.*

Your multinational company requires a total of 70 subnets. Although most of these will be relatively small, management foresees a requirement for 80,000 hosts on one of them. You are using the 10.0.0.0/8 internal intranet address specification (RFC 1918). Your technical director wants to know whether the hosts 10.2.4.213 and 10.6.1.14 will be on the same subnet. To implement the required subnet structure, proceed as follows:

1. Select the number of subnet bits. From Table 5.6, the choice of 7 subnet bits gives 126 networks, which meets the specification with room for expansion.

2. Check the number of hosts per subnet. A Class A network that has 7 subnet bits allows approximately 130,000 hosts per network. This is comfortably within specification.

3. Obtain the subnet mask. From Table 5.6, the second octet value (because it's a Class A network) is 254. The subnet mask is, therefore, 255.254.0.0 (or /15).

4. Apply the increment. From Table 5.6, this is 2. The subnets will therefore be 10.2.0.0/15, 10.4.0.0/15, 10.6.0.0/15, and so on.

5. Add the host address ranges. Host addresses can't be all ones or all zeros, so the address ranges are 10.2.0.1 to 10.3.255.254, 10.4.0.1 to 10.5.255.254, 10.6.0.1 to 10.7.255.254 and so on.

6. Examine the network structure that you have derived. Host 10.2.4.213 is on the 10.2.0.0 subnet, and host 10.6.1.14 is on the 10.6.0.0 subnet. They are, therefore, not on the same subnet.

Subnetting a Class B Network

Typically, an organization that's been allocated a Class B network or has implemented a private internal Class B network on its intranet will have subnetting requirements.

Your organization currently requires 28 subnets on its Class B network, 155.62.0.0. Currently, the maximum number of hosts on any one subnet is 250, and this number is most unlikely to exceed 500 in the foreseeable future. There's a requirement that hosts 155.62.10.6 and 155.62.15.230 do not share the same subnet. To implement the required subnet structure, proceed as follows:

1. Select the number of subnet bits. From Table 5.6, the choice of either 5 subnet bits (30 subnets) or 6 network bits (62 subnets) meets the specification, with the latter choice giving more room for expansion.

2. Check the number of hosts per subnet. If you choose 5 subnet bits, each subnet can accommodate approximately 2,000 hosts. The choice of 6 subnet bits limits the maximum number of hosts per subnet to approximately 1,000. Both figures are comfortably within specification.

3. Apply the increment. For 5 subnet bits, this is 8; for 6 subnet bits, it is 4. Thus, the choice of subnets is:

   • *5 subnet bits*—155.62.8.0/21, 155.62.16.0/21, 155.62.24.0/21, and so on.

   • *6 subnet bits*—155.62.4.0/22, 155.62.8.0/22, 155.62.12.0/22, and so on.

4. Apply the requirement stated in the specification. If you choose 5 subnet bits, then hosts 155.62.10.6 and 155.62.15.230 will both be on the 155.62.8.0/21 subnet. If, however, you choose 6 subnet bits, they will be on subnets 155.62.8.0/22 and 155.62.12.0/22, respectively. Therefore, your choice is 6 subnet bits.

5. Obtain the subnet mask. From Table 5.6, the third octet value (because it's a Class B network) is 252. The subnet mask is, therefore, 255.255.254.0.0 (or /22).

6. Add the host address ranges. Host addresses can't be all ones or all zeros, so the address ranges are 155.62.4.1 to 155.62.7.254, 155.62.8.1 to 155.62.11.254, 155.62.12.1 to 155.62.15.254 and so on.

Subnetting a Class C Network

Typically, a Class C network is more likely to be supernetted rather than subnetted. However, a small organization might be divided into a number of groups, each of which requires its own subnet.

Your small business requires a total of four subnets. There will never be more than 20 hosts on any one of these subnets. You have been allocated the Class C network 195.162.230.0/24. To implement the required subnet structure, proceed as follows:

1. Select the number of subnet bits. From Table 5.6, the choice of 3 subnet bits gives 6 networks, each with a maximum of 30 hosts. This meets the specification.

2. Obtain the subnet mask. From Table 5.6, the fourth octet value (because it's a Class C network) is 224. The subnet mask is, therefore, 255.255.255.224 (or /27).

3. Apply the increment. From Table 5.6, this is 32. The subnets will, therefore, be 195.162.230.32/27, 195.162.230.64/27, 195.162.230.97/27, and so on.

4. Add the host address ranges. Host addresses can't be all ones or all zeros, so the address ranges are 195.162.230.33 to 195.162.230.62, 195.162.230.65 to 195.162.230.94, 195.162.230.97 to 195.162.230.126 and so on.

TIP: *The final octet values in Class C subnetting sometimes cause confusion, because you're simultaneously applying the increment and the host address (with the all-ones and all-zeros restrictions) to the same octet. If you're puzzled, write it down in binary. You're dealing with only 8 bits, and the binary notation won't look daunting.*

Subnetting a VLSM Segment

Subnetting in the VLSM environment follows the same principles as normal subnetting. This procedure demonstrates both subnetting a VLSM segment and subnetting across a class boundary.

Your organization has implemented subnetting on a Class B network, as described in an earlier procedure. Now it wants to further subdivide the 155.62.12.0/22 subnet into the maximum possible number of sub-subnets, given the requirement that there can be a maximum of 40 hosts on each subnet. The internal subdivision of a backbone subnet requires that VLSM be deployed. You have checked that your organization uses a routing protocol that carries extended network prefix information with each route advertisement and that the network routers implement the longest match algorithm.

To further segment the backbone subnet 155.62.12.0/22, proceed as follows:

1. From Table 5.6, determine the subnet that meets the requirement for up to 40 hosts. This is a Class C network that has 2 subnet bits (a maximum of 62 hosts).

2. Obtain the subnet mask for this subnet. Following the subnetting principles used in all the other procedures, this mask is defined as 255.255.255.192, or /26.

3. Obtain the increment. Because we've crossed the class boundary into Class C, this increment will be applied to the fourth address octet. From Table 5.6, the increment is 64.

4. Apply the increment. The subnets are 155.62.12.64/26, 155.62.12.128/26, 155.62.12.192/26, 155.62.13.0/26, and so on, up to 155.62.15.128/26.

5. Add the host IDs. This gives address ranges of 155.62.12.65 to 155.62.12.126, 155.62.12.129 to 155.62.12.190, 155.62.12.193 to 155.62.12.254, 155.62.13.1 to 155.62.13.62 and so on.

6. To calculate the maximum number of sub-subnets, subtract the backbone subnet mask (/22) from the sub-subnet mask (/26). There are four extra subnet bits in the longer prefix. The number of sub-subnets is, therefore, 2^4-2, or 14.

Supernetting Class C Networks

Supernetting calculations are straightforward. The only restriction you need to remember is the boundary one. If you want to supernet two Class C networks, the value of the third octet of the lower address must be divisible by 2. If you want to supernet four networks, this value must be divisible by 4, and so on. Networks must be contiguous and are supernetted in groups of 2, 4, 8, 16 and so on (that is, powers of two).

Your company has been allocated four Class C networks, 207.23.68.0 to 207.23.71.0, and wishes to combine them into a single network. Check that this is possible and calculate the subnet mask and address range:

1. Check that the networks are contiguous (they are) and that the third octet value of the lowest network (68) is divisible by 4 (it is). The networks can, therefore, be combined.

2. Take the default Class B subnet mask (/24) and shorten it by the appropriate number of bits. To combine two networks, shorten it by one; to combine four, shorten it by two; to combine eight, shorten it by three, and so on. In this case we shorten it by two. The subnet mask is, therefore, /22, or 255.255.252.0.

3. The combined network is, therefore, 207.23.68.0/22. Add the host IDs to get the address range 207.23.68.1 to 207.23.71.254.

Chapter 6

Internet Layer Maintenance and Group Protocols

In Depth

This chapter discusses two protocols that provide support to the Internet Protocol (IP) at the Internet layer. Internet Control Management Protocol (ICMP), specified in RFC 792, is a maintenance protocol used to build and maintain route tables, perform router discovery, adjust flow control to prevent link or router saturation, and diagnose problems using the ping and tracert utilities. ICMP also assists in Path Maximum Transmission Unit (PMTU) discovery, which is discussed in Chapter 8.

Internet Group Management Protocol (IGMP) version 2 provides full support for IP multicasting, as described in RFC 1112 and RFC 2236. Windows 2000 implements router discovery using multicasts, and Windows Internet Name Service (WINS) servers use multicasting by default when attempting to locate replication partners.

Internet Control Message Protocol

ICMP is a required TCP/IP standard. IP hosts and routers use ICMP to report errors and to exchange control and status information. ICMP messages are sent in the following situations:

- An IP datagram can't reach its destination.
- An IP router can't forward datagrams at the current transmission rate.
- An IP router redirects the sending host to a preferred route.

One of the following types of ICMP message may be sent in these situations:

- Echo message
- Echo reply message
- Time exceeded message
- Parameter problem message
- Source quench message
- Redirect message
- Timestamp message
- Timestamp reply message
- Information request message

- Information reply message
- Destination unreachable message

In addition to these messages, ICMP implements router solicitation and adver-tisement messages if ICMP router discovery is enabled. Router solicitation and advertisement messages are specified in RFC 1265 rather than RFC 792 and are, therefore, discussed separately.

ICMP Packet Structure

Before discussing these messages, we'll consider the general structure of the ICMP packet. ICMP messages are encapsulated in IP datagrams. They don't, therefore, contain source and destination data, because packet routing is handled by IP. Figure 6.1 shows a typical ICMP package—in this case, an echo message.

The Type Field
This field identifies the ICMP message type, for example, 8 for an echo message, 0 for an echo reply message, 5 for a redirect message, and so on. This 8-bit field is common to all ICMP packages.

The Code Field
This field is used to indicate one of several possible functions within a given type. For example, in a destination unreachable message, the code field will differenti-ate between net unreachable (0), host unreachable (1), protocol unreachable (2), and so on. This 8-bit field is common to all ICMP packages.

The Checksum Field
This field contains a checksum that's used to verify the integrity of the ICMP packet. The IP encapsulation data has its own checksum, which is independent of the ICMP checksum. This 16-bit field is common to all ICMP packages.

6. Internet Layer Maintenance and Group Protocols

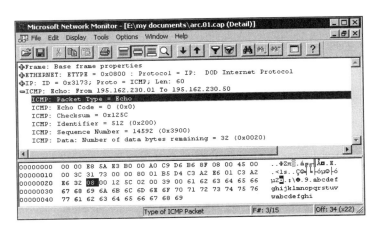

Figure 6.1   An ICMP package.

Type Specific Fields

The remaining fields are specific to the message type, although some of them, such as the Identifier and Sequence Number fields, are common to several message types. These fields will therefore be discussed when we look at specific messages. They include:

- Identifier
- Sequence number
- Pointer
- Gateway Internet address
- Timestamp
- Data

NOTE: *Although IP handles the routing for IP packages, some ICMP fields can contain IP address information. For example, if a redirect message is redirecting a host to an alternative gateway, the address of that gateway is contained in the gateway Internet address field.*

ICMP Messages

The primary function of ICMP is to generate messages. These messages are used to implement functions, such as flow control or router discovery, and command-line functions, such as ping and tracert.

The Echo and Echo Reply Messages

ICMP echo and echo reply messages are used to verify network connectivity, for example, in the ping utility. The data received in the echo message must be returned in the echo reply message. The echo sender can use an identifier and sequence number to match replies to echo requests.

The structure of the echo and echo reply messages is shown in Table 6.1.

Table 6.1   Echo and echo reply message structure.

Field	Value	Field Length
Type	8 (echo); 0 (echo reply)	8 bits
Code	0	8bits
Checksum	variable	16 bits
Identifier	variable	16 bits
Sequence number	variable	16 bits
Data	variable	variable

Time Exceeded Message

If the gateway processing a datagram discovers that the Time to Live (TTL) is zero, it discards the datagram and may also notify the source host that it has done so via a time exceeded message. If a host that's reassembling a fragmented datagram can't complete the reassembly because of missing fragments within its time limit, it discards the datagram and may send a time exceeded message.

The time exceeded message Data field contains the Internet Header (IH) plus the first 64 bits of the original datagram's data. If a higher-level protocol uses port numbers, they are assumed to be in the first 64 data bits of the original datagram's data. The structure of the time exceeded message is shown in Table 6.2.

The Parameter Problem Message

If a gateway or host that's processing a datagram encounters a problem with the header parameters such that it can't process the datagram, the datagram is discarded. The gateway or host may also send a parameter problem message to notify the source host.

The value in the Pointer field identifies the octet of the original datagram's header in which the error was detected. For example, a value of 1 indicates that something is wrong with the Type of Service (ToS).

The parameter problem message Data field contains the IH plus the first 64 bits of the original datagram's data. If a higher-level protocol uses port numbers, they are assumed to be in the first 64 data bits of the original datagram's data. The structure of the parameter problem message is shown in Table 6.3.

The Source Quench Message

ICMP source quench messages are used to implement *flow control*. If a host sends datagrams to a target at a rate that's saturating the routers or links between them, it may receive a source quench message asking it to slow down. Windows 2000 TCP/IP honors this message, provided that it contains the header fragment of one

6. Internet Layer Maintenance and Group Protocols

Table 6.2   Time exceeded message structure.

Field	Value	Field Length
Type	11	8 bits
Code	0 (TTL exceeded); 1 (fragment reassembly)	8bits
Checksum	variable	16 bits
Unused	0	32 bits
Data	variable	IH + 64 bits

Table 6.3 Parameter problem message structure.

Field	Value	Field Length
Type	12	8 bits
Code	0	8 bits
Checksum	variable	16 bits
Pointer	variable	8 bits
Unused	0	24 bits
Data	variable	IH + 64 bits

of its own datagrams. If a Windows 2000 computer is being used as a router and is unable to forward datagrams at the rate they are arriving, then it drops any datagrams that can't be buffered, but doesn't send source quench messages to the senders.

On receipt of a source quench message, the source host reduces the rate at which it is sending traffic until it no longer receives source quench messages from the gateway. The source host then gradually increases the rate at which it sends traffic to the target until it again receives source quench messages.

A gateway or target host may send the source quench message when it approaches its capacity limit instead of waiting until its capacity is exceeded. In this case, the data in the datagram that triggered the source quench message is delivered.

The source quench message Data field contains the IH plus the first 64 bits of the original datagram's data. If a higher-level protocol uses port numbers, they are assumed to be in the first 64 data bits of the original datagram's data. The structure of the source quench message is shown in Table 6.4.

The Redirect Message

Figure 6.2 illustrates the situation in which an ICMP redirect message may be sent. Host A sends a datagram to remote Host B via Gateway 1, its default gateway. Gateway 1 checks its routing table and obtains the address of Gateway 2 as

Table 6.4 Source quench message structure.

Field	Value	Field Length
Type	6	8 bits
Code	0	8 bits
Checksum	variable	16 bits
Unused	0	32 bits
Data	variable	IH + 64 bits

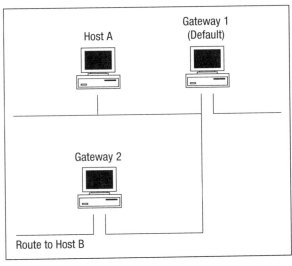

Figure 6.2   Situation in which a redirect message may be sent.

the next step on the route to the datagram's destination. Gateway 1 determines that Host A and Gateway 2 are on the same subnet and sends a redirect message to Host A, to advise it to send any future traffic for Host B directly to Gateway 2. Gateway 1 also forwards the original datagram to its destination.

The redirect message Code field can contain one of four values, as shown in Table 6.5.

The redirect message Gateway Internet Address field contains the address of the gateway to which traffic for the network that's specified in the original datagram's Internet Destination Network field should be sent.

The redirect message Data field contains the IH plus the first 64 bits of the original datagram's data. If a higher-level protocol uses port numbers, they are assumed to be in the first 64 data bits of the original datagram's data. The structure of the redirect message is shown in Table 6.6.

Table 6.5   Redirect message Code field values.

Value	Action
0	Redirect datagrams for the network.
1	Redirect datagrams for the host.
2	Redirect datagrams for the ToS and network.
3	Redirect datagrams for the ToS and host.

6. Internet Layer Maintenance and Group Protocols

Table 6.6   Redirect message structure.

Field	Value	Field Length
Type	5	8 bits
Code	see Table 6.5	8 bits
Checksum	variable	16 bits
Gateway Internet Address	variable	32 bits
Data	variable	IH + 64 bits

The Timestamp and Timestamp Reply Messages

Typically, timestamps are used in challenge/response dialogs that set up secure channels and authenticate users. For example, the Kerberos 5 protocol makes use of timestamps to counter replay attacks (see Chapter 11). The timestamp received in a timestamp message is returned in the reply together with an additional timestamp. A standard timestamp is given as the number of milliseconds since midnight, Universal Time (UT). The timestamp sender can use an identifier and sequence number to match replies from the echoer.

The Originate Timestamp is the time the sender last accessed the message before sending it, the Receive Timestamp is the time the echoer first accessed it on receipt, and the Transmit Timestamp is the time the echoer last accessed the message before sending a timestamp reply.

NOTE: RFC 792 defines timestamps as the time that the sender last touched the message before sending it and the time that the echoer first touched the message on receipt.

If the time isn't available in milliseconds or can't be provided with respect to midnight UT, then any time can be inserted in a timestamp, provided that the high order bit of the timestamp is set to one. This indicates a nonstandard value.

The structure of the timestamp and timestamp reply messages is shown in Table 6.7.

The Information Request and Reply Messages

An ICMP information message provides a mechanism for a host to discover the network number of the network that it's on. The request message is sent with the source network number set to zero in the IP header source and destination address fields. The responding IP module sends the reply with the addresses fully specified. The sender can use an identifier and sequence number to match replies.

The structure of the information request and information reply messages is shown in Table 6.8.

Table 6.7   Timestamp and timestamp reply message structure.

Field	Value	Field Length
Type	13 (timestamp); 14 (timestamp reply)	8 bits
Code	0	8 bits
Checksum	variable	16 bits
Identifier	variable	16 bits
Sequence number	variable	16 bits
Originate Timestamp	variable	32 bits
Receive Timestamp	variable	32 bits
Transmit Timestamp	variable	32 bits

Table 6.8   Information request and information reply message structure.

Field	Value	Field Length
Type	15 (request); 16 (reply)	8 bits
Code	0	8 bits
Checksum	variable	16 bits
Identifier	variable	16 bits
Sequence number	variable	16 bits

The Destination Unreachable Message

An ICMP destination unreachable message may be sent in the following circumstances:

- According to a gateway's routing tables, the network specified in the Internet destination field of a datagram is unreachable.

- The gateway is able to determine that the Internet destination host is unreachable.

- At the destination host, the IP module can't deliver the datagram because the indicated protocol module or port isn't active.

- A datagram must be fragmented in order to be forwarded by a gateway, but the Don't Fragment (DF) flag is set.

The destination unreachable message Code field can contain one of six values, as shown in Table 6.9.

The destination unreachable message Data field contains the IH plus the first 64 bits of the original datagram's data. If a higher-level protocol uses port numbers, they are assumed to be in the first 64 data bits of the original datagram's data. The structure of the destination unreachable message is shown in Table 6.10.

Table 6.9   Destination unreachable message Code field values.

Value	Meaning
0	Net unreachable
1	Host unreachable
2	Protocol unreachable
3	Port unreachable
4	Fragmentation needed and DF set
5	Source route failed

Table 6.10   Destination unreachable message structure.

Field	Value	Field Length
Type	3	8 bits
Code	see Table 6.9	8 bits
Checksum	variable	16 bits
Unused	0	32 bits
Data	variable	IH + 64 bits

ICMP Router Discovery

Internet Control Message Protocol (ICMP) router discovery uses ICMP router advertisement and router solicitation messages to discover the default gateway on a network segment, when a default gateway isn't configured manually or assigned using DHCP. Each enabled router periodically multicasts a router advertisement from each of its multicast interfaces, announcing the IP address of that interface. Hosts discover the addresses of neighboring routers by listening for advertisements. The default advertising rate is once every 7 to 10 minutes.

When a host attached to a multicast link boots up, it may multicast a router solicitation message, rather than waiting for the next periodic advertisement to arrive. If no advertisements are subsequently received, the host may retransmit the solicitation a small number of times (by default, three).

ICMP router discovery is enabled by default on Windows 2000 hosts. Configuring a Windows 2000 Server computer running the Routing and Remote Access service to support ICMP router discovery is discussed in the Immediate Solutions section of this chapter. ICMP router discovery is described in RFC 1256.

The Router Advertisement Message

The ICMP router advertisement message advertises one or more router addresses and includes a Preference Level field for each Router Address field. When a host has to choose a default router address, it will choose from those router addresses that have the highest preference level.

The Lifetime field specifies the maximum length of time that advertised addresses can be considered valid in the absence of further advertisements. The default lifetime is 30 minutes.

The value in the Num Addrs field indicates the number of addresses advertised in the message. The Addr Entry Size field indicates the number of 32-bit words required to hold each address and its associated preference level. For IP version 4 (Ipv4), this is 2.

The structure of a router advertisement message for two router addresses is shown in Table 6.11. A message with more router addresses would contain additional Router Address and Preference Level fields, and the value in the Num Addrs field would be amended accordingly.

The Router Solicitation Message

The IGMP router solicitation message contains the usual Code, Type, and Checksum fields, plus a 32-bit Reserved field that's currently sent as zero and ignored by the recipient. The structure of a router solicitation message is shown in Table 6.12.

Table 6.11   Router advertisement message structure.

Field	Value	Field Length
Type	9	8 bits
Code	0	8 bits
Checksum	variable	16 bits
Num Addrs	2	8 bits
Addr Entry Size	2	8 bits
Router Address (1)	variable	32 bits
Preference Level (1)	variable	32 bits
Router Address (2)	variable	32 bits
Preference Level (2)	variable	32 bits

Table 6.12   Router solicitation message structure.

Field	Value	Field Length
Type	9	8 bits
Code	0	8 bits
Checksum	variable	16 bits
Reserved	0	32 bits

The ICMP Command-Line Utilities

The use of the ICMP ping and tracert command-line utilities in troubleshooting is discussed in detail in Chapter 19. It is, however, appropriate to introduce them here and briefly discuss their syntax.

Ping

Pinging a host IP address verifies connectivity to that host. Pinging a host by name verifies both connectivity and address resolution. Ping uses ICMP echo and echo reply functionality. It places a unique sequence number on each packet it transmits and checks which sequence numbers it receives back, thus determining whether packets have been dropped, duplicated, or reordered. It uses checksums to detect damaged packets and places a timestamp on each packet to compute the Round Trip Time (RTT). You can use ping to report other ICMP messages. For example, it can tell you if a router is declaring a target host unreachable.

The syntax of the **ping** command is as follows:

```
ping [-t] [-a] [-n count] [-l length] [-f] [-i ttl] [-v tos] [-r count] [-s count] [[-j computer-list] | [-k computer-list]] [-w timeout] destination-list
```

Table 6.13 describes the function of each of the *ping* parameters.

Tracert

Tracert determines a route by sending ICMP echo packets with varying TTL values to the destination. When the TTL of a packet reaches zero, the router sends back an ICMP time exceeded message to the source system. Tracert determines the route by sending the first echo packet with a TTL of 1 and incrementing the TTL on each subsequent transmission, until either the target responds or the maximum TTL is reached. Tracert then determines the route by examining the time exceeded messages sent back by intermediate routers.

> **WARNING!**   *Some routers silently drop packets with expired TTL values and are, therefore, invisible to tracert.*

The syntax of the **tracert** command is as follows:

```
tracert [-d] [-h maximum_hops] [-j computer-list] [-w timeout] target_name
```

Table 6.14 describes the function of each of the *tracert* parameters.

Table 6.13   The ping parameters.

Parameter	Function
-t	Pings the specified computer until interrupted.
-a	Resolves addresses to computer names.
-n count	Sends the number of packets specified by *count*. The default is 4.
-l length	Sends packets containing the number of bytes of data specified by *length*. The default is 32 bytes; the maximum is 65,527.
-f	Sets the DF flag in the packet, so that the packet won't be fragmented by gateways on the route.
-i ttl	Sets the Time To Live field to the value specified by *ttl*.
-v tos	Sets the Type of Service field to the value specified by *tos*.
-r count	Records the route of the outgoing packet and the returning packet across a number of computers (between 1 and 9) specified by *count*.
-s count	Specifies the timestamp for the number of hops specified by *count*.
-j computer-list	Routes packets via the list of computers specified by *computer-list*. Consecutive computers can be separated by intermediate gateways.
-k computer-list	Routes packets via the list of computers specified by *computer-list*. Consecutive computers cannot be separated by intermediate gateways.
-w timeout	Specifies a time-out interval in milliseconds.
destination-list	Specifies the remote computers to ping.

Table 6.14   The tracert parameters.

Parameter	Function
-d	Disables the resolution of addresses to computer names.
-h maximum_hops	Specifies the maximum number of hops to search for a target.
-j computer-list	Specifies a route along *computer-list*. Consecutive computers can be separated by intermediate gateways.
-w timeout	Waits for a number of milliseconds, specified by *timeout*, for each reply.
target_name	Specifies the name of the target computer.

TIP: *Using the tracert* -d *parameter can significantly reduce the time taken to trace a route.*

IGMP and Multicasting

Windows 2000 provides full support for IP multicasting using IGMP version 2, as described in RFCs 1112 and 2236. IP multicasting is the transmission of an IP datagram to a host group that's identified by a single IP destination address. Hosts may join and leave groups at any time, and there's no restriction on the location or number of members in the group. Hosts join multicast groups by sending IGMP messages, and a host need not be a member of a group to send datagrams to it.

Multicast Addressing

IP multicast addresses are assigned from the Class D address range 224.0.0.0 through 239.255.255.255. A single IP address within this range identifies each multicast group. Each group's reserved IP address is shared by all host members of the group, who listen and receive any IP messages sent to the group's IP address. A *permanent* multicast host group has an assigned IP address. IP multicast addresses that aren't reserved for permanent groups are available for dynamic assignment to *transient* groups, which exist only as long as they have members.

> **NOTE:**   A permanent group may have any number of members (even zero) at any particular time. It's the address of the group that's permanent, not the membership.

Well-known Class D addresses reserved for Windows 2000 IP multicasting components are registered with the Internet Assigned Numbers Authority (IANA). These include the addresses specified in Table 6.15.

Table 6.15   *Reserved multicast addresses in Windows 2000.*

Address	Description
224.0.0.0	The base address.
224.0.0.1	The All Hosts multicast group. This contains all systems on the same network segment.
224.0.0.2	The All Routers multicast group. This contains all routers on the same network segment.
224.0.0.5	The Open Shortest Path First (OSPF) AllSPFRouters address. This is used to send OSPF routing information to all OSPF routers on a network segment. OSPF is discussed in Chapter 4.
224.0.0.6	The OSPF AllDRouters address. This is used to send OSPF routing information to OSPF designated routers on a network segment.
224.0.0.9	The Routing Internet Protocol version 2 (RIPv2) group address. This is used to send RIP routing information to all RIPv2 routers on a network segment. RIPv2 is discussed in Chapter 4.
224.0.1.24	The Windows Internet Name Service (WINS) server group address. This is used to support autodiscovery and dynamic configuration of replication for WINS servers. WINS is discussed in Chapter 15.

TIP: *A current listing of IP addresses that are reserved for multicasting can be obtained at **www.isi.edu/in-notes/iana/assignments/multicast-addresses**.*

An additional route is defined on a host that supports IP multicasting. This route specifies that if a datagram is being sent to a multicast host group, it should be sent to the IP address of the host group through the local interface card and not forwarded to the default gateway. Sending a packet to a host group using the local interface requires that the IP address be resolved to a Media Access Control (MAC) address.

IP multicast addresses are mapped to a reserved set of Ethernet MAC multicast addresses by placing the low-order 23 bits of the IP address into the low-order 23 bits of the MAC address 01-00-5E-00-00-00 (hex). Because there are 28 significant bits in an IP host group address (the first 4 bits identify the address as multicast), more than one host group address may map to the same MAC address.

For example, a datagram addressed to the multicast address 225.0.0.9 would be sent to the MAC address 01-00-5E-00-00-09—that is, 01-00-5E-00-00-00 combined with the 23 low-order bits of 225.0.0.9 (00-00-09).

Multicast Forwarding

Multicast forwarding enables a router to forward multicast traffic to networks where nodes are listening (or in directions where nodes are listening) and prevents the forwarding of multicast traffic to networks where no nodes are listening. Nodes and routers must be multicast-capable to enable multicast forwarding across an internetwork.

A multicast-capable node sends and receives multicast packets and registers the multicast addresses that the node is listening to with local routers, so that multicast packets can be forwarded to the node's network. All Windows 2000 computers are IP multicast-capable and can both send and receive. IP nodes use IGMP to register their interest in receiving IP multicast traffic from IP routers and send out an IGMP membership report message to notify their local routers that they are listening on a specific IP multicast address. IGMP messages are discussed later in this chapter.

A multicast-capable router listens for all multicast traffic on all attached networks and forwards received multicast packets to attached networks where nodes are listening or where downstream routers have nodes that are listening. Windows 2000 TCP/IP uses a *multicast forwarding table* to forward incoming multicast traffic. The router also listens for IGMP membership report message packets and updates the multicast forwarding table with the information they contain.

Multicast Routing

A multicast router should also be able to use a multicast routing protocol, such as Distance Vector Multicast Routing Protocol (DVMRP), to propagate multicast group listening information to other multicast-capable routers. Windows 2000 Server doesn't provide any multicast routing protocols (IGMP isn't a multicast routing protocol). However, IGMP router mode and IGMP proxy mode can provide multicast forwarding in a single router intranet or when connecting a single router intranet to the Internet.

NOTE: The Windows 2000 Routing and Remote Access service is an extensible platform and can support OEM multicast routing protocols.

If your intranet connects multiple networks using a single router, you can enable IGMP router mode on all router interfaces. This provides multicast forwarding support between multicast sources and multicast listening hosts on any network. IGMP router and proxy modes (and how they are enabled) are discussed later in this chapter.

If your Windows 2000 router is attached to the *MBone* (the multicast-capable part of the Internet) through an Internet Service Provider (ISP), you can use IGMP proxy mode to send and receive Internet multicast traffic to and from the Internet. This is accomplished by enabling IGMP proxy mode on the Internet interface and IGMP router mode on the intranet interface, as shown in Figure 6.3. Multicast hosts register themselves locally, and the IGMP proxy mode interface registers their memberships to the ISP. Multicast traffic from the Internet is forwarded to the ISP router, then to your Windows 2000 router, and finally to listening hosts on your intranet.

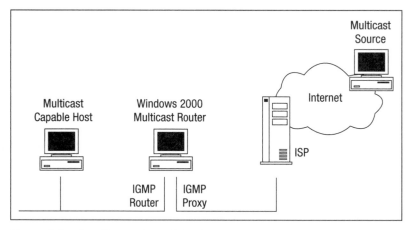

Figure 6.3   Sending and receiving Internet multicast traffic.

When multicast traffic is sent by an intranet host, it is forwarded over the IGMP proxy mode interface to the ISP router. The ISP router then forwards it to the appropriate downstream router and, hence, to an Internet host.

The IGMP Routing Protocol

The IGMP routing protocol maintains the entries in the TCP/IP multicast forwarding table. IGMP is installed using the Windows 2000 Routing and Remote Access service, and router interfaces are then added to IGMP. You can configure each interface in either IGMP router or IGMP proxy mode.

IGMP Router Mode

An interface running in IGMP router mode listens for IGMP membership report message packets and tracks group membership. You should enable IGMP router mode on the interfaces where listening multicast hosts are located.

IGMP Proxy Mode

An interface running in IGMP proxy mode sends IGMP membership report message packets on one interface for all such packets received on all other interfaces running in IGMP router mode. The upstream router that's attached to the network of the IGMP proxy mode interface receives the IGMP proxy mode membership report message packets and adds them to its own multicast tables. This enables the upstream router to forward multicast packets to the network segment of the IGMP proxy mode interface.

When the upstream router forwards multicast traffic to the IGMP proxy mode interface network, this traffic is forwarded to the appropriate hosts on the IGMP router mode interface. All nonlocal multicast traffic received on all interfaces running IGMP router mode is forwarded using the IGMP proxy mode interface. Multicast sources on networks attached to a Windows 2000 router can send multicast traffic to multicast hosts attached to upstream multicast routers using IGMP proxy mode.

IGMP proxy mode can pass IGMP membership report message packets from a single router intranet to the Internet multicast backbone (Mbone). With IGMP proxy mode enabled on the Internet interface, hosts on the single router intranet can receive multicast traffic from multicast sources on the Internet and send multicast traffic to hosts on the Internet.

IGMP Messages

IGMP messages exchange membership status information between IP routers that support multicasting and members of multicast groups. Individual member hosts report host membership in a multicast group, and membership status is polled by multicast routers. Table 6.16 lists the IGMP messages.

6. Internet Layer Maintenance and Group Protocols

Table 6.16   IGMP messages.

IGMP Message	Description
Host membership report	When a host joins a multicast group, it sends an IGMP host membership report message that declares its membership in a specific host group. IGMP host membership report messages are also sent in response to an IGMP host membership query that's sent by a router.
Host membership query	This is used by a multicast router to poll a network for group members.
Leave group	This is sent by a host when it leaves a host group and is the last member of that group on the network segment.

Multicast Boundaries

Boundaries create barriers to the forwarding of IP multicast traffic. If there are no boundaries, an IP multicast router forwards all appropriate IP multicast traffic. You can create multicast boundaries by specifying a range of IP addresses, known as a multicast scope, or by the value of the TTL field in the IP header.

Scope-Based Boundaries

Scope-based boundaries prevent the forwarding of IP multicast traffic with a specified group IP address or range of IP addresses. A scope-based boundary is specified by a base address and a subnet mask (255.255.255.255 specifies a single address). This specification follows the rules of Classless Interdomain Routing, or supernetting, discussed in Chapter 5—that is, the base address must have its final octet divisible by 2 if you're combining two addresses, by 4 if you're combining four addresses, and so on. Windows 2000 base boundary addresses must be in the range 239.0.0.0 through 239.254.255.255.

TTL-Based Boundaries

TTL-based boundaries prevent the forwarding of IP multicast traffic with a TTL that's less than a specified value; they apply to all multicast packets, regardless of the multicast group. They use more resource than scope-based boundaries and are not recommended by Microsoft.

By default, IP multicast datagrams are sent with a TTL of 1. Table 6.17 lists the restrictions to multicast datagrams associated with initial TTL settings.

Multicast Heartbeat

A Windows 2000 router can be set to listen for a regular multicast notification to a specified group address and, hence, verify that IP multicast connectivity is available on a network. This is known as *multicast heartbeat*. If the heartbeat isn't

Table 6.17   TTL threshold definitions.

Initial TTL Setting	Restriction
0	Restricted to the same host.
1	Restricted to the same subnet.
32	Restricted to the same site.
64	Restricted to the same region.
128	Restricted to the same continent.
255	Unrestricted.

received within a configured amount of time, the Windows 2000 router sets a flag on the configured interface. This flag setting is polled, and a notification is sent if the multicast heartbeat is no longer present.

6. Internet Layer Maintenance and Group Protocols

Immediate Solutions

Enabling ICMP Router Discovery

1. Access Start|Programs|Administrative Tools and select Routing and Remote Access.
2. Expand *server name*|IP Routing and click General.
3. In the details pane, right-click the interface you want to enable, then select Properties.
4. On the General tab, check the Enable router discovery advertisements checkbox.
5. In Advertisement lifetime (minutes), set a time period. If this amount of time has expired since its last router advertisement, the router is considered to be down.
6. In Minimum time (minutes), set the minimum time period between ICMP router advertisements.
7. In Maximum time (minutes), set the maximum time period between ICMP router advertisements. The actual time period between advertisements will fall between the maximum and minimum settings.
8. In Level of preference, click the arrows to set the router's level of preference as a default gateway. Your screen should look similar to Figure 6.4.
9. Click OK and exit from the MMC snap-in.

Configuring IP Multicast Support

Depending on the options chosen when a connection was set up using the Routing and Remote Access wizard, multicast support may already be enabled. To configure and (if necessary) enable multicast support, you need to complete the following steps:

- Add and configure the IGMP version 2, Router and Proxy routing protocol.
- Specify multicast scopes.
- Configure multicast boundaries.
- Configure multicast heartbeat.

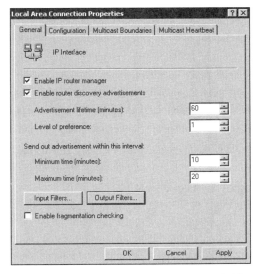

Figure 6.4   Enabling and configuring ICMP router discovery.

Adding and Configuring the IGMP Routing Protocol

In this set of procedures, you'll add the IGMP version 2, Router and Proxy routing protocol, and enable IGMP router and proxy modes by adding the Internal interface connection to the IGMP routing protocol and configuring it in IGMP router mode. You will also add the interface that represents the permanent connection to the Internet to the IGMP routing protocol and configure the interface in IGMP proxy mode. Finally, you'll configure the settings on the IGMP router.

TIP: *So that all of the procedures in this section are a standalone, I've specified that the Routing and Remote Access MMC snap-in be accessed at the start and closed at the end of each of them. If you're carrying out the procedures sequentially, keep the snap-in open.*

Adding the IGMP Routing Protocol

To add the IGMP protocol (assuming it's not already installed), proceed as follows:

1. Access Start|Programs|Administrative Tools and select Routing and Remote Access.

2. Expand *server name*|IP Routing and right-click General. If IGMP is in the IP Routing tree, the protocol is already installed. In this case, close the MMC snap-in. Otherwise, go on to step 3.

3. Select New Routing Protocol.

4. In the Select Routing Protocol dialog box, click IGMP Version 2, Router and Proxy, then click OK.

5. Close the MMC snap-in.

Enabling IGMP Router Mode on the Internal Connection

To enable IGMP router mode on the Internal connection, proceed as follows:

1. Access Start|Programs|Administrative Tools and select Routing and Remote Access.

2. Expand *server name*|IP Routing and click on IGMP.

3. If the Internal connection appears in the details pane, right-click it and select Properties. Otherwise, right-click General, select New Interface, click Internal, and click OK.

4. In the General dialog box, verify that the Enable IGMP checkbox is checked and the IGMP router radio button is selected. Also verify that Version 2 is selected in the IGMP protocol version drop-down list.

5. Click OK and exit from the MMC snap-in.

Enabling IGMP Proxy Mode on the Permanent Internet Connection

To enable IGMP proxy mode on the connection that you use for connection to the Internet (typically the Local Area Connection), proceed as follows:

1. Access Start|Programs|Administrative Tools and select Routing and Remote Access.

2. Expand *server name*|IP Routing and click IGMP.

3. If the connection you want to configure appears in the details pane, right-click it and select Properties. Otherwise, right-click General, select New Interface, select the appropriate interface connection, and click OK.

4. In the General dialog box, verify that the Enable IGMP checkbox is checked and select the IGMP proxy radio button.

5. Click OK and exit from the MMC snap-in.

TIP: You can enable IGMP proxy mode on only a single interface on the Windows 2000 router.

Configuring IGMP Router Settings

You don't usually need to modify the default IGMP router settings. You should do so only after you've made a careful analysis of your network. You can modify these settings only if IGMP router mode is enabled on the selected interface.

To modify the IGMP router settings, proceed as follows:

1. Access Start|Programs|Administrative Tools and select Routing and Remote Access.

2. Expand *server name*|IP Routing and click IGMP.

3. In the details pane, right-click the interface you want to configure and select Properties.

4. On the Router tab, configure the appropriate settings. Figure 6.5 shows the configuration settings available.

5. Click OK and exit from the MMC snap-in.

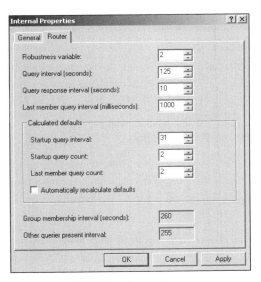

Figure 6.5   IGMP router settings.

Specifying a Multicast Scope

Scope-based boundaries prevent the forwarding of IP multicast traffic with a specified group IP address or range of IP addresses. The scope is specified by entering a base address (in the range 239.0.0.0 through 239.254.255.255) and a valid subnet mask. The subnet mask determines the number of addresses in the scope and must comply with CIDR boundary conditions. To specify a multicast scope, proceed as follows:

1. Access Start|Programs|Administrative Tools and select Routing and Remote Access.

2. Expand *server name*IP Routing and right-click General.

3. Select Properties.

4. On the Multicast Scopes tab, click Add.

5. In the Scoped Boundary dialog box, specify a multicast scope name, base address, and subnet mask.

6. Click OK. If you want to delete or edit a scope, highlight it and click the appropriate button.

7. Click OK and exit from the MMC snap-in.

Configuring Multicast Boundaries

The previous procedure specified a multicast scope. In this procedure, you'll add a specified multicast scope to an interface. This procedure also describes how to enable TTL scoping. You should, however, be aware that TTL scoping is not the recommended method of specifying a multicast scope.

1. Access Start|Programs|Administrative Tools and select Routing and Remote Access.

2. Expand *server name*IP Routing and click General.

3. In the details pane, right-click the interface on which you want to configure multicast boundaries, then select Properties.

4. On the Multicast Boundaries tab, select scope name in the Scope drop-down list, then click Add.

5. If you want to enable TTL scoping, check the Activate TTL boundary checkbox. A warning dialog box appears. If you're sure that you want to use this scoping method, click OK to close the box, then specify a TTL value and a rate limit (in kilobytes per second).

6. Click OK and exit from the MMC snap-in.

Configuring Multicast Heartbeat

Multicast heartbeat listens for periodic multicast traffic to confirm that the multicast structure is functioning normally. In this procedure, you'll configure the heartbeat for a multicast group, identified by IP address.

To configure multicast heartbeat, proceed as follows:

1. Access Start|Programs|Administrative Tools and select Routing and Remote Access.

2. Expand *server name*|IP Routing and click General.

3. In the details pane, right-click the interface on which you want to configure multicast heartbeat, then select Properties.

4. On the Multicast Heartbeat tab, check the Enable multicast heartbeat detection checkbox.

5. In the Multicast heartbeat group box, type the IP address of the multicast heartbeat group.

6. In the Quiet time before alerting (minutes) box, set the period of quiet time that can elapse before the multicast heartbeat sends an alert.

7. Click OK and exit from the MMC snap-in.

Using Network Shell Routing Commands

In addition to the facilities provided by the Routing and Remote Access snap-in, IGMP routing can be configured and tested from the command prompt using the network shell (netsh) utility. For example, the following command adds the static multicast group specified by the multicast IP address 239.192.230.10 to the Local Area Connection interface:

```
netsh routing ip igmp add staticgroup "Local Area Connection" 239.192.230.10
hostjoin
```

You can display the global IGMP logging level setting using:

```
netsh routing ip igmp show global
```

This will inform you whether errors, warnings, and information messages are being logged.

You can display the IGMP settings on an interface (for example, the Local Area Connection) using:

```
netsh routing ip igmp show interface "Local Area Connection"
```

The purpose of this procedure is to give examples of Network Shell routing commands. A full list of these commands can be found in Appendix D. To display the full syntax of any command, enter it at the command prompt, followed by a question mark, for example:

```
netsh routing ip igmp add interface ?
```

The netsh utility enables IGMP configuration commands to be placed in batch files and is useful when the same IGMP configuration parameters are specified on several machines.

Chapter 7

Internet Protocol Security

In Depth

The Windows 2000 Server operating system includes an implementation of the Internet Engineering Task Force (IETF) Internet Protocol Security (IPSec). IPSec exists below the transport level, and its security services are inherited transparently by applications. In today's business world, sensitive information constantly crosses networks. This traffic should be safe from interception and modification by unauthorized parties while en route. Such protocols as Secure Sockets Layer version 3/Transport Layer Security (SSL3/TLS) protect sensitive data but can be used only by applications, such as browsers, that understand them. A low-level protocol is needed that can provide security for all TCP/IP communications on both sides of an organization's firewall. IPSec addresses that need and provides data integrity, confidentiality, and authentication. IPSec also provides protection against replay attacks (see Chapter 11) and extends encryption support to Virtual Private Networks (VPNs).

Most security systems, such as firewalls and secure routers, provide protection against the outsider. An organization, however, can lose a great deal of sensitive information to internal attacks mounted by disgruntled staff members or contractors. IPSec provides protection against both internal and external attacks.

IPSec Features

IPSec uses an Authentication Header (AH) and an Encapsulated Security Payload (ESP). The AH provides data communication with source authentication and integrity checking. The ESP provides confidentiality. In an IPSec-protected communication, only the sender and recipient know the security key. If the authentication data is valid, the recipient knows that the communication came from the sender and wasn't changed in transit.

IPSec supports industry (IETF) standards and security protocols.

Supported Industry Standards

IPSec supports industry-standard cryptographic algorithms and authentication techniques, including the following:

- Diffie-Hellman (DH) technique
- Hash Message Authentication Code (HMAC)
- Data Encryption Standard Cipher Block Chaining (DES-CBC)

The Diffie-Hellman Technique

The DH technique (Whitfield Diffie and Martin Hellman) is a public key cryptography algorithm that allows two communicating entities to agree on a shared key. DH starts with two entities exchanging public information. Each entity then combines the other's public information with its own secret information to generate a shared-secret value.

Hash Message Authentication Code

HMAC is a secret key algorithm that provides integrity and authentication. The authentication method uses a keyed hash function to produce a digital signature for the packet, which can be verified by the receiver. If the message changes in transit, the hash value is different and the IP packet is rejected. IPSec uses one of two HMAC hash functions:

- *HMAC-MD5*—Message Digest function 95 (MD5) is a hash function that produces a 128-bit value.

- *HMAC-SHA1*—Secure Hash Algorithm (SHA) is a hash function that produces a 160-bit value. HMAC-SHA1 is slower than HMAC-MD5 but more secure.

MD5-Hash Security

While doubt has been cast on the security of the MD5 hash, particularly in an environment where collisions are possible (see Hans Dobbertin, "RIPEMD with two-round compress function is not collision-free," *Journal of Cryptology* 10(1): 51–70, Winter 1997), no such security concerns have been expressed for HMAC-MD5. Remember, however, that nothing is completely secure. Nor will any hashed information remain secure over time. There's nothing more dangerous than security that isn't secure any more, when users believe that it is. Also, security must always present a moving target.

Data Encryption Standard-Cipher Block Chaining

DES-CBC is a secret key algorithm used for confidentiality. A random number is generated and used with the secret key to encrypt the data.

TIP: *More information about DH may be found at **ftp://ftp.rsa.com/pub/pkcs/ascii/pkcs-3.asc**. HMAC is defined at **http://drax.isi.edu/in-notes/rfc/files/rfc2104.txt**, and DES-CBC at **http://www.kashpureff.org/nic/rfcs/1800/rfc1829.txt.html** and **http://info.internet.isi.edu:80/in-notes/rfc/files/rfc2405.txt**.*

The Windows 2000 IPSec implementation is compliant with the latest IETF drafts proposed in the IPSec working group. In addition, IPSec supports the Internet Security Association and Key Management Protocol (ISAKMP)—using the Oakley key determination protocol, which allows for dynamic rekeying. ISAKMP/Oakley is used to build Security Associations (SAs) between communicating computers. SAs are discussed later in this chapter.

Security Protocols

The Windows 2000 implementation of IPSec uses the following security protocols:

- Internet Security Association and Key Management Protocol
- Oakley Key Determination
- IP Authentication Header
- IP Encapsulating Security Protocol

Internet Security Association and Key Management Protocol

Before IP packets can be transmitted from one computer to another, an SA must be established between the two communicating parties using IPSec. ISAKMP defines a common framework to support the establishment of SAs, as discussed later in this chapter.

Oakley

Oakley is a key determination protocol that uses the DH key exchange algorithm. Oakley supports Perfect Forward Secrecy (PFS), which ensures that if a single key is compromised, access is permitted only to data protected by that single key. A key (or that key's original key-generation material) is never used to compute additional keys.

NOTE: *Oakley ensures that no key (or key-generation material) is ever reused. This applies to all keys, not merely those that we know are compromised. Otherwise, how can we be absolutely certain whether a key is compromised or not?*

IP Authentication Header

AH provides integrity, authentication, and anti-replay by using an algorithm to compute a keyed message hash (an HMAC) for each IP packet.

IP Encapsulating Security Protocol

ESP provides confidentiality, using the DES-CBC algorithm.

Security Associations

An SA defines the common security services, mechanisms, and keys used to protect a communication from source to destination. The Security Parameters Index (SPI) is a unique identifier used to distinguish between multiple SAs that exist at the receiving computer. Multiple SAs exist if a computer communicates securely with multiple computers simultaneously, such as when a file server or a remote access server serves multiple clients. In addition, multiple SAs can exist between two individual computers.

The IETF has established a standard method of security association and key exchange resolution to build SAs between computers. This method combines

ISAKMP and the Oakley key generation protocol. ISAKMP centralizes security association management and reduces connection time. Oakley generates and manages the authenticated keys used to secure the information.

This process also protects remote computers that are requesting secure access to a corporate network, or any situation in which the negotiation for the final destination computer (or *endpoint*) is performed by a security router or other proxy server. In the latter situation, referred to as *ISAKMP client mode*, the identities of the endpoints are hidden.

To ensure successful, secure communication, ISAKMP/Oakley performs a two-phase operation:

- The key exchange phase
- The data protection phase

The process assures confidentiality and authentication during each phase by using negotiated encryption and authentication algorithms that are agreed on by the two computers.

The Key Exchange Phase

During the key exchange phase, the two computers establish the ISAKMP SA. Oakley provides identity protection during this exchange, enabling total privacy. This helps prevent network attacks that hijack identities (for example, spoofing).

The security negotiation process during this phase is as follows:

1. The policy negotiation dialog determines the following:
   - The encryption algorithm (DES, 3DES, or none)
   - The integrity algorithm (MD5 or SHA1)
   - The authentication method (public key certificate, preshared key, or Kerberos 5)
   - The DH group
2. The key information exchange ensures that each computer has the necessary information to generate the shared-secret key (or master key) for the ISAKMP SA.
3. The computers authenticate the key information exchange. The master key is used, in conjunction with the algorithms negotiated in Step 1. Whatever authentication method is used, the payload cannot be intercepted or modified.

The initiating computer offers a list of potential security levels to the responding computer. The responder can't modify the offer; otherwise, the initiator will reject the responder's message. The responder sends a reply either accepting the offer or indicating that no offer was chosen. In the latter case, the process begins again.

The Data Protection Phase

Negotiation messages are automatically resent five times. After three seconds, a *soft* SA is established. If an ISAKMP response is received before the cycle times out, the soft SA is deleted and standard SA negotiation begins. A pair of SAs, referred to as *IPSec SAs*, is negotiated. This process is almost identical to the process discussed in the original key exchange negotiation. However, if the process to negotiate the SA pair times out for any reason, a renegotiation is attempted. If a message for the data protection phase is received without establishing an ISAKMP SA, it is rejected.

SA Lifetimes

When a key lifetime is reached for the master or session key, the associated SA is renegotiated and the old ISAKMP SA is marked as expired. This prevents a bogus IPSec SA from being formed from an old SA.

When the IPSec Policy Agent retrieves policy updates, it will update the IP filter list stored in the IPSec driver. Any SAs associated with old filters, which no longer exist in the policy, will be deleted, along with the old filters in the IPSec driver cache.

If the Windows 2000 power-save features cause the computer to hibernate or sleep, and the SA expires during this inactive period, the SA will be automatically renegotiated when the computer is reactivated. If Windows 2000 is shut down, Oakley deletes any remaining SAs, and new SAs are renegotiated. If Windows 2000 terminates abnormally, the old SAs might still be in place until the default time-out period is reached. If this occurs, the SAs must be manually deleted.

Monitoring IPSec Packets

You can use Network Monitor to view IPSec security protocol transmissions. The recommended method of capturing these packets is to configure a Network Monitor capture filter with the address pair of the source and destination computers. This procedure is described in the Immediate Solutions section of this chapter.

Authentication Header Packets

Network Monitor displays packets that are secured with AH as Transmission Control Protocol (TCP), Internet Control Message Protocol (ICMP), or User Datagram Protocol (UDP) packets with an AH header. In the Next Header field, AH is displayed as IP protocol number 51 (decimal).

Encapsulating Security Payload Packets

Because ESP encrypts the original header, Network Monitor displays ESP packets (rather than TCP, ICMP, or UDP). The data payload in the ESP packet won't be readable. In the Next Header field, ESP is displayed as IP protocol number 50 (decimal). IPSec creates a hash of the ICMP and Data fields of the frame and encrypts the data.

Viewing ISAKMP or Oakley Packets

ISAKMP/Oakley is displayed as UDP port number 500 (decimal) in the Next Header field. Figures 7.1, 7.2, and 7.3 show an unencrypted message, an ISAKMP encrypted message, and an ESP encrypted message, respectively. The important point here is that the contents of the message can be read in the first of these captures, but not in the others. Figure 7.1 was generated from the Network Monitor capture file arc1.cap (available on the CD-ROM). We saw how to capture an unencrypted (**ping**) message in Chapter 3. Figures 7.2 and 7.3 were generated from the Network Monitor capture file ipsec.cap (also available on the CD-ROM). We will see how to capture an encrypted message in the Immediate Solutions section of this chapter.

IPSec and the ping Command

Ping seldom works the first time between IPSec-enabled computers that are using Server (Request Security) or Secure Server (Require Security) policies. The ICMP packet sent by the **ping** command will match the IP filter list in these policies, and IPSec will attempt to apply security to the **ping** command. However, this process takes longer than the **ping** command normally waits for a response.

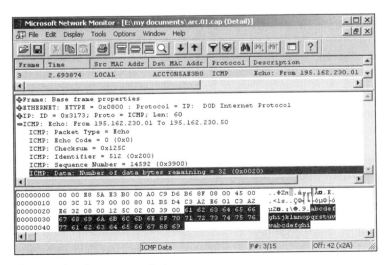

Figure 7.1   An unencrypted message.

Because of this, you may receive erroneous Destination Unreachable messages. One workaround is to exempt ICMP traffic in all of your IPSec policies. Alternatively, you can use the –w switch to increase the time-out value in the **ping** command—for example, **ping –w 500 195.162.230.50.**

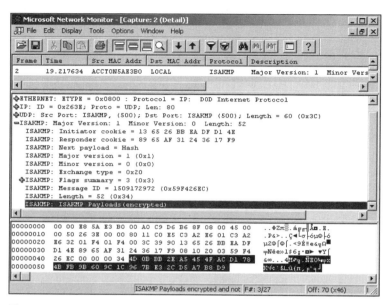

Figure 7.2   An ISAKMP encrypted message.

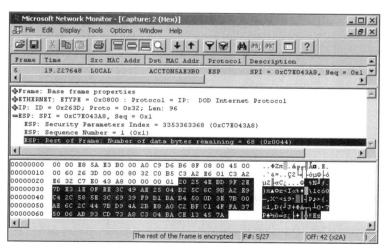

Figure 7.3   An ESP encrypted message.

Immediate Solutions

Analyzing IPSec Operation

Before you can specify IPSec settings and configure an IPSec policy, you need to understand how IPSec works. Suppose that a user on a computer called Laurel sends a message to a user on a computer called Hardy. The procedure is as follows:

1. The IPSec driver on Laurel checks the IP filter list in the active policy for a match with the address or traffic type of the outbound packets.

2. The IPSec driver notifies ISAKMP to begin security negotiations with Hardy.

3. The ISAKMP service on Hardy receives a request for security negotiations.

4. The two computers perform a key exchange and establish an ISAKMP SA and a shared-secret key.

5. The two computers negotiate the level of security for the data transmission, establishing a pair of IPSec SAs and keys for securing the IP packets.

6. Using the outbound IPSec SA and key, the IPSec driver on Laurel signs the packets for integrity and encrypts the packets if confidentiality has been negotiated.

7. The IPSec driver on Laurel transfers the packets to the appropriate connection type for transmission to Hardy.

8. Hardy receives the secured packets and transfers them to the IPSec driver.

9. Using the inbound SA and key, the IPSec driver on Hardy checks the integrity signature and decrypts the packets, if necessary.

10. The IPSec driver on Hardy transfers the decrypted packets to the TCP/IP driver, which transfers them to the receiving application.

The users don't see any of this process. Routers or switches in the data path between the computers don't require IPSec and will automatically forward the encrypted IP packets to the destination. However, if a router is functioning as a firewall, security gateway, or proxy server, you must enable special filtering so that the secured IP packets aren't rejected. In this case, input and output filters specified in Table 7.1 must be defined for Internet interface.

Refer to the router documentation for instructions on how to set up these filters.

Table 7.1   Router settings to enable IPSec traffic.

Filters	Settings
Input filters	IP Protocol ID of 51 (0x33) for inbound IPSec AH traffic
	IP Protocol ID of 50 (0x32) for inbound IPSec ESP traffic
	UDP port 500 (0x1F4) for inbound ISAKMP/Oakley negotiation traffic
Output filters	IP Protocol ID of 51 (0x33) for outbound IPSec AH traffic
	IP Protocol ID of 50 (0x32) for outbound IPSec ESP traffic
	UDP port 500 (0x1F4) for outbound ISAKMP/Oakley negotiation traffic

Specifying IPSec Settings

Depending on the sensitivity of the information, the relative vulnerability of the transmission carrier, and export restrictions applied to certain levels of encryption, you can specify the IPSec settings, or *attributes*, appropriate to your own situation.

Each configuration of IPSec attributes is called a *security policy*. Security policies are built on associated negotiation policies and IP filters and can be assigned to the domain, to individual computers, or to Organizational Units (OUs). IP filters determine which actions to take, based on the destination and protocol of individual IP packets.

TIP: *This procedure is a paper exercise. Nevertheless, it's an essential step toward a sound IPSec policy. Security policies should be planned on paper before going on to the deployment stage. The sign of a good network professional is that he or she plans everything very carefully on paper before going anywhere near a computer.*

To specify IPSec settings, proceed as follows:

1. Select a security level. The choices are as follows:

   • *Client (Respond Only)*—Sends unsecured requests, but responds securely to requests for IPSec-secured communications by securing the protocol and port traffic for such requests. Computers using this policy can't communicate with computers using the Secure Server policy.

   • *Server (Request Security)*—Accepts unsecured traffic, but attempts to secure further communications by requesting security from the sender. If the negotiation attempt times out (after 40 seconds), unsecured communication is permitted.

   • *Secure Server (Require Security)*—Rejects unsecured incoming traffic and secures all outgoing messages. Communication is blocked if a peer computer fails to negotiate security.

2. Specify Transport or Tunnel mode:

- *Transport Mode*—Secures communication between peer computers. This is the default mode for IPSec and provides end-to-end security between the sending computer and one or more recipient computers on the same network. Transport mode can be used by computers communicating through a Remote Access Server (RAS) and can be used across routers in an intranet. Its use is not indicated, however, if messages are required to cross foreign networks or hostile environments, such as the Internet.

- *Tunnel Mode*—Secures communication between remote networks. This enforces IPSec policies for Internet traffic and supports point-to-point traffic. It authenticates and encrypts data flowing within an IP tunnel created between two logical devices, typically computers or Windows 2000-enabled Routing and Remote Access Service (RRAS) routers. Either an IP address or a host name must be used to specify both tunnel endpoints.

WARNING! *IPSec tunneling specifies computers as endpoints and uses computer certificates rather than user certificates for validation. Any user with access to an endpoint computer has access to the tunnel, and this is a security risk. The workaround is to use either Point-To-Point Tunneling Protocol (PPTP) or Layer 2 Tunneling Protocol (L2TP) over IPSec.*

3. Specify the network type. The IPSec security rule must be applied to a network type. The options are as follows:

- All network connections
- Local Area Network (LAN)
- Remote access

4. Specify a machine authentication method. The three options are as follows:

- *Kerberos 5*—The Windows 2000 default. Windows 2000 and Unix computers running Kerberos 5 can use this method.

- *Public Key Certificates*—Any clients that access the Internet or business intranets using an X.509-compatible public key infrastructure can use this method.

- *Preshared Key*—Any clients that need a single peer-to-peer connection but aren't running Kerberos 5 can use this method. A preshared key is used only for authentication and doesn't encrypt data.

NOTE: *If certificates or preshared keys are used for authentication, the computer identity is protected. However, if the Kerberos 5 method is used, the computer identity remains unencrypted until the entire identity payload is encrypted.*

7. Internet
Protocol Security

5. Specify or configure an IP filter list. This defines the type of traffic for which the IPSec security rule applies. By default, you can specify all IP traffic or all Internet Control Message Protocol (ICMP) traffic. You can also define your own IP filter list. The options are as follows:

- *IP Traffic Source*—Specifies a source address. The choices are your IP address, any IP address, a specific DNS name, a specific IP address, or a specific IP subnet. The default is My IP Address.

- *IP Traffic Destination*—Specifies a destination address. The choices are your IP address, any IP address, a specific DNS name, a specific IP address, or a specific IP subnet. Unless you have a particular reason for restricting destination addresses, Microsoft recommends selecting Any IP Address.

- *IP Protocol Type*—Specifies the protocol used. A wide range is presented, including Exterior Gateway Protocol (EGP), Host Monitor Protocol (HMP), Internet Control Message Protocol (ICMP), Remote Desk Protocol (RDP), Transmission Control Protocol (TCP), User Datagram Protocol (UDP), and Xerox Network Systems Internet Data Protocol (XNS-IDP). If you specify a protocol, it must be installed on both the source and destination machines.

- *IP Protocol Port*—Specifies the source and destination ports, depending on the protocol selected.

6. Select a filter action for the IPSec security rule. The standard actions correspond to the security levels described in Step 1 of this procedure. You can, however, specify your own filter action. The settings are as follows:

- *General Options*—Sets the filter action behavior. *Permit* is a passthrough policy that ignores any incoming communications that don't negotiate IPSec security. *Block* stops all incoming and outgoing communications, both encrypted and nonencrypted, and *Negotiate security* gives the choice of communicating only with computers that support IPSec or falling back to unsecured communications.

- *IP Traffic Security*—Specifies a security method for IP traffic. *High* encrypts and authenticates data. *Medium* authenticates, but doesn't encrypt. You can also specify *Custom*, which gives the options shown in Figure 7.4.

7. Specify the authentication encryption scheme. The options are as follows:

- *SHA1*—Uses a 160-bit key. Specify this for high-security applications, such as U.S. government contracts.

- *MD5*—Uses a 128-bit key. This is sufficient for all normal commercial operations.

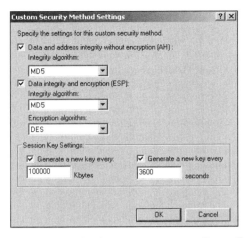

Figure 7.4   Setting a custom security method.

8. Specify the data encryption scheme. The options are as follows:

- *3DES*—Uses three 128-bit keys. Specify this for high-security communications.

- *DES*—Uses a single 56-bit key. This gives a much lower level of security.

Additional Encryption Schemes

For very high security, more sophisticated encryption schemes are available, such as dynamic key length (which uses an adjustable key length determined at runtime). Currently these aren't standard IPSec settings and will be encountered only in custom-built security systems. You should, however, be aware that they exist and may be used in future implementations.

9. Specify a DH level. The options are Low (1) or Medium (2).

10. Specify whether to deploy IPSec on individual computers, at the domain level, or for an OU. These options are discussed in the following sections.

Configuring IPSec on Individual Computers

In this procedure, you'll configure IPSec based on the decisions you made in the previous procedure, "Specifying IPSec Settings." When you carry out the procedure, you may wish to replace some of the settings with your own. The procedure remains the same.

7. Internet Protocol Security

You can configure IPSec on a single computer, configure IPSec domain policy on a Domain Controller (DC), or configure IPSec settings for an OU and place computers in that OU. To test IPSec policy, however, you need a minimum of two machines. To carry out the procedures as described, you should have access to a DC and two additional Windows 2000 computers on your network. You can then configure IPSec on the individual computers, test it, configure it for the domain, investigate the effect, and then configure it for an OU and place the non-DC computers in that OU.

To configure IPSec on an individual (non-DC) computer, proceed as follows:

1. Log on as an administrator.
2. Access Start|Run and enter **mmc**.
3. On the Console menu, select Add/Remove Snap-in.
4. In the Add/Remove Snap-in dialog box, click Add.
5. Select IP Security Policy Management. Click Add.
6. Verify that Local computer is selected. Click Finish.
7. Select Services. Click Add.
8. Verify that Local computer is selected. Click Finish.
9. Close the Add/Standalone Snap-in dialog box.
10. Click OK to close the Add/Remove Snap-in dialog box.
11. Select IP Security Policies on Local Machine. In the right pane, right-click Secure Server and then select Properties, as shown in Figure 7.5.
12. At this point, you can, optionally, select the General tab of the Secure Server (Require Security) Properties dialog box, click Advanced to see the Key Exchange Settings, and click Methods to see the Key Exchange Security methods. Don't change any of these settings at this stage. Click Cancel

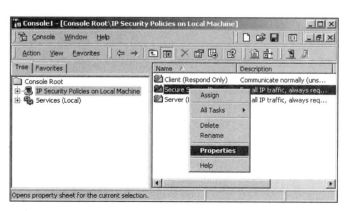

Figure 7.5   Accessing secure server properties.

on both dialog boxes to return to the Secure Server (Require Security) Properties dialog box.

13. Select the Rules tab of the Secure Server (Require Security) Properties dialog box and verify that all the IP Security Rules are checked. Click Add.

14. The Security Rule Wizard appears. Click Next.

TIP: *In the remainder of this procedure, you can implement your own settings, if you want to do so. If you need information about any of the settings, the F1 key provides in-context help.*

---

15. Select This rule does not specify a tunnel. Click Next.

16. Select All network connections. Click Next.

17. Select Use this string to protect the key exchange (preshared key), and then type a string, as shown in Figure 7.6. Click Next.

TIP: *Choose a string with both upper- and lowercase characters that you'll remember but that will be difficult for a third party to guess. You need not, of course, choose this authentication method. The reason I've chosen not to use the default Kerberos authentication is so that I can distinguish the policy I've configured from the default policies that already exist.*

---

18. Select All IP Traffic. Click Next.

19. Select Require Security. Click Next.

20. Click Finish to close the Security Rule Wizard.

21. In the Secure Server (Require Security) Properties dialog box, select only the rule that you've created, as shown in Figure 7.7.

22. Close the Secure Server (Require Security) Properties dialog box.

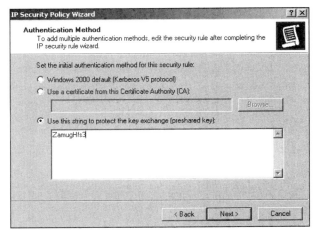

Figure 7.6   Setting preshared key authentication.

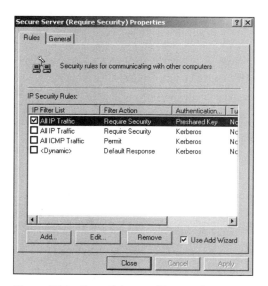

Figure 7.7   Specifying an IP security rule.

23. In the right pane of the MMC snap-in, right-click Secure Server and select Assign.

24. Save the MMC snap-in as IPSecSer. You'll be using it in subsequent procedures.

You have created and assigned a new security rule. To test it, you need to use a second machine.

Testing the IPSec Configuration

To test the IPSec configuration, proceed as follows:

1. Repeat the previous procedure on a second computer, so that you have two computers on your network with identical IPSec policies.

2. Take note of the second computer's IP address.

3. Log on to the first computer as an administrator.

4. Start the IPSecSer MMC snap-in that you created in the previous procedure. You should be able to access this through Start|Programs|Administrative Tools.

5. Select Services (Local).

6. In the right pane, right-click IPSEC Policy Agent and click Start (unless the service is already started).

7. Ping the second computer by IP address. You should receive responses telling you that IPSec is being negotiated. You may have to ping several times before you get through. A typical response is shown in Figure 7.8.

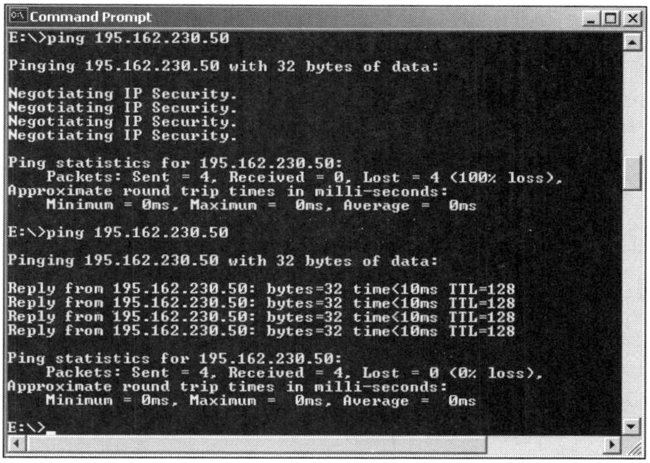

Figure 7.8   IPSec negotiation during the **ping** command.

8. Access Start|Run and enter **ipsecmon**. This starts the IP Security Monitor. This tool will give you information on the SAs that have been established, IPSec statistics, and the ISAKMP/Oakley statistics.

9. Close the IP Security Monitor and the MMC snap-in.

Removing the IPSec Assignment

In this procedure, you'll unassign the IPSec policy on both non-DC computers.

To unassign the IPSec policy, proceed as follows:

1. Log on as an administrator.

2. Start the IPSecSer MMC snap-in that you created in the previous procedure. You should be able to access this through Start|Programs|Administrative Tools.

3. Select IP Security Policies on Local Machine.

4. In the right pane, right-click Secure Server and select Un-assign.

Configuring IPSec for a Domain

In this procedure, you'll configure IPSec on a domain controller and apply it to an entire domain.

To configure IPSec for a domain, proceed as follows:

1. Log on to the DC as an administrator.
2. Create the IPSecSer MMC snap-in. The procedure for doing so is given in the previous section, "Configuring IPSec on Individual Computers." In this case, when adding the IP Security Policy Management snap-in, select Manage domain policy for this computer's domain.
3. Click IP Security Policies on Active Directory.
4. In the right pane, right-click Secure Server and select Properties.
5. Click Add to start the Security Rule Wizard.
6. Configure the settings specified in the "Configuring IPSec on Individual Computers" procedure earlier in this chapter, except in the Authentication Method window (refer to Figure 7.6), specify Use a certificate from this Certificate Authority (CA). If you're warned that Active Directory doesn't contain a shared certificate store when you click the Browse button, then click Yes to select a CA from the local machine certificate store.
7. Uncheck all the IP Security Rules, except for the one you've just created, and close the Secure Server (Require Security) Properties dialog box.

NOTE: If you configure IPSec in Active Directory, you don't need to assign it. You can check this by clicking Security Policies on Active Directory and right-clicking Secure Server in the right pane. In this case, no Assign option appears in the context menu.

---

8. Click Services (Local) in the MMC snap-in and start the IPSEC Policy Agent (unless the service is already started).

Testing Domain IPSec Policy

In this section, you attempt to assign local IPSec policy on a non-DC computer, when that computer is part of a domain with domain IPSec policy configured.

To assign local policy on a non-DC computer:

1. Log on to the computer as an administrator.
2. Open or create the IPSecSer MMC snap-in.
3. Click IP Security Policies on Local Machine. You should get an error message telling you that the domain controller has provided an IPSec policy. Click OK.
4. Right-click Secure Server in the right pane and select Assign.
5. You should receive a message stating that the policy has been assigned, but that domain policy is overriding.
6. Unassign the policy.

Capturing IPSec Traffic

This procedure assumes you've configured IPSec in Active Directory for the entire domain. In the procedure, you'll set up a Network Monitor capture filter on the DC and capture IPSec traffic between the DC and another computer on the domain. Typical IPSec traffic was illustrated in Figures 7.2 and 7.3, which show frames from the ipscec.cap file on the CD-ROM.

To capture IPSec Traffic, proceed as follows:

1. Log on to the DC as an administrator.
2. Log on to another computer in the domain using any domain account that has permission to access the Command Console.
3. On the DC, access Start|Programs|Administrative Tools and select Network Monitor.
4. On the Network Monitor Capture pull-down menu, select Filter.
5. In the Capture Filter dialog box, click Edit Addresses.
6. In the Address Database dialog box, click Add.
7. The Address Information dialog box appears. Select IP in the Type drop-down box and enter the name and IP address of the other computer that you logged on to in your domain. Click OK.
8. Close the Address Database dialog box.
9. In the Address Expression dialog box, select the DC as Station 1 and the other computer as Station 2. In the Direction box, select bidirectional (<··>). Click OK.
10. Click OK to close the Capture Filter dialog box.
11. On the Network Monitor Capture pull-down menu, select Start.
12. Ping the other computer using a timeout value of 500 milliseconds (**ping –w 500** *ip_address*). Continue to ping the computer until a reply is received. From the other computer, ping the DC.
13. On the Network Monitor Capture pull-down menu, select Stop and View. View the captured frames and save the capture.
14. Exit from Network Monitor.

Related solution:	Found on page:
Implementing a Capture Filter	101

Changing the Security Method

By default, the security method is a combination of 128-bit 3DES packet encryption and SHA1 authentication encryption with the DH level set to Medium (2). This is secure, but some locations may not be able to decrypt authentication or package information. In this case, you have to set your security to a lower level.

This procedure assumes you've configured IPSec in Active Directory for the entire domain. To change the security method, proceed as follows:

1. Log on to the DC as an administrator.

2. Access the IPSecSer MMC snap-in.

3. Select IP Security Policies on Active Directory. In the right pane, right-click Secure Server and select Properties.

4. On the General tab, click Advanced, then click Methods.

5. On the Key Exchange Security Methods page (see Figure 7.9), select the method of your choice and use the Move up button to place it at the top of the preference order. If you definitely won't be using one or more of the methods on the list, then remove them. If none of the standard methods is suitable, you can use the Edit button to design your own.

6. Click OK, click OK (again), and click Close to return to the MMC snap-in. Close the snap-in.

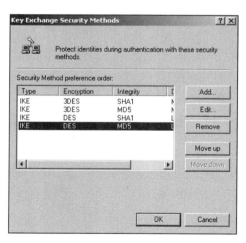

Figure 7.9   The Key Exchange Security Methods dialog box.

Configuring IPSec for an OU

In this procedure, you'll create an OU (or use one that's already in your DC's Active Directory), configure IPSec for that OU, and enable the settings on individual computers by placing them in that OU. This procedure stands on its own as a solution, but if you decided to implement the previous procedures in this chapter, you'll see how OU-based IPSec policy interacts with domain policy and policy set on individual computers.

NOTE: *In this procedure, I've specified IPSec settings that differ from those set in the previous procedures, both to distinguish between the various policies and to demonstrate how, for example, the IP Filter Wizard can be used to specify a filter list. You can use this procedure with whatever IPSec settings you decide are appropriate to your organization.*

To configure IPSec for an OU, proceed as follows:

1. Start the Active Directory Users and Computers MMC snap-in and add an OU called IPSec policies (or choose an already existing OU).

NOTE: *This procedure assumes that you're familiar with Active Directory and know how to create an OU and set Group Policy. If this isn't the case, refer to the product documentation.*

---

2. Right-click the OU and select Properties.

3. Add a Group Policy Object (GPO) called IPSec GPO. Edit this GPO.

4. Expand Computer Configuration|Windows Settings|Security Settings and click IP Security Policies on Active Directory.

5. Right-click Secure Server and select Properties.

6. On the Rules tab, click Add. The Security Rule Wizard appears.

7. Click Next. Select This rule does not specify a tunnel.

8. Click Next. Select All network connections.

9. Click Next. Select Use this string to protect the key exchange (preshared key) and type a preshared string.

10. Click Next. Click Add to specify a new IP filter.

11. Click Add. The IP Filter Wizard starts.

12. Click Next. Specify My IP Address for the source address.

13. Click Next. Specify Any IP Address for the destination address.

14. Click Next. Select Other in the drop-down box and then select TCP.

15. Click Next. Click Next (again) to accept the default IP Protocol Port assignment.

16. Click Finish.

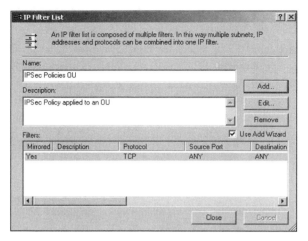

Figure 7.10   Specifying an IP filter.

17. Type a name and description for the new filter, as shown in Figure 7.10.

18. Click Close. Select the filter you've just created.

19. Click Next. Select Require Security.

20. Click Next. Click Finish.

21. Ensure that the new IPSec policy you've created is the only one that's checked.

22. Click Close. This returns you to the Group Policy MMC snap-in.

23. Right-click Secure Server and select Assign.

24. Exit from the Group Policy MMC snap-in.

25. Click Close. In the Active Directory Users and Computers MMC snap-in, add one or more non-DC computers (preferably the ones you configured earlier) to the IPSec Policies OU.

26. Check that these computers are now configured with the OU's IPSec settings.

Setting IPSec Policies

The rules for setting IPSec policies are as follows:

- Domain policy overrides individual computer policy.

- Policy set in an OU overrides domain policy.

- Policy set in a lower-level OU overrides policy set in an OU higher in the Active Directory tree.

- Set policies at as high a level as possible to simplify administration.

Chapter 8

Transmission Control Protocol

In Depth

Transmission Control Protocol (TCP) is a required TCP/IP protocol defined in RFC 793. It provides connection-based, reliable, byte-stream-oriented connections and is used for logon, file and print sharing, replication of information, transfer of browse lists, and other common functions in the Windows networking environment. TCP can be used only for one-to-one (or point-to-point) communications. This chapter first looks at standard TCP features and operation, then goes on to describe the enhancements and new features offered by Windows 2000. Because the majority of TCP/IP utilities and services use TCP, it's appropriate to summarize these in this chapter. Internetwork transport protocols, such as Hypertext Transport Protocol (HTTP) and File Transport Protocol (FTP), are described in Chapter 10.

Standard TCP Features and Operation

TCP is layered over the Internet Protocol (IP) service and is, arguably, the most significant transport protocol in the TCP/IP suite. It offers a reliable byte-stream transport method for programs that use session-based data transmission, and it guarantees delivery of IP datagrams. TCP implements reliable, efficient transport through a number of mechanisms, as described below.

Segmentation and Sequence Numbers

TCP segments and reassembles large blocks of data sent by programs and ensures correct sequencing and ordered delivery of segmented data. Sequence numbers are used to coordinate data transmission and reception, and TCP will arrange for retransmission if it determines that data has been lost. The protocol uses a 32-bit sequence number that counts octets in the data stream. Each TCP packet contains the starting sequence number of the data in that packet and the sequence number (or *acknowledgment number*) of the last byte received from the remote peer. Using this information, a *sliding-window* protocol is implemented, as described later in this chapter.

Forward and reverse sequence numbers are completely independent. TCP typically works in *full-duplex* mode, which means that it operates in both directions in an almost completely independent manner. There's no mechanism that associates forward and reverse byte-stream data. TCP exhibits *asymmetric behavior* (that is, data transfer in a single direction) only during connection start and close sequences.

TCP uses control flags to manage the connection. Some of these flags (such as the URG flag) pertain to a single packet. However, two flags (SYN and FIN) mark the beginning and end of the data stream and require reliable delivery. These flags are assigned spots in the sequence number space. TCP sends acknowledgments (ACKs) when data is received successfully. If Selective Acknowledgment (SACK) is enabled, TCP also sends negative acknowledgments when expected data isn't received. SACK is enabled by default in Windows 2000.

Checksums

Sequence numbers, control flags, and acknowledgments ensure that transmitted data has been received and reassembled in the correct sequence and that there are no missing segments. TCP also checks on the integrity of transmitted data by using checksum calculations. If the checksum is incorrect, the datagram is rejected and must be transmitted. Checksum calculation is complex. If you need to know the details, the following is a direct extract from RFC 793:

> The checksum field is the 16 bit one's complement of the one's complement sum of all 16 bit words in the header and text. If a segment contains an odd number of header and text octets to be checksummed, the last octet is padded on the right with zeros to form a 16 bit word for checksum purposes. The pad is not transmitted as part of the segment. While computing the checksum, the checksum field itself is replaced with zeros.

> The checksum also covers a 96 bit pseudo header conceptually prefixed to the TCP header. This pseudo header contains the Source Address, the Destination Address, the Protocol, and TCP length. This gives the TCP protection against misrouted segments. This information is carried in the Internet Protocol and is transferred across the TCP/Network interface in the arguments or results of calls by the TCP on the IP.

Flow Control

TCP ensures efficient transmission of data across a network through *flow control*. It dynamically discovers the network's delay characteristics and adjusts its operation to maximize throughput without overloading the network.

Each TCP connection endpoint has a buffer for storing data that is transmitted over the network before an application is ready to read that data. This enables network transfers to take place while applications are busy with other processing and improves overall performance. TCP manages traffic so its buffers don't overflow—fast senders are stopped periodically so slower receivers can catch up.

To avoid buffer overflow, TCP sets a *Window Size* field in each packet it transmits. This field indicates the amount of data that may be transmitted into the buffer. If the value in this falls to zero, the transmitting host sends no more data until it receives a packet that announces a non-zero value in the Window Size field.

Sometimes, the buffer space is too small for efficient transmission. This happens in networks that have limited bandwidth or slow links. The solution is to increase the buffer size, but there's a limitation to doing this that's imposed by the maximum Window Size that the protocol allows. Under these conditions, the network is termed a Long Fat Network (LFN). Windows 2000 TCP allows larger window sizes than did previous implementations.

NOTE: *LFN can stand for Long Fat Network or Long File Name. For Long File Name the acronym is pronounced "el-ef-en." For Long Fat Network, it's pronounced "elephant." Elephants are discussed in RFC 1072.*

One important factor governing the flow of information across a network is the period of time that a sending host waits for an acknowledgment before assuming the data is lost and retransmitting it. If this period is too short, packets are retransmitted unnecessarily; if it's too long, the connection can sit idle while the host waits to time out. TCP attempts to determine an optimum time-out period by monitoring the normal exchange of data packets. This process is called Round-Trip Time (RTT) estimation. Windows 2000 TCP provides an improved RTT algorithm that uses Timestamps. This is described later in this chapter.

TCP Sliding Windows

TCP implements flow control by using sliding window algorithms that permit multiple data packets to be in transit simultaneously. These algorithms place buffers between application programs and the network data flow. Data received from the network is stored in a buffer, and an application reads this data at its own pace, freeing up buffer space to accept more input from the network. The window is the amount of data that can be *read ahead* and is equal to the size of the buffer less the amount of valid data that's stored in it.

If the window size is larger than the packet size, then multiple packets can be transmitted, because the sender knows that buffer space is available on the receiver to hold them. Ideally, a steady-state condition is reached where the application is reading data from the buffer at the same rate that the sender is adding data to it. In this case, the buffer can be visualized as a window that slides smoothly along the data stream, keeping a series of data packets in transit and ensuring the efficient use of network resources. Each TCP host has two buffers, one for receiving data and one for sending it.

The size of the send and receive windows is set during the TCP three-way handshake. This is discussed later in this chapter.

TCP Sockets and Ports

TCP implements connections between hosts using sockets and ports. A socket is a network communications endpoint and can be active or passive. An active socket connects to a remote active socket via an open data connection. When the connection is broken, this destroys the active socket at each endpoint. A passive socket isn't connected, but instead awaits an incoming connection, which will spawn a new active socket.

A socket is associated with a port in a many-to-one relationship. Each port can have a single passive socket that awaits incoming connections and several active sockets that each correspond to an open connection on the port. A socket is an endpoint for network communication (similar to a file handle) and is created by specifying the IP address of its host, the type of service (TCP or UDP), and the port number being used.

All TCP connections are identified uniquely by two sockets—that is, two IP address and TCP port pairs (one for the sending host and one for the receiving host). TCP programs use reserved or *well-known* port numbers. Each server-side program that uses TCP ports listens for messages arriving on a well-known port number. All TCP server port numbers less than 1024 (and some higher numbers) are reserved and registered by the Internet Assigned Numbers Authority (IANA).

Table 8.1 lists well-known TCP server ports that are used by standard TCP-based programs. This list isn't exclusive, but contains the most commonly used ports.

TIP: *A complete list of currently registered well-known TCP ports is available at* **www.isi.edu/in-notes/iana/ assignments/port-numbers**.

Table 8.1 TCP server ports.

TCP Port Number	Description
20	File Transfer Protocol (FTP) server (data channel)
21	FTP server (control channel)
23	Telnet server
25	Simple Mail Transport Protocol (SMTP) server
53	Domain Name System (DNS) zone transfers
80	Hypertext Transport Protocol (HTTP) Web server
110	Post Office Protocol version 3 (POP3) server
139	NetBIOS session service

8. Transmission Control Protocol

229

The TCP Three-Way Handshake

TCP establishes connections by means of a handshake mechanism based on sequence numbers. Each connection requires a send sequence number and a receive sequence number. The initial send sequence number (ISS) is the current sequence number of the initiating TCP host, and the initial receive sequence number (IRS) is the current sequence number of the target TCP host.

For a connection to be established, TCP must synchronize the send and receive sequence numbers. This is done using the synchronize (SYN) control bit and the initial sequence numbers (ISNs). A SYN message (a message that has the SYN bit set) is acknowledged by an ACK message (a message that has the ACK or acknowledgment bit set). The entire procedure is known as the TCP *three-way handshake* and works as follows:

1. Host A sends a SYN message to Host B. This message contains Host A's sequence number (the ISS).

2. Host B sends an ACK message with the ISS incremented by one. This message also has the SYN flag set, and it contains Host B's sequence number (the IRS).

3. Host A acknowledges Host B's SYN message, using an ACK message with the IRS incremented by one and the data field empty. Notice that when Host A starts sending data, it won't increment Host B's sequence number as a result of this message. ACK messages that contain no data don't cause the receiver to increment the sender's sequence number. Otherwise, ACKs would continuously acknowledge other ACKs.

Figure 8.1 illustrates the three-way handshake.

The advantage of the three-way handshake is that Host A can check that the acknowledgment sent by Host B contains the sequence number it expects. It's possible, given a slow and unreliable internetwork (such as the Internet), that Host B could have received part of an old message that was sent by Host A and is out of synchronization. In this case, Host B's ACK would contain an erroneous sequence number, and the connection would not be established. Host A would send a message with the reset (RST) bit set, which would return Host B to the listening state.

The TCP three-way handshake is necessary because the protocol places no restriction on a particular connection's being used more than once. New instances of a connection are referred to as *incarnations*, and sometimes duplicate messages can be sent from previous incarnations, particularly if the connection is opened, closed, and reopened in quick succession or if the connection breaks with

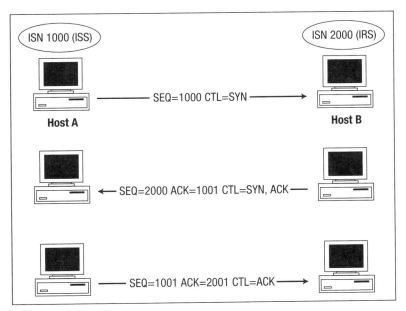

Figure 8.1 The TCP three-way handshake.

loss of memory and is then reestablished. The three-way handshake ensures that valid connections are established, even if a TCP host crashes and loses all knowledge of the sequence numbers it has been using.

The TCP Quiet Time Concept

On power-up, or when recovering from a crash in which sequence numbering information was lost, TCP keeps quiet (i.e., it doesn't assign any sequence numbers) for an interval equal to the Maximum Segment Lifetime (MSL). This ensures that a segment isn't created that carries a sequence number duplicated by an old segment remaining in the network. RFC 793 specifies an MSL of two minutes.

Sometimes a connection can be initiated from both hosts simultaneously. In this case, Host A sends a SYN packet to Host B, but instead of receiving a packet with both ACK and SYN set, it receives Host B's initiating SYN packet. If this happens, Host A resends its original SYN packet, and the three-way handshake proceeds as before.

TCP uses a similar handshake process before closing a connection. This verifies that both hosts have finished sending and receiving data.

Reliable Data Transfer

When a connection is established, TCP can transfer a continuous stream of data in both directions. The data is packaged into segments, and TCP on the sending and receiving hosts decides when to block and when to forward data.

TCP must be able to recover from situations in which data is damaged, lost, duplicated, or delivered out of order. This is achieved by assigning a sequence number when the connection is established, incrementing this by one for each octet of data that's transmitted, and requiring a positive acknowledgment (ACK) containing sequence number information from the receiving TCP host. If the ACK isn't received within a specified time, the data is retransmitted.

At the receiving host, the sequence numbers are used to reassemble segments in the order in which they were sent and to eliminate duplicates. Data corruption is handled by calculating a checksum for each segment transmitted, checking this checksum at the receiver, discarding damaged segments, and requiring retransmission of corrupted data. In this way, TCP ensures that transmission errors don't prevent the correct delivery of data and that network communication can recover from communication system errors.

Closing a TCP Connection

A TCP host closes a connection by sending a TCP packet with the FIN flag set. TCP communications are two-way (duplex), and the host that closes the connection is informing its peer that it has no more data to send. It can still receive data over the connection until its peer host also sends a closing FIN packet. Given that Host A and Host B are engaged in two-way TCP traffic, we have three possible scenarios.

Host A Initiates the Close

In this case, Host A places a FIN segment on the outgoing segment queue. No further data transmissions (SENDs) from Host A will be accepted by TCP, and Host A enters the *FIN-WAIT-1* state, in which incoming data segments (RECEIVEs) are allowed. If necessary, all segments preceding and including the FIN segment will be retransmitted until they're acknowledged. When Host B has acknowledged the Host A's FIN segment and sent a FIN of its own, Host A transmits an ACK segment to acknowledge this FIN. Host B receives this ACK segment, and the connection is closed.

Host A Receives a FIN Segment

In this case, Host A receives an unsolicited FIN segment from Host B. Host A ACKs the FIN (wonderful terminology), which tells Host B that the connection is closing. Host A will then send any remaining data to Host B, followed by a FIN statement. Host B, in turn, ACKs Host A's FIN, and the connection is closed. If Host A's FIN segment isn't acknowledged by Host B after a specified time-out period, the connection is aborted and Host B is informed.

Both Hosts Close Simultaneously

In this case, Hosts A and B exchange FIN segments. When all segments preceding the FINs have been processed and acknowledged, each host can ACK the FIN it received. Upon receipt of these ACKs, both hosts delete the connection.

The TCP Packet Structure

A TCP packet (or *segment*) is encapsulated by an IP header that specifies IP routing information, such as the source and destination addresses of the datagram, as shown in Figure 8.2. This figure illustrates a TCP SYN packet that's used to initiate a TCP three-way handshake. Because there's no data content in this packet structure, it also illustrates TCP header structure.

NOTE: *Figure 8.2 shows a packet from the Network Monitor capture file ftp.cap that's available on the CD-ROM.*

The TCP packet contains a number of fields, as described on page 234.

Source Port

This 16-bit field contains the source port number.

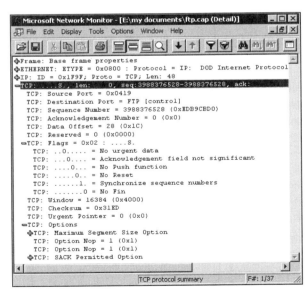

Figure 8.2   A TCP SYN packet.

Destination Port

This 16-bit field contains the destination port number. If, for example, the SYN packet were initiating a connection that's to be used by FTP, the value in this field would be 0x0015 (21 decimal).

Sequence Number

This 32-bit field contains either the ISN (for a SYN package) or the sequence number of the first data octet in the segment.

Acknowledgment Number

This 32-bit field contains the value of the next sequence number that the sender of the segment is expecting to receive. In an initiating SYN package, in which the ACK flag isn't set, the value in this field is zero.

Data Offset

This 4-bit field contains a value equal to the number of 32-bit words in the TCP header and indicates where the TCP data begins. The TCP header is always an integral number of 32-bit words long.

Reserved

This 6-bit field is reserved for future use and is set to zero.

Control Bits

This field contains six single-bit flags. Staring with the most significant bit, these are as follows:

- *URG*—Indicates whether urgent data is being transmitted. If this flag is set, the Urgent Pointer field (see below) points to the end of the urgent data in the segment.

- *ACK*—Indicates whether an acknowledgment is being sent. This flag is normally set, except in initial SYN packets. If the flag isn't set, the value in the Acknowledgment field is zero.

- *PSH*—Indicates that the data in the packet should be pushed through to the receiving host. If this flag is set, TCP will forward and deliver data promptly.

- *RST*—Resets the connection and puts the receiving host back into the listening state. Typically, this flag is set when an old, duplicate SYN message erroneously initiates the handshake process.

- *SYN*—Synchronizes sequence numbers. This flag is used during the TCP three-way handshake.

- *FIN*—Indicates that there is no more data from the sender.

Window

This 16-bit field specifies the number of data octets, beginning with the one indicated in the Acknowledgment field, that the sender of this segment is willing to accept. TCP hosts optimize transmission efficiency by negotiating window sizes.

Checksum

This 16-bit field contains the checksum value, calculated as described earlier in this chapter.

Urgent Pointer

If the packet contains urgent data and the URG flag is set, this 16-bit field holds the current value of the Urgent Pointer. This points to the sequence number of the octet following the urgent data and is held as a positive offset from the sequence number in the segment.

Options

The length of this field varies, depending on which options (if any) are specified, but is always a multiple of 8 bits. An option may begin at any octet boundary. An option may require only a single octet, specifying the *option-kind*. Alternatively, it may require several octets that hold values for *option-kind*, *option-length*, and the data contained in the option.

Standard TCP options include the following:

- *End of option list*—Indicates the end of the list of options, not the end of each option. This option requires a single octet that holds the *option-kind* value of 0. It's used only if the end of the options wouldn't otherwise coincide with the end of the TCP header.

- *No-Operation*—Used between options to align the beginning of a subsequent option to a 32-bit word boundary. This option requires a single octet that holds the *option-kind* value of 1. Not all senders use this option, and receivers must be able to process options even if they don't begin on a word boundary.

- *Maximum Segment Size*—Specifies the maximum receive segment size at the TCP host that sends the segment. This option requires four octets that hold the *option-kind* value of 2, the *option-length* value of 4, and the segment size data (two octets). Maximum Segment Size is specified only in SYN segments that initialize a three-way handshake (such as that shown in Figure 8.1). If the option isn't used, any segment size is permitted.

The SACK-Permitted option (*option-kind* 4, *option length* 2) is discussed later in this chapter.

Padding

TCP header padding is used to ensure that the header ends and data begin at a 32-bit boundary. The padding field has all octets set to zero.

NOTE: *The Options and Padding fields are sometimes combined into the Options and Padding field.*

Microsoft Enhanced TCP

Microsoft has rewritten the TCP/IP stack and introduced significant enhancements to TCP functionality. Not all of the enhancements described below were introduced in Windows 2000, but the Windows 2000 TCP/IP stack implements all of them (not always by default).

Checksum Offloading

Version 5 of the Network Driver Interface Specification (NDIS5) supports task offloading (see Chapter 2), and Windows 2000 TCP takes advantage of this by offloading TCP checksum calculations to the Network Interface Card (NIC), assuming that the NIC driver supports this function. This can result in performance improvements in very high-throughput environments.

Initial Sequence Number Generation

Windows 2000 TCP has been hardened against attacks such as *spoofing* (the sending of bogus messages). As part of this process, the ISN generation algorithm has been modified so that ISNs increase in random increments, using an RC4-based random number generator initialized with a 2,048-bit random key on system startup.

TIP: *RC4 is a Rivest-Sharmir-Adelman (RSA) algorithm. For more information on this and many other matters associated with security, access RSA's home page at* **www.rsasecurity.com**.

TCP Receive Window Size

The TCP receive window size is the amount of receive data (in bytes) that can be buffered at one time on a connection—that is, the amount of data that the transmitting host sends before waiting for an acknowledgment (and possibly a new window size) from the receiving host. Windows 2000 TCP uses larger default window sizes than earlier versions of Windows and matches the receive window size to even increments of the MSS that is negotiated during connection setup. This increases the percentage of full-sized TCP segments used during bulk data transmission.

The default receive window size is calculated rather than hard-coded. This value is calculated as follows:

1. The first connection request sent to a remote host advertises a receive window size of 16KB (16,384).

2. When the connection is established, the receive window size is rounded up to an even increment of the maximum TCP segment size (MSS) that was negotiated during connection setup.

3. If that is not at least four times the MSS, it is adjusted to that value. The maximum receive window size is 64KB, unless the RFC 1323 window scaling option (see below) is in effect.

For Ethernet, the window is normally set to 17,520 bytes (16KB rounded up to twelve 1,460-byte segments.). The receive window size can be set to a specific value by using the *TcpWindowSize* Registry parameter. This parameter can be specified either for all interfaces or on a per-interface basis. The setsockopt Windows Sockets (Winsock) function sets the receive window size on a per-socket basis. The use of *TcpWindowSize* is described in the Immediate Solutions section of this chapter. Winsock functions are described in Chapter 18.

NOTE: *Changing the* GlobalMaxTcpWindowSize *Registry parameter doesn't necessarily alter the receive window size on all interfaces. This parameter is a factor in the calculation of default window size (see Appendix A).*

RFC 1323 Window Scaling

RFC 1323 defines a method of supporting scalable windows by allowing TCP to negotiate a scaling factor for the window size at connection establishment. This allows for an actual receive window of up to 1GB, which improves performance on high-bandwidth, high-delay networks.

The Window Scale option, if enabled, appears in the TCP Options part of the TCP SYN segment as *option-kind* 3, *option-length* 3, *scale factor*. It indicates that the transmitting TCP host is prepared both to send and to receive window scaling and specifies a scale factor that can be applied to its receive window. The scale factor is expressed as a power of two, encoded logarithmically so it can be implemented by binary shift operations. For example, a scale factor of four offers possible window scaling of 2^4, or 16, which is implemented by a 4-byte shift of the value in the Window field. Suppose the Window field contained:

```
0100 0100 0111 0000 (17,520)
```

Then a scale factor of four would offer a possible window size of:

```
0100 0100 0111 0000 0000 (280,320)
```

A TCP host that's prepared to scale windows should send the Window Scale option, even if its own scale factor is 0. A scale factor of 0 gives a window scaling of 2^0, or 1. Both hosts must send Window Scale options in their SYN segments to enable window scaling in either direction. The scale factor does not need to sym-metrical and can be different for each direction of data flow.

The option can be sent in an initial SYN segment. It can also be sent in a SYN, ACK segment, but only if a Window Scale option was received in the initial SYN segment. The Window field in the SYN segment itself is never scaled.

Window scaling is implemented in Windows 2000 if *TcpWindowSize* is set to a value greater than 64KB and the *Tcp1323Opts* Registry parameter is set to either 1 or 3 (see Appendix A). By default, *Tcp1323Opt* is set to 0 and Window Scaling is disabled. The procedure for enabling Windows Scaling is described in the Immediate Solutions section of this chapter.

Delayed Acknowledgments

TCP uses delayed acknowledgments (ACKs) to reduce the number of packets sent. When data is received on a TCP connection, the Microsoft stack returns an ACK only if one of the following conditions is met:

- No ACK was sent for the previous segment received.

- A segment is received, but no further segments arrive on the connection within 200 milliseconds.

As a result, an ACK is sent for every second TCP segment received on a connection, unless the delayed ACK timer (set at 200 milliseconds by default) expires. This timer can be adjusted using the *TcpDelAckTicks* Registry parameter.

Delayed acknowledgments are specified in RFC 1122.

Selective Acknowledgment

Windows 2000 introduces support for SACK. This option is particularly advantageous for connections that use large TCP window sizes. Prior to SACK, a receiver could acknowledge only the latest sequence number of contiguous received data, or the *left edge* of the receive window. If SACK is enabled, the receiver can also acknowledge other blocks of received data individually. SACK uses TCP header options, as shown below. The SACK-Permitted option (*option-kind* 4, *option length* 2) can be sent in a SYN by a TCP host that can receive and process selective acknowledgments when the connection is opened. SACK-Permitted must not be sent on non-SYN segments.

The SACK option (*option-kind* 5, *option length* variable) conveys extended acknowledgment information from the sender to the receiver. Its data fields identify the left edge of the first block of data, the right edge of the first block of data, the left edge of the second block of data, and so on, up to the right edge of the final block of data in the segment.

When SACK is enabled (the Windows 2000 default), the receiver can inform the sender which data blocks have been received and where the holes in the data are if a packet (or series of packets) has been dropped. The sender then retransmits the missing data, but doesn't retransmit data blocks that have been successfully received. SACK is controlled by the *SackOpts* Registry parameter, which, by default, is set to 1 (True).

SACK is specified in RFC 2018.

Timestamps

Windows 2000 introduces support for TCP Timestamps, which (like SACK) are advantageous in connections that use large window sizes. Timestamps are used to measure RTT and adjust retransmission time-outs. The Timestamps option (*option-kind* 8, *option length* 10) contains two 4-byte data fields. The Timestamp Value field (TSval) contains the current value of the transmitting host's timestamp clock. The Timestamp Echo Reply field (TSecr) echoes the timestamp value that was sent by a peer TCP host in the TSval field. TSecr is valid only if the ACK bit is set in the TCP header; otherwise its value must be zero. The TSecr value will (generally) be from the most recent Timestamp option that was received.

A TCP host can send the Timestamps option in an initial SYN segment. It can send the option in other segments only if it received a Timestamp in the initial SYN segment for the connection.

The Timestamps option is disabled by default. Setting the *Tcp1323Opts* Registry parameter (normally 0) to either 2 or 3 enables the option. This procedure is described in the Immediate Solutions section of this chapter.

RFC 1323 specifies the use of timestamps and the Timestamps option.

Path Maximum Transmission Unit Discovery

When a connection is established, the TCP hosts exchange their MSS values, and the smaller of these values is used for the connection. Traditionally, the MTU is the negotiated MSS plus 40 bytes for the IP and TCP headers. However, support for additional TCP options, such as Timestamps, has increased the typical size of these two headers to a combined size of 52 bytes or more, which in turn increases the MTU size.

When TCP segments are sent to a nonlocal network, the Don't Fragment (DF) flag bit is set in the IP header. Any router or media along the path can have an

MTU that differs from that of the two hosts. If a media segment or router along the path has an MTU that is too small for the IP datagram being routed, the router attempts to fragment the datagram, but finds that the DF flag is set. At this point, the router should send an ICMP Destination Unreachable message to inform the transmitting host that the datagram can't be forwarded further without fragmentation.

Most routers also specify the MTU that's allowed for the next hop by putting its value in the low-order 16 bits of the ICMP "unused" header field (refer to RFC 1191 for details). Upon receiving this ICMP error message, the transmitting TCP host adjusts its MSS (and hence its MTU) so that any further packets sent on the connection can traverse the path without fragmentation. The minimum MTU permitted is 68 bytes.

Some noncompliant (or *black hole*) routers silently drop IP datagrams that can't be fragmented or don't report their next-hop MTU correctly. In this case, the PMTU detection algorithm in Windows 2000 may be reconfigured to work around the problem. Two Registry parameters are available:

- *EnablePMTUBHDetect*—Setting this parameter to 1 (True) instructs the PMTU discovery algorithm to attempt to detect black hole routers. Black hole router detection is disabled by default.

- *EnablePMTUDiscovery*—Setting this parameter to 0 (False) disables the PMTU discovery mechanism. When PMTU discovery is disabled, an MSS of 536 bytes is used for all remote destination addresses. PMTU discovery is enabled by default.

The PMTU between two hosts can be discovered manually using the **ping** command with the **-f** (don't fragment) switch. This technique can also detect black hole routers and is described in the Immediate Solutions section of this chapter. PMTU discovery is described in RFC 1191.

Dead Gateway Detection

Dead gateway detection enables a TCP host to detect the failure of the default gateway and to alter the IP routing table to use another default gateway. Microsoft 2000 stack uses the triggered reselection method (specified in RFC 816) with slight modifications based on customer feedback.

When a TCP connection attempts to send a TCP packet to the destination via the default gateway a number of times without receiving a response, the algorithm changes the Route Cache Entry (RCE) for that remote IP address to use the next default gateway in the list. The number of transmission attempts before this happens is equal to half the value specified in the Registry *TcpMaxData-Retransmissions* parameter. When 25 percent of the TCP connections have moved to the next default gateway, the algorithm changes the computer's default gateway to the one that the connections are now using.

If the second default gateway is also experiencing problems, the algorithm tries the next one on the list. When the search reaches the last default gateway, it returns to the beginning of the list. If a gateway transmits packages successfully, it will remain the default gateway until the computer is reinitialized.

Retransmission

TCP starts a retransmission timer when each outbound segment is passed down to IP. If an acknowledgment isn't received before the timer expires, the segment is retransmitted. For new connection requests, the retransmission timer is set to 3 seconds. This default can be altered on a per-adapter basis by changing the *TcpInitialRTT* Registry parameter.

If the request (SYN) segment isn't acknowledged, it's resent up to two times by default. The *TcpMaxConnectRetransmissions* Registry parameter can be used to alter this. For existing connections, the number of retransmissions is controlled by the *TcpMaxDataRetransmissions* Registry parameter, which is set to five by default. The retransmission time-out is adjusted to match the connection characteristics, using Smoothed Round Trip Time (SRTT) calculations (see RFC 793 for details). The timer for a segment is doubled after each retransmission. This algorithm enables TCP to tune to the normal delay of a connection.

Sometimes TCP retransmits data before the retransmission timer times out. The most common occurrence is because of the *Fast Retransmit* feature. When a receiver that supports Fast Retransmit receives data that has a sequence number beyond the one it expects, it assumes that data was dropped. In this event, the receiver sends an ACK with the ACK number set to the sequence number that it was expecting. It continues to do this for each additional TCP segment that contains data subsequent to the missing data in the incoming stream.

When the sender receives a stream of ACKs acknowledging the same sequence number, and that sequence number is earlier than the current sequence number being sent, it infers that one or more segments have been dropped. If the Fast Retransmit algorithm is supported, the transmitting TCP host immediately resends the segment that the receiver is expecting, without waiting for the retransmission timer to expire. This improves performance in an unreliable network environment.

By default, Windows 2000 resends a segment if it receives three ACKs for the same sequence number and that sequence number lags the current one. The number of ACKs is set in the *TcpMaxDupAcks* Registry parameter.

Keep-Alives

A TCP keep-alive packet is an ACK that has the sequence number set to one less than the current connection sequence number. A TCP host that receives one of these ACKs responds with an ACK for the current sequence number. Keep-alives are used to verify that the computer at the remote end of a connection is still online. The period between keep-alives is defined by the *KeepAliveTime* Registry parameter, which is 7,200,000 milliseconds, or two hours, by default.

If there's no response, the keep-alive packet is repeated once every second (by default). This time period is controlled by the *KeepAliveInterval* Registry parameter. NetBIOS over TCP/IP (NetBT) connections send NetBIOS keep-alives more frequently, and no TCP keep-alives are normally sent on a NetBIOS connection. TCP keep-alives are disabled by default, but Winsock applications can use the setsockopt function to enable them.

The Slow Start Algorithm and Congestion Avoidance

When a connection is established, TCP assesses the bandwidth of the connection. To avoid overflowing the receiving host or any other devices or links in the path, the send window is initially set to two TCP segments. If that's acknowledged, the window is incremented to three segments. If these are acknowledged, the window is incremented to four segments, and so on until the amount of per-burst data being sent reaches the size of the remote host's receive window.

At this point, the slow start algorithm is no longer used, and flow control is governed by the receive window. However, congestion can occur on a connection at any time during transmission. If regular retransmissions start to occur, a congestion-avoidance algorithm reduces the send window size temporarily, then lets it grow it back toward the receive window size. Slow start and congestion avoidance are defined in RFC 1122.

Silly Window Syndrome Avoidance

Silly Window Syndrome (SWS) is caused by a receiver's advancing the right window edge whenever it has any new buffer space available to receive data, and by the sender's using any incremental window (no matter how small) to send more data. This can result in tiny data segments being sent consistently, even though both sender and receiver have a large total buffer space for the connection.

Windows 2000 implements SWS avoidance by not sending additional data until the receiving TCP host advertises a window size that's sufficient to send a full TCP segment. It also implements SWS avoidance on the receive end of a connection by opening the receive window in increments of at least one TCP segment.

SWS is described in RFC 1122.

Nagle Algorithm

Like SWS avoidance, the purpose of the Nagle algorithm is to reduce the number of very small segments sent, especially on slow remote links. This algorithm allows only one small segment to be sent at a time without acknowledgment. If more small segments are generated before the ACK for the first one is received, these segments are coalesced into one larger segment. Full-sized segments are always transmitted immediately, assuming there's a sufficient receive window available. The Nagle algorithm is particularly effective in reducing the number of packets sent by interactive applications, such as Telnet, over slow links.

Winsock applications can disable the Nagle algorithm for their connections by setting the TCP_NODELAY socket option (see Chapter 18). However, this practice increases network utilization and should be avoided unless absolutely necessary. The Nagle algorithm isn't applied to loopback TCP connections for performance reasons, and it's disabled for NetBIOS over TCP connections and direct-hosted redirector/server connections. This can improve performance for applications that issue numerous small file manipulation commands (for example, applications that use file locking/unlocking frequently). The Nagle algorithm is described in RFC 896.

TIME-WAIT Delay

When a TCP connection is closed, the socket-pair is placed into the TIME-WAIT state. This implements a time delay before a new connection can use the same protocol, source IP address, destination IP address, source port, and destination port. The purpose of this delay is to ensure that any misrouted or delayed segments are not delivered unexpectedly on the new connection. RFC 793 specifies the delay as two MSLs, or four minutes, which is the default setting for Windows 2000. Sometimes, however, network applications that perform many outbound connections in a short time use up all available ports. In this case, it may be desirable to reduce the TIME-WAIT delay so that ports can be recycled more quickly.

Windows 2000 enables adjustments to be made to the TIME-WAIT delay using the *TcpTimedWaitDelay* Registry parameter. If required, the delay can be set as low as 30 seconds. Also, the number of user-accessible ports that can source outbound connections can be configured using the *MaxUserPort* Registry parameter. By default, a port number that has a value from 1024 through 5000 is specified when an application requests a socket to use for an outbound call. The *MaxUserPort* parameter can set the value of the uppermost port. Setting this value to (say) 9000 would more than double the number of available ports. See RFC 793 for details.

Additional Registry parameters that govern connection behavior include *MaxFreeTcbs*, which controls the available number of cached (or preallocated) Transport Control Blocks (TCBs). A TCB is a data structure that's maintained for each TCP connection. The parameter *MaxHashTableSize* controls how quickly the system finds a TCP control block. The value of *MaxHashTableSize* (512 by default) should be increased if the value of *MaxFreeTcbs* is increased from its default of 2,000 (Server) or 1,000 (Professional/Workstation).

NOTE: *If the value of* MaxHashTableSize *isn't a power of two, the system configures the hash table to the next power-of-two value. For example, a setting of 1,000 is rounded up to 1,024.*

Multihomed Computers

TCP connections to and from a multihomed host are made in several ways, depending on whether the host is local or remote and the name resolution service that's used.

Connections to a Multihomed Host

When TCP connections are made to a multihomed host, both the Domain Name Resolver (DNR) and the Windows Internet Name Service (WINS) client attempt to determine whether any of the destination IP addresses are on the same subnet as any of the interfaces in the local computer. Local addresses are placed at the top of the list so that the application can try them first. The *PrioritizeRecordData* TCP/IP Registry parameter can be used to prevent the DNR component from sorting local subnet addresses to the top of the list.

How remote IP addresses are handled depends on the type of name space that's being used. In the WINS name space, the WINS client is responsible for load balancing between the addresses provided. The WINS server always returns the list of addresses in the same order, and the WINS client picks one of them randomly for each connection.

In the Domain Name System (DNS) name space, the DNS server is typically configured to provide the addresses in a round-robin fashion. The DNR doesn't attempt to randomize the addresses further. In some situations, it is desirable to connect to a specific interface on a multihomed computer, and the best way to accomplish this is to provide the interface with its own DNS entry.

Connections from a Multihomed Host

If the connection from a multihomed host is a Winsock connection using the DNS name space, TCP attempts to connect from the best source IP address available once the target IP address for the connection is known. The route table is used to determine this address. If there's an interface on the local computer that is on the same subnet as the target IP address, its IP address is used as the source in the connection request. If there is no best source IP address, the system chooses one at random.

Little routing information is available at the application level for NetBIOS-based connections that use the Redirector. In this case, the Redirector places calls on all of the transports that are bound to it. If, for example, there are two interfaces on the computer and one protocol is installed, then two transports are available to the Redirector and calls are placed on both. NetBT submits connection requests to the stack, using an IP address from each interface.

If both calls succeed, the Redirector cancels one of them. The choice of which one to cancel depends on the Redirector *ObeyBindingOrder* Registry parameter. If this is set to 0 (the default value), the primary transport that's determined by binding order is preferred. In this case, the Redirector waits for the primary transport to time out before accepting the connection on the secondary transport. If *ObeyBindingOrder* is set to 1, the binding order is ignored. In this case, the Redirector accepts the first connection that succeeds and cancels the other(s).

TIP: *More information on Redirector Registry parameters is available in the Windows 2000 Resource Kit.*

Optimizing Link Throughput

Windows 2000 TCP is designed to provide optimum performance over most link conditions. Actual link throughput depends on a number of variables. The most important factors are:

- Link speed
- Propagation delay
- Window size
- Link reliability
- Network and intermediate device congestion

If you consider throughput unsatisfactory, a number of adjustments can be made. Tuning link performance is a complex operation and should be attempted only by experienced networking professionals. Some key considerations are as follows:

- A pipe is the connection between two TCP sockets. The capacity (or *bandwidth-delay product*) of a pipe is equal to bandwidth multiplied by the RTT. If the link is reliable, the window size should be greater than or equal to the capacity of the pipe so the sending stack can fill it. The Window field in a TCP segment is 16 bits long, and 65,535 bytes is, therefore, the largest window size that can be specified by this field. Window scaling, described earlier in this chapter, can negotiate larger windows.

- Throughput can never exceed window size divided by RTT.

- If the link is unreliable or badly congested and packets are being dropped, using a larger window size may not, by itself, improve throughput. In fact, increasing window size can sometimes degrade performance on a lossy network, because it results in the resending of larger packets. SACK can improve performance in environments that are experiencing packet loss, and Timestamps can be used to improve RTT estimation.

- Propagation delay is dependent on latencies in transmission equipment and, ultimately, on the speed of light. Transmission delay depends on the speed of the media. For a specified path, propagation delay is fixed, but transmission delay depends on the packet size. At low speeds, transmission delay is the limiting factor. At high speeds, the limiting factor may be the propagation delay.

To summarize, Windows 2000 TCP adapts to most network conditions and normally provides the optimum throughput and reliability on a per-connection basis. Attempts at manual tuning are often counterproductive unless an experienced network professional first performs a careful study of data flow.

TCP/IP Utilities and Services

Windows 2000 provides two types of TCP/IP-based utilities:

- *Connectivity utilities*—Interact with and use resources on a variety of Microsoft and non-Microsoft hosts (such as Unix systems).

- *Diagnostic utilities*—Detect and resolve networking problems.

Windows 2000 services provide printing and Web publishing services to TCP/IP-based clients. In addition, Windows 2000 provides a set of "Simple" TCP/IP protocol services, such as Echo and Quote of the Day. Tables 8.2 through 8.5 summarize the TCP/IP utilities and services.

> **WARNING!**   *Microsoft recommends that you do not install Simple TCP/IP protocol services unless you specifically need to support communication with other systems that use these services.*

Table 8.2   Connectivity utilities.

Utility	Description
Ftp	Transfers any size of files between Windows 2000 and a computer running FTP server software.
Lpr	Sends print jobs to remote Unix printers managed by Line Printer Daemon (LPD) print server software.
Rcp	Copies files between Windows 2000 and computers running Remote Copy Protocol (RCP) server software.
Rexec	Executes processes on remote computers.
Rsh	Runs commands on a computer running Remote Shell (RSH) server software.
Telnet	Uses terminal-based login to access remote network devices that are running Telnet server software.
Tftp	Transfers small files between Windows 2000 and computers running Trivial File Transfer Protocol (TFTP) server software.

Table 8.3   Diagnostic utilities.

Utility	Description
Arp	Displays and modifies the Address Resolution Protocol (ARP) cache. This cache is a local table used by Windows 2000 to resolve IP addresses to Media Access Control (MAC) addresses used on the local network.
Hostname	Returns the host name of the local computer.
Ipconfig	Displays the current TCP/IP configuration and can be used to release and renew TCP/IP configurations assigned by a Dynamic Host Configuration Protocol (DHCP) server.
Lpq	Obtains print queue status information from computers running Line Printer Daemon (LPD) print server software.
Nbtstat	Displays the local NetBIOS name table, a table of NetBIOS names registered by local applications, and the NetBIOS name cache, which is a local cache listing of NetBIOS computer names that have been resolved to IP addresses.
Netstat	Displays TCP/IP protocol session information.
Nslookup	Checks records, domain host aliases, domain host services, and operating system information by querying DNS servers.
Ping	Verifies configurations and tests IP connectivity.
Route	Displays or modifies the local routing table.
Tracert	Traces the route a packet takes to a destination.
PathPing	Traces the route a packet takes to a destination and displays information on packet losses for each router in the path. Pathping can also be used to troubleshoot Quality of Service (QoS) connectivity.

8. Transmission Control Protocol

Table 8.4   Windows 2000 services.

Service	Description
TCP/IP Printing Service	Enables Unix computers to use the Line Printer Remote (Lpr) utility to send print jobs to Windows 2000 computers.
Internet Information Services	Enables TCP/IP-based Web publishing services. These services, running on an IIS server, implement an Enterprise-ready Web server for use with an unlimited number of simultaneous connections.
Peer Web Services	Provided with Windows 2000 Professional to implement Web-publishing services similar to those offered by IIS, but for 10 simultaneous connections or fewer.

Table 8.5   TCP/IP Simple protocol services.

Protocol	Description	RFC
Character Generator (CHARGEN)	Sends the set of 95 printable ASCII characters. CHARGEN is used as a tool for testing or troubleshooting line printers.	864
Daytime	Returns messages containing the day of the week, month, day, year, current time (in *hh:mm:ss* format), and time-zone information. Daytime is used for debugging or monitoring variations in system clock time on different hosts or to reset system time.	867
Discard	Discards all messages received on a port without response or acknowledgment. Discard is used to implement a null port for receiving and routing TCP/IP test messages during network setup and configuration. Some programs can use it as a message discard function.	863
Echo	Echoes data from any messages it receives on this server port. Echo is used as a network debugging and monitoring tool.	862
Quote of the Day (QUOTE)	Returns a quotation as one or more lines of text in a message. Quotations are taken at random from *%systemroot%*\System32\Drivers\Etc\Quotes.	865

Immediate Solutions

Capturing TCP Traffic

Most Windows 2000 network communications generate TCP traffic. In this case, FTP and HTTP site access traffic between a Windows 2000 client and an IIS is captured using Network Monitor on the IIS. In order to reduce the capture size, a capture filter is set so that only traffic to and from the selected client computer is captured. The procedure assumes that both the HTTP and FTP sites on the IIS are activated. The captures thus obtained should be similar to capture files ftp.cap and http.cap on the CD-ROM.

To capture TCP traffic, proceed as follows:

1. Log on to the IIS server as an administrator.

2. Log on to another computer in the domain using any domain account that has permission to access the FTP and HTTP sites on the IIS server.

3. On the IIS server, access Start|Programs|Administrative Tools and select Network Monitor.

4. On the Network Monitor Capture pull-down menu, select Filter.

5. In the Capture Filter dialog box, click Edit Addresses.

6. In the Address Database dialog box, click Add.

7. The Address Information dialog box appears. Select IP in the Type drop-down box and enter the name and IP address of the other computer that you logged on to in your domain. Click OK.

8. Close the Address Database dialog box.

9. In the Address Expression dialog box, select the IIS server as Station 1 and the other computer as Station 2. In the Direction box, select bidirectional (<··>). Click OK.

10. Click OK to close the Capture Filter dialog box.

11. On the Network Monitor Capture pull-down menu, select Start.

12. On the other (non-IIS) computer, open a browser and browse to **ftp://*server-name***, where *server-name* is the name of the IIS server.

13. On the Network Monitor Capture pull-down menu (on the IIS server), select Stop and View. View the captured frames and save the capture (for example, as ftp.cap).

14. On the Network Monitor Capture pull-down menu, select Start.

15. On the other (non-IIS) computer, browse to **http://server-name**, where *server-name* is the name of the IIS server.

16. Close the browser.

17. On the Network Monitor Capture pull-down menu (on the IIS server), select Stop and View. View the captured frames, and save the capture (for example, as http.cap).

18. Exit from Network Monitor.

Related solution:	*Found on page:*
Implementing a Capture Filter	101

Configuring Windows 2000 TCP

The procedures in this section describe how to configure Windows 2000 TCP. They assume that you know what defaults you want to change and have worked out the probable consequences of such changes. Windows 2000 TCP provides optimum configuration in most environments, and changes should be made with care. Also, these procedures involve changing (*hacking*) the Registry. This should be done very carefully. Careless Registry hacks can seriously damage your operating system. Always save a subkey (using the Save Key command in the Registry pull-down menu) before changing it.

The Registry Editor program, regedt32.exe, is found in the *%Systemroot%*\System32 folder. For convenience, you may want to create a shortcut on your desktop or in the Administrative Tools menu. If you do so, be especially careful not to allow other users to have access to your machine while your account is logged on. The Registry Editor is not a tool to be left in the hands of an inexperienced user.

Setting TCP Receive Window Size

This procedure sets the TCP receive window size for a specific interface. The procedure to set the window size for all interfaces is similar, except that it's implemented in the /Tcpip/Parameters subkey rather than the /Tcpip/Parameters/Interfaces/*interface* subkey.

To set a receive window size, proceed as follows:

1. Start the Registry Editor.

2. Expand:

```
HKEY_LOCAL_MACHINE
    \SYSTEM
            \CurrentControlSet
                        \Services
                                \Tcpip
                                        \Parameters
                                                \Interfaces
```

3. Click the interface for which you want to specify a receive window size.

4. Select Add Value in the Edit pull-down menu.

5. Specify *TcpWindowSize* as a REG_DWORD data type, as shown in Figure 8.3.

6. Click OK. Enter a value in either hex or decimal in the DWORD Editor dialog box. The maximum permitted value is 3FFFFFFF (hex) or 1,073,741,823 (decimal).

7. Click OK. Close the Registry Editor.

Enabling the Window Scale Option and Timestamps

The Window Scale option and the use of Timestamps are enabled for all interfaces rather than on a per-interface basis. However, window scaling won't take effect on any interface where the receive window size is FFFF (hex) or less. Refer to the previous procedure for setting receive window size.

To enable the Window Scale option and the use of Timestamps, proceed as follows:

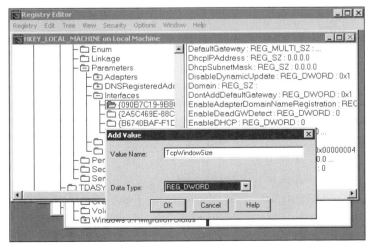

Figure 8.3   Specifying the TcpWindowSize data type.

1. Start the Registry Editor.

2. Expand:

```
HKEY_LOCAL_MACHINE
    \SYSTEM
            \CurrentControlSet
                    \Services
                            \Tcpip
```

3. Click Parameters.

4. Select Add Value in the Edit pull-down menu.

5. Specify *Tcp1323Opts* as a REG_DWORD data type.

6. Click OK. Enter a value from 1 to 3, depending on what you want to enable:

   • A value of 1 enables Window Scale only.

   • A value of 2 enables Timestamps only.

   • A value of 3 enables both Window Scale and Timestamps.

7. Click OK. Close the Registry Editor.

NOTE: *In this and the previous procedure, the full paths to the Tcpip/Parameters and Tcpip/Parameters/ Interfaces/interface Registry subkeys were specified. The rest of the procedures in this section use one or the other of these subkeys, and it seems pointless to specify the full path for each. In subsequent procedures, therefore, the full paths are abbreviated to Tcpip/Parameters and Tcpip/Parameters/Interfaces.*

Adjusting the Delayed Acknowledgment Timer

The delayed ACK timer is set at 2 (200 milliseconds) by default. To change this time-out value for an interface, proceed as follows:

1. Start the Registry Editor and expand the Tcpip/Parameters/Interfaces subkey.

2. Click the interface on which you want to change the delayed ACK timer.

3. Select Add Value in the Edit pull-down menu.

4. Specify *TcpDelAckTicks* as a REG_DWORD data type.

5. Click OK. Enter a value from 0 to 6. This specifies the number of 100 millisecond intervals before the timer times out. A value of 0 disables delayed acknowledgments, which causes the computer to acknowledge every packet it receives immediately.

6. Click OK and close the Registry Editor.

Disabling Selective Acknowledgment

If your network never uses large window sizes, you may want to disable SACK. This is unusual, and not normally advisable. However, the procedure to disable SACK is as follows:

1. Start the Registry Editor and click the Tcpip/Parameters subkey.
2. Select Add Value in the Edit pull-down menu.
3. Specify *SackOpts* as a REG_DWORD data type.
4. Click OK. Enter the value 0 to disable SACK.
5. Click OK and close the Registry Editor.

Enabling Black Hole Router Discovery

A black hole router discards a packet that has too large a window size and has the DF flag set, but doesn't send an ICMP Destination Unreachable message. The PMTU discovery mechanism can be set to detect such routers as follows:

1. Start the Registry Editor and click the Tcpip/Parameters subkey.
2. Select Add Value in the Edit pull-down menu.
3. Specify *EnablePMTUBHDetect* as a REG_DWORD data type.
4. Click OK. Enter the value 1 to enable black hole router discovery.
5. Click OK and close the Registry Editor.

Disabling Path Maximum Transmission Unit Discovery

It's possible to disable PMTU discovery completely. This is unusual, and not normally recommended, but you may want to do it if you never send large segments, or send segments over familiar networks where MTU sizes are known. When PMTU discovery is disabled, an MSS of 536 bytes is used for all remote destination addresses. To disable PMTU discovery, proceed as follows:

1. Start the Registry Editor and click on the Tcpip/Parameters subkey.
2. Select Add Value in the Edit pull-down menu.
3. Specify *EnablePMTUDiscovery* as a REG_DWORD data type.
4. Click OK. Enter the value 0 (zero) to disable PMTU discovery.
5. Click OK and close the Registry Editor.

Configuring TCP Retransmission Behavior

As described in the In Depth section of this chapter, TCP retransmission behavior can be configured and tuned using four Registry parameters:

8. Transmission
Control Protocol

- *TcpInitialRTT*
- *TcpMaxConnectRetransmissions*
- *TcpMaxDataRetransmissions*
- *TcpMaxDupAcks*

The *TcpMaxDataRetransmissions* parameter also configures dead gateway detection. All of these parameters have a REG_DWORD data type and need to be added to the Registry using the Add Value command in the Edit pull-down menu. *TCPInitialRTT* is specified on a per-interface basis, and the other three parameters are specified in the Tcpip/Parameters subkey. Given the information in Table 8.6, you can add and configure the parameters using the techniques described in the previous procedures.

> **WARNING!**   *The TcpInitialRTT parameter is applied exponentially, and a very small change can adversely affect performance (see Appendix A). A setting greater than 3 is not recommended.*

Configuring TCP Keep-Alives and the TIME-WAIT Delay

As described in the In Depth section of this chapter, TCP keep-alives can be configured and tuned using two Registry parameters:

- *KeepAliveTime*
- *KeepAliveInterval*

Both of these parameters have a REG_DWORD data type and specify values in milliseconds.

The TIME-WAIT delay can be configured using four Registry parameters:

- *TcpTimedWaitDelay*
- *MaxUserPort*
- *MaxFreeTcbs*
- *MaxHashTableSize*

All of these parameters have a REG_DWORD data type. **TcpTimedWaitDelay** specifies a value in seconds, and the other three parameters specify numbers.

Table 8.6   The TCP Retransmission parameters.

Parameter	Range	Default
TcpInitialRTT	0 to FFFF	3
TcpMaxConnectRetransmissions	0 to 255 (decimal)	3
TcpMaxDataRetransmissions	0 to FFFFFFFF	5
TcpMaxDupAcks	1 to 3	2

All of the keep-alive and TIME-WAIT parameters are added to the Tcpip/Parameters Registry subkey, by using the Add Value command in the Edit pull-down menu. Given the information in Table 8.7, you can add and configure the parameters using the techniques described in the previous procedures.

NOTE: *MaxHashTableSize should be a power of two. Refer to Appendix A.*

Table 8.7   The TCP keep-alives and TIME-WAIT parameters.

Parameter	Range	Default
KeepAliveTime	0 to FFFFFFFF	7,200,000 (decimal)
KeepAliveInterval	0 to FFFFFFFF	1,000 (decimal)
TcpTimedWaitDelay	30 to 300 (decimal)	240 (decimal)
MaxUserPort	5,000 to 65,534 (decimal)	5,000 (decimal)
MaxFreeTcbs	0 to FFFFFFFF	Server—2,000 (decimal), Professional—1,000 (decimal)
MaxHashTableSize	64 to 65,536 (decimal)	512 (decimal)

Discovering the PMTU Manually

The PMTU can be discovered using the **ping** command. The procedure is straightforward, if somewhat tedious. It supposes that you can ping a host on a remote network and want to discover the PMTU to that network.

The syntax of the **ping** command that you can use is:

```
ping -f -n <number of pings> -l <size> <destination ip address>
```

The **-f** switch sets the DF flag. The *size* parameter specifies the size of the data buffer that **ping** sends, not including headers. The ICMP header is 8 bytes, and the IP header is normally 20 bytes. The technique is to ping specifying the maximum data size that you know can be transmitted to the remote host, determined from Network Monitor captures, and to increase this value in subsequent pings until the command fails with the appropriate message.

TIP: *The MSS, negotiated during connection setup, gives a good indication of the initial value to be used in the* size *parameter.*

Suppose, for example, that you know you can ping remote host 142.24.234.66 with 1,600 bytes of data.

```
E:\>ping -f -n 1 -l 1600 142.24.234.66
Pinging 142.24.234.66 with 1600 bytes of data:
Reply from 142.24.234.66: bytes=1600 time<10ms TTL=128
Ping statistics for 142.24.234.66:
        Packets: Sent = 1, Received = 1, Lost = 0 (0% loss),
Approximate round trip times in milli-seconds:
        Minimum = 0ms, Maximum = 0ms, Average = 0ms
```

You continue to ping the same host, increasing the value of the *size* parameter until the ping fails.

```
E:\>ping -f -n 1 -l 1640 142.24.234.66
Pinging 142.24.234.66 with 1640 bytes of data:
Packet needs to be fragmented but DF set.
Ping statistics for 142.24.234.66:
        Packets: Sent = 1, Received = 0, Lost = 1 (100% loss),
Approximate round trip times in milli-seconds:
        Minimum = 0ms, Maximum = 0ms, Average = 0ms
```

In this example, the MTU to the specified host (or the PMTU for the path to that host) is 1,640 plus 28, or 1,668 bytes. If a black hole router had been in the path, the **ping** would have timed out, but no error message would have been returned.

Installing Simple TCP/IP Services

If you need to communicate with computers that have the Simple TCP/IP protocol services installed or if you have other reasons for installing them, the procedure to do so is as follows:

1. Log on as an administrator.

2. In Start|Settings|Control Panel, open Add/Remove Programs.

3. In the Add/Remove Programs dialog box, select Add/Remove Windows Components.

4. In the Windows Components Wizard, select Networking Services, then click Details.

5. Select Simple TCP/IP Services, then click OK.

6. Click Next.

7. If prompted, insert your installation CD-ROM or type the path where the Windows 2000 distribution files are located, then click OK.

8. Click Finish.

Chapter 9

User Datagram Protocol and Quality of Service

In Depth

User Datagram Protocol (UDP) is a required TCP/IP standard defined in RFC 768. It's an unreliable protocol that offers a connectionless, best-effort service and doesn't guarantee delivery or verify sequencing for any datagrams. It can be used for one-to-one unicast communications or for one-to-many communications that use broadcast or multicast IP datagrams. Microsoft networking uses UDP for logon, browsing, and name resolution. The protocol is used for the fast delivery of small messages to one or many recipients and in communications where speed of delivery is more important than reliability (such as real-time multimedia traffic).

Because delivery of UDP datagrams isn't guaranteed, applications that use UDP must supply their own mechanisms for reliability. If a network is congested, UDP packets may be dropped, and there is no mechanism for recovery. On a very busy network that has a high level of guaranteed Transmission Control Protocol (TCP) traffic, it's therefore possible that UDP packets are "crowded out" and that traffic loss becomes unacceptable. This is a particular problem for applications that rely on real-time network traffic, where the delays associated with TCP are unacceptable, but only a certain level of data loss can be tolerated. A mechanism must therefore be employed that reserves bandwidth and allows real-time traffic to coexist with traditional traffic on the same network. Windows 2000 Quality of Service (QoS) provides such a mechanism through the use of QoS Admission Control.

User Datagram Protocol

Like TCP, UDP relies on Internet Protocol (IP) for routing and is identified by a value of 17 (decimal) in the IP header's Protocol field (see RFC 1700). UDP messages are encapsulated and sent within IP datagrams. The protocol is transaction-based and connectionless and doesn't establish a session between hosts or initiate any handshake procedures. UDP provides the following additional functionality to IP:

- *Port numbers*—UDP provides 16-bit port numbers to let multiple processes use UDP services on the same host. A UDP address is the combination of an IP address and the 16-bit port number.

- *Checksums*—UDP uses checksums to ensure data integrity. The checksum algorithm is the same as that used by TCP (see Chapter 8). If the checksum is incorrect, the packet is discarded and no further action is taken.

> **NOTE:** Unlike TCP, use of the UDP checksum is optional. Some applications that normally run only on Local Area Networks (LANs) disable checksumming by sending a zero value in the Checksum field. This is not, however, normally considered good practice. No information is, in general, preferable to wrong information.

UDP is used where TCP is too complex or too slow. It doesn't segment a message, reassemble it at the other end, and check that the segments are in the correct order. It is, therefore, unsuitable for the reliable delivery of long messages. Network applications that exchange small data units (and, therefore, have very little message reassembling to do) use UDP rather than TCP. For example, Trivial File Transfer Protocol (TFTP) uses UDP for email applications.

UDP Ports

UDP ports provide a location for sending and receiving UDP messages. A UDP port functions as a single message queue that receives all datagrams intended for the program specified by the port number. UDP-based programs can, therefore, receive more than one message at a time. Server-side programs that use UDP listen for messages arriving on their well-known port number. All UDP server port numbers less than 1024 (and some higher numbers) are reserved and registered by the Internet Assigned Numbers Authority (IANA).

Table 9.1 lists the more commonly used well-known UDP server port numbers. A list of all reserved UDP port numbers can be obtained at **www.isi.edu/in-notes/iana/assignments/port-numbers**.

Name Resolution

NetBIOS name resolution is accomplished over UDP port 137, by means of either a unicast to a NetBIOS name server or subnet broadcasts. DNS-host-name to IP-address-resolution queries use UDP port 53. Both of these services use their own retransmission schemes if they receive no answer to queries. Because broadcast UDP datagrams aren't normally forwarded over IP routers, NetBIOS name resolution in a routed environment requires either a name server or static database files.

Table 9.1   UDP port numbers.

Port Number	Description
53	Domain Name System (DNS) name queries
69	TFTP
137	NetBIOS name service
138	NetBIOS datagram service
161	Simple Network Management Protocol (SNMP)
520	Routing Internet Protocol (RIP)

9. User Datagram Protocol and Quality of Service

Mailslots

A *mailslot* is a second-class, unreliable mechanism for sending a message from one computer to another over UDP, where both computers are identified by their NetBIOS names. Mailslot messages can be broadcast on a subnet or directed to the remote host. To direct a mailslot message, you must have some method of NetBIOS name resolution, such as the Windows Internet Name Service (WINS), available.

UDP Interlayer Communication

Like TCP, UDP exists at the transport layer of the TCP/IP four-layer model. If it receives any IP options (such as Source Route, Record Route, and Timestamp) from IP at the Internet layer, it passes them transparently to the application layer. UDP doesn't normally make any assumptions about the format or content of options it passes to or from applications. It will also pass all Internet Control Message Protocol (ICMP) error messages that it receives from the Internet layer to the application layer.

When a UDP datagram is received, its specific-destination address is passed up to the application layer. An application program either specifies the IP source address to be used for sending a UDP datagram or leaves it unspecified, in which case the networking software chooses an appropriate source address. A UDP datagram received with an invalid IP source address is discarded. When a host sends a UDP datagram, the source address is the source address of the host (or one of the host addresses if the host is multihomed).

UDP Packet Structure

Figure 9.1, obtained from the capture file login.cap on the CD-ROM, illustrates a UDP datagram. The packet structure is as follows:

- *Source port*—An optional 16-bit field that identifies the port of the sending process and is, by default, the port to which a reply should be addressed. If this field isn't used, a value of zero is inserted.

- *Destination port*—A 16-bit field that identifies the UDP port of the destination host and provides an endpoint for communications.

- *Length*—A 16-bit field that indicates the length of the datagram, including the header and subsequent data, in octets. The minimum value that this field can hold (assuming that there's no data) is 8.

- *Checksum*—A 16-bit field that contains the checksum and is used to check data integrity. A checksum value of zero means that the application on the sending host didn't generate a checksum.

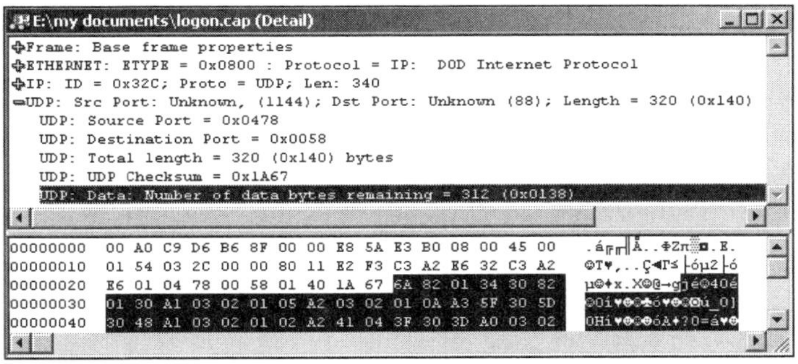

Figure 9.1   A UDP datagram.

Real-Time Multimedia Protocols

Multimedia traffic, which comprises a significant portion of potential unicast and (particularly) multicast traffic, possesses characteristics that differ from conventional network traffic and, therefore, has different requirements. If, for example, a receiver waits for a TCP retransmission, there's a noticeable and unacceptable gap in audio, video, or other delay-sensitive data reception. In addition, the slow-start TCP congestion-control mechanism (see Chapter 8) can interfere with the audio and video reception rate. Because there's no fixed path for datagrams to flow across the Internet, there's no mechanism in traditional TCP transmission for ensuring that the bandwidth needed for multimedia is available, and TCP doesn't provide timing information, a critical requirement for multimedia support.

Because of the unsuitability of TCP transmission, the use of UDP in real-time multimedia transmission, both on intranets and on the Internet, is of increasing importance. High-level protocols, such as Real-Time Transport Protocol (RTP), Real-Time Control Protocol (RTCP), and Real-Time Streaming Protocol (RTSP), typically operate over UDP, although their definitions don't exclude the use of other protocols. These protocols require guaranteed bandwidth and are described here in the context of both UDP and QoS. Resource Reservation Protocol (RSVP) is a QoS mechanism and is described, together with QoS, later in the chapter.

Real-Time Transport Protocol

RTP, defined in RFC 1889, provides end-to-end delivery services to support applications that transmit real-time data. RFC 1890 defines a profile for carrying audio and video traffic over RTP. Microsoft NetMeeting is one example of an RTP-based application.

RTP services include payload type identification, sequence numbering, and time stamping. The protocol offers end-to-end delivery services, but doesn't provide all of the functionality of a transport protocol. Typically, RTP runs on top of UDP and utilizes UDP's multiplexing and checksum services.

The RTP header provides timing information that's used to synchronize and display audio and video data. This information can also determine whether packets have been lost or have arrived out of order. The header also specifies the payload type, and multiple data and compression types are allowed. Auxiliary profile and payload format specifications configure RTP to a specific application—for example, a payload format can specify the type of audio or video encoding that's carried in the RTP packet. Encoded data can be compressed before delivery.

To set up an RTP session, an application defines a pair of destination transport addresses (one network address plus ports for RTP and RTCP). Each medium in a multimedia transmission is carried in a separate RTP session, enabling a recipient to select whether or not to receive a particular medium. RFC 1889 illustrates the use of RTP in an audio-conferencing scenario. Further information can be obtained from the RFC document.

RTP doesn't contain any mechanisms that ensure timely delivery or provide QoS guarantees. It doesn't guarantee delivery or check that packets are received in the order transmitted. Nor does it assume that the underlying network is reliable. Some adaptive applications do not require such guarantees, but for those that do, RTP must be supported by mechanisms that provide resource reservation, such as QoS Admission Control.

The RTP header contains the following fields:

- *Version*—This 2-bit field identifies the version of RTP, currently 2.

- *Padding*—This 1-bit field indicates whether the RTP packet contains one or more padding octets that aren't part of the payload. Padding may be required for encryption algorithms that have fixed block sizes or for carrying several RTP packets in a lower-layer protocol data unit.

- *Extension*—This 1-bit field indicates whether the fixed RTP header is followed by a header extension.

- *CSRC Count (CC)*—This 4-bit field specifies the number of Contributing Source (CSRC) identifiers that follow the fixed header.

- *Marker (M)*—This 1-bit field allows significant events, such as frame boundaries, to be marked in the packet stream. The precise interpretation of the Marker bit is defined by an RTP profile (see RFC 1889 for details).

- *Payload Type (PT)*—This 7-bit field identifies the format of the RTP payload and determines how it is interpreted by an application.

- *Sequence number*—This 16-bit field contains the sequence number, which increments by one for each RTP data packet sent and can be used by the receiver to detect packet loss and to restore packet sequence.

- *Timestamp*—This 32-bit field contains the timestamp, which reflects the sampling instant of the first octet in the RTP data packet. The timestamp is used in synchronization and jitter calculations. Calculation and use of the timestamp are complex. Refer to RFC 1889 for details.

- *SSRC*—This 32-bit field identifies the Synchronization Source (SSRC). This identifier is chosen randomly so that no two synchronization sources within the same RTP session have the same SSRC identifier.

- *CSRC list*—This field can contain from 0 through 15 items, each 32 bits in length. The CSRC list identifies the contributing sources for the payload contained in the packet. The number of identifiers is specified in the CC field.

NOTE: *The first 12 octets of the RTP header are present in every RTP packet, but the list of CSRC identifiers is present only if there are contributing sources.*

Real-Time Control Protocol

RFC 1889 also describes RTCP. Each participant in an RTP session periodically transmits RTCP packets to all other participants. Information fed back to the application can be used to control performance and for diagnostic purposes. RTCP performs the following functions:

- *Providing information to an application*—The primary function of RTCP is to provide information about the quality of data distribution to an application. Each RTCP packet contains sender and/or receiver statistics that include information about the number of packets sent, the number of packets lost, interarrival jitter, and so on. Senders, receivers, and third-party monitors use this reception-quality feedback. For example, senders can modify their transmissions; receivers can determine whether problems are local, regional, or global; and network managers can use the information to evaluate network performance.

- *Identifying the RTP source*—The transport-level identifier for an RTP source is known as the Canonical Name (CNAME). This is used to keep track of the participants in an RTP session. Receivers use the CNAME to associate multiple data streams in a set of related RTP sessions. For example, audio and video streams from the same source can be identified and synchronized.

- *Controlling the RTCP transmission interval*—Control traffic is limited to five percent of the overall session traffic. This prevents control traffic from overwhelming network resources and allows RTP to scale to a large number of session participants. Adjusting the rate at which RTCP packets are sent enforces this limit. Each participant sends control packets to everyone else and can, therefore, keep track of the total number of participants and use this number to calculate the rate at which to send RTCP packets.

- *Conveying minimal session control information*—RTCP can be used to convey a minimal amount of information to all session participants. For example, RTCP can carry a personal name to identify a participant on the user's display. This function is useful in (for example) teleconferencing sessions where participants enter and leave the session informally.

RTCP packet format is complex. RTCP packets are compounds of a number of packet types, as listed in Table 9.2.

The following is a direct quote from RFC 1889:

> Each RTCP packet begins with a fixed part similar to that of RTP data packets, followed by structured elements that may be of variable length according to the packet type but always end on a 32-bit boundary. The alignment requirement and a length field in the fixed part are included to make RTCP packets "stackable". Multiple RTCP packets may be concatenated without any intervening separators to form a compound RTCP packet that is sent in a single packet of the lower layer protocol, for example UDP. There is no explicit count of individual RTCP packets in the compound packet since the lower layer protocols are expected to provide an overall length to determine the end of the compound packet.

RFC 1889 is a highly detailed 75-page document that will give you all the information you need if you want to study RTCP and RTP in depth.

Real-Time Streaming Protocol

RTSP, defined in RFC 2326, streams multimedia data in one-to-many applications over unicast and multicast and supports interoperability between clients and servers from different vendors. Streaming breaks data into packets that are sized to reflect the available bandwidth between the client and server. User software can simultaneously play one packet, decompress another, and receive a third. A user can begin to listen to audio and watch video almost immediately, without having to download the entire media file. Data sources for streaming can include both live data feeds and stored clips.

Table 9.2   RTCP packet types.

Packet Type	Description
SR	Sender report, for transmission and reception statistics from participants that are active senders.
RR	Receiver report, for reception statistics from participants that aren't active senders.
SDES	Source description items, including CNAME.
BYE	Indicates end of participation.
APP	Application-specific functions.

RTSP controls multiple data delivery sessions and specifies a means for choosing delivery channels (such as UDP). It operates on top of RTP to control and deliver real-time content. Although RTSP can be used with unicast, it can help smooth the transition to IP multicasting with RTP. RTSP is an extremely complex and powerful text-based protocol. RFC 2326 is more than 90 pages long, and it's neither desirable nor appropriate to go into that amount of detail here. If you want more information, refer to the RFC document.

RTSP can be used with RSVP to set up and manage reserved-bandwidth streaming sessions. RSVP is described later in this chapter.

Quality of Service

Windows 2000 QoS is a set of service requirements that a network must meet to assure an adequate service level for data transmission. Implementing QoS enables real-time programs to make efficient use of network bandwidth. Because it provides a guarantee of sufficient network resources, QoS gives a level of service similar to that of a private network, to a network that's shared by RTP/UDP and traditional TCP traffic. The QoS guarantee indicates a service level that enables a program to transmit data in an acceptable way and within an acceptable time frame. The Windows 2000 implementation of QoS includes a Subnet Bandwidth Management (SBM) service for controlling bandwidth on a subnet and traffic control services for prioritizing and scheduling traffic.

Windows 2000 supports several QoS mechanisms, such as RSVP, Differentiated Services (DiffServ), the Institute of Electrical and Electronic Engineers (IEEE) 802.1p standard, and Asynchronous Transfer Media (ATM) QoS. These QoS mechanisms use a Generic QoS (GQoS) Applications Programming Interface (API) that's an extension to the Windows Sockets (Winsock) programming interface. GQoS provides applications with a method of reserving network bandwidth between client and server.

RSVP is a signaling protocol that's used to reserve bandwidth for individual flows on a network. It sets up a reservation for each and is therefore termed a *per-flow* QoS mechanism. RSVP is described in more detail later in this chapter. DiffServ defines 6 QoS bits in the IP header that determine how the IP packet is prioritized. DiffServ traffic can be assigned to one of 64 possible classes, known as Per Hop Behaviors (PHBs). IEEE 802.1p is a QoS mechanism that specifies how devices, such as Ethernet switches, prioritize traffic; it defines eight priority classes. DiffServ and 802.1p are termed *aggregate* QoS mechanisms, because they classify all traffic into a finite number of priority classes.

NOTE: *The 6 bits defined by DiffServ were previously known as the Type of Service (TOS) bits. Setting TOS bits through the Winsock interface is no longer supported, and all requests for IP TOS must be made through the GQoS API, unless the* DisableUserTOSSetting *Registry parameter (see Appendix A) is modified.*

Integrated Services over ATM (ISATM) automatically maps GQoS requests to ATM QoS on IP/ATM networks. Integrated Services over Low Bit Rate (ISSLOW) improves latency for prioritized traffic on slow WAN links. In addition, control and management applications can control traffic via the Traffic Control (TC) API, which allows a control or management application to provide some quality of service for non-QoS-enabled applications. Windows 2000 also provides a policy service called the QoS Admission Control Service (QoS ACS), which allows network administrators to control who gets QoS on the network.

For more detailed information, refer to RFC 2205.

Resource Reservation Protocol

RSVP (specified in RFC 2205, updated by RFC 2750) is a resource reservation setup protocol that's designed for an integrated services network. Applications invoke RSVP to request a specific end-to-end QoS for a data stream, and RSVP reserves guaranteed QoS resources. Resources provided through RSVP support unicast and multicast routing protocols and scale to large multicast delivery groups.

A receiving host uses RSVP to request a specific QoS for a particular data stream from a data source. An RSVP reservation request consists of a specification of a desired end-to-end QoS and a definition of the set of data packets to receive the QoS. RSVP is used in environments where QoS reservations are supported by reallocating rather than adding resources. For multicast traffic, a host sends Internet Group Management Protocol (IGMP) messages to join a host group, then sends RSVP messages to reserve resources along that group's delivery path(s). IGMP is described in Chapter 6.

RSVP provides access to internetwork integrated services, and all hosts, routers, and other network infrastructure elements between the receiver and sender must therefore support RSVP. If a router or switch is not RSVP-compliant, the reservation messages pass through the hop, and end-to-end QoS can't then be guaranteed.

If all elements on a route are RSVP-compliant, they each reserve system resources—such as bandwidth, CPU, and memory buffers—in order to satisfy the QoS request. RSVP QoS control request messages are also sent to reserve resources on all the nodes (routers and hosts) in the (reverse) delivery path to the sender. At each node along the receiver-sender path, RSVP makes a resource reservation for the requested stream. At each intermediate node, two actions are taken on a request:

- The request is granted or rejected according to admission and policy controls. Admission control determines whether the node has sufficient resources available, and policy control determines whether the user has authorization to make a reservation. If the reservation is rejected, RSVP returns an error message to the appropriate receiver(s), and the application determines whether to send the data now (using best-effort delivery) or to wait and repeat the request later. If the reservation can be accommodated, the node configures a *Packet Classifier* to select the appropriate incoming data packets and a *Packet Scheduler* to implement the desired QoS on the outgoing interface.

- The request is propagated to upstream nodes toward the appropriate senders.

The protocol also transmits teardown messages that relinquish resources.

RSVP is a *soft-state protocol* and requires that the reservation be refreshed periodically. The reservation information, or *reservation state*, is cached in each hop. If the network routing protocol alters the data path, RSVP automatically installs the reservation state along the new route. If refresh messages aren't received, reservations time out and are dropped.

The protocol is receiver-initiated, because sender initiation doesn't scale in large, multicast scenarios that have heterogeneous receivers. Each receiver makes its own reservation, and any differences among reservations are resolved by RSVP. If different receivers require different resources, both the sender and routers merge the reservation requests by taking the maximum values requested.

RSVP Messages

RSVP uses the message types listed in Table 9.3 to establish and maintain reserved traffic paths on a subnet.

An RSVP message consists of a common header, followed by a body that consists of a variable number of variable-length, typed objects. The message has a common header, and each object has a header of its own. The common RSVP header consists of the following fields:

- *Vers*—This 4-bit field contains the version number, currently 1.
- *Flags*—This 4-bit field is reserved for flags.
- *Msg Type*—This 8-bit field identifies the message type. Refer to Table 9.3 for the type values.
- *RSVP Checksum*—This 16-bit field contains the checksum. A value of zero means that no checksum was transmitted.
- *Send_TTL*—This 8-bit field contains the IP Time-to-Live value with which the message was sent.
- *RSVP Length*—This 16-bit field indicates the total length of the RSVP message in bytes, including the common header and the variable-length objects that follow that header.

Every RSVP object consists of one or more 32-bit words with a one-word header. The object header format is as follows:

Table 9.3   RSVP message types and type values.

Message Type	Function	Type Value
PATH	Carries the data flow information from the sender to the receiver. The PATH message reserves the path that requested data must take when returning to the receiver. It contains bandwidth requirements, traffic characteristics, and addressing information, such as source and destination IP addresses.	1
RESV	Carries the reservation request from the receiver. The RESV message contains the bandwidth reservation, the service level requested, and the source IP address.	2
PATH-ERR	Indicates an error in response to the PATH message.	3
RESV-ERR	Indicates an error in response to the RESV message.	4
PATH-TEAR	Removes the PATH state along the route.	5
RESV-TEAR	Removes the reservation along the route.	6
RESV-CONF	If a RESV message is sent with a confirmation object and there is sufficient bandwidth available to fulfill the request, then a RESV-CONF message is returned to the receiver. This doesn't guarantee the reservation, because a higher priority request might subsequently be received.	7

- *Length*—This 16-bit field contains the total object length in bytes. This is always a multiple of 4 bytes (32 bits), and the minimum value is 4.

- *Class-Num*—This 8-bit field identifies the object class. The object classes are NULL, SESSION, RSVP_HOP, TIME_VALUES, STYLE, FLOWSPEC, FILTER_SPEC, SENDER_TEMPLATE, SENDER_TSPEC, ADSPEC, ERROR_SPEC, POLICY_DATA, INTEGRITY, SCOPE, and RESV_CONFIRM. Refer to the RFC documents for descriptions of these classes and their corresponding values. The two high-order bits of this field are used to determine what action a node takes if it doesn't recognize an object class.

- *C-Type*—This 8-bit field identifies the object type. Each object type is unique within an object class, and the Class-Num and C-Type fields can therefore be used together as a 16-bit number that defines a unique type for each object.

Traffic Control

Traffic control is a QoS mechanism that starts when a client program requests QoS and performs the following tasks:

- It reduces delay and latency (accumulated delay) in the transmission of network traffic.

- It works with QoS Admission Control (see later in this chapter) and RSVP to provide the service level and priority required by the bandwidth request.

- It provides a service for subnet clients that aren't QoS Admission Control-enabled (although the client programs must be QoS-enabled).

- It controls data flow through devices that don't use RSVP.

The traffic control Dynamic-Link Library (DLL) configures and prioritizes traffic, using a process of packet classification and scheduling. The Packet Classifier determines the service class to which an individual packet belongs. Packets are then queued by service level to be serviced by the Packet Scheduler. The Packet Scheduler determines the delivery schedule of each packet queue and controls priorities when queued packets simultaneously need access to network resources. It takes information from the Packet Classifier, creates queues for each data flow, and then empties the queues at the rate specified by RSVP when the flow was created. The Immediate Solutions section of this chapter describes how to install the QoS Packet Scheduler.

Service Levels

QoS configures a service level as part of the traffic properties for each data flow. To determine what service level setting is required, we need to understand traffic patterns. These fall into two major groups:

- *Elastic traffic*—Delivery speed is a function of available bandwidth. Elastic traffic is slow when bandwidth is limited and fast when it is abundant. The data sender automatically tunes to the rate of the network. Transaction-oriented programs, such as bulk data transfers, typically generate elastic traffic.

- *Real-time traffic*—The arrival time interval between any two packets at the receiver must closely match their departure interval. Real-time traffic has limited ability to adapt to changing network conditions, and delays can significantly reduce intelligibility. For example, if video traffic experiences interpacket delays, the pictures become distorted and can't be viewed.

Windows 2000 QoS Admission Control (see below) supports three service levels:

- *Best effort*—A connectionless delivery model that's suitable for elastic traffic. Packets are sent with no guarantees of low delay or adequate bandwidth.

- *Controlled load*—A preferential service that is set up on a per-network element basis. A flow that receives controlled load service at a network element experiences little or no delay or congestion loss. End-to-end bandwidth allocation isn't, however, guaranteed.

- *Guaranteed service*—Allocates guaranteed bandwidth. When every host on the data path, including routers or switches, provides this service (that is, they are compliant with QoS and RSVP), end-to end bandwidth is guaranteed.

Best effort is suitable for elastic traffic, and the other two levels are suitable for real-time programs. Any unreserved bandwidth or reserved bandwidth not currently in use remains available for other traffic. Guaranteed service improves transmission quality, but impacts heavily on network resources and shouldn't be specified for elastic traffic.

QoS Admission Control

Real-time programs typically use RTP or UDP protocol to send data. Because RTP and UDP are connectionless protocols, the reliability of the delivery service is limited. To deploy real-time programs with an acceptable traffic rate, you must have some level of guaranteed availability of network resources. QoS Admission Control, working with Windows 2000 Quality of Service (QoS), provides this guarantee.

QoS Admission Control designates how, by whom, and when shared network resources are used. Any Windows 2000 server on a subnet can be configured as the QoS ACS host and will then control bandwidth for that subnet. A client on the subnet submits priority bandwidth requests to this host, which then determines if adequate bandwidth is available to meet this request, based on the current state of resource availability on the subnet and the QoS Admission Control user policy rights.

Windows 2000 clients are automatically configured to use QoS Admission Control. QoS Admission Control also supports clients on any other operating systems that are SBM-enabled.

Features of QoS Admission Control

Windows 2000 QoS Admission Control offers a number of features and benefits:

- It's transparent to the user.
- It can operate with different network configurations.
- It safeguards end-to-end delivery service with low-delay guarantees.
- It provides a QoS Admission Control console that enables an administrator to centralize policy and subnet configuration.
- It enables an administrator to use user and subnet identities as criteria for reserving network resources and setting priorities.
- It enables an administrator to partition network resources between low-priority and high-priority traffic.
- It supports multicast transmission of bandwidth reservation messages.
- It can process bandwidth reservation messages that are encrypted by Windows 2000 IP Security (IPSec).

How QoS Admission Control Works

In Figure 9.2, Clients A, B, and C make reservation requests to the QoS Admission Control host (Server 1), requesting 20Mbps of bandwidth. In this scenario, Clients A, B, and C are receivers that want to stream real-time data from Server 2. Server 1 is configured to allow a maximum reserved bandwidth of 50Mbps.

QoS Admission Control works as follows:

1. Server 1 multicasts *beacons*, which are messages that notify clients that a QoS ACS server is present and ready to receive requests. A client won't send a request to a host that isn't sending beacons.

2. Client A requests 20Mbps of reserved bandwidth.

3. On Server 1, Client A's identity is verified using the Kerberos 5 protocol (see Chapter 11), and the QoS Admission Control policy for Client A is retrieved from Active Directory.

4. Server 1 checks the policy to see if Client A has adequate rights for the request, then verifies that network resource levels are adequate.

5. Server 1 approves the request and grants the reservation of 20Mpbs of bandwidth to Client A.

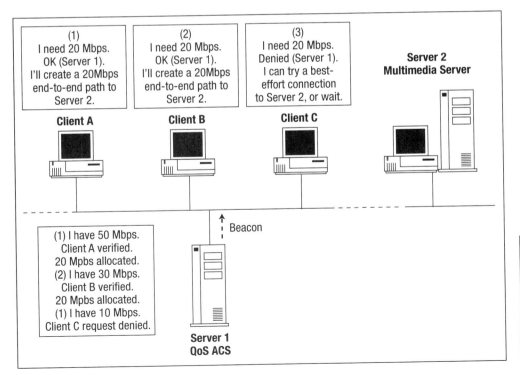

Figure 9.2   QoS Admission Control example.

6. Client A sends RSVP PATH messages to reserve end-to-end bandwidth between itself and Server 2. If there are one or more routers in the path between Client A and Server 2, bandwidth on these routers is also reserved (assuming they're QoS enabled).

7. The amount of reservable bandwidth that Server 1 can allocate is reduced by 20Mbps.

8. Client B requests 20Mbps of reserved bandwidth. The process is repeated.

9. Client C requests 20Mbps of reserved bandwidth. Because insufficient priority bandwidth is available at this time, Server 1 rejects the reservation. The application on Client C determines whether to request data from Server 2 now at a best-effort service level or wait until priority bandwidth becomes available.

This example assumes that Clients A, B, and C have the appropriate rights and that the same user policy applies to all three of them. In the next section, we'll look at how QoS Admission Control and Admission Control policies are implemented.

Implementing QoS Admission Control

QoS Admission Control requires network adapters that are compatible with the IEEE 802.1p standard and must be installed on a Windows 2000 Server in the domain that contains the subnet you intend to manage. Packet Scheduler should be installed on every end-system in the subnet that makes reservations with the QoS Admission Control. The procedures to install QoS Admission Control and Packet Scheduler are described in the Immediate Solutions section of this chapter.

TIP: *You can install the QoS Admission Control on multiple hosts on the same subnet. Only one QoS Admission Control host actually performs bandwidth management services at any time. The other QoS Admission Control hosts function as backups, one of which automatically becomes active if the primary QoS Admission Control host stops functioning.*

QoS Admission Control Policies

QoS Admission Control policy is a combination of two policies, the *Any Authenticated User enterprise policy* and the *Unauthenticated User enterprise policy*. All other QoS Admission Control policies that you create are exceptions to the general rules in the default enterprise policies. Policies are hierarchical, from most specific (a particular user on a specific subnet) to least specific (a user policy for all QoS Admission Control-managed subnets). You can use the QoS Admission Control console (see the Immediate Solutions section) to create enterprise and subnet policies centrally for all users.

Enterprise Policies

The enterprise settings specify the network-wide policies for users and apply to all QoS Admission Control-managed subnets. Configuring the default Any Authenticated User enterprise policy specifies these settings. This policy is applied to all authenticated users in the domain. If you have special user requirements, you should create exception polices for these users. Exception policies hold only those attributes that are different from the default policy.

An unauthenticated user is any user on a computer running Windows 2000 that isn't logged on under a domain account but is, nevertheless, connected to the network—for example, any user that logs on to a computer on the network using a local account. Configuring the default enterprise Unauthenticated User policy lets you specify the actions taken by the QoS Admission Control when an unauthenticated user makes a priority bandwidth request. The default settings for the enterprise policies are listed in Table 9.4.

Subnet Policies

Subnet settings contain a subnet object that represents the actual QoS Admission Control-managed subnet. By default, any subnet policy that you create uses the settings from the enterprise policies. You can create user policies for each QoS Admission Control subnet object, and these will then apply only to the subnet that contains them.

When a user requests priority bandwidth, the QoS Admission Control host first searches Active Directory for a subnet-level user policy for the subnet on which the user is requesting bandwidth, and then it searches for an enterprise-level user policy.

Subnet Configuration

Subnet properties shouldn't be confused with subnet-level user policies. A QoS Admission Control subnet object is created to set traffic limits for the subnet and also to set the QoS Admission Control Service properties for each QoS Admission Control host managing the subnet.

A subnet object is linked to the physical subnet and the QoS Admission Control hosts by the subnet IP address. The subnet object properties determine:

Table 9.4   QoS Admission Control default enterprise policy settings.

Traffic Property	Any Authenticated User	Unauthenticated User
Data Rate	500Kbps	64Kbps
Peak Data Rate	500Kbps	64Kbps
Number of Flows	2	1

9. User Datagram Protocol and Quality of Service

- The traffic limits for the subnet.
- The logging and accounting properties for the QoS Admission Control hosts.
- QoS Admission Control properties on each QoS Admission Control host.

After you create a QoS Admission Control subnet object, you can add subnet-level user policies.

User Policies

You can modify the enterprise-level Any Authenticated User policy to meet the general needs of users. You need to create additional policies only when a user has different requirements. In some cases, a particular user has unique resource requirements on a specific subnet. To meet special requirements, you can create user policies at the subnet settings level. Default unauthenticated and authenticated user policies are provided at this level and can be modified to meet the needs of users sending data on the subnet.

Enterprise settings apply to all subnets unless the user has a policy in subnet settings. If a user has a policy in enterprise settings and another policy in the subnet settings for Subnet A, then the enterprise policy applies *except* when the user sends or receives data on Subnet A.

Policy Hierarchy

The process of building the policy profile used by the QoS Admission Control for each user is cumulative. The initial user policy is determined by the global default. Then, the value of any attribute can be updated as each more specific policy is applied. If a user isn't recognized, the Unauthenticated User policy is applied. This enables you to create a policy that prevents visiting users from using reserved resources on the subnet.

When a user has a group profile defined, policies are applied in the following order:

1. User policy for the current subnet
2. Group policy on the current subnet
3. Authenticated user on the current subnet
4. User in the enterprise container
5. Authenticated user in the enterprise container

QoS Admission Control Logging

QoS Admission Control messages on a subnet can be tracked for network usage statistics and to verify that the subnet clients and the QoS Admission Control host are interacting correctly. Logging can also help with troubleshooting and verify that RSVP messages are being sent and received.

Accounting Logs

The QoS Accounting service can be configured to collect network resource usage information on a per-user basis. Accounting logs can help identify the causes of problems on your network and can assist in planning network usage. Accounting logs tell you who is using network resources and the dates and times of individual sessions. They will also give you addressing information for each session.

Table 9.5 lists the information fields contained in an Accounting log entry.

RSVP Logs

The logging service can also be configured to capture QoS Admission Control host RSVP messages. RSVP log information is typically used for troubleshooting. These logs identify the date and time of an RSVP message and address information for the sender and receiver of the message.

Table 9.6 lists the information fields contained in an RSVP log entry. Some of the field parameters are complex, and additional information may be obtained in RFCs 2205, 2210, 2215, and 2216. RFC 1700 contains a list of protocol IDs with matching protocol names.

Table 9.5   Accounting log fields.

Field	Description
Date/time	The date and time of the record in Greenwich Mean Time (GMT).
Session IP addressing information	The receiver's IP address, the port number on which the data is sent, and the decimal value of the protocol ID (see RFC 1700).
Record type	This can be one of the following: Start Sender, Start Receiver, Stop Sender, Stop Receiver, Reject Sender, or Reject Receiver.
User ID	The domain and username of the sender or receiver.
IP addressing information for the last hop	The IP address of the last hop and the port number on which the data is sent or the hexadecimal address of the network adapter (if the host relaying the message is a multihomed device).
Message status	This can be one of the following: New, Modify, Stop Sender reason, Reject Sender, or source IP address of the data flow.
Message detail	This can contain the sender's traffic information, the receiver's traffic information, the Stop Receiver reason, and the Reject Receiver reason.

Table 9.6   RSVP log fields.

Field	Description
Date/time	The date and time of the record in GMT.
Type of message	One of the following: PATH, RESV, PATH-ERR, RESV-ERR, PATH-TEAR, RESV-TEAR, with additional parameters Confirmation Request, Scope, and Reservation Style (see RFC 2205).
Session IP addressing information	The receiver's IP address, the port number on which the data is sent, and the decimal value of the protocol ID (see RFC 1700).
IP addressing information for the last hop	The IP address of the last hop and the port number on which the data is sent or the hexadecimal address of the network adapter (if the host relaying the message is a multihomed device).
Refresh interval	This value (in milliseconds) determines the frequency at which the message is sent.
Sender IP addressing information	The sender's IP address, the port number on which the data is sent, and the decimal value of the protocol used.
Bucket rate	The bucket data rate (see RFCs 2210, 2215, and 2216).
Bucket size	The size of the bucket in which packets are grouped for transmission.
Peak rate	The burst rate of the packets.
Packet size	The minimum packet size for transmission.
Maximum Transmission Unit (MTU) size	The maximum packet size for transmission. This field, plus the previous four fields, make up the *Tspec* parameters (see RFCs 2205, 2210, 2215, and 2216).
Adspec	The remaining fields in the record indicate the *Adspec* traffic parameters for the receiver.

Log Files

You can specify several options for RSVP and Accounting log files, including the number of files that are created and the directory in which they're placed. Both Accounting and RSVP log files are circular. If you specify a maximum file size and the file reaches that limit, one of two options can be specified:

- Unless the maximum number of log files is also reached, another log file is created. This option is useful if you want to examine the transaction history for a pattern.

- No new log files are created. The current file is overwritten each time the maximum file size is reached. In this case, examination of logged data is limited to current information.

New log entries are generated whenever a client requests bandwidth. The log file size or the number of log files grows as requests are made. It's important to balance the need for detailed data with the requirement to limit the size and number of the files. Large log files can compromise performance, and smaller log files are easier to search for specific events.

TIP: *You don't have to stop QoS Admission Control services to view log files.*

QoS Admission Control Internet Drafts

Internet Drafts contain the latest detailed technical information about RSVP, SBM, and traffic control. They provide a method of distributing documents that might eventually be submitted for publication as RFCs and of soliciting feedback.

The following Internet Drafts examine issues related to QoS Admission Control:

- Providing Integrated Services Over Low-Bit-Rate Links
- SBM (Subnet Bandwidth Manager): A Proposal for Admission Control Over IEEE 802-Style Networks
- A Framework for Providing Integrated Services Over Shared and Switched IEEE 802 LAN Technologies
- Integrated Services over IEEE 802.1D/802.1p Networks
- Integrated Service Mappings on IEEE 802 Networks
- RSVP Cryptographic Authentication
- RSVP Extensions for Policy Control
- Partial Service Deployment in the Integrated Services Architecture

These drafts can be obtained from the Internet Engineering Task Force (IETF) working group for quality of service at **www.ietf.org/html.charters/wg-dir.html**.

NOTE: *These documents are drafts at the time of writing. They may have become RFCs since then. For a list of the latest RFCs, access **http://info.internet.isi.edu/in-notes/rfc/files**.*

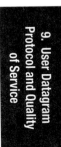

9. User Datagram Protocol and Quality of Service

Immediate Solutions

Capturing UDP Traffic

Microsoft networking uses UDP for logon, browsing, and name resolution. In this procedure, logon traffic from a client to a Domain Controller (DC) is captured. To reduce the capture size, a capture filter is set so that only traffic from the selected client computer is captured. A logon capture file (logon.cap) is available on the CD-ROM.

To capture a logon traffic that contains UDP datagrams, proceed as follows:

1. Log on to the DC as an administrator.

2. On the DC, access Start|Programs|Administrative Tools and select Network Monitor.

3. On the Network Monitor Capture pull-down menu, select Filter.

4. In the Capture Filter dialog box, click Edit Addresses.

5. In the Address Database dialog box, click Add.

6. The Address Information dialog box appears. Select IP in the Type drop-down box and enter the name and IP address of a client computer in your domain. Click OK.

7. Close the Address Database dialog box.

8. In the Address Expression dialog box, select the DC as Station 1 and the other computer as Station 2. In the Direction box, select unidirectional, from Station 2 to Station 1 ($<\cdots$). Click OK.

9. Click OK to close the Capture Filter dialog box.

10. On the Network Monitor Capture pull-down menu, select Start.

11. On the client (non-DC) computer, log on using any valid domain account.

12. On the Network Monitor Capture pull-down menu (on the DC), select Stop and View. View the captured frames and save the capture (for example, as logon.cap).

13. Exit from Network Monitor.

Related solution:	*Found on page:*
Implementing a Capture Filter	101

Installing QoS Admission Control

To install and configure QoS Admission Control, you need to be logged on as an administrator on the DC that you've chosen as the QoS ACS server. When QoS Admission Control is installed, it becomes available as an item on the Administrative Tools menu.

To install QoS Admission Control, proceed as follows:

1. Log on to the DC as an administrator.
2. In Start|Settings|Control Panel, open Add/Remove Programs.
3. In the Add/Remove Programs dialog box, select Add/Remove Windows Components.
4. In the Windows Components Wizard, select Networking Services, then click Details.

TIP: *Click on the words "Networking Services", not on the checkbox beside them.*

---

5. Check the QoS Admission Control Service checkbox, then click OK.
6. Click Next.
7. Click Finish.
8. Close the Add/Remove Programs dialog box and the Control Panel.

Creating and Configuring Subnets

In this set of procedures, you'll create a QoS Admission Control Subnet and configure the following:

- Traffic properties
- Servers
- Logging properties
- Accounting properties
- Advanced properties

Creating a QoS Admission Control Subnet

To create a QoS Admission Control Subnet, proceed as follows:

1. Log on to the QoS ACS server as an administrator.
2. Access Start|Programs|Administrative Tools and select QoS Admission Control.

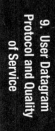

9. User Datagram Protocol and Quality of Service

3. In the console tree, click Subnetwork Settings.

4. On the Action pull-down menu, select Add subnetwork.

NOTE: *If you are reconfiguring a subnet rather than adding one, select Properties on the Action pull-down menu at this point.*

---

5. Type the IP address for the subnet, using the format *IP Address/subnet mask width in bits*—for example, 195.162.230.0/24 (see Chapter 5).

6. Click OK.

7. In the Subnet Properties dialog box, select the settings you want to apply to the subnet:

   • To configure data rates and service levels for the subnet, use the Traffic tab. Refer to "Configuring Traffic Properties."

   • To enable servers to act as QoS Admission Control hosts, use the Servers tab. Refer to "Configuring Servers."

   • To enable a QoS Admission Control host to log subnet RSVP messages, use the Logging tab. Refer to "Configuring Logging Properties."

   • To track network resource usage on the subnet by user, use the Accounting tab. Refer to "Configuring Accounting Properties."

   • To determine the behavior of the QoS Admission Control hosts managing the subnet, use the Advanced tab. Refer to "Configuring Advanced Properties."

8. Click OK to close the Subnet Properties dialog box.

9. Close the QoS Admission Control snap-in.

NOTE: *If you are carrying out this procedure in a child domain, the security settings in the parent domain (and ultimately the root domain) must be changed for the subnet object.*

Configuring Traffic Properties

To configure traffic properties for a subnet, proceed as follows:

1. Log on to the QoS ACS server as an administrator.

2. Access Start|Programs|Administrative Tools and select QoS Admission Control.

3. In the console tree, click Subnetwork Settings and select the subnet you want to configure.

4. On the Action pull-down menu, select Properties.

5. Select the Traffic tab. The Traffic configuration dialog box should appear, as shown in Figure 9.3.

6. Check the Enable Admission Control Service on this subnetwork checkbox to enable the service on the subnet.

7. Type a description in the Description of the subnetwork text box.

8. Click Add. The Limits dialog box (Figure 9.4) should appear.

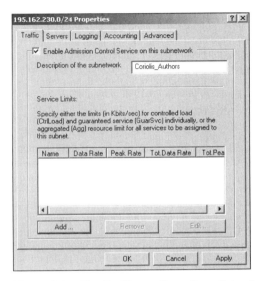

Figure 9.3   The Traffic configuration dialog box.

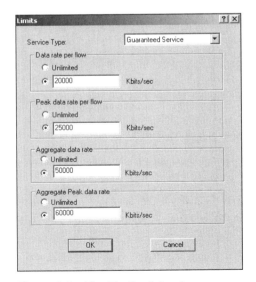

Figure 9.4   The Limits dialog box.

9. Configure the traffic limits as follows:

- In the Service Type drop-down box, select Aggregate, Controlled Load, or Guaranteed Service. If you previously set limits for Guaranteed Service on the subnet, this option won't be available.

- Set the maximum rate at which data can travel on the subnet by typing the value in the Data rate per flow box.

- Set the maximum rate allowed during a burst of packets on the subnet by typing the value in the Peak data rate per flow box. This value must be greater than or equal to the value in the Data rate per flow box.

- Set the maximum rate for all simultaneous flows on this subnet by typing the value in the Aggregate data rate box. This value must be greater than equal to the value in the Peak data rate per flow box.

- Set the maximum rate on all simultaneous flows during a burst of packets on this subnet by typing the value in the Aggregate Peak data rate box. This value must be greater than or equal to the value in the Aggregate data rate box.

10. Click OK to close the Limits dialog box. If a QoS Admission Control information box appears, click OK to close it.

11. Click OK to close the Subnet Properties dialog box.

12. Close the QoS Admission Control snap-in.

Configuring Servers

To add or remove servers or modify server passwords on a subnet, proceed as follows:

1. Log on to the QoS ACS server as an administrator.

2. Access Start|Programs|Administrative Tools and select QoS Admission Control.

3. In the console tree, click Subnetwork Settings and select the subnet you want to configure.

4. On the Action pull-down menu, select Properties.

5. Select the Servers tab. The Servers dialog box should appear, as shown in Figure 9.5.

6. Configure server properties for the subnet as follows:

- Click Add to add a server to the list of servers allowed to run QoS Admission Control on this subnet. Add a server to the list and specify the domain name and password.

Figure 9.5   The Servers dialog box.

- To remove a selected server from the list of servers allowed to run QoS Admission Control, click on the server name, then click Remove. You can deactivate the QoS ACS service on that server, in addition to removing it from the list (if you want to do so).
- To set a password, click on the relevant server, then click Change Password.

7. Click OK to close the Subnet Properties dialog box.

8. Close the QoS Admission Control snap-in.

Configuring Logging Properties

To configure RSVP logging properties for a subnet, proceed as follows:

1. Log on to the QoS ACS server as an administrator.

2. Access Start|Programs|Administrative Tools and select QoS Admission Control.

3. In the console tree, click Subnetwork Settings and select the subnet you want to configure.

4. On the Action pull-down menu, select Properties.

5. Select the Logging tab. The Logging configuration dialog box should appear, as shown in Figure 9.6.

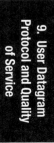

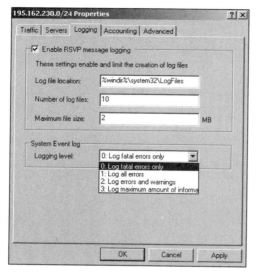

Figure 9.6   The Logging configuration dialog box.

6. Configure logging properties for the subnet as follows:

- Check Enable RSVP message logging if you want the QoS Admission Control host to record all RSVP messages in a log file.

- Specify where you want the log files to be created by typing the path in the Log file location box (or accept the default of %windir%\system32\LogFiles). The log file appears in the specified file location with the file name RSVPTRACExx.txt, where xx represents the number of the log file (in ascending order of creation).

- Specify the maximum number of circular log files QoS Admission Control can create by typing the value in the Number of log files box.

- Specify the maximum size of each circular log file by typing the value (in megabytes) in the Maximum file size box. If the RSVP log reaches the maximum file size, it creates a new file. If it reaches the maximum number of files, it overwrites the first log file.

- Determine the type of transactions that are tracked in the Windows 2000 Event Log by selecting the appropriate value in the Logging level box. Table 9.7 specifies the value for each logging level.

7. Click OK to close the Subnet Properties dialog box.

8. Close the QoS Admission Control snap-in.

Table 9.7   Logging levels.

Level	Description
0	Fatal errors only
1	All errors
2	All warnings and errors
3	All available information

Configuring Accounting Properties

To configure accounting properties for a subnet, proceed as follows:

1. Log on to the QoS ACS server as an administrator.

2. Access Start|Programs|Administrative Tools and select QoS Admission Control.

3. In the console tree, click Subnetwork Settings and select the subnet you want to configure.

4. On the Action pull-down menu, select Properties.

5. Select the Accounting tab. The Accounting configuration dialog box should appear, as shown in Figure 9.7.

6. Configure accounting properties for the subnet as follows:

    • Select Enable Accounting to record QoS Admission Control host information about network resource usage in a log file.

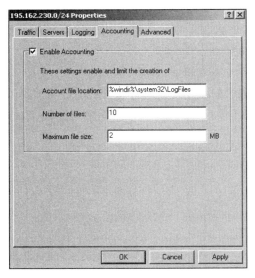

Figure 9.7   The Accounting configuration dialog box.

- Specify where you want the log files to be created by typing the path (for example, %windir%\system32\LogFiles) in the Account file location box. The log file appears in the specified file location with the file name ACSUSERSESSION*xx*.txt, where *xx* represents the number of the log file (in ascending order of creation).

- Specify the maximum number of circular log files QoS Admission Control can create by typing the value in the Number of files box.

- Specify the maximum size of each circular log file by typing the value in the Maximum file size box. If the accounting log reaches the maximum file size, it creates a new file. If it reaches the maximum number of files, it overwrites the first log file.

7. Click OK to close the Subnet Properties dialog box. If a QoS Admission Control information box appears, click OK to close it.

8. Close the QoS Admission Control snap-in.

Configuring Advanced Properties

To configure advanced properties for a subnet, proceed as follows:

1. Log on to the QoS ACS server as an administrator.

2. Access Start|Programs|Administrative Tools and select QoS Admission Control.

3. In the console tree, click Subnetwork Settings and select the subnet you want to configure.

4. On the Action pull-down menu, select Properties.

5. Select the Advanced tab. The Advanced configuration dialog box should appear, as shown in Figure 9.8.

6. Configure advanced properties for the subnet as follows:

- The Election Priority determines which host becomes the Designated Subnet Bandwidth Manager (DSBM) for the subnet. By default, the election priority is set to the same value on all QoS Admission Control hosts. The election is performed automatically. If the elected host goes offline, another is elected (assuming there's more than one host with QoS Admission Control installed).

- To specify how often the QoS Admission Control host transmits beacons on to the subnet, type a value (in seconds) in the Keep alive interval box.

- To set the interval (in seconds) following the last beacon, type a value in the Dead interval box. If this timeout occurs, another host is elected as the DSBM.

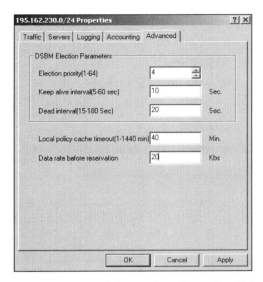

Figure 9.8   The Advanced configuration dialog box.

- To specify how often the QoS Admission Control host checks the directory service for new policy information, type a value (in minutes) in the Local policy cache timeout box.

- To specify the rate at which data is sent before the network reservation is complete, type a number (in Kbps) in the Data rate before reservation box. When the reservation is in place, this value is ignored, and the traffic properties set for the QoS Admission Control policy determine the data flow. (Refer to "Configuring Traffic Properties.")

7. Click OK to close the Subnet Properties dialog box.

8. Close the QoS Admission Control snap-in.

Installing QoS Packet Scheduler

The previous set of procedures installed and configured QoS ACS on a QoS Admission Control server. To enable QoS Admission Control clients to use the service, you need to install QoS Packet Scheduler on all client computers that make reservations on your QoS Admission Control subnet. To install Packet Scheduler on a client, proceed as follows:

1. Log on to the client PC as a domain administrator.

2. Access Start|Settings and select Control Panel.

3. Open Network and Dial-up Connections and click on the Local Area Connection on which you want to install QoS Packet Scheduler.

4. On the File pull-down menu, select Properties.

5. In the Local Area Connection Properties dialog box, click Install.

6. Select Service, then click Add.

7. Select QoS Packet Scheduler, then click OK.

8. Close the Local Area Connection Properties dialog box, then close the Control Panel.

NOTE: *The QoS ACS is configured on the QoS server. The client-side QoS Packet Scheduler is not configurable. The bandwidth that's requested by an application running on a client is a function of that application. The only way to check that your settings are correct is to monitor network traffic over an extended period using Network Monitor and the RSVP and Administration logs.*

Chapter 10

Application Level Protocols and Utilities

In Depth

This chapter looks at the protocols that are conceptually located at the lower part of the application layer in the TCP/IP four-layer model, or at the session layer of the Open Systems Interconnection (OSI) seven-layer model (see Chapter 1). These protocols use the transport layer protocols to implement information transfer and storage across intranets and the Internet. The chapter describes File Transport Protocol (FTP), which uses Transport Control Protocol (TCP) to transfer long files and to implement an FTP Internet site, and Trivial Transport Protocol (TFTP), which uses User Datagram Protocol (UDP) to transfer small amounts of data using best effort delivery.

Although Routing Internet Protocol (RIP) conceptually operates at the application layer, it's used by Internet Protocol (IP) for creating and maintaining routing tables and is therefore discussed with IP in Chapter 4. Simple Mail Transport Protocol (SMTP) exists at this layer and is described in this chapter, as is the Terminal Emulation (Telnet) protocol. Simple Network Management Protocol (SNMP) is used for network management and troubleshooting and (arguably) operates at a higher level in the application layer. SNMP is described in Chapter 19.

Chapter 8 lists the Windows 2000 connectivity utilities, which are described in more detail in this chapter, as are Hypertext Transport Protocol (HTTP), Network News Transport Protocol (NNTP), and Post Office Protocol version 3 (POP3). The Windows 2000 diagnostic utilities are described in Chapter 19.

File Transport Protocol

FTP, defined in RFC 959 updated by RFC 2228, is one of oldest Internet protocols and remains one of the most widely used. It uses separate command and data connections—the Protocol Interpreter (PI) implements the FTP protocol operations, and the Data Transfer Process (DTP) transfers the data. The protocol and the data transfer traffic use entirely separate TCP sessions. FTP servers listen on port 21, and the server initiates data connections from server port 20 to a specified port on the client. A data connection may be used in either direction and need not exist all the time.

The stated purposes of FTP are to shield users from variations in file storage systems on hosts and to transfer data reliably and efficiently. Although it can be used directly at a terminal by means of the **ftp** command, it's designed mainly for use by applications. FTP can transfer files that have differing data formats and word lengths. Data is packed into 8-bit transmission bytes on the sending host and unpacked into native format at the receiver.

FTP File Structures and Transmission Modes

FTP also allows the structure of a file to be specified. Three structures are defined:

- *File-structure*—There's no internal structure, and the file is considered to be a continuous sequence of data bytes.

- *Record-structure*—The file is made up of sequential records.

- *Page-structure*—The file is made up of independent indexed pages.

The default is file-structure, but both file- and record-structure are accepted for text files, such as ASCII (American Standard Code for Information Interchange) files, by all FTP implementations. The structure of a file affects both its transmission mode and its interpretation and storage. There are three transmission modes:

- *Stream mode*—The file is transmitted as a stream of bytes, with no restriction on the data type used. Record-structures are allowed. In a record-structured file, End-of-Record (EOR) and End-of-File (EOF) are identified by a 2-byte control code. In a file-structure, the sending host's closing the data connection indicates EOF. All bytes in a file-structure message are therefore data bytes.

- *Block mode*—The file is transmitted as a series of data blocks that are preceded by one or more header bytes. Header bytes contain a count field and a descriptor code. The *count field* contains the total length of the data block in bytes, thus marking the beginning of the next data block. The *descriptor code* defines block attributes, such as last block in the file (EOF), last block in the record (EOR), restart marker, or suspect data. Record structures are allowed in this mode, and any representation type may be used

- *Compressed mode*—Allows compression of data that consists of filler or replication bytes. The compressed mode header specifies a number of such bytes (up to 127). These are then sent compressed into a single byte.

NOTE: *The suspect data code isn't for error correction. It's used when sites exchange data (such as weather data) that may be prone to local error. The code indicates that all information should be exchanged, even though some parts of it are suspect.*

FTP also has two data transfer modes:

- *Ascii mode*—Uses standard 8-bit ASCII to transfer text files.

- *Binary mode*—Transfers binary files as a bit-by-bit process.

FTP uses TCP for error detection, but can initiate a transmission restart if a gross error occurs, such as a host going down. The standard protocol has no facilities for encrypting data or logon information, although RFC 2228 addresses this deficiency. For this reason, FTP communications are often set up to allow only anonymous access, which prevents usernames and passwords from being transmitted in clear text. FTP packet structure depends on file structure, transmission mode, and data transfer mode. Figures 10.1 and 10.2 show typical FTP frames using server ports 21 and 20, respectively. These figures were generated from the Network Monitor capture file ftp.cap that's provided on the CD-ROM. The procedure for generating a similar capture file is given in the immediate solution "Capturing TCP Traffic" in Chapter 8.

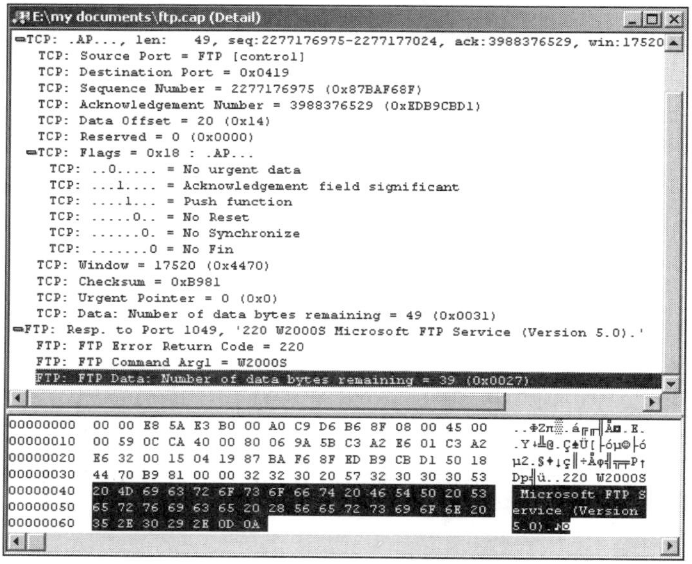

Figure 10.1   FTP traffic using control port 21.

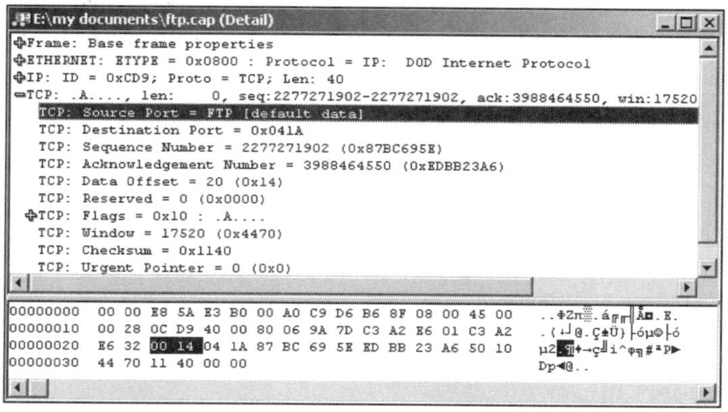

Figure 10.2   FTP traffic using data port 20.

A user can use the Command Console to key in FTP commands, such as **get** and **put** (see later in this chapter), or to run a script file that contains these commands. FTP is, however, normally used by applications to transfer data and by Internet Information Services (IIS), which implement FTP sites.

NOTE: *The acronyms IIS can also stand for Internet Information Server. In this chapter, however, it means the services that run on this server. IIS version 5 (IIS5) is described in Chapter 12.*

FTP commands issued from the Command Console can access an FTP site. A Web browser, such as Internet Explorer, can also access an FTP site, but with limited functionality. Full FTP access is typically implemented by using a commercial FTP access package (for example, CuteFTP).

Related solution:	*Found on page:*
Capturing TCP Traffic	249

Trivial File Transfer Protocol

TFTP, defined in RFC 1350 updated by RFCs 1783, 1785, 2347, and 2349, is a relatively simple protocol used to transfer files that (typically) are small and don't require much fragmentation. It's implemented on top of UDP, although its definition doesn't exclude the use of other datagram protocols. It lacks most of FTP's features—for example, it can't list directories or authenticate users—and its only purpose is to read files from and transmit files to a remote computer. Typically, TFTP is used by email applications.

A TFTP transfer starts with a file read or write request, which also requests a connection. The file is sent in fixed-length blocks of 512 bytes. An acknowledgment packet must acknowledge each data packet before the next packet can be sent. A data packet of less than 512 bytes indicates termination of the transfer. If a packet is lost, a timeout occurs at the intended recipient, which then requests the transmission of the lost packet. The packet retransmitted in this case is the final packet of the previous transmission, so the sender needs to retain only one packet for retransmission. Previous acknowledgments guarantee that packages sent previously have been received.

NOTE: *RFC 1783 defines a blocksize option that lets TFTP use a data packet size other than (usually larger than) 512 bytes.*

Each data packet has an associated block number. Block numbers are consecutive and begin with one, except for the positive response to a write request, which is an acknowledgment packet that has a block number of zero. Normally, an acknowledgment packet contains the block number of the data packet being acknowledged.

With one exception (described below), an error causes the connection to terminate. An error, indicated by an error packet, isn't acknowledged or retransmitted. Therefore, a timeout is used to detect a termination when the error packet has been lost.

If the source port of a received packet is incorrect, this error condition doesn't cause a termination. Instead, an error packet is sent to the originating host.

TFTP Transfer Modes

TFTP supports three data transfer modes, although only two of these are normally used:

- *Netascii*—Standard 8-bit ASCII, modified by the Telnet Protocol Specification (RFC 854).

- *Octet*—Used to transfer information on a bit-by-bit basis. This mode consists of "raw" 8-bit bytes and is similar to the FTP binary mode.

- *Mail*—Netascii characters sent to a user rather than a file. Although still supported, this mode is obsolete and shouldn't be implemented or used.

The RFC document doesn't make this list exclusive. Additional modes can be defined if both the sending and receiving hosts support them. By default, Windows 2000 supports only netascii and octet modes.

NOTE: *Microsoft defines the TFTP data transfer modes as binary (using the **-i** switch) and ascii. These modes are equivalent to the octet and netascii modes in the RFC 1350 specification.*

TFTP Packet Structure

TFTP supports five types of packets, each with its own operation code (opcode), as listed in Table 10.1.

RRQ and WRQ packets contain the following fields:

- *Opcode*—This 16-bit field contains the opcode, as specified by Table 10.1.

- *Filename*—This variable-length field contains the name of the file to be transferred as a sequence of netascii bytes.

- *Filename terminator*—This 8-bit field contains a zero value, which indicates the end of the Filename field.

Table 10.1   TFTP packet types.

Opcode	Packet Type
1	Read request (RRQ)
2	Write request (WRQ)
3	Data (DATA)
4	Acknowledgment (ACK)
5	Error (ERROR)

- *Mode*—This variable-length field contains "netascii", "octet", or (unusually) "mail" as a series of netascii bytes. The text may be uppercase, lowercase, or a combination of both.

- *Mode terminator*—This 8-bit field contains a zero value, which indicates the end of the Mode field.

NOTE: *The Filename terminator and Mode terminator fields are sometimes considered to be part of the Filename and Mode fields, respectively.*

RFC 2347 extends RRQ and WRQ packets, so sending and receiving hosts can negotiate additional TFTP options. A new type of TFTP packet, the Option Acknowledgment (OACK), is used to acknowledge a client's option negotiation request. RFC 2349 extends the RRQ and WRQ packets still further, to enable TFTP hosts to agree to timeout intervals and transfer sizes. Full details are given in the RFC documents.

DATA packets are used to send the specified file; they contain the following fields:

- *Opcode*—For DATA packets, this 16-bit field contains the value 3.

- *Block number*—This 16-bit field contains the block number. For DATA packages, this starts at 1 and increments by 1 with each block of data sent.

- *Data*—This variable-length field contains the data. For traditional TFTP, the field contains 512 bytes—unless the packet is indicating an end-of-transfer, in which case the Data field contains less than 512 bytes. If the blocksize option is negotiated, the field size for data transmission can be other than 512 bytes. End-of-transfer will, as before, be indicated by a smaller field size.

All packets other than duplicate ACKs and termination DATA packages are acknowledged, unless a timeout occurs. A DATA packet acknowledges the ACK packet of the previous DATA packet. ACK or ERROR packets acknowledge WRQ and DATA packets, and DATA or ERROR packets acknowledge RRQ and ACK packets. An ACK packet that has a block number of zero acknowledges a WRQ.

The ACK package contains the following fields:

- *Opcode*—For ACK packets, this 16-bit field contains the value 4.

- *Block number*—The block number in an ACK packet echoes the block number of the DATA packet that it's acknowledging. This field contains a zero value if the ACK is acknowledging a WRQ.

An ERROR packet can be the acknowledgment of any other type of packet. It contains the following fields:

- *Opcode*—For ERROR packets, this 16-bit field contains the value 5.

- *Error code*—This 16-bit field contains an error code, as defined in Table 10.2.

- *ErrMsg*—This variable-length field contains a human-readable error message in netascii.

- *ErrMsg terminator*—This 8-bit field contains a zero value and indicates the end of the error message. It's sometimes considered to be part of the ErrMsg field rather than a separate field.

A user can issue TFTP commands from the Command Console. Typically, however, they're used by TFTP-based applications such as email packages.

The Trivial File Transfer Protocol Daemon

The TFTP Daemon (TFTPD) is an example of a TFTP-based service used by Windows 2000. The Windows 2000 Remote Installation Services (RIS) server uses this service to download the files that it needs to begin the remote installation process.

Table 10.2   TFTP error codes.

Error Code	Meaning
0	Undefined. See error message (if any).
1	File not found.
2	Access violation.
3	Disk full or allocation exceeded.
4	Illegal TFTP operation.
5	Unknown transfer identity.
6	File already exists.
7	No such user.

Hypertext Transfer Protocol

HTTP version 1.1, documented in RFC 2068, is the de facto standard for transferring World Wide Web (WWW or Web) documents. The protocol is generic and stateless and is designed to be extensible to almost any document format. It operates over TCP connections, typically using port 80, although another port (such as 8080) may be specified. After a connection is established, the client transmits a request message to the server, which sends a reply. HTTP is normally used by such applications as browsers.

The simplest HTTP function, or *method*, is GET, which retrieves information stored in a Web site on a Web server. Fully featured information systems, however, require more functionality, including search, update, and annotation. HTTP provides a set of methods that indicate the purpose of a request. It uses a Uniform Resource Identifier (URI), either as a Uniform Resource Locator (URL) or Uniform Resource Name (URN), to indicate the resource to which a method is to be applied. Messages are passed in a format similar to that used by Internet mail, as defined by the Multipurpose Internet Mail Extensions (MIME) standard—refer to RFCs 2045 through 2049.

HTTP is also used for communication between user agents and gateways to other Internet systems, including those supported by SMTP, NNTP, and FTP. It thus enables basic hypermedia access to resources that are available from diverse applications.

HTTP Methods

RFC 2616 defines a set of common HTTP methods. The document doesn't exclude additional methods, but warns that methods outside the common list "may not share the same semantics for separately extended clients and servers." In other words, if you define and use additional methods, there could be incompatibilities between some hosts and some servers. The common HTTP methods are as follows:

- *OPTIONS*—Enables a client to determine the options and/or requirements associated with a resource or the capabilities of a server, without implying a resource action or initiating a resource retrieval.

- *GET*—Retrieves the information (in the form of an *entity*) that's identified by the requested URI. If the URI identifies a data-producing process, the produced data is returned as the entity. A *conditional GET* request message includes an If-Modified-Since, If-Unmodified-Since, If-Match, If-None-Match, or If-Range header field. This enables cached entities to be refreshed without requiring multiple transfers or requesting data already held by the client. A *partial GET* requests that only part of the entity, specified by a Range header field, be transferred.

- *HEAD*—Identical to GET, except that the server doesn't return a message-body in the response. This method obtains information about the entity without transferring the entity-body itself and is used to test hypertext links for validity, accessibility, and recent modification.

- *POST*—Requests that the servers accept the entity enclosed in the request as a new subordinate of the resource identified by the requested URI (in the same way that a file placed in a directory is said to be a new subordinate of that directory). POST is used for resource annotation, for message posting (for example to a bulletin board), for submitting form data, and for extending a database through an append operation. The function performed by the POST method is determined by the server and is usually dependent on the URI.

- *PUT*—Requests that the entity enclosed in the request be stored under the requested URI. If the resource referred to in the URI already exists, the transmitted entity is considered to be a modified version. If the URI doesn't point to an existing resource and the requesting user can define the URI as a new resource, then the resource is created on the server.

- *DELETE*—Requests that the server delete the resource identified by the URI.

- *TRACE*—Invokes a remote loopback of the request message. The final recipient of the request reflects the received message back to the client. TRACE lets the client see what's being received at the other end of the request chain. This information can be used for testing or fault finding.

- *CONNECT*—A method name reserved for use with a proxy that can dynamically switch to being a tunnel, using, for example, Secure Sockets Layer (SSL) tunneling. A *proxy* is an intermediary program that acts both as a server and as a client for the purpose of making requests on behalf of other clients.

HTTP Status Codes

HTTP status codes are either used by the methods during normal operation or sent to the user if an error occurs. There are five status-code classifications:

- *Informational (1xx)*—Indicates a provisional (usually intermediate) response. These codes indicate that a method is proceeding normally, and an expected event has occurred. If an HTTP 1.1 server detects an HTTP 1.0 client, it won't send informational messages because these aren't defined for HTTP 1.0.

- *Successful (2xx)*—Indicates that the client's request was successfully received, understood, and accepted.

- *Redirection (3xx)*—Indicates that the user agent needs to take further action in order to fulfill the request. The action may be carried out automatically by the user agent (if the method used is GET or HEAD) or may require user intervention.

- *Client Error (4xx)*—Indicates that there is, or appears to be, a client error. Except when responding to a HEAD request, the message includes an explanation of the error and informs the user whether it's temporary or permanent.
- *Server Error (5xx)*—Indicates that the server is aware that it has generated an error or that it's incapable of performing the request. Except when responding to a HEAD request, the message includes an explanation of the error and informs the user whether it's temporary or permanent.

> **NOTE:** Web sites hosted on the Windows 2000 IIS server can be configured to send user-friendly error messages. The procedure for doing this is described in Chapter 12.

Table 10.3 lists the HTTP status codes and messages. For details of what each message means, refer to Section 10 of RFC 2616.

Table 10.3   HTTP status codes and messages.

Status Code	Message	Status Code	Message
100	Continue	404	Not Found
101	Switching Protocols	405	Method Not Allowed
200	OK	406	Not Acceptable
201	Created	407	Proxy Authentication Required
202	Accepted	408	Request Time-out
203	Non-Authoritative Information	409	Conflict
204	No Content	410	Gone
205	Reset Content	411	Length Required
206	Partial Content	412	Precondition Failed
300	Multiple Choices	413	Request Entity Too Large
301	Moved Permanently	414	Request-URI Too Large
302	Found	415	Unsupported Media Type
303	See Other	416	Requested range not satisfiable
304	Not Modified	417	Expectation Failed
305	Use Proxy	500	Internal Server Error
307	Temporary Redirect	501	Not Implemented
400	Bad Request	502	Bad Gateway
401	Unauthorized	503	Service Unavailable
402	Payment Required	504	Gateway Time-out
403	Forbidden	505	HTTP Version not supported

HTTP Packet Structure

HTTP packets are, on the whole, exceptionally complex. RFC 2616 takes 51 pages to define the HTTP packet header structure (section 14, pages 100 through 150). It's pointless to reproduce that sort of detail here. Instead, a typical HTTP GET packet is illustrated in Figure 10.3. This figure is generated from the capture file http.cap on the CD-ROM. The procedure for generating a similar capture file is given in the immediate solution "Capturing TCP Traffic" in Chapter 8.

Related solution:	Found on page:
Capturing TCP Traffic	249

Secure HTTP (HTTPS)

The Web is used extensively for the exchange of information on a worldwide basis, particularly for business purposes. This raises a number of security issues:

- *Server authentication*—Clients need to verify that the server with which they are communicating is the one it purports to be.
- *Client authentication*—Servers need to verify a client's identity and use this as a basis for access-control decisions.
- *Confidentiality*—Encryption of data between client and server is needed to prevent the interception of sensitive information sent over public Internet links.

The SSL version 3 (SSL3) and Transport Layer Security (TLS) protocols play an important role in addressing these needs. SSL3 and TLS are flexible security protocols that can be layered on top of transport protocols, such as HTTP. They rely on Public Key (PK)-based authentication technology and use PK-based key

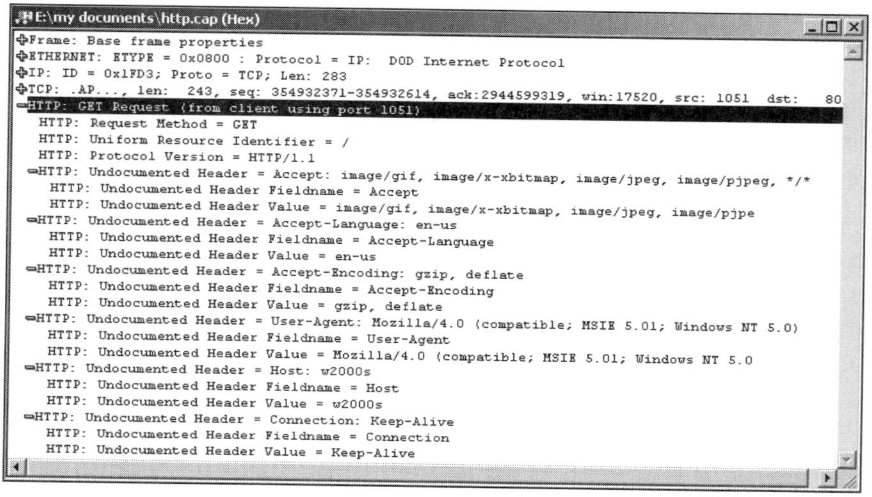

```
E:\my documents\http.cap (Hex)
+Frame: Base frame properties
+ETHERNET: ETYPE = 0x0800 : Protocol = IP:  DOD Internet Protocol
+IP: ID = 0x1FD3; Proto = TCP; Len: 283
+TCP: .AP..., len:  243, seq: 354932371-354932614, ack:2944599319, win:17520, src: 1051  dst:  80
-HTTP: GET Request (from client using port 1051)
  HTTP: Request Method = GET
  HTTP: Uniform Resource Identifier = /
  HTTP: Protocol Version = HTTP/1.1
 -HTTP: Undocumented Header = Accept: image/gif, image/x-xbitmap, image/jpeg, image/pjpeg, */*
   HTTP: Undocumented Header Fieldname = Accept
   HTTP: Undocumented Header Value = image/gif, image/x-xbitmap, image/jpeg, image/pjpe
 -HTTP: Undocumented Header = Accept-Language: en-us
   HTTP: Undocumented Header Fieldname = Accept-Language
   HTTP: Undocumented Header Value = en-us
 -HTTP: Undocumented Header = Accept-Encoding: gzip, deflate
   HTTP: Undocumented Header Fieldname = Accept-Encoding
   HTTP: Undocumented Header Value = gzip, deflate
 -HTTP: Undocumented Header = User-Agent: Mozilla/4.0 (compatible; MSIE 5.01; Windows NT 5.0)
   HTTP: Undocumented Header Fieldname = User-Agent
   HTTP: Undocumented Header Value = Mozilla/4.0 (compatible; MSIE 5.01; Windows NT 5.0
 -HTTP: Undocumented Header = Host: w2000s
   HTTP: Undocumented Header Fieldname = Host
   HTTP: Undocumented Header Value = w2000s
 -HTTP: Undocumented Header = Connection: Keep-Alive
   HTTP: Undocumented Header Fieldname = Connection
   HTTP: Undocumented Header Value = Keep-Alive
```

Figure 10.3 An HTTP GET packet.

negotiation to generate a unique encryption key for each client/server session. When SSL encryption is enabled for a Web site, the result is Secure HTTP, referred to as HTTPS. The procedure for setting up a secure Web site is described in the Immediate Solutions section of this chapter.

> **NOTE:** *IIS5 can be secured using protocols other than SSL3/TLS—for example, Fortezza, Digest Authentication, PKCS #7, and PKCS #10 (PKCS stands for Public Key Cryptography Standard). These are described in Chapter 12. The default Windows 2000 authentication protocol, Kerberos 5, is described in Chapter 11.*

Simple Mail Transport Protocol

SMTP, defined in RFC 821, is designed to transfer email reliably and efficiently. It's independent of the transmission protocol used and requires only a reliable ordered data stream channel. This means that SMTP will operate over (for example) the Network Control Program (NCP) transport service or the Network Independent Transport Service (NITS), as well as over TCP. SMTP, therefore, can relay mail across different transport service environments.

A transport service provides an Interprocess Communication Environment (IPCE) that can cover one network, several networks, or a subnetwork. Email is an interprocess communication that can send mail between hosts on different transport systems by relaying through a process connected to two (or more) IPCEs.

How SMTP Works

When a user makes an email request (i.e., sends an email message), the following sequence of events occurs:

1. The SMTP sender establishes a two-way transmission channel to a receiver-SMTP that may be either the ultimate or an intermediate destination.
2. The SMTP sender sends a MAIL command that indicates the sender of the mail.
3. If the SMTP receiver can accept mail, it responds with an OK reply.
4. The SMTP sender sends an RCPT command that identifies the recipient of the mail.
5. If the SMTP receiver can accept mail for that recipient, it responds with an OK reply; if not, it responds with a reply rejecting that recipient (but not the whole mail transaction, because the sender and receiver can negotiate several recipients).
6. When the recipients have been negotiated, the SMTP sender sends the mail data.
7. If the SMTP receiver processes the mail data successfully, it responds with an OK reply.

10. Application Level Protocols and Utilities

> **NOTE:** *The RFC document uses the terms "sender-SMTP" and "receiver-SMTP" rather than SMTP sender and SMTP receiver.*

If the sending and receiving hosts are connected to the same transport service, SMTP can transmit mail directly from sender to receiver. Otherwise, the message is transmitted via one or more SMTP relay servers. In the latter case, the SMTP relay server must receive the name of the ultimate destination host as well as the destination mailbox name.

SMTP can implement a forwarding service that's used when the path specified by the RCPT command is incorrect but the SMTP receiver knows the correct destination. In this case, one of the following replies is sent, depending on the identities of the sender and recipient and whether the SMTP receiver can take responsibility for forwarding the message:

- 251 User not local; will forward to *forward-path*.
- 551 User not local; please try *forward-path*.

The SMTP commands VRFY and EXPN, respectively, verify a username and expand a mailing list. Both commands have character strings as arguments. The string for the VRFY command is a username, and the response must include the user's mailbox and may include the full username.

The string for the EXPN command identifies a mailing list, and the response must include the user's mailbox and may include the full username.

> **NOTE:** *The RFC document is, quite deliberately, ambivalent about the term "username". In some email systems, the username is the same as the user's mailbox. If an email system chooses to use some other string as a username, then this is permitted by the specification, provided the strings for the VRFY command and EXPN response also identify the user's mailbox.*

Sending and Mailing

Some hosts deliver messages to a user's terminal (provided the user is active on the host) rather than to the user's mailbox. Delivery to a mailbox is called *mailing*; delivery to a terminal is called *sending*. The sending and mailing implementations are almost identical and are typically combined in SMTP. However, users should be able to control whether messages are written on their terminals, and RFC 821 defines sending commands (although they're not required for the minimum implementation).

The following commands can be used in a mail transaction instead of the MAIL command to support the sending function:

- *SEND*—Delivers mail data to the user's terminal. If the user isn't active on the host (or isn't accepting terminal messages), a 450 reply (see Table 10.5) may be returned.

- *SOML (send or mail)*—Delivers mail to the user's terminal if the user is active on the host and is accepting terminal messages. Otherwise, the mail is delivered to the user's mailbox.

- *SAML (send and mail)*—Delivers mail to the user's terminal if the user is active on the host and is accepting terminal messages. The mail is delivered to the user's mailbox whether or not it's delivered to the terminal.

SMTP Commands and Messages

Some of the SMTP commands have already been described when SMTP functionality was discussed. However, for convenience, all the SMTP commands are listed, with brief descriptions, in Table 10.4. Table 10.5 lists the messages, or *reply codes*, that can be generated during SMTP operation.

Additional SMTP RFCs

Additional RFC documents provide information about or propose extensions to, RFC 821. These either are proposed standards, or they are experimental or

Table 10.4 SMTP commands.

Command	Description
HELO	Initiates a connection and identifies the SMTP sender to the SMTP receiver.
MAIL	Initiates a mail transaction.
RCPT	Identifies an individual recipient.
DATA	Identifies the lines following the command as mail data from the sender.
RSET	Aborts the current mail transaction.
SEND	Delivers mail to a terminal.
SOML	Delivers mail to a terminal. If this operation fails, the mail is delivered to a mailbox.
SAML	Delivers mail to a terminal. The mail is also delivered to a mailbox.
VRFY	Verifies a username.
EXPN	Expands a mailing list.
HELP	Causes the receiver to send helpful information.
NOOP	Requires that the receiver send an OK reply, but otherwise specifies no actions.
QUIT	Requires that the receiver send an OK reply and then close the transmission channel.
TURN	Requests that the receiver take on the role of the sender. If an OK response is received, the sender then becomes the receiver.

Table 10.5   SMTP reply codes.

Reply code	Meaning
211	System status or system help reply.
214	Help message.
220	Service ready.
221	Service closing transmission channel.
250	Requested mail action okay, completed.
251	User not local; will forward to *forward-path*.
354	Start mail input.
421	Service not available, closing transmission channel.
450	Requested mail action not taken: mailbox unavailable.
451	Requested action aborted: local error in processing.
452	Requested action not taken: insufficient system storage.
500	Syntax error, command unrecognized.
501	Syntax error in parameters or arguments.
502	Command not implemented.
503	Bad sequence of commands.
504	Command parameter not implemented.
550	Requested action not taken: mailbox unavailable.
551	User not local; please try *forward-path*.
552	Requested mail action aborted: exceeded storage allocation.
553	Requested action not taken: mailbox name not allowed.
554	Transaction failed.

informational. For more information, refer to the following RFCs: 2645, 2554, 2502, 2487, 2442, 2197, 2034, 1985, 1891, 1870, 1869, 1846, 1845, 1830, 1652, and 1428.

Post Office Protocol

POP3, defined in RFC 1939 updated by RFCs 1957 and 2449, permits a client that may have limited resources to access a maildrop on a server dynamically and (typically) to retrieve mail that the server is holding for it. The protocol requires few resources and has limited functionality. Normally, mail is downloaded and then deleted, but not otherwise manipulated.

A client that wants to use the POP3 service establishes a connection to TCP port 110 on the POP3 server. When the connection is established, the POP3 server sends a welcome message. The client and server then exchange commands and responses (respectively) until the connection is closed or aborted. POP3 operation makes use of *states* and proceeds as follows:

1. The TCP connection is opened, and the client receives the welcome message.
2. The session enters the AUTHORIZATION state.
3. The client identifies itself to the server, which then acquires resources associated with the client's maildrop.
4. The session enters the TRANSACTION state.
5. The client requests that actions be carried out on the server.
6. The client issues the QUIT command.
7. The session enters the UPDATE state.
8. The POP3 server releases any resources acquired during the TRANSACTION state and sends a goodbye message.
9. The TCP connection is closed.

NOTE: *If the server has an autologout timer and that timer expires because of client inactivity, the server closes the TCP connection without removing any messages or sending any response to the client.*

POP3 Commands

Each POP3 command is valid in a specified state. Table 10.6 lists each command and the state in which it's valid, along with a brief description. The APOP, TOP, and UIDL commands are optional.

TIP: *MD5 is a Message Digest hash algorithm that compresses messages in a secure manner before encrypting them with a private key. Descriptions and source code for Message Digest algorithms are given in RFCs 1319 to 1321. More information is available from the Rivest-Sharmir-Adelman (RSA) Laboratories site at **www.rsasecurity.com/rsalabs**.*

POP3 Updates

RFC 1957 is informational. RFC 2595, however, adds two additional (optional) POP3 commands. The CAPA command can take a number of tags and will return information about the capabilities of a POP3 site (for example, the UIDL tag will indicate whether or not the UIDL command is enabled).

The AUTH command enables secure user authentication using the Simple Authentication and Security Layer (SASL) method, as specified in RFC 2222. Refer to the RFC documents for further details.

Table 10.6   POP3 commands.

Command	Valid State	Description
USER	AUTHORIZATION	Identifies a mailbox.
PASS	AUTHORIZATION	Supplies a server/mailbox-specific password.
QUIT	AUTHORIZATION	Terminates the session without entering the UPDATE state.
STAT	TRANSACTION	Provides information (for example, size and number of messages) about the maildrop. This is called the *drop listing*.
LIST	TRANSACTION	Specifies the message number and message size. This is called the *scan listing*.
RETR	TRANSACTION	The client sends a message number using this command. The server responds with the message content.
DELE	TRANSACTION	The client sends a message number using this command, and the server marks the message as deleted. The message isn't actually deleted until the transaction enters the UPDATE state.
NOOP	TRANSACTION	When the client sends this message, the server gives a positive response, but no other information.
RSET	TRANSACTION	Unmarks any messages that have been marked as deleted on the server.
QUIT	TRANSACTION	Causes the session to enter the UPDATE state. The client then sends a goodbye message, and the connection is closed.
APOP	AUTHORIZATION	Identifies a mailbox and an MD5 string for authentication and replay protection.
TOP	TRANSACTION	Specifies a message number and a number (*n*) of lines. The server returns the first (or top) *n* lines of the message.
UIDL	TRANSACTION	Provides a message number and unique identity, which together form the *unique-id listing* for the message.

Network News Transfer Protocol

NNTP, specified in RFC 977, is used for the distribution, browsing, retrieval, and posting of news articles using a reliable, stream-based transmission protocol (such as TCP) and SMTP-like commands and responses. TCP port 119 is used by the NNTP service.

News articles are stored in a central database, and subscribers select only those items they want to read. Indexing is enabled, as are cross-referencing and the expiry of old articles. Typically, NNTP operates in a client/server environment, with a single central depository for news information. However, servers exchanging news articles are provided with an interactive mechanism for deciding what to transmit.

Responses to NNTP commands can be either textual (the news articles) or status reports preceded by a three-digit number. Status reports are similar to the SMTP reply codes listed in Table 10.5 and are normally intercepted by the client software, which converts them to more user-friendly messages.

NNTP Commands

The NNTP commands are listed in Table 10.7. RFC 977 doesn't specify any optional commands.

As with SMTP and POP3 commands, NNTP commands are used by application programs rather than directly by the user. Details of command syntax and message reply codes are given in RFC 977. The structures for text-based protocols, such as SMTP, POP3, and NNTP, are defined in RFC 822, updated by RFCs 1123, 1138, 1148, 1327, and 2156.

> **NOTE:** SMTP, POP3, and NNTP server options for the Dynamic Host Configuration Protocol (DHCP) can be added to support DHCP clients that recognize them. These options are reserved and specified for use in RFC 2132, but are not currently predefined in Windows 2000 DHCP Manager. DHCP is described in Chapter 13.

Table 10.7   NNTP commands.

Command	Description
ARTICLE	Specifies an article by either number or title. The server returns the article (or an error code).
BODY	Specifies an article by either number or title. The server returns the article body text.
GROUP	Specifies the name of a newsgroup. The server returns the numbers of the first and last articles in the group and an estimate of the number of articles in the group.
HEAD	Specifies an article by either number or title. The server returns the article header.
HELP	Specifies a command. The server returns a brief description.
IHAVE	Informs the server that the client has an article (specified by a message identifier). The server informs the client whether or not it wants a copy.
LAST	Instructs the server to set the current-article pointer to the previous article in the current newsgroup.
LIST	Instructs the server to returns a list of valid newsgroups and associated information.
NEWSGROUPS	The server returns a list of newsgroups created since a specified date and time. Optionally, the command also specifies a list of distribution groups, and the server returns a list of newsgroups that match the distribution groups.
NEWNEWS	Specifies a date, time, and one or more newsgroups. The server returns a list of message identities of articles posted to or received by the specified newsgroup(s) since the date and time.

(continued)

Table 10.7   NNTP commands (continued).

Command	Description
NEXT	Instructs the server to set the current-article pointer to the next article in the current newsgroup.
POST	The client sends this command (without an argument) to apply for permission to submit an article. If permission is granted, the client posts the article, verbatim, to the sender.
QUIT	The server acknowledges this command, then closes the connection to the client.
SLAVE	Informs the server that the client connection is to a slave server, rather than a user. This function could (for example) be used to give priority to requests from slave servers because they are serving more than one user.
STAT	Specifies an article by either number or title. The server returns the article identity and sets the current article pointer.

NOTE: *The IHAVE command is intended for articles that have already been posted elsewhere, perhaps on another server, and that have a message identity. The POST command is normally used for new messages.*

Telnet

The Telnet protocol is defined in RFC 854, with options and enhancements specified in RFCs 855 through 861, 885, 927, 933, 946, 1041, 1043, 1053, 1073, 1079, 1091, 1096, 1372, 1411, 1412, 1416, 1572, 2066, and 2217, and further information provided in RFCs 1143, 1205, and 1571. It provides a bidirectional, 8-bit, byte-oriented communications facility and gives a standard method of interfacing terminal devices with terminal-oriented processes. Telnet is typically (but not exclusively) used for terminal emulation. The protocol has been greatly enhanced and extended since it was first introduced, and only the basic functionality is described here. The Windows 2000 telnet utility provides telnet client and server services and is described later in this chapter.

Telnet uses TCP to transmit data interspersed with Telnet control information. The Telnet server listens for connection requests on TCP port 23. When a connection is established, Telnet creates a Network Virtual Terminal (NVT) at both ends of the connection. This eliminates the need for the server and client hosts to store the characteristics of each other's terminals. All hosts map their local device characteristics and conventions so that they appear to be accessing an NVT over the network.

The protocol is readily extensible, with many options (hence the long list of RFCs). The client and server can negotiate the options to be used during the Telnet session, which enables servers to offer services, over and above those available within an NVT, to clients that have sophisticated terminals that can take advantage of these services. This process is known as *subnegotiation* and starts with the subnegotiation (SB) command.

Standard Telnet Functions

Telnet can connect a user to a wide variety of servers, which may have different methods of carrying out the same functions. It provides standard representations for five of the most common functions, as follows:

- *Interrupt Process (IP)*—Suspends, interrupts, aborts, or terminates the operation of a user process. This function is used, for example, when a process is in an unending loop.

- *Abort Output (AO)*—Allows a process that's generating output to run to completion without sending the output to the user's terminal. This function typically clears any output already produced, but not yet printed or displayed. If there are buffers external to the system that also need to be cleared, this is done using the Telnet Synch signal (see below).

- *Are You There (AYT)*—Provides the user with visible evidence that the system is still up and running.

- *Erase Character (EC)*—Deletes the last preceding undeleted character from the stream of data being supplied by the user. Typically, this function is used to edit keyboard input when typing mistakes are made.

- *Erase Line (EL)*—Deletes all the data in the current input line.

The Telnet Synch Signal

A Telnet Synch signal consists of a TCP Urgent notification (see Chapter 8) used with the Telnet DATA MARK (DM) command. In this mode, the data stream is immediately scanned for "interesting" signals; that is, IP, AO, or AYT (but not EC or EL) discarding intervening data. The DM command indicates that an interesting signal has been received, and the recipient can now process the data stream in the normal way. The DM command bytes are the final and typically the only data in the Synch signal.

One effect of the Synch signal is that all characters (except Telnet commands) that are currently buffered between the sender and recipient are deleted. This mechanism is the standard way to clear a data path.

Telnet Commands

Telnet commands consist of a sequence of at least 2 bytes. The first is an escape code (i.e., the nonprintable ASCII code 255) known as the Interpret as Command (IAC). This is followed by the code for the command. In commands that deal with option subnegotiation (WILL, WON'T, DO, DON'T), a third byte specifies the option. Table 10.8 lists the standard Telnet commands, with the ASCII code and a brief description of each.

Table 10.8   Telnet commands.

Command	ASCII Code	Description
SE	240	End of subnegotiation parameters.
NOP	241	No operation.
DM	242	Used in the Synch signal to indicate that normal data processing can recommence.
BREAK	243	Equivalent to a Break or Attention key code in a data sequence.
INTERRUPT PROCESS	244	Implements the IP function.
ABORT OUTPUT	245	Implements the AO function.
ARE YOU THERE	246	Implements the AYT function.
ERASE CHARACTER	247	Implements the EC function.
ERASE LINE	248	Implements the EL function.
GO AHEAD (GA)	249	When a process at one end of a Telnet connection can't proceed without input from the other end, it sends a GA command.
SB	250	Indicates the start of option subnegotiation.
WILL	251	Indicates that the sender wants to use or is currently using the specified option.
WON'T	252	Indicates that the sender refuses to use or to continue using the specified option.
DO	253	Requests that the receiver use or indicates that it's expected to use the specified option.
DON'T	254	Requests that the receiver stop using or indicates that it's no longer expected to use the specified option.

The Windows 2000 Connectivity Utilities

The Windows 2000 TCP/IP connectivity utilities enable files to be transferred from one Microsoft host to another and between Microsoft hosts and foreign TCP/IP systems (such as Unix hosts). These utilities include the following:

- *Ftp*—Transfers any size of files between Windows 2000 and a computer running FTP server software.
- *Tftp*—Transfers small files between Windows 2000 and a computer running TFTP server software.
- *Telnet*—Uses terminal-based login to access remote network devices that are running Telnet server software.
- *Rexec*—Executes processes on remote computers.

- *Rsh*—Runs commands on a computer (typically a Unix host) running Remote Shell (RSH) server software.

- *Rcp*—Copies files between Windows 2000 and computers running Remote Copy Protocol (RCP) server software (typically Unix hosts).

- Lpr—Sends print jobs to remote Unix printers managed by Line Printer Daemon (LPD) print server software.

- Lpq—Views print queues on remote Unix printers managed by LPD print server software.

The FTP Utility

This utility provides a command-line interface that uses FTP to transfer files to and from a computer running an FTP server service (for example, a Windows 2000 IIS5 server). The **ftp** command establishes a connection and creates a subenvironment in which you can use the subcommands provided by the ftp utility—that is, you enter these subcommands from the ftp> prompt. You can then return to the Windows 2000 command prompt by using either the **quit** or **bye** subcommand. The syntax of the **ftp** command is:

```
ftp [-v] [-n] [-i] [-d] [-g] [-s:filename] [-a] [-w:windowsize] [computer]
```

where the parameters are as follows:

- *-v*—Suppresses the display of remote server responses.

- *-n*—Suppresses auto-logon on initial connection. A user who subsequently enters a subcommand that requires authorization will be prompted to log on with a username and password.

- *-i*—Turns off interactive prompting during multiple file transfers.

- *-d*—Displays all ftp subcommands passed between the client and server. This feature is used for debugging.

- *-g*—Disables file name *globbing*. Globbing permits the use of wildcard characters (* and ?) in local file and path names.

- *-s:filename*—Specifies a text file containing ftp subcommands that run automatically after a connection is established.

- *-a*—Enables the data connection to use any local interface.

- *-w:windowsize*—Overrides the default transfer buffer size of 4096.

- *computer*—Specifies the computer name or IP address of the remote computer. This must be the last parameter on the line.

The ftp subcommands are listed in Table 10.9. Sometimes two commands implement the same function; this is for compatibility with other systems.

Table 10.9   Ftp subcommands.

Command	Parameters	Description
!	None	Returns to the Windows 2000 command shell. Used to access MS-DOS commands without exiting the ftp subsystem (for example, **!dir** lists the local directory).
?	*Subcommand name*	Describes the subcommand, or lists all the subcommands if used without a parameter. Identical to the **help** subcommand.
append	*Local file, remote file*	Appends a local file to a file on the remote computer. If the remote file isn't specified, it's assumed to have the same file name as the local file.
ascii	None	Sets the file transfer mode to ascii (the default).
bell	None	Toggles a bell (or beep), which indicates that a transfer command is completed. By default, the bell is off.
binary	None	Sets the file transfer mode to binary.
bye	None	Ends the FTP session with the remote computer and exits the ftp subsystem. Identical to **quit**.
cd	*Directory name*	Changes the working directory on the remote computer.
close	None	Ends the FTP session with the remote computer and returns to the ftp subsystem.
debug	None	Toggles debugging. When debugging is on, each FTP command (protocol commands rather than ftp subcommands) sent to the remote computer is printed. Debugging is off by default.
delete	*Filename*	Deletes files on the remote computer.
dir	*Remote directory, local file*	Lists the remote directory's files and subdirectories to a local file or to the screen (if a local file isn't specified). If a remote directory isn't specified, the current directory is listed.
disconnect	None	Disconnects from the remote computer and returns to the ftp subsystem. Identical to **close**.
get	*Remote file, local file*	Copies a remote file to the local computer using the current file transfer type. If a local file isn't specified, the destination file name will be the same as the source file name.

(continued)

***Table 10.9   Ftp subcommands* (continued).**

Command	Parameters	Description
glob	None	Toggles file name globbing. Globbing is on by default (unless the **-g** switch is used in the ftp command).
hash	None	Toggles the printing of a hash mark (#) for each 2,048-byte data block transferred. Hash mark printing is off by default.
help	*Subcommand name*	Describes the subcommand or lists all the subcommands (if used without a parameter). Identical to the **?** subcommand.
lcd	*Directory name*	Changes the working directory on the local computer. By default, this is the directory from which the ftp session was started.
literal	*Argument*	Sends arguments, verbatim, to the remote FTP server.
ls	*Directory name*	Displays an abbreviated list of the files and subdirectories in a remote directory. If no directory name is specified, the contents of the current remote working directory are listed.
mdelete	*Remote files*	Deletes files on the remote computer.
mdir	*Remote directories, local file*	Lists the contents of one or several remote directories. The listing is placed in the local file specified. To list the current remote directory, specify "-" for the *remote directories* parameter. To list to the screen, specify "-" for the *local file* parameter.
mget	*Remote files*	Copies one or more remote files to the local computer using the current file transfer type.
mkdir	*Directory name*	Creates a remote directory.
mls	*Remote files, local file*	Generates an abbreviated list of the files and subdirectories in a remote directory and places the list in a local file. Specify the remote files as "-" to use the current working directory on the remote computer. Specify the local file as "-" to display the list on the screen.
mput	*Local files*	Copies one or more local files to the remote computer using the current file transfer type.

(continued)

Table 10.9   Ftp subcommands (continued).

Command	Parameters	Description
open	*Computer, port*	Connects to an FTP server specified by IP address or computer name. Optionally, a port number on the server can also be specified.
prompt	None	Toggles prompting. By default, ftp prompts during multiple file transfers to allow you to retrieve or store files selectively. If prompting is turned off, **mget** and **mput** transfer all files.
put	*Local file, Remote file*	Copies a local file to the remote computer using the current file transfer type. If no remote file is specified, the remote file takes the same file name as the local file.
pwd	None	Displays the current directory on the remote computer.
quit	None	Ends the FTP session with the remote computer and exits ftp. Identical to **bye**.
quote	*Argument*	Sends arguments, verbatim, to the remote FTP server. Identical to **literal**.
recv	*Remote file, local file*	Copies a remote file to the local computer using the current file transfer type. If a local file isn't specified, the destination file name will be the same as the source file name. Identical to **get**.
remotehelp	*Command name*	Displays help for remote commands. If the command name isn't specified, a list of all remote commands is displayed.
rename	*Filename, new filename*	Renames remote files.
rmdir	*Directory*	Deletes a remote directory.
send	*Local file, Remote file*	Copies a local file to the remote computer using the current file transfer type. If no remote file is specified, the remote file takes the same file name as the local file. Identical to **put**.
status	None	Displays the current status of FTP toggles and connections.
trace	None	Toggles packet tracing. Trace displays the route that each packet takes during an ftp subcommand. Tracing is off by default.

(continued)

Table 10.9   Ftp subcommands (continued).

Command	Parameters	Description
type	*Ascii* or *binary*	Specifies the file transfer mode (or type). If no parameter is specified, the current transfer mode is displayed.
user	*User name, password, account*	Specifies the username, with password and user account, used to log on to the remote computer.
verbose	None	Toggles verbose mode. By default, verbose mode is on and all ftp responses are displayed, as are statistics regarding the efficiency of the transfer when the transfer completes.

Creating a new FTP site, logging on to an FTP site, and using the ftp utility are all described in the Immediate Solutions section of this chapter.

The Tftp Utility

The tftp utility uses UDP to transfer files to and from a remote computer running the TFTP service, without establishing a connection. The syntax of the command is:

```
tftp [-i] computer [get | put] source_filename [destination_filename]
```

where the parameters are as follows:

- *-i*—Specifies binary image transfer mode (also called octet). If this parameter isn't specified, the transfer mode is ascii (or netascii). The mail transfer mode isn't supported by the Windows 2000 tftp utility.

- *computer*—Specifies the local or remote computer by IP address or computer name.

- *get*—Copies the file *source_filename* on the remote computer to the file *destination_filename* on the local computer.

- *put*—Copies the file *source_filename* on the local computer to the file *destination_filename* on the remote computer.

- *source_filename*—Specifies the file to transfer.

- *destination_filename*—Specifies where to transfer the file. If *destination_filename* is omitted, it's assumed to be the same name as *source_filename*.

Because TFTP doesn't support user authentication, the user must be logged on using an account recognized by the remote computer and must have the appropriate read/write permissions to the files accessed on the remote computer.

The Telnet Utility

The Windows 2000 telnet utility enables a user on a telnet client to connect to a telnet server, log on to the server, and use command-line, character-mode applications on the server as if he or she were sitting in front of it.

Telnet client supports NT LAN Manager (NTLM) authentication. If this option is enabled, integrated Windows 2000 security can be used and authentication can occur without usernames and passwords being sent in clear text. If the user is logged on to a telnet client workstation using an account that's authenticated in the server's domain, then he or she won't be prompted for a username and password when using the telnet client utility to log on to a telnet server. The user must, of course, have logon rights to that server.

TIP: *If you're setting up an account on a telnet server to enable a user to log on from a telnet client, disable the User must change password at next logon feature. Otherwise, logon from the telnet client fails, and the user needs to log on directly to the server (or to the server's domain) to change the password.*

An administrator can use the telnet server admin utility to start or stop telnet server, obtain telnet server information, get a list of current users, terminate a user's session, or change telnet server Registry settings. Table 10.10 lists the telnet server admin options. Table 10.11 gives details of the Registry settings you can change.

WARNING!   *Careless Registry editing can severely damage your operating system.*

If you change the default domain account, the setting takes effect only when the telnet server is restarted. Starting and stopping the telnet server is described in the Immediate Solutions section of this chapter, as is changing the authentication mode.

Table 10.10   Telnet server admin options.

Option	Name	Description
0	Quit this application	Ends the telnet server admin session.
1	List current users	Lists the connected telnet clients by username, domain, remote computer, session ID, and log time.
2	Terminate session	Terminates the selected user's session.
3	Display/change Registry settings	Puts the utility into Registry settings mode. See Table 10.11.
4	Start	Starts telnet server.
5	Stop	Stops telnet server.

Table 10.11   Telnet server admin Registry setting options.

Option	Name	Description and Allowed Values	Default Value
0	Exit this menu	Returns to the original telnet server admin utility options.	N/A
1	AllowTrustedDomain	If set to 1, allows access to domain users from domains with a trust relationship; if set to 0, these users are forbidden access	1
2	AltKeyMapping	Allows for ALT key functionality (VT100 terminals only). If set to 1, Ctrl+-A is treated as Alt for these terminals.	1
3	DefaultDomain	May be set to any domain that has a trust relationship with the local domain. If AllowTrustedDomain is set to 1 and you want the local domain to be the default, set this value to ".".	Null
4	DefaultShell	Sets the path location for the shell installation.	%Systemroot%\System32\Cmd.exe /q /k
5	LogonScript	Sets the path location for the (optional) telnet server logon script.	%Systemroot%\System32\login.cmd
6	MaxFailedLogins	Sets the maximum number of failed logon attempts before a connection is terminated.	3
7	NTLM	Authentication options. If 0, NTLM authentication isn't used; if 1, the server tries NTLM authentication first and, if it fails, prompts for a username and password; if 2, only NTLM authentication is used.	2
8	TelnetPort	Sets the port on which the telnet server listens for telnet requests.	23

> **NOTE:**   *The Windows 2000 telnet server supports a maximum of two telnet clients at any given time. The Microsoft Services for Unix add-on pack supports a maximum of 63 clients. More details about this add-on pack can be found at* ***www.microsoft.com/WINDOWS2000/sfu/default.asp***.

The Rexec Utility

The Windows 2000 rexec (remote execute) utility executes commands on remote computers running the REXEC service. The **rexec** command authenticates the username on the remote computer before executing the specified command. Rexec can be used, for example, to run diagnostic utilities on a computer that has a faulty keyboard or keyboard driver. The syntax of the command is

```
rexec computer [-l username] [-n] command
```

where the parameters are as follows:

- *computer*—Specifies the remote computer on which to run the command specified by **command**.

- *-l username*—Specifies the username on the remote computer. If this parameter is omitted, the logged-on username is used.

- *-n*—Redirects the input of the **rexec** command to NULL.

- *command*—Specifies the command to run.

The Rsh Utility

The Windows 2000 rsh (remote shell) utility runs commands on remote computers running the RSH service—typically computers that have Posix-compliant operating systems, such as Unix. The syntax of the command is

```
rsh computer [-l username] [-n] command
```

where the parameters are the same as those of the **rexec** command (see above).

The Rcp Utility

The Windows 2000 rcp (remote copy) utility copies files between a Windows 2000 computer and a system running the Remote Shell Daemon (RSHD). RSHD is available on Unix computers, and the Windows 2000 computer participates only as the system from which the **rcp** command is issued. The syntax of the command is

```
rcp [-a | -b] [-h] [-r] source1 source2 ... sourceN destination
```

where the parameters are as follows:

- *-a*—Specifies ascii transfer mode (the default).

- *-b*—Specifies binary image transfer mode.

- *-h*—Transfers hidden source files. If this parameter isn't specified, files marked with the hidden attribute on the Windows 2000 computer are treated as if they don't exist.

- *-r*—Copies the contents of all subdirectories on the source to the destination recursively. Both the source and destination must be directories. If the source isn't a directory, there will be no recursion.

- *source*—Specifies one or more source files. This parameter takes the form [*computer*[.*user*]:]*filename* (note the "." and ":" separators). If the [*computer*[.*user*]:] portion is omitted, the computer is assumed to be the local computer. If the [.*user*] portion is omitted, the username of the currently logged-on Windows 2000 user is assumed.

- *destination*—Specifies the destination file. This takes the same form as the source parameter.

The Lpr Utility

The lpr (line printer remote) connection utility is used to print a file to a computer running the Line Printer Daemon (LPD) service. In Windows 2000, this is a utility that enables a Windows 2000 host to send jobs to (for example) a Unix print server. A TCP/IP printer can also be installed on a Windows 2000 print server. In this case, a Unix client can use the **lpr** command to send a print job to the Windows 2000 print server. The command syntax is

```
lpr -Sserver -Pprinter [-Cclass] [-Jjobname] [-Ooption] filename
```

where the parameters are as follows:

- *-Sserver*—Specifies the computer name or IP address of the print server.
- *-Pprinter*—Specifies the name of the printer.
- *-Cclass*—Specifies a class. This parameter is used for banner pages.
- *-Jjobname*—Specifies the name of the job.
- *-Ooption*—Specifies the type of file. By default, this is ascii. A binary file type is specified by Ol (lower case "l").
- *filename*—Specifies the name of the file to be printed.

The Lpq Utility

The lpq (line printer queue) utility is used to obtain the status of a print queue on a print server running the LPD service. The command syntax is

```
lpq -Sserver -Pprinter [-l]
```

where the parameters are as follows:

- *-Sserver*—Specifies the computer name or IP address of the print server.
- *-Pprinter*—Specifies the name of the printer.
- *-l*—Specifies that a detailed status report should be given.

Immediate Solutions

Transferring Files Using the FTP Utility

In this set of procedures you'll use the ftp utility to transfer files from and to an FTP site and to list the contents of the site's default directory. To do this, you'll first bind an additional IP number to your Network Interface Card (NIC) and use this to set up a new FTP site. If you already have an FTP site that you can use for this purpose, then you don't need to carry out the first two procedures.

These procedures accept the default FTP site configuration. The FTP site Properties dialog box, used for site configuration, is described in Chapter 12.

Binding an Additional IP Address to an NIC

To bind an additional IP address to the NIC of your IIS5 server, proceed as follows:

1. Log on to the IIS5 server as an administrator.
2. Access Start|Settings|Network and Dial-up Connections and click Local Area Connection.
3. Click Properties and select Internet Protocol (TCP/IP).
4. Click Properties. The Internet Protocol (TCP/IP) Properties dialog box appears.
5. Click Advanced. On the IP Settings tab, click the Add button under the IP addresses box.
6. Specify an additional IP address and subnet mask, as shown in Figure 10.4. Click Add.
7. Click OK to close each of the dialog boxes.

Related solution:	*Found on page:*
Configuring TCP/IP for a Local Area Connection	24

Creating an FTP Site

To create a new FTP site for use with the ftp utility, proceed as follows:

1. Log on to the IIS5 server as an administrator.
2. Access Start|Programs|Accessories and start Windows Explorer.

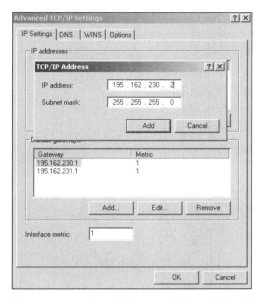

Figure 10.4   Specifying an additional IP address.

3. Create a new folder called (for example) ftpfold. This will be the default directory for your new site and is typically (but not necessarily) a subfolder of %Systemroot%\InetPub.

4. Create a number of files in this folder, either by copying them from other folders or by using the Windows Explorer File menu. Create more than two text (.TXT) files and ensure that one of these is called fred.txt. Ensure that none of the .TXT files are called mary.txt.

5. Access Start|Programs|Administrative Tools and click Internet Services Manager.

6. Right click *server-name*, click New, and select FTP Site.

7. Type a description for the new site. Click Next.

8. In the IP address drop-down box, select the IP address that you bound to the NIC in the previous procedure. Click Next.

9. Click Browse and specify the folder that you created in Step 3 as the default folder. Click Next.

10. Ensure that both the Read and Write checkboxes are checked. Click Next.

11. Click Finish. Ensure that the new site is present in the left pane of the MMC snap-in and that the site is started.

12. Exit from the MMC snap-in.

> ***WARNING!*** *This procedure assumes that you're creating a private FTP site for internal use. You create a public Internet site in the same way, but in this case the site name and IP address must be registered with the Internet Network Information Center (InterNIC) at **www.internic.net.***

Transferring Files to and from an FTP Client

The previous two procedures set up an FTP site that you can transfer files to and from. To use the ftp file transfer utility, proceed as follows:

1. Log on to a Windows 2000 computer in your domain, other than the IIS5 server.

> ***NOTE:*** *You don't need to log on as an administrator to use the ftp utility. You can log on as an ordinary user, and/or you can log on to a host in another domain. If you want to, you can carry out this procedure on the IIS5 server itself, but this never seems quite so convincing.*

---

2. Access Start|Programs|Accessories and start Windows Explorer.

3. Create a new folder called (for example) myfolder.

4. Create the text file mary.txt in that folder.

5. Access Start|Programs|Accessories and click Command Prompt.

6. Use the MSDOS **cd** command to navigate to the folder that you created in Step 3.

7. Enter **ftp *ipnumber***, where *ipnumber* is the IP number of the new FTP site that you created in the previous procedure.

8. You're prompted for a username. Enter **anonymous**.

9. You're prompted for a password. Press the Enter key (blank password).

10. You're informed that the Anonymous user has been logged in. Enter **dir**. The directory listing for the default FTP directory appears.

11. Enter **get fred.txt**. The file fred.txt is copied to your local folder.

12. Enter **!dir** to list the local directory. Check that fred.txt is listed. Figure 10.5 shows the output for a successful **get** operation (or download).

13. Enter **bell**.

14. Enter **mget *.txt**. The rest of the text files in the FTP site's default directory are copied to your local folder. You're prompted for each file. A "bell" sounds when all the text files are transferred.

15. Enter **prompt**.

16. Enter **mget ***. All the files in the FTP site's default directory are copied to your local folder without prompting.

```
Command Prompt - ftp 195.162.230.2                              _ □ ×
G:\myfolder>ftp 195.162.230.2
Connected to 195.162.230.2.
220 W2000S Microsoft FTP Service (Version 5.0).
User (195.162.230.2:(none)): anonymous
331 Anonymous access allowed, send identity (e-mail name) as password.
Password:
230 Anonymous user logged in.
ftp> dir
200 PORT command successful.
150 Opening ASCII mode data connection for /bin/ls.
05-15-00  10:38AM                  0 alf.txt
05-15-00  10:38AM                  0 fred.txt
06-04-99  12:13AM                342 help.gif
05-15-00  10:38AM                  0 sid.txt
226 Transfer complete.
ftp: 194 bytes received in 0.00Seconds 194000.00Kbytes/sec.
ftp> get fred.txt
200 PORT command successful.
150 Opening ASCII mode data connection for fred.txt(0 bytes).
226 Transfer complete.
ftp> !dir
 Volume in drive G has no label.
 Volume Serial Number is B080-5E55

 Directory of G:\myfolder

05/15/2000  06:53p    <DIR>          .
05/15/2000  06:53p    <DIR>          ..
05/15/2000  06:53p                 0 fred.txt
05/15/2000  06:48p                 0 mary.txt.txt
               2 File(s)            0 bytes
```

Figure 10.5   Downloading a file as the Anonymous user.

17. Enter **put mary.txt**. The file mary.txt is uploaded to the FTP site.

18. Enter **dir** to list the FTP site's default directory. Figure 10.6 shows the output from a successful **put** operation (or upload).

19. Enter **close**.

20. Experiment with the other subcommands listed in Table 10.9. Enter **bye** to close the connection and exit from the ftp subsystem.

21. Close the Command Console and Windows Explorer.

NOTE: *The purpose of the previous procedure is to demonstrate the use of the Windows 2000 ftp utility with simple **put** and **get** commands. To become completely familiar with the utility, experiment further. You could, for example, restrict access to the FTP site's default directory and open the connection with various usernames and passwords, or you could create a file containing ftp subcommands and experiment with the **-s** parameter.*

```
Command Prompt - ftp 195.162.230.2                             _ □ ×
ftp> put mary.txt
200 PORT command successful.
150 Opening ASCII mode data connection for mary.txt.
226 Transfer complete.
ftp> dir
200 PORT command successful.
150 Opening ASCII mode data connection for /bin/ls.
05-15-00  10:38AM                  0 alf.txt
05-15-00  10:38AM                  0 fred.txt
06-04-99  12:13AM                342 help.gif
05-15-00  11:11AM                  0 mary.txt
05-15-00  10:38AM                  0 sid.txt
226 Transfer complete.
ftp: 243 bytes received in 0.00Seconds 243000.00Kbytes/sec.
ftp>
```

Figure 10.6   Uploading a file to an FTP site.

Using SSL3 to Secure a Web Site

HTTP and HTTPS have no associated command-line utility, and an HTTP site (or Web site) is accessed through a Web browser. A Web site is configured to use SSL encryption (and hence to become an HTTPS Web site) using the Internet Services Manager snap-in. In this procedure, a new Web site is added and then configured. If you already have a Web site that you want to configure to use SSL, then you don't need to set up a new site.

This procedure assumes that you already have an administrator security certificate that you can use for SSL encryption. Typically, an administrator certificate is installed by default by the domain's Certificate Server when a Windows 2000 Certificate Authority is set up. If you don't have Certificate Server running on your domain or if a Certificate Authority isn't set up, you can obtain third-party security certificates from suppliers, such as VeriSign or Thawte.

TIP: *The VeriSign Web site is at **www.verisign.com**. Thawte, a VeriSign company, can be found at **www.thawte.com**.*

The procedure also assumes that you have bound an additional IP address to your NIC, as described earlier in this chapter. Host headers (see Chapter 12) don't work with secure Web sites.

An SSL-enabled Web site is set up as follows:

1. Log on to the IIS5 server as an administrator.
2. Access Start|Programs|Accessories and start Windows Explorer.
3. Create a new folder called (for example) secfold. This will be the default directory for your new site and is typically (but not necessarily) a subfolder of %Systemroot%\InetPub.
4. Create a Hypertext Markup Language (HTML) file in this folder, either by copying one from another folder or by using a hypertext editor (such as Microsoft Word). Name the file default.htm.
5. Access Start|Programs|Administrative Tools and click Internet Services Manager.
6. Right-click *server-name*, click New, and select Web Site.
7. The Web Site Creation Wizard starts. Click Next.
8. Type a description for the new site. Click Next.
9. In the IP address drop-down box, select the additional IP number that you bound to the NIC to identify this site. Click Next.

10. Browse to the folder you created in Step 4. Click Next.

11. Set the Web site access permissions according to your requirements. Click Next.

12. Click Finish. Check that the new site has been created and is started.

13. Right-click the new site and select Properties.

14. On the Directory Security tab, under Secure communications, click Server Certificate.

15. The Web Server Certificate Wizard starts. Click Next.

16. Select Assign an existing certificate. Click Next.

17. Select a certificate from the list. Click Next.

18. Check that you've selected the correct certificate. Click Next.

19. Click Finish. This returns you to the Directory Security tab of the Site Properties box.

20. The Edit button in the Secure communications section is now active. Click this button.

21. Check Require secure channel (SSL). Do not check Require 128-bit encryption unless you're absolutely sure that all clients can support this encryption strength.

Encryption Export Regulations

On the very day of writing this I received a news bulletin announcing that the U.S. Department of Commerce Bureau of Export Administration (BXA) has issued new encryption export regulations that implement the new approach announced by the Clinton Administration in September 1999. This move permits U.S. companies to export any encryption product around the world under a license exception. There are certain caveats, and the U.S. government will review the workability of the new regulation, receiving public comments for 120 days.

By the time you read this, 128-bit encryption may be available overseas. Nevertheless, it may not be implemented on many international sites. The same advice applies—don't enable 128-bit encryption unless you're certain that all clients can support it.

22. Click OK to exit from the Secure Communications dialog box.

23. Click OK to exit from the Site Properties dialog box.

24. Close the MMC snap-in.

25. Access the site from a browser using **https** rather than **http**. As this procedure stands, you can access it by IP address only. Chapter 14 describes how to allocate a friendly site name. If the site is on the Internet, both the IP address and the site name must be registered with InterNIC.

WARNING!   You shouldn't enable SSL encryption on a site unless you have a very good reason for doing so. SSL encryption slows site operation considerably and uses a lot of CPU resources. SSL-enabled sites are used for secure operations, such as sending your name and credit card number over the Internet.

Starting and Stopping Telnet Server

Telnet server may be started and stopped either from the Computer Management MMC snap-in or from a command prompt. Both of these procedures assume you're logged on to the Telnet server as an administrator.

Using the Computer Management Tool

To start and stop telnet server using the Computer Management MMC snap-in tool, proceed as follows:

1. Access Start|Programs|Administrative Tools and click Computer Management.
2. Expand Services and Applications and click Services.
3. In the details pane, right-click Telnet, then select Start or Stop as required.
4. Exit from the MMC snap-in.

Using the Command Prompt

To start and stop telnet server using the command prompt, proceed as follows:

1. Access Start|Programs|Accessories and click Command Prompt.
2. Enter either **net start tlntsvr** or **net stop tlntsvr**, depending on whether you want to start or stop the service.
3. Close the Command Console.

Configuring the Telnet Service

In this procedure, you'll use the telnet server admin tool to configure authentication on the telnet server. This tool also provides another method of starting and stopping the service. To configure authentication on the telnet server, proceed as follows:

1. Log on to the telnet server as an administrator.
2. Access Start|Programs|Accessories and click Command Prompt.
3. Access Start|Run and enter **tlntadmn**.
4. Select option 4 to start the telnet server (unless it's already started).
5. Select Display/change registry settings (option 3).
6. Select NTLM (option 7).
7. Refer to Table 10.11 for the authentication Registry settings. In a Windows 2000 domain, you would typically set the value to 2 (the default) for NTLM-only.
8. Exit from the Registry settings menu (option 0).
9. Stop and restart the telnet server.
10. Quit the application and close the Command Console.

Using Telnet Client

You may want to set the telnet clients on your network to use NTML-only authentication. This prevents names and passwords from being transmitted in clear text, but has the disadvantage that clients won't be able to establish connections with telnet servers that don't support this type of authentication. In this procedure, you'll use the telnet client to set authentication and to establish a telnet session with the FTP site you created on the IIS5 server in previous procedures. If you didn't create a new FTP site, then you can establish a connection with your domain's default FTP site.

To use telnet client, proceed as follows:

1. Log on to the telnet client as an administrator.
2. Access Start|Run and enter **telnet**.
3. Enter **set NTLM**.
4. Enter **set LOCAL_ECHO**. This lets you see the commands that you enter after you've established a telnet connection.
5. Enter **open *ipaddress* 21** where *ipaddress* is the additional IP address that you bound to your NIC in a previous procedure (or the IP address of the IIS5 server if you didn't carry out this procedure). Figure 10.7 shows the telnet commands that set authentication and establish a connection.
6. You now have a telnet connection to the FTP control port of the server for which you specified the IP address. Enter **user anonymous**.

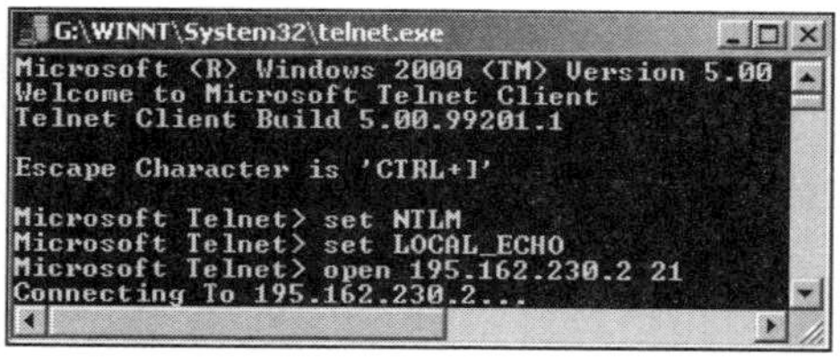

Figure 10.7   Telnet authentication and connection establishment.

7. You're prompted for a password. Enter **pass** with no arguments to specify a blank password.

8. Enter **stat**. The FTP Server status is returned, as shown in Figure 10.8.

9. Enter **quit**.

10. Close the Command Console.

NOTE: *The last procedure demonstrated the use of the telnet client to perform a few simple functions. To become familiar with the telnet client, experiment further. The functionality of a connection depends on the host and the port that you're connected to. You could, for example, connect to port 80 on a Web server to access an HTTP site.*

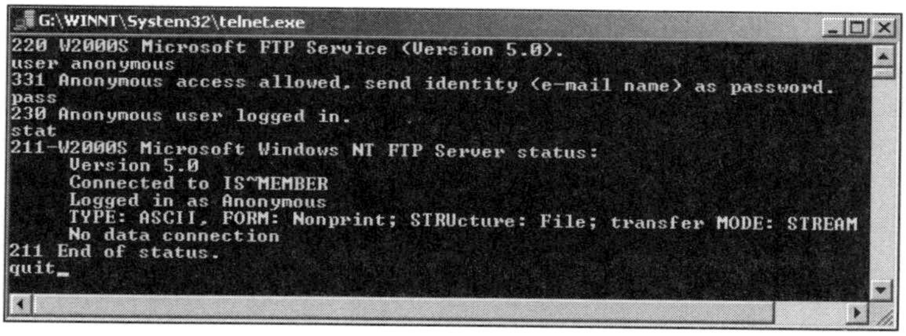

Figure 10.8   Telnet session used to determine FTP Server status.

Using TCP/IP Printing

There are two situations in which you would use TCP/IP printing—when you want to send print jobs to an RFC 1179 compliant Unix print server and when you have (for example) Unix hosts on your network that send print jobs to your Windows 2000 print server, but can't use Windows 2000 printing. In both cases, you need to install Print Services for Unix. This set of procedures installs this service, adds an LPR port to a Windows 2000 host so it can send jobs to a Unix print server, and sets up a Windows 2000 print server so that it can receive print jobs from a Unix host.

Installing Print Services for Unix

To install Print Services for Unix, proceed as follows:

1. Log on as an administrator.
2. Access Start|Settings and select Control Panel.
3. Double-click Add/Remove Programs.
4. Click Add/Remove Windows components.
5. Select Other Network File and Print Services and click Details.
6. Check Print Services for Unix. Click OK.
7. Click Next. If prompted, insert the Windows 2000 setup CD-ROM (or specify a path to installation files) and click OK.
8. Click Finish. Click Close.
9. Close the Control Panel.

Connecting to a TCP/IP Printer on Your Subnet

Connecting to a TCP/IP printer on your local subnet—that is, one that you can locate through browsing—is similar to connecting to any other type of printer. The only difference is that the client host must have Print Services for Unix installed in order to use the **lpr** command.

To connect to a TCP/IP printer on your subnet, proceed as follows:

1. Log on to the Windows 2000 host. You can carry out this procedure logged on as an ordinary user.
2. Access Start|Settings and click Printers.
3. Double-click Add Printer.
4. The Add Printer Wizard starts. Click Next.
5. Clear the Automatically detect my printer checkbox, select Network printer, then click Next.
6. Select Type the printer name or click Next to browse for a printer. Ensure that the box beside the radio button is clear. Click Next.
7. Browse for the TCP/IP printer. Highlight it and click Next.
8. Specify whether you want to use the printer as a default printer (you probably don't). Click Next.
9. Click Finish. Close the Printers window.
10. Send jobs to the printer using the command **lpr –S*ipaddress* –P*printername filename***, where *ipaddress* is the IP address of the Unix print server, *printername* is the network name of the printer, and *filename* is the name of the file you want to print.

Connecting to a TCP/IP Printer by Adding an LPR Port

In this procedure, you set up a Windows 2000 host so it can send print jobs to a TCP/IP printer that you can't locate by browsing. The printer either can be one that's installed on a Unix print server, or it can be an LPD-enabled network printer. You do this by creating an LPR port on the host and specifying the network printer or Unix print server. The procedure is as follows:

1. Log on to the Windows 2000 host as an administrator.
2. Access Start|Settings and click Printers.
3. Double-click Add Printer.
4. The Add Printer Wizard starts. Click Next.
5. Clear the Automatically detect my printer checkbox, select Local printer, then click Next.
6. Click Create a new port and select LPR Port in the Type drop-down box. Click Next.
7. Provide the following information:
   - In the Name or address of server providing lpd box, type the host name or IP address of the host for the printer you're adding (or of an LPD-enabled network printer).
   - In Name of printer or print queue on that server, type the name of the printer. This is either a network printer name or the name of a printer on the Unix print server.
8. Click OK.
9. Specify the manufacturer and model of the remote printer. Click Next.
10. Specify a printer name. This is the same as the name you specified in Step 7. Click Next.
11. Select Do not share this printer. Click Next.
12. Insert information in the Location and Comment boxes. Click Next.
13. Select Do not to print a test page. Click Next.
14. Click Finish. An icon for the new printer appears in the Printers window.
15. Close the Printers window.
16. Send jobs to the printer using the command **lpr –S*ipaddress* –P*printername filename***, where *ipaddress* is the IP address of the Unix print server, *printername* is the network name of the printer, and *filename* is the name of the file you want to print.

Installing a TCP/IP Printer on a Windows 2000 Print Server

In this procedure, you'll install a TCP/IP printer on a Windows 2000 print server so Unix clients can send jobs to that printer. The procedure assumes that Print Services for Unix is installed on the print server and that the LPD service is running. It also assumes that the appropriate printer driver is installed on the Unix client.

1. Log on to the Windows 2000 print server as an administrator.

2. Access Start|Settings and click Printers.

3. Double-click Add Printer.

4. The Add Printer Wizard starts. Click Next.

5. Select Local printer, clear the Automatically detect my printer checkbox, then click Next.

6. Click Create a new port and select LPR Port in the Type drop-down box. Click Next.

7. Type the print server name or IP address in the Name or address of server providing lpd box. Specify a printer name (such as tcpprt) in the Name of printer or print queue on that server box. Click OK.

8. Select the manufacturer and model of your printer. Click Next.

9. Specify a printer name. Make this the same as the name you specified in Step 7. Click Next.

10. Select Share as. By default, the share name is the same as the printer name. Change this only if your printer name is more than eight characters long or contains one or more spaces. Click Next.

11. Insert information in the Location and Comment boxes. Click Next.

12. Select whether or not to print a test page. Click Next.

13. Click Finish. An icon for the new printer appears in the Printers window.

14. Close the Printers window.

Chapter 11

Kerberos 5

In Depth

Kerberos version 5 (Kerberos 5) is, strictly speaking, a Windows 2000 TCP/IP feature rather than an integral part of the TCP/IP stack. Nevertheless, it's a very important feature, used by default for authentication and trust relationships. An understanding of security, and the methods by which endpoints are authenticated and messages are protected, is an essential component of the administrator's toolkit. Kerberos 5 isn't as immediately configurable as most protocols. Only a limited number of its parameters can be changed, but the implications of any change can be considerable. This chapter, therefore, contains more in-depth theory and less in the way of immediate solutions than the rest of the book. I make no apology for this—a sound knowledge of security is (in my opinion) an essential.

Comparing NT LAN Manager and Kerberos 5

Kerberos 5 is the default Windows 2000 authentication protocol, but the NT LAN Manager (NTLM) legacy protocol is also supported to provide backward compatibility with previous Microsoft Network Operating Systems (NOS), such as Windows NT4 and LAN Manager. The NTLM security provider authenticates by a challenge/response procedure. The security provider knows the password of the user (or, more precisely, the *MD4 hash* of the password). It encrypts a randomly generated block of data using the MD4 hash and sends it back to the client (the challenge). The client then decrypts the data block and returns it to the server. If the client also knows the correct password, the decryption is successful and the server registers that the client has been authenticated. The NTLM security provider then generates a unique access token, which it returns to the client for future use. For future authentication, the client uses the token, and the NTLM security provider doesn't have to repeat the challenge/response authentication.

TIP: *MD2, MD4, and MD5 are Message Digest algorithms developed for digital signature applications where a large message has to be "compressed" in a secure manner before being signed with a private key. Description and source code for the three algorithms can be found in RFCs 1319 through 1321. More detail is available at RSA Laboratories' Web site at **www.rsasecurity.com/rsalabs/**. In particular, there is a Frequently Asked Questions (FAQ) Web page at **www.rsasecurity.com/rsalabs/faq/3-6-6.html**.*

Kerberos 5 security uses the concept of *proxy tickets*. Consider, for example, a process (A) that calls an application (B). B then "impersonates" A—that is, B acts as A in certain ways. However, if B calls another application (C) while acting as A, C will, by default, impersonate B, not A, because the security privileges of A are not delegated to C. True delegation, as implemented by the Kerberos 5 Security Service Provider (SSP), means that if application B—which is the acting A thread—calls another application, C, then C can impersonate A. Application B holds the proxy ticket for A, which enables it to impersonate A even when calling other applications.

Computers running Windows 3.11, Windows 95, Windows 98, or Windows NT4 will use the NTLM protocol for network authentication in Windows 2000 domains. Computers running Windows 2000 will use NTLM when authenticating to servers with Windows NT4 and when accessing resources in Windows NT4 domains. But, the protocol of choice in Windows 2000 is Kerberos 5. The benefits of using Kerberos 5 authentication are as follows:

- *Mutual authentication*—NTLM allows a server to verify the identities of its clients, but doesn't allow clients to verify a server's identity or one server to verify the identity of another. Kerberos 5 ensures that parties at both ends of a network connection know that the party on the other end is who it claims to be.

- *Faster connections*—With NTLM authentication, an application server must connect to a domain controller (DC) to authenticate each client. Using Kerberos 5 authentication, the server doesn't need to go to a DC, but can instead authenticate the client by examining the client's credentials. Clients can obtain credentials for a particular server just once and then reuse them throughout a network logon session.

- *Simplified trust management*—One of the main benefits of mutual authentication in the Kerberos 5 protocol is that trust relationships between Windows 2000 domains are two-way and transitive by default. In a multidomain tree, credentials issued by any domain are accepted throughout the tree.

NOTE: *A transitive trust means that if A trusts B and B trusts C, then A trusts C. Kerberos 5 trusts are transitive, but NTLM trusts are not.*

- *Delegated authentication*—Both NTLM and Kerberos 5 provide the information that a service needs to impersonate its client locally, but some distributed applications are designed so that a front-end service must impersonate clients when connecting to back-end services on other computers. Kerberos 5 has a proxy mechanism that allows a service to impersonate its client when connecting to other services. NTLM doesn't.

- *Interoperability*—Microsoft's implementation of the Kerberos 5 protocol is based on specifications recommended to the Internet Engineering Task Force (IETF). As a result, the implementation of the protocol in Windows 2000 provides a foundation for interoperability with other networks (particularly Posix-compliant networks) in which Kerberos 5 is used for authentication.

Kerberos 5 provides a mechanism for mutual authentication between a client and a server, or between one server and another, before a network connection is opened between them. The protocol assumes that initial transactions between clients and servers take place on an open network, where most computers aren't physically secure and attackers can monitor and modify packets at will—rather like the Internet. Kerberos 5 ensures that the sender knows who the receiver is, and vice versa—and ensures that no third party can impersonate either.

Shared Secrets Authentication

Kerberos uses an authentication technique involving *shared secrets*. If only two people know a secret, either person can verify the identity of the other by confirming that the other person knows that secret. Suppose, for example, that Bonnie often sends messages to Clyde, who needs to be sure that a message from Bonnie is genuine before he acts on its information. They decide to solve their problem by selecting a password and agreeing not to share it with anyone else. If Bonnie's messages show that the sender knows the password, Clyde will know that the sender is Bonnie.

So, how will Bonnie show that she knows the password? She could include it somewhere in her messages, such as in a signature block at the end. This is simple and efficient, but will be secure only if Bonnie and Clyde can be certain that no one else is reading their mail. Unfortunately, their messages pass over a network used by the Sheriff, who has a network analyzer. So, Bonnie can't prove that she knows the secret simply by saying it, and hence revealing it to the Sheriff. To keep the password secret, she must show that she knows it without putting it on the network.

Kerberos 5 solves this problem with *secret-key cryptography*. Rather than share a password, communication partners share a cryptographic key and use knowledge of this key to verify one another's identity. The shared key must be *symmetric*—in other words, a single key must be capable of both encryption and decryption. One party proves knowledge of the key by encrypting a piece of information, and the other proves knowledge of the key by decrypting that piece of information. Secret-key authentication begins when someone presents an *authenticator* in the form of a piece of information encrypted in the secret key. The information in the authenticator must be different each time the protocol is executed—otherwise, an old authenticator could be reused by anyone who happens to overhear the communication. On receiving an authenticator, the recipient decrypts it. If decryption is successful, the recipient knows that the person presenting the authenticator has the correct key. Only two people have the correct key—the recipient is one of them, so the person who presented the authenticator must be the other.

WARNING!   *This assumes that two* and only two *persons have the secret key or, to employ the appropriate terminology, use the same key pad. A secret key that's known by a third person is no longer secret.*

Where information is downloaded from a trusted source, the recipient must ensure that the source is who it purports to be and that the information hasn't been tampered with en route. Although this is by no means a straightforward problem, the parameters are fixed and *adequate* solutions can be found. (Note that, in the security context, solutions are *adequate*, never *perfect*.) When, however, communication is two-way and mutual authentication is required, a whole new set of problems arises, particularly when it comes to sharing secret keys, and new techniques have to be employed to solve these problems.

To provide mutual authentication, the recipient can extract part of the information from the original authenticator, encrypt it in a new authenticator, and return the new authenticator to the sender, who can then decrypt the recipient's authenticator and compare the result with the original. If there's a match, the sender will know that the recipient was able to decrypt the original and has the correct key.

Suppose, for example, Bonnie and Clyde decide that each will use a shared secret key to verify the identity of the party at the other end of the connection before transferring any information. Therefore, they agree on the following protocol:

1. Bonnie sends Clyde a message that contains her name in plaintext and an authenticator encrypted in the secret key she shares with Clyde. In this protocol, the authenticator is a data structure that has two fields. One field contains information about Bonnie—for example, "Parker". The second field contains the current time on Bonnie's workstation.

2. Clyde receives the message and uses the key he shares with Bonnie to decrypt the authenticator. He extracts and evaluates the field that contains the time on Bonnie's workstation.

3. Assume that both Bonnie and Clyde use a network time service to keep their clocks fairly close. Thus, Clyde can compare the time from the authenticator with the current time on his clock. If the difference is outside a specified limit, he'll reject the authenticator.

4. If the time is within the allowable skew, the authenticator probably came from Bonnie, but Clyde still doesn't have proof of this. The Sheriff might have been watching network traffic and might now be replaying an earlier attempt by Bonnie to establish a connection. However, if Clyde has recorded the times of authenticators received from Bonnie, he can defeat attempts to replay earlier messages by rejecting any message that has a time that is the same as or earlier than the time of the last authenticator.

11. Kerberos 5

> **TIP:** *The previous paragraph describes a* replay attack. *This is a term worth remembering, because such attacks are a matter of some concern to the Internet community.*

5. Clyde uses the key he shares with Bonnie to encrypt the time taken from Bonnie's message and sends the result back to her. He doesn't send back all the information taken from Bonnie's authenticator—just the time. If he sent back everything, Bonnie would have no way of knowing whether someone posing as Clyde had simply copied the authenticator from her original message and sent it back to her unchanged. Clyde chooses the time, because that's the one piece of information that's sure to be unique in Bonnie's message to him.

6. Bonnie receives Clyde's reply, decrypts it, and compares the result with the time in her original authenticator. If the times match, she can be confident that her authenticator reached someone who knows the secret key needed to decrypt it and extract the time. She shares that key only with Clyde, so it must be Clyde who received her message and replied. Both sender and receiver can be confident in the connection. Figure 11.1 shows the mutual authentication process.

Using a Key Distribution Center

The preceding procedure has one major weakness—it doesn't explain how or where Bonnie and Clyde got the secret key to use in sessions with each other. For clarity, the procedure is presented as if Bonnie and Clyde are both people, who could meet and agree on a shared secret. In practice, Bonnie is likely to be a client program running on a workstation, and Clyde is likely to be a service running on a network server. Another problem is that the client, Bonnie, talks to many servers and thus needs keys for each of them—and Clyde talks to many

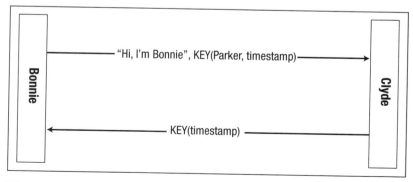

Figure 11.1   Mutual authentication.

clients and thus needs keys for each of them. If each client needs to have a key for every service and each service needs a key for every client, key distribution could quickly become complex and pose a considerable security risk.

NOTE: *Throughout this chapter, and elsewhere in this book where the Bonnie and Clyde analogy is used, Bonnie is referred to as "her" and Clyde as "him". As stated in the previous paragraph, Bonnie and Clyde could be programs or services, and the analogy would still apply. The use of "her" and "him" doesn't necessarily imply that Bonnie and Clyde are people.*

The Kerberos 5 protocol solves this problem by identifying three entities: a client, a server, and a trusted third party to mediate between them. The trusted intermediary in the protocol is known as the Key Distribution Center (KDC). This three-entity structure gave the protocol its name—Kerberos, the three-headed dog that guards the gates of the Underworld.

TIP: *There's currently an expanding market for third-party companies that provide and manage key pads and act as trusted intermediaries. If you have an entrepreneurial streak and are considering commercial opportunities, then this is one well worth thinking about.*

The KDC service runs on a physically secure server and maintains a database that has account information for all security principals in its *realm* (the Kerberos 5 equivalent of a Windows 2000 domain). Along with other information about each security principal, the KDC stores a cryptographic key known only to the security principal and the KDC. This key is used in exchanges between the security principal and the KDC and is known as a *long-term key*. Usually, it's derived from the security principal's logon password.

A client who wants to talk to a server sends a request to the KDC, which then distributes a unique, short-term *session key* for the two parties to use when they authenticate each other. The server's copy of the session key is encrypted in the server's long-term key. The client's copy of the session key is encrypted in the client's long-term key.

In theory, the KDC could send the session key directly to each of the security principals involved, but in practice, that procedure would be extremely inefficient. It would require the server to retain its copy of the session key in memory while it waited for the client to call. Moreover, the server would need to remember a key not just for this client, but for every client who might ask for service. Key management would consume a disproportionate amount of server resources, and the solution wouldn't scale. Kerberos solves this problem by using session tickets.

Session Tickets

The KDC responds to a client request by sending both server and client session key copies to the client, as shown in Figure 11.2. The client copy of the session key is encrypted with the key that the KDC shares with the client. The server copy is embedded, along with information about the client, in a data structure called a *session ticket*, and the entire structure is then encrypted with the key that the KDC shares with the server. The client then uses the ticket when it contacts the server.

The KDC doesn't keep track of its messages to make sure they reach the intended address—it merely grants the ticket. Security isn't compromised if the KDC's messages fall into the wrong hands. Only someone who knows the client's secret key can decrypt the client copy of the session key, and only someone who knows the server's secret key can read what's inside the ticket.

The client extracts the ticket and the client's copy of the session key and puts them into a secure cache (located in memory, not on disk). When the client wants to connect to the server, it sends a message that consists of the ticket and an authenticator encrypted with the session key. The ticket (which is still encrypted with the server's secret key) and the authenticator together form the client's credentials to the server.

The server decrypts the session ticket with its secret key, extracts the session key, and uses the session key to decrypt the client's authenticator. If everything checks out, the server knows that the client's credentials were issued by the KDC, which is a *trusted authority*. If mutual authentication is required, the server uses its copy of the session key to encrypt the timestamp from the client's authenticator and returns the result to the client as the server's authenticator, as shown in Figure 11.3.

Notice that the server doesn't have to store the session key that it uses in communicating with a client. The client is responsible for holding a ticket for the server

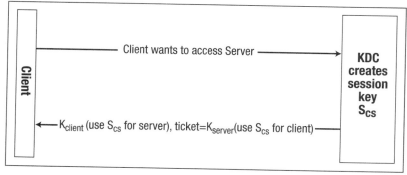

Figure 11.2   Key distribution.

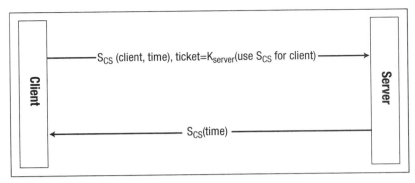

Figure 11.3   Mutual authentication (client/server).

in its credentials cache and presenting the ticket each time it wants access to the server. When the server no longer needs the session key, it can discard it.

Also, the client doesn't need to go back to the KDC each time it wants access to this particular server, because session tickets can be reused—unless they have expired. How long a ticket is valid depends on Kerberos policy for the domain—typically, tickets are good for eight hours. When the user logs off the client machine, the credentials cache is flushed and all session tickets and session keys are destroyed.

Ticket-Granting Tickets

Bonnie logs on. First, the Kerberos client on her workstation converts her password to a cryptographic key by using a one-way hashing function—Kerberos 5 supports the DES-CBC-MD5 hashing algorithm, although other algorithms are permissible. Then, the Kerberos client requests a session ticket and session key that it can use in subsequent transactions with the KDC during this logon session. The KDC searches its database for Bonnie, pulls up her account record, and takes her long-term key from a field in the record. This process—computing one copy of the key from a password and fetching another copy of the key from a database—takes place only once, when a user initially logs on to the network.

The KDC responds to the client's request by returning a special type of session ticket, called a Ticket-Granting Ticket (TGT), for itself. Like an ordinary session ticket, a TGT contains a copy of the session key that the service (in this case, the KDC) will use in communicating with the client. The package that returns the TGT to the client also includes a copy of the session key that the client can use in communicating with the KDC. The TGT is encrypted in the KDC's long-term key, and the client's copy of the session key is encrypted in the user's long-term key.

In all subsequent exchanges with the KDC, the client uses the session key (the cryptographic key derived from the user's password isn't needed and can be discarded). Like any other session key, this key is temporary, valid only until the TGT expires or the user logs off. For that reason, it's called a *logon session key*.

Before it attempts to connect to any service, the client checks its credentials cache for a session ticket to that service. If it doesn't have one, it checks the cache again for a TGT. If it finds a TGT, the client fetches the corresponding logon session key from the cache, uses this key to prepare an authenticator, and sends both the authenticator and the TGT to the KDC, along with a request for a session ticket for the service. Thus, gaining admission to the KDC is no different from gaining admission to any other service in the domain—it requires a session key, an authenticator, and a ticket (in this case, a TGT).

Kerberos 5 Subprotocols

Kerberos 5 is comprised of three subprotocols:

- *Authentication Service (AS) Exchange*—Used when the KDC gives the client a logon session key and a TGT.

- *Ticket-Granting Service (TGS) Exchange*—Used when the KDC distributes a service session key and a session ticket for the service.

- *Client/Server (CS) Exchange*—Used when the client presents the session ticket for admission to a service.

To see how the three subprotocols work together, consider how Bonnie, a user at a workstation, gets access to Clyde, a service on the network.

AS Exchange

The AS information exchange proceeds as follows:

1. Bonnie logs on to the network. The Kerberos 5 client on Bonnie's workstation converts her password to an encryption key and saves the result in its credentials cache.

2. The Kerberos 5 client sends the KDC's authentication service a Kerberos Authentication Service Request (KRB_AS_REQ). The first part of this message identifies the user, Bonnie, and the name of the service for which she is requesting credentials—the ticket-granting service. The second part of the message contains *preauthentication data* that proves Bonnie knows the password. This is usually a timestamp encrypted with Bonnie's long-term key.

3. The KDC receives the KRB_AS_REQ.

4. The KDC looks up the user Bonnie in its database, gets her long-term key, decrypts the preauthentication data, and evaluates the timestamp contained therein. If the timestamp is acceptable, the KDC can be assured that

the preauthentication data was encrypted with Bonnie's long-term key and that the client is genuine.

5. The KDC creates credentials that the Kerberos client on Bonnie's workstation can present to the ticket-granting service, as follows:

   - It creates a logon session key and encrypts a copy of it with Bonnie's long-term key.
   - It embeds another copy of the logon session key in a TGT, along with other information about Bonnie, such as her authorization data.
   - It encrypts the TGT with its own long-term key.
   - It sends both the encrypted logon session key and the TGT back to the client in a Kerberos Authentication Service Reply (KRB_AS_REP).

6. When the client receives the message, it uses the key derived from Bonnie's password to decrypt her logon session key and stores the key in its credentials cache. Then, it extracts the TGT from the message and stores that in its credentials cache as well.

Figure 11.4 illustrates the AS information exchange.

TGS Exchange

After the AS information exchange process is complete, the TGS exchange process proceeds as follows:

1. The Kerberos client on Bonnie's workstation requests credentials for the service Clyde by sending the KDC a Kerberos Ticket-Granting Service Request (KRB_TGS_REQ). This message includes the user's name, an authenticator encrypted with the user's logon session key, the TGT obtained in the AS information exchange, and the name of the service for which the user wants a ticket.

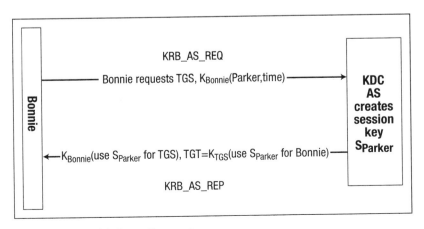

Figure 11.4   AS information exchange.

2. The KDC receives the KRB_TGS_REQ and decrypts the TGT with its own secret key—extracting Bonnie's logon session key, which it uses to decrypt the authenticator.

3. If the authenticator is valid, the KDC extracts Bonnie's authorization data from the TGT and creates a session key for the client (Bonnie) to share with the service (Clyde).

4. The KDC encrypts one copy of this session key with Bonnie's logon session key; embeds another copy in a ticket, along with Bonnie's authorization data; and encrypts the ticket with Clyde's long-term key.

5. The KDC sends these credentials back to the client in a Kerberos Ticket-Granting Service Reply (KRB_TGS_REP).

6. When the client receives the reply, it uses Bonnie's logon session key to decrypt the session key to use with the service and stores the key in its credentials cache. Then, it extracts the ticket to the service and stores that in its cache also.

Figure 11.5 illustrates the TGS information exchange.

CS Exchange

After the TGS information exchange is complete, the CS information exchange proceeds as follows:

1. The Kerberos 5 client on Bonnie's workstation requests service from Clyde by sending Clyde a Kerberos Application Request (KRB_AP_REQ). This message contains an authenticator encrypted with the session key for the service, the ticket obtained in the TGS information exchange, and a preconfigured flag that indicates whether the client wants mutual authentication.

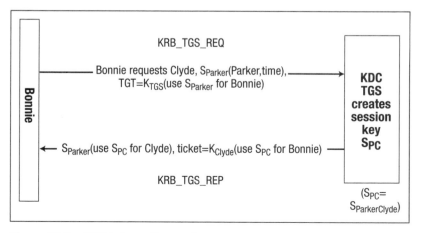

Figure 11.5   TGS information exchange.

2. Clyde receives the KRB_AP_REQ, decrypts the ticket, and extracts Bonnie's authorization data and the session key.

3. Clyde uses the session key to decrypt Bonnie's authenticator and evaluates the timestamp inside.

4. If the authenticator is valid, Clyde looks for a mutual authentication flag in the client's request.

5. If the flag is set, the service uses the session key to encrypt the time from Bonnie's authenticator and returns the result in a Kerberos Application Reply (KRB_AP_REP).

6. When the Kerberos 5 client on Bonnie's workstation receives the KRB_AP_REP, it decrypts Clyde's authenticator with the session key it shares with Clyde and compares the time returned by the service with the time in the client's original authenticator.

7. If the times match, the client knows that the service is genuine, and the connection proceeds. During the connection, the session key can be used to encrypt application data—or the client and server can share another key for this purpose.

Figure 11.6 illustrates the CS information exchange.

Logon Authentication

When you log on to a network that uses the Kerberos 5 protocol for authentication, the first thing that happens is that you get a TGT you can present when requesting session tickets for other services in the domain. When you log on to a Windows 2000 domain, you always need at least one session ticket—a ticket for the computer where you are logging on. Computers running Windows 2000 have their own accounts in the domain—think of them as service accounts. Interactive users can access resources in a Windows 2000 domain by submitting

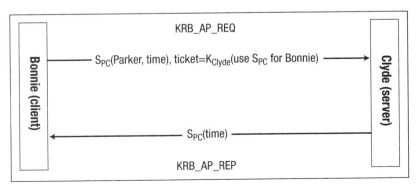

Figure 11.6   CS information exchange.

requests to the computer's Workstation service, whereas remote users submit requests to its Server service. Before you can gain admission to either service— or to any other service running as Local System—you must present a session ticket for the computer.

Suppose Bonnie has a network account in a domain called West and is logging on to a computer, Clyde, which also has an account in West. Bonnie starts with the Secure Attention Sequence (SAS) Ctrl+Alt+Delete. Clyde's WinLogon service switches to the logon desktop and accesses the Graphical Identification and Authentication (GINA) dynamic link library (DLL), msgina.dll (known as MSGINA), that's responsible for collecting logon data from the user, packaging it in a data structure, and sending everything to the Local Security Authority (LSA) for verification.

Bonnie types her username and password and selects West from the Domains drop-down list. When she clicks OK to end the dialog, MSGINA returns her logon information to WinLogon, which sends the information to the LSA for validation by calling **LsaLogonUser**.

On receiving a data structure that has Bonnie's logon data, the LSA immediately converts her clear-text password to a secret key by passing it through a one-way hashing function. The result is saved in the credentials cache, where it can be retrieved when needed for TGT renewal or for NTLM authentication to servers that aren't capable of Kerberos 5 authentication.

To validate Bonnie's logon information and set up her logon session on the computer, the LSA must obtain a TGT that's good for admission to the ticket-granting service and a session ticket that's good for admission to the computer. The LSA gets these tickets by working through the Kerberos 5 SSP, which exchanges messages directly with the KDC in West.

The message sequence is as follows:

1. The LSA sends a KRB_AS_REQ to the KDC in West. The message includes:
   - The user principal name, Bonnie.
   - The name of the account domain, West.
   - Preauthentication data encrypted with the secret key derived from Bonnie's password.

2. If the client's preauthentication data is correct, the KDC replies with a KRB_AS_REP. The message includes:
   - A session key for Bonnie to share with the KDC, encrypted with the secret key derived from Bonnie's password.
   - A TGT for the KDC in West, encrypted with the KDC's secret key. The TGT includes a session key for the KDC to share with Bonnie, as well as

authorization data for Bonnie. This authorization data contains the Security Identifier (SID) for Bonnie's account, SIDs for security groups in the domain West that include Bonnie, and SIDs for universal groups in the enterprise that include either Bonnie or one of her domain groups.

3. The LSA sends a KRB_TGS_REQ to the KDC in West. The message includes:

   • The name of the target computer, Clyde.

   • The name of the target computer's domain, West.

   • Bonnie's TGT.

   • An authenticator encrypted with the session key Bonnie shares with the KDC.

4. The KDC replies with a KRB_TGS_REP. The message includes:

   • A session key for Bonnie to share with Clyde, encrypted with the session key Bonnie shares with the KDC.

   • Bonnie's session ticket to Clyde, encrypted with the secret key Clyde shares with the KDC. The session ticket contains a session key for Clyde to share with Bonnie and authorization data copied from Bonnie's TGT.

When it receives Bonnie's session ticket, the LSA decrypts it with the computer's secret key and extracts her authorization data. It then queries the local Security Accounts Manager (SAM) database to discover whether Bonnie is a member of any security groups local to the computer and whether she has been given any special privileges on the local machine. It adds any SIDs returned by this query to the list taken from the ticket's authorization data. The entire list is then used to build an access token, and a *handle* to the token is returned to WinLogon, along with an identifier for Bonnie's logon session and confirmation that her logon information was valid.

WinLogon creates a window station and several desktop objects for Bonnie, attaches her access token, and starts the shell process that she uses to interact with the computer. Any application process that Bonnie starts during her logon session subsequently inherits her access token.

Notice that, during the preceding process, the same key is used for both encryption and decryption. Shared secret keys, used for password logon, are therefore *symmetric*.

Smart Card Logon

To support smart card logons, Windows 2000 implements a public key extension to the Kerberos protocol's initial AS information exchange. Public key cryptography is *asymmetric*—two different keys are needed, one to encrypt and the other to decrypt. Together, the keys make up a private key/public key pair. The private key is known only to the owner of the pair and is never shared. The public key can be made available to anyone with whom the owner wants to exchange confidential information.

When a smart card is used in place of a password, a private key/public key pair, stored on the user's smart card, is substituted for the shared secret key derived from the user's password. In the public key extension to the Kerberos 5 protocol, the initial AS information exchange is modified so that the KDC encrypts the user's logon session key with the public half of the user's key pair. The client decrypts the logon session key with the private half of the pair.

The logon process using a smart card proceeds as follows:

1. The user inserts a smart card into a card reader attached to the computer. When computers with Windows 2000 are configured for smart card logon, a card-insertion event provides the SAS.

2. WinLogon dispatches to MSGINA, which displays a Logon Information dialog box.

3. The user types in a Personal Identification Number (PIN).

4. MSGINA sends the user's logon information to the LSA by calling **LsaLogonUser**.

5. The LSA uses the PIN to access the smart card, which stores the user's private key and an X.509v3 certificate that contains the public half of the key pair. All cryptographic operations that use these keys take place on the smart card.

6. The Kerberos SSP on the client computer sends the user's public key certificate to the KDC as preauthentication data in its initial authentication request, KRB_AS_REQ.

7. The KDC validates the certificate and extracts the public key, which it uses to encrypt a logon session key. In its reply to the client (KRB_AS_REP), it returns the encrypted logon session key and a TGT.

8. If the client is in possession of the private half of the key pair, it uses the private key to decrypt the logon session key.

Both the client and the KDC then use the logon session key in all further communications with each other. No other deviation from the standard protocol is necessary.

By default, the Kerberos 5 SSP on a client computer sends the KDC preauthentication data in the form of an encrypted timestamp. On systems configured for smart card logon, the Kerberos 5 SSP sends preauthentication data in the form of a public key.

Authentication across Domain Boundaries

The functions of the KDC are split into two services: an Authentication Service that issues TGTs and a Ticket-Granting Service (TGS) that issues session tickets. This allows the Kerberos 5 protocol to operate across domain boundaries. A client can get a TGT from the Authentication Service of one domain and use it to get session tickets from the TGS of another domain.

First, consider a network that has two Windows 2000 domains, East and West. If a trust relationship is set up, authentication across domain boundaries is implemented by sharing an interdomain key. The TGS of each domain is registered as a security principal with the other domain's KDC, and the TGS in each domain can treat the TGS in the other domain as just another service for which properly authenticated clients can request and receive session tickets.

When a user that has an account in East wants access to a server that has an account in West, the authentication process proceeds as follows:

1. The Kerberos 5 client on the user's workstation sends a request for a session ticket to the TGS in the East domain.

2. The TGS in East sees that the desired server isn't a security principal in its domain and replies by sending the client a *referral ticket*—a TGT encrypted with the interdomain key that the KDC in East shares with the KDC in West.

3. The client uses the referral ticket to prepare a second request for a session ticket and this time sends the request to the TGS in the West domain.

4. The TGS in West uses its copy of the interdomain key to decrypt the referral ticket. If decryption is successful, it sends the client a session ticket to the desired server in its domain.

Where a domain tree exists, a client in one domain can get a ticket to a server in another domain by traveling a referral path through one or more intermediate domains. This is illustrated in the example shown in Figure 11.7.

The company where Bonnie works has a parent domain, **coriolis.com**, and two children domains, **east.coriolis.com** and **west.coriolis.com**. Bonnie logs on to her domain account in **west.coriolis.com** and collects a TGT for the KDC in this domain. She decides that she needs to access a document stored in a public share on Clyde, a server in the **east.coriolis.com** domain. Because Bonnie's domain is different from the file server's domain, the SSP on Bonnie's workstation must obtain a TGT for the **east.coriolis.com** domain and use that TGT to get a ticket for the server. This involves the following referral process:

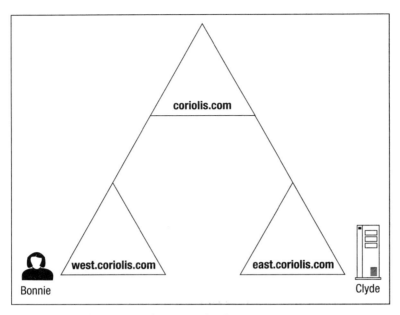

Figure 11.7   Cross-domain authentication.

1. Bonnie's workstation sends a KRB_TGS_REQ to the KDC in **west.coriolis.com**. The message includes:
   - The name of the target computer, Clyde.
   - The name of the target computer's domain, **east.coriolis.com**.
   - A TGT for admission to the KDC in **west.coriolis.com**.
   - An authenticator encrypted with the session key Bonnie shares with that KDC.

2. The KDC in **west.coriolis.com** sends a KRB_TGS_REP. The message includes:
   - A session key for Bonnie to share with the KDC in the parent domain, **coriolis.com**, encrypted with Bonnie's logon session key.
   - A TGT for admission to the KDC in **coriolis.com**, encrypted with the secret key for the trust relationship between the two domains.

3. Bonnie's workstation sends a KRB_TGS_REQ to the KDC in **coriolis.com**. The message includes:
   - The name of the target computer, Clyde.
   - The name of the target computer's domain, **east.coriolis.com**.

- A TGT for admission to the KDC in **coriolis.com**.

- An authenticator encrypted with the session key Bonnie shares with that KDC.

4. The KDC in **coriolis.com** sends a KRB_TGS_REP. The message includes:

  - A TGT for admission to the KDC in **east.coriolis.com**, encrypted with the secret key for the trust relationship between the two domains.

  - A session key for Bonnie to share with that KDC, encrypted with the session key Bonnie shares with the KDC in **coriolis.com**.

5. Bonnie's workstation sends a KRB_TGS_REQ to the KDC in **east.coriolis.com**. The message includes:

  - The name of the target computer, Clyde.

  - The name of the target computer's domain, **east.coriolis.com**.

  - A TGT for admission to the KDC in **east.coriolis.com**.

  - An authenticator encrypted with the session key Bonnie shares with that KDC.

6. The KDC in **east.coriolis.com** sends a KRB_TGS_REP. The message includes:

  - A session key for Bonnie to share with Clyde, encrypted with the session key Bonnie shares with the KDC in **east.coriolis.com**.

  - A session ticket for admission to Clyde, encrypted with the secret key Clyde shares with the KDC. The session ticket contains a session key for Clyde to share with Bonnie, authorization data copied from Bonnie's TGT, and data for the local domain, **east.coriolis.com**. The authorization data includes the SID for Bonnie's account, SIDs for groups in **west.coriolis.com** that include Bonnie, SIDs for universal groups that include either Bonnie or one of her groups in **west.coriolis.com**, and SIDs for groups in **east.coriolis.com** that include Bonnie, one of her groups in **west.coriolis.com**, or one of her universal groups.

7. Bonnie's workstation sends a KRB_AP_REQ to Clyde. The message includes:

  - The user principal name, Bonnie.

  - A ticket to Clyde.

  - An authenticator encrypted with the session key Bonnie shares with Clyde.

8. Clyde replies with a KRB_AP_REP. The message includes an authenticator encrypted with the session key Clyde shares with Bonnie.

Kerberos 5 Tickets

An understanding of the contents of Kerberos 5 tickets and the method used to calculate expiration times is important when configuring Kerberos 5 policy settings. This section lists the fields in a ticket and briefly describes the information they contain. The exact data structures for tickets can be found in RFC 1510. Table 11.1 lists the first three fields in a ticket. These aren't encrypted—the information is in plaintext so that the client can use it to manage tickets in its cache.

The remaining fields are encrypted with the server's secret key. These fields are listed in Table 11.2.

Table 11.1   Plaintext ticket fields.

Field Name	Description
Tkt-vno	The version number of the ticket format, currently 5.
Realm	The name of the realm (domain) that issued the ticket. A KDC can issue tickets only for servers in its own realm, so this is also the name of the server's realm.
Sname	The name of the server.

Table 11.2   Encrypted ticket fields.

Field Name	Description
Flags	Ticket options.
Key	Session key.
Crealm	The name of the client's realm (domain).
Cname	The client's name.
Transited	A list of the Kerberos realms that took part in authenticating the client to whom the ticket was issued.
Authtime	The time of initial authentication by the client. The KDC places a timestamp in this field when it issues a TGT. When it issues tickets based on a TGT, the KDC copies the authtime of the TGT to the authtime of the ticket.
Starttime	The time after which the ticket is valid.
Endtime	The ticket's expiration time.
Renew-till	The maximum endtime that may be set in a ticket with a RENEWABLE flag (optional).
Caddr	One or more addresses from which the ticket can be used. If this is omitted, the ticket can be used from any address (optional).
Authorization-data	Privilege attributes for the client. Kerberos doesn't interpret the contents of this field. Interpretation is done by the service (optional).

The Flags field is a bit field in which options are set by turning a particular bit on (1) or off (0). Although the field is 32 bits long, only a few of the ticket flags are of interest. These are listed in Table 11.3.

Clients need to know some of the information that's inside tickets and TGTs in order to manage their credentials cache. When the KDC returns a ticket and session key as the result of an AS or TGS information exchange, it packages the client's copy of the session key in a data structure that includes the information in the ticket fields Flags, Authtime, Starttime, Endtime, and Renew-till. The entire structure is encrypted in the client's key and returned with KRB_AS_REP or KRB_TGS_REP.

Ticket Lifetimes

Kerberos 5 tickets have a start time and an expiration time. Between these times, a client that holds a ticket for a service can present that ticket and gain access to the service, no matter how many times the client has used the ticket before. To reduce the risk of having a ticket or the corresponding session key become compromised, administrators can set a maximum lifetime for tickets.

When a client asks the KDC for a ticket to a service, it may request a specific start time. If this time is missing from the request or is a time in the past, the KDC sets the ticket's Starttime field to the current time.

Whether or not clients specify a start time, their requests must include a desired expiration time. The KDC determines the value of a ticket's Endtime field by adding the maximum ticket life fixed by Kerberos policy to the value of the ticket's

Table 11.3   Ticket flags.

Flag Name	Description
FORWARDABLE	Tells the TGS that it can issue a new TGT with a different network address based on the presented TGT (TGT only).
FORWARDED	Indicates either that a TGT has been forwarded or that a ticket was issued from a forwarded TGT.
PROXIABLE	Tells the TGS that it can issue tickets with a different network address than the one in the TGT (TGT only).
PROXY	Indicates that the network address in the ticket is different from the one in the TGT used to obtain the ticket.
RENEWABLE	Used in combination with the Endtime and Renew-till fields to cause tickets that have long life spans to be renewed periodically at the KDC.
INITIAL	Indicates that this is a TGT (TGT only).

Starttime field. It then compares the result with the requested expiration time. Whichever time is sooner becomes the ticket's expiration time.

The KDC doesn't notify clients when session tickets or TGTs are about to expire. If a client presents an expired session ticket when requesting a connection to a server, the server returns an error message, and the client must then request a new session ticket from the KDC. After a connection is authenticated, however, it doesn't matter whether the session ticket expires during that session. Session tickets are used only to authenticate new connections with servers, and ongoing operations aren't interrupted if the session ticket expires.

If a client presents an outdated TGT when requesting a session ticket from the KDC, the KDC responds with an error message. The client must then request a new TGT and needs the user's long-term key. If the client didn't cache this key during the initial logon process, it may have to ask the user for a password.

Renewable Kerberos Tickets

One defense against attacks on session keys is to set Kerberos 5 policy so that the maximum ticket life is relatively short. Another defense is to allow renewable tickets. When tickets are renewable, session keys are refreshed periodically without issuing a completely new ticket. If Kerberos 5 policy permits renewable tickets, the KDC sets a RENEWABLE flag in every ticket it issues and sets two expiration times in the ticket. The first expiration time limits the life of the current instance of the ticket, and the second expiration time sets a limit on the cumulative lifetime of all instances of the ticket.

The expiration time for the current instance of the ticket is held in the Endtime field. A client that holds a renewable ticket must send it to the KDC for renewal before the endtime is reached, also presenting a fresh authenticator. When the KDC receives a ticket for renewal, it checks the second expiration time held in the Renew-till field and ensures that the renew-till time hasn't yet arrived. It then issues a new instance of the ticket with a later endtime and a new session key.

This means that administrators can set Kerberos 5 policy so that tickets must be renewed at relatively short intervals. When tickets are renewed, a new session key is issued, minimizing the damage that could result from a compromised key. Administrators can also set the cumulative ticket life for a relatively long period. At the end of that time, the ticket expires and is no longer valid for renewal.

Delegation of Authentication

In multitier client/server applications, a client connects to a server, which in turn must then connect to a second, back-end server. For this to happen, the first server must have a ticket to the second server. Ideally, the ticket should limit the first server's access on the second server to whatever the client—rather than the first server—is authorized to do.

Kerberos 5 deals with this situation through a mechanism known as *delegation of authentication,* in which the client delegates authentication to a server by telling the KDC that the server is authorized to represent the client. This is a concept similar to impersonation in Windows 2000.

Delegation can be done in either of two ways:

- *Proxy tickets*—The client gets a ticket for the back-end server and then gives it to the front-end server. The difficulty with proxy tickets is that the client must know the name of the back-end server.

- *Forwarded tickets*—The client gives the front-end server a TGT that it can use to request tickets, as needed.

The Kerberos 5 policy may use either of these methods, but not both.

Proxy Tickets

When the KDC issues a TGT to a client, it checks Kerberos 5 policy to see whether proxy tickets are allowed. If they are, the KDC sets the PROXIABLE flag in the TGT that it issues to the client.

The client obtains a proxy ticket by presenting a TGT to the TGS and asking for a ticket to the back-end server. The client's request includes a flag signaling that it wants a proxy ticket and also includes the name of the server that will represent the client. When the KDC receives the client's request, it creates a ticket for the back-end server, sets the PROXY flag in the ticket, and sends it back to the client. The client then sends the ticket to the front-end server, which uses the ticket to access the back-end server.

Forwarded Tickets

If a client wants to delegate the task of obtaining tickets for back-end servers to a front-end server, it asks the KDC for a forwardable TGT. It does this through an AS Exchange request, indicating to the KDC the name of the server that will act on its behalf. If Kerberos 5 policy permits forwarding, the KDC creates a TGT for the front-end server to use in the client's name, sets the FORWARDABLE flag, and sends the TGT back to the client. The client then forwards the TGT to the front-end server.

When the front-end server requests a ticket to the back-end server, it presents the client's TGT to the KDC. When the KDC issues a ticket, it sees the FORWARDABLE flag in the TGT, sets the FORWARDED flag in the ticket, and returns the ticket to the front-end server.

11. Kerberos 5

The Security Support Provider

The Security Support Provider has been mentioned a few times in this chapter without a full explanation of what it is. The SSP is a DLL that's supplied with the operating system and implements the Kerberos 5 authentication protocol. Windows 2000 also includes an SSP for NTLM authentication and, by default, both are loaded by the LSA on a Windows 2000 computer when the system boots. Either SSP may be used to authenticate network logons and client/server connections—the one that's used depends on the capabilities of the computer on the other side of the connection. The Kerberos SSP is always the first choice.

After the LSA establishes a security context for an interactive user, a process running in the user's security context to support the signing and sealing of messages may load another instance of the Kerberos SSP.

The Security Support Provider Interface

System services and transport-level applications access SSPs through the Microsoft Security Support Provider Interface (SSPI). The SSPI is the Win32 interface between transport level applications and network security service providers. It implements methods for enumerating the providers available on a system, selecting one and using it to obtain an authenticated connection. SSPI APIs integrate authentication, message integrity, and privacy into distributed applications. The Distributed Component Object Model (DCOM) application framework and authenticated Remote Procedure Calls (RPCs) take advantage of SSPI services from higher-level interfaces. SSPI security services are also integrated with application-level interfaces, such as Winsock2 and WinInet.

The SSPI provides an abstraction layer between application-level protocols and security protocols. SSPI services can be used in a number of ways:

1. Traditional socket-based applications can call SSPI routines directly and implement the application protocol that carries SSPI security-related data, using request and response messages.

2. Applications can use DCOM to call security options that are implemented using authenticated RPC and SSPI APIs at lower levels. Applications don't call SSPI APIs directly.

3. Winsock2 extends the Windows Sockets interface to allow transport providers to expose security features. This approach integrates the SSPI security provider into the network stack and provides both security and transport services through a common interface.

4. WinInet is an application protocol interface that's designed to support Internet security protocols, such as Secure Sockets Layer (SSL). WinInet security support uses the SSPI interface to the Secure Channel security provider.

Scripting languages, such as vbscript and jscript, allow the applications developer access to the SSPI APIs. If you want to try your hand at coding, look first at the examples provided in the Windows 2000 Software Development Kit (SDK).

The SSPI provides a common interface between transport-level applications, such as Microsoft RPC or a file system redirector, and security providers. It also provides a mechanism by which a distributed application can call one of several security providers to obtain an authenticated connection without knowledge of the details of the security protocol. Details of the SSPI interfaces and functions (or *methods*) that applications can use are given in the Immediate Solutions section of this chapter.

Security Providers and Security Packages

A Security Provider is a DLL that implements the SSPI and makes one or more *security packages* available to applications. A security package SSP maps the SSPI functions to an implementation of the security protocol specific to that package, such as NTLM, Kerberos 5, or Secure Sockets Layer (SSL). The name of the security package is used in the initialization step to identify a specific package.

The SSPI allows an application to use any of the available security packages on a system without changing the interface to use security services. The SSPI doesn't establish logon credentials because that's generally a privileged operation handled by the operating system.

An application can use the package-management functions to list the security packages available and select one to support its needs. The application then uses the credential-management functions to obtain a *handle* to the credentials of the user on whose behalf they are executing. With this handle, the application can use the context-management functions to create a security context to a service. A *security context* is an opaque data structure that contains the security data relevant to a connection, such as a session key, the duration of the session, and so on. Finally, the application uses the security context with the message-support functions to ensure message integrity and privacy during the connection.

The capabilities of the security package determine what services it provides to the application. These include, for example, support for client-only authentication or mutual authentication or support for message integrity and message privacy. In addition, some packages are designed for use only on reliable transport protocols and not for use on datagram transports.

The security package capabilities available from a specific package are obtained by accessing the **QuerySecurityPackageInfo** function within an application. Security package capabilities can be classified as follows:

1. Authentication-related capabilities:
   - Client-only authentication
   - Multileg authentication required
   - Supports Windows impersonation
2. Transport-related capabilities:
   - Datagram-style transports
   - Connection-oriented transports
   - Data-stream connection semantics
3. Message-related capabilities:
   - Supports message integrity
   - Supports message privacy

Applications typically select security packages based on the type of security capabilities available to meet their needs.

Immediate Solutions

Configuring Kerberos 5 Domain Policy

In Windows 2000, Kerberos 5 policy is defined at the domain level and implemented by the domain's KDC. Kerberos 5 policy is stored in Active Directory as a subset of the attributes of domain security policy. By default, policy options can be set only by members of the Domain Administrators group. To Set Kerberos 5 domain policy, proceed as follows:

1. Log on to a domain controller as a domain administrator.

2. Access Start|Programs|Administrative Tools and select Domain Users and Computers.

3. Right-click the domain name and select Properties.

4. On the Security tab, click Domain Policy GPO, then click Edit.

5. Expand Computer Configuration|Windows Settings|Security Settings| Account Policy and then click Kerberos Policy, as shown in Figure 11.8.

6. You can now configure the following settings:

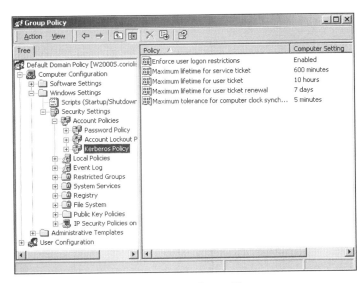

Figure 11.8   Kerberos domain policy settings.

- *Enforce user logon restrictions*—When this option is enabled, the KDC validates every request for a session ticket by examining the user rights policy on the target computer to verify that the user has the right either to log on locally or to access this computer from the network. Verification is optional, because the extra step takes time and may slow network access to services. The default is Enabled.

- *Maximum lifetime for service ticket*—A *service ticket* is a session ticket. Settings are in minutes. The setting must be greater than 10 minutes and less than or equal to the setting for *Maximum lifetime for user ticket*. The default is 600 minutes (10 hours).

- *Maximum lifetime for user ticket*—A *user ticket* is a TGT. Settings are in hours. The default is 10 hours.

- *Maximum lifetime for user ticket renewal*—Settings are in days. The default is 7 days.

- *Maximum tolerance for computer clock synchronization*—Settings are in minutes. The default is 5 minutes.

WARNING!   The Windows 2000 defaults are adequate for most situations and should be changed only after careful analysis of your security requirements. If your domain doesn't have any slow links and you're concerned about replay attacks, you may want to reduce the clock synchronization time. In a high-security environment, you may want to reduce ticket lifetimes. If security isn't a particular concern and you want to speed up access to services, consider disabling the Enforce user logon restrictions option.

Using the Security Support Provider Interface

Application programs can make use of the SSPI interfaces and methods. The Windows 2000 platform SDK, available at **www.microsoft.com**, provides details on how to access the SSPI, together with sample programs. The SSPI consists of four types of interfaces, each with a number of methods:

1. *Credential-management interfaces*—Provide access to credentials (password data, tickets, and so on) or free such access. The following methods are available:

   - **AcquireCredentialsHandle**—Acquires a handle to the reference credentials.

   - **FreeCredentialsHandle**—Releases a credential handle and associated resources.

- **QueryCredentialAttributes**—Allows queries on various credential attributes, such as associated name, domain name, and so on.

2. *Context-management interfaces*—Provide methods for creating and using security contexts. The contexts are created on both the client and the server side of a communication link and can then be used later with the message support interfaces. The following methods are available:

    - **InitializeSecurityContext**—Initiates a security context by generating an opaque message (security token) that can be passed to the server.

    - **AcceptSecurityContext**—Creates a security context, using the opaque message received from the client.

    - **DeleteSecurityContext**—Frees a security context and associated resources.

    - **QueryContextAttributes**—Allows queries on various context attributes.

    - **ApplyControlToken**—Applies a supplemental security message to an existing security context.

    - **CompleteAuthToken**—Completes an authentication token. This is necessary because some protocols, such as Distributed Computing Environment Remote Procedure Call (DCE RPC), need to revise the security information after the transport has updated certain message fields.

    - **ImpersonateSecurityContext**—Attaches the client's security context to the calling thread as an impersonation token.

    - **RevertSecurityContext**—Ceases impersonation and defaults the calling thread to its primary token.

3. *Message-support interfaces*—Provide communication integrity and privacy services based on a security context. The following methods are available:

    - **MakeSignature**—Generates a secure signature based on a message and a security context.

    - **VerifySignature**—Verifies that the signature matches a received message.

4. *Package-management interfaces*—Provide services for various security packages that the security provider supports. The following methods are available:

    - **EnumerateSecurityPackages**—Lists available security packages and their capabilities.

    - **QuerySecurityPackageInfo**—Queries an individual security package for its capabilities.

Chapter 12

Internet Information Services

In Depth

Internet Information Services (IIS) is a well-established product, providing a set of services that enable fully featured World Wide Web (WWW or Web) and File Transport Protocol (FTP) sites to be set up for a wide variety of organizations—of all sizes and with varying requirements. It's also used for information storage and dissemination within organizations through company intranet sites. Version 5 (IIS5) provides new features that improve reliability, security, manageability, and performance. The new version introduces Web Distributed Authoring and Versioning (WebDAV), and application developers can take advantage of improvements to Active Server Pages (ASP). IIS5 runs as an enterprise service within Windows 2000 and makes use of Windows 2000 security and Active Directory services.

New Features and Improvements

IIS4 provided full support for Internet standards and offered a number of enhanced security and programmability features. Where IIS4 made its major step forward, however, was its improved administration features—it was the first Microsoft product to use the Microsoft Management Console (MMC), which subsequently became the main administration engine for Windows 2000. IIS5 improves the product still further in the following areas:

- *Security*—IIS5 supports industry-standard security protocols, such as Digest Authentication, Server Gated Cryptography (SGC), Kerberos 5, Transport Layer Security (TLS), and Fortezza.

- *Reliability*—The reliable restart feature makes IIS5 faster and easier to restart and enables an administrator to restart Web services without rebooting the computer. Application Protection provides the ability to run applications in a pool, separate from the Web services. Central Processing Unit (CPU) Throttling and Socket Pooling are mainly performance enhancements, but can also improve reliability.

- *Performance*—CPU Throttling and Socket Pooling enable administrators to tune performance and resource usage. Application developers are presented with a number of performance tools, such as scriptless ASP processing, ASP self-tuning, and performance-enhanced ASP objects.

- *Management*—IIS5 provides a simplified installation process, flexible remote administration, a facility to account for the time used by processes, custom error messages, and new security task wizards.

- *File management*—Although part of the management topic, file management, particularly the management of remote files during collaborative projects through WebDAV, is an area where IIS5 offers significant new facilities. It is therefore discussed separately.

- *Application development*—In addition to the ASP enhancements mentioned above, IIS5 expands the development environment by building on new technologies included in Windows 2000 Server, such as Active Directory and the expanded Component Object Model (COM+).

Security

Security is an essential feature for any Internet server, because that server is normally an organization's primary interface to the public (and often dangerous) Internet. IIS5 takes advantage of Internet-standard security features that are fully integrated with Windows 2000. Securing an Internet site (whether Web, FTP, or email) involves a number of multistep procedures that use these standard security features. This chapter describes these procedures and how they make use of the security features. IIS5 introduces three new task wizards to make it easier for administrators to configure security, and these are described in this section.

Security Protocols and Features

Some of these security features were implemented in IIS4; others are introduced in the new version. The security features and protocols supported by IIS5 are described below.

Secure Sockets Layer Version 3

SSL3 is used to verify content integrity and user identity and to encrypt network transmissions. The protocol uses security certificates, which are described later in this chapter. Hypertext Transfer Protocol (HTTP) that uses SSL3 encryption is known as Secure Hypertext Transfer Protocol (HTTPS). The immediate solution "Using SSL3 to Secure a Web Site" in Chapter 10 describes how SSL3 encryption can be applied to an HTTP Web site. Procedures for setting up a Certificate Authority (CA) and obtaining a certificate are described in the Immediate Solutions section of this chapter.

Transport Layer Security

TLS is based on SSL3 and enables cryptographic user authentication. The protocol provides a mechanism that lets a programmer write TLS-enabled code that can exchange cryptographic information with a process written by another programmer, without the programmers needing to be familiar with each other's code. TLS provides a framework that can be used by new public key and bulk encryption methods as they emerge and improves performance by reducing network traffic and providing an optional session caching scheme. This reduces the number of connections that need to be established from scratch. The Proposed Standard RFC 2246 describes TLS.

Public Key Cryptography Standard Protocols

IIS5 supports two of these protocols:

- *PKCS #7*—Describes the format of encrypted data, such as digital signatures that identify a user and digital envelopes that securely contain information. Further information is available in RFC 2315.

- *PKCS #10*—Describes the format of requests for certificates that are submitted to CAs. Further information is available in RFC 2314.

Fortezza

IIS5 introduces support for the U.S. government's Fortezza security standard, which satisfies the Defense Message System security architecture requirements. Fortezza offers a cryptographic mechanism that provides message confidentiality, integrity, authentication, nonrepudiation, and access control to messages, components, and systems. These features are implemented in both server and browser software and on Personal Computer Memory Card International Association (PCMCIA) card hardware.

Kerberos 5

Kerberos 5 (see Chapter 11) is the default Windows 2000 authentication protocol and is used when IIS5 user authentication is integrated with Windows authentication. Integrated Windows Authentication, described in the next section, uses Kerberos 5 if supported by the client, failing which it uses NT LAN Manager (NTLM) protocol—sometimes known as Windows NT Challenge/Response protocol.

Authentication

Authentication mechanisms confirm the identity of a user that's requesting access to your Internet sites. IIS5 supports several types of authentication.

Anonymous Authentication

Anonymous Authentication gives users access to the public areas of a Web or FTP site without prompting for a username or password. If Anonymous Authentication is enabled, IIS5 always tries to use it first. When an anonymous user connects to a public Web or FTP site, the IIS5 server assigns the user to the user account IUSR_*computername*, where *computername* is the IIS5 server name.

If your IIS5 sever hosts multiple sites or if you have areas of your site that require different access privileges, you can create multiple anonymous accounts. You can then give these accounts different access permissions or assign them to different Windows user groups. In this way, you can grant users anonymous access to several areas of your public Web and FTP sites and give them permissions appropriate to the area that they access.

Basic Authentication

Basic Authentication is included in the HTTP 1 specification, as discussed in the Informational RFC 1945. Older browsers that aren't RFC 2616 (HTTP 1.1) compliant can, therefore, use it. The Basic Authentication method sends passwords over networks in Base64 encoded format and is a widely used, industry-standard method for collecting username and password information. However, Web browsers that use Basic Authentication transmit passwords in an unencrypted form, and a malicious third party can intercept and decipher these passwords by using a network sniffer. Basic Authentication is not recommended unless you are confident that the connection between the user and your Web server is secure.

Digest Authentication

IIS5 introduces Digest Authentication, which offers the same features as Basic Authentication but passes authentication credentials through a one-way process known as hashing. The result of this process is called a *hash*, or *message digest*, and the original text can't (in theory) be deciphered from the hash. The server generates additional information (such as a timestamp) that's added to the password before hashing so the password hash can't be captured and used to impersonate the true client in a *replay attack* (see Chapter 11).

> **TIP:** *Nothing, and I mean nothing, is totally secure, especially on a network. When choosing a security method, you're looking for an appropriate level of security. Perfect security doesn't exist.*

Digest Authentication can be used across proxy servers and other firewall applications and is available to WebDAV. If a noncompliant browser makes a request on a server that requires Digest Authentication, the server will reject the request and send the client an error message. Digest Authentication can be used only with newer browsers, such as Internet Explorer version 5 (IE5) or later.

Basic FTP Authentication

When Basic FTP Authentication is used, users log on with a username and password corresponding to a valid Windows user account. If the FTP server can't verify the user's identity, an error message is returned. Basic FTP authentication transmits the password and username across the network in an unencrypted form and is therefore insecure.

Anonymous FTP Authentication

If your FTP site is configured to allow Anonymous FTP Authentication, IIS5 will always try to use it first, even if Basic Authentication is also enabled. If you select Anonymous Authentication for a resource, all requests for that resource will be accepted without prompting the user for a username or password. Access to the resource can be limited by IP filtering, but otherwise the resource is available to any user. Resource permissions are therefore likely to be minimal.

Integrated Windows Authentication

Integrated Windows Authentication allows users who have domain accounts, or accounts in trusted domains, to use resources to which they have appropriate permissions without needing any additional authentication. In previous versions of Microsoft Windows (such as NT4), Windows Authentication used NTLM (or Windows NT Challenge/Response) authentication, in which the username and password are not sent across the network. Windows 2000 supports NTLM authentication for backward compatibility and use in mixed domains. The default method of Windows 2000 authentication, however, is Kerberos 5.

Kerberos 5 is a feature of the Windows 2000 Distributed Services architecture. Windows 2000 IIS5 Web services are fully integrated with the Kerberos security infrastructure, which provides fast, single logon to Windows 2000 Server and is the primary security protocol for access to resources within or across Windows 2000 domains. For Kerberos 5 authentication to be successful, both the client and server must have a trusted connection to a Key Distribution Center (KDC) and be Active Directory compatible. If this isn't the case, the Integrated Windows Authentication mechanism will fall back to using NTLM authentication.

Only certain browsers support Integrated Windows Authentication, and the mechanism doesn't work over HTTP proxy connections. Integrated Windows Authentication is best suited for an intranet environment, where both the client and Web server computers are in the same domain and where a standard browser can be specified for all users.

Certificates

Certificates are digital identification documents that are used extensively by Windows 2000 as a mechanism for verifying user identities and allowing both servers and clients to authenticate each other. Until Microsoft introduced Certificate Services, certificates had to be obtained from commercial certificate authorities, such as VeriSign or Thawte. Although this is a straightforward procedure for most types of certificates, it's more convenient to use a CA in your own domain.

A certificate is required for both the IIS server and the client browser to set up an SSL3 connection over which encrypted information can be sent. Server certificates typically contain information about the organization that provides the Internet service and the organization that issued the certificate (which may be the same organization). Client certificates typically contain information about the user and the organization that issued the certificate.

The certificate-based SSL3 features in IIS5 consist of a server certificate, an optional client certificate, and digital keys. Procedures for setting up a CA and obtaining a certificate are described in the Immediate Solutions section of this chapter.

Certificate Authentication

An SSL3-enabled Web server can carry out two types of authentication. A server certificate enables users to authenticate a Web site before they transmit personal information, such as a credit card number; a client certificate is used by the Web site to authenticate users that are requesting information.

Certificate Mapping

Client certificates can be associated with, or *mapped* to, Windows 2000 domain user accounts on a Web server. Each time a user logs on with a mapped client certificate, the Web server automatically associates that user with the appropriate user account and thus authenticates the user without requiring Basic, Digest, or integrated Windows authentication.

A single client certificate can be mapped to one user account. Alternatively, you can map many client certificates to a single account. If, for example, your company has a business partner or associated company whose employees require access to specific Web resources, you can map all of the client certificates of that associate to a user account that has the appropriate access permissions. The associate company then issues certificates to its employees, and any employee of that company has the appropriate access permissions to your Web site without further administrative effort on your part.

A second associate company can have its certificates mapped to another user account in your domain, and its employees will have a different set of access permissions. User certificates can be installed on *smart cards*, which are validated using a Personal Identity Number (PIN). This avoids many of the known weaknesses of username/password authentication.

TIP: *If you want to learn more about certificates, certificate mapping, and smart cards, refer to Chapters 7, 8, and 9 of* Windows 2000 Security Little Black Book, *published by The Coriolis Group, © 2000: ISBN 1-57610-387-0. The book is written by one Ian McLean, and I think it's wonderful (but I would, wouldn't I?).*

Certificate Storage

IIS5 certificate storage is integrated with Windows 2000 Cryptographic Application Programming Interface (CryptoAPI) storage. Administrators can use the Windows Certificate Manager tool to store, back up, and configure server certificates.

Encryption

Encryption is used to protect information as it passes over a network. In a Windows 2000 intranet, Internet Protocol Security (IPSec) provides protection at the transport layer level that's invisible to the user (see Chapter 7). Over the Internet, SSL3 provides a secure method of establishing an encrypted communication link with users so that private information, such as credit card numbers, can be transmitted. Encryption scrambles the information before it's sent, and decryption unscrambles it after it's received. SSL3 confirms the authenticity of your secure Web site and (optionally) the identity of users accessing that site.

Certificates include encrypted keys that are used to establish an SSL3 connection. A key is a unique identifier that's used to authenticate the server and the client. SSL3 uses a public key/private key pair. The Web server uses the key pair to negotiate a secure connection with the user's browser and to determine the level of encryption required for securing communications. Private key/public key encryption is termed *asymmetric* because the private and public keys aren't the same (compare symmetric secret key encryption, as described in Chapter 11). A slightly simplistic description of asymmetric encryption is as follows:

1. You want to send me your credit card number. You want to be sure that it's read by me and only me.

2. I send you my public key. This isn't confidential. My private key, on the other hand, is known only to me.

3. You encrypt the information with my public key and send it to me. I decrypt it with my private key.

4. Because I can decrypt the information with my private key, I know it's been encrypted with my public key.

5. If anyone else intercepts the signal, they can't decrypt it because they don't know my private key.

Of course, it's not as simple as that. How do you know the public key that I sent you actually came from me? How do I know the message that I got back came from you? Is a third party intercepting and replaying information? Other data, such as timestamp information, is used in the transaction to generate a *session key* that's actually used for encryption and decryption. At the end of the transaction, the session key is deleted so that it can't be discovered and used later by another party.

SSL3 encryption requires that both the Web server and the user's browser have compatible encryption and decryption capabilities. The session key's degree of encryption, or *strength*, is measured in bits—the greater the number of bits, the greater the level of encryption and security. Each extra bit doubles the encryption strength. The downside is that strong encryption requires a lot of server resources, particularly processing power.

A Web server session key is typically 40 bits long, but can be up to 128 bits long, depending on the level of security required. For some time, U.S. export restrictions limited the 128-bit key strength encryption feature to the U.S. and Canada. Server-Gated Cryptography (SGC) allowed financial institutions that had export versions of IIS5 to use strong (128-bit) encryption internationally, provided they obtained an SGC certificate. This, however, is no longer the case. 128-bit encryption can now be exported under a license exception, and SGC certificates should no longer be necessary. Nevertheless, don't specify 128-bit encryption unless you're certain that all your Web site clients can support it.

WARNING!   If you specify 128-bit encryption on your secure Web site (it's a simple check in a checkbox) and you don't have a 128-bit certificate, your site will be disabled.

Access Control

IIS5 uses two types of access control, Web permissions and New Technology Filing System (NTFS) permissions. Web permissions apply to all HTTP clients and define the HTTP verbs, or *methods*, that can be used to access server resources (see Chapter 10). NTFS permissions define the level of access that individual user accounts have to directories and files on the server.

IIS5 implements the WebDAV standard (described later in this chapter). WebDAV facilitates file and directory manipulation over an HTTP connection and is an extension of HTTP 1.1. It enables properties to be added to and read from files and directories, and files and directories can also be created, deleted, moved, or copied remotely. Additional access control can be configured through both Web server and NTFS permissions.

Auditing

The easy part of auditing consists of creating audit policies that record directory and file access or server events. The difficult part is finding time to inspect the security logs on a regular basis. Auditing enables you, for example, to detect access attempts by unauthorized persons and to monitor your site's usage. You can configure security logs to record information about directory and file access and server events. You can use the integrated Windows utilities (such as Event Viewer) or the logging features built into IIS5. ASP applications can be designed to create auditing logs to your own requirements.

> **TIP:**   Directory and file access auditing requires that these files and directories reside on a volume of your hard disk that's formatted as NTFS. You can convert from the File Allocation Table (FAT) to the NTFS file system without losing any data (back it up first anyway) by accessing Start|Run and entering **convert x: /FS:NTFS,** where x is the drive letter of the volume. This is a one-way conversion.

You can monitor server-wide events, such as logging on and off the Web server, changing Web server security policies, and shutting down the server computer. You can also monitor attempts to access your Web or FTP sites, virtual directories, or files.

Security Wizards

IIS5 provides three new security wizards, which are described in this section.

The Certificate Wizard

The Certificate Wizard performs certificate administration tasks, such as creating certificate requests and managing the certificate life cycle. It simplifies the task of setting up SSL-enabled Web sites and makes it easier to establish and maintain SSL encryption and client certificate authentication. The wizard can detect whether a server certificate has already been installed and if it is about to expire. You can use the wizard to replace the server certificate with another one from an external CA, from an online CA, or from a file previously obtained from Key Manager. You can also reassign a certificate from one Web site to another. The Certificate Wizard is used in the Immediate Solutions section of this chapter.

The Permission Wizard

The Permission Wizard simplifies the task of setting up and managing a Web or FTP site that requires authenticated access to its content. This wizard takes a walk-through approach. You select the standard configuration that most closely resembles your site's needs, and the wizard sets all of the access permissions and authentication schemes for you. This ensures that site and NTFS permissions are properly coordinated and that the correct authentication scheme is used. You can then fine-tune the permissions to your particular requirements using the IIS MMC snap-in. The standard configurations are:

- *Public Web site*—The information on the site is intended for public consumption over the Internet. This configuration uses anonymous authentication and allows users to view all files and access ASP applications on the site. It gives administrators complete control over the site.

- *Secure Web site*—This configuration is used for corporate *extranets*, which are intranets accessed over the Internet. It uses Basic, Digest, or Integrated Windows authentication and allows only authorized users to view all files and access ASP applications. It gives administrators complete control over the site.

The Certificate Trust List Wizard

The Certificate Trust List (CTL) Wizard is used to configure lists of trusted CAs for a particular directory. Configuring these CTLs enables certificates issued by one CA to be used while prohibiting the use of certificates from another CA. CTLs are used (for example) by Internet Service Providers (ISPs) that host several Web sites on the one server and need to have a different list of approved CAs for each site. CTLs aren't available for FTP sites.

Performance and Reliability

Performance and reliability features are discussed together in this section, because features that determine performance often have reliability implications, and vice versa. Some of the features that are new in IIS5 can't be configured. For example, operation speed has been increased through coding refinements, and the Reliable Restart feature lets you restart the server more quickly. However, IIS5 also introduces features that you can use and configure to improve the speed and reliability of Web and FTP sites.

Application Protection

In earlier versions of IIS, all Internet Server Application Programming Interface (ISAPI) applications (including ASP) shared the resources and memory of the server process, and unstable components could cause the server to crash. This made it difficult to develop and debug new components. Also, in-process components couldn't be unloaded unless the server was restarted. This meant that modifying existing components affected all sites that shared the same server, whether they were directly affected by the upgrade or not.

IIS4 allowed applications to run either in the same process as Web services (inetinfo.exe) or in a process that's separate from Web services (dllhost.exe). IIS5 provides a third option—applications can be run in a pooled process in dllhost.exe. These three options provide varying levels of protection, each of which impacts performance. The more processes you choose to isolate, the slower your performance.

WARNING!   Don't run more than 10 isolated applications. To do so could adversely affect performance.

By default, Web services (inetinfo.exe) will run in its own process, and other applications will be run in a single, pooled process (dllhost.exe). If one application in the pool fails, it takes down all the applications in the pool, but the core Internet services still run. Optionally, you can set critical applications to run as isolated processes by using another instance of dllhost.exe.

You can also choose to run one or more applications in inetinfo.exe. Applications running in inetinfo.exe will run faster, but a faulty application can crash the core Internet services. The recommended configuration is to run inetinfo.exe in its own process, run mission-critical applications in their own processes, and run remaining applications in a shared pooled process, as shown in Figure 12.1.

Reliable Restart

Windows 2000 introduces the IIS Reliable Restart feature, which implements a one-step restart process. There's no need to reboot, nor is it necessary to start four separate services manually, as was the case with former versions of IIS. You can restart IIS by right-clicking Internet Information Services in the IIS MMC snap-in and selecting Restart IIS. The Windows 2000 Service Control Manager automatically restarts IIS Services if the inetinfo process terminates unexpectedly.

Hosting Multiple Sites

IIS4 extends the capability of IIS4 to host multiple sites on a single server. This is a useful feature for a company that wants to host different sites for different departments or for an ISP that hosts multiple sites for different customers. Each site has a unique, three-part identity that it uses to receive and to respond to requests—a port number, an IP address, and a site name. The name of the default site is (normally) the host name or Fully Qualified Domain Name (FQDN) of the IIS server, but additional Web sites can be assigned alternative *host header* names. Multiple Web sites can be hosted on a single server by assigning different ports, different IP addresses, or different host header names.

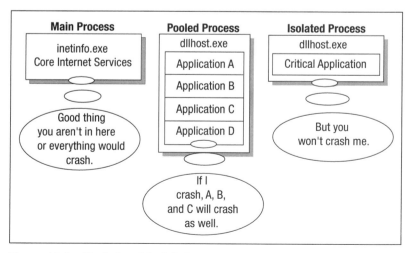

Figure 12.1   Pooled and isolated processes.

Port Numbers

If you specify port numbers other than the default, you can append each of them to the IP address of the default site and thus identify a number of sites. If, for example, the IP address of your Web server were 195.162.230.20 (the appended default port 80 is understood), you could identify sites 195.162.230.20:2000, 195.162.230.20:2001, and so on.

Clients that want to reach these sites would have to type in the actual IP address and port number, rather than the more user-friendly Uniform Resource Locator (URL) that Internet users are accustomed to. Port numbers provide a less than user-friendly method of hosting multiple sites and wouldn't normally be used for public Internet sites. They do, however, provide a primitive level of security for sites that you want only a limited number of selected people to access. Anyone who doesn't know both the IP address and the port number won't be able to access the site.

Multiple IP Addresses

You can bind multiple IP addresses to a single Network Interface Card (NIC) and use these addresses to differentiate between sites on your server. There's no need to add additional NICs. (Although a server that has more than one NIC can host more than one site, additional NICs are normally installed for routing rather than for multiple site access.) You can then specify a host name for the site and add that host name and its corresponding IP address to your name resolution system. The host name becomes the URL for the site. If the site is on the public Internet, you must also register the host name with the Internet Network Information Center (InterNIC), either directly or through an ISP.

Host Header Names

Host header names can be used with a single IP address to host multiple sites. You don't need multiple addresses, and users don't need to type in IP and port numbers to access the site. As with the previous method, you need to add the host header names to your name resolution system, and you need to register the host header names with InterNIC if they are implementing Internet sites. Host headers provide the simplest method of multiple site hosting and require fewer resources than do separate IP addresses.

There are, however, limitations to this method. Host headers can't be used with FTP sites, nor can they be used for SSL3-encrypted sites, because the host header is encrypted and the site can't, therefore, be accessed. Older browsers (prior to Microsoft Internet Explorer 3 and Netscape Navigator 2) can't pass host header names back to IIS. As a result, visitors using older browsers will reach the default site for the IP address rather than the correct site.

Socket Pooling

A *socket* consists of a node address, a port number that identifies the service, and a protocol. For example, TCP port 80 on an Internet node represents a Web server. In previous versions of IIS, sites that were bound to different IP addresses on the same server each had their own socket, which was created when the site started and consumed a significant amount of nonpaged RAM. This limited the number of such sites that could be created on a single machine. In particular, FTP sites that couldn't use host headers and needed separate IP addresses were affected by this limitation.

In IIS5, sites that are bound to different IP addresses but share the same port number also share the same set, or *pool*, of sockets. Sockets from this pool can be allocated flexibly to all of the sites that are started. This reduces resource consumption and lets you allocate more sites to a single IP address. Socket pooling is enabled by default and shouldn't be disabled unless you have a mission-critical site that shares pooled sockets with other, less critical sites. In this case, disable socket pooling at site level, so the less critical sites can continue to share the socket pool.

Clustering

Clustering is available in Windows 2000 Advanced Server. It allows multiple servers to be connected through clustering software so they appear as one computer to users of the Web site. Server clusters increase a site's fault tolerance, because another server can pick up the request load if one server stops working. This is known as *failover* and is particularly important in mission-critical systems. Linked servers can also share the workload so no single server (or clustering *node*) is either overloaded or underutilized. This is known as *load balancing*. Server clusters can share clustered disks that contain (for example) a database that's frequently accessed by users.

The Windows 2000 Cluster Service provides two clustering technologies that can be used with IIS5:

• *Network load balancing clusters*—Provide both high scalability and availability with clusters of up to 32 servers. Load balancing is implemented by distributing client connections among multiple server nodes. Availability is provided by failover fault tolerance. Typically, these clusters are configured for both load balancing and fault tolerance.

- *Server clusters*—Provide high availability through the failover clustering of two connected servers. These clusters provide static load balancing through the assignment of Web or FTP sites, either manually or programmatically, to a specific preferred server node.

Cluster Node Replication

To enable clustered servers to offer mission-critical failover support, content and configuration settings must be copied, or *replicated*, from one server node to other nodes. In this way, all servers can offer the same resources to users. Configuration settings for all nodes must be replicated, whether they share content or not. There's no need to replicate content when nodes share a data storage device, such as a disk drive. IIS5 provides the command-line utility iissync.exe to replicate configuration settings (such as IIS *metabase* settings) from one computer to any number of other computers.

NOTE: *The IIS metabase is a hierarchical structure for storing IIS configuration settings. It provides easier administration and requires less disk space than the Registry.*

If you need to replicate both content and settings, you can use the Content Deployment Service (formerly known as the Content Replication System, or CRS) provided by Microsoft Site Server.

Throttling

IIS5 servers, like most server computers, carry out a number of functions. An IIS5 server could also be hosting email or news services or could be running applications other than Web applications. It is often important to restrict, or *throttle*, the amount of resources used by one function so the performance of other (possibly time-critical) functions isn't adversely affected. Throttling affects only static HTML files, not dynamic ASP files or any other kind of dynamic content. IIS5 offers two throttling modes.

Process Throttling

Process throttling (sometimes referred to as Process Limits, CPU Limits, or Job Object Limits) lets you limit the amount of processor time that a single Web site's applications are permitted to use. This is useful if the IIS5 server hosts multiple Web sites or if there are other applications running on the same server. This feature, new in IIS5, also enables you to limit the use of the CPU by *out-of-process* applications that run in a separate memory space from the core IIS process.

Per Web Site Bandwidth Throttling

If a Web server's network connection is also used by such services as email or news, it's sometimes desirable to limit the bandwidth used by Web services. Per Web Site Bandwidth Throttling, introduced in IIS5, lets you regulate the amount of server bandwidth on a per-site basis bandwidth. An ISP, for example, would use this type of throttling to guarantee a predetermined amount of bandwidth to each site.

NOTE: *If you are using socket pooling (described above), throttling the bandwidth on one site also throttles all other sites sharing that port number. Socket pooling is enabled by default.*

HTTP Compression

HTTP compression allows faster transmission of pages between the Web server and compression-enabled clients and is particularly useful where bandwidth is limited. It is, however, expensive in terms of processor resources. If your server generates a large volume of dynamic content, the additional processing cost of compression may not be one you can reasonably afford. If the %Processor Time counter in Performance Monitor is consistently at 80 percent or more, HTTP compression may be contraindicated.

FTP Restart

Windows 2000 Server supports the FTP Restart protocol, which speeds and smoothes information downloading. If an interruption occurs during data transfer from an FTP site, the download can continue where it left off, and it's not necessary to download the entire file over again.

Management

IIS5 builds on the management tools, such as the MMC, introduced by IIS4, and addresses reported weaknesses in IIS management. For example, the IIS5 installation process is built into the Windows 2000 Server setup. There are three new security wizards, discussed earlier in this chapter, and IIS5 provides improved command-line administration scripts and additional built-in management scripts.

Integrated Setup and Upgrade

IIS5 installs by default as a Windows 2000 Server networking service. A setup wizard helps you install a new copy of IIS5 or upgrade from an older version. Default Web and FTP sites are created when you install Windows 2000 Server, making initial site setup a straightforward file-copying operation. You can add or remove IIS5 or select additional components by using the Add/Remove Programs tool in the Control Panel.

Local Administration

IIS5 is managed using the IIS MMC snap-in, which is accessed from the Server Applications and Services section of the Computer Management Tool. The Internet Services Manager tool also opens the IIS snap-in, but the Computer Management tool lets you access other Windows 2000 administrative functions.

Right-clicking the appropriate site object and selecting Properties accesses the Properties dialog boxes of Web sites, FTP sites, and virtual directories. The Simple Mail Transport Protocol (SMTP) virtual server is an additional IIS5 component that's installed by default. Its property dialog box is accessed in the same way.

As shown in Figure 12.2, the Default Web Site Properties dialog box has 10 tabs:

- *Web Site*—Lets you specify a description, IP address, and port number for your Web site. The Advanced button lets you specify multiple site identities using TCP ports, IP addresses, and host header names. You can specify the maximum number of connections allowed and the connection timeout. You can also enable or disable HTTP Keep-Alives, which allow a client to maintain an open connection with your server rather than reopening the connection with each new request. You can enable logging and specify a log format.

- *Operators*—Lets you specify which Windows user accounts have operator privileges for the site.

- *Performance*—Lets you tune performance to the number of daily connections that you anticipate for the site. You can also enable and configure bandwidth and process throttling.

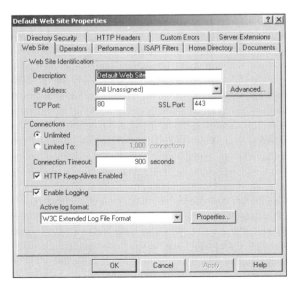

Figure 12.2   The Default Web Site Properties dialog box.

- *ISAPI Filters*—Lets you add, remove, enable, disable, and edit ISAPI filters. An ISAPI filter is a program that responds to events during the processing of an HTTP request.

- *Home Directory*—Lets you specify a path to the site's home directory and set the Web site permissions. You can configure application settings, set execute permissions, and specify the level of Application Protection.

- *Documents*—Lets you define your site's default Web page and append a footer to the site's documents. If you specify several default documents, a browser will attempt to connect to the first document. If the connection attempt fails, the browser will attempt to connect to the second document, and so on down the list.

- *Directory Security*—Lets you specify the authentication methods allowed by the site and use IP filtering to permit or deny access by IP address. You can install a certificate on the site. Once this certificate this has been installed, you can set SSL authentication, specify client certificate requirements, enable client certificate mapping, and configure CTLs.

- *HTTP Headers*—Lets you set values returned to the browser in the header of the HTML page. You can enable and configure content expiration, which is useful if the page contains time-sensitive information, such as special offers or event announcements. You can use a custom HTTP header to send instructions that aren't supported in the current HTML specification. Content ratings are used when sites contain potentially objectionable content. You can configure Multipurpose Internet Mail Extensions (MIME) mappings, which set the file types that the Web server returns to browsers.

- *Custom Errors*—Lets you specify a path to a custom error message. Specifying custom error messages is described in the Immediate Solutions section of this chapter.

- *Server Extensions*—Lets you specify FrontPage Server Extensions, which are publishing controls for a Web site that's been extended using Microsoft's FrontPage publishing software.

As shown in Figure 12.3, the Default FTP Site Properties dialog box has five tabs:

- *FTP Site*—Lets you specify a description, IP address, and port number for your FTP site. You can specify maximum connections allowed and connection timeout, enable logging, and specify a log format.

- *Security Accounts*—Lets you specify whether anonymous access is allowed, whether only anonymous access is allowed, and the name of the account used for anonymous connections. You can specify which Windows user accounts have operator privileges for the site.

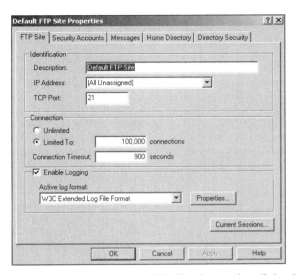

Figure 12.3   The Default FTP Site Properties dialog box.

- *Messages*—Lets you specify welcome and exit messages and, also, the message sent to clients who attempt to connect to the site after the maximum connection limit has been reached.

- *Home Directory*—Lets you specify a path to the home directory, set FTP site permissions, and specify the style for listing the directory contents.

- *Directory Security*—Lets you use IP filtering to permit or deny access by IP address.

As shown in Figure 12.4, the SMTP Virtual Server Properties dialog box has six tabs:

- *General*—Lets you specify a server name and IP address, specify connection parameters, enable logging, and specify a logging format.

- *Access*—Lets you specify authentication methods, install a certificate and use SSL3 encryption, grant or deny access to the site by IP address or domain name, and grant or deny permission to relay email through the virtual server.

WARNING!   If you grant permission to relay email through the virtual server, your email clients could receive unsolicited mail, sometimes of a dubious nature.

- *Messages*—Lets you specify session, message, and recipient limits, the path to the Badmail directory, and the mailbox that Non-Delivery Reports (NDRs) are sent to.

- *Delivery*—Lets you specify retry intervals, delay notifications, and expiration timeouts. The Outbound Security button lets you set authentication, configure

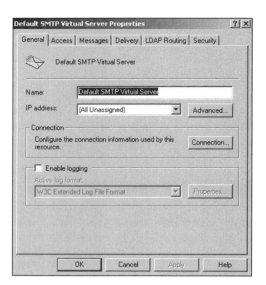

Figure 12.4   The default SMTP Virtual Server Properties dialog box.

the Windows security package, and enable TLS encryption. The Advanced button lets you specify a Masquerade domain, which replaces the local domain name in the mail-from listing. On the Advanced dialog box, you can also specify a smart host. Mail will be sent to this host for onward transmission rather than directly to the recipient. Reverse DNS (Domain Name System) lookup checks the IP address from which an email message is received against the domain or host specified in the message. Finally, this dialog box lets you specify the maximum hop count.

- *LDAP Routing*—Lets you specify the identity and properties of the directory services server used by the virtual server to store information about mail clients and their mailboxes. The SMTP virtual server uses Lightweight Directory Access Protocol (LDAP) to communicate with directory services.

- *Security*—Lets you specify which Windows user accounts have operator privileges for the virtual server.

Remote Administration

Windows 2000 provides Web-based administration tools that let you manage a server remotely from almost any browser. The browser-based administration tool, Internet Services Manager (HTMLA), lets you administer IIS5 remotely over an intranet, over the Internet, or through a proxy server. You can also access the IIS MMC snap-in remotely from a Windows 2000 client, provided that there are no firewall restrictions that prevent you from doing so, and you can use Terminal Services to access either the MMC or HTMLA administration tools. This last approach requires that the server have Terminal Services installed and that the client is running the Remote Access Service (RAS).

Delegated Administration

You can set up Web Site Operators accounts with limited administration privileges on Web sites to help distribute the administrative workload. Web Site Operators can configure properties that affect only their respective sites and don't have access to properties that affect overall IIS5 operation.

For example, a Web Site Operator can set Web site access permissions, enable logging, change the default document or footer, set content expiration, and enable the content ratings features. However, he or she can't change the identification of Web sites, configure the anonymous username or password, throttle bandwidth, create virtual directories or change their paths, or alter application isolation. Web Site Operators can't browse the file system remotely and, therefore, can't set properties on directories and files unless they specify a Universal Naming Convention (UNC) path. The procedure for adding and removing Web Site Operators is described in the Immediate Solutions section of this chapter.

Process Accounting

IIS5 introduces Process Accounting, which lets you monitor and log how Web sites use CPU resources on the server. You can use this information to discover which sites are demanding disproportionately high CPU resources and to determine whether process throttling should be enabled. Process Accounting can also identify sites that may have malfunctioning scripts or Common Gateway Interface (CGI) processes. Accountants can use the information to accurately charge the cost of hosting a Web site and/or application to the appropriate department within an organization.

Process Accounting is enabled on a per-server basis and records information on a per-Web site basis. It doesn't provide details about the CPU usage of each individual application, nor can it log information about applications that share the same process (inetinfo.exe) as the Web server. It adds fields to the W3C Extended log file, and these fields are recorded only when W3C Extended log file format is selected. Process accounting isn't available for FTP sites.

Command-Line Administration Scripts

IIS5 provides command-line scripts to automate the management of common Web server tasks. You can use them to create and control Web sites, applications, and directories and as models if you want to create your own custom scripts. The scripts are written in Microsoft Visual Basic Scripting Edition (VBScript) and are typically used with the cscript.exe command-line scripting utility, which should be registered for running .VBS files.

Administration Scripts can be run using the .VBS files that are installed by default in the Inetpub\adminscripts directory. An executable version of the script file adsutil.vbs (adsutil.exe) is installed in the same directory and accepts the same parameters as adsutil.vbs. This sample file demonstrates how to manipulate the metabase using the Active Directory Service Interfaces (ADSI) in C/C++.

NOTE: *Adsutil.vbs is used in the immediate solution, "Restoring IIS Configuration," later in this chapter.*

Configuration Back Up and Restore

The IIS MMC snap-in can be used to back up your IIS5 configuration metabase settings, so you can, if necessary, restore the configuration to a safe, known state. This won't back up content files or Registry settings, and the method won't implement a full configuration backup if you reinstall IIS5. You can't use the resulting backup files to restore or configure IIS5 settings on other computers.

You can also back up an IIS5 configuration by using the browser-based Internet Services Manager (HTMLA), but you must use the IIS snap-in to restore the configuration. Backing up and restoring an IIS5 configuration is described in the Immediate Solutions section of this chapter.

Custom Error Messages

If an HTTP error occurs when a user attempts to connect to a Web site, an error code and message are sent back to the client browser. These error codes are subsets of the HHTP status codes 401, 403 through 407, 412, 414, 500, 501, and 502 listed in Chapter 10, Table 10.3. The messages provide somewhat cryptic error descriptions. Table 12.1 lists the error codes and generic error messages.

Some of these generic messages aren't particularly helpful. Fortunately, IIS5 lets you customize the generic HTTP error messages through the Custom Errors tab on the site Properties dialog box. The procedure for customizing HTTP error messages is described in the Immediate Solutions section of this chapter.

Table 12.1   HTTP error codes and generic messages.

Error Code	Error Message
400	Bad request
401.1	Log on failed
401.2	Log on failed due to server configuration
401.3	Unauthorized due to ACL on resource
401.4	Authorization failed by filter

(continued)

Table 12.1 ***HTTP error codes and generic messages*** **(continued).**

Error Code	Error Message
401.5	Authorization failed by ISAPI/CGI application
403.1	Execute access forbidden
403.2	Read access forbidden
403.3	Write access forbidden
403.4	SSL required
403.5	SSL 128 required
403.6	IP address rejected
403.7	Client certificate required
403.8	Site access denied
403.9	Too many users
403.10	Invalid configuration
403.11	Password change
403.12	Mapper denied access
403.13	Client certificate revoked
403.14	Directory listing denied
403.15	Client Access Licenses exceeded
403.16	Client certificate untrusted or invalid
403.17	Client certificate has expired or is not yet valid
404	Not found
404.1	Site not found
405	Method not allowed
406	Not acceptable
407	Proxy authentication required
412	Precondition Failed
414	Request-URL too long
500	Internal server error
500.12	Application restarting
500.13	Server too busy
500.15	Requests for Global.asa not allowed
500-100.asp	ASP error
501	Not implemented
502	Bad gateway

File Management

There have been many millions of documents published on the Internet and millions more on private intranets. It's easy to read a document published on a Web site, but not so easy to change it. For most documents, that's probably just as well (RFCs would devalue very quickly if everyone could alter them). If, however, you want to set up collaborative projects in which a group of remote authors move, search, edit, or delete files and directories (and may want to change file and directory properties), the inflexibility of Web site access becomes a limiting factor.

IIS5 addresses this problem by providing full support for WebDAV, as described below. IIS5 also makes use of the Microsoft Distributed file system (Dfs). Dfs was available in NT 4, but was (in my opinion) grossly underused, possibly because it wasn't part of the original release. However, it ships with Windows 2000 and can be used by IIS5 (and other services) to simplify file management and allow administrators to treat the directories of multiple servers as if they were all part of the same directory namespace.

WebDAV

WebDAV is an extension of the HTTP 1.1 standard that's used to expose storage media, such as file systems, over an HTTP connection. If you set up a WebDAV directory on your Web server, you can let users share documents over the Internet or an intranet, while taking advantage of the Windows 2000 security and file access features to lock and unlock resources as required. WebDAV is configured using the Web server permission settings and addresses such issues as file access permissions, offline editing, file integrity, and conflict resolution when competing changes are made to a document.

Because it's integrated into IIS5, WebDAV provides the following facilities:

- *Resource manipulation*—Users with the appropriate permissions can copy and move files in a WebDAV directory.

- *Property modification*—Users can write to and retrieve a file's property information.

- *Resource locking*—Multiple users can read a file concurrently, but only one person at a time can modify it.

- *File searching*—Users connected to a WebDAV directory can search the files for both content and properties. For example, a user can search for all files that contain a specified phrase or for all files written by a specific author.

Setting up a WebDAV publishing directory is similar to setting up a virtual directory through the IIS snap-in—see the immediate solution "Creating a Publishing

Directory" later in this chapter. Users with the appropriate permissions can then publish documents to the server and manipulate files in the directory. The directory can be accessed via a Windows 2000 client, an Office 2000 client, IE5, or any other client that supports the industry-standard WebDAV protocol.

A Windows 2000 client connects to a WebDAV server through the Add Network Place Wizard and displays the contents of a WebDAV directory as if it were part of the local computer's file system. Once connected, you can drag and drop files, retrieve and modify file properties, and do other file-system tasks. IE5 lets you browse to a WebDAV directory and do the same file-system tasks as you can through Windows 2000. Office 2000 creates, publishes, edits, and saves documents directly into a WebDAV directory through any Office 2000 application.

WebDAV uses all of the security features offered by both Windows 2000 and IIS5, including the IIS permissions specified in the IIS snap-in and the Discretionary Access Control Lists (DACLs) that specify NTFS permissions. IIS5 reinforces integrated Windows authentication by adding support for Kerberos 5. In addition, IIS5 uses Digest Authentication to provide tighter security for passwords and for transmitting information across the Internet.

Web Folders

Shortcuts to shared files that are created using WebDAV and stored on Web servers are known as *Web folders* or *HTTP folders*. Web folders are created automatically in My Network Places whenever you open resources on a WebDAV-compliant server on which you have Read and Write access. They let users navigate to a server and view the content as if it were part of the same namespace as the local system. Users can (for example) drag and drop files and retrieve and modify file property information. When you view the contents of a Web folder, you see a list of files and folders as if they were on your local disk, except that you also see their associated Internet addresses.

The Distributed File System

Dfs also unites files on different computers into a single namespace, but isn't limited to WebDAV files. It lets system administrators build a single, hierarchical view of multiple file servers and file server shares on the network and makes it easier for users to access and manage network files and folders. Users no longer need to know and specify the actual physical location of files in order to access them.

You can use Dfs as the filing system for IIS5 by selecting the root for the Web site as a Dfs root. This lets you move resources within the Dfs tree without affecting any HTML links.

Application Development

The ASP technology provided with IIS5, combined with the data access and component services offered by Windows 2000 Server, gives powerful support for application development. Enhanced flow control and error handling, Windows script components, and other improvements make ASP easier to use for both scriptwriters and Web application developers. Features such as scriptless ASP, ASP self-tuning, and performance-enhanced objects, as well as improvements within the Windows 2000 operating system, increase the speed of ASP applications.

> **NOTE:**   *This book is about protocols and services, not programming. I intend, therefore, to list the programming resources available and describe them only briefly. Programmers can take it from there. The Windows 2000 Help files give a considerable amount of additional information on ASP scripting and provide an excellent ASP tutorial.*

Active Server Pages

ASP is a server-side scripting environment that's used to create and run dynamic, interactive Web server applications. It lets you combine HTML pages, script commands, and Component Object Model (COM) components to create interactive Web pages or Web-based applications. IIS5 offers a number of new ASP features, such as additional flow control and error-handling capabilities. Other new features, such as scriptless ASP processing, improve the performance of ASP pages.

Flow Control

New ASP flow control capabilities reduce the number of round trips required between a client and server. A round trip occurs when a server sends an HTTP response to a browser indicating the location of the new URL. The browser leaves the server's request queue and submits a new HTTP request for this URL. The server then adds this request to the request queue. This process, known as Response.Redirect, can waste bandwidth and reduce server performance—especially when the browser is redirected to a file located on the same sever.

The ASP Server object offers two new methods that control program flow, Server.Transfer and Server.Execute. The Server.Transfer method is used to transfer from one ASP file to another file located on the same server. Using Server.Transfer, you can transfer requests for ASP files directly without leaving the server request queue.

The Server.Execute method is used to transfer to a file, execute its content, and then return to the file that initiated the transfer. If you're familiar with VBScript, think of Server.Execute as being similar to a procedure call, except that you're executing an entire ASP file instead of executing a procedure.

The Browser Capabilities Component

The ASP Browser Capabilities component is used to make Web applications more responsive to a particular user's browser by determining the exact capabilities of that browser. When a browser sends a cookie describing its capabilities, an instance of the Browser Capabilities component retrieves the browser's properties as returned by the cookie and creates a Browser Type object that can be used in ASP scripts.

When a browser connects to a Web server, it automatically sends an HTTP User Agent header, which comprises an ASCII string that identifies the browser and its version number. The Browser Type object compares the header to entries in the browscap.ini file. If it finds a match, it assumes the properties of the browser listing that matched the User Agent header. If it doesn't find an exact match, it searches for the closest match using the * and ? wildcards. If a match still can't be found, it uses the default browser settings. You can add properties or new browser definitions to the Browser Capabilities component by updating the browscap.ini file.

Error Handling

ASP offers improved error-handling capabilities that help trap errors in Web applications and send information to the programmer by means of a custom error-message ASP file. The Server.GetLastError method displays such information as an error description or the line number where the error occurred. The ASPError object is used to obtain information about an error condition that has occurred in script in an ASP page and is returned by the Server.GetLastError method.

Scriptless ASP

In earlier IIS versions, ASP pages were processed as though they included script. Pages without script were channeled through the ASP parser before being presented to the client, even though they didn't need server-side processing. As a result, pages coded as static HTML rather than ASP were processed faster. If developers wanted to avoid an unneeded call to the ASP parser, they had to code scriptless pages as HTML and use the .ASP extension only on pages that included script.

IIS5 examines an ASP page to see if it includes server-side scripting before sending it to the parser. If a page doesn't include script, it's served without a trip to the parser. Although HTML pages still process more quickly than ASP pages, ASP pages that don't include scripting are served more quickly than they were in the past.

Performance-Enhanced Objects

IIS5 ASP includes performance-enhanced versions of its installable components that scale reliably in a wide range of Web publishing environments. These components are used to carry out such tasks as rotating advertisements (adrot.dll) and determining a browser's capabilities (browscap.dll).

Self-Tuning

IIS5 ASP detects when external resources block an executing request. If the ASPThreadGateEnabled property in the IIS5 metabase is enabled, ASP automatically provides more threads to execute additional requests simultaneously and to continue normal processing. If the CPU becomes overburdened, ASP reduces the number of threads.

IIS5 performs thread gating to dynamically control the number of concurrently executing threads. Thus, thread numbers vary in response to changing load conditions. The default settings for the ASPThreadGateEnabled property and for the other thread gating properties are designed to be appropriate to the majority of server configurations and traffic conditions. Changing these settings can lead to significant performance degradation. To put this another way, thread usage is self-tuning and shouldn't be tampered with unnecessarily.

The Web service setting for the ASPThreadGateEnabled property is applicable to all in-process and pooled out-of-process application nodes, at all levels. Metabase settings at the Web server level or lower will be ignored for in-process and pooled out-of-process applications. However, settings at the Web server level or lower will be used if that node is an isolated out-of-process application.

Extensible Markup Language Integration

Extensible Markup Language (XML) provides semantic rules that describe the complex structure of data or documents in the same way that HTML describes the format of a Web document. XML-formatted data can be shared across a variety of applications, clients, and servers. You can use the Microsoft XML Parser, included with IE4 or later, to create server-side applications that enable your Web server to exchange XML-formatted data with browsers or servers that have XML parsing capabilities.

Windows Script Components

IIS5 ASP supports the Windows Script Components scripting technology, which lets developers turn business logic script procedures into reusable COM components for use in Web applications and in other COM-compliant programs.

Script components provide a method of creating COM components using scripting languages such as VBScript. You can use script components as COM components in such applications as the Windows Scripting Host (WSH) and any other applications that support COM components.

Encoded ASP Scripts

Web developers can now apply an encoding scheme to both client- and server-side scripts that makes the programmatic logic appear as unreadable ASCII characters. Encoded scripts are decoded at runtime by the script engine. Although the feature isn't intended as a secure, encrypted solution, it can prevent casual users from browsing or copying scripts.

Component Services

IIS5 and COM+ (or Component Services) work together to form a basic architecture for building Web applications. In Windows 2000, COM+ provides the transaction support formerly implemented by Microsoft Transaction Server (MTS), in addition to a number of other component development and deployment features. IIS5 uses the functionality provided by Component Services to isolate applications into distinct processes, manage communication between COM components, and coordinate transaction processing for transactional ASP applications.

IIS5 and Active Directory

Windows 2000 Active Directory stores and manages network resource information, which simplifies network management and makes it easier for users to find resources. Active Directory also makes it easier for developers to write applications that require the current version of significant information. Active Directory Service Interfaces (ADSI) is a COM-based directory service model that allows ADSI-compliant client applications to access a wide variety of directory protocols, including Active Directory and LDAP, while using a single, standard set of interfaces.

An ADSI provider makes itself available to ADSI client applications, exposing data organized in a custom namespace that's defined by the provider. The provider also can implement the ADSI schema, which supplies metadata about the namespace structure and objects that are provided by the ADSI provider. Application developers can add custom objects, properties, and methods to the existing ADSI provider, giving administrators more flexibility in configuring sites.

Immediate Solutions

Installing a Certification Authority

In Chapter 10, you used a certificate to enable SSL3 on a Web site. That procedure assumed that a certificate already existed that could be used for this purpose. The aim of the procedure was to demonstrate the setting up of an HTTPS site rather than the installation of a certificate.

Later in this chapter, you'll be using the IIS5 Certificate Wizard to install a certificate that a Web site can use for authentication. In order to do this, you need to have a CA installed in your domain. This procedure installs a CA. If a suitable CA already exists on your domain, you don't need to carry out the procedure.

There are four types of CAs:

- *Enterprise root CA*—The root of a Windows 2000-based corporate CA hierarchy.

- *Enterprise subordinate CA*—Issues certificates within a corporation, but isn't the most trusted CA in that corporation.

- *Standalone root CA*—The root of a CA trust hierarchy. It can issue certificates outside a corporation's enterprise network.

- *Standalone subordinate CA*—Operates as a solitary certificate server or exists in a CA trust hierarchy. You should set up a Standalone Subordinate CA when you are issuing certificates to entities outside a corporation.

NOTE: *The procedure described next installs an Enterprise root CA on your IIS5 server. This assumes that IIS5 is installed on a domain controller. If your requirements differ from this configuration—you may want your CA on another machine on your network or you may want to set up a CA hierarchy—then amend the procedure accordingly. Remember, however, that the Web Server Certificate Wizard won't recognize a standalone Certificate Server on the same machine.*

To install an Enterprise root CA, proceed as follows:

1. Log on to the IIS5 server as an administrator.
2. Access Start|Settings and select Control Panel.

3. Double-click Add/Remove Programs. The Add/Remove Programs dialog box appears.

4. Click Add/Remove Windows Components to start the Windows Components Wizard.

5. Check the Certificate Services checkbox. Click OK to clear the message box. Ensure that the IIS checkbox is checked. Click Next.

TIP: *Normally the IIS checkbox will be checked, but grayed. This means that IIS5 is installed, but that some optional IIS components are not. Provided there's a tick in the box, you can proceed with installing Certificate Services.*

6. The wizard prompts you to specify the type of CA that you want to set up. Enterprise root CA should be selected by default. Click Next.

NOTE: *If the two Enterprise options are disabled, then no Active Directory has been detected. If the Enterprise subordinate CA is selected by default, then an Enterprise root CA is already registered in Active Directory.*

7. The wizard prompts you to supply identifying information appropriate for your site and organization, as shown in Figure 12.5. Type in this information and click Next.

8. A warning box appears, informing you that the Distinguished Name(s) will be encoded as Unicode strings. Click Yes to clear the box.

9. A dialog box defines the locations of the certificate database, database log, and configuration information. Specify the storage locations for your information, then click Next.

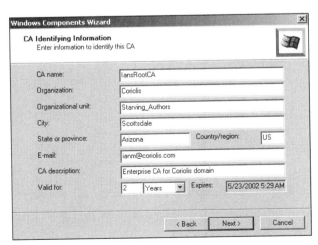

Figure 12.5   Identifying a CA.

TIP: *You are recommended to check the Shared folder checkbox and specify the location of a folder in which configuration information for the CA will be stored. You should make this folder a UNC path and have all of your CAs point to the same folder. Then the administration tools can use this folder to determine CA configuration if Active Directory isn't available.*

---

10. A message box may appear informing you that a folder will be created. Click Yes to clear the box.

11. If IIS is running, a message will appear requesting that you stop the service. Click OK to stop IIS.

12. Installation now occurs. You may be prompted to insert the Windows 2000 Server installation CD-ROM. Click Finish to close the wizard.

Creating an IIS Snap-in Tool

Microsoft recommends using the IIS MMC snap-in rather than the Internet Services Manager tool. This procedure accesses the snap-in and then saves the MMC configuration as IIStool. In the rest of the procedures in this chapter, the IIS snap-in can be started by accessing Start|Programs|Administrative tools and selecting IIStool.

To create an IIS snap-in tool, proceed as follows:

1. Log on to the IIS server as an administrator.

2. Access Start|Run and enter **mmc**.

3. On the Console pull-down menu, select Add/Remove Snap-in.

4. Click Add and select Computer Management.

5. Click Add. Check that Local computer is selected and click Finish.

6. Click Close. Click OK.

7. Expand Computer Management (local).

8. Expand Services and Applications.

9. Expand Internet Information Services.

10. On the Console pull-down menu, select Save As.

11. Save the MMC snap-in as IIStool. The snap-in tool should look similar to Figure 12.6.

12. Close the snap-in.

13. For any procedures in this chapter that require it, open the IIS snap-in by accessing Start|Programs|Administrative tools and selecting IIStool.

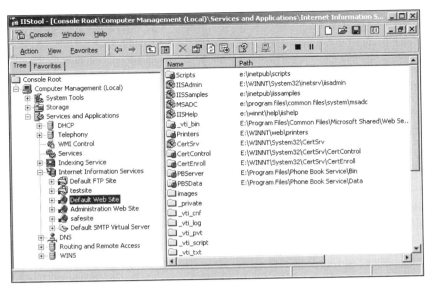

Figure 12.6   The IIStool snap-in.

Obtaining a Certificate for a Web Site

A Web site can use a certificate for a number of purposes, such as user authentication or SSL3 encryption. In this procedure, the IIS5 Certificate Wizard is used to obtain such a certificate. This procedure assumes that there's a CA available to issue certificates and that the IIStool has been created (see the previous two procedures).

The procedure can be carried out on any Web site. However, if the purpose of the certificate is to enable SSL3 encryption, the Web site can't be identified by a host header. To obtain a certificate for a Web site, proceed as follows:

1. Log on to the IIS5 server as an administrator and open the IIS snap-in.

2. Right-click the Web site for which you want to obtain a certificate and select Properties.

3. In the Secure communications section of the Directory Security tab, click Certificate.

4. The Web Server Certificate Wizard starts. Click Next.

5. Select Create a new certificate. Click Next.

6. Select Send the request immediately to an online certification authority. Click Next.

7. Type in the certificate name. Specify an encryption strength. The higher strength should be chosen only if you are certain that all clients can support it. Do not check the SGC option. Click Next.

8. Type in Organization and Organizational Unit (OU) information or accept the site defaults. Click Next.

9. Specify the Common name for the site. This can be a DNS name or a NetBIOS name. Click Next.

10. Type in Geographical information or take the site defaults. Click Next.

11. Specify the path to the CA. If you've installed a root Enterprise CA (see the previous procedure), this should be specified by default. Click Next.

12. Check that the Certificate Request Submission information is OK. Click Next.

13. Click Finish. This returns you to the Directory Security tab of the Web site Properties dialog box.

14. You can view the certificate or access the Secure communications dialog box by clicking View Certificate and Edit, respectively.

15. Close the IIS snap-in.

Related solution:	Found on page:
Using SSL3 to Secure a Web Site	324

Adding a Virtual Directory

A virtual directory appears to client browsers as though it were a subfolder of the home directory, but it can be located elsewhere on the directory tree, on another volume, on another computer in the domain, or even on a remote host identified by a URL. Web browsers access a virtual directory by means of its alias. Because users know only the alias, they don't know where the virtual directory is physically located and can't use that information to access and modify its files.

Virtual directories let administrators distribute large sites over multiple computers, only one of which need be an IIS server. They allow administrators to change the location of files without having to change the URL that clients use to access the directory. All that needs to be changed is the mapping between the alias and the physical location of the directory.

This procedure specifies a folder on the IIS5 server as the virtual directory location. If you specify a network share at a remote location, you need to provide the username and password of an account that has access to the network resource.

To add a virtual directory, proceed as follows:

1. Log on to the IIS5 server as an administrator.
2. Create or select a folder to use as your virtual directory location.
3. Open the IIS snap-in.
4. Right-click the FTP or Web site to which you want to add a virtual directory, click New, and select Virtual directory.
5. The Virtual Directory Creation Wizard starts. Click Next.
6. Specify an alias for the virtual directory. Click Next.
7. Click Browse and select the directory location. Click OK. Click Next.
8. Set the access permissions and click Next.
9. Click Finish.
10. Right-click the new virtual directory and click Properties. You can change the directory properties using the dialog box tabs provided. The Virtual Directory tab, shown in Figure 12.7, lets you specify a new directory location and change access and applications settings.
11. Click OK. Close the IIS snap-in.

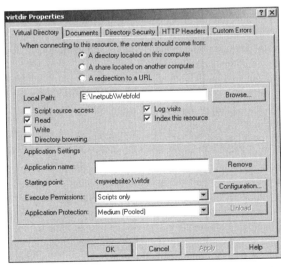

Figure 12.7   The Virtual Directory Properties dialog box.

Setting Web Server Permissions

Unlike NTFS permissions, Web server permissions apply to all users accessing your Web and FTP sites. NTFS permissions control access to physical directories on your server, whereas Web and FTP permissions control access to virtual directories on your Web or FTP site.

By default, Web and FTP access permissions use the Windows account IUSR_*computername*, which is the account used by clients who access your site, using anonymous authentication. By default, IUSR_*computername* is given NTFS permissions by IIS5 for the actual folders that comprise the Web or FTP site. Because these permissions are given to IUSR_*computername* and not to individual user accounts, they apply to all anonymous site users and are therefore known as Web server permissions.

You can change these Web server permissions to control whether users visiting your Web site are allowed to view a particular page, upload information, or run scripts on the site. If Web server permissions and NTFS permissions differ for a directory or a file, the more restrictive settings are used.

To set Web server permissions for Web content, proceed as follows:

1. Log on to the IIS5 server as an administrator and open the IIS snap-in.
2. Right-click an FTP site, Web site, virtual directory, or file and select Properties.
3. On the Home Directory, Virtual Directory, or File property sheet, select or clear any of the following checkboxes (if available):

   - *Read*—Users can view directory or file content and properties (selected by default).
   - *Write*—Users can change directory or file content and properties.
   - *Script Source Access*—Users can access source files. If Read is selected, the source can be read; if Write is selected, the source can be written to. Script Source Access includes access to the source code for scripts, such as the scripts in an ASP application. This option isn't available if neither Read nor Write is selected.
   - *Directory browsing*—Users can view file lists and collections.
   - *Log visits*—A log entry is created for each visit to the Web site.
   - *Index this resource*—Allows Indexing Service to index the resource. This allows searches to be carried out.

NOTE: *For FTP content, only Read, Write, and Log visits are available.*

4. In the Execute Permissions drop-down list, select the appropriate level of script execution:

   - *None*—Don't run scripts (such as ASP applications) or executables on the server.

   - *Scripts only*—Run only scripts on the server.

   - *Scripts and Executables*—Run both scripts and executables on the server.

5. Click OK. Close the snap-in.

WARNING! *If you enable Script Source Access, users may be able to obtain sensitive information, such as usernames and passwords, from the scripts in an ASP application. They can also change source code that runs on your server. It's usually advisable to disable this Web server permission and allow access to scripts only to individual (nonanonymous) user accounts that are authenticated by methods such as Digest or Integrated Windows Authentication.*

Adding and Removing Web Site Operators

Web Site Operators are Windows user accounts that have limited administration privileges on a Web site.

Adding a Web Site Operator

To add a Web Site Operator, proceed as follows:

1. Log on to the IIS5 server as an administrator and open the IIS snap-in.

2. Right-click the Web site and select Properties.

3. On the Operators tab, click Add. This opens the Select Users and Groups window.

4. Select a user account. Click Add.

5. Click OK. Click OK again to close the Properties box, then close the snap-in.

Removing a Web Site Operator

To remove a Web Site Operator, proceed as follows:

1. Log on to the IIS5 server as an administrator and open the IIS snap-in.

2. Right-click the Web site and select Properties.

3. On the Operators tab, select the user and click Remove.

4. Close the snap-in.

Tracking Processor Use

Process accounting is enabled on a per-server basis and records information on a per-Web site basis. It doesn't provide details on CPU usage of individual applications or CGI applications. Process accounting requires that the W3C Extended log file format is selected (the default).

To enable process accounting, proceed as follows:

1. Log on to the IIS5 server as an administrator and open the IIS snap-in.
2. Right-click the Web site and select Properties.
3. On the Web Site tab, click Properties.
4. On the Extended Properties tab, check the Process Accounting checkbox.
5. Click OK. Click OK again to close the Properties box, then close the snap-in.

NOTE: Process accounting isn't available for FTP sites.

Backing Up and Restoring IIS Configuration

You can back up your IIS configuration so that it's easy to return to a previous state. The steps to restore a configuration differ, depending on whether or not you removed and reinstalled IIS.

Backing Up IIS Configuration

The next procedure creates a backup file that can be used to restore IIS configuration if IIS is not removed and reinstalled. The file can assist in restoring the configuration of a reinstalled IIS, but in this case you need to take some additional steps. The procedure doesn't back up content files.

To create an IIS backup file, proceed as follows:

1. Log on to the IIS5 server as an administrator and open the IIS snap-in.
2. Right-click Internet Information Services and select Backup/Restore Configuration.
3. Click Create backup, choose a name for your backup file, and click OK. By default, the backup file will be stored in the \Winnt\system32\inetsrv\MetaBack directory.
4. Click Close. Close the snap-in.

WARNING! *The backup file can be used to restore the configuration only on the IIS server that was backed up. It can't be used to restore an IIS configuration on another computer.*

Restoring IIS Configuration

If IIS hasn't been reinstalled, the following procedure will restore the IIS configuration:

1. Log on to the IIS5 server as an administrator and open the IIS snap-in.

2. Right-click Internet Information Services and select Backup/Restore Configuration.

3. From the Backups list, select the backup file that you created in the previous procedure and click Restore. When asked whether to restore your configuration settings, click Yes.

4. Click Close. Close the snap-in.

Restoring IIS Configuration after Reinstalling IIS

The next procedure uses the adsutil.vbs script file to obtain parameter values that you can use to complete IIS configuration restoration. In order to run adsutil.vbs, you need to have Windows Script Host (WSH) installed.

To restore the IIS configuration after removing and reinstalling IIS, proceed as follows:

1. Log on to the IIS5 server as an administrator and open the IIS snap-in.

2. Right-click Internet Information Services and select Backup/Restore Configuration.

3. From the Backups list, select the backup file that you created in the backup procedure and click Restore. Although an error message states that the restoration has failed, a part of your backed-up configuration will be restored.

4. Access Start|Programs|Accessories and select Command Prompt.

5. Enter **cscript *x*:\InetPub\AmdinScripts\adsutil.vbs enum w3svc**, where *x* is the letter of the drive where IIS is installed. From the settings listed, find the WAMUserName and the associated WAMUserPass value.

NOTE: *Depending on how security is set up on the server, you may find that WAMUserPass is blanked out by asterisks. In this case, the rest of the configuration has to be done manually.*

---

6. Access Start|Programs|Administrative Tools. If your IIS server is a domain controller, select Active Directory Users and Computers. Otherwise, select Computer Management and expand Local Users and Groups.

TIP: *On a non-domain controller, you can access Local Users and Groups from the IIStool snap-in, which is already open. I prefer to open the Computer Management snap-in at this point because it can be confusing having two different dialog boxes open in the same snap-in tool.*

---

7. Click Users. Right-click the IWAM_*computername* user account and select Reset Password. Type the WAMUserPass value retrieved from Step 6 and click OK.

8. In the Backup/Restore Configuration dialog box, in the Backups list, select the backup file that you created in the backup procedure and click Restore. Your configuration will now be fully restored.

9. Close the snap-ins and the Command Console.

Adding a Custom Error Message

Custom error messages can be in the form of a mapping to a file or to a URL. Either of these can be implemented by using the Custom Errors property sheet in the IIS snap-in.

Customizing an Error Message by Mapping to a File

You can customize an error message for an HTTP error by placing the error message in a file and setting the HTTP error properties to point to that file. This is the recommended method if you're using static HTML files. The procedure for doing this is as follows:

1. Log on to the IIS5 server as an administrator.

2. Create an HTML file that contains your custom error message and place it in a folder. You can use any folder for this purpose (although it's a good idea to avoid using Web or FTP default directories).

TIP: *You can type a message in Microsoft Word and save it as an HTML file.*

---

3. Access the IIS snap-in, right-click the Web site, virtual directory, directory, or file for which you would like to customize HTTP error messages, and select Properties.

4. Select the Custom Errors tab.

5. Select the HTTP error that you would like to change.

6. Click the Edit Properties button.

7. Select File from the Message Type box.

8. Type the path and file name that points to your customized error message or use the Browse button to locate the file and click Open.

9. If prompted, select any child nodes that should inherit the new message location and click OK.

10. Click OK.

11. Click OK to close the Properties dialog box and close the snap-in.

Customizing an Error Message by Mapping to a URL

You can configure the HTTP error properties to point to a custom message in virtual directory identified by a URL, rather than a local file. This is the recommended method if you're using ASP files to create dynamic error-handling routines. To use a virtual directory to hold your error message, proceed as follows:

1. Log on to the IIS5 server as an administrator.

2. Create a file that contains your custom error message and place it in a virtual directory.

3. Access the IIS snap-in, right-click the Web site, virtual directory, directory, or file for which you would like to customize HTTP error messages, and select Properties.

4. Select the Custom Errors tab.

5. Select the HTTP error that you would like to change.

6. Click the Edit Properties button.

7. Select URL from the Message Type box.

8. Type the local absolute URL path that points to your customized error message, beginning with the virtual directory name (for example, /virtdir/sorry404.htm).

9. If prompted, select any child nodes that should inherit the new message location and click OK.

10. Click OK.

11. Click OK to close the Properties dialog box and close the snap-in.

TIP: *If you're using IE5, then the browser may replace some custom error messages with its own HTTP error messages. The workaround is to ensure that the file sizes of your custom error messages are always greater than 512 bytes.*

Creating a Publishing Directory

This procedure sets up a publishing directory called WebDAV for use in collaboration projects. It assumes that the collaborators have accounts in your domain and are members of a collaboration group. You can also set up collaboration groups containing accounts from trusted domains or users that are validated by certificates mapped to a single user account. Technically, you can include anyone that can access your site by giving permissions to the Everyone group and allowing anonymous access. This is not recommended.

To set up a publishing directory, proceed as follows:

1. Log on to the IIS5 server as an administrator.
2. Create a folder called WebDAV in the Inetpub directory.

NOTE: *You don't have to create this folder under Inetpub. You can put it anywhere you want, except under the wwwroot directory. This is because the default DACLs on wwwroot are different from those on other directories. The folder should, however, be on an NTFS partition.*

---

3. Assign appropriate user permissions to that directory. Don't forget to remove the Everyone group.

TIP: *It's a good idea to grant Read permission only to the collaboration group initially and to grant Write permission to a few selected users. This lets you test the collaboration setup before assigning Write permission more widely.*

---

4. Open the IIS snap-in and create a virtual directory. You can do this on the default Web site, or you may choose to do it on a Web site you've set up for the purpose. Refer to the immediate solution, "Creating a Virtual Directory," earlier in this chapter.
5. Type WebDAV as the alias for this virtual directory and link it to the physical directory you created in Step 2.
6. Enable Read, Write, and Browse access permissions on the virtual directory.

NOTE: *Granting Write access doesn't give clients the ability to modify ASP files or any other script-mapped files. If you want users to be able to modify these files, you must grant Write permission and Script source access after creating the virtual directory. For information about setting these permissions, refer to the immediate solution, "Setting Web Server Permissions."*

---

7. Right-click the WebDAV virtual directory and select Properties.
8. In the Anonymous access and authentication control section of the Directory Security tab, click Edit.

9. Specify the authentication settings using the following guidelines:

   - Clear Anonymous access (unless you have a very good reason for not doing so).

   - Don't use Basic authentication. This is insecure.

   - Use Integrated Windows Authentication for collaboration within your own intranet.

   - Use Digest Authentication for collaboration over the Internet, provided all collaborating clients can support this form of authentication.

10. Click OK.

11. Click OK to close the WebDAV Properties dialog box and close the snap-in.

Publishing Files on a WebDAV Directory

When you have set up a WebDAV virtual directory, you can allow clients to publish to it. This can be done using a Windows 2000 client, IE5, or an Office 2000 client.

Publishing through Windows 2000

You can publish to a WebDAV directory from a Windows 2000 Professional (that has Web services installed), a Windows 2000 Server, or a Windows 2000 Advanced Server that is able to connect to a WebDAV publishing directory. The procedure for doing so is as follows:

1. Log on to a Windows 2000 client with a user account that has permission to publish to the WebDAV directory.

2. Double-click My Network Places on the desktop.

3. Double-click Add Network Place.

4. In the Add Network Place Wizard, type the URL of the WebDAV directory that you want to connect to.

5. Click Next.

6. Type a friendly name for the directory that you're connecting to.

7. Click Finish.

8. A Window opens with the friendly name that you specified in the title bar. You can add folders to the collaboration directory and read, create, edit, or delete files within these folders.

9. Open My Network Places any time you want to access the collaboration directory.

Publishing through IE5

You can connect to a WebDAV directory through IE5 from any Microsoft Windows client (Windows 2000, Windows NT4, Windows 98, or Windows 95) that has the browser installed. The procedure for doing so is as follows:

1. From the File menu in IE5, click Open.

2. In the Open box, type the URL for the WebDAV directory that you want to connect to.

3. Select the Open as Web Folder box and click OK.

Publishing through Office 2000

You can use Office 2000 to create, download, amend, and save documents in a WebDAV collaboration directory. This procedure assumes that you've either created a shortcut to the directory (see "Publishing through Windows 2000" above) or that you know the URL for the directory.

Creating a Document in a WebDAV Directory

To create a document in a WebDAV directory from Office 2000, proceed as follows:

1. Create a document using any Office 2000 application.

2. From the File pull-down menu, select Save As.

3. In the left column of the Save As dialog box, click My Network Places.

4. Either select the shortcut to the WebDAV directory or type the URL, then click OK.

Editing a Document in a WebDAV Directory

To edit an existing document in a WebDAV directory from Office 2000, proceed as follows:

1. Start the appropriate Office 2000 application for the file you want to edit.

2. On the File pull-down menu, select Open.

3. In the left column of the Open dialog box, click My Network Places.

4. Either select the shortcut to the WebDAV directory or type the URL, then click OK.

5. When you've edited the document, save it in the normal way.

6. Close the document. This releases the lock you've placed on the document and enables your collaborators to access it.

Chapter 13

Dynamic Host Configuration Protocol

In Depth

Dynamic Host Configuration Protocol (DHCP), defined in RFCs 2131 and 2132, provides a service that dynamically configures a host's Internet Protocol (IP) address and subnet mask while that host is booting on a TCP/IP network. It can also change these settings while the host is attached. This lets all available IP addresses be stored in a central database along with associated configuration information. DHCP can also specify parameters such as the subnet mask, default gateway, alternative gateway addresses, and the address of Domain Name System (DNS) and Windows Internet Name Service (WINS) servers. It reduces the complexity of administering networks and avoids the errors inherent in manual configuration.

The DHCP Myths

DHCP has sometimes been viewed with suspicion and mistrust, although (in my experience) more by managers than by administrators. There have been myths built up about the service that bear little resemblance to reality:

- *DHCP does **not** alter IP addresses frequently*—DHCP can be set to allocate configuration information with a long lease time. This means that a host will normally retain an allocated lease. You can set permanent leases, which means that when a lease is allocated, the host retains the configuration permanently, unless the host is removed from the network or the configuration is released manually.

- *DHCP does **not** conceal IP identities*—Address leases can be viewed, linked to both computer name and Media Access Control (MAC) address. So, if you detect misuse of a host identified by its IP address, you can tell exactly which host has been used. In Windows 2000, this information can be accessed (but not altered) by nonadministrative users. DHCP is more secure than static configuration in this respect. A statically configured host (particularly a Windows 9x host) can have its IP address changed and then changed back by a computer-literate user intent on mischief.

- *DHCP **does** let you allocate a particular IP address to a particular host*— You can reserve a lease so that a specific host, identified by computer name and MAC address, is allocated a specific IP address. This is (in effect) the same as a static configuration, except that subnet mask, gateway, DNS server, and WINS server information can all be configured dynamically, and you don't have to visit a host (which may be some distance from your office) in order to configure it.

- *DHCP is **not** difficult to set up or administer*—Overlap problems associated with multiple address ranges (or *scopes*) and multiple servers were never particularly difficult to resolve, especially when compared to the problems of configuring a few thousand hosts manually. Windows 2000 provides tools for checking interscope consistency and detecting rogue DHCP servers, so any IP address overlaps can be quickly detected and resolved.

- *DHCP does **not** generate a lot of broadcast traffic*—When it first comes on to a network, a host will broadcast for a DHCP server and receive a broadcast response. These are not large broadcast packets and will occur again only if the DHCP lease either expires or reaches its *rebinding state* (when seven-eighths of the lease time has expired), if the host is moved to another network, or if the configuration is released and renewed manually. DHCP traffic typically takes up only a small proportion of network bandwidth.

NOTE: *DHCP leases are also renewed when a client reboots halfway through the lease period. In these cases, however, the client attempts to renew its lease from the DHCP server that it obtained the lease from before, rather than going through the full DHCP Discover process (see later in this chapter).*

Some networks will have hosts that can't be DHCP clients, and some computers—such as DHCP servers themselves, Domain Controllers (DCs), routers, DNS servers, WINS servers, Internet Information Services (IIS) servers, and significant BackOffice servers—should be configured statically or at least be given permanent DHCP reservations. Nevertheless, many of the problems associated with networks can be solved through DHCP configuration.

DHCP Address Allocation

DHCP has its origins in the Bootstrap Protocol (BOOTP), defined in RFCs 951 and 1084. BOOTP allowed the dynamic assignment of IP addresses. In addition to IP addresses, DHCP supplies all the configuration data required by TCP/IP, plus additional data for specific servers.

The full address allocation process occurs in the following situations:

- When a host first comes online.
- When a host's DHCP lease has either expired or reached its rebinding state.
- When a host's configuration has been manually released and renewed using the **ipconfig /release** and **ipconfig /renew** commands.
- When a host can't access either its DHCP server or its default gateway on reboot.
- When a host receives a DHCP negative acknowledgment (DHCPNAK) message from a DHCP server that tells it that its lease can't be renewed.

IP configuration through DHCP involves four steps:

1. *DHCP Discover*—The DHCP client broadcasts a DHCPDISCOVER configuration request packet, supplying its MAC address and host name. If the client previously had an IP address allocated to it, it also sends this information in the Requested Address option field. In this way, a client often retains the same address even if it has been powered down for longer than its lease duration.

2. *DHCP Offer*—Every DHCP server that receives the request replies with a DHCPOFFER broadcast packet that contains an offered IP address (if it has one or more unassigned) and its own IP address. DHCP servers on the far side of a router can respond to a DHCPDISCOVER broadcast, provided that the router is enabled to pass DHCP broadcast traffic.

3. *DHCP Request*—The DHCP host accepts the first offer that it gets and requests the address that was sent with that offer. The DHCPREQUEST packet is a broadcast packet because the client hasn't yet been officially allocated the offered IP address. The packet contains the IP address of the chosen DHCP server and the IP address offered by this server.

4. *DHCP Acknowledge*—The DHCP server officially assigns the requested address to the client in a DHCPACK broadcast packet and stores the information in its database as an allocated lease.

DHCPDISCOVER, DHCPOFFER, DHCPREQUEST, and DHCPACK packets are illustrated in Figures 13.1 through 13.4, respectively. These packets are contained in the Network Monitor capture file dhcp.cap on the CD-ROM.

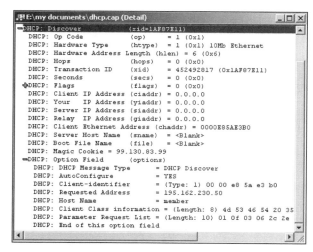

Figure 13.1   DHCPDISCOVER.

In addition to the IP address, the DHCP server will send other information to the host, such as a subnet mask and IP addresses of gateways and of WINS and DNS servers. There is a wide range of additional options that can be allocated through DHCP. These are defined in RFC 2132.

The DHCP server specifies a lease duration. Halfway through the lease duration, or whenever it reboots, the DHCP client requests a lease renewal with a DHCPREQUEST message and the DHCP server extends the lease with a DHCPACK

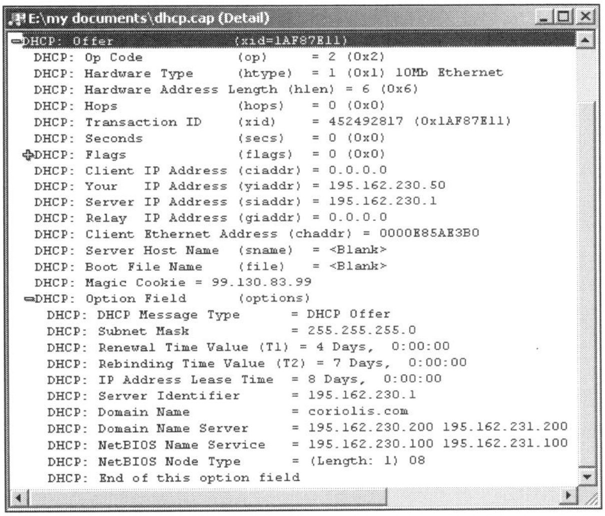

Figure 13.2 DHCPOFFER.

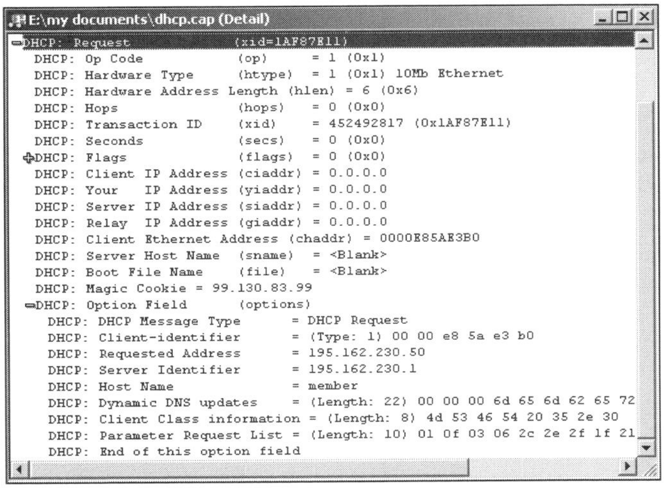

Figure 13.3 DHCPREQUEST.

```
E:\my documents\dhcp.cap (Detail)                                    _ □ ×
DHCP: ACK              (xid=1AF87E11)
   DHCP: Op Code            (op)    = 2 (0x2)
   DHCP: Hardware Type      (htype) = 1 (0x1) 10Mb Ethernet
   DHCP: Hardware Address Length (hlen) = 6 (0x6)
   DHCP: Hops               (hops)  = 0 (0x0)
   DHCP: Transaction ID     (xid)   = 452492817 (0x1AF87E11)
   DHCP: Seconds            (secs)  = 0 (0x0)
   DHCP: Flags              (flags) = 0 (0x0)
   DHCP: Client IP Address (ciaddr) = 0.0.0.0
   DHCP: Your   IP Address (yiaddr) = 195.162.230.50
   DHCP: Server IP Address (siaddr) = 0.0.0.0
   DHCP: Relay  IP Address (giaddr) = 0.0.0.0
   DHCP: Client Ethernet Address (chaddr) = 0000E85AE3B0
   DHCP: Server Host Name  (sname)  = <Blank>
   DHCP: Boot File Name    (file)   = <Blank>
   DHCP: Magic Cookie = 99.130.83.99
   DHCP: Option Field      (options)
      DHCP: DHCP Message Type    = DHCP ACK
      DHCP: Renewal Time Value (T1) = 4 Days,  0:00:00
      DHCP: Rebinding Time Value (T2) = 7 Days,  0:00:00
      DHCP: IP Address Lease Time = 8 Days,  0:00:00
      DHCP: Server Identifier    = 195.162.230.1
      DHCP: Subnet Mask          = 255.255.255.0
      DHCP: Dynamic DNS updates  = (Length: 3) 00 ff 00
      DHCP: Domain Name          = coriolis.com
      DHCP: Domain Name Server   = 195.162.230.200 195.162.231.200
      DHCP: NetBIOS Name Service = 195.162.230.100 195.162.231.100
      DHCP: NetBIOS Node Type    = (Length: 1) 08
      DHCP: End of this option field
```

Figure 13.4   DHCPACK.

message. If the client doesn't obtain a lease renewal from the DHCP server, it retains its configuration information, unless it detects that it has been moved to another network. The DHCP traffic generated by a client reboot is contained in the Network Monitor capture file dhcp1.cap on the CD-ROM.

If a client is moved to another network and Media Sense is enabled (see later in this chapter), it releases its configuration. It then broadcasts for a DHCP server on the new network using a DHCPDISCOVER message. It either obtains a new configuration through DHCP or configures itself with a private address through Automatic Private IP Addressing (APIPA—see later in this chapter).

If, on the other hand, a client retains its original IP configuration when it's moved to another network, it requests a lease renewal with a DHCPREQUEST message. If there's a DHCP server on the new network, that server won't recognize the client's current IP address and will refuse the renewal request by sending a DHCPNAK message. The client then releases its IP configuration and broadcasts a DHCPDISCOVER message.

If a client is moved to a subnet that has no DHCP server and that client retains its current configuration, it broadcasts a DHCPREQUEST, but obtains no reply. It then pings its default gateway. When this ping fails, it deduces that it has been moved to a private subnet and configures itself using APIPA. It broadcasts a DHCPDISCOVER message every five minutes and is reconfigured through DHCP if a DHCP server is subsequently installed on the network.

If the DHCP client is moved to another subnet or if it is taken out of service, the DHCP lease will expire on the server, which will then tombstone the IP address and eventually return it to its list of allocable addresses. In this case, it's good practice to release the IP configuration manually at the client before it's moved or retired.

DHCP Servers

On a Windows 2000 network, the DHCP server can be a Domain Controller (DC), a member server, or a standalone workgroup server (for peer-to-peer networks). In a mixed environment, Microsoft recommends upgrading all servers to Windows 2000 before deploying Windows 2000 DHCP. The server must have a static IP configuration and have DHCP installed, authorized, and configured (see the Immediate Solutions section of this chapter).

Installing DHCP automatically installs the DHCP snap-in tool (sometimes referred to as DHCP Manager). If a domain has more than one DHCP server, each one is authorized in Active Directory and added to the DHCP console, so the entire DHCP configuration can be controlled from a single server. A DHCP server also maintains a database for managing the assignment of IP addresses and other configuration parameters.

TCP/IP configuration parameters that can be assigned dynamically through DHCP include:

- IP addresses for each network adapter in a client computer.
- Subnet masks.
- Gateways. More than one gateway can be defined for the purpose of dead gateway detection.
- Additional configuration parameters, such as IP addresses for DNS or WINS servers.
- Options. Most options are predefined through RFC 2132, but the DHCP server also enables custom options to be defined and added.

DHCP Clients

Hosts running the following Microsoft operating systems can act as DHCP clients:

- Windows 2000 Server (all versions)
- Windows 2000 Professional
- Windows NT Server (all versions)
- Windows NT Workstation (all versions)
- Windows 98
- Windows 95

13. Dynamic Host Configuration Protocol

- Windows for Workgroups version 3.11 with the Microsoft 32-bit TCP/IP Virtual Driver (VxD) installed

- Microsoft Network Client version 3 for MS-DOS with the real-mode TCP/IP driver installed

- LAN Manager version 2.2c

Non-Microsoft clients running TCP/IP and compliant with RFC 2132 may also support DHCP client software. Windows 2000 DHCP offers additional support to BOOTP clients through Dynamic BOOTP (see later in this chapter).

BOOTP Relay Agents

Routers don't automatically forward broadcast traffic. An RFC 2131-compliant router, however, can be configured to act as a BOOTP relay agent and pass DHCP broadcasts to the subnets it controls, so you don't need a DHCP server on each physical network. User Datagram Protocol (UDP) server port 67 is enabled to allow a router to pass DHCP broadcast traffic.

If the routers on a network can't be configured as BOOTP relay agents, then a host computer (typically a Windows 2000 server) can be configured to listen for DHCP broadcast messages and direct them to one or more DHCP Servers using directed IP datagrams. In other words, the host computer rather than the router is the BOOTP relay agent. Figure 13.5 illustrates both scenarios. Relay agents direct local DHCP client requests to remote DHCP servers and return the server responses to the clients.

Windows 2000 Enhancements

Windows 2000 DHCP introduces a number of enhancements. These are described below.

Automatic Client Configuration

Windows 2000 can configure an IP address and subnet mask automatically if the client is installed on a small private network where no DHCP server is available to assign addresses. In this scenario, the client attempts to locate a DHCP server and obtain a configuration from it. If a Windows 2000 DHCP client fails in its first attempt to locate a DHCP server after installation, it will use the APIPA feature (see below) to obtain a private IP address and subnet mask.

If the DHCP client previously obtained a lease from a DHCP server, it attempts to renew its unexpired lease on reboot. If it fails to locate the DHCP server, the client attempts to ping the default gateway listed in its lease. If this succeeds, the client assumes it hasn't been moved to another network and retains the lease. The client then seeks to renew the lease after half of the lease duration has expired.

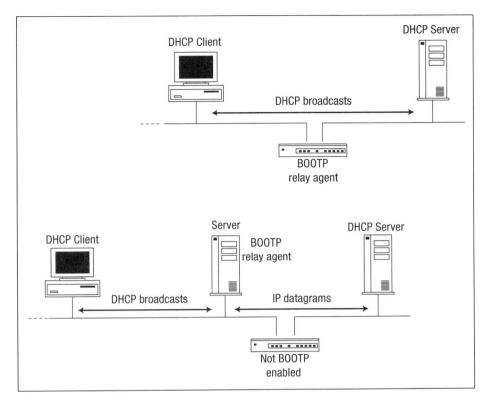

Figure 13.5   BOOTP relay agents.

If the attempt to ping its default gateway fails, the client assumes that it has been moved to a network that has no DHCP services currently available, such as a small intranet or a home network. It then uses APIPA to configure itself automatically.

APIPA

APIPA automatically configures a host using the Internet Assigned Numbers Authority (IANA)-reserved range 169.254.0.0/16 (that is, 169.254.0.1 to 169.254.255.254, subnet mask 255.255.0.0—see Chapter 5). If a host detects an address conflict with another host on the network, it will automatically reconfigure itself with another address in the reserved range, for as many as 10 addresses. A host that's configured through APIPA tries to find a DHCP server every five minutes. If a DHCP server is found, the host is reconfigured through DHCP.

NOTE: *APIPA can be disabled using the* IPAutoconfigurationEnabled *Registry key. The subnet and subnet mask that's used can be controlled using the* IPAutoconfigurationSubnet *and* IPAutoconfigurationMask *Registry keys (see Appendix A).*

Media Sense

Support for Media Sense was introduced in version 5 of the Network Driver Interface Specification (NDIS5—see Chapter 2). It enables the Network Interface Card (NIC) to notify the protocol stack of media connect and disconnect events. These notifications assist in addressing a problem that was apparent in NT4. If a portable computer that's a DHCP client on an NT4 Ethernet subnet is moved to another subnet without rebooting, the protocol stack receives no indication of the move and the configuration parameters become stale. IP configuration on the laptop could then conflict with settings on the subnet.

Also, if a computer on an NT4 network is powered down, carried home, and rebooted, the protocol stack isn't aware of these events and stale configuration parameters remain. This can be a problem, because subnet routes, default gateways, and so on can conflict with dial-up parameters.

In Windows 2000, Media Sense allows the protocol stack to react to events and invalidate stale parameters. If a Windows 2000 DHCP client is unplugged from the network and its NIC supports Media Sense, TCP/IP will invalidate the stale parameters after a damping period implemented in the stack (currently 20 seconds).

TIP: If a host that's statically configured is moved to another network, it needs to be reconfigured before it can be used on that network (whether it's rebooted or not). This is another example of the advantages of DHCP.

Rogue DHCP Server Detection

Windows 2000 DHCP prevents unauthorized, or *rogue*, DHCP servers from creating address assignment conflicts. Windows 2000 requires an additional authorization step before a DHCP server can become active on the network. The enterprise administrator—that is, the administrator of the first DC installed on the domain—typically carries out authorization. In a domain tree, the enterprise administrator for the root domain is responsible for this step. These administrators can delegate DHCP management rights, but they should choose their delegates carefully.

When a DHCP server initializes on a domain, Active Directory verifies its status. If the server is unauthorized, it can't respond to DHCP requests. On initialization, the server connects to Active Directory and finds out whether or not it's part of the domain. If it is, it determines whether it's in the list of authorized servers. If authorized, it sends out a DHCPINFORM message to find out if there are other directory services running and makes sure that it is valid in these services also.

If the server can't connect to Active Directory or doesn't find itself in the authorized list, it assumes that it isn't authorized and doesn't respond to client requests.

When a DHCP server that's not a domain member server (such as a member of a workgroup) initializes, it broadcasts a DHCPINFORM message on the network.

Any other server that receives this message responds with a DHCPACK message and provides the name of the domain that it is part of. If a workgroup DHCP server detects a DHCP domain member server on the network, it assumes itself to be unauthorized and doesn't service requests.

If the workgroup DHCP server detects the presence of another workgroup server, it ignores it. There can, therefore, be multiple workgroup servers active at the same time. Even if a workgroup server initializes and finds that it's permitted to run, it continues to broadcast DHCPINFORM messages every five minutes. If an authorized DHCP domain member server is detected, the workgroup server becomes unauthorized and stops its service.

Vendor-Specific Options

Windows 2000 DHCP server allows vendor-specific options to be defined. This means that such options can be supported even though they haven't yet been approved as standard options by the Internet Engineering Task Force (IETF). Vendor classes are defined by specific vendors and are identified by data bits that determine whether a given option class is standard or vendor-specific.

When an option class is identified as vendor-specific, DHCP looks up the configuration as specified for that vendor. Hardware from multiple vendors on a network can use different option numbers for different functions. Vendor classes and vendor options are described in detail in RFC 2132, which contains descriptions of BOOTP vendor extensions previously defined in RFC 1497 (superceded by RFC 2132).

User Class Support

User classes enable a DHCP client to specify what type of client it is—for example, a desktop, a laptop, and so on. An administrator can configure the DHCP server to assign different options, depending on the type of client they're assigned to. For example, shorter leases could be assigned to laptop clients, or configuration could be tailored to client functionality. A workstation that is running multimedia software can be given a different set of configuration options from one that is used mainly for word processing, and a file and print server can be configured differently from both. These variations can include lease duration, WINS and DNS settings, and the various DHCP options. If user class options are unused, default settings are assigned.

Enhanced Monitoring and Statistical Reporting

This new feature provides notification if the number of allocable IP addresses falls below a user-defined threshold. For example, an alert can be triggered when 90 percent of IP addresses in a particular scope have been assigned, and a second alert can be triggered when the IP address pool is exhausted. An icon changes to yellow on the remaining addresses if the allocable address pool falls below a defined level. The icon changes to red if the address pool is completely depleted.

The DHCP manager supports Simple Network Management Protocol (SNMP) and Management Information Bases (MIBs), which provide a graphical display of statistical data. This helps administrators monitor system status, providing such information as the number of available versus the number of depleted addresses or the number of leases being processed per second. Additional statistical information about the operation of the DHCP service can also be provided. This includes the number of messages and offers processed and the number of requests, acknowledgments, declines, negative status acknowledgment messages (NACKs), and releases received.

You can also view the total number of scopes and addresses on the server, the number used, and the number available. These statistics can be provided for a particular scope or at the server level—which shows the aggregate of all scopes managed by that server.

Multicast Address Allocation and MADCAP

A multicast address is a single IP address that identifies a group of computers. Multicast scopes are supported through the use of Multicast Address Dynamic Client Allocation Protocol (MADCAP), which is built on a client/server model that enables MADCAP clients to request dynamic multicast address allocation services from MADCAP servers. Windows 2000 MADCAP clients support client-side Application Programming Interfaces (APIs) that applications use to request, renew, and release multicast addresses.

Typically, a MADCAP client might also be a Multicast Server (MCS) that's used to support IP multicasting. An MCS manages the group use of an allocated multicast IP address and streams data traffic to members of the specified group address. Multicast clients that have registered their membership with the MCS can receive streams sent to this address. The MCS also manages the multicast group list so that all current members receive multicast traffic.

NOTE: *RFC 2771 gives more details about the allocation and use of multicast addresses. The RFC document is informational and isn't a required standard.*

Typical applications for multicasting are video conferencing or real-time audio (see Chapter 9), which traditionally required users to configure multicast addresses manually. Windows 2000 DHCP server, however, can assign multicast addresses in the same fashion as unicast addresses, allowing complete utilization of the existing infrastructure.

An administrator configures multicast scopes and corresponding multicast IP ranges as described in the Immediate Solutions section of this chapter. The multicast addresses are then managed on the server in the same manner as normal IP addresses, and client applications call the APIs to request a multicast address from a scope.

Windows Clustering

Windows Clustering is supported by Windows 2000 Advanced Server. It allows two or more servers to be managed as a single system and can improve the availability, manageability, and scalability of DHCP servers. Clustering can detect the failure of an application or service automatically and restart it quickly on another server in the cluster, so users experience only a momentary pause in service. Administrators can inspect the status of all cluster resources and move workload to different servers within the cluster. This facility is used for load balancing and for performing updates on the servers without taking important data and applications offline.

Clustering allows DHCP servers to be *virtualized*. A virtual IP address is defined using the Cluster Administrator tool. This address must be static. The Windows 2000 DHCP server service is then bound to this virtual IP address. If one of the clustered nodes crashes, its namespace and all of its services are transparently reconstituted on the second node. The client sees no change and obtains or refreshes a lease from what appears to be the same server as before, identified by the same IP address.

Traditionally, network administrators implemented failover protection by splitting scopes between servers, so if one server went down at least some of the allocable addresses remained available. Clustering removes the need to split scopes and makes more efficient use of IP addresses. A Windows Clustering database on a remote disk tracks address assignment and other activity, and if the active cluster node goes down, the second node becomes the DHCP server, with complete knowledge of what has been assigned and with access to the complete scope of addresses. Only one node at a time runs as a DHCP server, with the database providing transparent transition when needed.

Because Windows Clustering works with all clustering-enabled Windows services, the same cluster servers used for DHCP support high availability for all other clustering-enabled Windows services that run on them.

DNS Integration

DNS servers resolve host names and Fully Qualified Domain Names (FQDNs) to IP addresses (see Chapter 14). Windows 2000 introduces Dynamic DNS (DDNS), which addresses the problems that are traditionally associated with the static

DNS database. DHCP is integrated with DNS and, particularly, with DDNS, so the DNS database can be updated with new or altered IP addresses allocated dynamically to host computers in the DNS zone.

Dynamic DNS updates are described in RFC 2136. Every time there is an address event (new address or renewal), the DHCP client sends a DHCP option code (option code 81) and its FQDN to the DHCP server and requests that the server register a DNS pointer (PTR) resource record on its behalf. The dynamic update client normally handles the address (A) resource record registration without reference to the DHCP server, because only the client knows which IP address or addresses on the host map to that FQDN.

Optionally, the DHCP server can be configured to register both PTR and A records on behalf of the client. In this case, the server will instruct the client accordingly as part of the initial configuration process. Registry parameters associated with the DNS update client are listed in Appendix C.

If a Windows 2000 DHCP client obtains configuration information from a down-level (e.g., NT4) DHCP server that doesn't implement option 81, the client itself registers PTR and A records with the DDNS server, as does a statically configured host.

A DHCP server can act as a proxy for clients, such as Windows 9x and Windows NT4, for the purpose of DDNS registration. The DHCP server can differentiate between Windows 2000 clients and other clients and will implement DNS registration depending on the type of client it's configuring and the way it has itself been configured.

If a legacy (static) DNS server is employed on your network, DHCP can't update the DNS database dynamically, and failed DNS lookups can occur. Here are some workarounds for this problem:

- Enable WINS lookup for DHCP clients that use the Network Basic Input/Output System (NetBIOS).
- Assign IP address reservations that have a permanent (infinite) lease duration for DHCP clients that use DNS only and don't support NetBIOS.
- Wherever possible, upgrade or replace static DNS servers with Windows 2000 DNS servers that support DDNS.

Dynamic BOOTP

Windows 2000 DHCP provides support for BOOTP clients through dynamic BOOTP. This is an extension of the BOOTP protocol that enables a DHCP server to configure BOOTP clients, rather than using explicit fixed address configurations. This feature provides easier administration of large BOOTP networks by enabling dynamic distribution of IP addresses without needing to change client-side behavior.

The DHCP Tool

Windows 2000 DHCP introduces the DHCP Microsoft Management Console (MMC) snap-in tool, which provides a standard Graphical User Interface (GUI) for DHCP server administration and configuration. Single-seat management of all the DHCP servers in a domain or in a domain tree can be implemented. The DHCP service on any server can be started or stopped, DHCP scopes and options can be configured, and the DHCP database can be *reconciled* (checked for errors and inconsistencies), all from the same GUI.

DHCP can also be administered using the Command Line Network Shell (netsh) utility (see Appendix D). Configuring and administering the DHCP server using both the Command Line and the GUI tool are described in the Immediate Solutions section of this chapter.

DHCP Terminology

DHCP administrators can define global and scope-specific configuration settings that identify routers and set DHCP client configurations. Before I describe how these settings are applied, it's appropriate to define the terms used.

DHCP Scope

A DHCP scope is a range of IP addresses that can be assigned on a specific network. If you prefer, the Microsoft definition is "an administrative grouping that identifies the full consecutive ranges of possible IP addresses for all DHCP clients on a physical subnetwork." A scope defines the subnet for which DHCP services are offered and allows the server to identify configuration parameters to be given to all DHCP clients on the subnet.

Inherent in the scope definition is the subnet mask that accompanies the range of addresses. A typical scope might be "195.162.230.100 through 195.162.230.199, subnet mask 255.255.255.0."

Exclusion Range

An exclusion range is a sequence of IP addresses within a scope range that are not to be offered to DHCP clients. For example, within the scope defined above, you might want to exclude 195.162.230.150 through 195.162.230.160.

Address Pool

When a DHCP scope is defined and exclusion ranges applied, the remaining IP addresses within the scope form the available address pool. As addresses are allocated, they're removed from the pool; if they're released, they're added to it again. The address pool defines the IP addresses that are currently available for dynamic allocation to a DHCP client.

Reservation

A reservation allows a specified IP address to be permanently assigned to a specified hardware device (usually identified by its MAC address). Reservations are typically made for network printers or for host computers that you want always to have the same IP address but don't want to configure statically.

TIP: *Use the command **ipconfig /all** to obtain a Windows NT (including Windows 2000) client's MAC address. On Windows 9x clients, run winipcfg.exe and view the Adapter Address field. If the client already has an IP address that you want to convert into a permanent reserved lease, you can ping the client from the server, then use the **arp -a** command.*

Superscope

If you've configured a number of scopes, it's often convenient to group them together into a single administrative entity. This entity or grouping is known as a *superscope*. Superscopes are described in more detail later in this chapter.

Lease

Microsoft defines a lease as the amount of time that a DHCP client can retain its configuration information if it isn't refreshed in the interim. I find it clearer to refer to this as the lease duration, especially when an *active lease* is defined as a lease (meaning a full IP configuration) that's assigned to a client. When you view a client lease (see the Immediate Solutions section of this chapter), you view the entire configuration, not merely the duration. This, of course, is merely my opinion.

Options

DHCP Options are client-configuration parameters other than IP address and subnet mask that a DHCP server can assign to clients. For example, IP addresses for gateways, WINS servers, and DNS servers are typically provided either for a single scope or globally for all scopes managed by the server. Additional options are predefined in RFC 2132 (see later in this chapter) or are defined and added as custom options.

Deploying DHCP

The Immediate Solutions section of this chapter describes how to install, authorize, and configure DHCP. As with almost everything else (whether it has to do with computers or not), a planning stage is advisable before going ahead with the practical implementation. This section discusses the basic considerations of DHCP deployment and advises on best practice.

Determining the Number of DHCP Servers

DHCP scopes can't have overlapping IP addresses. This makes the concept of a "backup" DHCP server difficult. Windows Clustering (supported by Windows 2000 Advanced Server) provides backup and failover support by having an offline node that shares information with the online DHCP server and comes online if that server fails.

Otherwise, it's necessary to have two nonoverlapping scopes on two DHCP servers on a network, so that if one server fails there's still an address pool available on the other. This solution works better if the two servers are on either side of a BOOTP-enabled router, rather than on the same physical subnet.

One online DHCP server and one backup DHCP server (however implemented) can support a large number of clients. The actual number depends on hardware specifications (disk capacity and CPU speed) and other issues, such as the lease duration and whether hosts move frequently. Other factors to be considered when determining how many servers you need are the location of routers, the physical size of the network, the speed of links between distant segments, and whether you want a DHCP server in each subnet.

Although there's no theoretical limit to the maximum number of clients that can be served by a single DHCP server, there are practical constraints. Here are some things you should consider:

- What is the IP address class of the network?

- If remote segments are connected by slow links, do you intend to have a DHCP server on both sides of the link? It's usually a good idea to do so.

- Are your network routers capable of being BOOTP relay agents? It's generally considered good practice to enable routers to relay BOOTP/DHCP messages if possible, rather than using a host as a relay agent. Many routers employ vendor-specific router commands or configurable router settings to enable BOOTP/DHCP traffic, such as the IP HELPER command used in some Cisco routers. If a router doesn't support this functionality, a router upgrade may be available from the vendor.

There's no easy way of determining the optimum number of DHCP servers. The best you can do is to make an informed decision based on the various factors discussed above.

Planning Scopes

You need to create a scope for each physical subnet. The scope is then used to define parameters used by clients on that subnet. Scopes can be planned based on the needs of particular groups of users, with appropriate lease durations and option settings. You can specify one or more exception ranges that contain the IP addresses of all the computers and other devices on the subnet that either aren't DHCP-capable or that you want to configure statically.

You need to plan reservations. You can reserve IP addresses for permanent lease assignment to specified computers or devices on a network. Reservations can be made only for devices that are DHCP-enabled. For example, you may want to reserve specific IP addresses for WINS and DNS servers, for BackOffice servers, or for DHCP-enabled network printers.

There may be administrative rather than technical reasons for ensuring that a particular host has a specific IP address. A reservation guarantees that the host that is allocated the reserved IP address will always obtain configuration settings even if the address pool is exhausted. You also need to decide where you should use reservations and where static configuration is more appropriate.

You also need to plan the lease duration. The default is currently eight days. If you have a stable, fixed network where scope address space is plentiful (you may, for example, be using the 10.0.0.0/8 private address range) and configurations rarely change, increasing the lease duration lowers the frequency of lease renewal queries. A longer lease period (say, 24 days) also ensures that the IP address of a DHCP client on the network normally remains unaltered.

If IP addresses are limited and either client configurations or network locations change frequently, then reducing the lease duration ensures that IP addresses not currently in use are returned more quickly to the available address pool for reassignment. Short lease durations may, for example, be appropriate in a sales organization, where laptop computers are issued to traveling personnel.

You don't need to set the same lease duration for all scopes on a given DHCP server. User class support gives you the option, for example, of assigning a scope with a short lease duration to laptop computers and a second scope with a longer lease to the less mobile desktop clients.

Using Superscopes

A superscope is an administrative grouping of scopes that offers a number of advantages:

- It supports DHCP clients on a *multinet*—that is, a single physical network segment that has multiple logical subnets.
- It supports remote DHCP clients located on the far side of BOOTP relay agents, where the remote network uses multinets.

Superscopes may be used when a network expands and more hosts are added than were initially planned for, when a network is renumbered (possibly with private IP addresses), or when two or more DHCP servers manage separate logical subnets on the same physical network segment. Superscope configuration is described in the Immediate Solutions section of this chapter.

TIP: *You don't have to create a superscope just because you have two scopes on a DHCP server. The usual situation is that a server has one scope of addresses for allocation on its local subnet and another scope for allocation to clients on a remote subnet accessed through a BOOTP relay agent. In this case, there's no need to create a superscope.*

DHCP Options

RFC 2132 lists and describes more than 60 options that can be stored in a DHCP message. These include BOOTP vendor extensions, IP layer parameters per host, IP layer parameters per interface, link layer parameters per interface, Transmission Control Protocol (TCP) parameters, application and service parameters, and DHCP extensions. The RFC document also gives details of the packet structure for each option.

It's neither practicable nor desirable to replicate all of these details here. I've therefore included only those options that are provided by default by Windows 2000 DHCP server. These fall into four of the classes listed above, BOOTP vendor extensions (Table 13.1), IP layer parameters per interface (Table 13.2), application parameters (Table 13.3), and DHCP extensions (Table 13.4). Windows 2000 DHCP server provides IP layer parameters per interface to Windows 2000 DHCP clients only. The other options are provided to all DHCP clients.

A detailed list of the preconfigured options is available in RFC 2132. Configuring user options is described in the Immediate Solutions section of this chapter.

Table 13.1   BOOTP vendor extensions.

Option Code	Option Name	Description
1	Subnet mask	Defines the subnet mask (compulsory).
3	Router	Specifies a list of IP addresses for routers on the client's subnet. The router gateway addresses are listed in order of preference, so the first is the default gateway.
6	DNS servers	Specifies a list of IP addresses for DNS name servers available to the client. These are listed in order of preference.
15	Domain name	Specifies the DNS domain name that the client should use for DNS host name resolution.

Table 13.2   IP layer parameters per interface (Windows 2000 clients only).

Option Code	Option Name	Description
31	Perform router discovery	Specifies whether the client solicits routers using the router discovery method defined in RFC 1256.
33	Static route	Specifies a list of static routes that the client installs in its routing cache. Multiple routes to the same destination are listed in descending order of priority.

Table 13.3   Application and service parameters.

Option Code	Option Name	Description
44	WINS/NBNS servers	Specifies a list of IP addresses for NetBIOS name servers (NBNS), such as WINS servers. These are listed in order of preference.
46	WINS/NBT node type	Allows configurable NetBIOS over TCP/IP clients to be configured as described in RFCs 1001 and 1002, where 0x1=b-node, 0x2=p-node, 0x4=m-node, and 0x8=h-node.
47	NetBIOS scope ID	Specifies a string for the NetBIOS over TCP/IP scope identity for the client, as specified in RFCs 1001 and 1002.

Table 13.4   DHCP extensions.

Option Code	Option Name	Description
51	IP address lease time	Used to negotiate and exchange lease-time information between DHCP clients and servers. The option can be specified by the client in a DHCPDISCOVER or a DHCPREQUEST message or specified by the server in a DHCPOFFER message.
53	DHCP message type	Used in all DHCP messages to convey the type of message (DHCPDISCOVER, DHCPOFFER, and so on).
54	Server identifier	The IP address of a selected DHCP server. Used by the client to distinguish between multiple lease offers and to identify the offer that's being accepted.
58	Lease renewal time	Typically half of the full lease duration.
59	Lease rebinding time	Typically seven-eighths of the full lease duration.

Immediate Solutions

Installing and Authorizing DHCP

The DHCP Server service can be, and very often is, implemented on a DC. On a busy network, however, it may be appropriate to run DHCP from a member server. On a peer-to-peer workgroup, DHCP (if used) will be implemented on a standalone server. After you have selected the server that will offer the DHCP Server service, you then have to install and (possibly) authorize the service.

WARNING!   In a mixed environment where DHCP servers are placed in the DnsUpdateProxy security group, running the DHCP service on a DC can pose a security risk (see Chapter 14). In this situation, Microsoft's recommendation is to install DHCP on a member server, not a DC.

The server should have a fixed IP address, and procedure assumes that TCP/IP has been configured statically on the server host. Refer to the immediate solution "Configuring TCP/IP" in Chapter 1.

The account you use to install, authorize, and administer DHCP must have the appropriate rights. In a domain tree, DHCP is typically administered from the root domain, in which case an enterprise administrator account must be used. Implementing DHCP within a domain requires domain administrator rights. If a domain has several DCs, you must have administrative rights on the first DC that was created on that domain.

WARNING!   If your domain is a mixed environment, Microsoft (strongly) recommends that you upgrade your domain controllers to Windows 2000 Server before installing the Windows 2000 DHCP Server service on your network.

To install and authorize the DHCP Server service, proceed as follows:

1. Log on to the server as an administrator.
2. Access Start|Settings and select Control Panel.
3. Double-click Add/Remove Programs. The Add/Remove Programs dialog box appears.
4. Click Add/Remove Windows Components to start the Windows Components Wizard.
5. Select Networking Services and click Details.

6. Check Dynamic Host Configuration Protocol (DHCP) and click OK.

7. Click Next.

8. If prompted, insert the Windows 2000 CD-ROM or type the path to the Windows 2000 distribution files, then click Continue.

9. Click Finish and close the Add/Remove Programs window.

NOTE: *Microsoft's documentation states that the DHCP software can then be used "after restarting the system." If you're creating the first scope on a DC, a reboot isn't normally necessary. If you're creating a scope on a member server that you're authorizing in Active Directory, you should reboot that server.*

---

10. Access Start|Programs|Administative Tools and select DHCP.

11. Expand the server node.

12. If the server is unauthorized (indicated by a red down-arrow), select and then right-click the server, then select Authorize. The authorization process can take some time. Check the authorization status by pressing F5. A green up-arrow indicates that the process is complete.

NOTE: *If you're installing another DHCP server on a domain that already has a DHCP server activated, you need to authorize the additional server in Active Directory. Refer to the immediate solution following this one.*

---

13. Select and then right-click the server, then select All Tasks. Ensure that the service is started. You can start, stop, pause, and resume the service from the All Tasks pop-up menu. Restart stops and then automatically restarts the service.

14. Close the DHCP snap-in.

TIP: *You can also start, stop, pause, and resume the DHCP service from the Command Console by using the **net start dhcpserver**, **net stop dhcpserver, net pause dhcpserver**, and **net continue dhcpserver** commands, respectively.*

Authorizing a DHCP Server in Active Directory

If an additional DHCP server is added to a domain or domain tree, it must be authorized in Active Directory. This adds the server to the DHCP tree and enables single-seat administration of the DHCP service.

To authorize a DHCP server in Active Directory, proceed as follows:

1. Log on to the first DHCP server in the domain or the root DHCP server in a domain tree (not the additional DHCP server that you want to authorize) as an administrator.
2. Access Start|Programs|Administative Tools and select DHCP.
3. Select and then right-click the DHCP icon at the root of the console tree, then select Manage authorized servers.

TIP: *If the DHCP server that you want to authorize is also a DC, you don't usually need to carry out Steps 4, 5, and 6 of this procedure. In this case, the server appears in the Manage Authorized Servers list and is authorized when you add it to the DHCP console (Step 7). You need to carry out the full procedure only if you've installed the DHCP service on a member server or if the new DHCP server doesn't appear automatically on the list.*

---

4. Click Authorize.
5. Type the name or IP address of the DHCP server that you want to authorize and click OK.
6. Check that the new DHCP server's details are correct and click Yes.
7. In the Manage Authorized Servers dialog box, highlight the server that you've just authorized and click OK. This adds the server to the DHCP console.
8. Close the DHCP snap-in.

TIP: *In addition to adding the newly installed DHCP server to the DHCP console on the root or original DHCP server, you can add the root or original DHCP server to the console on the new DHCP server. You don't need to authorize it, just highlight it in the Manage Authorized Servers list and click OK. That way you can fully administer DHCP from either server.*

Disabling Service Bindings

If you install the DHCP Server service on a multihomed computer that has more than one network connection, you need to disable the service bindings for any connections that aren't used to provide the service to clients.

NOTE: *If a single network connection has more than one IP address configured, only the first configured IP address is used by the DHCP server bindings.*

To disable service bindings on a network connection, proceed as follows:

1. Log on to the DHCP server as an administrator.
2. Access Start|Programs|Administative Tools and select DHCP.
3. Select and then right-click the server on which you want to disable bindings, then select Properties.

4. On the Advanced tab, click Bindings.

5. On the Connections and server bindings list in the Bindings dialog box, uncheck the checkbox for any statically configured network connection that you want to disable. Ensure that those that should be enabled remain checked.

6. Click OK. Click OK (again) to close the Properties dialog box.

7. Exit from the DHCP snap-in.

Delegating DHCP Administration

You can allow two levels of access to the DHCP database. If you add a user or group as a DHCP User, then that user, or a member of the group, can view the DHCP database. This is useful if a manager in your organization wants to know what IP numbers are currently leased to which hosts. You can also create DHCP administrators, who can administer the DHCP service without having any other administrative rights. The procedures for delegating DHCP administration (or rather the tools used to implement the procedures) depend on whether the DHCP Server service is installed on a DC or on a member server.

Adding DHCP Users

A DHCP User can view the DHCP database. To enable a DHCP User, you add the user account to the DHCP User group as follows:

1. Log on to the DHCP server as an administrator.

2. The next step depends on whether or not the DHCP server is a DC:

   • If the DHCP server is a DC, access Start|Programs|Administative Tools and select Active Directory Users and Computers, expand the server icon, and click Users.

   • If the DHCP server is a domain member server or a standalone workgroup server, access Start|Programs|Administative Tools and select Computer Management. Under Computer Management (Local), expand System Tools, expand Local Users and Groups, and click Groups.

3. Select and then right-click the DHCP Users group, then select Properties.

4. The DHCP Users Property box appears. On the Members tab (for a DC) or on the General tab (for a non-DC server), click Add.

5. In the Look in drop-down box, select the computer or domain that contains the user or group accounts that you want to add (or select Entire Directory).

6. Click the users and/or groups to be added. On a DC, you can also select a computer account if you want to enable any user logged in locally on that computer to view the database. Click Add.

7. Click OK.

8. Click OK to close the DHCP Users Property box. Close the console.

Adding DHCP Administrators

A member of the DHCP Administrators group has administrative access to the DHCP Server service. The procedure for adding accounts to this group is the same as the procedure for adding accounts to the DHCP Users group in the previous procedure, except that in Step 3 you right-click the DHCP Administrators group and select Properties.

However, you probably won't want to add group accounts to the DHCP Administrators group, and you almost certainly won't want to add computer accounts. Members of this group can change settings, and membership should be strictly limited.

13. Dynamic Host Configuration Protocol

Creating and Configuring a DHCP Scope

A DHCP scope contains a list of IP addresses that can be allocated to DHCP clients. Selected addresses within the scope range can (if required) be excluded from the scope and won't, therefore, be allocated. The DHCP Server service also allocates a subnet mask to clients and can be used to specify the IP addresses of gateways and of DNS and WINS servers. A Time-to-Live (TTL) can be specified for DHCP leases, and specific IP numbers can be allocated to individual hosts, identified by their MAC addresses.

A DHCP server can be configured with several scopes, provided that there's no *conflict*—that is, the same IP address doesn't occur in more than one scope. If an enterprise has more that one DHCP server, there must also be no conflict between the scopes on these servers. If a scope on one server holds an IP address, then that IP address shouldn't be held in any other scopes on any of the DHCP servers. Scopes can be activated and deactivated individually.

This procedure assumes that the DHCP Server service is installed and activated. To create and configure a DHCP scope, proceed as follows:

1. Log on to the DHCP server as an administrator.

2. Access Start|Programs|Administrative Tools and select DHCP.

3. Select and then right-click the server, then select New Scope.

4. The New Scope Wizard starts. Click Next.

5. Type a name and description for the new scope. Click Next.

6. Set up the scope range and enter the subnet mask, as shown in Figure 13.6. The subnet mask can specified by setting the number of network bits in the Length box or by typing in the dotted decimal value (refer to Chapter 5). Altering the Length box automatically alters the number in the Subnet mask box, but if you type a number into the Subnet mask box it won't alter the value in the Length box unless you click on that box.

7. Click Next. If required, you can exclude one or more addresses within the DHCP scope from being leased, as shown in Figure 13.7.

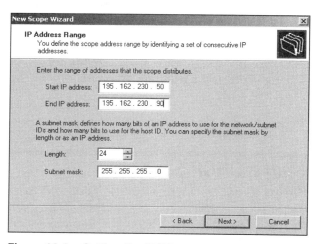

Figure 13.6   Setting the DHCP scope and the subnet mask.

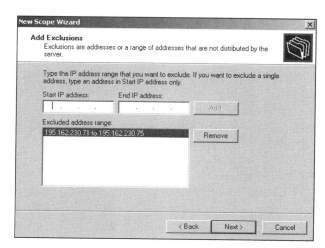

Figure 13.7   Excluding addresses within the DHCP scope.

8. Click Next. Set the lease duration. A DHCP client will attempt to renew its lease halfway through the lease period and each time it reboots. The default of eight days is suitable for most purposes.

9. Click Next. If you want to, you can set up a scope now and apply the values later. Usually, however, the default of configuring the options now is chosen.

10. Click Next and specify the IP addresses of the gateways on routers that are used by the DHCP clients. The first IP address specified is the default gateway.

11. Click Next. DHCP clients can be supplied automatically with the IP addresses of one or more DNS servers and with a parent domain name, as shown in Figure 13.8. More than one DNS server address can be specified in order of preference.

TIP: *If a DNS server has already been configured, clicking on Resolve will automatically generate the IP number information for the dialog box shown in Figure 13.8.*

---

12. Click Next. One or more WINS servers can be specified in order of preference.

13. Click Next. You can choose whether to activate the scope now or later.

14. Click Next. Click Finish. A red down-arrow indicates an inactive scope. If the scope node has no arrow displayed, the scope is activated.

15. Close the console.

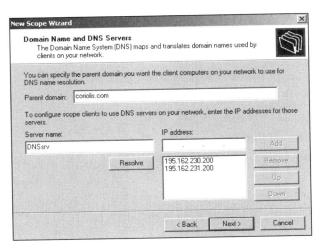

Figure 13.8   Specifying DNS server information.

Enabling DDNS Updates

DHCP is integrated with DDNS so the DNS database can be updated with new or altered IP addresses allocated dynamically to host computers in the DNS zone. To enable DHCP to integrate with DDNS and update the DNS database, proceed as follows:

1. Log on to the DHCP server as an administrator.

2. Access Start|Programs|Administative Tools and select DHCP.

3. In the console tree, select and then right-click the server on which you want to enable DDNS updates, then select Properties.

4. On the DNS tab, check the Automatically update DHCP client information in DNS checkbox.

NOTE: *There are a number of other options on this dialog box that aren't fully explained at this point. DNS is described in detail in Chapter 14.*

---

5. Click OK. Close the console.

Reconciling the DHCP Database

You can use the DHCP tool to identify and repair any inconsistencies in the DHCP database. This can be done for a single scope or for all the scopes on a server.

1. Log on to the DHCP server as an administrator.

2. Access Start|Programs|Administative Tools and select DHCP.

3. The next step depends on whether you want to reconcile a single scope or all of the scopes on a server.

   • To reconcile a single scope, expand the server node, select and then right-click the scope you want to reconcile, then select Reconcile.

   • To reconcile all of the scopes on a server, select and then right-click the server, then select Reconcile all scopes.

4. Click Verify.

5. If the database is consistent, click OK.

6. If the database isn't consistent, select the displayed addresses that need to be reconciled, then click Reconcile to repair inconsistencies. Click Verify. Click OK.

7. Close the Reconcile dialog box. Close the console.

Adding a Client Reservation

You can reserve a specific IP address for a client that's identified by computer name and MAC address. This procedure assumes that you have the appropriate client information. To add a client reservation, proceed as follows:

1. Log on to the DHCP server as an administrator.

2. Access Start|Programs|Administative Tools and select DHCP.

3. Expand the appropriate scope in the console tree, select and then right-click Reservations, then select New Reservation.

4. Type in the client details, as shown in Figure 13.9.

5. Click Add.

6. If you want to make any more reservations, repeat Steps 4 and 5 for each one that you want to make. Click Close when you have finished.

7. Close the console.

TIP: *You can view a client reservation by selecting and right-clicking the reservation in the console tree and selecting Properties. The dialog sheet lets you make changes to the client name and MAC address (convenient if you've installed a new NIC). If, however, you want to change the IP address for the client, you need to delete and re-create the reservation.*

Enabling Address Conflict Detection

If conflict detection is enabled, the DHCP server pings an IP address a specified number of times and leases that address to a client only if all the ping attempts time out. If a ping succeeds, the IP address is already in use on the network and won't be allocated. A possible scenario is that there is a statically configured host on the network, and the administrator has failed to include that host's address in the exclusion list for the scope.

WARNING! *This is not infallible. The statically configured host could (for example) be powered down when the DHCP server pings for its IP address. There will then be an address conflict when the host initializes. Make sure that you include all your network's static IP addresses in your exclusion list.*

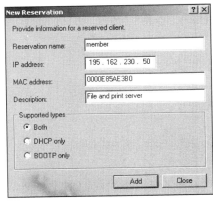

Figure 13.9   Adding a client reservation.

To enable address conflict detection, proceed as follows:

1. Log on to the DHCP server as an administrator.
2. Access Start|Programs|Administative Tools and select DHCP.
3. Select and then right-click the server, then select Properties.
4. Select the Advanced tab.
5. Specify a number greater than zero in the Conflict detection attempts box. The number you specify determines how many times the DHCP server pings an IP address before leasing it to a client.
6. Click OK. Close the snap-in.

TIP: *Don't specify more than two conflict detection attempts. Otherwise, DHCP server performance may become unacceptably slow.*

Creating a Superscope

A superscope is an administrative grouping of scopes that enables you to perform scope operations on several scopes at once. For example, you can display address allocation statistics for all the scopes within the superscope.

This procedure assumes that you've added all the DHCP servers that you administer into the DHCP console so you can administer all of them from a single seat. Refer to the immediate solution "Authorizing a DHCP Server in Active Directory." To create a superscope and add scopes to it, proceed as follows:

1. Log on to a DHCP server as an administrator.
2. Access Start|Programs|Administative Tools and select DHCP.
3. Select and then right-click the appropriate server, then select New Superscope.

NOTE: *This menu option appears only if at least one scope that's not currently part of a superscope exists on the server.*

4. The New Superscope Wizard appears. Click Next.
5. Specify a superscope name. Click Next.
6. Select the scopes that you want to add to the superscope. Click Next.
7. Click Finish. Close the console.

Adding Scopes to a Superscope

You can add scopes to a superscope retrospectively. Ensure that any scope you choose to add has been fully configured before you add it. To add scopes to a superscope (in addition to those you specified when the superscope was created), proceed as follows:

1. Log on to a DHCP server as an administrator.

2. Access Start|Programs|Administative Tools and select DHCP.

3. In the console tree, expand the server node that holds the scope you want to add to the superscope. This doesn't need to be the same server you created the superscope on.

4. Select and then right-click the scope you want to add, then select Add to Superscope.

5. In the Available superscopes list, click the superscope to which you want to add the scope.

6. Click OK.

7. Close the console.

WARNING! *Don't deactivate a superscope unless you intend to retire all of its member scopes permanently. Do not use deactivate to pause a superscope.*

Creating a Multicast Scope

Windows 2000 DHCP can allocate multicast IP addresses in the same way as unicast addresses. A multicast Time-to-Live (TTL) isn't the same as the lease duration of a unicast scope. The multicast TTL value specifies the number of routers (hops) that multicast traffic is permitted to pass through before expiring on the network. To create a multicast scope, specify the multicast TTL, and set a finite lifetime for the scope itself, proceed as follows:

1. Log on to a DHCP server as an administrator.

2. Access Start|Programs|Administative Tools and select DHCP.

3. Select and then right-click the appropriate server, then select New Multicast Scope.

4. The New Multicast Scope Wizard appears. Click Next.

5. Specify a name and description. Click Next.

6. Specify a start and end address and a TTL, as shown in Figure 13.10. Click Next.

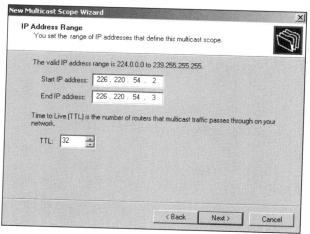

Figure 13.10   Specifying a multicast scope and TTL.

7. If you want to specify an exclusion range, type the start and end addresses, then click Add.

8. Click Next.

9. Specify a lease duration. Click Next.

10. Choose whether or not to activate the scope now. Click Next.

11. Click Finish. Close the console.

Setting a Multicast Scope Lifetime

By default, the lifetime of a multicast scope is infinite. If the scope is being created for a specific, time-limited purpose, however, it's sometimes convenient to specify a lifetime so you don't have to remember to delete the scope when you're finished with it.

To set a multicast scope lifetime, proceed as follows:

1. Log on to a DHCP server as an administrator.

2. Access Start|Programs|Administative Tools and select DHCP.

3. Expand the appropriate server node, select and then right-click the multicast scope, and select Properties.

4. On the Lifetime tab, select Multicast scope expires on.

5. Specify an expiry date and time, then click OK.

6. Close the console.

Configuring and Managing Options

Windows 2000 DHCP lets you assign a large number of configuration options through DHCP. These options can be assigned on a per-server or per-scope basis. They can also be assigned to an individual reserved client. You can select options that are specific to a particular vendor or user class. In addition to the standard options and classes, you can add new options and new vendor and user classes and amend option properties.

Specifying Server, Scope, or Reserved Client Options

To specify configuration options on either a per-server or per-scope basis, proceed as follows:

1. Log on to a DHCP server as an administrator.

2. Access Start|Programs|Administative Tools and select DHCP.

3. Expand the console tree. Select and then right-click either Server Options or Scope Options for the appropriate server or scope, or an individual client reservation, as shown in Figure 13.11. Select Configure Options.

4. On the General tab, you are presented with a list of more than 70 options. These are the DHCP standard options for the default user class. Check any option you want to configure on the DHCP clients and specify the configuration details in the Data entry section of the dialog box, as shown in Figure 13.12.

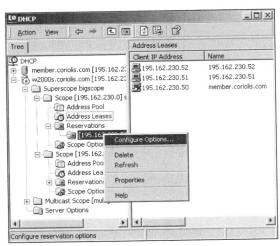

Figure 13.11   Selecting a client reservation for option configuration.

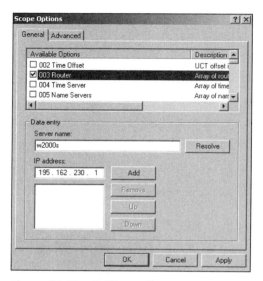

Figure 13.12   Setting options.

5. Select the Advanced tab. This lets you select a Vendor class (such as Microsoft Windows 2000 Options) and a User class (such as Default Routing and Remote Access Class) and configure user and/or vendor class-specific options, as shown in Figure 13.13.

6. When you have specified all the options you require, click OK.

7. Close the console.

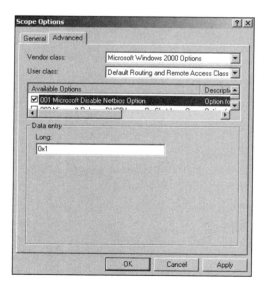

Figure 13.13   Setting user- and vendor class-specific options.

TIP: *Options specified at scope level override the same options specified at server level. Options specified for a client reservation override the same options specified at scope level.*

Adding a New User or Vendor Class

User and vendor classes are defined on a per-server basis. To add a new vendor or user class, proceed as follows:

1. Log on to a DHCP server as an administrator.
2. Access Start|Programs|Administative Tools and select DHCP.
3. Select and then right-click the appropriate server, then select either Define User Classes or Define Vendor Classes.

Class Identity

The Class ID section in the User or Vendor Class dialog box lets you type in class identity data that's used by the DHCP Server service to match the Class ID provided by DHCP clients. The data is entered as octet (8-bit) values using one of two methods:

- *As ASCII text characters*—To use this method, click the right side of the edit box.
- *As hexadecimal bytes*—To use this method, click the left side of the edit box.

Windows 2000 DHCP clients are configured to use the Class ID that you specify when setting up a new vendor or user class by using the **ipconfig /setclassid** command. For more details, enter **ipconfig /?** in the Command Console.

4. Click Add. Enter the relevant information in the New Class dialog box (refer to the Class Identity sidebar), then click OK.
5. Click Close. Close the console.

TIP: *You can use the New Class dialog box accessed in the above procedure to edit or delete a class that you've added. You can't edit or delete the vendor or user classes that are there by default.*

Adding an Option

You can add an existing option to an option class or define a new option within an option class. This latter facility allows options that are specific to vendor hardware to be configured on Windows 2000 DHCP clients before such options have gone through the standards process, been defined as RFCs, and been added to the list of predefined options. Linking the vendor-supplied code to the option definition is outside the scope of this book. The procedure assumes that if you're adding a new option, you know what the data type and code are for that option.

Options are added on a per-server basis. To add an option, proceed as follows:

1. Log on to a DHCP server as an administrator.
2. Access Start|Programs|Administative Tools and select DHCP.
3. Select and then right-click the appropriate server, then select Set Pre-defined Options.
4. Select the class to which you want to add an option, then click Add.
5. Type the option name, code, and description in the corresponding boxes. Select the data type and, if required, check the Array checkbox. Click OK.

TIP: If you're adding standard options into a new class, you can get all these details by selecting the option in the DHCP Standard Options class and clicking Edit. The Edit button also lets you edit any new options that you add. For standard options, you can change only the name and description. The Delete button lets you remove options, but you can't delete standard options in the DHCP Standard Options class.

---

6. Click OK to close the Predefined Options and Values dialog box. Close the console.

Administering Client Leases

You can view client leases at a DHCP server and determine which IP address is leased to which client. If a client has been retired or moved to another subnet, you can delete the client lease and return the allocated IP address to the address pool. At the client, you can release and renew a lease, set a Class ID, and view Class ID information.

Viewing and Deleting Leases at a Server

To view client leases and delete a lease at the server, proceed as follows:

1. Log on to a DHCP server as an administrator.
2. Access Start|Programs|Administative Tools and select DHCP.
3. Expand the console tree and select Address Leases. The details pane gives you the following information:
   - Client IP address
   - Lease expiration date (or whether the lease is a permanent reservation)
   - Type of lease (DHCP or BOOTP)
   - Unique ID (normally the client's MAC address)
   - Description (if specified)

4. Right-click Address Leases. The Export List option on the context menu lets you export the address lease information to a text file for further analysis.

5. In the details pane, select and right-click any lease you want to delete. Select Delete in the context menu. Click Yes.

TIP: *Deleting a client lease on the server is effective only if the client has been retired or is permanently off the network. If you delete an active lease held by a client on the network, that client will retain its configuration and renew the lease on reboot or halfway through the lease period. In this case, the client has to release the configuration (see the next procedure). If you don't want that client to be reallocated the released IP address, then you must either add the address to the exclusion list or reserve it for another client.*

---

6. Close the console.

Viewing, Releasing, and Renewing a Lease at a Client

To view, release, or renew a client's lease, proceed as follows:

1. Log on to the client as a user with sufficient rights to access the Command Console.

2. Access Start|Programs|Accessories and select Command Prompt.

3. To view the configuration, enter **ipconfig /all**.

4. To release a configuration, enter **ipconfig /release**.

5. To renew a configuration, enter **ipconfig /renew**.

6. Close the Command Console.

Adding and Viewing Class ID Information at a Client

This procedure views DHCP Class ID information for the Local Area Connection and adds the user Class ID "LaptopID" that I predefined, using the procedure "Adding a New User or Vendor Class" described earlier in this chapter. Please amend this procedure to your own requirements.

To specify and view Class ID information on a client, proceed as follows:

1. Log on to the client as an administrator.

2. Access Start|Programs|Accessories and select Command Prompt.

3. To view Class ID information, enter **ipconfig /showclassid "Local Area Connection"**.

4. To add a Class ID, enter (for example) **ipconfig /setclassid "Local Area Connection" LaptopID**.

5. Close the Command Console.

Monitoring DHCP Server Statistics

This procedure enables DHCP server logging and sets server properties so statistics are refreshed automatically. It also describes how to view statistics and refresh them manually.

To monitor DHCP server statistics, proceed as follows:

1. Log on to a DHCP server as an administrator.
2. Access Start|Programs|Administative Tools and select DHCP.
3. Select and then right-click the appropriate server, then select Properties.
4. On the General tab, check the Automatically update statistics checkbox and specify a time period. Ensure that the Enable DHCP audit logging checkbox is checked.
5. On the Advanced tab, specify the path for the audit log file. Click OK.
6. Right-click the server and select Display Statistics. You can now view the server statistics.
7. Click Refresh to refresh the statistics manually.
8. Click Close. Close the console.

TIP: *You can also view and manually refresh the statistics for scopes, multicast scopes, and superscopes. Automatic refresh, however, is specified on a per-server basis.*

Administering DHCP Server from the Command Console

Windows 2000 provides a wide range of options that let you administer the DHCP Server service from the Command Console using the Network Shell utility. This utility is described in detail in Appendix D.

To administer the DHCP server service from the Command Console, proceed as follows:

1. Log on to the client as an administrator.
2. Access Start|Programs|Accessories and select Command Prompt.
3. Enter **netsh**.
4. At the netsh> prompt, enter **dhcp**.

5. At the dhcp> prompt, enter either **server *servername*** or **server *ipaddress***, where *servername* and *ipaddress* specify the name and the IP address of the server you want to manage.

6. You should receive the message "You have Read and Write access to the server *servername*".

7. Use the Network Shell DHCP subcommands and options documented in Appendix D.

NOTE: *You can also use netsh subcommands in script files. In this case, you need to use the fully qualified command syntax* **netsh dhcp server [\\servername] subcommand**.

---

13. Dynamic Host Configuration Protocol

Chapter 14

The Domain Name System

In Depth

The Domain Name System (DNS) resolves host names—both local host names and Fully Qualified Domain Names (FQDNs)—to Internet Protocol (IP) addresses. DNS uses a hierarchical, extensible database and the concept of hierarchical domain name space. The system was first defined in 1984 and was one of the major factors in the creation of the World Wide Web.

Windows 2000 DNS Compatibility

Windows 2000 DNS is the name system of choice for Windows 2000 operating systems in both native and mixed environments. Although other DNS implementations, such as Berkeley Internet Name Domain (BIND) version 8.1.2, are compatible with Windows 2000 requirements, Windows 2000 DNS is fully integrated with Active Directory and uses multi-master replication.

Down-level clients, such as Windows NT4, use Network Basic Input Output System (NetBIOS) name resolution, particularly for locating Domain Controllers (DCs). These clients rely on broadcasts and the NetBIOS Name Services (NBNSs), such as the Windows Internet Name Service (WINS). Windows 2000 DNS is WINS-aware and uses WINS integration in mixed environments to locate network services and resources. Windows NT4 clients can register in Windows 2000 WINS, and Windows 2000 clients can register in Windows NT4 WINS.

Windows 2000 clients use DNS for name resolution and service location, including locating DCs. Because Windows 2000 DNS supports dynamic updates—that is, Dynamic DNS or DDNS functionality—integration with WINS isn't required for local host name resolution in a native environment. Windows 2000 DNS is integrated with Windows 2000 Dynamic Host Configuration Protocol (DHCP), and IP address assignments made through DHCP are entered in the DNS database (see Chapter 13).

DNS Standards

Windows 2000 DNS supports a number of standards and draft standards. Table 14.1 lists supported Internet Engineering Task Force (IETF) Request for Comments (RFC) standards, and Table 14.2 lists supported IETF drafts. Some of the IETF drafts may have become standards by the time you read this book, and some may have expired.

Table 14.1   Supported RFCs.

RFC	Title
1034	Domain Names—Concepts and Facilities
1035	Domain Names—Implementation and Specification
1123	Requirements for Internet Hosts—Application and Support
1886	DNS Extensions to Support IP Version 6
1995	Incremental Zone Transfer in DNS
1996	A Mechanism for Prompt DNS Notification of Zone Changes
2136	Dynamic Updates in the Domain Name System (DNS UPDATE)
2181	Clarifications to the DNS Specification
2308	Negative Caching of DNS Queries (DNS NCACHE)

Table 14.2   Supported drafts.

Draft	Title
Draft-ietf-dnsind-rfc2052bis-02.txt	A DNS RR for Specifying the Location of Services (DNS SRV)
Draft-skwan-utf8-dns-02.txt	Using the UTF-8 Character Set in the Domain Name System
Draft-ietf-dhc-dhcp-dns-08.txt	Interaction between DHCP and DNS
Draft-ietf-dnsind-tsig-11.txt	Secret Key Transaction Signatures for DNS (TSIG)
Draft-ietf-dnsind-tkey-00.txt	Secret Key Establishment for DNS (TKEY RR)
Draft-skwan-gss-tsig-04.txt	GSS Algorithm for TSIG (GSS-TSIG)

14. The Domain Name System

An RR is a resource record, UTF stands for UCS Transfer Format (where UCS is Unicode Character Set), and GSS stands for Generic Security Services. Internet drafts and RFCs can be accessed at **www.ietf.org**. A full list of the RFCs currently available on the Internet can be found at **http://info.internet.isi.edu/in-notes/rfc/files**.

The Domain Name Space

DNS is implemented as a hierarchical distributed database that contains various types of data, including host names and domain names. These names form a hierarchical tree structure called the domain name space.

An FQDN uniquely identifies a host's position within the DNS name space by specifying a list of dot-delineated names—for example, **authors.coriolis.com**. The root and top level (i.e., com, gov, edu, and so on) parts of the name space are managed on the Internet by a name registration authority such as the Internet

Network Information Center, InterNIC (at **www.internic.net**), whose designated representative is Network Solutions, Inc. (at **www.networksolutions.com**).

Organizations such as companies and educational establishments register domain names and IP addresses and administer their own part of the name space without the need to refer back to the name registration authority. Figure 14.1 illustrates the hierarchical domain name space.

Domain names comply with the International Standard ISO 3166. Reserved abbreviations are shown in Table 14.3.

Reverse DNS resolves an IP address to an FQDN and is used, for example, by Internet security applications (see Chapter 12).

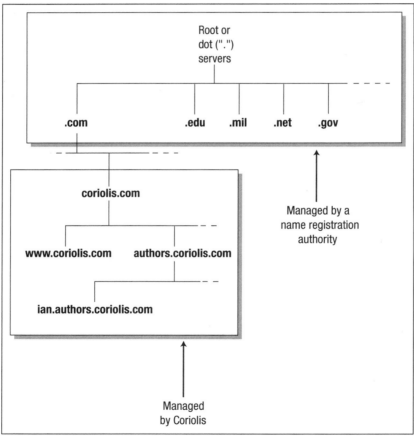

Figure 14.1 The hierarchical domain name space.

Table 14.3   DNS abbreviations.

Abbreviation	Organization Type
com	Commercial
edu	Educational
org	Nonprofit
net	Backbone networks
gov	Government, nonmilitary
mil	Government, military
num	Telephone numbers
arpa	Reverse DNS
xx	Country code (e.g., uk, fr, aus)

The DNS Database

The DNS database holds RRs in zone files. A DNS zone is an administrative entity that doesn't necessarily map to a domain. There can be several zones in a domain, and there can be more than one domain in a zone. A primary zone file can be copied to a secondary, read-only zone file for the purposes of backup and failover protection. The files can be held in various types of DNS name servers. The DNS database can be queried for name resolution using recursive or iterative queries. An understanding of DNS database structure and operation is central to an understanding of the Name System itself, and all of these topics are described in this section.

NOTE: *A DNS name server is sometimes referred to simply as a Name Server and given the acronym NS. This is because the NS RR in the DNS database (see below) identifies a DNS name server. Be careful about using this terminology, however. A WINS server is also a name server.*

DNS Resource Records

Various types of RRs are required for host name resolution, reverse resolution, and other administrative purposes. The most common types of RR are described below.

Start of Authority

An SOA RR identifies the DNS zone (or zone of authority). It contains the following data fields:

- *Owner name*—The host name of the primary DNS name server that's authoritative for the zone.

- *Responsible person*—The email address of the person that's responsible for administering the zone. A period (.) is used instead of an at sign (@) in this email address.

- *Serial number*—The zone file revision number. This number increments each time an RR in the zone changes.

- *Refresh Interval*—The time, in seconds, that a secondary DNS server waits before querying its master for the zone to attempt renewal of the zone information. The default for this field is 900 (15 minutes).

- *Retry Interval*—The time, in seconds, that a secondary server waits before reattempting a failed zone transfer. The default for this field is 600 (10 minutes).

- *Expire Time*—The time, in seconds, before a secondary server stops responding to queries after the refresh interval has lapsed and zone information hasn't been refreshed or updated. After this time has expired, the secondary server considers that its local data is unreliable. The default for this field is 86,400 (24 hours).

- *Minimum TTL*—A Time-to-Live (TTL), in seconds, that's applied to all RRs in the zone that have unspecified record-specific TTLs. This value determines how long an RR provided in an answer should be cached (see later in this chapter). The default for this field is 3600 (1 hour).

Host

A Host or Address (A) RR contains a host name (or DNS name) and the corresponding IP address (Ipv4). This is the simplest and most common type of record in a DNS database. An A record is required for any host that shares resources on the network.

Ipv6 Host

An Ipv6 Host or AAAA record is the same as an A record except that it maps a host name to a 128-bit IPv6 address (see Chapter 20).

NOTE: *Other Host records exist that aren't described here, for example, the Andrew File System Database (AFSDB) RR and the Asynchronous Transfer Mode Address (ATMA) RR. For more details, refer to RFC 1183 and* **ftp://ftp.atmforum.com/pub/approved-specs/**, *respectively.*

Name Server

A Name Server (NS) RR identifies a DNS name server and is used to assign authority to a specified server for a DNS zone in one of two ways:

- It establishes an authoritative name server for the zone and identifies that server to others that request information about the zone.

- It identifies an authoritative DNS server for any subzone that's *delegated* from the zone (see later in this chapter).

NS RRs contain the name of a domain or zone (the owner name) and the FQDN of the DNS name server that's authoritative for the zone.

NOTE: *If a name server is specified in an NS RR as being authoritative for a delegated zone, it will have an out-of-zone name. An A RR may be required to resolve this out-of-zone name. This A RR is known as a glue record.*

Canonical Name

A Canonical Name (CNAME) RR provides an alias for a host name by mapping an alternate DNS domain name specified in its *owner* field to a canonical or primary DNS domain name specified in its *canonical_name* field.

Pointer

A Pointer (PTR) RR links the DNS name in its *owner* field to another location in DNS namespace, as specified by its *targeted_domain_name* field. PRT RRs are typically used to link DNS names with records in the in-addr.arpa domain tree to provide reverse lookups of address-to-name mappings.

Mail Exchanger

A Mail Exchanger (MX) RR enables messages that are sent to the domain name, specified in its *owner* field, to be routed to a mail exchanger host, specified in its *mail_exchanger_host* field. A two-digit preference value indicates the preferred order when multiple exchanger hosts are specified. Each exchanger host must have a corresponding A RR.

Mailbox

A Mailbox (MB) RR maps a domain mailbox name, specified in its *owner* field, to a mailbox host name, specified in its *mailbox_hostname* field. The mailbox host name must be the same as a valid Address (A) RR already used by a host in the same zone.

NOTE: *Other email-associated RR types include Mail Group (MG), Mailbox Mail List Information (MINFO), and Mailbox Renamed (MR). Refer to the Windows 2000 documentation for details.*

Service Locator

The Service Locator (SRV) RR enables multiple servers that provide a similar TCP/IP-based service to be located using a single DNS query operation. SRV RRs maintain a list of servers for well-known server ports and transport protocol types for a DNS domain name. The list is ordered by preference. For example, it could locate DCs that use the Lightweight Directory Access Protocol (LDAP) service over TCP port 389. These RRs have a complex structure that has a large number of fields. Refer to the Windows 2000 documentation for details.

Host Information

A Host Information (HINFO) RR specifies the type of CPU and operating system (OS) for the host DNS domain name specified in the *owner* field. This information is held in the *cpu_type* and *os_type* fields, respectively.

NOTE: *Other RRs that provide general information include Responsible Person (RP), Route Through (RT), Text (TXT), Well-Known Service (WKS), Integrated Services Digital Network (ISDN), and X25. Refer to the Windows 2000 documentation for details.*

Windows Internet Name Service Forward Lookup

The Windows Internet Name Service Forward Lookup (WINS) RR is used to provide resolution of DNS queries for names not found in the zone by querying WINS servers configured and listed using this record. The WINS record applies only to the topmost level within a zone and not to subdomains used in the zone. See Chapter 15 for more details.

Windows Internet Name Service Reverse Lookup

The Windows Internet Name Service Reverse Lookup (WINS –R) RR is used in a reverse lookup zone to provide further resolution for reverse queries not found in the zone, by using a NetBIOS adapter node status query in WINS for the queried IP addresses. See Chapter 15 for more details.

DNS Zones

A zone is a portion of the DNS database that contains the RRs for the owner names that belong to a contiguous portion of the DNS namespace. A single DNS server can be configured to host one or more (or sometimes zero) zones.

Each zone is defined by a specific domain name, referred to as the root domain. If, for example, a zone's root domain were **coriolis.com**, it would contain information about all FQDNs that end with **coriolis.com** (any local host name in the **coriolis.com** domain has an FQDN that ends with **coriolis.com**). A DNS server is considered authoritative for a name if it loads the zone file containing that name. The SOA RR for the zone identifies the zone's primary DNS name server as the best source of information for the data within that zone and as the server that processes the updates for the zone.

Names within a zone can be delegated to other zone(s). For example, names in the domain **authors.coriolis.com** end with **coriolis.com** and would, by default, be members of the **coriolis.com** zone. Responsibility for these names can, however, be delegated to the zone **authors.coriolis.com**, which would then have its own zone of authority, its own SOA RR, and possibly its own primary DNS name server.

Delegation is the process of assigning responsibility for a portion of a DNS namespace to a separate entity. This entity could be a department or workgroup within a company or a company within a large organization. Delegation is implemented by using an NS RR that specifies both the delegated zone and the DNS name of the server that's authoritative for that zone. Delegating across multiple zones was one of the original design goals of DNS back in 1984. The authors of the original RFCs 882 and 883 (now superceded) identified several reasons for delegating a DNS namespace:

- A need to delegate management of a DNS domain to a number of organizations or departments within an organization.

- A need to distribute the load of maintaining one large DNS database among multiple name servers to improve the name resolution performance and create a DNS fault tolerant environment.

- A need to allow for host's organizational affiliation by including it in an appropriate domain.

NS RRs are contained in all forward and reverse lookup zones and assist delegation by identifying the DNS servers for each zone. Whenever a DNS server needs to access a record in a delegated zone (known as crossing a delegation), it will refer to the NS RRs to identify DNS servers in the target zone.

In Figure 14.2, the management of the **coriolis.com** domain is delegated across two zones, **coriolis.com** and **authors.coriolis.com**.

NOTE: *Typically, the zone file for a delegated zone will be loaded on to more than one DNS name server, and the top-level name server for the domain will, therefore, hold multiple NS RRs identifying the DNS name servers that are available for querying. In this situation, Windows 2000 DNS selects the closest DNS name server based on the round-trip intervals measured over time for each of the subsidiary DNS name servers.*

Database Replication

There are two types of DNS zones, *primary* and *secondary*, that have corresponding primary and secondary zone files. All zone record updates are made in the primary zone. A secondary zone is a read-only copy of the primary zone. Any changes made to the primary zone file are replicated to the secondary zone file. Secondary zones provide failover protection and can speed name resolution on remote network segments.

It's possible for a DNS name server to hold the primary zone file (or master copy of the zone file) for one zone and the secondary zone file (or read-only copy of the

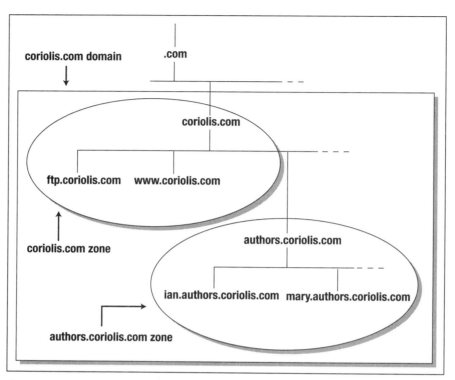

Figure 14.2   Delegated zones.

zone file) for another. The server would, in this case, be the primary DNS name server for the first zone and a secondary DNS server for the second zone.

The process of replicating a zone file to multiple name servers is called *zone transfer*. This is achieved by copying the zone file information from a *master* server to a *secondary* server (sometimes called a *slave* server), where the master server is the source of the zone information. The master server can be primary or secondary. If the master server is primary, then the zone transfer comes directly from the source. If the master server is secondary, the file received from the master server by means of a zone transfer is a copy of the secondary zone file. Figure 14.3 illustrates this distinction.

Master and Primary DNS Name Servers

The distinction between a master and a primary DNS sever can be a source of confusion. Primary and secondary refer to the type of zone. A DNS name server that holds a primary (updateable) zone file is the primary server for that zone. DNS name servers that hold a secondary (read-only) zone file are the secondary servers for that zone.

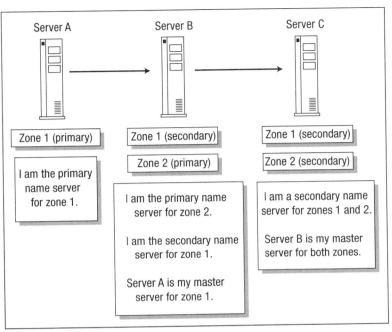

Figure 14.3   Master, primary, and secondary DNS name servers.

Master servers are part of the zone transfer process. If Server C receives DNS zone information from Server B, then Server B is the master and Server C is the secondary for that zone transfer. Any replicated information is read-only at the recipient. Server B could hold the primary file for one particular zone and the secondary file for another. Server C would get secondary files for both.

If the secondary zone file held on Server B is replicated from Server A, which holds the primary file for that zone, then Server A would be the master and Server B the secondary in this zone transfer. Refer to Figure 14.3.

The zone transfer is initiated in one of the following ways:

- The master server sends a *notification* to the secondary server(s) that the zone file has changed. RFC 1996 describes this process in detail.

- When the secondary server's DNS service starts, or when the secondary server's *refresh interval* has expired, it queries the primary server for the changes. The refresh interval is specified in the SOA RR and is 15 minutes by default.

There are two types of zone file replication:

- *Full zone transfer (AXFR)*—Replicates the entire zone file. There are two types of AXFR. One transfers a single record per packet, and the other allows multiple records per packet. Windows 2000 DNS supports both. By default it uses multiple records per packet, unless it's configured differently for compatibility with legacy DNS servers, such as BIND versions 4.9.4 and earlier, that support only a single record per packet. Windows NT4 supports multiple records per packet AXFR.

- *Incremental zone transfer (IXFR)*—Replicates only the changed records of the zone. Windows 2000 DNS supports IXFR; Windows NT4 does not. IXFR protocol is described later in this chapter.

Caching-Only Servers

All DNS name servers cache the queries they have resolved. You can, however, install a DNS name server specifically as a caching-only server. A *caching-only* server performs queries, caches the answers, and returns the results. It's not authoritative for any zone and contains only information that has been cached while resolving queries.

If you have a site with a large volume of DNS traffic or if you have satellite sites, such as branch offices, that use a slow-speed WAN link, a caching-only server can be used for load balancing and for reducing network traffic. A caching-only server doesn't perform zone transfers, which can be network intensive in WAN environments.

Windows 2000 DNS introduces the concept of a client-side *caching resolver*. This is described later in this chapter.

DNS Queries

DNS queries are sent from a DNS client (the resolver) to a DNS name server (the *name server*). Also, one name server can send a query to another name server. DNS queries are typically, but not exclusively, name resolution queries. For example, a query can request all host RRs with a particular name.

There are two types of DNS queries:

- *Recursive*—Requires the name server to return either a successful response or a failure message. Typically, a resolver makes a recursive query. The resolver then takes no further part in the query process, but instead waits for a response. A name server can send a recursive query to its *forwarder*, which is another name server that's specifically configured to handle requests forwarded to it.

- *Iterative*—The queried name server provides the best available information about the query. Typically, if the queried server isn't authoritative for the zone it will send a *referral*, which is a list of one or more name servers that may be able to satisfy the query or provide more information about it. The querying name server then sends the query to one of the servers on the referral list, and the query process continues as a series of iterations until the query is resolved. If a name server doesn't have any available information regarding the query, it sends a negative response.

Figure 14.4 illustrates the query process. This is a slightly simplistic example because it doesn't take into account queries to the cache of any of the resolving participants. Nor does it describe the use of WINS servers (or other NBNS servers) or broadcasts to resolve local host names, as would occur in legacy or mixed domains. The example describes DNS name resolution only.

In the example, a client (the resolver) in a remote domain wants to resolve **www.coriolis.com** to an IP address. This would typically occur if the client browser were attempting to connect to a URL.

1. The resolver sends a recursive query to its local name server for the FQDN **www.coriolis.com**.

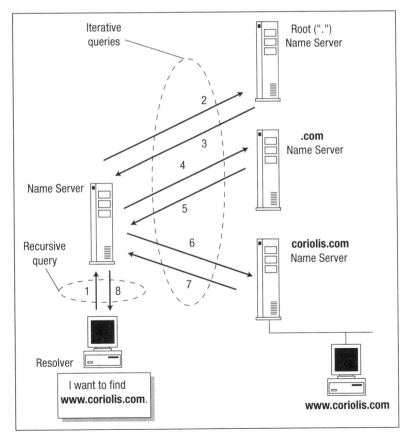

Figure 14.4   DNS name resolution.

2. The local name server can't resolve the FQDN from its own database. It therefore *parses* the FQDN. All FQDNs are understood to end with a dot. This isn't normally entered, but its assumed presence is essential for FQDN parsing. The local name server parses the final dot and understands that this stands for a root server (sometimes called a dot server) in the domain name space. All implementations of DNS incorporate a cache file (or root server hints) that contains IP addresses of root servers for the Internet domains. The local name server sends an iterative query to a root server asking it to resolve **www.coriolis.com**.

TIP: *The latest version of the root server cache file can be downloaded from InterNIC at **ftp://rs.internic.net/ domain/named.cache**.*

---

3. The root server can't resolve **www.coriolis.com**, but it *can* resolve **com**. It therefore sends a referral back to the local name server with a list of the IP addresses of name servers in the **com** namespace.

4. The local name server sends an iterative query to a **com** name server asking it to resolve **www.coriolis.com**.

5. The **com** name server can't resolve **www.coriolis.com**, but it *can* resolve **coriolis.com**. It sends a referral back to the local name server giving the IP address of the authoritative name server for **coriolis.com**.

6. The local name server sends an iterative query to the **coriolis.com** name server, which *can* resolve **www.coriolis.com**.

7. The **coriolis.com** name server returns the IP address of **www.coriolis.com** to the local name server.

8. The local name server satisfies the recursive query by sending the IP address for **www.coriolis.com** to the resolver.

Forwarders

If you don't want a DNS name server to use iterative queries (either at all or by default), you can configure it to use a *forwarder*. A forwarder is a DNS name server that handles iterative requests for other DNS name servers and returns the results to these servers. A DNS name server that can't resolve a request from its own zone information can send a recursive request to the forwarder. The forwarder is therefore said to provide *recursive service* to the requesting server.

Forwarders are typically used when access to remote DNS name servers is via a slow link. For example, you could be administering a high-speed internal network linked to the Internet over a relatively low-speed connection, in which case you may choose to use a DNS name service provided by your Internet Service Provider (ISP) for iterative queries. This could significantly reduce your network traffic.

A DNS name server that uses a forwarder can have iteration disabled completely. Alternatively, you can specify a forwarder and a time delay. In the latter case, the server sends a recursive request to its forwarder first, then it attempts iteration if the forwarder can't satisfy the request within the specified time.

You can also use a forwarder to share remote name resolution information. Suppose, for example, your organization has several DNS name servers. Rather than having each server send queries to the Internet (probably through a firewall), all your DNS servers can be configured to submit queries to a single forwarder. The forwarder builds up a cache of Internet DNS names from the responses it receives and can satisfy a query from one server from cached information resulting from a query from another.

Configuring a DNS name server to use a forwarder is described in the Immediate Solutions section of this chapter.

NOTE: *A DNS name server installed on a root server in a domain can't use forwarders.*

Resource Record Time-to-Live

When a query is resolved, both the resolver and the name server can cache the information and use cached responses to answer subsequent queries. The cached data has a limited lifetime that is specified in the TTL parameter returned with the data. This ensures that DNS doesn't keep information for so long that it becomes out of date. A cache TTL can be set on the DNS database, either for an individual RR by setting the TTL field of the record, or for a zone by setting the minimum TTL field of the SOA record. A cache TTL can also be set on a resolver.

There are two competing factors to consider when setting a TTL. If the TTL is short, the likelihood of information's becoming stale is reduced, but network traffic and DNS name server utilization are increased. If the TTL is long, the client could be given false answers to queries, but DNS name server utilization and network traffic are reduced. If a query is answered with an entry from cache, the TTL of the entry is sent with the response, so the resolvers that receive the response know for how long it's valid. The resolvers honor the TTL from the responding server and don't set it again based on their own TTL.

Updating the Database

Windows 2000 DNS supports both static and dynamic updates of the DNS database. Static updates are implemented using the DNS Microsoft Management Console (MMC) snap-in tool. Use of this tool is described extensively in the Immediate Solutions section of this chapter. Dynamic update is a Windows 2000 DNS enhancement and is described in the next section.

Windows 2000 Enhancements

The user interface to Windows 2000 DNS is through an MMC console snap-in. This provides consistency with other Windows 2000 services and provides the administrator with a consistent, easy-to-use management tool. In addition to simplified management, Windows 2000 DNS offers a number of enhancements and new features. These include:

- Active Directory integration
- Dynamic update, including secure dynamic update
- Record aging and scavenging
- Incremental Zone Transfer (IXFR)
- Caching resolver
- Unicode character support
- Enhanced domain locator

Active Directory Integration

Windows 2000 can use Active Directory services as its data storage and replication engine. A DNS zone that uses Active Directory integration must be loaded on a DC and is known as a Directory Service (DS)-integrated zone. DS-integrated zones provide the following benefits:

- Multi-master DNS replication is performed by Active Directory, and there's no need to support a separate replication methodology for DNS information.
- Active Directory service replication provides whatever replication granularity is required, right down to per-property replication.
- Active Directory service replication is secure, and secure DDNS updates can be implemented.
- A primary DNS server is eliminated as a single point of failure. An update can be made to any DNS name server DC, and the change is propagated to other DCs.

Active Directory integration simplifies the administration of the DNS namespace, while at the same time supporting standard zone transfer to non-Windows 2000 DNS name servers.

Multi-Master Replication

Zone update information for DS-integrated zones is written to Active Directory, and the Active Directory service is responsible for replicating the data. DNS name servers running on other DCs will poll for updates from the Active Directory service. DNS updates can be written to any DS-integrated DNS server, and the data will automatically be replicated across all DCs using multi-master replication.

Multi-master replication has a number of implications. The ability to write to Active Directory from several DCs simultaneously can create a conflicting situation in which changes are made to the same object on two or more different DNS name servers. This conflict will eventually be resolved in favor of the last update made to the object, based on the timestamps of the updates. The same rule applies if two or more nodes that have the same name are created on two or more DNS servers. Until the conflict is resolved and the DNS server that contains the invalid update polls the valid data from Active Directory, it's possible that requests for the same object made to two different DNS servers will be resolved differently. That's why the Active Directory service database is described as *loosely consistent*.

> **WARNING!** If a DS-integrated zone is converted to an original (non-DS-integrated) primary zone file, the DNS server loading the new primary zone must be the single primary source of authority for the zone. Therefore, the converted zone has to be deleted from Active Directory—that is, from all DCs that were previously authoritative for the zone. Otherwise, outdated or incorrect information will be replicated.

Reducing Latency in Zone Transfer Information

If a DNS zone has been updated, but this update has yet to be replicated to other DNS name servers, then name servers that hold different information exist for the zone. To reduce latency in propagation of changes to a DNS database, Windows 2000 DNS uses the NOTIFY extension, which actively notifies name servers that a change has occurred. A NOTIFY packet, sent by a master server, doesn't contain any zone change information. It merely notifies the other party that a zone transfer needs to be initiated.

Dynamic Update (DDNS)

DNS was originally designed to support queries by using a statically configured database, in which the frequency of changes was expected to be low. In this situation, all updates were implemented as external edits to a primary zone master file.

Dynamic IP address allocation using DHCP made manual updating of DNS information insufficient, as did the increasing size of both internal intranets and the Internet. Windows NT4 addressed this problem by integrating WINS and DNS, but this was at best a partial solution that relied on host and NetBIOS names being the same (or sufficiently similar) for resolution to work. In Windows 2000, the automatic assignment of addresses through DHCP is integrated with dynamic DNS updates. This capability, known as dynamic update, or DDNS, is defined in RFC 2136. The RFC introduces a new *opcode* or *message format* called UPDATE. The *update message* can add and delete RRs from a specified zone and test for prerequisite conditions. Updating is an *atomic* operation—that is, all prerequisites must be satisfied. Otherwise, no update will take place.

The zone update must be implemented on a primary name server for that zone. If a secondary server receives an update, that update is forwarded through the replication topology until it reaches the primary server. In a DS-integrated zone, an update may be sent to any DNS server running on a DC on which the zone is loaded. While a zone transfer is taking place, the zone is locked and can't receive any updates. This can be a problem in a large zone that's implementing DDNS and is locked frequently for the purpose of zone transfer. Windows 2000 DNS addresses this problem by queuing the update requests that arrive during zone transfer and processing them after zone transfer is complete.

Every Windows 2000 host attempts to register its A and PTR records through the DHCP client service. This service runs on every host, whether it's configured as a DHCP client or not. The dynamic update algorithm differs depending on the type of client that's supplying RR information to the dynamic update process. The client could be one of the following:

- A DHCP client
- A statically configured client
- A Remote Access Service (RAS) client

DHCP Client

When a Windows 2000 DHCP client obtains its IP configuration, it negotiates the DNS dynamic update procedure with the DHCP server. By default, the DHCP client always proposes that it update the A RR and that the DHCP server update the PTR RR.

The Windows 2000 DHCP server can be configured to respond in one of two ways:

- Update DNS server according to client request (default).
- Always update forward and reverse lookups.

If the DHCP server is configured to always update forward and reverse lookups, it will update both A and PTR RRs itself regardless of the DHCP client's request.

If dynamic updates are disabled on the DHCP server, the DHCP client will attempt to update both A and PTR RRs itself. Figure 14.5 shows the dialog box for configuring dynamic updates on a DHCP server. The DHCP MMC snap-in tool (DHCP Manager) is described in Chapter 13.

When an IP address lease expires, the associated A and PTR records must be removed. Dynamic cleanup requires that the records be deleted by the hosts—in this case the DHCP client and/or server—that created them. If the host that created an A or PTR RR is disconnected from the network before the DHCP lease expires, the corresponding RRs may become stale. Because the DHCP server is the owner of the IP address, it's recommended that DHCP servers register PTR records whenever possible.

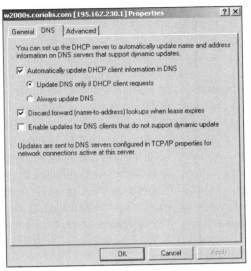

Figure 14.5   Configuring dynamic updates on a DHCP server.

In a mixed environment, a Windows 2000 DHCP client may attempt to negotiate the dynamic update procedure with a Windows NT4 DHCP server. In this case, the Windows 2000 DHCP client will update both the A and PTR RRs itself. If a down-level (for example, Windows NT4 or 9x) client obtains a lease from a Windows 2000 DHCP server, the server will register both the A and PTR records in DNS, provided the Do updates for down-level DHCP clients option is selected.

When a DHCP client's lease expires, A Windows 2000 DHCP server will remove the client's PTR RR. The server will also remove the corresponding A RR if the Discard forward lookups when leases expire option is set.

Statically Configured Client
A statically configured Windows 2000 client dynamically updates both A and PTR RRs every time it reboots, changes its IP address, or changes its domain name.

RAS Client
A Windows 2000 RAS client attempts to dynamically update both A and PTR RRs and to delete both records before closing the connection. If, however, the dynamic update fails (for example, the DNS server wasn't running at the time) or if the remote connection goes down unexpectedly, the records become stale. In this case, the RAS server attempts to deregister the corresponding PTR record.

Reregistration
DDNS provides a certain level of fault tolerance. The DHCP server reregisters DNS RRs upon lease renewal, and Windows 2000-based clients reregister their DNS RRs every 24 hours. Reregistration refreshes any RRs that have become corrupted since the last registration.

TIP: The DefaultRegistrationRefreshInterval *Registry parameter specifies the interval between client reregistrations.*
See Appendix C for details.

Name Conflicts

If a DDNS client discovers that its name is already registered in DNS with an IP address that belongs to another host, it (by default) deletes the existing registration and registers its own RRs. This behavior can be disabled in the client's Registry, resulting in the client's not registering the RR and logging the error in the Event Viewer. Apart from the inconvenience of hacking every client's Registry, this solution isn't totally satisfactory. The default behavior removes stale records but is vulnerable to malicious attacks. Altering this behavior protects against attacks, but stale records need to be removed manually. The solution is to use secure dynamic updates (see below), which ensure that only the owner of the existing record can update it.

Secure Dynamic Update

DS-integrated zones can be configured to use secure dynamic update. Active Directory maintains Access Control Lists (ACLs) that specify groups or users who are permitted to update RRs in such zones. The Windows 2000 DNS implementation of secure dynamic update uses the algorithm defined in the IETF draft "GSS Algorithm for TSIG (GSS-TSIG)." This algorithm is based on the Generic Security Service Application Program Interface (GSS-API) specified in RFC 2078.

A client that attempts a dynamic update on a DNS server can be configured to use one of the following approaches:

- Attempt a nonsecure dynamic update first. If this fails, negotiate a secure dynamic update (default).

- Always negotiate a secure dynamic update.

- Attempt only a nonsecure dynamic update.

Microsoft recommends the default approach because it allows clients to register with DNS servers that don't have the secure dynamic update capability.

ACLs can be specified for an entire zone or modified for specific names. By default any authenticated user can create A or PTR RRs in any zone. Once an owner name has been created, however, only users or groups specified in the ACL with write permission for that name can modify records that correspond to it. While this is normally what is required, there are situations where other user or computer accounts may be given permissions to modify secure dynamic update records. To address these situations, Windows 2000 provides the DnsUpdateProxy and DnsAdmins security groups.

DnsUpdateProxy Group

In a mixed environment, a DHCP server can be configured to register A and PTR records dynamically for down-level clients. In this situation, the default secure update configuration can cause stale records. When a DHCP server performs a secure dynamic update on a name, it becomes the owner of that name. If that DHCP server subsequently went down, a backup DHCP server couldn't update the record because it doesn't own it. Also, if the down-level client were subsequently upgraded to Windows 2000, it couldn't update its own RRs because it doesn't own them.

This problem is addressed by the use of the DnsUpdateProxy security group. Any object created by a member of this group has no security, and the first entity that's not a member of this group and that accesses the object becomes its owner. Every DHCP server that registers A records for down-level clients is put in the DnsUpdateProxy group. These servers create the records, but don't own them, and the problem is eliminated.

This solution, however, results in any DNS names that are registered by a DHCP server in the DnsUpdateProxy group being insecure. This is of particular concern if the DHCP service is installed on a DC. In this case, all SRV, A, and CNAME records registered by the Netlogon service for that DC are insecure. To minimize the problem, Microsoft recommends that DHCP servers, particularly in a mixed environment, should not be installed on DCs. Another argument against installing the DHCP service on a DC is that it gives the DHCP server full control over all DNS objects stored in the Active Directory, because the DHCP server is running under the computer (DC) account.

DnsAdmins Group

The DnsAdmins group has, by default, full control of all zones and records in a Windows 2000 domain. This security group lets a domain administrator delegate DNS administration without granting group members administrative privileges to other services and resources.

NOTE: *The procedures for adding accounts to the DnsUpdateProxy and DnsAdmins groups are described in the Immediate Solutions section of this chapter.*

Aging and Scavenging

If you use dynamic update, records are automatically added to the zone when computers and DCs are added. In some cases, they aren't deleted automatically and may become stale. Stale resource records take up space on the server and may give incorrect information in response to a query. Windows 2000 DNS *scavenges* stale records. You can specify the records that *must* be scavenged if they become stale, the zones that can be scavenged, and the servers that can scavenge these zones.

WARNING!   Do not enable scavenging unless you are certain that you understand all the parameters. Otherwise, you might accidentally configure the server to delete important records that it should retain.

By default, the scavenging mechanism is disabled. You can enable or disable aging and scavenging manually on a per-server, per-zone, or per-record basis. If you enable scavenging on a record that isn't dynamically updated, that record will be deleted unless it's refreshed periodically.

If you enable scavenging on a standard zone, and scavenging was previously disabled, the server doesn't scavenge records that existed before you enabled scavenging. To enable scavenging of such records, use the dnscmd utility supplied with the Windows 2000 Resource Kit. For more information, access **http:// windows.microsoft.com/windows2000/reskit**.

Windows 2000 DNS server uses a record timestamp and configurable scavenging parameters to determine when to scavenge records. You can set scavenging parameters on a per-zone or a per-server basis.

Per-Zone Scavenging Parameters

The aging and scavenging parameters that can be configured on a per-zone basis are as follows:

- *No-refresh interval*—The time during which the server doesn't accept refreshes for a record after the last time that the record's timestamp was refreshed. During the *no-refresh interval*, the server still accepts updates. When a DS-integrated zone is created, this parameter is set to the DNS server's *DefaultNoRefreshInterval* parameter.

- *Refresh interval*—The time during which the server accepts refreshes after the expiry of the *no-refresh interval*. After the *refresh interval* expires, the DNS server may scavenge records that haven't been refreshed during or after the refresh interval. When a DS-integrated zone is created, this parameter is set to the DNS server's *DefaultRefreshInterval* parameter.

- *Enable scavenging*—Indicates whether aging and scavenging are enabled for the records in the zone. When a DS-integrated zone is created, this parameter is set to the DNS server's *DefaultEnableScavenging* parameter.

- *Scavenging servers*—Determines which servers can scavenge records in the zone. This parameter isn't configurable through the DNS MMC snap-in tool, but can be configured using the dnscmd utility.

NOTE: *The* StartScavenging *parameter isn't directly configurable, but is set during the scavenging process. The scavenging algorithm for this process is described later in this section.*

Per-Server Aging and Scavenging Parameters

Per-server aging and scavenging parameters determine the default parameters for any zones that are created on that server. These parameters are as follows:

- *DefaultNoRefreshInterval*—Specifies the *no-refresh interval* that's used by default for a DS-integrated zone created on the server. The parameter is set in the No Refresh Interval box on the DNS console. The default setting is 7 days.

- *DefaultRefreshInterval*—Specifies the *refresh interval* that's used by default for a DS-integrated zone created on the server. The parameter is set in the Refresh Interval box on the DNS console. The default setting is 7 days.

- *DefaultEnableScavenging*—Specifies the *enable scavenging* parameter that's used by default for a DS-integrated zone created on the server. This parameter is enabled (set to 1) by checking the Enable scavenging checkbox on the DNS console. The default setting is 0 (disabled).

- *EnableScavenging*—Specifies whether a DNS server can scavenge stale records. If scavenging is enabled on a server, it automatically scavenges records with a frequency specified by the *ScavengingPeriod* parameter. The *EnableScavenging* parameter is enabled (set to 1) by checking the Enable automatic scavenging of stale records checkbox on the Advanced View tab of the DNS console. The default setting is 0 (disabled).

- *ScavengingPeriod*—Specifies how often a DNS server performs scavenging. The parameter is set in the Scavenging Period box on the Advanced View tab of the DNS console. The default setting is 7 days.

Scavenging Algorithm

A server can be configured to perform scavenging automatically at regular intervals, and scavenging can also be triggered manually. The server attempts to scavenge all primary zones and succeeds if all the following conditions are met:

- The *EnableScavenging* parameter is set to 1 for both the server and the zone.

- Dynamic update is enabled on the zone.

- The zone *ScavengingServers* parameter is either not specified or contains the IP address of the server.

- The current time is greater than the value in the zone *StartScavenging* parameter.

The server sets a time in the *StartScavenging* parameter when any one of the following events occur:

14. The Domain
Name System

- Dynamic update is turned on.
- The zone *EnableScavenging* parameter is changed from 0 to 1.
- The zone is loaded.
- The zone is resumed.

The time in the *StartScavenging* parameter is equal to the time at which the trigger event occurs plus the period of time specified in the refresh interval for the zone. This prevents a zone from being scavenged and valid records from being lost when a client can't refresh records because the zone isn't available—for example, when the zone is paused or the server is offline.

When a server scavenges a zone, it examines all the records in the zone. If a record's timestamp isn't zero, and the current time is later than the time specified in the timestamp plus the no-refresh and refresh intervals for the zone, the record is deleted.

Configuring Scavenging

If you're using the Windows 2000 DHCP service, the default scavenging and aging values are usually acceptable. If, on the other hand, you are using another DHCP source (such as a Windows NT4 DHCP server), you may need to modify the defaults. If you decide to reconfigure the scavenging parameters, ensure that the refresh interval is greater than the refresh period for each record subjected to scavenging within a zone. This, in turn, ensures that no records are deleted before the dynamic update client has time to refresh them. Many different services can refresh records at different intervals. For example:

- The Netlogon service refreshes records once an hour.
- Cluster servers typically refresh records every 15 to 20 minutes.
- DHCP servers refresh records whenever IP address leases are renewed.
- Windows 2000 hosts refresh their A and PTR resource records every 24 hours.

The longer you make the no-refresh and refresh intervals, the longer stale records remain. Therefore, you should make those intervals as short as you sensibly can. If, however, you make the no-refresh interval too short, you might cause unnecessary Active Directory replication.

Incremental Zone Transfer

AXFR isn't an efficient means of propagating changes to a zone because it transfers the entire zone file. IXFR transfers only changes in the zone information and is, therefore, a more efficient mechanism. IXFR, defined in RFC 1995, is implemented in Windows 2000 DNS. It works in the following way:

1. An IXFR client initiates a zone transfer by sending an IXFR message containing the SOA serial number of its copy of the zone.

2. The IXFR server that responds to the IXFR request stores a record of the newest version of the zone and files that contain the differences between that copy and several older versions. For performance reasons, only a limited number of recent changes to the zone are kept on the server. When an IXFR request that has an older serial number is received, the IXFR server sends only those changes that are required to make the IXFR client's version current.

In the following cases, a full zone transfer may be implemented:

• The number of changes is larger than the number of records in the entire zone.

• The client's serial number is lower than the one the server has as its oldest change record.

• The name server that responds to the IXFR request doesn't recognize the query type (that is, the server isn't an IXFR server). In this case, the IXFR client automatically initiates an AXFR.

Figure 14.6 illustrates the IXFR mechanism.

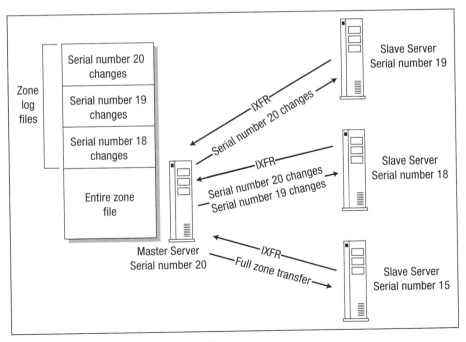

Figure 14.6   Incremental zone transfer.

In a DS-integrated environment, changes to a DNS zone can be made at any master server. Therefore, different master servers will contain zone changes applied in a different order. This causes a problem when the master IXFR server that previously provided the zone changes to an IXFR client isn't currently available. If the IXFR client selects another master server that has zone changes applied in a different order, the integrity of the IXFR client's zone may be compromised after the incremental transfer. In this case, the IXFR client initiating the zone transfer will request AXFR.

Caching Resolver

Windows 2000 DNS introduces a client-side caching resolver for DNS name resolution. Caching resolver is a Windows 2000 service that improves name lookup performance and reduces network traffic associated with name lookups by minimizing the number of name resolution round-trips. It runs in the context of the Service Control Manager and can be turned on and off like any other service.

The Windows 2000 DNS caching resolver service includes the following features:

- General caching of queries.
- Negative caching.
- Removal of previously resolved names from the cache based on negative acknowledgement.
- Keeping track of transient (Plug and Play) network adapters and their IP configuration.
- Keeping a record of each adapter's domain name.
- Managing unresponsive name servers.
- Prioritizing multiple A RRs returned from the DNS server, based on their IP address. If the resolver sends a query specifying prioritization, the DNS server finds the A records with IP addresses from the network to which the resolver is directly connected and places them first in its response. This feature prevents Round Robin from working properly and can be disabled through the *PrioritizeRecordData* Registry parameter. See Appendix C for details.

Round Robin

Round Robin is the allocation of multiple IP addresses to the same host name on the DNS database. Typically it's used for a frequently accessed service, such as the Internet Information Service (IIS). If your home page is held on a number of IIS servers, you can assign the same alias to all of them and then link all their IP addresses to that alias. This provides load balancing and failover protection.

- Accepting responses from nonqueried IP addresses. This feature is enabled by default and can be disabled through the *QueryIpMatching* Registry parameter. See Appendix C for details.

- Automatically reloading the updated local hosts file into the resolver's cache. As soon as a hosts file is changed, the resolver's cache is updated.

- Initiating a network failure timeout. If all of a resolver's queries are timed out, it assumes network failure and doesn't submit any queries for a period of time (30 seconds by default). The time period is specified using the *NetFailureCacheTime* Registry parameter. Setting this parameter to 0 disables the feature. See Appendix C for details.

If a DNS name server doesn't respond to a query, it moves down the priority list. This prevents the resolver from repeatedly querying a nonresponsive server. If a server that didn't respond previously is tried again and does respond, it moves back up the priority list.

Negative Caching
Negative caching is the storage of the fact that the requested information doesn't exist. This is useful because it reduces the response time for negative answers. It also reduces the number of messages that have to be sent between resolvers and name servers, as well as network traffic generated by these messages.

The Windows 2000 implementation of negative caching is based on RFC 2308. Setting the *NegativeCacheTime* Registry parameter to 0 disables negative caching. See Appendix D for details.

Disabling the Caching Resolver
The caching resolver is disabled using one of two methods:

- Enter **net stop dnscache** at the command prompt. This disables all the caching resolver features, resulting in Windows NT4-like name resolution.

- Set the *MaxCacheEntryTtlLimit* Registry parameter to 0 (see Appendix C for details). The value in this parameter specifies the maximum amount of time that the positively answered lookup is cached. Setting this value to 0 eliminates the RR caching, but doesn't disable DNS name server ordering or support for Plug and Play.

Unicode Character Support
Originally, DNS names were restricted to the character set specified in RFCs 952 and 1123—that is, a-z, 0-9, and a few additional characters. NetBIOS names can use a much broader character set than original DNS names. The difference in the character sets used by the two name services was foreseen as a problem during

upgrade from Windows NT4 NetBIOS names to DNS names used in Windows 2000. It wasn't considered practical to rename all the Windows NT4 NetBIOS names to adhere to then-existing DNS standards. Instead, the DNS character set was extended.

RFC 2181 enlarges the character set allowed in DNS names. It specifies that a DNS label can be any binary string that doesn't necessarily have to be interpreted as ASCII. Windows 2000 DNS supports the UTF-8 character set as specified in RFC 2044. This is a superset of ASCII and a translation of the UCS-2 (or Unicode) character encoding. The UTF-8 character set includes characters from most of the world's written languages, allowing a far greater range of possible names and allowing names to use characters that are relevant to a particular locality.

> **WARNING!**   *Take care when implementing a DNS system using UTF-8 character encoding, because some protocols place restrictions on the characters allowed in a name. In addition, names that are intended to be visible globally (refer to RFC 1958) should contain only the characters specified in RFC 1123.*

A Windows 2000 DNS server can be configured to allow or disable the use of UTF-8 characters on a per-server or per-zone basis. A DNS server that doesn't support UTF-8 may accept a zone transfer of a zone containing UTF-8 names, but it may not be able to write those names back to a zone file or reload those names from a zone file. Be very careful when transferring a zone containing UTF-8 names to another DNS server. Check if the target server is UTF-8 aware. If it isn't, check that all the records have been transferred correctly. If problems occur, you may have to disable the use of UTF-8 characters.

Enhanced Domain Locator

The Windows 2000 domain locator is implemented in the Netlogon service. It enables a client to locate a DC, and it contains the IP/DNS-compatible and Windows NT4-compatible locators. This provides interoperability in a mixed environment.

The DC location algorithm is implemented as follows:

1. The client collects the information needed to select a DC. This can include:

   - The DNS domain name of the client's Active Directory domain.
   - The Globally Unique Identifier (GUID) of the queried domain. Typically, this will be known only if the domain being queried is the client's primary domain. If the domain GUID isn't known, it's left blank.
   - The site name. This is obtained either from a previous query or manual site-configuration information. If neither is available, the site name is left blank.

2. The NetLogon service calls the DNS server using the IP/DNS Compatible Locator.

3. DNS calls the DnsQuery service, specifying the selection criteria listed in Step 1.

4. The service either supplies a list of one or more DCs that satisfy the criteria or returns the message that a DC can't be located.

5. The IP/DNS Compatible Locator pings the DCs in random order (to implement load balancing) and waits for 100 milliseconds for a response. The pinging continues until a positive response has been received or until all the DCs have been tried.

6. When a DC responds to the ping, the parameters supplied in the response are compared with the parameters required by the client. If the information doesn't match, the response is ignored.

7. The first DC to respond to a ping and satisfy the client's requirements is used by the client.

8. If the machine running Netlogon service isn't configured to use the IP/DNS Compatible Locator or if IP/DNS failed to discover a DC, the NetLogon service performs DC discovery using the Windows NT4 Compatible Domain Locator—that is, using broadcast or WINS.

9. The discovered DC information is returned to the client.

10. The NetLogon service caches the discovered DC to aid in resolving future requests.

Interoperability

Windows 2000 DNS is fully interoperable with all other RFC-compliant DNS servers. However, in a mixed environment with non-Microsoft DNS servers, some of the additional features that Windows 2000 DNS offers could raise interoperability issues. In particular, WINS and WINS-R records aren't supported by non-Microsoft DNS implementations, and the UTF-8 character set may also be unrecognized.

WINS and WINS-R Records

Currently, only Microsoft DNS name servers support the WINS and WINS-R RRs. Microsoft recommends disabling replication of these records if at least one of the secondary zones resides on a non-Microsoft DNS name server. The implication of doing this is that the RRs won't then be replicated to secondary zones residing on Microsoft DNS secondary name servers and that manual input is required.

The UTF-8 Character Format

The Windows 2000 DNS server can be configured to allow or disable the use of UTF-8 characters on a per-server or per-zone basis. A DNS name server that doesn't support UTF-8 may accept a zone transfer of a zone containing UTF-8 names, but may not be able to write back those names to a zone file or reload those names from a zone file. It may therefore be necessary to disable UTF-8 if secondary DNS name servers don't support it.

Non-RFC-Compliant Data

If a Windows 2000 DNS name server supports a secondary zone and receives non-RFC-compliant RRs, it drops these RRs and continues zone replication. It also drops circular CNAME RRs (X is the alias for Y and Y is the alias for X) if it receives them.

Immediate Solutions

Installing and Configuring DNS

DNS can be installed on a domain member server. However, if you want to take advantage of Active Directory integration, you should install it on a DC. When installed, the server can be configured to your requirements. The procedures assume that all the servers on which you're installing and configuring DNS have static IP configurations. This is the recommended practice.

Installing DNS

To install DNS, proceed as follows:

1. Log on to the server as an administrator.
2. Access Start|Settings and select Control Panel.
3. Double-click Add/Remove Programs. The Add/Remove Programs dialog box appears.
4. Click Add/Remove Windows Components to start the Windows Components Wizard.
5. Select Networking Services and click Details.
6. Check Domain Name Service (DNS) and click OK.
7. Click Next.
8. If prompted, insert the Windows 2000 CD-ROM or type the path to the Windows 2000 distribution files, then click Continue.
9. Click Finish and close the Add/Remove Programs window.

NOTE: *Microsoft recommends rebooting the server after you've installed DNS. The service works without a reboot, but it's advisable to reboot at this point.*

Configuring a Newly Installed DNS Name Server

After you've installed DNS, you need to configure the DNS name server. The procedure to do this is as follows:

1. Log on to the DNS name server as an administrator.
2. Access Start|Administrative Tools and select DNS.
3. Right-click the server and select Configure the server.

4. When the Configure DNS Server Wizard starts, click Next.

5. Wait for the server to collect setup information. This can take some time.

6. Specify whether or not this is the first DNS server on the network. If one or more DNS servers are already running on the network, you need to supply the IP address of one of them. Click Next.

7. Select Yes, create a forward lookup zone (unless you have a good reason for not doing so). Click Next.

8. Select whether your DNS name server is to be Active Directory-integrated (DCs only), a Standard Primary, or a Standard secondary. If possible, the recommendation is to install DNS on a DC and integrate it with Active Directory. Click Next.

NOTE: *An Active Directory-integrated zone is the same as a DS-integrated zone. This nomenclature is chosen here because it's used in the dialog boxes.*

---

9. Type the name of the zone. Click Next.

10. If you specify a Standard secondary name server, you'll be prompted for the IP address of the server that provides the zone information. Use the Add button to add one or more servers in order of preference. Click Next.

11. Select whether or not to create a reverse lookup zone. It's normal practice to do so. Click Next.

12. Select the type of zone that you want to create. If possible, the recommendation is to store the zone in Active Directory.

13. If you chose to create a reverse lookup zone, you'll be asked for a zone name or network identity (ID). Type in the information and click Next.

14. If you're configuring a Standard secondary name server, you'll be asked to specify the DNS server(s) from which you want to copy reverse zone information. This step is similar to Step 10. Click Next when you have finished.

15. Ensure that the configuration information is correct and click Finish.

16. Close the console.

Adding a Secondary DNS Server for an Existing Zone

If you install DNS on a server (typically a non-DC server) that already has another DNS name server on its network, you can configure the newly installed server as a secondary DNS name server by using the previous procedure.

Sometimes, however, you can have two DNS name servers already configured on a network, possibly both primaries for separate zones, and you want to make one the secondary server for the other's primary zone. This procedure adds a zone to a DNS name server as a secondary zone.

This procedure is normally carried out from the computer that you want to act as the secondary DNS name server. If you prefer, you can carry out the procedure from the primary DNS name server. To do this, access the DNS snap-in, right-click the DNS icon at the root of the console tree, and select Add Computer to add the new DNS server to the console. This lets you administer both DNS name servers from the same console. (You can also add the primary DNS name server to the DNS console on the secondary DNS server using the same technique.)

1. Log on to the DNS name server as an administrator.
2. Access Start|Administrative Tools and select DNS.
3. Right-click the appropriate server and select New Zone.
4. The New Zone Wizard starts. Click Next.
5. Select Standard secondary. Click Next.
6. Select either Forward lookup zone or Reverse lookup zone, depending on the type of secondary zone you want to create. If you want to create a secondary for both types of zones, you need to carry out the procedure twice. Click Next.
7. Type the zone name or use the Browse button. Click Next.
8. Specify the DNS server from which you want to copy zone information. This is normally the primary DNS name server, but it doesn't have to be. You can, if you want to, specify an already existing secondary DNS name server as your master server. Click Add.
9. Optionally, you can repeat Step 8 to specify several DNS name servers in order of preference. Click Next when you have finished.
10. Ensure that the configuration information is correct and click Finish.
11. Close the console.

Adding a New Zone

The last procedure used the New Zone Wizard to add a zone that already exists on one DNS name server to a second DNS name server that then acts as a secondary. You can use the same procedure to add a new zone to a DNS name server. In this case, the zone can be Active Directory-integrated (on a DC) or Standard primary and either a forward or reverse lookup zone. Other than this information, all you need is a name for the zone.

Installing a Caching-Only DNS Server

Caching-only DNS name servers don't host any zones. They build a local cache of names learned while performing recursive queries on behalf of their clients.

14. The Domain Name System

This information is then available from cache when answering subsequent client queries.

The procedure for installing a caching-only server is very straightforward:

1. Install DNS on the server as described in the procedure "Installing DNS."

2. Don't do anything else. A DNS name server that isn't configured acts as a caching-only server by default.

Configuring a DNS Server to Use a Forwarder

Forwarders are DNS servers that provide recursive service for other DNS servers. When forwarders are specified, they attempt to resolve any DNS names that can't be answered by the requesting server.

To configure a DNS server to use a forwarder, proceed as follows:

1. Log on to the DNS name server as an administrator.

2. Access Start|Administrative Tools and select DNS.

3. Select the appropriate server (not a root server), right-click it, and select Properties.

4. On the Forwarders tab, check the Enable forwarders checkbox. Add the IP address of the forwarder. If required, you can specify several forwarders in order of precedence.

5. Either check the Do not use recursion checkbox or specify a Forward timeout in seconds. In the first case, the server won't attempt iterative queries. In the second case, it will attempt iterative name resolution if it times out without a response from its forwarder.

6. Click OK. Close the console.

Delegating DNS Administration

You can delegate DNS administration by adding users or groups to the DnsAdmins security group. Members of this group have the right to carry out DNS administration tasks and have no other administrative-level rights in the domain. Nevertheless, the membership of this group should be severely limited and chosen carefully.

Typically, users are added to these groups at a DC that's also a DNS name server, and the procedure for doing this is described here. You can also add users to these groups at a member server, in which case you would use the Computer Management tool rather than the Active Directory Users and Computers tool. To add an account to the DnsAdmins group, proceed as follows:

1. Log on to the DNS (DC) server as an administrator.

2. Access Start|Programs|Administative Tools and select Active Directory Users and Computers.

3. Expand the server icon and click Users.

4. Select and then right-click the DnsAdmins group, then select Properties.

5. The Group Property box appears. On the Members tab, click Add.

6. In the Look in drop-down box, select the computer or domain that contains the user or group accounts that you want to add (or select Entire Directory).

7. Click the users and/or groups to be added. You can also select a computer account. However, it's unlikely that you'll want to add a computer account (and possibly not even a group account) to DnsAdmins. Click Add.

8. Click OK.

9. Click OK to close the Group Property box. Close the console.

Adding Accounts to the DnsUpdateProxy Group

Members of the DnsUpdateProxy group can perform dynamic updates on behalf of other clients but don't own the RRs that they create. The function of this group is to allow a DHCP server to create RRs but to prevent these RRs from becoming stale if that DHCP server goes down and (optionally) to enable clients that are upgraded to Windows 2000 to take ownership of their own A and PTR RRs. In a mixed environment, DHCP server computer accounts are added to this group. In this situation, don't install DHCP servers on DCs.

The procedure must be carried out on a DC. It's the same as the previous procedure for adding users to the DnsAdmins group, except that the DnsUpdateProxy group is selected and the computer accounts of the DHCP servers are added.

Configuring and Managing Zones

When you have installed DNS, configured your DNS name servers, and created the zones you require, your next task is to configure and manage these zones. This set of procedures describes how to modify zone properties (including enabling dynamic updates), create a delegated zone, and initiate zone transfers from a secondary DNS name server.

Modifying Zone Properties

This procedure describes how the Properties dialog box for a zone can be used to do the following:

• Change the zone name

• Change the zone type

• Allow dynamic updates

• Allow only secure dynamic updates

• Specify other DNS servers as authoritative

• Set the aging and scavenging parameters

• Adjust the refresh, retry, and expire intervals and other SOA parameters

• Enable DNS to use WINS resolution

• Modify security for an Active Directory-integrated zone

To modify the properties of a zone, proceed as follows:

1. Log on to a DNS name server as an administrator.

2. Access Start|Administrative Tools and select DNS.

3. Expand the appropriate server icon.

4. Expand either Forward Lookup Zones or Reverse Lookup Zones and click the zone that you want to configure.

5. Right-click the selected zone and select Properties. Figure 14.7 shows the Zone Properties dialog box for a standard primary zone.

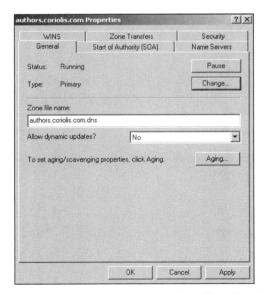

Figure 14.7   The Zone Properties dialog box for a standard primary zone.

6. On the General tab, click Pause. It's good practice to pause the zone while making changes.

7. If required, change the zone name. This option isn't available if the zone is Active Directory-integrated.

8. Click Change. If required, change the zone type in the Change Zone Type dialog box. The Active Directory-integrated zone type is available only on a DC. Click OK.

9. In the Allow dynamic updates dialog box, specify whether or not you want the zone to be updated dynamically. If the zone is a standard secondary zone, this feature isn't available in the dialog box. If the zone is Active Directory-integrated, you can also choose to allow only secure dynamic updates.

10. If the zone is a standard secondary, you can add or remove authoritative servers from which the zone receives update information. Clicking the Find Names button searches for the names of master servers in the address list and adds the search results to the list display.

11. If the zone isn't a standard secondary, click Aging. If required, check the Scavenge stale resource records checkbox. The dialog box gives descriptions of the no-refresh interval and refresh interval—more detail is available in the In Depth section of this chapter. Read the descriptions and set the intervals accordingly. Click OK.

12. Select the Start of Authority (SOA) tab, as shown in Figure 14.8. In a standard secondary zone, this tab is present, but the parameters are grayed out.

13. If required, adjust the refresh, retry, and expiry intervals. You can also change the minimum TTL, the TTL for the SOA record, the Primary server, and the Serial number. If you browse for a Responsible person, the search will return any RP records in the zone.

14. Select the Name Servers tab. This lets you specify additional name servers that will load the zone.

15. Select the Zone Transfers tab. You can choose whether to allow zone transfers and to what servers they can be sent. Clicking Notify lets you specify secondary servers that are notified when zone information is updated.

16. Select the WINS tab. This lets you specify whether WINS forward lookup is enabled. This is used in a mixed domain where NetBIOS is required for local host name resolution and DC identification. You can also specify whether to replicate the WINS record or, in the case of a standard secondary zone, whether to use a local WINS resource record. Clicking Advanced lets you adjust WINS cache timeout and lookup timeout. You can also use the WINS tab to specify WINS servers.

14. The Domain
Name System

483

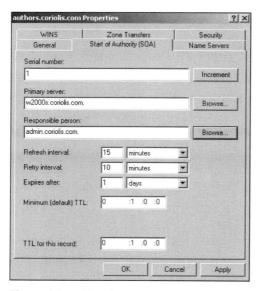

Figure 14.8   The Start of Authority (SOA) tab.

17. The Security tab is available only for Active Directory-integrated zones. Selecting this tab accesses the Active Directory Access Control List (ACL) editor. For information on setting Active Directory security, refer to the Windows 2000 Server documentation.

18. When you've made all the changes you require, click Start on the General tab to restart the zone. Click OK to close the Zone Properties dialog box.

19. Close the console.

Creating a Delegated Zone

This procedure delegates responsibility for a portion of the **coriolis.com** namespace to the **authors.coriolis.com** subdomain. This example is used for the sake of clarity. Substitute your own domain and subdomain names in the procedure.

To create a delegated zone, proceed as follows:

1. Log on to a DNS name server as an administrator.
2. Access Start|Administrative Tools and select DNS.
3. Expand the appropriate server icon.
4. Expand either Forward Lookup Zones or Reverse Lookup Zones and click the zone on which you want to create a new delegation. In this example, this is **coriolis.com**.
5. Right-click the selected zone and select New Delegation.

6. The New Delegation Wizard starts. Click Next.

7. Type in the name of the delegated domain. In this example, this is **authors.** Click Next.

8. Click Add, then specify the server name and IP address of a DNS name server that you want to host the delegated zone. Click OK.

9. Repeat Step 8 for each server you want to add. When you've finished, click Next.

10. Click Finish. Click the new delegated zone and check that it contains at least one name server record.

11. Close the console.

Initiating a Zone Transfer Manually

Normally, a secondary zone is updated automatically with an update frequency determined by the refresh interval and by how often changes are made to its primary zone. Sometimes, however, it's necessary to initiate a manual refresh—for example, if you've made an important amendment to the primary that you want replicated to the secondary immediately. This procedure is normally implemented at the secondary DNS name server, but if you've added that server to the DNS console at the primary, you can carry it out from either computer.

To initiate a manual zone transfer, proceed as follows:

1. Log on to a DNS name server as an administrator.

2. Access Start|Administrative Tools and select DNS.

3. Expand the appropriate secondary server icon.

4. Expand either Forward Lookup Zones or Reverse Lookup Zones and click the target zone.

5. Right-click the selected zone and select Transfer from master.

6. In the details pane of the console, check that the zone information has been updated.

7. Close the console.

Adding a Domain to a Zone

A DNS zone can span several domains. A domain can be added only to a primary zone, because the primary is authoritative for that zone. To add a domain to a zone of authority, proceed as follows:

1. Log on to a DNS name server as an administrator.

2. Access Start|Administrative Tools and select DNS.

3. Expand the appropriate server icon.

4. Expand either Forward Lookup Zones or Reverse Lookup Zones and click the appropriate zone.

5. Right-click the selected zone and select New Domain.

6. Type the domain name. This should be a local domain name and can't contain a dot.

7. Click OK.

8. Close the console.

Adding Records to a Zone

Dynamic updates in Windows 2000 DNS dramatically reduce the number of records that need to be added manually to a DNS database, as does WINS integration in NT4 and mixed domains. Nevertheless, there are occasions where manual update may be required—for example, if a client can't register with DDNS or WINS. You may also want to add an RR type, such as RP or ISDN, that isn't entered dynamically.

Adding a Host Record

You can add a Host (A) record to a primary forward lookup zone. To do so, proceed as follows:

1. Log on to a DNS name server as an administrator.

2. Access Start|Administrative Tools and select DNS.

3. Expand the appropriate server icon.

4. Expand Forward Lookup Zones and click the appropriate zone.

5. Right-click the selected zone and select New Host.

6. Type a host name. This should be a local host name and can't contain a dot. Type a corresponding IP address. If you want to create a corresponding PTR record in the reverse lookup zone, check the checkbox. Click Add. Click OK.

7. Repeat Steps 5 and 6 for each host that you want to add. Click Done when you've finished.

8. Check that the records in the details pane are correct.

9. Expand Reverse Lookup Zones and click the corresponding reverse lookup zone to select it.

10. Right-click the selected zone and select Refresh.

11. Check that PTR records have been created for the corresponding A records (assuming that this option was enabled when the A records were created).

12. Close the console.

Adding an Alias

You can add an Alias (or CNAME) record in either a forward or reverse lookup primary zone, although this type of record is normally added to a forward lookup zone. To add an alias, proceed as follows:

1. Log on to a DNS name server as an administrator.

2. Access Start|Administrative Tools and select DNS.

3. Expand the appropriate server icon.

4. Expand either Forward Lookup Zones or Reverse Lookup Zones and click the appropriate zone.

5. Right-click the selected zone and select New Alias.

6. Type an alias name. This can't contain a dot.

7. Type an FQDN or use the Browse button.

8. Click OK.

9. Check the details pane to ensure that the alias has been added.

10. Close the console.

Adding a Mail Exchanger Record

A Mail Exchanger (MX) record can be added to a primary forward lookup zone. An A record for the mail exchanger host must already exist in the zone. Where there are multiple mail exchangers within a zone, a two-digit preference value is used to indicate the order of preference.

1. Log on to a DNS name server as an administrator.

2. Access Start|Administrative Tools and select DNS.

3. Expand the appropriate server icon.

4. Expand Forward Lookup Zones and click the appropriate zone.

5. Right-click the selected zone and select New Mail Exchanger.

6. Type a host or domain name. This can't contain a dot.

7. Type the FQDN of the mail server or use the Browse button.

8. Type a preference value.

9. Click OK.

10. Check the details pane to ensure that the MX record has been added.

11. Close the console.

14. The Domain Name System

487

Adding a Pointer Record

A Pointer (PTR) record can be added to a primary reverse lookup zone. Typically, this happens automatically when A records are created. You can, however, add a PTR record manually. The A record must already exist in the associated forward lookup zone. You can create PTR records automatically when you create A records, but the reverse doesn't apply.

To create a PTR record, proceed as follows:

1. Log on to a DNS name server as an administrator.
2. Access Start|Administrative Tools and select DNS.
3. Expand the appropriate server icon.
4. Expand Reverse Lookup Zones and click the appropriate zone.
5. Right-click the selected zone and select New Pointer.
6. Specify an IP address and either type in or browse for the FQDN of the corresponding host. Click OK.
7. Check that the new PTR record in the details pane is correct.
8. Close the console.

Adding Additional Resource Records

You can add additional RRs by using the New Other Records menu item. This menu item is available on both reverse and forward lookup zones, but these records are typically added to the forward lookup zone. There would be little point, for example, in creating an AAAA record in a reverse lookup zone. Records can be created only in primary zones.

To create RRs, proceed as follows:

1. Log on to a DNS name server as an administrator.
2. Access Start|Administrative Tools and select DNS.
3. Expand the appropriate server icon.
4. Expand Forward Lookup Zones and click the appropriate zone.
5. Right-click the selected zone and select New Other Records. The Resource Record Type dialog box appears.

TIP: *Accessing the Resource Record Type dialog box is a good method of viewing all the record types and obtaining a description for each of them.*

---

6. Select a resource record type and click Create Record. Supply the requested information, then click OK.

7. When you have entered all the records you require, click Done.

8. Check that the records appear in the details pane. Close the console.

Administering a Client from the Command Console

You can enter commands at the command prompt to view and clear a client resolver's cache and renew DNS client registration. An administrator normally (but not necessarily) carries out these tasks. The procedures assume that the client is running Windows 2000 and that the DNS Client service is started.

NOTE: *The **nslookup** command is also used for DNS administration. However, this command is mainly for troubleshooting and is therefore discussed in Chapter 19.*

To administer a client using the Command Console, proceed as follows:

1. Log on to the client as an administrator.

2. Access Start|Programs|Accessories and select Command Prompt.

3. To display the client's resolver cache, enter **ipconfig /displaydns|more**. Use the spacebar to scroll the screen.

4. To flush the client's resolver cache, enter **ipconfig /flushdns**. This removes all dynamically added entries, including negative cache entries. It doesn't remove entries that are preloaded from the local hosts file.

5. To renew DNS registration at the client, enter **ipconfig /registerdns**. This initiates dynamic registration manually, refreshes all DHCP address leases, and registers all related DNS names configured and used by the client computer. This option assumes that the DHCP client service is running on the computer. By default, this service runs on all Windows 2000 clients, whether they're enabled for dynamic IP address configuration or not.

TIP: *You can use the **ipconfog /registerdns** command option on a per-adapter basis. To find out what adapters are available on the client for use with this option, enter **ipconfig** without any parameters.*

Chapter 15

The Windows Internet Name Service

In Depth

The concept of the Windows Internet Name (or Naming) Service (WINS) is a straightforward one. It provides a dynamic, centralized database that holds Network Basic Input/Output System (NetBIOS) names mapped to their corresponding IP addresses. A host computer on a network announces its NetBIOS name-to-IP address mapping to a WINS server, and when another host wants to discover the first host's IP address it looks in the WINS database to find it.

Because it uses a dynamic database, WINS addresses many of the problems associated with static Domain Name System (DNS) mappings. Dynamic Host Configuration Protocol (DHCP) assigns IP addresses dynamically, and dynamic address resolution is therefore required. WINS provides a method of implementing this function, although the solution isn't ideal because DNS host names aren't exactly the same as NetBIOS names. WINS also addresses the problems of domain controller (DC) discovery and resource browsing across a router, where these functions can't be implemented by broadcasts.

When Dynamic DNS (DDNS) was introduced in Windows 2000, many predicted the demise of WINS. A native Windows 2000 environment can use DNS for dynamic name registration and resolution and for DC discovery. If such a network can also use broadcasts to fulfill its browsing needs and doesn't access BackOffice services that use NetBIOS names, then NetBIOS and WINS aren't required and NetBIOS over TCP/IP (NetBT) can be disabled. However, such networks are still the exception rather than the rule. WINS is alive and well and performing a useful function in mixed environments, as it will for some time to come. Microsoft's continuing support for WINS is evidenced by the Windows 2000 WINS enhancements that address known problems with the service.

NetBIOS

WINS is a NetBIOS Name Service (NBNS). To understand WINS, we need to look at the basic concepts of NetBIOS and the methods of NetBIOS name resolution, as well as the use of NetBT. The first consideration is that NetBIOS isn't a protocol. It's a system that specifies a software interface and a naming convention.

In 1983, Sytec Inc. (currently Hughes LAN Systems) developed the NetBIOS interface for IBM. NetBIOS was designed with a flat namespace, which means that names can be used only once within a network. Originally, this wasn't a problem because IBM's PC network accommodated a maximum of 72 connected devices. NetBIOS wasn't designed to scale to large networks. Other vendors, including Microsoft, used the NetBIOS interface to design their networking system components and programs.

Windows 2000 provides NetBIOS name support in two ways:

- All Windows 2000 computers that use TCP/IP provide, by default, client-side support for registering and resolving NetBIOS names. This support is provided through NetBIOS over TCP/IP (NetBT) and can be disabled manually.

- Windows 2000 Server provides server-side support through WINS. This is a cost-effective solution in mixed networks. Windows NT4 clients can register in Windows 2000 WINS, and vice versa.

NetBIOS Names

NetBIOS names are 16 characters (or bytes) in length. These names are dynamically registered when computers start up, services start, or users log on. NetBIOS names can be *unique names* (one address mapped with a name) or *group names* (more than one address mapped to a name).

The first 15 characters of each name are user-specified; the 16th character is used as a name suffix to identify the name and to indicate the resource that the name is registering on the network. If a user specifies less than 15 characters in a NetBIOS name, the "+" character is used as a filler. Unique names are used to send network communications to a specific process on a computer. Group names are used to send information simultaneously to multiple computers.

Tables 15.1 and 15.2 list unique and group NetBIOS names, respectively.

Table 15.1   Unique NetBIOS names.

Unique Name	Service
computername [00h]	Workstation service
computername [03h]	Messenger service
computername [06h]	Remote Access Service (RAS) server service
computername [1Fh]	Network Dynamic Data Exchange (NetDDE) service
computername [20h]	Server service
computername [21h]	RAS client service
computername [BEh]	Network Monitor agent
computername [BFh]	Network Monitor application
username [03]	Messenger service (names of logged-on users)
domainname [1Bh]	Domain master browser

Table 15.2   Group NetBIOS names.

Group Name	Service
domainname [00h]	Domain name
domainname [1Ch]	Domain controllers (up to 25)
domainname [1Dh]	Master browser (one per subnet)
domainname [1Eh]	Browser service elections
__MSBROWSE__[01h]	Registered by the master browser for each subnet

TIP: *To list the NetBIOS names held in the database of a WINS server, enter **nbtstat -n** from the Command Console.*

Lmhosts Files

The lmhosts file is a static file that can be used for remote NetBIOS name resolution. It contains NetBIOS name-to-IP addresses mappings. To resolve a NetBIOS name, a host first checks its NetBIOS name cache. Normally, the cache contains only those names that were resolved recently. However, static NetBIOS name-to-IP address mappings that are entered in the lmhosts file using the #PRE notation are preloaded into the NetBIOS name cache and used to resolve a name query before a NetBIOS subnet broadcast or a WINS query is tried.

If a NetBIOS name can't be resolved from cache, the host attempts to use a WINS server or a subnet broadcast. The order in which these methods are used can be preconfigured through DHCP or by editing the host's Registry. By default, WINS is tried first. If these methods fail, the host may return to the lmhosts file and access the entries that aren't preloaded. These are, typically, entries for remote hosts, because local names would already have been resolved by the broadcast (or by WINS).

The lmhosts file is static, and entries must be updated if the name or IP address of a target host changes. Also, it's typically held on a per-computer basis. Lmhosts files therefore require a lot of administrative effort, and their use is limited. In Windows 2000, the WINS console supports a setting that enables you to import static mappings from an lmhosts file into a WINS server database.

NetBIOS Name Resolution

Windows 2000 uses a number of methods to locate NetBIOS resources:

- NetBIOS name cache
- NetBIOS name server (typically a WINS server)
- Subnet broadcasts

- Lmhosts file
- Hosts file (optional)
- DNS (optional)

NOTE: *The use of the hosts file and DNS in NetBIOS name resolution is controlled by the* EnableDns *Registry parameter. Refer to Appendix B for details.*

The order in which the above methods are applied depends on the node type (DHCP option 46) and the system configuration. The following node types are supported:

- *B-node*—Uses subnet broadcasts (broadcast node).
- *P-node*—Uses an NBNS (such as WINS).
- *M-node*—Tries subnet broadcasts first, but switches to p-node if it receives no answer (mixed node).
- *H-node*—Tries to use an NBNS first. If a name server can't be located, it switches to b-node. It continues to poll for name server and switches back to p-node when one becomes available (hybrid node).
- *Microsoft-enhanced*—Uses the local lmhosts file or WINS proxies plus Windows Sockets (Winsock) calls (see Chapter 18), in addition to standard node types. This node type is supported for backward compatibility with legacy (pre-NT4) systems.

NetBT

NetBT, specified in RFCs 1001 and 1002, implements the NetBIOS programming interface over the TCP/IP protocol, extending the reach of NetBIOS client and server programs to Wide Area Networks (WANs) and providing interoperability with other operating systems. In Windows NT4, the Workstation, Server, Browser, Messenger, and NetLogon services are all direct NetBT clients that use the Transport Driver Interface (TDI) to communicate with NetBT. Both Windows NT4 and Windows 2000 include a NetBIOS emulator, which takes standard NetBIOS requests from NetBIOS applications and translates them to equivalent TDI primitives. The TDI is described in detail in Chapter 17.

Windows 2000 uses NetBT to communicate with legacy systems, such as Windows NT4 and Windows 95. However, Windows 2000 redirector and server components now support *direct hosting* to communicate with other computers running Windows 2000, which means that they use DNS for name resolution. Direct hosting uses TCP port 445, instead of the NetBIOS TCP port 139.

By default, both NetBT and direct hosting are enabled, and both are tried in parallel when a new connection is established. The first to succeed in connecting is used for any subsequent attempt. In a native Windows 2000 environment, NetBT can be disabled to force all network traffic to use direct hosting. The procedures for doing this on both DHCP and non-DHCP clients are described in the Immediate Solutions section of this chapter.

WARNING!   *If you disable NetBT, applications and services that depend on NetBIOS no longer function. Make sure that no clients or applications need NetBIOS support before you take this action.*

WINS Components

WINS clients register their NetBIOS name-to-IP address mappings in a WINS server's database and query the database for NetBIOS name resolution. WINS servers handle name registration requests from WINS clients and respond to NetBIOS name queries submitted by clients. A client that's not WINS-enabled can make limited use of WINS through a WINS proxy.

WINS Servers

When a WINS-enabled client computer initializes on the network, its NetBIOS name and IP address are sent in a registration request directly to its configured *primary* WINS server. Because this primary server registers the clients, it's said to be the *owner* for the client's WINS records.

A client uses a WINS server as either a primary or secondary. (Windows 2000 and Windows 98 clients can be configured with a list of up to 12 WINS servers.) All WINS servers are functionally identical. The distinction between primary and secondary is made at the client, which is typically configured with an ordered list of WINS servers. The client's primary server is the first server on this list.

The client contacts its primary WINS server for all of its NetBIOS name service functions (name registration, name renewal, name release, and name query and resolution). Secondary WINS servers are accessed only when the primary WINS server is offline or is unable to resolve a name-resolution request. In this case, the client requests the same service from its secondary WINS server(s). If more than two WINS servers are configured at the client, the additional WINS servers are tried until the list is exhausted or until one of the secondary WINS servers succeeds in processing the request. If a secondary WINS server is used, the client attempts to switch back to its primary WINS server for future service requests.

WARNING!   *Don't overuse the option of listing more than two WINS servers. Processing a query request in WINS takes incrementally longer to achieve for each additional WINS server listed. This can delay the processing of the name query substantially before alternative resolution methods are tried.*

In addition to registering clients' NetBIOS name-to-IP address mappings and re-solving name queries, WINS servers can replicate the contents of their databases to other WINS servers. WINS replication is described later in this chapter.

WINS Clients

WINS clients are configured to make direct use of a WINS server. Typically a WINS client registers several NetBIOS names for use on the network. These names identify types of network service, such as the Messenger or Workstation service. Refer to Table 15.1 for a list of NetBIOS names and associated services.

Microsoft WINS supports clients running on the following platforms:

- Windows 2000 Server
- Windows 2000 Professional
- Windows NT Server
- Windows NT Workstation
- Windows 98
- Windows 95
- Windows for Workgroups
- Microsoft LAN Manager
- MS-DOS
- OS/2
- Linux and Unix (with Samba installed)

NOTE: *The list of clients given here is the official list given in the Microsoft documentation. It may or may not include every current WINS client.*

Clients that aren't WINS-enabled can make limited use of WINS through WINS proxies.

WINS Proxies

A WINS proxy is a WINS client that's configured to act on behalf of other hosts that can't use WINS directly. WINS proxies can resolve NetBIOS name queries that can't be resolved by subnet broadcasts—i.e., for computers located on routed TCP/IP networks.

Most non WINS-enabled computers use broadcasts to resolve NetBIOS name que-ries and register their NetBIOS names on the network. You can configure a WINS proxy to listen for broadcasts from these computers and to query a WINS server for names not resolved by these broadcasts.

WINS proxies work in the following way:

- When a b-node client attempts to register its name and IP address, the proxy checks the name against the WINS server database. If the name already exists in the WINS database, the proxy sends a negative registration response back to the b-node client. Otherwise, the proxy stores the client's NetBIOS name-to-IP address mapping in its remote name cache.

- When a b-node client broadcasts a name query, the proxy attempts to resolve the name using either information in its remote name cache or information it obtains from the WINS server.

- When a b-node client releases its name, the proxy deletes the client name from its remote name cache.

WINS proxies are required for broadcast-only (or b-node) clients. On most networks, WINS-enabled clients are the norm and WINS proxies aren't required. For more information about WINS proxies, refer to the Windows 2000 Resource Kit (access **http://windows.microsoft.com/windows2000/reskit**).

TIP: *Static mappings for non-WINS-enabled hosts can be entered manually into the WINS database. In this way, WINS-enabled clients can resolve the names of non-WINS-enabled clients (but not vice versa).*

Figure 15.1 illustrates the various WINS components. In this figure, Host B can resolve Hosts D's NetBIOS name through WINS and vice versa, even though they're on different subnets and Host D isn't WINS-enabled.

WINS Replication

If your network contains multiple WINS servers, they can be configured to replicate their database records with each other. In this way, consistent WINS information is maintained and distributed throughout the network. Each WINS server must be configured with at least one other WINS server as its replication partner. This ensures that a name registered with one WINS server is eventually replicated to all other WINS servers in the network. A replication partner can be added and configured as a push partner, a pull partner, or (by default) a push/pull partner. WINS replication is always incremental; only the changes in the database are replicated, rather than the entire database.

A latency period exists before a client mapping from any given server is propagated to all other WINS servers in the network. This latency is known as the *convergence time* for the entire WINS system. The latency or convergence time can depend on the type of operation being carried out as well as the replication settings specified on the WINS servers. For example, a name release request by a client won't propagate as fast as a name registration request. This is because it's normal for client names to be released, then reused with the same mapping as computers are periodically shut down and restarted.

When a WINS client computer is shut down improperly, the registered names of the computer aren't released and a name release request isn't sent to the WINS

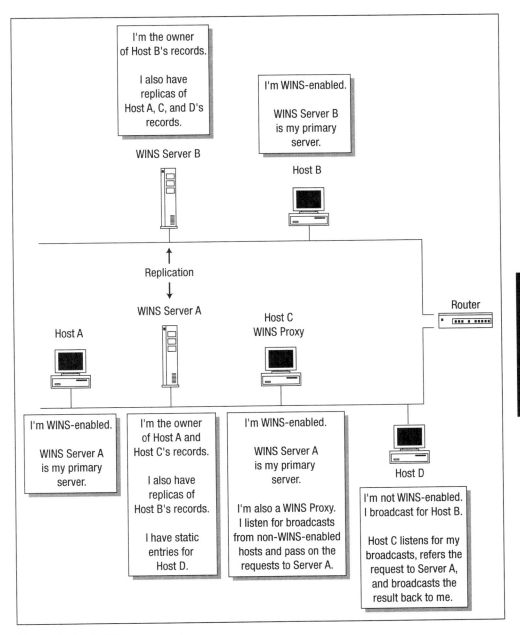

Figure 15.1 **WINS components.**

15. The Windows
Internet Name Service

server. Therefore, the presence of a client record in the WINS database doesn't necessarily mean that the client computer is still using the name or its associated IP address.

Pull Partners

A pull partner is a WINS server that pulls or requests replication of updated WINS database entries from other WINS servers at preconfigured intervals, or whenever WINS starts. The pull partner requests entries with a higher version ID than the last entry it received from its configured partner.

The amount of time between pull replications is indicated in the *replication interval*, which can be specified globally for all pull partners or individually for specific partners. When the replication interval elapses, the WINS server sends a pull replication trigger to its partners. The partners then respond with any changes that have been made since the last time replication occurred. Configuring a pull partner and setting start times and replication intervals are described in the Immediate Solutions section of this chapter.

All WINS servers maintain an internal table that maps record owners to version IDs. This table is built dynamically at server startup and is held in memory. The owner-version mappings are used by WINS to determine the state of the database at any point in time before or after replication and to determine which records should be replicated when pull replication is triggered. The table can also be used to determine update consistency between databases. A WINS server that owns a record should have the latest version ID of that record, because the client will send updates to the owner, which is that client's primary server by definition. If this isn't the case (maybe the owner has been offline for a while), WINS takes the appropriate corrective action.

TIP: Because WINS uses a higher version ID during replication to determine which version is more recent between two servers storing the same record, increasing the starting version ID can be useful where you are attempting to force update and replication between servers.

Push Partners

A push partner notifies other WINS servers that its database has been updated and that it needs to replicate these changes. You can enable WINS to notify configured partners that push replication is required when one of the following events occurs:

- The WINS server starts.
- A change is made in the WINS server database.
- A specified number of changes have been made.

You can configure push parameters for all push partners or for a specific partner. Configuring these parameters is described in the Immediate Solutions section of this chapter. How push replication is configured is largely dependent on whether a persistent connection exists between partners. If a partner is configured with a persistent connection, you can set to zero the number of changes that have to occur before a push replication trigger is sent. This will result in every change triggering a push request. If there's no persistent connection, a minimum of 20 changes to the version ID is required before push replication is triggered.

Push replication can be specified so that the replication trigger is propagated to all partners. If, for example, Server A pushes changes to Server B and Server B pushes changes to Server C, there could be an unacceptable delay in updating Server C with changes made at Server A. Push with propagation ensures that Server B will send a push replication trigger to Server C as soon as it receives updated information from Server A.

TIP: Both push and pull replication can be initiated manually.

Blocking Replication Partners

If a WINS server is removed from a network, that server's records can continue to be distributed to other servers in a replicated WINS environment. In some cases, stale records aren't deleted at all; in others, they are deleted eventually, but can remain in the WINS database for an extended period of time. The reasons for this are as follows:

- Static mappings originally made at the inactive WINS server replicate indefinitely among the other active WINS servers in the network, unless manually deleted or tombstoned.

- Dynamic mappings originally registered at the inactive WINS server aren't immediately removed from the WINS database. In the case of dynamic entries, WINS must check with an owner server before entries are deleted. If a WINS server is no longer in use, other WINS servers retain records they can't verify as expired on that owner server. Typically, an extinction period of 36 days passes before a record is fully removed from the database through the scavenging process.

To address this problem, the WINS console offers the "Block records for these owners" feature. This functionality was previously available in Windows NT4 WINS, using the *PersonaNonGrata* Registry parameter. It provides a method of blocking replication of entries owned by inactive servers by allowing you to specify these servers' IP addresses so their records are removed from the WINS database in a timely manner. Because it can prevent further replication of unwanted or stale records between active, this feature is useful when you need to remove WINS servers from your network.

15. The Windows
Internet Name Service

WINS Name Registration and Resolution

Each NetBIOS name has an entry in the WINS database. It's owned by the WINS server that it registered with and is replicated on all WINS partner servers. Each entry has an associated state—active, released, or extinct (tombstoned). Entries are also assigned a version ID that's used in the replication process.

WINS also allows you to register static names for clients that aren't capable of dynamic name registration.

Registering Names

Name registration occurs when a WINS client requests the use of a NetBIOS name on the network. The request can be for a unique or group name. NetBIOS applications can also register one or more names. WINS accepts or rejects the name registration request and issues either a positive or negative name registration response, depending on whether the name already exists on the network, what the name state is, and whether or not the name is unique.

New Registration

If the name is accepted as a new registration, the following steps occur:

1. The NetBIOS name-to-IP address mapping is entered into the WINS database with a new version ID and marked with the owner ID of the WINS server.

2. The record's timestamp is calculated, based on adding the value of the renew interval (six days by default) that's set on the WINS server to the current date and time on the server.

3. A positive registration response is sent back to the host with a Time-to-Live (TTL) value equal to the timestamp recorded for the new record.

Name Registered for the Same IP Address

If the name already exists in the database with the same IP address as that being requested, the action taken depends on the state and ownership of the existing name.

- If the entry is marked as active and is owned by the WINS server, the server updates the timestamp for the record and returns a positive response back to the client.

- If the entry is marked as being either released or tombstoned or if another WINS server owns the entry, the registration is treated as a new registration. Timestamp, version ID, and ownership are all updated and a positive response is returned.

Name Registered for a Different IP Address

If the name exists in the WINS database but is associated with a different IP address than that being requested, the WINS server avoids duplicate names. If the database entry is in the released or tombstoned state, the WINS server can assign the name to the new IP address. If, however, the entry is in the active state, the node holding the name is challenged to determine if it still exists on the network. If the challenge receives a positive response, the WINS server sends a negative name registration response back to the requesting client, rejecting the name registration.

If a positive response isn't received back from the first challenge, two subsequent challenges are made. After three attempts with no response, the challenge process is complete, a positive registration response is returned to the requesting client, and the new NetBIOS name-to-IP address mapping is inserted into the WINS database.

Releasing Names

When a WINS client computer finishes using a particular name or when an orderly shutdown occurs, the name is released. The WINS client notifies its WINS primary server that it's no longer using its registered name. The WINS server takes two actions:

- The WINS server marks the related database entry as released. If the entry remains released for a specified time period, the WINS server marks the entry as tombstoned, updates the version ID for the entry, and notifies other WINS servers of the change.
- The WINS server returns a release confirmation message to the WINS client.

If a name entry is marked as released, the WINS server can immediately update or revise that name entry when a new registration request arrives from a WINS client with the same name but with a different IP address. This can happen, for example, when a DHCP-enabled client changes subnets.

However, name release is most frequently used when clients shut down and restart on the network. If a computer releases its name during shutdown, the WINS server doesn't challenge the name when the computer reconnects. If, on the other hand, a proper shutdown doesn't occur, a name registration with a new IP address causes the WINS server to challenge the previous registration. When the challenge fails (because the client computer is no longer using the old IP address), the registration succeeds.

Name Renewal

WINS client computers renew their NetBIOS name registrations periodically with the WINS server. The WINS server treats name renewal requests in a similar fashion to new name registrations. When a client first registers with a WINS server, the server returns a TTL value that indicates when the client registration needs to be renewed. If renewal doesn't occur by that time, the name registration expires on the WINS server and the name entry is (eventually) removed from the WINS database. Static name entries don't expire and don't need to be renewed.

The default TTL, or *renew interval*, for entries in the WINS database is six days. WINS clients attempt to renew their registrations when 50 percent of the TTL value has elapsed.

It's the responsibility of the client to refresh its name before the renew interval expires. If the WINS server doesn't respond to the refresh request, the client increases the frequency at which it attempts to refresh its name.

TIP: *Always set the same renew interval for all replication partners when multiple WINS servers are used.*

Name Resolution

Name resolution is transparent to the user. By default, Windows 2000 WINS clients use the following procedure for resolving a name query:

1. Determine if the name is longer than 15 characters (the 16th NetBIOS byte isn't counted) or if it contains periods. If so, query DNS for the name.
2. Determine if the name is stored in the client's remote name cache.
3. Contact configured WINS servers to attempt to resolve the name using WINS.
4. Use local IP broadcasts to the subnet.
5. Check the lmhosts file (if Enable LMHOSTS Lookup is checked in the TCP/IP properties for the connection).
6. Check the hosts file (if the *EnableDns* Registry entry is appropriately configured).
7. Query a DNS server (if the *EnableDns* Registry entry is appropriately configured).

For more details, refer to the Windows 2000 Server Resource Kit Networking Guide.

Enabling WAN Browsing Using WINS

The Browser service identifies resources on a network and maintains a resource list so browse clients can access these resources. Although browsing relies mainly on broadcast communication, there are occasions when it's necessary to browse for resources over routed networks. There are three methods of implementing WAN browsing:

- *Enable routers to pass NetBIOS broadcasts*—This leads to an unacceptable increase in network traffic over WAN links and is *not* a recommended solution.

- *Use lmhosts files*—This is a partial solution and can require a lot of administrative effort.

- *Use WINS*—This is the preferred solution.

A WINS-enabled domain master browser, such as a Windows 2000 DC or a Windows NT4 or NT3.5 Primary Domain Controller (PDC), periodically registers its [1Bh] NetBIOS name with its primary WINS server. This information is replicated through the WINS database. Each domain master browser on the internetwork queries WINS periodically (every 12 to 15 minutes) and obtains a list of all the [1Bh] domain names and corresponding IP addresses of domain master browsers whose records are stored in the WINS database. This isn't a list of all the resources in remote domains, merely a list of master browsers.

When a client needs to access a resource in a remote domain, the process is as follows:

1. The client tries a subnet broadcast. This fails to return a positive response.

2. The client queries WINS and obtains the [1Bh] NetBIOS name and IP address of the master browser for the required domain.

3. The client uses the IP address to send a direct request to the remote domain master browser, asking for a list of backup browsers for the requested domain.

4. The remote domain master browser responds with a list of up to three backup browser NetBIOS names.

5. The client randomly selects one of the backup browsers from the list and queries WINS for the IP address corresponding to the NetBIOS name.

6. The client sends a request directly to the remote backup browser, asking for a copy of the browse list for the remote domain.

7. The remote backup browser returns the browse list for the remote domain to the client.

Sometimes this method fails at Step 2 when WINS can't supply a domain master browser name. This can happen if the remote domain master browser isn't WINS-enabled, or if the resource isn't on another domain (it may be in a workgroup). In this case, the client will access its local master browser and attempt to obtain the name of the master browser that advertised the domain or workgroup. The client then resolves the master browser name through WINS and makes a connection with that master browser to request a list of servers in the domain or workgroup. The list of servers in the domain or workgroup is then returned to the client.

Locating DCs Using WINS

Windows 2000 domains are established in Active Directory, which uses DNS to locate Windows 2000 DCs. However, if your internetwork contains legacy Windows NT4 or NT3.5 PDCs or Backup Domain Controllers (BDCs), then clients will use either WINS or subnet broadcasts (or possibly lmhosts files) to locate these computers.

Each time a PDC or BDC comes online, it registers its *domainname* [1Ch] name in WINS. This record is replicated to other WINS servers located throughout the network. [1Ch] NetBIOS names are group names and can be associated with the IP addresses of up to 25 DCs. The first IP address on the list is the PDC.

There is, however, another (quicker) way of locating a PDC through WINS. The *domainname* [1Bh] entry is a unique name that identifies the domain master browser. Because the PDC is always the domain master browser, this record identifies the PDC.

When a user at a client computer logs on to a domain, a DC must be located to authenticate the username and password. If the client is WINS-enabled it will query its primary WINS server for *domainname* [1Ch] records. The WINS server returns a list of IP addresses ordered so that logon verification will be attempted first at a local DC owned by that WINS server. When a PDC needs to replicate changes in the Security Accounts Manager (SAM) database to BDCs, it will obtain a list of BDCs using the same method.

If a user changes his or her password, or if an administrator or account operator adds or amends a user account, then this change must be implemented at the PDC. In this case, a WINS-enabled client will query its primary WINS server for the *domainname* [1Bh] record to locate the PDC.

Clients that aren't WINS-enabled can locate DCs using subnet broadcasts. Remote DCs are located using #DOM entries in the lmhosts file.

Windows 2000 Enhancements

The Windows 2000 implementation of WINS provides a number of enhancements:

- *Persistent connections*—WINS servers can be configured to maintain persistent connections with one or more replication partners. This eliminates the overhead involved in opening and terminating connections and increases the speed of replication.

- *Enhanced filtering and record searching*—You can locate records that meet specified filter criteria. This is particularly useful when analyzing large WINS databases.

- *Dynamic record deletion and multi-select*—Both dynamic and static records can be deleted, and the point-and-click interface lets you delete files whose names contain non-alphanumeric characters that can't be specified from the command line.

- *Manual tombstoning*—When a record is marked for deletion, its tombstone state can be replicated across all WINS servers. The record can then be scavenged from all servers, and undeleted copies of the record on different server databases won't propagate. This feature is particularly useful if a WINS server is decommissioned.

- *Record verification and version ID validation*—Database consistency checking between WINS servers is enhanced. The IP addresses returned for a NetBIOS name query from different WINS servers can be compared, and owner address-to-version ID mapping tables can be examined.

- *Burst handling*—WINS servers can support handling of high-volume (burst) server loads. Bursts occur when a large number of WINS clients simultaneously register their local names in WINS. Burst handling was first introduced in Windows NT4, Service Pack 3. The WINS console lets you configure the level of burst handling by modifying the size of the burst queue to accommodate a low, medium, or large burst situation.

- *WINS partner autodiscovery*—WINS servers announce their presence on the network periodically. If a WINS server has the autodiscovery feature enabled, it listens for these announcements and learns about other WINS servers on the network.

- *Export function*—You can export WINS database records to a text file that can then be imported into analysis and reporting tools.

- *Increased fault tolerance*—Windows 2000 Professional (and Windows 98) clients can specify up to 12 WINS servers per interface. This improves fault tolerance because name-resolution requests can still be answered even if both the primary and the first secondary WINS servers go down.

- *Dynamic re-registration*—WINS clients can re-register their NetBIOS name-to-IP address mapping without rebooting.

- *Improved management tools*—The WINS console (or WINS Manager) is fully integrated with the Microsoft Management Console (MMC), providing a consistent, user-friendly management tool. WINS servers can be added to the console, enabling single-seat management of most WINS functions.

15. The Windows Internet Name Service

NOTE: *Some functions, such as WINS installation, de-installation, and restoring the WINS database, require that you log on locally to the appropriate WINS server.*

Persistent Connections

Windows 2000 WINS introduces persistent connections between WINS server replication partners. The WINS database is managed collectively by a set of WINS servers, each of which has a copy of the WINS database. The servers replicate records to keep these copies consistent. Each new host installed on the network registers its name and IP address with a WINS server, which in turn propagates the new record to its replication partners.

Earlier versions of WINS required that new connections be established between the WINS servers whenever replication occurred. As a result, WINS servers using push replication were configured to accumulate a number of record changes prior to establishing connections with replication partners. This caused updating delays, resulting in inconsistency between replication partners. Typically, networks were configured so that 20 or more changes occurred before push replication took place. The effects on pull replication were less obvious, but the need to re-establish a connection for each replication used resources, and resulted in intervals that were longer than the ideal being specified between pull cycles.

Windows 2000 WINS can be configured so that a server requests persistent connections with its replication partners. Persistent connections increase the speed of replication because a server immediately sends updated records to its partners without needing to establish a temporary connection. In push replication, the number of changes stored prior to replication can be set to zero, resulting in every new or amended record being immediately updated across the network. The bandwidth used by persistent connections is minimal, because the connection is usually idle.

TIP: *The number of changes stored prior to push replication can be set to zero. It doesn't have to be. On a busy network, or when replicating over slow WAN links, you may decide to increase this number. It will, however, have a lower value than it would otherwise have had prior to persistent connection.*

Enhanced Filtering and Record Searching

The WINS console provides two methods of finding and displaying WINS database records:

- *Find by Name*—Queries the database and filters the results to display NetBIOS name records that start with a specified set of one or more characters. Before this feature (sometimes known as *quick find*) was introduced, it was necessary to display the entire WINS database.

- *Find by Owner*—Displays WINS server data for one or more owners (WINS servers). This feature also introduces a filtering feature that allows the displayed results to show only records of selected NetBIOS name record suffix types. You can, for example, display all the DC records (type 1C) or all the master browser records (type 1D). NetBIOS name types are described earlier in this chapter.

Dynamic Record Deletion and Multi-Select

Individual dynamic records in a Windows 2000 WINS database can be deleted. Previous versions allowed only the deletion of individual static records. Manual tombstoning (see below) prevents records that you deleted from the database on one server from reappearing because they've been replicated from the database on another server.

You can multi-select records for deletion using the Ctrl and Shift keys with the left mouse button, in exactly the same way as you select multiple files in Windows Explorer. Point-and-click record deletion is particularly useful when you want to delete files whose names contain non-alphanumeric characters.

Manual Tombstoning

If you tombstone a record manually, it's marked for deletion and its delete status is propagated across all participating WINS servers. WINS is a distributed environment and each server holds the entire database, so the removal of unwanted records was difficult in legacy WINS servers. If Server A had a record marked for deletion, but Server B pushed information to Server A rather than vice versa, then the deletion information could be overwritten and the record would remain.

Windows 2000 WINS introduces the manual tombstoning option to address this problem. The lifetime of the tombstoned state exceeds the propagation delay of replication across the network. When the time limit is reached, tombstoned records are removed on all servers. This feature is available from both the WINS console and the WINS Network Shell command-line interface. Manual tombstoning requires a Windows 2000 WINS server, but tombstoned records can replicate to Windows NT3.51 and Windows NT4 WINS servers.

Record Verification and Version ID Validation

Record verification enables an administrator to verify WINS records by sending name queries to each server and ensuring that IP addresses returned for a NetBIOS name are the same for every server.

Version ID validation ensures that version IDs are consistent between servers. It obtains the owner address to version ID mappings from different WINS servers and ensures that a WINS server holds the highest version ID for any records that it owns. If Server A owns a record, updates to that record are made at Server A. If Server B holds the same record with a higher version ID than that on Server A, a replication operation from Server B can cause changes to the record to be overwritten. Windows 2000 DNS version ID validation identifies and corrects this problem.

In addition to verifying a single record and validating its version ID, Windows 2000 WINS offers the ability to check the consistency of all records in the database. Consistency checking can be initiated manually from the WINS console, and you can enable automatic consistency checking and configure the frequency with which WINS databases are compared.

To perform a consistency checking operation, a WINS server replicates all of a particular owner's records from one of its replication partners and checks them to determine whether its database is synchronized with its partner's for that owner. Consistency checking is bandwidth-intensive and should be scheduled to occur at times when network traffic is expected to be light.

Burst Handling

Typically, a burst can happen after a power failure. When power is restored, a large number of users simultaneously reboot and register their names on the network, creating a high level of WINS traffic. Burst mode support enables a WINS server to respond positively to these client requests.

Burst mode uses a burst queue size as a threshold value (500 by default) that determines how many name registration and name refresh requests sent by WINS clients are processed normally before burst handling is started. When burst handling starts, the WINS server answers additional client requests immediately with positive responses that include a modified TTL.

If, for example, the burst queue size is 500 entries and more than 500 requests are active, the next 100 WINS client registration requests will be answered with a starting TTL of 5 minutes. For each additional 100 client requests, 5 minutes more are added to the TTL, up to a maximum of 50 minutes. If WINS client traffic still arrives at burst levels, the next round of 100 client requests is answered with the initial TTL value of 5 minutes, and the entire process is repeated until the WINS server reaches its maximum intake level of 25,000 name registration and refresh queries. At this point it begins to drop queries.

WINS Partner Autodiscovery

The autodiscovery feature, which can be set from the WINS console, enables a WINS server to discover its replication partners automatically. WINS servers periodically announce their presence on the network, and a WINS server that has autodiscovery turned on listens for these announcements, learns about other WINS servers on the network, and automatically adds them to its partners list as push/pull partners. WINS announcements are sent by multicast on the reserved multicast address 224.0.1.24. Autodiscovery shouldn't be used if there are more than three WINS servers on a network.

Export Feature

You can use a WINS console command to export the contents of the Active Reservations container to a comma-delimited text file. This text file is subsequently imported into Microsoft Excel, reporting tools, scripting applications, and other files. This lets you use any tool that you want to for analysis and reporting.

Increased Fault Tolerance

Windows 2000 and Windows 98 provide an extra measure of fault tolerance by allowing a client to specify more than two WINS servers (up to a maximum of 12) per interface, either statically or through DHCP. The additional WINS server addresses are used to resolve names only if both the primary and first-choice secondary WINS servers fail to respond. Nonprimary server name resolutions are cached and used again the next time the primary WINS server fails to resolve the name. The client, however, always attempts to use its primary server first for the purposes of name registration and resolution.

Dynamic Re-registration

Windows 2000 WINS clients can re-register their NetBIOS name-to-IP address mappings without rebooting. This is useful if incorrect static entries exist or if a WINS database is restored with an old record. Updating the version ID on the server triggers re-registration.

Improved Management Tools

Windows 2000 WINS can be managed interactively from the Command Console using the Network Shell (netsh) utility (see Appendix D). Network Shell commands can also be used in script files to automate administrative tasks.

Interactive administration, however, is normally implemented using the WINS MMC console (or WINS Manager). This provides a standard interface that's consistent with other Windows 2000 interface tools. A server's replication partners can be added to the WINS console on that server, enabling single-seat administration of most of the WINS functions.

The WINS console offers resizable windows, and multiple WINS console windows can be open simultaneously. A multithreaded user interface allows background tasks to take place while a foreground task is being performed. You can, for example, select the Active Registration node to display the database (which can take some time) and carry out other administrative tasks while you're waiting for the information to appear.

The database records window (in the details pane) features resizable display columns. You can resize columns to accommodate their current tasks and use the list view to sort information according to column type. The WINS console is used extensively in the Immediate Solutions section of this chapter.

Immediate Solutions

Installing WINS

WINS is typically installed on a member server on a domain, although you can install it on a DC if you want to. To install WINS, proceed as follows:

1. Log on to the server as an administrator.

2. Access Start|Settings|Control Panel and double-click Add/Remove Programs.

3. Click Add/Remove Windows Components.

4. Select Network Services, then click Details.

5. Check the Windows Internet Name Service (WINS) checkbox, then click OK.

6. If prompted, insert the Windows 2000 Server CD-ROM or type the path to the distribution files, then click Continue.

7. Click Finish. Close the Add/Remove Programs dialog box.

8. Close the Control Panel.

9. Reboot the server.

Managing WINS Servers

When WINS is installed, the local server is added to the WINS console. If there are additional WINS servers on a network, you can add them to your console. This lets you manage them from a single seat. You can then start, stop, pause, resume, and restart the WINS service on any server. You can also delete a WINS server. This doesn't stop it from running WINS; it merely deletes its icon from your console.

If you want to stop using a server for WINS name resolution, it isn't good practice simply to uninstall WINS. The WINS server may have replicated its database with other servers, and stale records could remain on these machines. The correct procedure is to decommission the WINS server. This ensures that records held in that server's WINS database are tombstoned and replicated to its WINS partners so they can be scavenged. After this has been done, WINS can be removed from the decommissioned server.

Before you decommission a WINS server, ensure that hosts that are configured as that server's clients are reconfigured to point to other servers, assuming that you want these hosts to continue to use WINS name resolution.

In addition to stopping, starting, and removing WINS servers, the WINS console can be used to configure server properties. These include backup settings, record management settings, database verification settings, logging and burst handling properties, the WINS database path, and the starting version ID. If you don't have any hosts on your network that run LAN Manager, you can disable LAN Manager compatibility in the Server Properties box.

From the WINS console, you can view and reset server statistics and export console data to a text file.

Adding, Stopping, Starting, and Pausing a WINS Server

To add, stop, start, and pause a WINS server, proceed as follows:

1. Log on to a WINS server as an administrator.

2. Access Start|Programs|Administrative Tools and select WINS.

3. To add a server, right-click the WINS icon at the top of the console tree and select Add Server. Either identify the server by NetBIOS name or IP address or click Browse. In the latter case, select a server and click OK. Click OK to close the Add Server dialog box.

4. To start, stop, pause, resume, or restart WINS on a server, expand the console tree, select the appropriate server, right-click it (or click the Action menu), and click All Tasks. If you select Restart, WINS is stopped and then automatically restarted.

5. Close the WINS console.

Decommissioning a WINS Server

To decommission a WINS server, proceed as follows:

1. Log on to a WINS server. This is normally the server that you're decommissioning, because you can subsequently uninstall WINS on that server.

2. Expand the console tree. Expand the icon for the server that you want to decommission and select Active Registrations.

3. Right-click Active Registrations and select Delete Owner.

4. In the Delete Owner dialog box, select the IP address of the WINS server you want to decommission.

NOTE: *If the WINS server isn't the computer that you're logged on to, it might take some time to load the records.*

15. The Windows Internet Name Service

5. Select Replicate deletion to other WINS servers (tombstone), then click OK.

6. When prompted to confirm tombstoning, click Yes.

7. Select and right-click Replication Partners, then select Replicate Now.

8. Verify that the tombstoned records have been replicated to partner servers.

9. Stop, then remove WINS on the decommissioned server. The procedure for removing WINS is the same as for installing it, except that the Windows Internet Name Service (WINS) checkbox is unchecked.

NOTE: *If tombstone status doesn't replicate properly, you need to delete the records manually at each WINS replication partner.*

Modifying Server Properties

To modify server properties, proceed as follows:

1. Log on to a WINS server as an administrator.

2. Access Start|Programs|Administrative Tools and select WINS.

3. Expand the console and select the appropriate WINS server.

4. Right-click the selected server (or access the Action menu) and select Properties. You can then modify server properties as follows:

   - On the General tab, you can modify the update frequency, specify the path to the folder where you want to store the backup file, and specify whether to back up the WINS database when the WINS server is stopped.

   - On the Interval tab, you can alter the frequency at which records are renewed, deleted, and verified. Refer to the In Depth section of this chapter for descriptions of the renew, extinction, and verification intervals and of the extinction timeout.

TIP: *For most networks, the default interval settings are acceptable and don't require modification.*

   - On the Database Verification tab, specify the settings you require for verifying database consistency. Ensure that database consistency is checked at a time that the network is quiet, usually at night.

   - On the Advanced tab, check the Log detailed events to Windows event log checkbox if you require this feature. When the checkbox is checked, WINS logs additional detailed information to the system event log, and this information can be viewed by using Event Viewer. Detailed logging can degrade system performance and is disabled by default. The feature is normally used for troubleshooting.

- On the Advanced tab, enable or disable burst handling as required, and set the appropriate level. Burst handling is described in the In Depth section of this chapter.

- On the Advanced tab, modify the database path if required. On this tab, you can also adjust the starting version ID and enable or disable LAN Manager compatibility.

WARNING! *If you modify the database path, run WINS backup again to archive the database with the updated path information. Otherwise, WINS can't restore previously archived copies of the database.*

5. Click OK to close the Server Properties box.
6. Close the WINS console.

Viewing and Resetting Statistics

To view WINS statistics and reset them if necessary, proceed as follows:

1. Log on to a WINS server as an administrator.
2. Access Start|Programs|Administrative Tools and select WINS.
3. Expand the console and select the appropriate WINS server.
4. Right-click the selected server (or access the Action menu) and select Display Server Statistics.
5. Click Refresh. This ensures that the statistics are up to date.
6. If you want to reset the statistics, click Reset.
7. Close the Server Statistics box.
8. Close the WINS console.

Viewing Console Data and Exporting It to a Text File

You can view and export the data associated with any node in the console tree. This is, however, normally done for the Active Registrations node, and that procedure is therefore described here. The procedure is the same for any other node. To view and export Active Registrations node data, proceed as follows:

1. Log on to a WINS server as an administrator.
2. Access Start|Programs|Administrative Tools and select WINS.
3. Expand the appropriate WINS server icon and select Active Registrations.
4. Right-click Active Registrations (or access the Action menu) and select either Find by Name or Find by Owner.
5. If you select Find by Name, type sufficient information to identify the server name uniquely, specify whether or not to match case, then click Find Now.

6. If you select Find by Owner, specify a particular owner or select All owners, specify the record types that you want to find, then click Find Now.

7. A typical Active Registrations details pane is shown in Figure 15.2. To export this data, right-click Active Registrations and select Export List.

8. Specify a file name and path, then click Save.

9. If the file already exists, click Yes to replace it.

10. Close the WINS console.

11. Use a text editor to view the data file. The file can be imported into Microsoft Excel and other reporting and analysis packages.

Active Registrations	Items found for the owner 195.162.230.1: 17		
Record Name	Type	IP Address	State
--__MSBROWSE__-	[01h] Other	195.162.230.50	Released
ADMINISTRATOR	[03h] Messenger	195.162.230.1	Active
CORIOLIS	[00h] Workgroup	195.162.230.50	Active
CORIOLIS	[1Bh] Domain Maste...	195.162.230.1	Active
CORIOLIS	[1Ch] Domain Contr...	195.162.230.1	Active
CORIOLIS	[1Eh] Normal Group...	195.162.230.50	Active
INet~Services	[1Ch] Domain Contr...	195.162.230.50	Active
IS~MEMBER------	[00h] WorkStation	195.162.230.50	Active
IS~W2000S------	[00h] WorkStation	195.162.230.1	Active
MEMBER	[00h] WorkStation	195.162.230.50	Active
MEMBER	[03h] Messenger	195.162.230.50	Active
MEMBER	[20h] File Server	195.162.230.50	Active
W2000S	[00h] WorkStation	195.162.230.1	Active
W2000S	[03h] Messenger	195.162.230.1	Active
W2000S	[20h] File Server	195.162.230.1	Active
WORKGROUP	[00h] Workgroup	195.162.230.50	Released
WORKGROUP	[1Eh] Normal Group...	195.162.230.50	Released

Figure 15.2   Active Registrations data.

Configuring WINS Clients

DHCP clients automatically receive their WINS information from the DHCP server, provided the appropriate options are set up in DHCP. Non-DHCP clients need to be configured statically. WINS client configuration can be checked from the client's Command Console, and registrations can be released and refreshed.

If you migrate your name-resolution system from WINS to DNS, you should disable WINS/NetBT name resolution. This is done through static configuration for non-DHCP clients or through the DHCP console for DHCP clients.

Configuring WINS for Non-DHCP Clients

If a client doesn't get its WINS configuration from DHCP, it must be configured manually on a per-network connection basis. This procedure specifies an administrator account for logging on. If you prefer, you can log on with any account that has permission to configure a client's network connections. This will vary from client to client, but an administrator should be able to configure any of them.

1. Log on to the client as an administrator.
2. Access Start|Settings and select Network and Dial-up Connections.
3. Double-click the connection you want to configure, then click Properties.
4. Select Internet Protocol (TCP/IP), then click Properties.
5. Click Advanced and select the WINS tab.
6. Click Add. Specify the IP address of the client's primary WINS server.
7. Click Add to close the TCP/IP WINS Server dialog box.
8. Repeat Steps 6 and 7 to add secondary WINS servers in order of preference.
9. When you've finished adding WINS servers, click OK to close the Advanced TCP/IP Settings dialog box.
10. Click OK to close the TCP/IP Properties dialog box.
11. Click OK to close the Connection Properties dialog box.
12. Click Close to close the Connection Status box.
13. When you've configured all the connections that you need to, close Network and Dial-up Connections.

WARNING! *If you manually configure a list of WINS servers for a host that's later configured to use DHCP, the static list supercedes WINS servers provided dynamically through DHCP. In this case, you need to remove the static WINS servers from the connection configuration.*

Related solution:	See page:
Configuring TCP/IP	24

Configuring WINS for DHCP Clients

WINS information automatically provided to clients in a DHCP scope is specified at the DHCP server as follows:

1. Log on to a DHCP server as an administrator.
2. Access Start|Programs|Administrative Tools and select DHCP.
3. Expand the appropriate server and scope icons and select Server Options.
4. Right-click Server Options (or access the Action menu) and select Configure Options.
5. In the Available Options list on the General tab, check 044 WINS/NBNS Servers.

NOTE: *If you want to specify these options for a specific user class (see Chapter 13), use the Advanced tab.*

---

6. Either type the primary WINS Server name and click **Resolve**, or type the primary WINS Server IP address. Click **Add**.

7. Repeat Step 6 for all the WINS servers you want to add.

8. In the Available Options list, check 046 WINS/NBT Node type.

9. Specify the node type. In a Microsoft network, this is normally 0x8 (hybrid node).

10. Click OK to close the Server Options dialog box.

11. Close the DHCP console.

Related solution:	*See page:*
Configuring and Managing Options	439

Verifying WINS Registration

To verify WINS registration and detect any conflicts, proceed as follows:

1. Log on as an administrator to the WINS client that you want to verify.

2. Access Start|Programs|Accessories and select Command Prompt.

3. Enter **nbtstat –n**.

4. A list of registrations is returned, as shown in Figure 15.3.

5. Verify that each name indicates Registered in the Status column.

6. If the status column indicates Registering, enter **nbtstat –RR**. This releases and refreshes NetBIOS name registration.

TIP: *Remember that the **nbtstat** switches are case sensitive. Entering **nbtstat –rr** displays resolution and registration statistics.*

Figure 15.3   Client registrations.

15. The Windows Internet Name Service

7. If the status column indicates Conflict, try one of the following:

   - For Windows 2000 WINS clients, disconnect and reconnect the network connection in the Network and Dial-up Connections folder.

   - For clients running earlier versions of Windows, shut down and restart the computer.

8. Close the Command Console.

Disabling WINS/NetBT Name Resolution on Non-DHCP Clients

If a client doesn't obtain its WINS information from DHCP, WINS/NetBT resolution is disabled manually on a per-connection basis. To do this, proceed as follows:

1. Log on to the client as an administrator.

2. Access Start|Settings and select Network and Dial-up Connections.

3. Double-click the connection that you want to configure, then click Properties.

4. Select Internet Protocol (TCP/IP), then click Properties.

5. Click Advanced and select the WINS tab.

6. Select Disable NetBIOS over TCP/IP.

TIP: *If you intend reconfiguring the client to use DHCP, you can, alternatively, select the Use NetBIOS setting from the DHCP server. In this case, you can configure DHCP to disable NetBIOS over TCP/IP, as described in the next procedure.*

7. Click OK to close the Advanced TCP/IP Settings dialog box.

8. Click OK to close the TCP/IP Properties dialog box.

9. Click OK to close the Connection Properties dialog box.

10. Click Close to close the Connection Status box.

11. When you've configured all the connections you need, close Network and Dial-up Connections.

Disabling WINS/NetBT Name Resolution through DHCP

You can disable WINS/NetBT name resolution for all the DHCP clients in a particular scope as follows:

1. Log on to a DHCP server as an administrator.

2. Access Start|Programs|Administrative Tools and select DHCP.

3. Expand the appropriate server and scope icons and select Server Options.

4. Right-click Server Options (or access the Action menu) and select Configure Options.

5. Select the General tab, unless options have been specified for a particular user class.

6. In the Available Options list, uncheck 044 WINS/NBNS Servers.

7. In the Available Options list, uncheck 046 WINS/NBT Node type.

8. Select the Advanced tab.

9. In the Vendor class, select Microsoft Options. If required, select a user class (other than the default).

10. Under Available Options, check 001 Microsoft Disable NetBIOS Option.

11. Specify the data entry as 0x2.

12. Click OK to close the Server Options dialog box.

13. Close the DHCP console.

Related solution:	**See page:**
Configuring and Managing Options	439

Administering the WINS Database

The WINS database is dynamic and, therefore, requires comparatively little administrative effort. Occasionally, however, you may want to initiate backup, restore, or scavenging manually, or delete and tombstone either an individual record or all the records owned by a server. The version IDs of the server databases (among other factors) control WINS replication, and you can check version consistency manually. You can also check database consistency manually.

It's good practice to administer a server's database from that server. Some operations, such as restoring the database, require local logon. The procedure, therefore, asks you to log on to the WINS server whose database you want to administer.

You should always perform manual backups using the same database path that you use for dynamic backups. This path is set on the Server Properties sheet. Refer to the procedure "Modifying Server Properties" earlier in this chapter. You need to know what the backup path is before carrying out this procedure.

To administer the WINS database, proceed as follows:

1. Log on as an administrator to the WINS server whose database you want to administer.

2. Access Start|Programs|Administrative Tools and select WINS.

3. Double-click the appropriate server icon. This both selects and expands the server node.

4. Right-click the selected server or access the Action menu. This lets you perform the following tasks:

   - To scavenge the database, select Scavenge Database. Click OK to clear the message box. Event ID 4328 in the System log in Event Viewer indicates that scavenging was initiated.

   - To verify database consistency, select Check Database Consistency. Click Yes, then click OK to clear the message boxes.

   - To verify version ID consistency, select Check Version ID Consistency. Click Yes to close the message box, check that there are no consistency errors, and click Close. If you need to change the server's version ID, refer to the "Modifying Server Properties" procedure earlier in this chapter.

TIP: *Consistency checking (database or version ID) is resource intensive. If possible, perform manual consistency checks at a time when there isn't heavy WINS traffic.*

   - To delete and tombstone records, refer to the procedure "Decommissioning a WINS Server" earlier in this chapter. This procedure deletes and tombstones all of an owner's records. If you want to delete an individual record, select it on the details pane and press the Delete key.

   - To back up a database, select Back Up Database. Specify the database backup path. Click OK to clear the dialog box when backup is complete.

   - To restore a database, you first have to stop the WINS service on the server. Select All Tasks, then click Stop. On the same menu, select Restore Database and specify the path to the backup file. Click OK to clear the dialog box. The procedure restarts the WINS service automatically.

5. Close the WINS console.

TIP: *You can sometimes repair WINS database corruption by incrementing the starting version ID for the WINS server and then restarting the server.*

---

15. The Windows Internet Name Service

Implementing and Configuring WINS Replication

Two or more WINS servers can be set up to replicate database information. This is done to provide failover protection and to improve name-resolution performance over slow WAN links. You can set up replication properties on your WINS server that become defaults for any partner that you add, you can add a partner and modify these defaults, and you can configure your WINS server to replicate with any nonpartner WINS server that it locates on your network.

Partner configuration can be set to be automatic. If you decide you don't want to replicate your database with another WINS server, you can remove that WINS server as a replication partner. You can also specify a WINS server that you don't want to replicate with. If you want to, you can trigger replication manually.

These procedures assume that you have the necessary permissions to carry them out. By default, a domain administrator has these permissions. If you get access denied messages, check the network policy settings. You can carry out the procedures from any WINS server if you have added all WINS servers on your network to the WINS console. However, for simplicity, the procedures ask you to log on to the WINS server for which you want to implement and configure replication partners.

Configuring Server Replication

In this procedure, you set the replication properties of your WINS server. The values you specify are the values for your server and the default values for any partner you subsequently add. The procedure for doing this is as follows:

1. Log on as an administrator to the WINS server you want to configure.

2. Access Start|Programs|Administrative Tools and select WINS.

3. Expand the appropriate server icon and select Replication Partners.

4. Either right-click Replication Partners or access the Action menu. Select Properties. You can configure the server replication properties as follows:

   - On the General tab, you can specify whether you want replication to occur only with partners. Clearing the Replicate only with partners checkbox enables database replication with any WINS server on the network. If you check the Overwrite unique static mappings at this server (migrate on) checkbox, then static mappings will be treated as if they were dynamic (i.e., overwritten) when they conflict with a new name registration or replica.

   - On the Push Replication tab, you can specify when to start push replication, specify a value in the Number of changes in version ID before replication box, and specify whether a persistent connection is used.

If a persistent connection is used, the number of changes is typically (but not necessarily) zero. If a persistent connection isn't used, this number should be at least 20. Persistent connections are discussed in the In Depth section of this chapter.

- On the Pull Replication tab, you can specify the start conditions, the replication interval, the number of retries, and whether a persistent connection is used.

- On the Advanced tab, you can specify whether automatic partner configuration is enabled. This works through multicasting, and you can specify the multicast interval and TTL. If you click the Add key, you can specify WINS servers with which you want to block replication.

TIP: *If you're administering a mixed environment and want to implement record blocking on a Windows NT4 WINS server, adjust the* PersonaNonGrata *Registry parameter on that server.*

---

5. Click OK to close the Replication Partners Properties box.

6. Close the WINS console.

Adding and Configuring a Replication Partner

This procedure adds a replication partner, defines it as it as a push, pull, or push/pull partner (by default it's a push/pull partner), and configures its replication properties. These properties can be left at the default values that were set in the previous procedure, but there's no requirement to do so. Server A can pull information from Server B (for example) more frequently than Server B pulls information from Server A. In the case of pull partners, it's good practice to alter the partner properties so that partners don't try to pull information from each other at the same time.

To add and configure a replication partner, proceed as follows:

1. Log on as an administrator to the WINS server that you want to add a partner to.

2. Access Start|Programs|Administrative Tools and select WINS.

3. Expand the appropriate server icon and select Replication Partners.

4. Either right-click Replication Partners or access the Action menu. Select New Replication Partner.

5. Either enter the name or the IP address of the WINS server that you want to add as a replication partner or click Browse, select the server, then click OK.

6. Click OK to close the New Replication Partner dialog box.

7. In the details pane, right-click the new replication partner and select Properties. Select the Advanced tab, as shown in Figure 15.4.

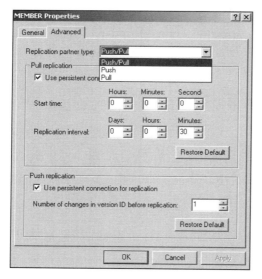

Figure 15.4   Configuring a replication partner.

8. In the Replication partner type pull-down box, select the replication partner type.

9. If pull replication is used, set the start time and interval. Give these settings some thought, and arrange the times so that the partner isn't trying to pull information from your server at the same time that your server is pulling information from the partner. You can also specify whether to use a persistent connection.

10. If push replication is used, specify a value in the Number of changes in version ID before replication box. You can also specify whether to use a persistent connection.

11. Click OK.

12. Close the WINS console.

Deleting a Replication Partner

To delete a replication partner, proceed as follows:

1. Log on as an administrator to the WINS server whose replication partner you want to delete.

2. Access Start|Programs|Administrative Tools and select WINS.

3. Expand the appropriate server icon and select Replication Partners.

4. In the details pane, right-click the replication partner you want to remove and select Delete.

5. Click Yes to confirm that you want to delete the partner.

6. Specify whether or not you also want to purge all references to the selected WINS server from the database.

7. Close the WINS console.

Triggering Replication Manually

You can start WINS database replication manually, either with all of your server's replication partners or with a selected partner. If you choose to replicate with all of your partners, they must all be push/pull partners. The procedure to force manual replication is as follows:

1. Log on as an administrator to the appropriate WINS server.

2. Access Start|Programs|Administrative Tools and select WINS.

3. Expand the server icon and select Replication Partners. Trigger replication as follows:

   • To replicate with all partners, right-click Replication Partners (or access the Action menu) and select Replicate Now. Click Yes to confirm the instruction. Click OK to close the WINS dialog box.

   • To replicate with one partner, right-click the partner in the details pane. Depending on how the partner is configured, you can trigger either push or pull replication. If the partner is configured for push/pull, you can choose either option. Click Yes to confirm. Click OK to close the status box.

4. Close the console.

Using Static Mappings

Static mappings are used when you have hosts that can't register themselves with WINS. NetBIOS name/IP address pairs for these hosts can be entered directly into a WINS database, or they can be imported from an lmhosts file, in which they're held as #PRE entries. Static mappings should be used only when essential and should be mapped only to computer names. They can override dynamic mappings and can be difficult to remove when they've been replicated to other servers.

NOTE: *Static mappings could cause serious problems in Windows NT4, particularly when a non-WINS-enabled host was retired and replaced. Windows 2000 allows static mappings to be treated as dynamic during replication, which means they can be overwritten by dynamic information. In other words, they cause less problems than they used to, but their use should nevertheless be minimized. Refer to the procedure "Modifying Server Properties" earlier in this chapter.*

To add, delete, modify, and import static mappings, proceed as follows:

1. Log on to a WINS server as an administrator.

2. Access Start|Programs|Administrative Tools and select WINS.

3. Expand the appropriate server icon and select Active Registrations.

4. Right-click Active Registrations (or access the Action Menu). Static mappings can be managed as follows:

   - To add a static mapping, select New Static Mapping. In the dialog box, specify a computer name and IP address. The Type should be either Unique or Multihomed. Other types can be specified, but should be avoided. NetBIOS scopes aren't widely used. If your network uses them, then also specify the scope for the NetBIOS name. If you're adding more records, click Apply. Click OK when you've finished.

   - To edit a static mapping, you can double-click it in the details pane and amend it. However, there are likely to be at least three entries for every host. It's usually easier to select all the entries (use the Ctrl key), press the Delete key, choose to tombstone the records at other servers (another advantage of this method), and click Yes to close the message box. Then add the mapping again.

WARNING! *Each record is added when you click Apply. You can't go back and change them from the New Static Mapping dialog box. So make sure that the details are correct before you click the Apply button.*

   - To import static mappings from an lmhosts file, select Import LMHOSTS File. Specify the path to the lmhosts file and click Open. Click OK to close the message box.

TIP: *The lmhosts file is normally stored in the %Systemroot%\System32\Drivers\Etc folder.*

5. Close the WINS console.

Administering WINS from the Command Console

Windows 2000 provides a range of options that let you administer WINS from the Command Console using the Network Shell (netsh) utility. This utility is described in detail in Appendix D. You can administer WINS from the Command Console on the server that you want to administer, but typically this utility is used to enable administration of the server from a WINS client.

15. The Windows Internet Name Service

You can also stop, start, pause, and resume WINS from the Command Console of the appropriate WINS server.

Using the Network Shell Utility

To administer the WINS from the Command Console using the netsh utility, proceed as follows:

1. Log on to a WINS client as an administrator.

2. Access Start|Programs|Accessories and select Command Prompt.

3. Enter **netsh**.

4. At the netsh> prompt, enter **wins**.

5. At the wins> prompt, enter either **server *servername*** or **server *ipaddress***, where *servername* and *ipaddress* specify the name and the IP address of the server that you want to manage.

6. You should receive the message "You have Read and Write access to the server *servername*".

TIP: If you're logged on to the server that you're administering, you can skip Steps 5 and 6.

7. Use the Network Shell DHCP subcommands and options documented in Appendix D.

*NOTE: You can also use netsh subcommands in script files. In this case, you need to use the fully qualified command syntax **netsh wins server [\\servername] subcommand**.*

Stopping, Starting, Pausing, and Resuming WINS

To stop, start, pause, or resume WINS from the Command Console, proceed as follows:

1. Log on to the WINS server as an administrator.

2. Access Start|Programs|Accessories and select Command Prompt.

3. Stop, start, pause, or resume WINS as follows:

   - To stop WINS, enter **net stop wins**.
   - To start WINS after it has been stopped, enter **net start wins**.
   - To pause WINS, enter **net pause wins**.
   - To resume WINS after it has been paused, enter **net continue wins**.

NOTE: The Restart function is available only from the WINS console. To replicate this function from the Command Console, stop WINS, then start it again.

Chapter 16

The Remote Access Service

In Depth

The Windows 2000 Remote Access Service (RAS) is part of the integrated Routing and Remote Access Service (RRAS) and is administered from the RRAS console. Although interrelated, routing and remote access are two separate services. A Windows 2000 RRAS server is typically multihomed to provide access to your organization's intranet, but a router won't necessarily (or normally) provide a remote access service.

Routing was described in Chapter 4, where we looked at the Routing Internet Protocol (RIP) and the Open Shortest Path First (OSPF) protocol. This chapter discusses RAS. The term "RRAS server" is used throughout the chapter because it's standard Microsoft terminology and because RAS can't be installed separately from RRAS.

RAS Concepts

RAS connects remote users to their organization's network. These users can be roaming (salespersons connecting from a laptop in a hotel room) or static (home workers or staff at a branch office). RAS users work as if their computers were physically connected to their organization's network. Their usernames and passwords—or certificates and Personal Identification Numbers (PINs) if they use smart cards—are authenticated, and they can be given the same permissions as any other domain users. For security purposes, however, remote access is sometimes limited to files held on the RRAS server. All services typically available to a connected Local Area Network (LAN) user (including file and print sharing, Web server access, and messaging) can be enabled by means of the RAS connection.

RAS users access resources by using standard tools. Windows Explorer may be used to make drive connections and to connect to printers. Connections are persistent, and users don't need to reconnect to network resources during their remote sessions. Because mapped drives and Universal Naming Convention (UNC) names are supported by RAS, most commercial and custom applications work without modification.

NOTE: *A RAS user is the person using the RAS connection. A RAS client (or host) is the computer that he or she uses.*

A RAS client can implement a connection to an organization's central RRAS server in one of two ways:

- *Dial-up networking*—The RAS client makes a nonpermanent, dial-up connection to a physical port on the RRAS server through a telecommunications provider, such as an analog telephone line, Integrated Services Digital Network (ISDN), or X.25. Dial-up networking creates a direct physical connection between the dial-up networking client and the dial-up networking server. Data sent over the connection can be encrypted if required.

- *Virtual private networking*—A secure, point-to-point connection, known as a Virtual Private Network (VPN) connection, is made (typically) across a public network, such as the Internet. A VPN client uses TCP/IP-based *tunneling* protocols to ensure that the connection remains both private and secure. Data sent over the connection must be encrypted. In addition to implementing connections across the Internet, VPNs can also be used to create secure communication channels through a large private intranet.

Dial-up connections and VPNs are described in more detail later in this chapter.

RAS Client Configuration

RAS clients are configured to obtain their IP configurations dynamically. Configuration information can be provided by one of three methods:

- *Dynamic Host Configuration Protocol*—When the RAS client makes a connection, it's allocated an IP address and subnet mask (and possibly other configuration options) by a DHCP server.

- *Static address pool*—The RRAS server can be configured with a pool of IP addresses that it can allocate to RAS clients. If the rest of the network uses DHCP, you must ensure that these addresses aren't in the DHCP scope. Typically, the RRAS server is multihomed, and the addresses in the static address pool are on a separate network from the addresses that are used in the organizational intranet. This is the usual method of configuring RAS clients.

- *Automatic Private IP Addressing (APIPA)*—If the RRAS server is configured to use DHCP for IP address allocation and no DHCP server is available, then an address from the address range 169.254.0.1 through 169.254.255.254 is allocated. If the DHCP service later becomes available, the client is reconfigured using DHCP.

RAS Protocols

RAS protocols control data transmission over Wide Area Network (WAN) links. Additional tunneling protocols are described later in this chapter when we look at VPNs. The RAS protocols supported by Windows 2000 are:

16. The Remote Access Service

- Point-to-Point Protocol (PPP)
- Serial Line Internet Protocol (SLIP)
- Microsoft RAS Protocol

PPP

PPP is a set of industry-standard framing and authentication protocols. The protocol set is defined in RFCs 1334, 1378, 1549, 1552, 1570, 1661, 1877, 1990, 1994, 2097, 2118, and 2125. PPP enables Windows 2000 RAS clients to access remote networks through any server that complies with the PPP standard. PPP compliance also enables a Windows 2000 RRAS server to receive calls from and provide network access to other vendors' RAS software. The PPP architecture enables RAS to use (almost) any combination of Internetwork Packet Exchange (IPX), TCP/IP, Network Basic Input/Output System Extended User Interface (NetBEUI), and AppleTalk. (Microsoft clients don't support the use of the AppleTalk protocol over a RAS connection.)

When you connect to a remote computer, a process known as *PPP negotiation* takes place. This proceeds as follows:

1. Framing rules are established between the remote computer and server. This allows frame transfer to occur.

2. The remote access server then authenticates the remote user by using PPP authentication protocols (described later in this chapter). The protocols that are invoked depend on the security configurations of the remote access client and server.

3. If callback is enabled, the remote access server hangs up and calls the remote access client.

4. The required LAN protocols, such as TCP/IP, IPX, and NetBEUI, are enabled and configured on the remote access client.

When the PPP connection sequence has completed successfully, the remote access client and server can transfer data from programs written to standard programming interfaces, such as Windows Sockets (Winsock).

SLIP

SLIP, defined in RFC 1055 supplemented by RFC 1144, is typically used by Unix RAS servers. Windows 2000, NT4, and NT3.5 RAS clients support SLIP and can connect to a RAS server using the SLIP standard. A Windows 2000 RRAS server doesn't support SLIP clients (neither does an NT4 RAS server). SLIP is both slower and less secure than PPP.

Microsoft RAS Protocol

The Microsoft RAS protocol supports the Network Basic Input/Output System (NetBIOS) standard and is used by Windows NT3.1, Windows for Workgroups, MS-DOS, and LAN Manager RAS clients. These clients use the NetBEUI protocol, and the RRAS server acts as a NetBIOS gateway, providing access to resources over the NetBEUI, NetBIOS over TCP/IP (NetBT), or NetBIOS over IPX protocols.

Authentication Protocols

PPP, the Windows 2000 RAS protocol of choice, uses a number of authentication protocols, such as Password Authentication Protocol (PAP), Challenge Handshake Authentication Protocol (CHAP), and Microsoft Challenge Handshake Authentication Protocol (MS-CHAP). Microsoft's implementation of tunneling protocols (see later in this chapter) also uses Extensible Authentication Protocol (EAP), in particular EAP Transaction Level Security (EAP-TLS). EAP is a new feature in Windows 2000. The authentication methods available for Windows 2000 RAS are as follows:

- *PAP*—An authentication scheme that returns the username and password in clear text (unencrypted). PAP isn't secure and provides no protection against replay attacks or against client impersonation if the user's password is compromised.

- *CHAP*—An encrypted authentication mechanism that avoids transmission of the actual password on the connection. The Network Access Server (NAS) sends a challenge, consisting of a session ID and an arbitrary string, to the remote client. The remote client uses the Message Digest function 95 (MD5) hash to return the username and an encryption of the challenge, session ID, and client password. CHAP protects against replay attacks by using an arbitrary challenge string for each authentication attempt and protects against remote client impersonation by sending repeated challenges unpredictably to the remote client throughout the duration of the connection.

- *MS-CHAP*—An encrypted authentication mechanism very similar to CHAP, except that it provides an additional level of security because it allows the server to store hashed passwords rather than clear-text passwords. MS-CHAP authentication is required to enable Microsoft Point-To-Point Encryption (MPPE) data encryption (described later in this chapter).

- *MS-CHAP v2*—Similar to MS-CHAP, but runs only on Windows 2000 RRAS servers. Downstream Microsoft RAS clients (such as Windows NT4 and Windows 98) can support MS-CHAP v2 if they have the appropriate service packs installed. MS-CHAP v2 can be used over dial-up connections, but it was designed specifically for VPNs.

- *SPAP (Shiva PAP)*—Used in a mixed environment to support clients using Shiva LAN Rover software.

- *EAP-TLS*—A strong authentication method based on public key certificates. A client presents a user certificate to the server, and the server presents a server certificate to the client. The first certificate provides user authentication to the server; the second provides assurance that the user has reached the correct server. The user's certificate can be stored either on the client computer or on a smart card.

- *EAP-MD5 CHAP*—Uses the same challenge handshake protocol as CHAP, but the challenges and responses are sent as EAP messages.

NOTE: *You also have the option of allowing remote users to connect with no authentication. This option is used when third-party authorization and authentication systems, such as Dialed Number Identification Service (DNIS) authorization and Automatic Number Identification/Calling Line Identification (ANI/CLI) authentication, are in force. It's also used for guest authentication.*

Multilink and Bandwidth Allocation Protocol (BAP)

Multilink allows multiple physical links to be combined so they appear as a single logical data transmission link over which data is sent and received. For example, both B channels of an ISDN-2 Basic Rate Interface (BRI) connection can be aggregated. Multilink must be supported on both sides of the connection.

TIP: *You can also combine, or bond, ISDN B channels through hardware support. This method, however, is specific to the ISDN adapter. Multilink is the recommended method of combining multiple B channels of a BRI connection, because you can use it for any ISDN adapter.*

Multilink combines multiple links, but it doesn't provide a mechanism to adapt to changing bandwidth conditions by adding links if they're needed or terminating them if they're not. This capability is provided by BAP, which manages links dynamically over a multilink connection. When the utilization of a connection rises to a configured level, the RAS client sends a BAP request message to request an additional link. This message specifies the type of link required, such as analog telephone, ISDN, or X.25. The RRAS server returns a BAP response message that contains the telephone number of an available port of the same type as that specified in the BAP request, and multilink implements the additional link. If utilization subsequently falls below a preconfigured level (normally lower than the configured connection level) for a specified length of time, then the additional link is disconnected.

For more information about BAP and the associated Bandwidth Allocation Control Protocol (BACP), refer to RFC 2125. BAP and BACP are new features in Windows 2000.

> **WARNING!** *When multilink and BAP are used in combination with callback, and callback is set to always call back to the same number, a concentrator that can distribute incoming calls to the same number on various ports must be installed on the caller side.*

The Remote Authentication Dial-in User Service

The Remote Authentication Dial-In User Service (RADIUS), defined in RFCs 2138 and 2139, runs over the User Datagram Protocol (UDP) and can be used to manage remote user authentication and authorization. RADIUS servers provide a proxy service that forwards authentication requests to other RADIUS servers in distant locations. Many Internet service providers (ISPs) have formed consortia that allow roaming subscribers to use local services from the nearest ISP for dial-up access to the Internet. If an ISP recognizes a username as being a subscriber to a remote network, it uses a RADIUS proxy to forward the access request to the appropriate network.

A RADIUS client, typically a dial-up server used by an ISP, sends user and connection information to a RADIUS server. The RADIUS server authenticates and authorizes the RADIUS client request. Windows 2000 RRAS server includes a RADIUS client so that ISPs or RAS users who use RADIUS as their authentication or accounting scheme can use the server. You can configure multiple RADIUS servers so that if the primary RADIUS server becomes unavailable, secondary RADIUS servers are used automatically.

The RADIUS protocol provides a suite of call-accounting requests. A RADIUS server generates accounting records at the start and end of a call and at predetermined intervals during the call. An accounting RADIUS server can be configured regardless of whether RADIUS is used for authentication.

Windows 2000 Server also provides the Internet Authentication Service (IAS). IAS is a RADIUS server that the RRAS server can use as its authentication or accounting provider. An IAS server is used to implement centralized authentication, authorization, accounting, and management of RAS policies. If your network has a number of RRAS servers and you want to take advantage of centralized remote access policies, accounting, and logging, configure the RRAS servers as RADIUS clients of a single Windows 2000 RADIUS server running IAS.

RADIUS and IAS are new features in Windows 2000 RAS.

Authentication vs. Authorization

It's important to distinguish between authentication and authorization when you're configuring RAS policy or working out why connection attempts are accepted or denied. The distinction is as follows:

- *Authentication* is the verification of the connection attempt's credentials. The process consists of sending credentials from the RAS client to the RRAS server in either plain-text or encrypted form by using an authentication protocol.

- *Authorization* occurs after successful authentication. It's the verification that the connection attempt is allowed.

For a connection to be accepted, credentials must be authenticated and the connection attempt authorized. If an RRAS server is configured for Windows authentication, Windows 2000 security is used to verify the credentials for authentication, and the dial-in properties of the user account and locally stored RAS policies are used to authorize the connection. It's possible for a connection attempt to be authenticated by using valid credentials, but not authorized. In this case, the connection attempt is denied.

RAS Logging

A Windows 2000 RRAS server supports three types of logging:

- *Event logging*—Records events in the Windows 2000 System Event Log, which is accessed through the Event Viewer administrative tool. Event log entries are typically used for troubleshooting or for notifying network administrators when specific events have occurred. For more details, refer to Chapter 19.

- *Local authentication and accounting logging*—Records authentication and accounting information for RAS connections in local log files when Windows authentication or Windows accounting is enabled. This information is used to track RAS usage and authentication attempts. The RAS policy that either accepted or rejected a connection is identified for each authentication attempt. This is useful for troubleshooting RAS policy issues. Logged information is stored in a configurable log file (or files) located in the %Systemroot%\System32\LogFiles folder. The log files are saved in IAS 1 or Open Database Connectivity (ODBC) format, so any ODBC-compliant database program (such as SQL 2000) can read the log file directly.

- *RADIUS-based authentication and accounting logging*—Records authentication and accounting information for RAS connections at a RADIUS server when RADIUS authentication and accounting are enabled. This information can be used to track RAS usage and authentication attempts. If the RADIUS server is a Windows 2000 computer running IAS, then authentication and accounting information is stored in log files on the IAS server.

NOTE: *Authentication and accounting logging, whether local or RADIUS-based, is known as* PPP logging.

Windows 2000 RAS Enhancements

In this chapter, the enhancements and additional features provided by Windows 2000 are discussed in context. Nevertheless, at this point it's appropriate to look briefly at Windows 2000 RAS enhancements.

Windows 2000 RAS provides the following new features:

- *Integration with Windows 2000 Active Directory*—A Windows 2000 RRAS server that's part of a Windows 2000 domain can access user dial-in settings (such as RAS permissions and callback options) that are stored in Active Directory.

- *MS-CHAP v2*—Specifically designed for authenticating VPN connections.

- *EAP*—Typically used for the deployment of smart cards. EAP allows other authentication modules to plug into the Windows 2000 RAS PPP implementation. Windows 2000 supports EAP-MD5 CHAP, EAP-TLS, and the passing of EAP messages to a RADIUS server.

- *BAP*—Makes multilink more efficient by adding or dropping additional links dynamically to accommodate changes in traffic flow. BAP is particularly useful in operations that have carrier charges based on bandwidth utilization.

- *RAS policies*—A set of conditions and connection settings that allow more flexibility in setting RAS permissions and connection attributes.

- *RADIUS client*—Windows 2000 RRAS server can act as a RADIUS client to an IAS server that provides centralized authentication, authorization, and accounting functions and a central location to configure RAS policies.

- *L2TP*—Used in conjunction with Internet Protocol Security (IPSec) to create secure VPN connections.

- *AppleTalk RAS client support*—Windows 2000 supports dial-up connections to Apple Macintosh RAS clients that use AppleTalk protocol with PPP.

- *IP multicast support*—An RRAS server can use Internet Group Management Protocol (IGMP—see Chapter 6) to forward IP multicast traffic between connected RAS clients and the Internet or a corporate network.

- *Account lockout*—Denies access after a predefined number of failed authentication attempts. Account lockout helps prevent dictionary attacks, in which an unauthorized user attempts to log on by using a known username and a list of common words as the password. Account lockout is disabled by default.

RAS Security

Security is an important consideration in any remote communication. Windows NT4 authorization was based on the "Grant dial-in permission to user" option. Callback options were also configured on a per-user basis. Windows 2000 RAS expands the security features of its predecessor and offers a number of levels of authentication checking and authorization requirements.

In Windows 2000 RAS, authorization is granted based on the dial-in properties of a user account *in addition to* RAS policies. Callback can provide additional security, as can security hosts. Account lockout provides a defense against dictionary attacks, and the authentication protocols described under "Authentication Protocols" earlier in this chapter let you set the strength of your authentication method. Data can be encrypted over dial-up connections and must be encrypted over VPNs. IPSec provides a level of security below the network layer that's invisible to the user. Certificates can be used for authentication, particularly for smart card users, and RADIUS can help implement consistent, centrally stored security policies over an intranetwork.

RAS Policies

RAS policies consist of a set of conditions and connection settings that give network administrators more control over the authorization of connection attempts. Windows 2000 RRAS and Windows IAS both use RAS policies to determine whether to accept or reject connection attempts. In both cases, the RAS policies are stored locally, either on the RRAS server or, if IAS is used, on the IAS server. Policies stored on the IAS server can be applied to a number of RRAS servers that are set up as RADIUS clients.

For example, RAS policies enable you to grant or deny authorization by the time of day, day of the week, the Windows 2000 security group to which the RAS user belongs, and the type of connection being requested. You can configure settings that limit the maximum session time, specify the authentication and encryption strengths, and configure BAP settings. A connection is authorized only if its settings match at least one of the RAS policies that you specify. If they don't, the connection attempt is denied regardless of the dial-in properties of the user account.

RAS policies can be centralized at an IAS server. If you configure a Windows 2000 RRAS server as a RADIUS client to an IAS server, the local RAS policies stored on the RRAS are no longer used.

User Account Dial-in Properties

You can configure both standalone and Active Directory-integrated RRAS servers to apply a set of properties that allow or deny a connection attempt made by any user.

The dial-in properties configurable for a user account are as follows:

- *Remote Access Permission (Dial-in or VPN)*—Determines whether remote access is explicitly allowed, denied, or determined through RAS policies. Even if access is explicitly allowed by this setting, RAS policy conditions, user account properties, or profile properties can still deny the connection attempt. The "Control access through Remote Access Policy" option for this property is available only for user accounts in a Windows 2000 native-mode domain or for local accounts on Windows 2000 standalone RRAS servers.

- *Verify Caller ID*—Causes the RRAS server to verify the caller's telephone number. If the caller's number doesn't match the configured number, the connection attempt is denied. Caller ID must be supported by the caller's client machine, by the telephone system between the caller and the RRAS server, and by the RRAS server itself.

- *Callback Options*—Causes the RRAS server to call the client back during connection establishment, either at the caller's current telephone number or at a specific telephone number set by the network administrator. The latter option provides a form of security and is often used for dial-up home workers. If I want to log in to your organization's network using your account, not only do I have to learn your username and password, I also have to break into your house and use your telephone.

- *Assign a Static IP Address*—If this property is enabled, you can assign a specific IP address to a user when a connection is made. The term "static" is rather confusing here. The IP configuration is released when the connection is terminated.

- *Apply Static Routes*—Lets you define a series of static IP routes that are added to the routing table of the RRAS server when a connection is made. This setting is designed for user accounts that Windows 2000 routers use for demand-dial routing.

RAS Policy Conditions

RAS policy conditions consist of one or more attributes that are compared to the settings of the connection attempt. If there are multiple conditions, then all of the conditions must match. The IAS server uses most of these conditions when policies are stored and applied centrally. Table 16.1 lists the condition attributes that can be set for a RAS policy.

Table 16.1   RAS policy condition attributes.

Attribute	Description
NAS IP Address	In Windows 2000, the NAS is the RRAS server. This attribute is used by the IAS server.
Service Type	The type of service being requested, such as framed (for PPP connections) and login (for Telnet connections). This attribute is used by the IAS server.
Framed Protocol	The framed protocol that's used, for example, PPP, SLIP, or Frame Relay. This attribute is used by the IAS server.
Called Station ID	The telephone number of the NAS.
Calling Station ID	The telephone number used by the caller.
NAS Port Type	The type of media used by the caller, for example, analog telephone line, ISDN, or VPN.
Day and Time Restrictions	The day of the week and the time of day of the connection attempt.
Client IP Address	The IP address of the RADIUS client. This attribute is used by the IAS server.
Client Vendor	The vendor of the NAS that's requesting authentication. You can use this attribute to configure separate policies for different NAS manufacturers who are RADIUS clients to an IAS server. This attribute is used by the IAS server.
Client Friendly Name	The name of the RADIUS client computer that's requesting authentication. This attribute is used by the IAS server.
Windows Groups	The names of the Windows 2000 groups to which the user that's attempting the connection belongs.
Tunnel Type	The type of tunnel being created by the requesting client. Tunneling is discussed later in this chapter.

RAS Policy Profile

A RAS policy profile is a set of properties that are applied to a connection when that connection is authorized. A profile consists of the following:

- Dial-in constraints
- IP properties
- Multilink
- Authentication
- Encryption
- Advanced properties

Dial-in Constraints

You can set the following dial-in constraints:

- *Idle disconnect time*—The time after which a connection is disconnected if there's no activity. By default, the RRAS server doesn't disconnect an idle connection.

- *Maximum session length*—The maximum amount of time that a connection is maintained by the RRAS server. By default, the RRAS server has no maximum session limit.

- *Day and time limits*—The days of the week and hours of each day that a connection is allowed. By default, the RRAS server has no day or time limits.

- *Dial-in number*—The specific telephone number that a caller must call for a connection to be allowed. By default, the RRAS server allows all dial-in numbers.

- *Dial-in media*—The specific types of media that a caller must use for a connection to be allowed. By default, the RRAS server allows all dial-in media types.

IP Properties

You can set IP properties that specify whether the client can request a specific IP address for a connection. By default, the RRAS server automatically allocates an IP address and the client isn't allowed to request a specific IP address.

You can also define RAS policy profile filtering. IP packet filters define the allowed traffic across a connection after that connection has been made. You can configure IP traffic that's allowed out of the connection (to the client) or into the connection (from the client). RAS policy profile filtering applies to all connections that match the RAS policy.

Multilink

You can enable multilink and specify the maximum number of ports that a multilink connection can use. Also, you can set BAP policies that determine when extra links are created and dropped. Multilink and BAP properties are specific to Windows 2000 RAS and are disabled by default.

Authentication

You can specify the types of authentication that are allowed for a connection and the EAP type that must be used. By default, MS-CHAP and MS-CHAP v2 are enabled. The RRAS server must have the corresponding authentication types enabled for the authentication properties of the profile to be enforced.

Encryption

You can set encryption properties as follows:

- *No Encryption*—Allows a nonencrypted connection. If encryption is required, clear the No Encryption option.

- *Basic Encryption*—MPPE with a 40-bit key is used for dial-up and Point-to-Point Tunneling Protocol (PPTP) VPN connections. 56-bit DES encryption is used for Layer 2 Tunneling Protocol (L2TP) over IPSec VPN connections. PPTP, L2TP, and DES are described when we look at tunneling later in this chapter. IPSec is described in Chapter 7.

- *Strong Encryption*—MPPE with a 56-bit key is used for dial-up and PPTP VPN connections. 56-bit DES encryption is used for L2TP over IPSec VPN connections.

- *Strongest Encryption*—MPPE with a 128-bit key is used for dial-up and PPTP VPN connections. Triple DES (3DES) encryption is used for L2TP over IPSec VPN connections. This option is now available (almost) worldwide, but make sure that all clients can support it.

Advanced Properties

Advanced properties specify the RADIUS attributes that are sent back to a RADIUS client by an IAS server. RADIUS attributes are specific to RADIUS authentication and are ignored by the RRAS server. By default, Framed Protocol is set to PPP and Service Type is set to Framed.

Default RAS Policy

A default RAS policy named "Allow access if dial-in permission is enabled" is created when you initialize RRAS. The default policy has the following configuration:

- The day and time restrictions are set to all times and all days.

- Permission is set to "Deny remote access permission".

- All profile properties are set to their default values—that is, Framed Protocol is set to PPP, and Service Type is set to Framed.

Security Hosts

A security host is an authentication device that verifies whether a user at a RAS client is authorized to connect to an RRAS server. It sits between the client and the server and provides an extra layer of security by requiring a hardware key to provide authentication. You can choose from a variety of security hosts to augment RAS security.

For example, you could select a system that uses a security host and a security card. The security host is installed between the RRAS server and its modem. The security card displays a different access number every minute, and this is synchronized with the same number on the security host. When connecting, the remote user sends the number on the security card to the security host, which allows connection to the RRAS server only if the number is correct.

Other security hosts require username and password authentication that's separate from the authentication required by Windows 2000. This gives an additional layer of security, but the user needs to remember two usernames and passwords.

The security host is configured to allow the RRAS server to initialize the modem that's connected to the security host before the security host's functions take effect. Otherwise, the security host might interpret the RRAS server's initializing the modem as an attempt to dial out.

Account Lockout

RAS account lockout is an additional security feature that isn't related to the "Account locked out" feature in Windows 2000, although you can set either feature to lock out an account after a configurable number of failed logon attempts. RAS account lockout is specifically designed as a defense against malicious persons who attempt to access an organization's intranet through the Internet by means of password attacks, and the feature is, therefore, typically implemented on VPN connections. During a dictionary attack, the attacker uses a known username and a list of passwords (usually a very large number of passwords) based on common words or phrases.

If RAS account lockout is enabled, the user account is locked after a specified number of failed attempts. After each failed attempt, a failed attempts counter for the user account is incremented. A successful authentication resets the failed attempts counter. The failed attempts counter must also be reset periodically to prevent inadvertent account lockouts because of normal mistakes made by users when typing their passwords.

Changing Registry settings on the Windows 2000 computer that provides the authentication enables the RAS account lockout feature. If the RRAS server is configured for Windows authentication, modify the Registry on that computer. If the RRAS server is configured for RADIUS authentication and IAS is used, modify the Registry on the IAS server.

The number of failed logins before an account is locked out is specified in the *MaxDenials* Registry parameter. By default, this parameter is set to zero, which disables RAS account lockout.

The period of time between resets of the failed attempts counter is specified in the *ResetTime (mins)* Registry parameter. By default, this parameter is set to 0xb40, or 2880 minutes (48 hours).

The *MaxDenials* and *ResetTime (mins)* parameters are located in the Registry subkey:

```
HKEY_LOCAL_MACHINE\
        SYSTEM\
            CurrentControlSet\
                Services\
                    RemoteAccess\
                        Parameters\
                            AccountLockout
```

To reset a user account that has been locked out, delete the Registry subkey that corresponds to the user's account name. This subkey is created in the Registry when a lockout occurs and is found under:

```
HKEY_LOCAL_MACHINE\
        SYSTEM\
            CurrentControlSet\
                Services\
                    RemoteAccess\
                        Parameters\
                            AccountLockout\
                                domainname:username
```

> **WARNING!**   *There's no truth in the rumor that careless Registry editing will destroy civilization as we know it. The consequences are usually much worse than that. Seriously, take extreme care when editing the Registry. Always save the Registry key that you intend to edit prior to changing it, and ensure that all valuable data is backed up.*

Dial-up Connections

Windows 2000 RAS provides dial-up connections to support home users or mobile users who dial in to organization intranets. Dial-up equipment installed on a Windows 2000 RRAS server answers incoming connection requests from dial-up clients, authenticates and authorizes the callers, and transfers data between the dial-up networking clients and the organization's intranet.

Dial-up connections are typically used to enable home workers to connect to their organization's network. Often, these workers can use the Public Switched Telephone Network (PSTN) to connect using local calls on analog telephone lines. ISDN can be used for links that carry higher levels of network traffic, and Asymmetric Digital Subscriber Lines (ADSLs) can be used to advantage because home workers usually download significantly more information than they upload. Mobile workers can use dial-up connections, but if they typically connect via long-distance telephone calls, VPNs may provide the cheaper option.

Dial-up connections can be implemented over dedicated X25 or Asynchronous Transfer Mode (ATM) lines to provide high-bandwidth links over long distances. This is an expensive solution in comparison to (for example) the use of VPNs and should be chosen only when traffic levels justify it. Dial-up RAS can also provide an appropriate method of connecting a computer to a network through line-of-sight infrared transmission, a null-modem cable, or a parallel connection.

You can configure Windows 2000 RRAS server to provide dial-up networking access to an entire network or restrict access to the shared resources of the RRAS server only. Windows 2000 logon and domain security, security hosts, data encryption, RADIUS, smart cards, RAS policies, and callback can all be used to provide secure network access for dial-up clients.

Windows 2000 dial-up RAS supports the standard LAN protocols—TCP/IP, IPX, AppleTalk, and NetBEUI, which enable access to Unix, Apple Macintosh, and Novell NetWare resources and to the Internet. It also supports the standard remote access protocols—PPP, SLIP, and the Microsoft RAS Protocol.

You can configure a Windows 2000 RRAS server to access an ISP that offers dial-up Internet connections to PPP clients. A Windows 2000 RAS client can dial into an Internet-connected computer running Windows NT Server 3.5 or later or into any industry-standard PPP- or SLIP-based Internet server.

Dial-up can use MPPE encryption, and IPSec encrypts information while it's in transit on a network. Data encryption is optional in Windows 2000 RAS using dial-up connections.

Dial-up Clients

Windows 2000 RAS can support a wide variety of clients through dial-up connections, although not every type of client has access to every feature. A client must have a modem, access to a WAN link (such as an analog telephone line), and the appropriate remote access software. Clients can be subdivided into Microsoft PPP clients, non-Microsoft PPP clients, and Microsoft RAS Protocol clients.

Microsoft PPP Clients

Microsoft PPP clients can access a Windows 2000 RRAS server by using TCP/IP, IPX, or NetBEUI. They can't use AppleTalk protocol. The RRAS server automatically negotiates authentication with PPP clients.

Table 16.2 lists the levels of support provided for each type of client.

Non-Microsoft PPP Clients

Non-Microsoft PPP clients can access a Windows 2000 RRAS server by using TCP/IP, IPX, NetBEUI, or AppleTalk. The RRAS server automatically negotiates authentication with PPP clients. No special configuration of the Windows 2000 RRAS

Table 16.2   Support for Microsoft PPP clients over dial-up connections.

Client	Supported Features	Unsupported Features
Windows 2000	Multilink, PAP, SPAP, CHAP, MS-CHAP, MS-CHAP v2, EAP, and BAP.	None
Windows NT4	Multilink, PAP, SPAP, CHAP, and MS-CHAP. MS-CHAP v2 is supported if Service Pack 4 (or later) is installed.	EAP and BAP
Windows NT3.5x	PAP, SPAP, CHAP, and MS-CHAP.	Multilink, MS-CHAP v2, EAP, and BAP
Windows 98	Multilink, PAP, SPAP, CHAP, and MS-CHAP. MS-CHAP v2 is supported if Service Pack 1 (or later) is installed.	EAP and BAP
Windows 95	PAP, SPAP, CHAP, and MS-CHAP (with the Windows Dial-Up Networking 1.3 Performance and Security Upgrade for Windows 95).	Multilink, MS-CHAP v2, EAP, and BAP

server is required for non-Microsoft PPP clients, except that it must be configured with the LAN and authentication protocols that are used by the client.

Microsoft RAS Protocol Clients

Windows 2000 RAS supports clients that can't use PPP through the Microsoft RAS Protocol. These clients access the Windows 2000 RRAS server by using NetBEUI. SLIP clients can't connect to a Windows 2000 RRAS server, although a Windows 2000 client can connect to a SLIP server. The following non-PPP clients can connect to a Windows 2000 RRAS server provided they have the appropriate remote access client software installed:

- Windows NT3.1
- Windows for Workgroups
- MS-DOS
- LAN Manager

Because these clients don't support PPP, they can't use applications that run directly over TCP/IP or IPX. For example, these clients can't access Web servers or Novell NetWare servers across a dial-up networking connection.

Dial-up Servers

A Windows 2000 RRAS server that's accessed through dial-up connections must have at least one modem or a multiport adapter and access to WAN links, such as analog telephone lines or other WAN connections. If the server provides access to a network, you need a separate Network Interface Card (NIC) for that network.

When you configure a Windows 2000 RRAS server for dial-up connection, you must specify the protocols to use on the LAN (IPX, TCP/IP, AppleTalk, and/or NetBEUI) and whether access through each of these protocols is to the entire network or to the RRAS server only. You must also select authentication and encryption options. The procedure to configure a Windows 2000 RRAS server is described in the Immediate Solutions section of this chapter.

Virtual Private Networks

VPNs allow users to connect securely to a remote corporate server using a public internetwork (such as the Internet). A VPN can also provide a secure channel through a large corporate intranet. The nature of the intermediate internetwork is irrelevant to the user, because it appears as if the data is being sent over a dedicated private link.

Using VPN technology, a roaming user can connect to the nearest ISP and set up a secure channel from almost any location. If home workers can't connect using local telephone calls, then VPNs may be more cost effective than dial-up connections. Branch offices—connected to the Internet through a persistent connection, such as a T1 or T3 line—are provided with a secure, on-demand connection to corporate headquarters at a cost considerably less than that of a dedicated long-haul circuit. Sensitive information can pass securely through a corporate network, protected (as much as anything ever can be) from attacks by malicious insiders.

NOTE: *An RRAS server that's configured to use VPNs is referred to as a VPN server. This convenient terminology is used throughout this chapter—even though it isn't technically accurate, because VPN isn't a service.*

VPN connections can be one-way or two-way. This doesn't refer to the information flow, which is always two-way, but rather to how the communication is initiated. A roaming user will initiate a connection session with the central office, and a branch office typically will initiate a connection with corporate headquarters. These are examples of one-way connections, with the central office or corporate headquarters accepting connections through a VPN server—for example, a Windows 2000 RRAS server enabled for VPN connections—known as the *answering router*. In the branch office case, the client machines probably will connect through their own, local RRAS server, known as the *calling router*.

In some cases, however, an organization may wish to initiate communications from corporate headquarters. In this case, the VPN servers at either end of the VPN link, or *tunnel*, are set up as each other's clients—that is, they are each both calling and answering routers.

NOTE: *The answering router must use a dedicated connection—it must be listening 24 hours a day for incoming VPN traffic.*

Tunneling

Tunneling is a method of transferring data for one network over a second, intermediate network. The data to be transferred (or *payload*) is split into packets. A tunneling protocol encapsulates each packet in an additional header, which provides routing information so that the encapsulated payload can traverse the intermediate network. After the encapsulated data reaches its destination, or tunnel endpoint, on the intermediate network, the information is unencapsulated and forwarded to its final destination. Tunneling encompasses the entire process of encapsulation, transmission, and unencapsulation.

> **NOTE:**   *A frame consists of a header associated with a specific protocol, the frame data and associated headers, and a cyclic redundancy check (CRC). Layer 2 (data link layer) tunneling protocols encapsulate frames. Layer 3 (network layer) tunneling protocols encapsulate packets.*

Tunnels can be created in two ways:

- *Voluntary tunnels*—A client issues a VPN request to configure and create a voluntary tunnel. In this case, the client computer is a tunnel endpoint. In the examples given above, a roaming user or a home worker creates a voluntary tunnel when connecting to his or her central office.

- *Compulsory tunnels*—A VPN-capable access server configures and creates a compulsory tunnel. In this case, the client computer isn't a tunnel endpoint. In the branch office example, compulsory tunnels would typically be created between each branch and its central office.

Tunneling can be based on either a Layer 2 or a Layer 3 tunneling protocol (or both). Layer 3 protocols assume that all the configuration issues have been handled elsewhere and provide network-level security that's invisible to the user. Such protocols typically have no tunnel maintenance phase. An exception to this is the IPSec Internet Security Association and Key Management Protocol (ISAKMP) negotiation, which provides mutual authentication of the tunnel endpoints. If Layer 2 protocols are used, however, a tunnel must be created, maintained, and then terminated. Windows 2000 supports the following tunneling protocols:

- *Point-to-Point Tunneling Protocol (PPTP)*—Allows IP, IPX, or NetBEUI traffic to be encrypted, encapsulated in an IP header, then sent across an IP network, such as the Internet. PPTP is a Layer 2 protocol.

- *Layer 2 Tunneling Protocol (L2TP)*—Allows IP, IPX, or NetBEUI traffic to be encrypted, then sent over any medium that supports point-to-point datagram delivery, such as IP, X.25, Frame Relay, or ATM. L2TP is a Layer 2 protocol.

- *IPSec Tunnel Mode*—Allows IP payloads to be encrypted, encapsulated in an IP header, then sent across an IP network, such as the Internet. IPSec is a Layer 3 protocol.

NOTE: *Typically, a tunneling strategy uses a combination of Layer 3 and Layer 2 protocols to provide both network-level protection and tunnel maintenance. By default, Windows 2000 uses L2TP over IPSec. This overcomes a potential security weakness inherent in using IPSec alone—it supports only computer-based certificates, and any user with access to a tunnel endpoint computer has access to the tunnel.*

PPTP and L2TP are based on PPP and provide the following features:

- *User authentication*—PPTP and L2TP inherit the user authentication protocols supported by PPP, which were described earlier in this chapter (under "Authentication Protocols"). These protocols can support a wide variety of authentication methods, including one-time passwords, cryptographic calculators, and smart cards.

NOTE: *Layer 3 tunneling protocols also support user authentication. For example, IPSec defines public key certificate authentication in its ISAKMP/Oakley negotiation.*

- *Dynamic address assignment*—PPTP and L2TP support dynamic assignment of client addresses based on the Network Control Protocol (NCP) negotiation mechanism.
- *Data compression*—Microsoft implementations of both PPTP and L2TP use Microsoft Point-to-Point Compression (MPPC).
- *Data encryption*—The Microsoft implementation of PPTP optionally supports the use of MPPE, based on the Rivest-Sharmir-Adelman (RSA) RC4 algorithm. The Microsoft implementation of the L2TP protocol uses IPSec encryption to protect the data stream.

TIP: *Bookmark www.rsasecurity.com. This site (RSA Laboratories) contains a wealth of information about security algorithms, hashes, and ciphers.*

- *Key management*—MPPE employs the initial key generated during user authentication and refreshes it periodically. IPSec explicitly negotiates a common key during the ISAKMP exchange and also refreshes it periodically.
- *Multiprotocol support*—PPTP and L2TP can support multiple protocols (although PPTP requires TCP/IP). IPSec Tunnel Mode supports only target networks that use the IP protocol.

NOTE: *IPSec is still under development and may, in time, support many of the features currently implemented by PPTP and L2TP. For details of the latest Internet Engineering Task Force (IETF) IPSec drafts, access www.ietf.org/html.charters/ipsec-charter.html.*

At the network layer, IPSec defines data encryption and data integrity, using an Authentication Header (AH) to provide source authentication and integrity without encryption and the Encapsulated Security Payload (ESP) to provide authentication and integrity along with encryption.

IPSec can be seen as a layer below the TCP/IP stack that's controlled by a security policy on each computer and a negotiated security association between the sender and receiver. The policy consists of a set of filters and associated security behaviors. If a packet's IP address, protocol, and port number match a filter, the packet is subject to the associated security behavior. IPSec is described in Chapter 7.

Comparing PPTP and L2TP

PPTP uses a TCP connection for tunnel maintenance and Generic Routing Encapsulation (GRE) encapsulated PPP frames for tunneled data. The payloads of the encapsulated PPP frames can be encrypted and/or compressed.

L2TP encapsulates PPP frames to be sent over IP, X.25, Frame Relay, or ATM networks. It can be used as a tunneling protocol over the Internet and can also be used directly over various WAN media (such as Frame Relay) without an IP transport layer. The protocol uses UDP for tunnel maintenance and to send L2TP-encapsulated PPP frames as the tunneled data. The payloads of encapsulated PPP frames can be encrypted and/or compressed.

Both PPTP and L2TP use PPP to provide an initial envelope for data, then append additional headers for transport through the internetwork. The two protocols are similar, but do have some differences:

- PPTP requires an IP network. L2TP requires only that the tunnel media provide packet-oriented point-to-point connectivity.

- PPTP can support only a single tunnel between endpoints. L2TP allows for the use of multiple tunnels.

- When header compression is enabled, L2TP operates with 4 bytes of overhead, as compared to 6 bytes for PPTP.

- L2TP provides tunnel authentication; PPTP does not. However, when either protocol is used over IPSec, IPSec provides tunnel authentication.

NOTE: *PPTP is documented in the draft RFC "Point-to-Point Tunneling Protocol" (pptp-draft-ietf-pppext-pptp-02.txt). L2TP is documented in the draft RFC "Layer 2 Tunneling Protocol L2TP" (draft-ietf-pppext-l2tp-09.txt). For details, access **www.ietf.org/ids.by.wg/pppext.html**. It's possible that these drafts may be RFC standards by the time you read this book.*

VPN Clients

Microsoft VPN clients that connect to a Windows 2000 RRAS server can be Windows 2000, Windows NT4, Windows 95, or Windows 98 clients. The client must be able to send TCP/IP packets to the server. Either a NIC or a modem with an analog telephone line or other WAN connection is required.

Table 16.3 lists the tunneling protocols supported by Microsoft VPN clients.

Table 16.4 lists the authentication protocols supported by Microsoft VPN clients. The main differences between VPN and dial-up client support (refer to Table 16.2) are that Windows NT3.5x isn't a VPN client and that the Windows 95 VPN client with the Windows Dial-Up Networking 1.3 Performance and Security Upgrade supports MS-CHAP v2, but the Windows 95 dial-up client doesn't.

Non-Microsoft VPN Clients

Non-Microsoft VPN clients that use PPTP or L2TP with IPSec can access a Windows 2000 RRAS server. No special server configuration is required for non-Microsoft VPN clients, but the clients must support the appropriate encryption methods. MPPE must be supported for PPTP, and IPSec must be supported for L2TP.

Table 16.3 *Tunneling protocols supported by Microsoft VPN clients.*

Client	Supported Protocols	Unsupported Protocols
Windows 2000	PPTP and L2TP.	None
Windows NT4	PPTP.	L2TP
Windows 98	PPTP.	L2TP
Windows 95	PPTP (with the Windows Dial-Up Networking 1.3 Performance and Security Upgrade for Windows 95).	L2TP

Table 16.4 *Authentication protocols supported by Microsoft VPN clients.*

Client	Supported Protocols	Unsupported Protocols
Windows 2000	PAP, SPAP, CHAP, MS-CHAP, MS-CHAP v2, and EAP.	None
Windows NT4	PAP, SPAP, CHAP, and MS-CHAP. MS-CHAP v2 is supported if Service Pack 4 (or later) is installed.	EAP
Windows 98	PAP, SPAP, CHAP, and MS-CHAP. MS-CHAP v2 is supported if Service Pack 1 (or later) is installed.	EAP
Windows 95	PAP, SPAP, CHAP, MS-CHAP, and MS-CHAP v2 (with the Windows Dial-Up Networking 1.3 Performance and Security Upgrade for Windows 95).	EAP

16. The Remote Access Service

VPN Servers

A VPN server typically has a permanent connection to the Internet. A nonpermanent connection is possible if the ISP supports demand-dial connections and the connection is created when traffic is delivered to the VPN server. This, however, isn't a common configuration. If the server provides access to a network, such as a company intranet, you need a separate NIC for that network.

When you configure a Windows 2000 VPN server, you must specify whether access is to the entire network or to the remote access server only. You must also select authentication and encryption options. The procedure to configure a Windows 2000 VPN server is described in the Immediate Solutions section of this chapter.

Specifying a VPN Strategy

A RAS configuration using dial-up to let locally based home workers access the corporate network is relatively straightforward to design. You need only specify the protocols to be used (often determined by the available remote clients), the authentication methods, whether you need to use data encryption, the multilink and callback settings, and whether to allow access to the entire network or only the RRAS server.

If you use VPN connections, however, you need to give the overall strategy rather more thought. You're implementing your connections through a foreign, and probably very hostile, network (typically the Internet). You'll be servicing roaming clients that could be connecting from anywhere in the world and transmitting sensitive information. You may have to cater to branch offices or to major overseas offices that communicate with corporate headquarters. You need to decide what you can ask your ISP to do and what should be implemented in-house. Security is a major consideration. What type and level of encryption should you use? What Internet attacks (replay, dictionary, and so on) should you anticipate and attempt to counter?

Very few of us have the luxury of specifying a new network from scratch. Your VPN implementation decisions will be based on your organization's current network structure, the requirements for remote access, the level of security considered appropriate, and future expansion plans. Every situation has its own unique features, and no universally applicable rules exist. You will be required to make a number of decisions concerning RAS and VPN.

Topology

You should specify a topology that's based on your organization's structure. Figures 16.1 through 16.4 illustrate typical scenarios.

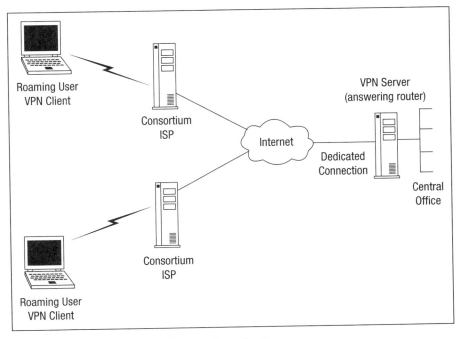

Figure 16.1   Remote access by roaming clients.

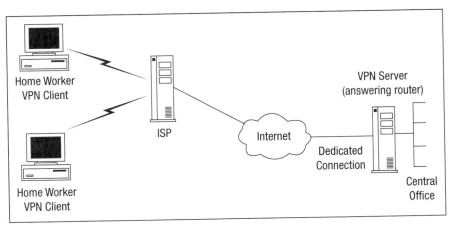

Figure 16.2   Remote access by home workers.

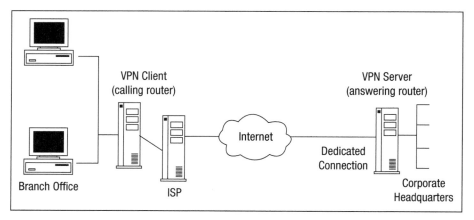

Figure 16.3   Remote access by a branch office.

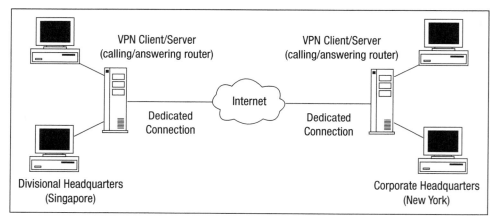

Figure 16.4   Two-way communication between major sites.

Internet Connection Mechanism

You need to specify the Internet connection mechanism. Several issues are involved:

- *ISP*—Remote roaming users will connect directly to an ISP. Many ISPs form consortia. This means that your users can connect to any one consortium ISP anywhere in the world to make a connection, resulting in wide geographical coverage with no additional configuration overhead. Home workers that use VPN connections will also connect directly to an ISP. A branch office connecting with corporate headquarters might consider connecting via its own Web server.

- *Calling router*—Will each computer in a branch office be a VPN client, or should you set up a router-to-router connection? The latter is the more usual option for all but the very smallest branch offices.

Client Connections

You need to specify client connection parameters. Several factors should be considered:

- *Port connections*—How many PPTP or L2TP ports must you set up to accommodate the maximum number of client connections?

- *User accounts*—Who will be permitted to log in to your network remotely? Will all remote users have the same rights and permissions? Will you be creating a single group for all remote users, or will there be several categories?

- *Restrictions*—What particular restrictions will you set up for remote users? You may want to prohibit access to certain parts of your intranet. In a high-security environment, you may consider putting on to the VPN server all the resources that remote users need to access, and limiting remote user access only to that machine.

- *Client authentication*—You need to specify how the VPN server will authenticate the client. Active Directory or RADIUS authentication can be used.

Router-to-Router Connections

You need to specify router-to-router connections. You have several choices to make:

- *Connection technology*—How will you implement your persistent connection to the Internet? Will the volume of router-to-router traffic justify the cost of, for example, leasing all or part of a T1 line?

- *Demand dialing*—Will demand dialing be implemented to automate the initiation of the connection between locations?

- *Connection type*—Should you set up one-way or two-way VPN connections? Will corporate headquarters ever initiate a connection?

- *Mutual authentication*—How will the RRAS servers authenticate each other? RADIUS or Active Directory verification can be used. If the latter, all RRAS servers should be in a security group.

Encryption

You need to specify the encryption method to be used. The tunneling protocols support several encryption methods. Currently, IPSec will secure network traffic, but won't provide a full VPN solution. Therefore, the choice is between the following:

- *PPTP using MPPE*—Make this choice if you are operating in a mixed environment, if a machine-based certificate infrastructure doesn't exist, or if user-based authentication is sufficient and machine-based authentication isn't required.

- *L2TP over IPSec*—Make this choice if all of your tunnel endpoint computers are running Windows 2000, a machine-based certificate infrastructure (such as Kerberos 5) exists, and you want the additional security of machine-based authentication. This is the Windows 2000 default.

You also need to choose the encryption strength. 128-bit encryption gives a high level of security and is now available outside North America, but you have to check that all parts of your organization and all your remote clients support it.

Authentication

You need to specify the authentication method. Authentication methods are described earlier in this chapter. To summarize:

- *EAP*—Methods include MD5 challenge and Smart Card or other Certificate. EAP is mainly used for smart card authentication.

NOTE: *The actual method is EAP-TLS, but the Setup dialog box specifies merely "EAP". Configuring the authentication method is described in "Configuring an RRAS Server" in the Immediate Solutions section later in this chapter.*

- *MS-CHAP v2*—Provides encrypted authentication support for Windows 2000 clients. Support for other Microsoft clients will depend on the level of service pack or upgrade that's installed on the client.

- *MS-CHAP*—Provides encrypted authentication support for Windows 95, Windows 98, Windows NT4, and Windows 2000 clients.

- *CHAP*—Provides encrypted authentication support for clients using diverse operating systems.

- *SPAP*—Provides encrypted authentication support for clients using Shiva LAN Rover software.

- *PAP*—Provides unencrypted authentication. This is used when the client can't support any of the other protocols.

- *Unauthenticated access*—Allows remote systems to connect without authentication. This is used when third-party authentication systems are in force, or for guest access.

IP Configuration

How will clients obtain their IP addresses and other configuration information? The VPN server can be allocated a static pool of IP addresses, or DHCP can be used. Problems can occur if static IP addresses are used for VPN clients.

Firewall Considerations

How should you position the VPN server in relation to the firewall? If a firewall, such as Microsoft Proxy server, protects your corporate network, then you can decide to position the VPN server outside or inside the firewall protection:

- *Outside the firewall*—Place the VPN server outside the firewall if the additional risk of exposing the server directly to the Internet doesn't compromise security, and all sensitive data is placed behind the firewall, with remote access through the firewall limited to the VPN server. Placing the VPN server outside the firewall can solve security problems associated with allowing access to the entire VPN IP address range through the firewall. Where a VPN server is placed outside a firewall, the functions of VPN and RRAS are separated; in other words, there's an RRAS server inside the firewall connected to the VPN server.

TIP: *When a VPN server is positioned outside a firewall, provide an IPSec tunnel between the VPN server and the RRAS server inside the firewall and configure the firewall to allow communication only through this tunnel. Encrypt all data between the servers with the strongest possible encryption and configure the VPN server as a standalone server to reduce the exposure of the Active Directory database.*

- *Inside the firewall*—Place the VPN server inside the firewall if the risk of exposing the server directly to the Internet is unacceptable, and the risk associated with allowing access to the entire VPN IP address range through the firewall is acceptable. In this case, configure the firewall to allow all PPTP and L2TP traffic across the entire VPN address range.

Network Address Translation Integration

If you have a Network Address Translation (NAT) server on your network, then problems can arise in integrating it with your VPN server, because some application servers directly record the IP address and port number of the RAS client. Such applications need a translation table on the NAT device to operate properly. PPTP doesn't encrypt IP headers and works with any NAT device. IPSec with AH encryption, however, encrypts IP headers. Thus, using L2PT over IPSec may not work with applications that require NAT translation tables.

RADIUS

You should decide whether to implement RADIUS client on your VPN servers and use an IAS server. Situations in which this would be an advantage include the following:

- You need to authenticate remote user accounts through methods other than Windows 2000 authentication (if, for example, you have Unix clients).

- You have multiple VPN and/or dial-up RRAS servers and want to configure them to share a common policy.

- You require centralized accounting of logon status.

Multiple VPN Servers

Do you need more than one VPN server? Multiple VPN servers can provide high availability of network resources and failover support. You can configure multiple servers by using either of the following:

- *Windows clustering*—Provides VPN server redundancy and centralized administration. All servers in the same cluster should have high-speed, persistent connections. Clustering is resource-intensive. Failover is automatic, and remote access clients don't get timeout messages when attempting to connect to a failed VPN server. You need to install Windows 2000 Advanced Server to support clustering.

- *Domain Name System (DNS) round-robin*—This technique uses the same fully qualified domain name, but several IP addresses, for a group of VPN servers. Round-robin provides availability and redundancy and uses significantly less system resources than does clustering. Failover isn't automatic, and users will receive timeout messages when attempting to connect to a failed VPN server.

Immediate Solutions

Enabling RRAS

By default, RRAS is installed when you install Windows 2000 Server, and the local server is added to the RRAS console. However, the service isn't enabled. You should enable RRAS on the server that you want to use as your RRAS server. If you intend to allow RAS clients access to your organization's intranet, the RRAS server should be a multihomed domain member server. If you intend to allow access only to resources on the RRAS server itself, you can enable RRAS on a standalone server.

RRAS *can* be enabled on a domain controller (DC), but this is *not* recommended.

When you enable RRAS, you're presented with a number of configuration options. Those relevant to this chapter are the VPN server and Remote Access (dial-in) server options. The next two procedures are mutually exclusive. You can't use the Routing and Remote Access Server Setup Wizard to enable the same server to be both a VPN and a dial-in RRAS server.

Enabling RRAS for a RAS Dial-in Server

To enable RRAS and configure the server connections as dial-up connections (a dial-in server is one that supports dial-up connections), proceed as follows:

1. Log on as an administrator on the Windows 2000 server you intend to use for remote access.

2. Access Start|Programs|Administrative Tools and select Routing and Remote Access.

3. Right-click the local server name and select Configure and Enable Routing and Remote Access.

4. The Routing and Remote Access Server Setup Wizard starts. Click Next.

5. Select Remote Access Server. Click Next.

6. If all the communication protocols that you require are listed, then select Yes, all of the available protocols are on this list. Otherwise, select No, I need to add protocols. Any protocol that you decide to add must already be installed on your computer. This procedure assumes that all the necessary protocols are on the list.

7. Click Next.

8. RAS can allocate IP addresses from a specified range, or a DHCP server can be used to allocate addresses. Choose the option that you want to use. Click Next.

9. If you've chosen to allocate addresses from a specified range (or *static pool*), Click Add, specify the IP address range in the New Address Range dialog box, and click OK. Click Next.

10. If you have multiple RRAS servers and you want to manage them centrally, then you can specify a RADIUS server to do this. If you select this option, you'll be asked to provide the name of the primary and alternate RADIUS servers on your network and the shared secret (password) required for access. Either select No, I don't want to set up this server to use RADIUS now, or select Yes, I want to use a RADIUS server and provide the relevant information.

TIP: *You can specify RADIUS servers retrospectively.*

---

11. Click Next. Click Finish.

12. A message appears that advises you to configure your DHCP relay agent with the address of your DHCP server. Click OK to close the message box.

13. Expand the Routing and Remote Access tree, as shown in Figure 16.5. Right-click DHCP Relay Agent and select Properties.

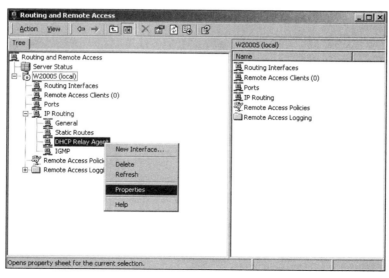

Figure 16.5   Configuring a DHCP relay agent.

14. Add the IP address of your DHCP server to the DHCP Relay Agent Properties list. Click OK.

15. Close the RRAS console.

Enabling RRAS for a VPN Server

Typically, a VPN is established either between a remote client and an RRAS server or between two RRAS servers. The next procedure sets up an RRAS server that's configured to use VPNs via either your domain's Internet Information Service (IIS) server or an ISP.

Much of this procedure is similar to the previous procedure, "Enabling RRAS for a RAS Dial-In Server." However, because the two procedures are mutually exclusive and you'll be carrying out either one or the other (but not both) on any one Windows 2000 server, this procedure is given in full.

To enable RRAS for a VPN Server, proceed as follows:

1. Log on as an administrator on the Windows 2000 server you intend to use for remote access.

2. Access Start|Programs|Administrative Tools and select Routing and Remote Access.

3. Right-click the local server name and select Configure and Enable Routing and Remote Access.

4. The Routing and Remote Access Server Setup Wizard starts. Click Next.

5. Select Virtual private network (VPN) server. Click Next.

6. If all the communication protocols that you require are listed, then select Yes, all of the available protocols are on this list. Otherwise, select No, I need to add protocols. Any protocol that you decide to add must already be installed on your computer. This procedure assumes that all the necessary protocols are on the list.

7. Click Next.

8. Specify the Internet connection that the server uses. Connection can be via an IIS on your network or via an ISP. Click Next.

9. RAS can allocate IP addresses from a specified range, or a DHCP server can be used to allocate addresses. Choose the option that you want to use. Click Next.

10. If you've chosen to allocate addresses from a specified range (or *static pool*), Click Add, specify the IP address range in the New Address Range dialog box, and click OK. Click Next.

11. If you have multiple RRAS servers and you want to manage them centrally, then you can specify a RADIUS server to do this. If you select this option,

you'll be asked to provide the name of the primary and alternate RADIUS servers on your network and the shared secret (password) required for access. Either select No, I don't want to set up this server to use RADIUS now, or select Yes, I want to use a RADIUS server and provide the relevant information.

12. Click Next. Click Finish.

13. A message appears that advises you to configure your DHCP relay agent with the address of your DHCP server. Click OK to close the message box.

14. Expand the Routing and Remote Access tree (refer to Figure 16.5). Right-click DHCP Relay Agent and select Properties.

15. Add the IP address of your DHCP server to the DHCP Relay Agent Properties list. Click OK.

16. Close the RRAS console.

Configuring an RRAS Server

When RRAS has been enabled on a server to use either dial-up connections or VPNs, you need to make a number of configuration decisions. The procedures for configuring a RAS dial-in server and a VPN server are identical, although some of the choices you make will depend on the type of server that you're configuring.

This procedure doesn't specify particular options, but instead tells you where they can be found and discusses the implications of changing them.

To configure an RRAS server, proceed as follows:

1. Log on to the RRAS server as an administrator.

2. Access Start|Programs|Administrative Tools and select Routing and Remote Access.

3. Right-click the server name and select Properties.

4. The General tab lets you enable the computer as a router and specify LAN-only or LAN and demand-dial routing. If you want remote users to have access to your organization's intranet, you need to enable routing, and the server needs to be multihomed. You can also disable RAS on this tab.

NOTE: *The defaults on this tab differ, depending on your connection type. For a dial-in RAS server, routing is disabled. For a VPN server, routing is enabled for both LAN and demand-dial connections.*

5. Select the Security tab.

6. Access the Authentication provider drop-down box. The provider can be Windows or RADIUS. If you didn't specify a RADIUS server during RRAS setup or if you've just set one up on your network, you can specify it here.

TIP: *RADIUS authentication can authenticate remote users through methods other than Windows 2000 authentication. For example, an RRAS server can use RADIUS to authenticate remote users by accessing a user account database on a Unix system.*

---

7. Access the Accounting provider drop-down box. The Accounting provider maintains a list of connection requests and settings. The options are Windows, RADIUS, or none.

8. Click the Authentication Methods button. You can select one or more authentication methods, as shown in Figure 16.6. Click OK.

9. Select the IP tab. On this tab, you can add addresses to the static pool, enable DHCP for address assignment, enable or disable IP routing, and enable or disable IP-based remote access and demand-dial connections.

10. Select the PPP tab. You can enable or disable the following on this tab:

    - *Multilink*—If multilink is enabled, you also have the option of enabling dynamic bandwidth control.

    - *Link Control Protocol (LCP) extensions*—Clearing this checkbox prevents LCP from sending Time-Remaining and Identification packets and requesting callback during LCP negotiation. For more details, see RFC 1570.

    - *Software compression*—Specifies whether the server uses MPPC to compress data.

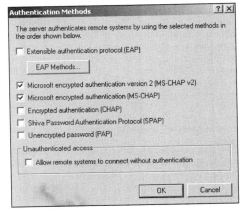

Figure 16.6   Selecting authentication methods.

11. Select the Event Logging tab, on which you can set the event logging level and enable PPP logging. The PPP log is a useful debugging tool if you're having problems with remote connections.

12. When you've made your selections, click OK. If a dialog box appears referring you to the help files, then click No to close it (or click Yes if you need more information).

13. Close the RRAS console.

Configuring a RAS Client

A RAS client can be a workstation, possibly a laptop, that's carried from place to place by (typically) a salesperson and used to access an ISP from wherever its user is located. The client computer could also be a static machine, possibly in a branch office, that accesses the VPN directly through an intranet or Internet connection. More typically, such computers will access the VPN via an RRAS server set up at the branch office. In this case, the remote RRAS server (or calling router) is the VPN client. The RAS client can also be a static (or possibly a laptop) computer that accesses the RRAS server through a dial-up connection.

To configure a RAS client, proceed as follows:

1. Log on to the client computer.

2. Access Start|Settings|Network and Dial-up Connections and double-click Make New Connection.

3. If this is the first new connection that you've created for this computer, you'll be prompted for location information. In this case, supply the information and click OK. If you want to specify more than one location or set up a calling card, you can click New on the Phone and Modem Options dialog box. Otherwise, click OK to close this dialog box.

4. The Network Connection Wizard starts. Click Next.

5. The Network Connection Type dialog box appears, as shown in Figure 16.7. Select the connection type as follows:

    • *Dial-up user*—Select Dial-up to private network. Click Next. Specify the telephone number to dial (using dialing rules lets you select the country/region code and area code from drop-down boxes). Click Next.

    • *VPN user connecting through an ISP*—Select Dial-up to the Internet. Click Next. On the Internet Connection Wizard (see Figure 16.8), make the appropriate selection depending on whether or not you have an existing Internet account. Click Next. Supply the necessary information, as prompted. Click Finish to close the Internet Connection Wizard.

- *Static VPN client or calling router*—Select Connect to a private network through the Internet. Click Next. If prompted, specify whether or not you want Windows 2000 to dial the initial connection automatically, then click Next. Specify the answering router. Click Next.

6. If you're setting up the connection for an individual client computer, then select Only for myself. Otherwise, select For all users. Depending on the default remote access policy set up for your server, you may be asked

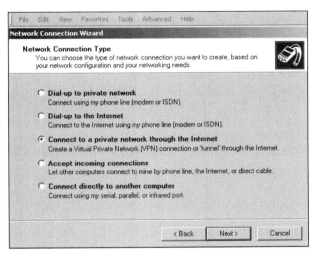

Figure 16.7   Selecting the network connection type.

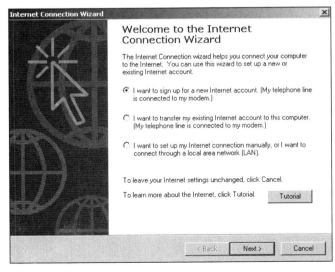

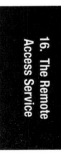

Figure 16.8   The Internet Connection Wizard.

whether you want to enable Internet connection sharing. If so, go on to Step 7. Otherwise, click Next and go directly to Step 9.

7. If you want other computers on the LAN to access resources through the connection (which you probably do if you're setting up a tunneling endpoint), check Enable Internet Connection Sharing for this connection. This gives you the option of enabling demand dialing. Click Next.

8. If you've enabled Internet Connection Sharing, you'll get a warning that you may lose connectivity with other computers on your network if they are set up with static addresses. This warning is given because you may be obtaining your IP address from the remote RRAS server's static address pool or through DHCP. In this case, you should ensure that these computers are set up to obtain their IP addresses automatically. Click Yes to implement Internet Connection Sharing.

9. Specify a name for the connection (or take the default), then click Finish.

10. To connect to the VPN, type your name and password in the Connect Virtual Private Connection dialog box, then click Connect. Your account must be enabled for remote access.

11. Click OK to close the Connection Complete dialog box.

Organizing Remote Access User Accounts

Enabling dial-in permission for a user account is done on an account-by-account basis. However, it's good practice to group such accounts so that you can apply group policies (for example, audit policies). Accounts used for remote access are placed in one or more groups, depending on whether some remote users require wider access to resources than do others. Typically, you'll place this group (or these groups) in an Organizational Unit (OU) and apply security policies to that OU. If your remote access accounts are staff at a branch office, they may already be in an OU.

This procedure assumes that RRAS is enabled on a member server in a Windows 2000 domain. If it's enabled on a standalone server, carry out the same procedure logged on to that sever and use the Computer Management administrative tool rather than Active Directory Users and Computers.

To organize remote access accounts, proceed as follows:

1. Log on to a DC as an administrator.

2. In the Administrative Tools menu, select Active Directory Users and Computers.

3. Right-click the domain object, or an OU further down the domain tree, and create a new OU. Typically, this might be called Home Workers.

4. Right-click the new OU and create a group. Typically, this might be called Ordinary Home Workers. You might add other groups in this OU later, such as Administrative Home Workers.

5. Right-click the new OU and select Properties.

6. In the Group Policy tab, create a Group Policy Object (GPO). Edit this GPO to define the Group Policy to be applied to home workers.

7. Select all the remote access accounts, move them to the Home Workers OU, and place them in the Ordinary Home Workers group. Note that you can perform these operations on several accounts simultaneously, as shown in Figure 16.9. If the accounts don't already exist, create them in the Home Workers OU.

8. Right-click each account and select Properties. On the Dial-in tab, you can check Allow access if you want to permit the user to access remotely through a dial-in connection. If a remote access policy is set, which might (for example) limit the hours during which a remote user could log on or limit the maximum connection period, then you can instead check Control Access through Remote Access Policy. Remote access policies are set up in the Routing and Remote Access snap-in, as described in the next procedure. If the user account uses a dial-up connection, you can set callback on this tab.

9. Click OK. Close the Active Directory Users and Computers console.

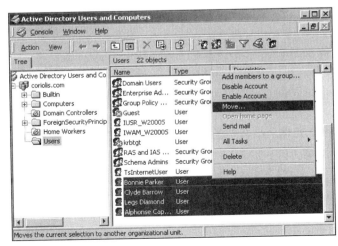

Figure 16.9   Moving user accounts in a block.

Creating a Router-to-Router VPN Connection

In previous procedures, you set up RRAS servers as either dial-in RAS or VPN servers, set up the RAS clients appropriately, and assigned dial-in rights to RAS users. The next set of procedures deals with the situation where you have a router-to-router VPN connection (refer to Figures 16.3 and 16.4). The procedures assume that RRAS is enabled on a domain member server for both the calling routers and the answering router, and that the routers are either in the same domain or in domains linked by trust relationships. This is the normal setup.

Creating a Router-to-Router RAS Policy

This procedure creates a RAS policy for a VPN topology that requires router-to-router connections, which use a specific authentication method and encryption strength.

You can adapt this procedure to your own requirements. The general process of setting up a RAS policy will be the same.

The procedure to create the RAS policy that's described above is as follows:

1. Log on to a DC as an administrator.
2. Access Start|Programs|Administrative Tools and select Active Directory Users and Computers.
3. Right-click the Computers container and create a global security group called VPN-Routers.
4. Add the accounts of the calling routers that initiate router-to-router VPN connections to this group.
5. Close the Active Directory Users and Computers console and log out from the DC.
6. Log on to the answering router as an administrator.
7. Access Start|Programs|Administrative Tools and select Routing and Remote Access.
8. Double-click the icon for the answering router. Right-click Remote Access Policies and select New Remote Access Policy.
9. Specify a policy name, such as Router-to-Router. Click Next.
10. Click Add. Click NAS-Port-Type. Click Add.
11. Click Virtual (VPN). Click Add. Click OK.
12. In the Remote Access Policy dialog box, click Add. Click Windows Groups.

13. Click Add. The Groups dialog box appears. Click Add.

14. Select the VPN-Routers group. Click Add. Click OK. Click OK (again) to close the Groups dialog box.

15. Click Next.

16. Select Grant remote access permission. Click Next.

17. Click Edit Profile. On the Authentication and Encryption tabs, specify an appropriate authentication method and encryption strength.

18. Click OK. If a box appears referring you to the help files, click No to close it.

19. Click Finish.

20. Close the RRAS console.

TIP: *You can also use this procedure to create separate remote access policies for PPTP and L2TP connections. In the Add Remote Access Policy dialog box, select Tunnel-Type. Set the Tunnel-Type to (for example) Point-to-Point Tunneling Protocol, grant remote access permission, and then use the Edit Profile button to specify the authentication and encryption settings.*

Enabling Mutual Authentication

With two-way initiated connections, either router can be the VPN server or the VPN client, depending on who is initiating the connection (refer to Figure 16.4). Both routers must be configured to initiate and accept a VPN connection. Two-way initiated router-to-router VPN connections require that user accounts be added for both routers, so that the authentication credentials for the calling router are accessed and validated by the answering router.

Demand-dial interfaces, with the same name as the user account that's used by the calling router, must be fully configured at both routers, including settings for the host name or IP address of the answering router and user account credentials to authenticate the calling router.

To set up mutual authentication for a two-way initiated connection, proceed as follows:

1. Set up both routers as VPN servers. Refer to the procedures "Enabling RRAS for a VPN Server" and "Configuring a RRAS Server," earlier in this chapter. Ensure the same encryption and authentication settings are used on both machines.

2. Set up both routers as VPN clients, specifying each other as VPN servers. Refer to the procedure "Configuring a RAS Client," earlier in this chapter.

3. If certificates are used for machine-level authentication, then both routers will require a computer certificate issued by an enterprise certificate

authority (CA). These certificates can be issued automatically. The procedure to set this up is described next.

TIP: If VPN clients are dialing in to a VPN server running Windows NT4 that's a member of a Windows 2000 mixed-mode domain, verify that the domain has been enabled for Windows NT4 RAS authentication. Use the **netsh ras show domainaccess** command on a DC to view the current state of the domain. Use the **netsh ras set domainaccess** command on a DC to enable the domain to perform authentication for remote access servers running Windows NT4.

Obtaining a Computer Certificate Automatically

The use of machine certificates for machine-level authentication of VPN clients and VPN servers is required for L2TP over IPSec-based VPN connections. To create an L2TP-over-IPSec connection, you must install a machine certificate, also known as a *computer certificate*, on both the VPN client and the VPN server computers. There are two methods of doing this:

• Configure the automatic allocation of computer certificates to computers in a Windows 2000 domain.

• Use Certificate Manager to obtain a computer certificate.

Where you have a number of VPN clients, the second (manual) method can be tedious, and it tends to be used only where an enterprise Certificate Authority (CA) isn't available in the domain. Installing an enterprise CA is described in detail in Chapter 12. This procedure assumes that you have an enterprise CA installed in your domain.

1. Log on to a DC as an administrator.

2. Access Start|Programs|Administrative Tools and select Active Directory Users and Computers.

3. Right-click the icon for the root DC and select Properties.

4. On the Group Policy tab, select Default Domain Policy, then click Edit.

5. Expand Computer Configuration|Windows Settings|Security Settings|Public Key Policies and right-click Automatic Certificate Request Settings.

6. From the context menu, select New and click Automatic Certificate Request. This starts the Automatic Certificate Request Setup Wizard. Click Next.

7. Select the Computer certificate template. Click Next.

8. Select an enterprise CA (typically, there will be only one on the list). Click Next.

9. Click Finish to create the automatic certificate request. Click OK to edit the Default Domain Policy GPO.

10. Close the Active Directory Users and Computers console.

11. To create a computer certificate for a VPN server or client, either restart the computer or type **secedit /refreshpolicy machine_policy** from the Windows 2000 Command Console.

Related solution:	Found on page:
Installing a Certificate Authority	392

Adding L2TP and PPTP Ports

By default, 128 ports are enabled for L2TP and PPTP traffic on a VPN server (5 for each protocol on a RAS dial-in server). If you have more than 128 VPN clients (for example, in the scenarios that are illustrated in Figures 16.1 and 16.2), you need to add more ports.

To add PPTP or L2TP ports, proceed as follows:

1. Log on to the VPN server as an administrator.
2. In the Administrative Tools menu, select Routing and Remote Access.
3. Expand server name, right-click Ports, and select Properties.
4. Select either WAN Miniport (PPTP) or WAN Miniport (L2TP), depending on the protocol you're using. Click Configure.
5. In Maximum ports, type the number of ports (up to 30,000) and click OK.
6. Click OK (again). Close the RRAS console.

Setting Up a RADIUS Client

A RADIUS server uses the IAS to provide authentication and accounting support in networks that have a number of RRAS and VPN servers. The RADIUS solution scales up to large multinational WANs, and a RADIUS server might, typically, be implemented on a Windows 2000 Advanced Server, which must also be running IIS.

To set up a RADIUS server, proceed as follows:

1. Log on to your domain's IIS server as an administrator.
2. Install IAS using Add/Remove Programs in Control Panel (unless it's already installed). IAS is a component of Networking Services.
3. Access Start|Programs|Administrative Tools and select Internet Authentication Service.

4. Right-click Internet Authentication Service and select Properties.

5. On the Service tab, select both options for event logs.

6. On the RADIUS tab, specify the RADIUS authentication and accounting UDP ports to be used.

7. If the realm names used at the ISPs to access the corporate network are different from those required to access the corporate domains, specify text replacement rules for manipulating the realm names on the Realms tab.

8. Click OK. In the console tree, right-click Clients. Select New Client.

9. Follow the prompts to add and specify information about each RADIUS client.

TIP: *If your RADIUS server is reachable only through your Internet interface, add an input filter and output filter to the Internet interface for UDP port 1812 (or UDP port 1645 for older RADIUS servers) for RADIUS authentication. For RADIUS accounting, add an input filter and output filter to the Internet interface for UDP port 1813 (or UDP port 1646 for older RADIUS servers).*

Using the Network Shell Utility

To administer the RRAS from the Command Console using the netsh utility, proceed as follows:

1. Log on to an RRAS server as an administrator.

2. Access Start|Programs|Accessories and select Command Prompt.

3. Enter **netsh**.

4. At the netsh> prompt, enter **ras**.

5. At the ras> prompt, use the Network Shell RAS subcommands (for example, **ip show config**) that are documented in Appendix D.

Chapter 17
The Transport Driver Interface

In Depth

The Transport Driver Interface (TDI) is an abstraction layer that's similar in concept to the Network Driver Interface Specification version 5 (NDIS5) layer that was described in Chapter 2. NDIS5 forms a buffer between the low-level Network Interface Card (NIC) drivers and transport providers (or protocols), such as TCP/IP and NWLink. TDI forms a buffer between the transport providers and high-level application interfaces, such as the Network Basic Input Output System (NetBIOS) interface and the Windows Socket (Winsock) interface. TDI also gives a layer of abstraction between the transport providers and services, such as the Server Service, File and Printer Sharing for Microsoft Networks, Gateway (and Client) Services for Netware, Services for Macintosh, and so on.

This chapter is mainly of interest to programmers who want to write transport drivers. Other than the (often important) facility of reconfiguring bindings between protocols and services, there's very little that a nonprogramming administrator can configure in TDI. Nevertheless, a discussion of the TCP/IP stack would be incomplete without mention of the abstraction layers, and more and more administrators are turning to programming to give them more flexibility in controlling their networks.

TDI Components and Features

TDI provides a set of components, features, and functions that are of particular interest to designers of transport drivers. Because all transport drivers make procedure calls to (or *expose*) a single common interface, TDI simplifies the task of transport driver development. It also simplifies the task of developing client applications by minimizing the amount of transport-specific code that needs to be written.

Figure 17.1 shows where TDI is located in the Windows 2000 operating system. The TDI layer defines a kernel-mode network interface that's exposed at the upper edge of all transport protocol stacks. The highest-level protocol driver in every stack supports TDI for higher-level kernel-mode network clients.

TDI Components

TDI includes the following components:

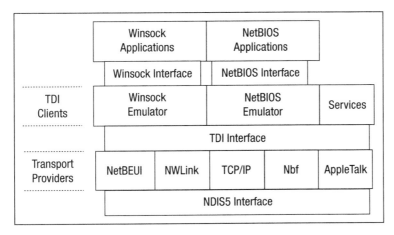

Figure 17.1   The TDI abstraction layer.

- A set of standard kernel-mode intermediate driver *dispatch routines* that are exported by each TDI transport driver. Clients submit Input/Output (I/O) Request Packets (IRPs) by making calls to kernel-mode support routines, such as IoCallDriver.

- A set of ClientEvent*Xxx callback routines* that are exported by each TDI client. These routines can be registered with the underlying transport driver to receive notifications of specific network events when they occur.

- A set of ClientPnP*Xxx* callback routines that are exported by TDI clients. These routines can be registered with TDI to receive notifications of dynamic binding, network address, and power-state changes from Plug and Play (PnP)-aware Windows 2000 transports.

- Parameters, structures, I/O controls (IOCTLs), and procedural rules associated with TDI transport ClientEvent*Xxx* and ClientPnP*Xxx* routines.

- A set of system-supplied Tdi*Xxx* functions that transports and clients can call to communicate with each other.

- A set of system-supplied TdiBuild*Xxx* macros and functions that clients can use to set up I/O requests to be submitted to their underlying transports.

> **NOTE:**   *TDI dispatch routines, callback routines, parameters, structures, IOCTLs, macros, functions, and transports are described briefly in this chapter and in considerably more detail in the documentation that's downloaded with the Windows 2000 Driver Development Kit (DDK).*

Windows 2000 includes interface modules for network interfaces, such as Winsock and NetBIOS. Each of these modules exposes a set of low-level (or *primitive*) functions that are accessible through standard calls from user mode. When it's called, the interface module maps the function and its associated parameters and procedural rules to one or more calls to the underlying TDI transport driver.

TDI Features

The Windows 2000 TDI implementation offers a number of features:

- *32-bit code*—All TDI transports and their clients use 32-bit code. TDI-defined structures and parameters use 32-bit pointers and values.

- *Asynchronous operation*—Most kernel-mode TDI operations are asynchronous. They use client-supplied callback routines to indicate asynchronous network events as they occur, and they also complete asynchronously most of the client-initiated operations submitted as IRPs.

- *Extensible communication*—TDI transports can use TDI_ACTION IOCTL to support a set of transport-determined operations initiated by requests from their clients. This allows a client to submit transport-specific driver requests that aren't expressly defined by TDI to the underlying transport.

- *Extensible address mechanism*—TDI doesn't prescribe a particular address format. Instead, it features an extensible mechanism that allows many address formats to be identified and used.

- *Event notification*—TDI transports can notify their clients when "interesting" events occur on the network without requiring a client to submit an explicit I/O request. For certain types of events (connects, disconnects, and receives), the transport driver can indicate data along with the event notification.

- *PnP event notification*—Windows 2000 transports can notify their clients of certain PnP events, such as the availability of underlying NICs and the creation/deletion of connections on local network addresses.

- *System power-state change notification*—Windows 2000 transports can notify their clients of proposed system power-state changes. This gives the client the option of keeping an active connection powered up.

- *Granularity*—TDI is granular in nature, with several small TDI-defined requests that can accommodate mapping from existing network-interface functions. It therefore can accommodate all the primitive functions (*primitives*) and conventions from existing popular network interfaces.

Optional Features

The TDI transport driver supports the following features as additional options:

- *Data transfer modes*—Data can be sent and received as discrete messages (message mode) or as a stream of bytes (byte-stream mode). Support for either mode (or both modes) depends on the protocol used and how the driver is designed.

- *Expedited delivery*—A client can flag particular messages as *expedited*. The underlying transport sends these messages ahead of nonexpedited messages. When expedited messages are received, they're indicated to the recipient client before and/or separate from nonexpedited messages.

- *Chained receive indications*—If an underlying NDIS5 miniport supports multipacket receive indications, a TDI transport can give its clients direct read-only access to a full Transport Service Data Unit (TSDU) in a single call. The client can then retain control of the buffer containing the TSDU until it has completed all the appropriate operations on (or *consumed*) the indicated data. This improves the performance of both the transport and the client by cutting down on call overhead.

- *Internal buffering*—The TDI client can set and query the driver's internal buffer sizes, request nonblocking send operations, receive notification of available buffer space, and look at (*peek*) buffered data before receiving it.

- *Management options*—Transports maintain information about their features, limits, and runtime statistics. This allows each client dynamically to query and, in some cases, to set transport-provider static information, statistics, and configuration parameters. The extensible TDI_ACTION IOCTL enables a TDI transport driver to implement unique network-management features that can be accessed by its clients through action requests to the transport.

- *Quality of Service (QoS)*—TDI-defined connection-establishment and datagram-send requests include the *Options* and *OptionsLength* parameters that allow a TDI client to include a transport-specific, variable-length string specifying QoS options. This supports both QoS negotiation and QoS for connectionless datagram transmission.

TIP: *The* Options *and* OptionsLength *parameters can be used to pass any transport-specific connection-related or datagram-related options to the transport driver, not just QoS specifications.*

TDI File Objects

A TDI file object can represent a physical device, a virtual device, a data file, or any logical target of I/O requests that can be opened by a particular process. Open file objects are process-specific. For example, the I/O Manager creates a file object for each process that opens a particular data file.

TDI uses file objects to represent entities that exist in any network communication environment. In particular, file objects represent the following types of TDI-defined entities:

- Transport addresses that are opened by specific processes or groups of processes on a network node.

- Connection endpoints that identify specific endpoints associated with particular transport addresses that are opened to set up endpoint-to-endpoint connections with remote-node peer processes.

- Control channels that identify transport providers that are opened for the purpose of setting and querying global configuration, features, limits, and/or statistical information that's maintained by the underlying transport.

A TDI transport driver and the underlying NDIS5 drivers provide a mechanism by which data can be transferred from a process on one network node to one or more processes, either on the same node or on other network nodes. For example, when the Windows 2000 redirector process sends Server Message Block (SMB) messages to a server process on a remote node and receives messages back from that server process, it opens two file objects, one representing a transport address, and the other, a connection endpoint associated with that address.

Transport Address File Objects

TDI supports both unreliable connectionless and reliable connection-oriented data transfers (see Chapters 8 and 9). Unreliable connectionless data can be sent to one process or a group of processes that have opened a particular transport address on a remote node. When sending unreliable connectionless data as datagrams, the sender need identify only the target remote-node address for the process or group of processes.

Reliable connection-oriented data transfers can be sent between two processes if an endpoint-to-endpoint connection—also called a *virtual connection (VC)*—has been established between them. A VC is a one-to-one association between two, and only two, processes. To establish such a connection, each process must open a transport address and a connection endpoint on its respective network node and associate its connection endpoint with the open transport address.

The TDI entity that's used to identify a specific process is a file object that represents a particular transport address. This file object contains transport-supplied pointers to a driver-maintained *state* that identifies the specific process and the node on which that process resides. Routable transports, such as TCP/IP, AppleTalk, or NWLink, maintain a state that also contains information to identify the network (or subnet) on which the node resides.

Some TDI-defined transport address types contain information that indicates whether the address identifies a single process (unique address) or a group of processes (group address). In the case of a group address, the TDI-defined address can contain information that identifies the specific processes (that is, the node on which the process resides) and the network (or subnet) on which the node resides.

TDI supports a number of address types. There are three commonly used TDI address types, as described below.

TDI_ADDRESS_NETBIOS

The NetBIOS address type consists of a 16-character NetBIOS name and information (an address-type *member*) that indicates whether the name is registered as a unique name or as a group name. Because a unique name is used by only one process on the network at any one time, it not only identifies the process but also implicitly identifies the node on which that process resides. If the registered name is a group name, it can be an address that's registered by many processes on many stations. A group name identifies all processes that registered the name, as well as the nodes on which those processes reside.

TDI_ADDRESS_IP

The IP address type consists of a port number and a standard IP address. Because TCP/IP allows the same port number to be registered by processes on many nodes, the IP address identifies the node and the port number identifies the process on that node. For connectionless data transfer using the User Datagram Protocol (UDP), many processes can register the same port number on the same station. Also, certain IP addresses can be used by more than one node. Data sent to a TDI address that consists of this type of port number and IP address will be received by all nodes to which the IP address applies. On those nodes, the data will be passed to all processes that have registered the specified (UDP) port number.

TDI_ADDRESS_IPX

The Internetwork Packet Exchange (IPX) address type consists of a 4-byte network number, a 6-byte node number, and a 2-byte port number. Because IPX allows the same port number to be registered by processes on many nodes, the IPX address identifies the network and the node, and the port number identifies the process on that node.

Connection Endpoint File Objects

A file object that represents an open connection endpoint identifies a specific connection on which local and remote-node peer processes are communicating (or will communicate) with each other. This file object must be associated with another open file object that represents a particular transport address. The transport address identifies the process.

The transport uses the local connection endpoint file object to maintain a state about the remote-node peer process, such as the remote-node transport address that its local-node client establishes an endpoint-to-endpoint connection with.

A client process can establish many endpoint-to-endpoint connections between itself and other processes on remote nodes. For example, the Windows 2000 redirector establishes separate connections between itself and each remote Windows 2000 server with which it communicates.

When a process wants to send data over an endpoint-to-endpoint connection, it must be able to identify which connections the data is to be sent over. Each open file object that represents a connection endpoint is used to differentiate between established endpoint-to-endpoint connections of the same process.

Control Channel File Objects

A network management process queries or defines global configuration or statistical information concerning a specific transport provider. The process must therefore have a means of identifying a particular transport among several possible transport providers. The client process opens a file object that represents a control channel so that it can query the appropriate transport. For example, a client might issue a query to determine the transport's limit on datagram size so it can size the buffers that it will subsequently use to send and receive datagrams.

A TDI transport maintains global state information about its features and current statistics, rather than process-specific state information tied to a particular open file object. For example, a client queries the current state of its open transport address and passes a pointer to a client-specific file object representing that address, but the transport returns information common to all clients that currently have the same address open.

TDI Device Objects

Windows 2000 transports support PnP and power management (see Chapter 2) by creating device objects to represent their respective bindings to underlying NICs. Each transport registers itself with TDI during system startup as a network provider. This ensures that PnP-aware transports are available to potential clients when the underlying network hardware comes online.

Potential clients of these PnP-aware transports register their respective ClientPnP*Xxx* callbacks with TDI. This enables them to receive notifications of the availability of active transport-to-NIC bindings and of transport-established network addresses on which they can subsequently send and receive data over the network.

A transport establishes a binding to an underlying NIC by using the ProtocolBindAdapter function that the lowest module in the transport stack (the *monolithic transport driver*) registers with NDIS5. By this means, the TDI transport driver creates a named device object to represent its binding to the underlying NDIS miniport.

During system startup, a PnP-aware transport registers each named device object it creates with TDI and sets up its per-binding state. The transport also registers known network addresses on each binding with TDI and thus sets up its per-registered-address state. When NDIS5 calls the ProtocolPnPEvent function at the bottom of the transport stack with the PnP event code NetEventBindsComplete, the transport notifies TDI that it's ready to transfer data over the network on at least one transport-to-NIC binding.

TDI enables a network client that has registered its ClientPnP*Xxx* handlers to bind itself to a transport-created device object by calling ZwCreateFile from the client's registered ClientPnPBindingChange routine. TDI subsequently calls its registered ClientPnPAddNetAddress routine with each network address that the underlying transport has already registered for its device object. It also notifies registered clients when any transport indicates that it's ready to carry out network transfers and when all startup-time transport-to-NIC bindings have been established.

At runtime, PnP-aware transports continue to call TDI whenever a dynamic binding change occurs and whenever the transport makes or breaks a connection to a remote-node network address. This can happen in the following situations:

- *A new NIC is enabled*—NDIS5 calls the ProtocolBindAdapter function at the bottom of each transport stack, thereby enabling each transport to bind itself to the new NIC, to create another device object to represent its new binding, and to register its new device object with TDI. As each such transport-created device object is registered, TDI calls the set of currently registered ClientPnPBindingChange routines and enables the clients to open the new bindings.

- *A new device object is registered*—The transport that registers the object also registers any known network addresses on its new binding with TDI, which calls the set of registered ClientPnPAddNetAddress routines. These calls enable clients to open a connection to a registered address (or to a binding). Whenever a transport breaks a connection to a remote node, it calls TDI to deregister the corresponding network address.

- *Before a NIC is disabled*—NDIS5 calls the ProtocolPnPEvent function at the bottom of the transport stack to check whether it's safe to remove the NIC. The transport notifies TDI of the request to remove the NIC, and TDI notifies the clients with calls to their registered ClientPnPPowerChange routines. If no client objects to the NIC's removal, NDIS5 calls the ProtocolUnbindAdapter function at the bottom of the transport stack and the transport releases (or *tears down*) its binding. The transport calls TDI to deregister all the network addresses that it formerly registered on the binding and to deregister the device object that it created to represent that binding. TDI notifies clients of these unbinding operations by making calls to their registered ClientPnPDelAddress and ClientPnPBindingChange routines.

17. The Transport Driver Interface

- *A binding change*—If a user initiates a binding change in the network connections folder, NDIS5 calls TDI directly to notify registered network clients of the proposed binding change. If no client objects, NDIS5 calls the appropriate ProtocolPnPEvent, ProtocolBindAdapter, or ProtocolUnbindAdapter function at the bottom of the transport stack. If, on the other hand, a client objects to the binding change, the user is prompted to cancel it.

- *A power-state change*—TDI notifies the clients of PnP-aware transports about proposed system power-state changes for underlying NICs. When the system power manager calls NDIS5 to power a NIC up or down, NDIS5 calls the ProtocolPnPEvent function at the bottom of each transport stack that's currently bound to the NIC. Each transport notifies TDI of the proposed power-state change, and TDI forwards the notification to the transport's clients for their approval or rejection.

Transport Driver Routines

TDI-compliant transport drivers are *standard intermediate drivers* that export a number of entry points in response to the I/O Manager's calls. Some TDI transport driver routines initialize and unload the driver itself. Others are standard *dispatch routines* that the I/O Manager calls when TDI clients call system support routines, such as ZwCreateFile and IoCallDriver.

A TDI transport driver's DriverEntry routine sets up one or more driver-supplied dispatch routines to handle various types of I/O requests passed in as IRPs. A TDI driver can export a single dispatch routine to handle all incoming IRPs or a separate Dispatch*Xxx* routine to handle each IRP_MJ_*Xxx* that the driver supports. TDI-specific requirements for dispatch routines are summarized later in this chapter. More details are available in the DDK documentation.

When a TDI transport completes an operation that's requested by its client, the I/O Manager calls any IoCompletion routine that the client set in the IRP before it submitted that IRP to the underlying transport. The transport driver also calls the TDI client at preregistered entry points within the client's code when specific network events occur. These client-supplied event handlers are summarized later in this chapter.

Client Interactions

A TDI client interacts with its underlying transport driver as described below.

Creating TDI File Objects

A client calls ZwCreateFile to create or open a file object that represents a transport address, a connection endpoint, or a control channel. The I/O Manager allocates an IRP, transfers the client-supplied parameters into that IRP, and passes the IRP to the underlying transport driver's TdiDispatchCreate routine. When the transport driver has set up the state it maintains for the newly created file object, it calls IoCompleteRequest (or TdiCompleteRequest) with the IRP and STATUS_SUCCESS. ZwCreateFile then returns to the TDI client with a handle to the file object.

Each time a client process calls to ZwCreateFile, it creates a separate file object. A successful call to ZwCreateFile opens a transport address, a connection endpoint, or a control channel, depending on the *EaXxx* parameters that the client passes in its call.

Submitting Requests

After the appropriate file objects have been created, the client can submit requests that reference those objects. For example, after it opens a file object that represents a particular transport address, the client can submit an address-information query or a "send datagram from this address" request. All such requests use standard I/O system mechanisms and conventions, as follows:

1. The client prepares an IRP with an IRP_MJ_*Xxx* opcode that identifies what operation the transport driver is to perform. The client supplies all appropriate parameters for the given IRP_MJ_*Xxx* and, optionally, sets up its own IoCompletion routine that will be called when the request is completed by the transport. The TdiBuild*Xxx* macros can be linked into client code and used to prepare IRPs for TDI-defined IOCTL requests. The TdiBuildInternalDeviceControl function allocates the IRP.

2. The client calls IoCallDriver with pointers to the IRP; to the file object that represents the address, connection endpoint, or control channel; and to the transport driver's device object. The I/O Manager passes the IRP directly to the transport driver's appropriate TdiDispatch*Xxx* routine.

3. The transport driver completes the requested operation and then calls TdiCompleteRequest or IoCompleteRequest. The I/O Manager calls the client-supplied IoCompletion routine for the IRP.

Handling Event Notifications

If a client preregisters its entry point(s) for one or more event handlers, the transport driver calls each event handler routine when the corresponding network event occurs. For example, if the client registers a ClientEventReceive handler on an address associated with an endpoint-to-endpoint connection, the transport calls this handler when data sent by a remote-node peer process is received on the local node.

Deleting TDI Objects

A client calls ZwClose to delete a file object when it no longer needs the address, connection endpoint, or control channel. The close request is forwarded to the transport's TdiDispatchCleanup and (subsequently) TdiDispatchClose routines.

17. The Transport Driver Interface

TDI Event Notification

Interfaces, such as NetBIOS and Winsock, are primarily one-way. A client can call the underlying transport driver, but the transport driver can't call the client. The only thing that the transport driver can communicate to its client is an error code from a client-initiated request. TDI, however, provides an *event-notification* mechanism that allows a TDI transport to call a kernel-mode client whenever a specific network event occurs, provided that the client has registered its ClientEvent*Xxx* handler with the transport for that type of event. The TDI client-supplied callback then takes the appropriate action and returns control to the transport driver.

TDI also provides a means for PnP-aware Windows 2000 transports to notify their clients whenever the transport performs one of the following operations:

- Binding itself to an underlying NIC
- Unbinding itself from an underlying NIC
- Establishing a connection to a remote node on a binding
- Breaking a connection to a remote node on a binding

The transport also notifies the client whenever a system power-state change is proposed and/or made by the Power Manager. The transport's clients register a set of ClientPnP*Xxx* handlers with TDI to receive these of notifications.

When a TDI transport driver calls a client's registered ClientEvent*Xxx* handler, it can pass a limited amount of data as a call parameter. This allows the client to receive messages from the transport without having to allocate a buffer.

When, for example, the Windows 2000 redirector sends an SMB request to the server service, the underlying TDI transport driver calls the redirector's registered ClientEventReceive handler with an SMB response message. The redirector can view (but not necessarily copy) the indicated message and note the SMB response status indicator. In this transaction, the redirector receives the SMB response message without having to allocate a buffer.

TDI Routines, Macros, and Callbacks

The previous section described the general operation and features of TDI transport routines. This section goes into more detail about specific transport routines, functions, and macros and the callback routines exported by TDI kernel-mode clients. In particular, the section covers the following:

- Transport driver initialization and dispatch routines
- TDI-defined IOCTLs that kernel-mode clients issue to their underlying transports

- Event handlers that clients register with their underlying transports during TDI client callbacks
- The set of system-supplied TDI library functions and macros that TDI transports and their clients can use

Transport Driver Initialization

Every transport driver must provide an initialization routine that's named DriverEntry. The driver should also provide all the TdiDispatch*Xxx* routines and internal driver functions that it requires to satisfy the I/O requests of its kernel-mode clients. A TDI transport driver, or one of the underlying protocol drivers in its transport stack, must provide the required NDIS5 driver lower-edge functions.

When the transport is loaded, DriverEntry is declared in the driver code. This enables the transport to be loaded automatically. The I/O Manager loads the driver, creates a driver object to represent the transport, and passes a pointer to the driver object when it calls the DriverEntry routine. Then, the DriverEntry routine does the following:

- If required, it reads the Registry (using kernel-mode support routines) to retrieve configuration information created by the transport's information (INF) file.
- It sets all the driver's TdiDispatch*Xxx* entry points in the driver object. The TdiDispatch*Xxx* routines will be called later by the I/O Manager to handle requests from TDI clients.
- It calls TdiRegisterProvider to notify TDI about the transport's PnP and power management support.
- It creates at least one named device object for itself by using IoCreateDevice. Some transport drivers, such as NWLink, create only one named device object no matter how many NICs they bind themselves to. Others, such as TCP/IP, create one or more named device objects and export a set of device interfaces for each device object. Some transport drivers, such as NetBEUI frames (Nbf), create a separate named device object for each bound NIC.
- It performs other initialization tasks, such as binding to underlying NDIS5 intermediate and/or NIC drivers.
- As it establishes bindings to each underlying NIC, a PnP-aware Windows 2000 transport also calls TdiRegisterDeviceObject with the named device object that the transport creates. It then makes one or more calls to TdiRegisterNetAddress to register all known network addresses associated with the transport-created device object for its newly established binding. When it has completed its initialization on at least one binding, the transport calls TdiProviderReady, typically as a consequence of an NDIS5 call to the ProtocolPnPEvent function at the lower edge of the transport stack.

A TDI transport driver must provide an unload routine unless the driver can't be unloaded without making the system unusable. Most TDI transport drivers declare an unload routine, and their DriverEntry routines set its entry point in the driver object.

Driver Registration

A TDI transport driver registers with the NDIS5 library and binds itself to an underlying NDIS5 NIC driver by calling NdisRegisterProtocol. The PnP manager calls NDIS5 to initialize each NIC, and NDIS5 calls the registered ProtocolBindAdapter functions at the lower edge of the appropriate TDI transport drivers or transport stacks to give each transport the opportunity to bind itself to the appropriate NDIS5 miniports.

When a TDI transport driver is bound to an NDIS5 miniport or is layered above an NDIS5 protocol driver that has bound itself to a miniport, the TDI driver can respond to any registered TDI client that submits a request to open any registered network address on that binding. Consequently, a PnP-aware TDI transport doesn't call TdiProviderReady until it has set up its per-device-object and per-address state for each initialization call that it makes to TdiRegisterDeviceObject and TdiRegisterNetAddress.

The transport calls TdiRegisterProvider and TdiProviderReady only once each during system startup, but it can make many runtime calls to TDI-provided PnP and power-management functions, such as TdiRegister/DeregisterDeviceObject, TdiRegister/DeregisterNetAddress, and TdiPnPPowerRequest.

Driver Deregistration

Before a NIC is removed from the machine, the TDI transports bound to that NIC first notify their clients that the NIC is going to be disabled and removed (unless the removal is unexpected, for example, due to circuit failure). NDIS5 calls the ProtocolPnPEvent function at the lower edge of each transport that's bound to the NIC by using the input NetEventQueryRemoveDevice code. Each TDI transport then forwards this notification to its clients by calling TdiPnPPowerRequest.

The transport doesn't tear down its binding or make calls to TdiDeregisterNetAddress and TdiDeregisterDeviceObject until NDIS5 has called the ProtocolUnbindAdapter function at the lower edge of the transport stack. Also, a transport driver can't be unloaded until it has released all its bindings to all underlying NICs.

After a NIC is removed from the machine, the system can unload a TDI transport driver that was either bound directly to the NIC's driver (and only to that driver) or layered over an NDIS5 protocol driver that was bound to the NIC's driver. To accomplish this, the system calls the TDI transport's unload routine, which frees all remaining driver-allocated resources.

A PnP-aware TDI transport driver must make a call to TdiRegisterProvider from its unload routine. If the TDI driver exports a set of NDIS-defined Protocol*Xxx* functions, it also must call NdisDregisterProtocol from its unload routine.

I/O Requests and Dispatch Routines

I/O requests are formatted as IRPs, either by the I/O Manager or by a TDI client, and submitted to the transport driver by calling IoCallDriver. Completed IRPs are returned to the caller when the transport driver calls IoCompleteRequest or TdiCompleteRequest. Any kernel-mode TDI client can set its IoCompletion routine for an IRP before it calls IoCallDriver.

There are five IRP_MJ_*Xxx* codes (known as MajorFunctionCodes) that are used to send I/O requests to TDI transport drivers. The entry points in the TDI drivers call one or more dispatch routines that handle these IRP_MJ_*Xxx* requests. Because a TDI client communicates with the driver only through IRPs, the driver has one or more TdiDispatch*Xxx* routines that determine what operation to carry out. Usually, these TdiDispatch*Xxx* routines pass the client requests to the appropriate internal driver functions for further processing.

A TDI transport driver exports all its TdiDispatch*Xxx* entry points by setting them in the driver object passed to its DriverEntry routine. The I/O Manager calls a TdiDispatch*Xxx* routine whenever a client makes an I/O request. A transport driver can have a separate TdiDispatch*Xxx* to handle each of the possible IRP_MJ_*Xxx* opcodes, a single TdiDispatch routine that processes IRPs with all possible IRP_MJ_*Xxx* opcodes, or a number of TdiDispatch*Xxx* routines that handle discrete subsets of the IRP_MJ_*Xxx* opcodes.

The transport drivers handle incoming IRPs in which the MajorFunctionCode is one of those listed in Table 17.1. The table also lists the dispatch routine normally associated with the request MajorFunctionCode. The dispatch routines are described briefly below and in more detail in the DDK documentation.

The TDI dispatch routines are described in Table 17.2.

TIP: *Because all dispatch entry points are exported by address in the driver object rather than by name, you don't have to give the dispatch routines the names listed here when you're designing transport drivers. You can call them anything you want to.*

17. The Transport
Driver Interface

Table 17.1   I/O request MajorFunctionCodes and dispatch routines.

MajorFunctionCode	Description	Dispatch Routine
IRP_MJ_CREATE	Opens a named device object created by the transport, then opens a transport address, connection endpoint, or control channel in the underlying transport. This request originates in a client's call to ZwCreateFile.	TdiDispatchCreate
IRP_MJ_INTERNAL_DEVICE_CONTROL	Specifies kernel-mode client requests (TDI IOCTLs) for which internal transport functions handle operations other than opening and closing file objects. This request usually originates in a client's call to a TdiBuild*Xxx* macro, followed by its call to IoCallDriver.	TdiDipatchInternalDeviceControl
IRP_MJ_DEVICE_CONTROL	Specifies user-mode-visible IOCTL requests issued by a transport-dedicated application. Except for any transport-defined "private" IOCTLs, these requests are forwarded to the same internal driver functions that handle internal-device control requests. This request originates in a call by a transport-dedicated user-mode application to DeviceIoControl.	TdiDispatchDeviceControl
IRP_MJ_CLEANUP	Closes an open address, connection endpoint, or control channel when the executive is closing the last handle for the corresponding file object. This request originates in a client's call to ZwClose.	TdiDispatchCleanup

(continued)

Table 17.1 *I/O request MajorFunctionCodes and dispatch routines* (continued).

MajorFunctionCode	Description	Dispatch Routine
IRP_MJ_CLOSE	Closes an address, connection endpoint, or control channel if the executive is removing its last reference to the file object handle. When no outstanding file object handles are open, the request closes a transport-created device object. This request follows an IRP_MJ_CLEANUP request on the same file object.	TdiDispatchClose

Table 17.2 *TDI dispatch routines.*

Dispatch Routine	Description
TdiDispatchCreate	Opens a file object that represents an address, connection endpoint, or control channel, and sets up a driver-allocated state to track I/O operations on the open file object.
TdiDispatchInternalDeviceControl	Handles TDI_*Xxx* device-control requests from kernel-mode clients. The routine returns STATUS_SUCCESS if it completes the requested operation successfully. Otherwise, it returns a driver-determined error status, such as STATUS_INVALID_DEVICE_REQUEST or STATUS_INVALID_DEVICE_STATE.
TdiDispatchDeviceControl	Processes IRPs set with the major function code IRP_MJ_DEVICE_CONTROL. Typically, the routine calls TdiMapUserRequest and, if this routine returns STATUS_SUCCESS, TdiDispatchDeviceControl calls the transport's TdiDispatchInternalDeviceControl function with the input DeviceObject and IRP pointers.
TdiDispatchClose	Closes an address, connection endpoint, or control channel. The routine runs when the I/O Manager is releasing its last reference to the handle of the file object representing an address, connection endpoint, or control channel. The file object is deallocated when this last reference to the file handle has been released.
TdiDispatchCleanup	Completes any outstanding IRPs for an address, connection endpoint, or control channel that's about to be closed. The routine runs when the I/O Manager is closing the last handle to an open file object representing an address, connection endpoint, or control channel, and is responsible for completing any IRPs currently held in the transport that reference the open file object.

17. The Transport Driver Interface

IOCTL Requests

TDI transport drivers respond to the TDI_*Xxx* IOCTL requests issued by their kernel-mode clients. Each IRP submitted to the driver's TdiDispatchInternalDeviceControl routine has the MajorFunctionCode of IRP_MJ_INTERNAL_DEVICE_CONTROL and a MinorFunctionCode that specifies one of these TDI_*Xxx* codes.

Typically, a transport's TdiDispatchInternalDeviceControl routine uses the TDI_*Xxx* IOCTL request code to route each incoming kernel-mode client request to an internal driver function for further processing. The IOCTL request codes are described in Table 17.3.

Table 17.3   IOCTL request codes.

Request Code	Description
TDI_ACCEPT	Requests the underlying TDI transport driver to accept an incoming connection from a remote-node peer, and thus to enable data transfer on an endpoint-to-endpoint network connection between the client and the remote-node peer.
TDI_ACTION	Requests the underlying TDI transport driver to make transport-specific extensions available to the client. The successful completion of any client's action request makes the transport-provided extension applicable to that client, but not to any other TDI clients or drivers.
TDI_ASSOCIATE_ADDRESS	Requests the underlying TDI transport driver to make an association between a particular open local-node address and an open connection endpoint. A kernel-mode client must make an associate-address request before it makes an endpoint-to-endpoint connection to the remote node either with a TDI_LISTEN request, optionally followed by a TDI_ACCEPT request, to the transport driver or with a TDI_CONNECT request to the transport driver.
TDI_CONNECT	Requests the underlying TDI transport driver to offer a connection on a particular local-node connection endpoint to a remote-node peer. For a local-node client to establish an endpoint-to-endpoint connection with a remote-node peer, it must associate an idle local connection endpoint with an open transport address before making a TDI_CONNECT request. If the specified local endpoint is active or nonexistent, the transport fails the connect request.

(continued)

Table 17.3   IOCTL request codes (continued).

Request Code	Description
TDI_DISASSOCIATE_ADDRESS	Requests the underlying TDI transport driver to break an established association between a particular local-node address and a connection endpoint. A client makes this request to disassociate a connection endpoint for an inactive connection from the associated local-node address, whether that client initiated the disconnection from its remote-node peer or vice versa.
TDI_DISCONNECT	Requests the underlying TDI transport driver to make a disconnect indication to the remote node, to acknowledge a disconnect indication from the remote node for an established endpoint-to-endpoint connection, or to reject an offered connection by a remote-node peer. During a disconnect operation, the underlying transport driver usually refuses any incoming requests for an established connection and stops all activity at the specified connection endpoint, unless the transport supports controlled disconnects. By default, TDI_DISCONNECT requests the disconnection of an endpoint-to-endpoint connection that's not a controlled-disconnect operation, and the transport need not complete outstanding I/O requests on the connection before it completes the disconnect request and returns control.
TDI_LISTEN	Requests the underlying TDI transport driver to listen for an offer to make an endpoint-to-endpoint connection from a remote node. Depending on whether TDI_QUERY_ACCEPT is set in RequestFlags, the transport completes the listen request either by accepting an offered remote-node connection on behalf of its local-node client or by deferring acceptance or rejection of such an offer to that client. To initiate a listen request successfully, the local-node client must have its transport address already associated with an idle connection endpoint.
TDI_QUERY_INFORMATION	Requests the underlying TDI transport driver to return information of a client-specified type, such as a broadcast address, the transport's capabilities, or its current statistics for I/O on a particular connection.
TDI_RECEIVE	Requests the underlying TDI transport driver to indicate a normal or expedited TSDU on an established endpoint-to-endpoint connection.
TDI_RECEIVE_DATAGRAM	Requests the underlying TDI transport driver to indicate a TSDU as a datagram on a specified address. Because a datagram is never associated with an endpoint-to-endpoint connection, the transport must return the address of the remote-node client to the receiving client along with each datagram.

(continued)

Table 17.3 IOCTL request codes (continued).

Request Code	Description
TDI_SEND	Requests the underlying TDI transport driver to transmit a normal or expedited TSDU on a specified connection endpoint to its remote-node peer. The local-node TDI transport driver can queue any number of send requests on a particular connection, but it must process them in first-in-first-out (FIFO) order, unless the client issues an expedited send. Each expedited send request must be queued and transmitted ahead of any normal send requests that the transport is holding queued, and each expedited send also must be transmitted in FIFO order for the client.
TDI_SEND_DATAGRAM	Requests the underlying TDI transport driver to transmit a TSDU, as a datagram, to a specified remote-node address. A TDI transport doesn't send fragmented datagrams. Consequently, its client makes one send-datagram request to send each datagram.
TDI_SET_EVENT_HANDLER	Requests the underlying TDI transport driver to call the specified ClientEvent*Xxx* routine whenever the corresponding network event occurs.
TDI_SET_INFORMATION	Requests the underlying TDI transport driver to set a client-specified information type on a particular address, connection, or control channel.

Callback Routines

TDI defines a set of callback routines that clients register with the underlying TDI transport to receive notifications when network events of interest occur. These consist of system-defined ClientEvent*Xxx* callback routines and ClientPnP*Xxx* notification routines. A client registers a ClientEvent*Xxx* callback by setting up an IRP for the underlying transport driver. These *event handlers* use the TdiBuildSetEventHandler function to hold the TDI_SET_EVENT_HANDLER code and call IoCallDriver. ClientPnP*Xxx* routines are notified with TdiRegisterPnPHandlers.

The names of client-supplied callback routines and PnP notification routines are *metanames*, chosen to describe their basic functionality. Because a client passes only the entry points for these event handlers in calls to TdiBuildSetEventHandler and/or TdiRegisterPnPHandlers, you can give callback routines any names you want when you're writing transport drivers. The client-supplied callback routines are described in Table 17.4.

Library Functions and Macros

Windows 2000 TDI provides a number of library functions as a kernel-mode dynamic link library (the tdi.sys export library) with which TDI drivers and kernel-mode clients link. Most of the system-supplied TdiBuild*Xxx* functions called by kernel-mode clients are, however, implemented as macros.

Table 17.4   Callback routines.

Callback Routine	Description
ClientEventChainedReceive	Called by the underlying TDI transport in response to an incoming receive from a remote node with which the client has an established endpoint-to-endpoint connection. The transport calls this handler, rather than ClientEventReceive, when it's forwarding a full TSDU that's indicated to the transport by an NDIS5 miniport and the client can be given direct read-only access to the buffered TSDU until the client has consumed the data.
ClientEventChainedReceiveDatagram	Called by the underlying TDI transport in response to an incoming receive from a remote node that was directed to a local-node transport address opened by the client. The transport calls this handler, rather than ClientEventReceiveDatagram, when it's forwarding a full TSDU that's indicated to the transport by an NDIS5 miniport and the client can be given direct read-only access to the buffered TSDU until the client has consumed the data.
ClientEventChainedReceiveExpedited	Called by the underlying TDI transport in response to an incoming expedited receive from a remote node with which the client has an established endpoint-to-endpoint connection. The transport calls this handler, rather than ClientEventReceiveExpedited, when it's forwarding a full TSDU indicated to the transport by an NDIS5 miniport and the client can be given direct read-only access to the buffered TSDU until the client has copied all the data.
ClientEventConnect	Called by the TDI driver in response to an incoming endpoint-to-endpoint connection offer from a remote node. This call notifies the local-node client of an incoming connection offer from a remote-node peer process.
ClientEventDisconnect	Called by the underlying TDI transport in response to an incoming disconnection notification from a remote node. A call to this event handler notifies the local-node client that its remote-node peer is closing their established endpoint-to-endpoint connection.
ClientEventError	Called by the underlying TDI transport in response to an error, either in the transport itself or in a lower-level network driver, that makes I/O on a particular local transport address unreliable or impossible. A call to this event handler notifies the local-node client of an error condition in the underlying TDI transport, in one of the lower protocol layers of the transport stack, or in the underlying NDIS5 NIC driver to which the transport stack is bound.

(continued)

17. The Transport Driver Interface

Table 17.4   Callback routines (continued).

Callback Routine	Description
ClientEventErrorEx	Called by the underlying TDI transport in response to an error, either in the transport itself or in a lower-level network driver, that makes I/O on a particular local transport address unreliable or impossible. A call to this event handler notifies the local-node client of an error condition in the underlying TDI transport, in one of the lower protocol layers of the transport stack, or in the underlying NDIS5 NIC driver to which the transport stack is bound.
ClientEventReceive	Called by the underlying TDI transport in response to an incoming receive from a remote node with which the client has an established endpoint-to-endpoint connection. This is usually a normal TSDU, unless the client hasn't registered a ClientEventReceiveExpedited handler.
ClientEventReceiveDatagram	Called by the underlying TDI transport in response to an incoming receive from a remote node that was directed to a local-node transport address that the client has opened.
ClientEventReceiveExpedited	Called by the underlying TDI transport in response to an incoming expedited receive from a remote node with which the client has an established endpoint-to-endpoint connection. This handler is almost identical to ClientEventReceive, except that expedited data flow supersedes normal data flow.
ClientEventSendPossible	When the underlying TDI transport (which buffers sends internally, but returns STATUS_DEVICE_NOT_READY for the client's preceding TDI_SEND request) has internal buffer space available to accept a resubmitted send request from the client, it calls this event handler.
ClientPnPAddNetAddress	Called by the underlying TDI transport as following the client's call to TdiRegisterPnPHandlers. Subsequently, TDI calls ClientPnPAdd-NetAddress as a consequence of any transport's call to TdiRegisterNetAddress or (rarely) as a consequence of the client's call to TdiEnumerateAddresses.
ClientPnPBindingChange	Called by the underlying TDI transport following the client's call to TdiRegisterPnPHandlers. At system startup, TDI calls ClientPnPBindingChange as a consequence of the underlying transports' calls to TdiRegisterDeviceObject, TdiProviderReady, and TdiDeregisterDeviceObject. Subsequent to system startup, TDI calls ClientPnPBindingChange whenever a transport to which the client is bound calls TdiRegisterDeviceObject and TdiDeregisterDeviceObject.

(continued)

Table 17.4 *Callback routines* (continued).

Callback Routine	Description
ClientPnPDelNetAddress	Called by the underlying TDI transport as a consequence of a transport's call to TdiDeregisterNetAddress.
ClientPnPPowerChange	Called by the underlying TDI transport as a consequence of a transport's call to TdiPnPPowerRequest or, for a user-initiated network reconfiguration, as a consequence of a call by NDIS5.

After the client has set up an IRP with a TdiBuild*Xxx* macro, it submits the request to the underlying TDI driver by passing the IRP to IoCallDriver. Each of the macros fills in the relevant components, or *members*, of the client-provided IRP, except for the Status and Information members, which the underlying transport fills in after processing its client's request.

Parameters to these macros always include pointers or handles to file objects representing addresses, connection endpoints, or control channels already opened with calls to ZwCreateFile. A successful call to ZwCreateFile returns a handle to an open file object, from which the client can obtain a pointer to that file object by calling ObReferenceObjectByHandle.

The TDI library routines are described in Table 17.5 and the macros in Table 17.6.

Table 17.5 *TDI library routines.*

Library Routine	Description
TdiBuildInternalDeviceControlIrp	Allocates an IRP to be passed to a TdiBuild*Xxx* macro and then to IoCallDriver when a kernel-mode client makes a request to its underlying transport on its own behalf.
TdiBuildNetbiosAddressEa	Sets up a buffered Extended Attribute (EA) that describes a NetBIOS address with which the client of a NetBIOS transport can subsequently call ZwCreateFile.
TdiBuildNetbiosAddress	Sets up a NetBIOS address for the client of a NetBIOS transport.

Table 17.6 *TDI macros.*

Macro	Description
TdiBuildAccept	Sets up an internal device control IRP for a TDI_ACCEPT request to the underlying transport in which a local-node client has already opened a connection endpoint and associated it with a local-node address and to which the client has already issued a TDI_LISTEN request.

(continued)

Table 17.6   TDI macros (continued).

Macro	Description
TdiBuildAction	Sets up an internal device control IRP for a TDI_ACTION request to the underlying transport in which a local-node client has already opened an address, connection endpoint, or control channel to which the requested action applies.
TdiBuildAssociateAddress	Sets up an internal device control IRP for a TDI_ASSOCIATE_ADDRESS request to the underlying transport in which a local-node client has already opened an address and a connection endpoint.
TdiBuildConnect	Sets up an internal device control IRP for a TDI_CONNECT request to the underlying transport in which a local-node client has already associated an address and a connection endpoint.
TdiBuildDisassociateAddress	Sets up an internal device control IRP for a TDI_DISASSOCIATE_ADDRESS request to the underlying transport in which a local-node client has already associated an address and a connection endpoint.
TdiBuildDisassociateAddress	Sets IRP_MJ_INTERNAL_DEVICE_CONTROL as the MajorFunction Code and TDI_DISASSOCIATE_ADDRESS as the MinorFunction Code in the transport's I/O stack location of the given IRP. A kernel-mode client makes this request to disassociate a connection endpoint for an inactive connection from the associated address object, whether that client initiated the disconnection from its remote-node peer or vice versa. If this request is successful, the client can reassociate the connection endpoint with another local-node address or the local-node address with another connection endpoint by setting up another IRP for the underlying transport with TdiBuildAssociateAddress.
TdiBuildDisconnect	Sets up an internal device control IRP for a TDI_DISCONNECT request to the underlying transport through which a local-node client has already established an endpoint-to-endpoint connection with a remote-node peer or to which that client previously made a listen request in anticipation of establishing such a connection.
TdiBuildInternalDeviceControlIrp	Allocates an IRP for a client-initiated internal device control request. After it returns from this macro, the client calls another TdiBuild*Xxx* macro with the returned IRP to set up the I/O stack location of the underlying transport driver before making the request with IoCallDriver.
TdiBuildListen	Sets up an internal device control IRP for a TDI_LISTEN request to the underlying transport in which the local-node client has already associated an address and a connection endpoint.

(continued)

Table 17.6   TDI macros (continued).

Macro	Description
TdiBuildNetbiosAddress	Sets up a TA_NETBIOS_ADDRESS structure for the caller.
TdiBuildNetbiosAddressEa	Sets up a buffered NetBIOS address that the caller can pass subsequently to ZwCreateFile as the EaBuffer parameter.
TdiBuildNetbiosAddressEa	Returns STATUS_SUCCESS if it set up the given EA buffer. Otherwise, it can return STATUS_UNSUCCESSFUL if the given buffer is too small, or (possibly) it can return a propagated error status if attempting to access the given parameters raised an exception.
TdiBuildQueryInformation	Sets up an internal device control IRP for a TDI_QUERY_INFORMATION request to the underlying transport in which the local-node client has already opened a file object representing an address, a connection endpoint, or a control channel. A TDI client can use the query request to ask its underlying transport for information, such as connection-status information, a broadcast address it can use, or the features of the transport (such as its size limits for sends, datagrams, and user-connect data).
TdiBuildReceive	Sets up an internal device control IRP for a TDI_RECEIVE request to the underlying transport in which the local-node client has established an endpoint-to-endpoint connection with a remote-node peer.
TdiBuildReceiveDatagram	Sets up an internal device control IRP for a TDI_RECEIVE_DATAGRAM request to the underlying transport in which the local-node client has already opened a file object representing an address.
TdiBuildSend	Sets up an internal device control IRP for a TDI_SEND request to the underlying transport in which the local-node client has already opened a file object representing a connection endpoint and established an endpoint-to-endpoint connection with a remote-node peer.
TdiBuildSendDatagram	Sets up an internal device control IRP for a TDI_SEND_DATAGRAM request to the underlying transport in which the local-node client has already opened a file object representing an address.
TdiBuildSetEventHandler	Sets up an internal device control IRP for a TDI_SET_EVENT_HANDLER request to the underlying transport in which the local-node client has already opened a file object representing an address.
TdiBuildSetInformation	Sets up an internal device control IRP for a TDI_SET_INFORMATION request to the underlying transport in which the local-node client has already opened a file object representing an address, connection endpoint, or control channel.

NOTE: *Where macro names are listed more than once their operation varies depending upon context. For example, the operation of TdiBuildDisassociateAddress depends upon whether it's used by a local-node or kernel-node client.*

TDI Functions

Windows 2000 TDI provides a set of system-supplied Tdi*Xxx* functions called by transport drivers and/or by their kernel-mode clients. Some of these functions have already been mentioned in this chapter, but are described here for convenience. The standard TDI functions are listed in Table 17.7.

Table 17.7   Standard TDI functions.

Function	Description
TdiCompleteRequest	Completes a given IRP with a transport-supplied status. The function sets the given status value in the IoStatus.Status member of the given IRP and completes the IRP with the system-defined IO_NETWORK_INCREMENT priority boost to the thread that originally made the I/O request.
TdiCopyBufferToMdl	Copies data from a buffer range into a set of one or more destination buffers mapped by a given Memory Descriptor List (MDL) chain. The function always copies as much data as possible from the source buffer to the destination buffer(s), even if it returns STATUS_BUFFER_OVERFLOW.
TdiCopyLookaheadData	Safely copies receive data, which is indicated in a lookahead buffer by the underlying NDIS5 driver, to the transport protocol. This function can be called by a transport's ProtocolReceive function.
TdiCopyMdlToBuffer	Copies data from a set of buffers mapped by a given MDL chain into a caller-supplied destination buffer range. The function always copies as much data as possible from the given mapped source buffers into the given destination buffer range, even if it returns STATUS_BUFFER_OVERFLOW.
TdiDeregisterNetAddress	This is the reciprocal of TdiRegisterNetAddress. It removes a transport-supplied network address from the list of valid network addresses registered with TDI.
TdiDeregisterPnPHandlers	This is the reciprocal of TdiRegisterPnPHandlers. It disables further PnP and power-state notifications to a set of ClientPnP*Xxx* routines that were previously registered with TdiRegisterPnPHandlers on a particular transport-to-NIC binding. A successful call to TdiDeregisterPnPHandlers stops further PnP/power, bind, unbind, and net-address-change notifications from being sent as calls to the ClientPnP*Xxx* routines.
TdiDeregisterProvider	This is the reciprocal of TdiRegisterProvider. PnP-supporting transports call this function when they're being unloaded. A transport must free all the TDI-associated resources that it has allocated before it calls TdiDeregisterProvider.
TdiEnumerateAddresses	Provides information to a client about the currently registered network addresses on a particular transport-to-NIC binding. When a client calls this function, it initiates a sequence of calls to the ClientPnPAddNetAddress routine, which the client previously registered with TdiRegisterPnPHandlers. Each such call to the ClientPnPAddNetAddress routine supplies a currently active network address provided and registered with TDI by the underlying transport.

(continued)

Table 17.7   *Standard TDI functions* (continued).

Function	Description
TdiMapUserRequest	Converts a given IRP in which MajorFunctionCode is set to IRP_MJ_DEVICE_ CONTROL into an IRP_MJ_INTERNAL_DEVICE_CONTROL request if it recognizes the IOCTL_TDI_*Xxx* code specified in the input IRP. For the majority of system-defined IOCTL_TDI_*Xxx* codes that can be set in IRPs passed to a transport's TdiDispatchDeviceControl routine, TdiMapUserRequest converts the current I/O stack location into the format of the corresponding kernel-mode TDI_*Xxx* request.
TdiPnPPowerComplete	Indicates that the client has completed the processing of a power-state-change notification for which the client originally returned STATUS_PENDING to TDI. If the input status is anything other than STATUS_SUCCESS, this function notifies the transport that its attempt to change the power state has failed.
TdiPnPPowerRequest	Forwards a power-state change notification from the transport to all its clients on a particular transport-to-NIC binding. When NDIS5 notifies a transport of a power-state-change event with a call to the ProtocolPnPEvent function, the transport is responsible for notifying its higher-level clients of any power-state changes that might affect their current network operations with a call to TdiPnPPowerRequest.
TdiProviderReady	Notifies TDI clients that a particular transport has established binding(s) to one or more underlying NICs and is now available to send and receive data over the network.
TdiRegisterDeviceObject	Notifies a transport's clients that the transport has created a new device object to represent the target of its clients' network I/O requests on a particular transport-to-NIC binding.
TdiRegisterNetAddress	Notifies a transport's clients that it has just established a connection to a remote node with a particular network address or that the transport has just created a new network address for the computer on which it's running.
TdiRegisterPnPHandlers	Registers a set of client-supplied ClientPnP*Xxx* routines that are to receive subsequent notifications of dynamic PnP events. These events can include the discovery of a new NIC in the machine, the removal of an existing NIC from the machine, system power-state changes, and the arrival and departure of network addresses registered and deregistered by the underlying transport(s).
TdiRegisterProvider	Notifies the TDI that a PnP-supporting transport driver is initializing and that the transport will make a subsequent call to TdiProviderReady when it has established its bindings to one or more underlying NDIS5 NIC miniports and it's ready to carry out network I/O operations.

(continued)

17. The Transport Driver Interface

Table 17.7   Standard TDI functions **(continued).**

Function	Description
TdiReturnChainedReceives	Returns an array of TSDU descriptors for one or more chained receive indications that were previously forwarded to a transport's client, which returned STATUS_PENDING for each such chained receive indication. To achieve faster network throughput, a TDI transport gives its clients direct (but read-only) access to a chain of NDIS5 miniport-allocated buffers containing a received network packet.

Obsolete Functions

The following functions are obsolete in Windows 2000 TDI:

- TdiDeregisterAddressChangeHandler
- TdiRegisterNotificationHandler
- TdiDeregisterNotificationHandler
- TdiMapBuffer
- TdiRegisterAddressChangeHandler
- TdiUnmapBuffer

TDI Structures

TDI structures contain the information (or *elements*) that are used by TDI routines and macros or describe the way in which that information is stored. The structures used by TDI transport drivers and/or by their kernel-mode clients are listed in Table 17.8.

Table 17.8   TDI structures.

Structure	Description
TRANSPORT_ADDRESS	Contains a specified number of elements of type TA_ADDRESS. For certain TDI_ADDRESS_TYPE_*Xxx* values, transports, and their kernel-mode clients can use system-defined substructures for Address and corresponding TDI_ADDRESS_LENGTH_*Xxx* constants for AddressLength. For convenience, TDI defines TA_ADDRESS_*Xxx* structures that specify a single address of a certain TDI_ADDRESS_TYPE_*Xxx* type.
TA_APPLETALK_ADDR	Contains a single AppleTalk transport address, suitable for use as a TRANSPORT_ADDRESS. TDI defines this structure for convenience in situations requiring a single TDI_ADDRESS of type TDI_ADDRESS_TYPE_APPLETALK.

(continued)

Table 17.8 **TDI structures (continued).**

Structure	Description
TA_ADDRESS_IP	Contains a single IP transport address, suitable for use as a TRANSPORT_ADDRESS. TDI defines this structure for convenience in situations requiring a single TDI_ADDRESS of type TDI_ADDRESS_TYPE_IP.
TA_ADDRESS_IPX	Contains a single IPX transport address, suitable for use as a TRANSPORT_ADDRESS. TDI defines this structure for convenience in situations requiring a single TDI_ADDRESS of type TDI_ADDRESS_TYPE_IPX.
TA_NETBIOS_ADDRESS	Contains a single NetBIOS transport address, suitable for use as a TRANSPORT_ADDRESS. TDI defines this structure for convenience in situations requiring a single TDI_ADDRESS of type TDI_ADDRESS_TYPE_NETBIOS.
TA_ADDRESS_NS	Contains a single Xerox Network System (XNS) transport address, suitable for use as a TRANSPORT_ADDRESS. TDI defines this structure for convenience in situations requiring a single TDI_ADDRESS of type TDI_ADDRESS_TYPE_NS.
TA_ADDRESS_VNS	Contains a single Banyan VINES (VNS) transport address, suitable for use as a TRANSPORT_ADDRESS. TDI defines this structure for convenience in situations requiring a single TDI_ADDRESS of type TDI_ADDRESS_TYPE_VNS.
TDI_ACTION_HEADER	The initial structure in any client-supplied action parameter block passed in a TDI_ACTION request to the underlying transport driver. The remainder of an action parameter block is a transport-specific extension to the TDI interface. The transport driver defines the structure and required contents for the remainder of the buffer that its kernel-mode clients must supply in each TDI_ACTION request.
TDI_ADDRESS_8022	Contains an 802.2 netcard-level address, correctly packed and aligned.
TDI_ADDRESS_APPLETALK	Contains an AppleTalk address, correctly packed and aligned.
TDI_ADDRESS_INFO	Defines the structure of the information returned for a TDI_QUERY_INFORMATION request in which the IrpSp->Parameters.QueryType is set to TDI_QUERY_ADDRESS_INFO. A single transport address can have many associated file objects at any particular time.
TDI_ADDRESS_IP	Contains an IP address, correctly packed and aligned.
TDI_ADDRESS_IPX	Contains an IPX address, correctly packed and aligned.
TDI_ADDRESS_NETBIOS	Contains a NetBIOS address, correctly packed and aligned.

(continued)

17. The Transport Driver Interface

Table 17.8   TDI structures (continued).

Structure	Description
TDI_ADDRESS_NETBIOS_EX	Contains an extended NetBIOS address, correctly packed and aligned.
TDI_ADDRESS_NETONE	Contains a Net/One address, correctly packed and aligned.
TDI_ADDRESS_OSI_TSAP	Contains an ISO TP4-compliant TSAP address, correctly packed and aligned.
TDI_ADDRESS_VNS	Contains a Banyan VINES IP address, correctly packed and aligned.
TDI_CONNECTION_INFO	Defines the structure of the information returned for a TDI_QUERY_ INFORMATION request in which the IrpSp-->Parameters.QueryType is set to TDI_QUERY_CONNECTION_INFO.
TDI_CONNECTION_INFORMATION	Defines the structure of information that a kernel-mode client passes to or receives from the underlying transport for a subset of the TDI_Xxx internal device control requests, particularly those relevant to endpoint-to-endpoint connections.
TDI_DATAGRAM_INFO	Defines the structure of the information returned for a TDI_QUERY_ INFORMATION request in which the IrpSp-->Parameters.QueryType is set to TDI_QUERY_DATAGRAM_INFO.
TDI_MAX_DATAGRAM_INFO	Defines the structure of the information returned for a TDI_QUERY_ INFORMATION request in which the IrpSp-->Parameters.QueryType is set to TDI_QUERY_MAX_DATAGRAM_INFO.
TDI_PNP_CONTEXT	Defines the structure of buffered information passed to transport clients that register themselves with TdiRegisterPnPHandlers to receive notifications of PnP (binding) and power-state changes, as well as dynamic notifications of network address additions and deletions. The information passed in this structure is both context-dependent, as indicated by the ContextType value, and protocol-dependent.
TDI_PROVIDER_INFO	Defines the structure of the information returned for a TDI_QUERY_ INFORMATION request in which the IrpSp-->Parameters.QueryType is set to TDI_QUERY_PROVIDER_INFO or TDI_QUERY_PROVIDER_ INFORMATION.
TDI_PROVIDER_STATISTICS	Defines the structure of the information returned for a TDI_QUERY_ INFORMATION request in which the IrpSp-->Parameters.QueryType is set to TDI_QUERY_PROVIDER_STATISTICS.
TDI_REQUEST	Contains information common to most TDI requests. Transport drivers can use this structure to pass request-specific information between internal driver routines.

(continued)

Table 17.8 **TDI structures** (continued).

Structure	Description
TDI_REQUEST_KERNEL	Defines a parameter format common to certain kernel-mode TDI_*Xxx* IOCTL requests.
TDI_REQUEST_STATUS	Contains status information that a TDI driver function sets when it completes its operation. Transport drivers can use this structure to pass request-specific information between internal driver routines.
TRANSPORT_ADDRESS	Defines the general format for an array of TDI driver-specific transport addresses.

TDI Operations

Many TDI runtime operations involve an endpoint-to-endpoint connection between a local-node client and a remote-node client. These TDI operations are *connection-oriented* and include the following:

- Opening a transport address
- Opening a local-node connection endpoint
- Requesting a connection
- Accepting a connection
- Sending connection-oriented data
- Receiving connection-oriented data
- Disconnecting
- Closing a local-node connection endpoint
- Closing a transport address

TDI also permits *connectionless* communications between network nodes. This type of operation doesn't require that the local-node client establish an endpoint-to-endpoint connection with a remote-node client. Connectionless operations are faster but less reliable than connection-oriented communications. TDI connectionless operations include the following:

- Sending a datagram
- Receiving a datagram

The remaining TDI operations are common to both connection-oriented and connectionless communication and include the following:

- Packaging and submitting an IOCTL request
- Setting and querying information

17. The Transport Driver Interface

- Receiving error notification
- Requesting transport-specific actions if the underlying transport supports extensions to the TDI interface for its clients

---

NOTE: *The descriptions of TDI operations given in this chapter are summaries. They don't, for example, describe the various error procedures that occur when the operations go wrong. For comprehensive descriptions, refer to the DDK documentation.*

Opening a Transport Address

A TDI client typically initiates communication with its local-node transport by opening a file object that represents a transport address, as follows:

1. The client calls ZwCreateFile, passing the address specification in the EA buffer.

2. The I/O Manager creates a client-process-specific file object to represent the address.

3. The file object calls the TDI transport driver TdiDispatchCreate routine with an IRP containing the parameters that the client supplied to ZwCreateFile.

4. TdiDispatchCreate parses the EA information, and the transport sets up internal state for the open address and returns a file handle to the client.

5. The client obtains a pointer to the file object by calling ObReferenceObjectByHandle, and makes TDI_*XXX* IOCTL requests to its underlying transport. The client must decide whether to register one or more of its ClientEvent*Xxx* handlers and whether it will use the open address to communicate with a remote-node peer process, in which case the client also must open a connection endpoint.

6. If the client wants to receive notifications of various network events, it registers its ClientEvent*Xxx* handler for each type of event by submitting one or more TDI_SET_EVENT_HANDLER requests to the underlying transport.

7. The client either opens a connection endpoint, as described below, or begins connectionless communication, as described later in this chapter.

Opening a Connection Endpoint

A connection endpoint is opened as follows:

1. The client passes a client-supplied context for the connection in the EA buffer parameter to ZwCreateFile.

2. The I/O Manager to creates a client-process-specific file object to represent the connection endpoint.

3. The file object calls the TDI transport driver TdiDispatchCreate routine with an IRP containing the parameters that the client supplied to ZwCreateFile.

4. TdiDispatchCreate parses the EA information, and the transport sets up internal state for the open connection endpoint and returns a file handle to the client.

5. The client obtains a pointer to the file object by calling ObReferenceObject-ByHandle, and makes TDI_*XXX* IOCTL requests to its underlying transport to establish an endpoint-to-endpoint connection with a remote-node peer.

Requesting a Connection

A local-node client requests a connection to a remote-node peer process as follows:

1. The client submits a TDI_CONNECT request, set up with TdiBuildConnect, to its underlying transport.

2. The transport determines the client-specified target remote-node address from its client's connect request and transmits the connection offer to the corresponding remote-node transport.

3. The remote-node transport notifies its client of the incoming connection offer, either by satisfying a TDI_LISTEN request previously submitted by its client or by calling the previously registered ClientEventConnect handler.

4. The remote-node client accepts or rejects the offered connection if both transports support *delayed-connection acceptance*, as described below.

Accepting or Rejecting a Connection

A local-node client can listen passively for connection requests from remote-node peers by submitting a TDI_LISTEN request, set up with TdiBuildListen, to its underlying transport. However, in Windows 2000 TDI, the local-node client typically uses event handling to communicate with the underlying TDI transport driver. In this case, the procedure for accepting (or rejecting) a connection is as follows:

1. The transport receives a connection offer from a remote-node client that's directed to the open transport address of the local-node client.

2. The transport calls the local-node client's registered ClientEventConnect handler with the transport address of the offering client and any connect data that the transport received with the connection offer.

3. The ClientEventConnect handler accepts or rejects the connection.

Sending Connection-Oriented Data

When an endpoint-to-endpoint connection has been accepted, data is sent across it as follows:

1. The local-node client issues a send request by submitting a TDI_SEND IOCTL request to its transport. This IRP, which the client sets up with TdiBuildSend, contains a pointer to a client-supplied buffer containing a stream-oriented or message-oriented TSDU.

2. The client's call to IoCallDriver with the TDI_SEND IRP forwards the IRP to the underlying transport's TdiDispatchInternalDeviceControl routine.

3. The transport either queues the client-supplied data in its internal buffers or sends the specified data through the network.

Receiving Connection-Oriented Data

A local-node client receives a TSDU on a connection as follows:

1. The client makes a TDI_RECEIVE request to the underlying transport. This IRP, which the client sets up with TdiBuildReceive, contains a pointer to a client-supplied buffer into which the transport copies all or part of the TSDU data it received from the client's remote-node peer.

2. The client's call to IoCallDriver with the TDI_RECEIVE IRP forwards the IRP to the underlying transport's TdiDispatchInternalDeviceControl routine, which transfers received data into the client-supplied buffer until the buffer is full or until the received TSDU data is exhausted.

NOTE: *Connection-oriented data can be flagged as expedited. Expedited data will always be sent before normal data.*

Disconnecting

Disconnection behavior is transport-specific. When a connection-oriented TDI client initiates a disconnect between nodes, both nodes typically participate in the disconnection operation. In this case, the operation is as follows:

1. One client on an endpoint-to-endpoint connection initiates a disconnection operation by submitting a TDI_DISCONNECT request, set up with TdiBuildDisconnect, to its underlying transport.

2. The transport notifies the remote-node transport driver that a disconnection is in progress.

3. If the responding remote-node client registered its ClientEventDisconnect handler, the TDI transport driver notifies the client when the disconnect occurs by calling this handler.

4. The ClientEventDisconnect handler acknowledges the disconnection by making a TDI_DISCONNECT request to its underlying transport. This notification allows the responding client to clear the endpoint-to-endpoint connection promptly.

NOTE: *A disconnection operation doesn't close either client's open connection endpoints or transport addresses. After TDI_DISCONNECT requests have been satisfied, both clients can reuse the file objects representing these open resources in their underlying transports. Until each client closes the file objects representing its respective connection endpoint and the associated transport address, these resources remain allocated to the client and available for client-submitted IOCTL requests to the underlying transport.*

Closing a Local-Node Connection Endpoint

After an endpoint-to-endpoint connection has been disconnected, a client closes the connection as follows:

1. The client passes the file object pointer that was returned by ObReference-ObjectByHandle to ObDereferenceObject.

2. The client passes the file handle that was returned by ZwCreateFile when the connection endpoint was opened to ZwClose.

3. The I/O Manager submits IRPs to the transport's TdiDispatchCleanup and TdiDispatchClose routines. These routines close the connection endpoint and free all associated transport driver resources.

Closing an Open Transport Address

When a client no longer has any use for an open transport address, it closes the address as follows:

1. The client passes the file object pointer returned by ObReferenceObject-ByHandle to ObDereferenceObject.

2. The client passes the file handle that was returned by ZwCreateFile when the connection endpoint was opened to ZwClose.

3. The I/O Manager submits IRPs to the transport's TdiDispatchCleanup and TdiDispatchClose routines, which close the transport address and free all associated client-specific transport driver resources.

Sending and Receiving a Datagram

A client can engage in connectionless communication by sending data over the network as soon as it has successfully opened a transport address in the underlying TDI transport. To receive connectionless data, the client must register its ClientEventReceiveDatagram and (possibly) ClientEventChainedReceive-Datagram handlers with the underlying transport or issue an explicit

TDI_RECEIVE_DATAGRAM request to the underlying transport. Sending and receiving datagrams is very similar to sending and receiving data over an endpoint-to-endpoint connection, except for the following:

- The sending client submits a TDI_SEND_DATAGRAM request to its underlying transport on an open transport address, instead of a send request on an established endpoint-to-endpoint connection.

- The receiving client submits a TDI_RECEIVE_DATAGRAM request to its underlying transport on its open transport address, instead of a receive request on an established endpoint-to-endpoint connection.

Packaging and Submitting an IOCTL Request

A client prepares its own IOCTL IRPs for communication with the underlying transport driver by using one of the TdiBuild*Xxx* macros summarized earlier in this chapter. When the IRP has been packaged using the macro, it's submitted as follows:

1. The client calls IoCallDriver to submit its IOCTL request to its underlying transport.

2. The transport's TdiDispatchInternalDeviceControl routine receives the client-supplied IRP from IoCallDriver, completes the requested operation, sets the I/O status block in the IRP with the results of the operation, and calls either TdiCompleteRequest or IoCompleteRequest with the IRP when the client's request has been satisfied.

Setting and Querying Information

A client can query information held in its underlying transport, and, if appropriate, set information parameters as follows:

- To query information, the client submits a TDI_QUERY_INFORMATION request, set up with TdiBuildQueryInformation, to the underlying transport, passing pointers to the file object that represents the address or connection endpoint and to a client-supplied buffer in which the transport returns the requested information.

- To set information, the client submits a TDI_SET_INFORMATION request, set up with TdiBuildSetInformation.

For each of these operations, the client also passes a system-defined TDI_QUERY_*XXX* value as the QType or SType parameter to the TdiBuild*Xxx*-Information macros to specify the information to be queried and set.

Receiving Error Notification

To receive a notification of unexpected error conditions in an underlying driver or in the underlying physical medium, the client registers its ClientEventError or ClientEventErrorEx handler with its underlying transport. If the transport, or any lower-level driver that the transport depends on to carry out client communications over the network, encounters an error condition, it calls the handler. This call notifies the client that network I/O on the client's open transport address is no longer reliable (or possible). The client then notifies its own higher-level clients of the network failure and cleans up all TDI-client-allocated resources for pending operations on the affected open transport address.

Requesting Transport-Specific Actions

A TDI client can send special or proprietary extension requests to a TDI transport driver that defines a set of transport-specific action codes for these operations. These extensions apply only to the calling client and not to any other TDI transport clients or drivers. To request a transport-defined operation over an open address, connection endpoint, or control channel, the client uses TdiBuildAction to set up a TDI_ACTION request. A client-supplied buffer contains the transport-defined action code and corresponding action parameter block for the requested operation.

17. The Transport
Driver Interface

Immediate Solutions

The immediate solutions presented in this chapter are almost identical to those in Chapter 2. As with the NDIS5 abstraction layer, the TDI layer lets you adjust bindings and binding order. The difference is that the bindings are between the upper edges of the transports (or protocols) and services.

If you already downloaded the DDK in Chapter 2, you don't have to do so again. The procedure is repeated here for convenience. The tools to build and debug transport drivers that are provided in the DDK are the same tools as those described in Chapter 2 for building and debugging miniport drivers.

Installing Network Protocols

The Windows 2000 default installation installs TCP/IP as the connection protocol. If you want to use other protocols and optimize the binding order, you must first install those protocols.

To install additional network protocols:

1. Log on as an administrator.
2. Access Start|Settings and double-click Network and Dial-up Connections.
3. Right-click the connection to which you want to add a protocol, then select Properties.
4. Click Install.
5. Select Protocol, then click Add.
6. Select the protocol you want to install. If prompted, insert the Windows 2000 CD-ROM or specify a path to the installation files.
7. Depending on the protocol you've installed, you may be prompted to reboot the computer. If you want to install additional protocols, click No at this stage and repeat the procedure. After you've installed all the protocols you need, reboot the machine.

17. The Transport
Driver Interface

Related solution:	*See page:*
Installing Network Protocols	61

WARNING!   A newly installed protocol will be placed at the top of the bindings list. This is not usually what is wanted, so always check and reconfigure your binding order after installing a network protocol.

Configuring Bindings

Bindings between protocols and services can be enabled or disabled, and the binding order can be changed. If, for example, most of the traffic on your subnet is local, with very few packets being sent to the router for onward transmission, you may want NetBEUI to be used as a first-choice protocol on both your workstations and servers, rather than TCP/IP. If most of the clients on your subnet are NetWare hosts running the Internetwork Packet Exchange/Sequenced Packet Exchange (IPX/SPX) protocol, then you may want to move NWLink up the binding order on your servers.

WARNING!   Changing the binding order, particularly on workstations, can improve performance dramatically. Selecting the incorrect binding order can, therefore, cause an equally dramatic performance drop. Take care when reconfiguring bindings; always carry out a traffic analysis first, using Network Monitor.

To configure bindings, proceed as follows:

1. Log on as an administrator.
2. Access Start|Settings and double-click Network and Dial-up Connections.
3. Select the connection you want to configure.
4. On the Advanced pull-down menu, select Advanced Settings.
5. Select a protocol bound to a service and use the up or down arrow to change its binding order. Unchecking the checkbox to the left of the protocol will disable the binding. Figure 17.2 shows the Advanced Settings dialog box.
6. Click OK. Close Network and Dial-up Connections.

Related solution:	*See page:*
Configuring Bindings	61

17. The Transport Driver Interface

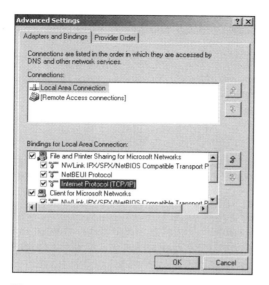

Figure 17.2   Configuring bindings.

Using the Windows 2000 Driver Development Kit

The amount of user configuration of TDI settings possible through administrative tools is limited. The remainder of this chapter is therefore of interest only if you currently write or intend to write transport drivers; it covers the installation of the DDK, using predefined macros to build drivers, using the driver verifier tool, and using debugging tools, such as breakpoints.

The purpose of the procedures in this section is to outline the tools and facilities available in the DDK and discuss the methodology provided to generate driver source code. It is neither practical nor desirable to attempt in-depth treatment of these topics here. Detailed documentation can be downloaded with the DDK, in addition to sample code.

TIP: *Unless you're already an experienced C++ programmer and have driver development experience, the best way to start is with the sample programs supplied with the DDK. Study the way these programs are built, use the driver verifier tool, and implement breakpoints.*

Installing the Driver Development Kit

To develop and debug transport drivers, you'll need at least two machines: one as the driver-development PC and the second as a driver-testing machine. Your driver-testing machine should have a Windows 2000 OS installed and should have at least 128MB RAM. (Although Microsoft claims that you can use a 64MB PC, I really wouldn't recommend it.)

The driver-development PC requires the following:

- Windows 2000.

TIP: *It's possible to develop Windows 2000 drivers on a Windows NT4 or Windows 98 machine and test them on a Windows 2000 system. This is not, however, a wholly satisfactory development strategy. In some circumstances, such as when you're carrying out kernel debugging on a driver that's under development, two Windows 2000 machines are necessary.*

- Microsoft Visual C++ 5 or later (preferably later). You'll need the Professional or Enterprise edition. The Academic and Standard editions are not supported.
- The latest Visual C++ service pack for the version you're using.
- A CD-ROM drive or Internet access.
- At least 128MB of RAM. Again, Microsoft specifies a 64MB minimum. My development PC has 256MB and sometimes struggles.
- 1GB free hard disk space. You can install the DDK on 200MB, but you'll need 750MB if you intend to compile all the samples. Then, of course, you'll need some space for your own routines.

TIP: *Ensure that all the devices on both PCs are fully compatible with Windows 2000. Check your PC specification against the hardware compatibility list, available at **www.microsoft.com/hcl**.*

You require administrator rights for the installation. You also need a clean PC that doesn't already have a previous version of the DDK installed (if so, uninstall it).

> ***WARNING!** **Do not install the Windows 2000 DDK over previous Windows 2000 DDKs or over DDKs for other OSs.***

To install the Windows 2000 DDK:

1. If you have the CD-ROM from the Microsoft Developers Network (MSDN&trade), run setup.exe from the CD-ROM. Otherwise, access the Microsoft Driver Development Kit Web site at **www.microsoft.com/ddk** and download and run X86DDK.exe (for x86 systems). The file is 42MB and takes some time to download.
2. Click Next.
3. Read and accept the license conditions.

17. The Transport Driver Interface

Resources for Developers

MSDN&trade, the Microsoft Developers Network, is accessed at **http://msdn.microsoft.com**. It provides tools and information to assist software development. This information includes downloads for service packs or patches for Microsoft development tools; platform SDK releases; access to user groups, chats, and event information; and the MSDN online library.

The Microsoft Driver Development Kit Web site at **www.microsoft.com/ddk** provides resources for driver development, including the latest version of the Windows 2000 DDK for download, the latest DDK documentation, news about DDK developments, a feedback form, a Frequently Asked Questions (FAQ) page, and extended release notes.

4. Choose the components you want to install. Unless you're an experienced driver programmer, I recommend that you install all of them.

5. Decide whether you want a free build or debugging environment. Initially, you will almost certainly require the latter. The environments are as follows:

   • *Free build*—The end-user version of the operating system. The system and drivers are built with full optimization, and debugging is disabled. A free build system or driver is smaller, faster, and uses less memory than the equivalent checked build implementation. Free build is sometimes known as *retail build*.

   • *Checked build*—Used when testing and debugging drivers. Checked build contains error checking, argument verification, and debugging information that's not available in free build. A checked system or driver can help isolate and track down problems that can cause unpredictable behavior, memory leaks, or improper device configuration. Checked build consumes more memory and disk space than free build, and system and driver performance is slower.

6. From Programs|Development Kits|Windows 2000 DDK, select either a free or checked console window.

7. From the console command prompt, run setenv.bat. Note that this will close all Windows programs. Also, the batch file won't run unless Visual C++ is installed.

8. From the Command Console prompt, enter **build -cZ**. This compiles and links all drivers in the source tree of the current directory. Note that any directory in which you run **build -cZ** must contain a file called *sources*. If this file doesn't exist in the directory, then the directory doesn't contain any driver source files.

TIP: *You can verify your installation by running **build -cZ** from the \destination\src subdirectory. This builds a complete set of installed drivers. The process can take about 30 minutes.*

Building Drivers

The DDK provides a set of macros that are recognized by the build utility. These are split into sources file macros, which specify the components for a build product or products; and dirs file macros, which enable the build utility to create an entire source tree from several sources files in directories that are subdirectories of the dirs file subdirectory. In addition, a set of build environment variables is provided. Sample code is available from the DDK.

The format for macro definitions is:

```
MACRONAME=value
```

where *value* is a text string. For example:

```
TARGETNAME=mylibrary
```

To specify the components for a build product:

1. Create a directory tree. Source directories should be subdirectories of a source code tree, the root of which will contain the dirs file.

2. In each source directory, create a file called sources. A text editor can be used to create this file, and the file shouldn't have a file type extension.

3. Place your source code in the sources file. The macros available are shown in Table 17.9.

4. Reference environmental variables as required using the syntax $(*VariableName*). The available environmental variables are shown in Table 17.10.

5. Create a dirs file in the root directory of the source code tree. Like the sources file, this file can be created using a text editor and shouldn't have a file type extension. The macros shown in Table 17.11 can be defined in the dirs file.

6. Run the build utility. If, for example, directory1 and directory2 were specified in the OPTIONAL_DIRS macro, then the command is **build -cZ directory1 directory2**.

Table 17.9   *Macros used in the sources file.*

Macro	Function
TARGETNAME	Specifies the name of the library being built.
TARGETPATH	Specifies the name of the destination directory for all build products (EXE, DLL, LIB files, and so on). Build creates platform-specific subdirectories under this directory. Note that build always creates an \obj subdirectory (\objfre or \onbjchk) under the directory that contains the sources file.

(continued)

Table 17.9   Macros used in the sources file (continued).

Macro	Function
TARGETPATHLIB	Specifies a file path and destination directory for import libraries created by the build operation. If the file path isn't specified, import libraries are placed in the same subdirectory as other build product files.
TARGETTYPE	Specifies the type of product being built. This is typically LIBRARY or DYNLINK (for DLLs).
TARGETEXT	Specifies the file name extension for DLLs (for example, CPL). The default file name extension for DLLs is DLL.
TARGETLIBS	Specifies the set of import libraries with which your driver must be linked.
INCLUDES	Contains a list of paths to be searched for header files during compilation. Build also searches for header files in a default list of directories. The paths specified by INCLUDES are searched before the default paths.
SOURCES	Contains a list of source file names with extensions. These files must reside in the directory in which the sources file resides. Source files that contain a main function are listed using UMAPPL or UMTEST rather than SOURCES.
UMTYPE	Specifies the type of product being built. The choices are Win32 (user mode), kernel mode, and Win32 console.
UMAPPL	Contains a list of source files that contain a main function. If you use UMAPPL, build will automatically create executable files.
UMTEST	Contains a list of source files that contain a main function. If you use UMTEST, you must identify the files you want built by listing them in the build command line.
UMAPPLEXT	Specifies the file name extension for executable files (for example, COM). The default file name extension for executable files is EXE.
UMLIBS	Contains a list of path names of libraries to be linked to the files specified by UMTEST or UMAPPL. The library specified by SOURCES should be included here. The path names must be absolute.
NTPROFILEINPUT	Enables you to use a file that lists the order in which the linker should access functions. This file should be in the same directory as the sources file and should be named *TargetName*.prf, where *TargetName* is the file name specified by the TARGETNAME macro. NTPROFILEINPUT is set to one (binary) if the PRF file is to be used.
DLLORDER	Enables you to specify a file that lists the order in which the linker should access functions. The macro must be set to the name of the file that contains the order list. You can use this macro instead of NTPROFILEINPUT.
386_WARNING_LEVEL	Specifies the compiler warning level.

Table 17.10   Environmental variables.

Environmental Variable	Function
BASEDIR	Contains the base of the build product's source tree (i.e., the directory that contains the dirs file).
BUILD_ALT_DIR	Appends specified characters to the \obj subdirectory name. The free and checked build environments use this variable to create the \objfre and \objchk subdirectories.
BUILD_DEFAULT	Contains a list of default parameters to pass to the build utility.
BUILD_DEFAULT_TARGETS	Contains a list of default target switches.
BUILD_MAKE_PROGRAM	Contains the name of the make utility used by build. This variable must take the value "nmake.exe".
CRT_INC_PATH	Contains the path to a directory that contains Windows 2000 header files.
CRT_LIB_PATH	Contains the path to a directory that contains Microsoft-supplied C import libraries.
DDK_INC_PATH	Contains the path to a directory that contains DDK-specific, Microsoft-supplied header files.
DDK_LIB_PATH	Contains the path to a directory that contains DDK-specific, Microsoft-supplied C import libraries.
DDK_LIB_DEST	Contains the path to the destination directory for a DDK-specific import library that's a build product.
OAK_INC_PATH	Contains the path to a directory that contains Microsoft-supplied header files.
SDK_LIB_DEST	Contains the path to the destination directory for an import library that's a build product.
SDK_LIB_PATH	Contains the path to a directory that contains Microsoft-supplied C import libraries.
WDM_INC_PATH	Contains the path to a directory that contains Microsoft-supplied, WDM-specific header files.
C_DEFINES	Defines switches that are passed to compilers.
O	Identifies the subdirectory into which build product files will be placed.
NTDEBUG	Set to "ntsd" in the checked environment. This causes the compiler to create symbolic debugging information.
BUILD_OPTIONS	Can be initialized by the user. This variable contains a list of optional subdirectories that should be scanned during a build operation. These are the subdirectories identified by the OPTIONAL_DIRS macro in the dirs file.

Table 17.11   Macros used in the dirs file.

Macro	Description
DIRS	Contains a list of subdirectories to be built by default.
OPTIONAL_DIRS	Contains a list of subdirectories to be built only if specified in the build command.

Verifying Drivers

The driver verifier will check that a driver unloads properly and releases any memory it has used (i.e., it's not "leaky"). It will check memory overruns, reveal paging violations, test the driver's response to a low-memory condition, and monitor I/O handling. The verifier.exe utility can be used from the command line using command-line switches, but it's more convenient to use the Driver Verifier Manager Graphical User Interface (GUI) provided.

To use the Driver Verifier Manager to verify a driver, proceed as follows:

1. Start the Driver Verifier Manager from the Start|Programs|Development Kits|Windows 2000 DDK menu or run verifier.exe from a command line with no switches specified. The verifier.exe file is located in the Ntddk\tools subdirectory.

NOTE: *This file won't run, nor will the Driver Verifier Manager appear on the appropriate menu, unless the DDK has been fully installed and the build environment set up (refer to the previous procedure).*

---

2. The Driver Status tab appears by default. This lists the drivers that are loaded and are being verified and indicates which driver verifier options are active. The Global flags section shows which driver verifier options are enabled. The Verified drivers section lists all drivers that driver verifier has been instructed to verify and their current verification status. Refresh frequency for this screen can be set using the radio buttons. Selecting Manual disables automatic updates. The Refresh Now button causes the Status column to be refreshed immediately. Figure 17.3 shows the Driver Status tab.

3. Select the Global Counters tab. This screen displays statistics that monitor the driver verifier's actions. The Allocations counters monitor memory pool use by standard kernel-mode drivers. Figure 17.4 shows the Global Counters tab.

4. Select the Pool Tracking tab. This screen displays information on paged and nonpaged memory pool allocations. The Individual counters section displays statistics for one driver at a time, specified in the drop-down box at the top of this section. In the Global counter section, the Not tracked allocations

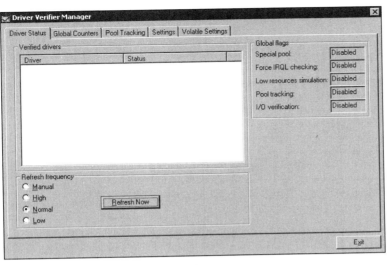

Figure 17.3   Driver status verification.

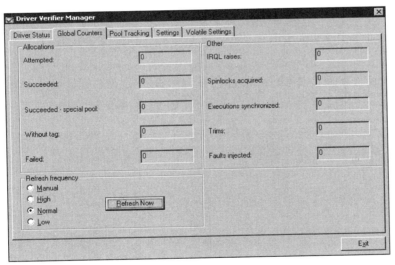

Figure 17.4   Global counters used by the driver verifier.

counter displays the number of untracked allocations from all the drivers currently being verified. Figure 17.5 shows the Pool Tracking tab.

5. Select the Settings tab. This screen enables you to select the drivers to be verified. You can set the verification type and the level of I/O verification. Right-clicking on a driver lets you control verification from a pop-up menu. The Verify these additional drivers after next reboot text box lets you enter the names of drivers not currently loaded on the system. If Verify all drivers

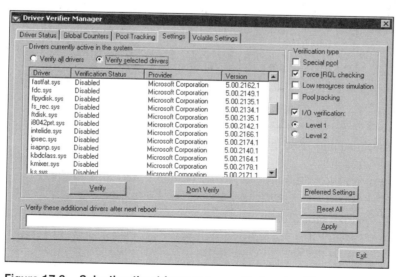

Figure 17.5 Tracking memory pool allocation.

is selected, the driver verifier will verify all drivers after reboot. When this radio button is selected, the list of drivers and the Verify and Don't Verify buttons are grayed out. The Preferred Settings button is a quick way to turn on the most commonly used options. When settings are made using this screen, click Apply, exit from the Driver Verifier Manager, and reboot the computer. The changed settings won't take effect until after a reboot. Figure 17.6 shows the Settings tab.

Figure 17.6 Selecting the drivers to be verified and setting the verification type and level.

6. Select the Volatile Settings tab. This screen enables you to make alterations to the driver verifier settings immediately (rather than after a reboot). Special memory pool, Force IRQL checking, and Low resources simulation can be enabled or disabled for all the drivers being verified. The new settings take effect immediately when the Apply button is clicked. Figure 17.7 shows the Volatile Settings tab.

7. Make the changes you require on all the screens described and close the Driver Verifier Manager. Reboot if necessary.

Debugging Drivers

Newly written drivers (or any other type of program) seldom work the first time. The Windows 2000 DDK provides extensive debugging facilities, including such routines as OutputDebugString and DebugBreak for user-mode drivers and DbgPrint, KdPrint, DbgBreakPoint, DgbBreakPointWithStatus, KdBreakPoint, KdBreakPointWithStatus, ASSERT, and ASSERTMSG for kernel-mode drivers. These routines can be inserted into source code for debugging purposes. Syntax details and samples are available from the DDK.

There is, however, a more user-friendly tool available—the Windows Debugger (WinDbg). This procedure looks at the facilities available from this GUI. To access and use the Windows debugger, proceed as follows:

1. Access Start|Programs|Development Kits|Windows 2000 DDK|Debugging Tools and select WinDbg. The Windows Debugger GUI appears, as shown in Figure 17.8.

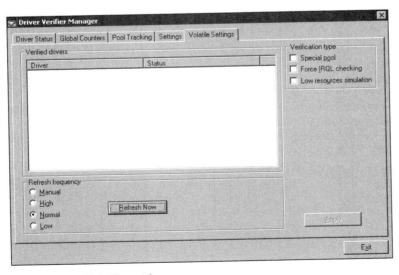

Figure 17.7   Volatile settings.

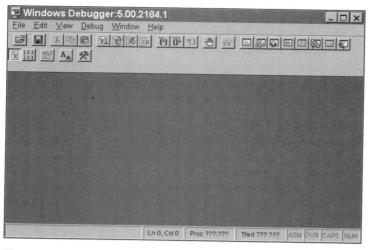

Figure 17.8   The Windows Debugger.

2. The File menu enables you to open a source file, an executable file, or a crash dump. You can also manage your workspace from this menu.

3. In the Edit menu, select Breakpoints. The Breakpoint drop-down box lists the breakpoint options available, as shown in Figure 17.9. Make the selection you require, then click OK.

4. In the View menu, you have a choice of view items, such as registers, memory, and call stack. Figure 17.10 shows the memory view options available.

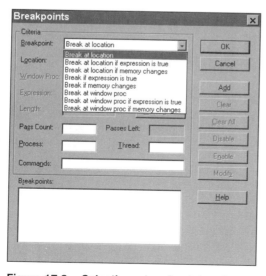

Figure 17.9   Selecting a breakpoint option.

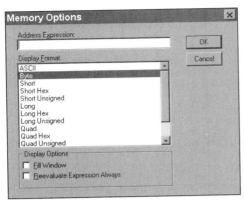

Figure 17.10 The memory view display format options.

5. In the Debug menu, you can start or stop debugging, step into a routine or step over a breakpoint, enable or disable source mode (disabling source mode starts the disassembler), and set exceptions, as shown in Figure 17.11.

6. The tool also has a number of buttons that provide shortcuts to menu items. The Options button, for example, provides the same functionality as View|Options. Explore all the tabs on this dialog box. Figure 17.12 (for example) shows the Debugger tab.

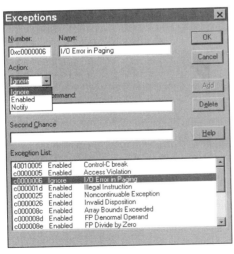

Figure 17.11 Setting exceptions.

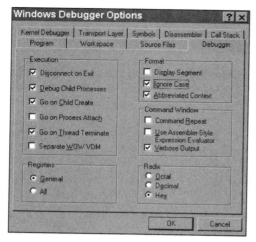

Figure 17.12   The Windows Debugger Options dialog box.

Related solution:	See page:
Using the Windows 2000 Driver Development Kit	64

As stated previously, the purpose of describing the DDK-related procedures in this chapter is to explore the facilities available for generating, verifying, and debugging driver programs. A full treatment of how to write C++ source code and use all the DDK facilities would take a book at least as big as this one. Fortunately, extensive documentation is available with the DDK (if you choose to download it), as are sample programs.

Chapter 18

Network Application Interfaces

In Depth

Network applications can communicate with the Windows 2000 TCP/IP protocol stack in a number of ways. Some work through the network redirector, which is part of the Workstation service. Others are written to the application interfaces provided by the Windows 2000 operating system (OS). Two application interfaces are used for this purpose, the Network Basic Input/Output System (NetBIOS) interface and the Windows Sockets version 2 (Winsock2) interface.

The NetBIOS interface is supported by NetBIOS over TCP/IP (NetBT). Some older applications use this interface, and therefore it's still supported. The current Windows 2000 network application interface of choice is Winsock2. This chapter looks briefly at the NetBIOS interface, then describes the Winsock2 interface in rather more detail. The Windows platform software development kit (SDK) contains the Winsock2 functions for use by application developers.

The Windows 2000 Driver Development Kit (DDK) contains a Dynamic Link Library (DLL) that provides user-mode Windows Sockets Helper (WSH) DLL files, and these are also described. As with Chapter 17, this chapter is mainly of interest to programmers rather than nonprogramming administrators.

The NetBIOS Interface

We looked at NetBIOS in Chapter 15 and saw that it isn't a protocol, but rather a system that specifies a software interface and a naming convention. Sytec Inc. (currently Hughes LAN Systems) developed the NetBIOS interface for IBM in 1983. NetBIOS was designed to use 16-character (or byte) NetBIOS names in a flat namespace, which means that names can be used only once within a network. The system wasn't designed to scale to large networks.

Figure 18.1 illustrates the NetBIOS interface. Windows 2000 supports NetBIOS in two ways:

- By default, all Windows 2000 computers that use TCP/IP provide client-side support for registering and resolving NetBIOS names. This support is provided through NetBIOS over TCP/IP (NetBT).

- Windows 2000 Server provides server-side support through the Windows Internet Name Service (WINS).

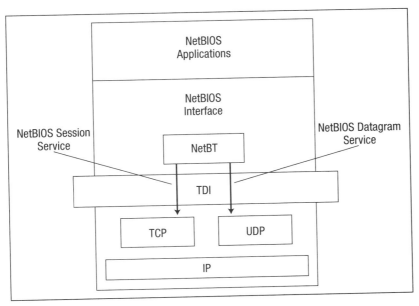

Figure 18.1   The NetBIOS interface.

NetBIOS Names

NetBIOS names are registered dynamically when computers boot up, when services start, or when users log on. NetBIOS names can be *unique names* (one address mapped with a name) or *group names* (more than one address mapped to a name).

The first 15 characters of each name are user-specified; the 16th character is used as a name suffix to identify the name and to indicate the resource that the name is registering on the network. If a user specifies fewer than 15 characters in a NetBIOS name, the "+" character is used as a filler. Unique names are used to send network communications to a specific process on a computer. Group names are used to send information simultaneously to multiple computers.

Tables 18.1 and 18.2 list unique and group NetBIOS names, respectively.

NetBIOS name resolution and the various resolution methods (WINS, lmhosts, and so on) and resolution modes are a function of the TCP/IP stack and its related services rather than the NetBIOS network application interface. Name resolution is described in depth in Chapter 15. The NetBIOS name service uses UDP port 137.

Table 18.1   Unique NetBIOS names

Unique Name	Service
computername [00h]	Workstation service
computername [03h]	Messenger service
computername [06h]	Remote Access Service (RAS) server service
computername [1Fh]	Network Dynamic Data Exchange (NetDDE) service
computername [20h]	Server service
computername [21h]	RAS client service
computername [BEh]	Network Monitor agent
computername [BFh]	Network Monitor application
username [03]	Messenger service (names of logged-on users)
domainname [1Bh]	Domain master browser

Table 18.2   Group NetBIOS names

Group Name	Service
domainname [00h]	Domain name
domainname [1Ch]	Domain controllers (up to 25)
domainname [1Dh]	Master browser (one per subnet)
domainname [1Eh]	Browser Service Elections
__MSBROWSE__ [01h]	Registered by the master browser for each subnet

NetBT

NetBT, specified in RFCs 1001 and 1002, implements the NetBIOS programming interface over the TCP/IP protocol, extending the reach of NetBIOS client and server programs to Wide Area Networks (WANs) and providing interoperability with other operating systems. Windows 2000 includes a NetBIOS emulator that takes standard NetBIOS requests from NetBIOS applications and translates them to equivalent Transport Driver Interface (TDI) primitives (see Chapter 17).

Windows 2000 uses NetBT to communicate with legacy systems, such as Windows NT4 and Windows 9x. However, Windows 2000 redirector and server components now support *direct hosting* to communicate with other computers running Windows 2000. Direct hosting uses TCP port 445, instead of the NetBIOS TCP port 139.

NetBT in Multihomed Computers

NetBT binds to only one IP address per Network Interface Card (NIC), and a computer is multihomed to NetBT only if it has more than one NIC installed. When a name registration packet is sent from such a computer, it's flagged as a multihomed name registration so it doesn't conflict with the same name registered by another interface in the same computer.

If a multihomed machine receives a broadcast name query, all NetBT interface bindings receiving the query respond with their addresses. By default, the client chooses the first response and connects to the address supplied by it. This behavior can be controlled by the *RandomAdapter* Registry parameter (see Appendix B). When a directed name query is sent to a WINS server, the WINS server responds with a list of all IP addresses that were registered with WINS by the multihomed computer.

Choosing the IP address to connect to on a multihomed computer is a client function. The selection is made using the following algorithm:

1. If one of the IP addresses in the name query response list is on the same logical subnet as the calling computer, that address is selected. If more than one of the addresses meets this criterion, one is picked at random.

2. If one of the IP addresses in the list is on the same classless network (see Chapter 5) as the calling computer, that address is selected. If more than one of the addresses meets this criterion, one is picked at random.

3. If one of the IP addresses in the list is on the same logical subnet as any NetBT binding on the calling computer, that address is selected. If more than one of the addresses meets this criterion, one is picked at random.

4. If none of the IP addresses in the list is on the same logical subnet as any NetBT binding on the calling computer, an address is selected at random from the list.

This algorithm balances connections to a server across multiple NICs, but favors direct connections. When a list of IP addresses is returned, they're sorted into the best order, and NetBT pings each of the addresses in the list until one responds. If no addresses respond, a connection attempt is made to the first address in the list anyway, because there may be a firewall or other device that filters Internet Control Message Protocol (ICMP) traffic.

The Service Message Block (SMB) Device

By default, Windows 2000 attempts to make connections using both NetBIOS and non-NetBIOS methods, so it can support connections to down-level computers. However, in Windows 2000 native environments you can disable NetBT (see Chapter 15) so that NetBIOS namespace isn't used at all.

The Windows 2000 interface that makes this possible is called the *SMB device*. It appears to the redirector and server as another interface. At the TCP/IP stack, however, the SMB device is bound to ADDR_ANY and uses the Domain Name System (DNS) namespace natively. Calls placed on the SMB device will result in a standard DNS lookup to resolve the name to an IP address, followed by a single outbound connection request (even on a multihomed computer) using the best source IP address and interface, as determined by the route table. There's no NetBIOS session set up on top of the TCP connection. By default, the redirector places calls on both the NetBIOS device(s) and the SMB device, and the file server receives calls on both. The file server SMB device listens on TCP port 445 instead of the traditional NetBIOS over TCP port 139.

Windows 2000 also offers two additional methods of connecting to a NetBT resource:

- Using the command **net use *ip_address**share_name***
- Using the command **net use *fully_qualified_domain_name**share_name***

It's also possible to use direct hosting (see earlier in this chapter) to establish redirector or server connections between Windows 2000 computers without using the NetBIOS namespace.

NetBIOS Session Service

The NetBIOS session service (sometimes known as NetBIOS over TCP) provides delivery of NetBIOS messages that's connection-oriented, reliable, and sequenced. When (for example) a Windows 2000 Professional client makes a file-sharing connection to a server using NetBIOS over TCP/IP, the following sequence of events takes place:

1. The server's NetBIOS name is resolved to an IP address.
2. The server's IP address is resolved to a Media Access Control (MAC) address.
3. A TCP connection is established from the workstation to the server, using TCP port 139.
4. The workstation sends a NetBIOS session request to the server name over the TCP connection. If the server is listening on that name, it responds and a session is established.

When the NetBIOS session has been established, the workstation and server negotiate which level of the SMB protocol to use. Microsoft networking uses only one NetBIOS session between two names at any one time. Additional file- or print-sharing connections are multiplexed over the same NetBIOS session.

NetBIOS *keep-alives* are used on each connection to verify that both the server and workstation are still able to maintain their session. If a workstation is shut down ungracefully, the server cleans up the connection and associated resources (and vice versa). NetBIOS keep-alives are controlled by the *SessionKeepAlive* Registry parameter, which defaults to once per hour (see Appendix B).

NetBIOS Datagram Service

Datagrams are sent from one NetBIOS name to another over UDP port 138. Datagrams can be sent to a unique name or to a group name. Group names resolve either to a list of IP addresses or to a broadcast. If the datagram is broadcast, all hosts on the subnet pick it up and process it. On hosts that are running the NetBIOS datagram service, UDP hands the datagram to NetBT on port 138. NetBT checks the destination name to see if any application has posted a datagram receive and, if so, passes the datagram up. If no receive is posted, the datagram is discarded.

If support for NetBT is disabled, the NetBIOS datagram service isn't available.

The Winsock Interface

Winsock is based on the Socket interface designed by the University of California at Berkeley. The original Winsock specification was the result of a collaboration of more than 20 vendors in the TCP/IP community. The project, led by Martin Hall of the JSB Corporation, was initiated at a "Birds of a Feather" session at the 1991 Interop conference. As a result of this project, version 1.1 of the specification was released in January 1993. Version 2 was published in May 1996. Windows 2000 supports version 2, commonly referred to as Winsock2, and provides a set of extensions that take advantage of the message-driven nature of Microsoft Windows.

Like NetBIOS, Winsock2 is an interface, *not* a protocol, and doesn't need to be used on both ends of a communications link. It provides a protocol-independent interface capable of supporting emerging networking capabilities, such as real-time multimedia communications.

There are many Winsock2 applications available, including several of the utilities that ship with Windows 2000, such as the File Transfer Protocol (FTP) client and server, the Dynamic Host Configuration Protocol (DHCP) client and server, Telnet client, and so on. Some higher-level programming interfaces, such as the Windows Internet Application Programming Interface (WinInet) that's used by Internet Explorer, also rely on Winsock2.

The Sockets Paradigm

The concept of communications sockets, or the sockets paradigm, was first introduced in the early 1980s and was used by Berkeley's BSD Unix. The paradigm was initially designed as a local Interprocess Communication (IPC) mechanism, but evolved into a network IPC mechanism for TCP/IP.

A socket defines a bidirectional endpoint for communication between processes and has three primary components:

- The interface to which it is bound (specified by an IP address).
- The port number or identity (ID) to which it will send, or from which it will receive, data.
- The type of socket, either stream or datagram (see below).

Typically, a server application listens on a well-known port over all installed network interfaces, and a client initiates communication on a specific interface from any available port. The type of the socket (stream or datagram) depends on the needs of the application.

The Winsock2 model provides service for both connection-oriented and connectionless protocols. In TCP/IP, TCP stream sockets provide connection-oriented service, and UDP datagram sockets provide connectionless service.

NOTE: *The term "stream socket" is historical. It refers to the AT&T Streams environment. Microsoft Windows implements a native TDI implementation of this functionality, because Streams imposes a performance overhead on all transactions. The term is retained in the socket name.*

Blocking Functions

A blocking function is one that doesn't return control until the associated operation has completed. Problems can arise when the operation takes a long time to complete. The default behavior in the Berkeley sockets model is for a socket to operate in blocking mode unless the programmer explicitly requests that operations be treated as nonblocking. Winsock1.1 environments couldn't assume preemptive scheduling, in which a thread that wants access to a Central Processing Unit (CPU) can take control from the thread currently accessing that CPU. Therefore, programmers were strongly recommended to use nonblocking (asynchronous) operations. Because this was not always possible, the pseudo-blocking facilities were provided.

In pseudo-blocking, the service provider initiates the operation, then enters a loop in which it checks for the completion of the Winsock function. If the function has completed, or if WSACancelBlockingCall has been invoked, the blocking function completes. In this situation, a service provider must allow installation of a *blocking hook* function that prevents messages from being processed, in order to avoid the possibility of re-entrant messages occurring while a blocking operation is outstanding.

Because of the difficulty in managing this condition safely, particularly in 16-bit operations, Winsock1.1 doesn't permit an application to make more than one nested function call. The only exceptions are the functions WSAIsBlocking and WSACancelBlockingCall, provided to assist the programmer in this situation.

Winsock2 runs only on preemptive 32-bit operating systems, where deadlocks aren't a problem. Function calls can be nested, and pseudo-blocking is unnecessary. Winsock2 doesn't support blocking hooks (because it doesn't need to). This impinges (slightly) on the source compatibility between Winsock1.1 and Winsock2, as described later in this chapter.

Name and IP Address Resolution

Winsock applications generally use the gethostbyname function to resolve a host name to an IP address. By default, this function uses the following lookup sequence:

1. It checks the hosts file for a matching name entry.

2. If a DNS server is configured, it queries it.

3. If no match is found, it tries NetBIOS name-resolution methods (such as WINS).

Some applications use the gethostbyaddr function to resolve an IP address to a host name. By default, this function uses the following lookup sequence:

1. It checks the hosts file for a matching address entry.

2. If a DNS server is configured, it queries it using reverse lookup.

3. It sends a NetBIOS adapter status request to the IP address being queried. If this request returns a list of NetBIOS names registered for the adapter, the function parses the list for the computer name.

The Backlog Parameter

Winsock server applications generally create a socket, then use the listen function to listen for connection requests. One of the parameters that are passed when calling listen is the backlog of connection requests that the application wants Winsock to queue. This parameter controls the number of unaccepted connections that can be queued. Once an application accepts a connection, that connection is moved out of the backlog.

Windows 2000 and Windows NT4 Servers accept a backlog of 200. Windows 2000 Professional and Windows NT4 Workstation accept a backlog of 5 (to reduce demands on memory).

Push Bit Interpretation

TCP can transmit data with the PSH control bit (the push bit) set. This indicates that the data in the packet should be pushed through to the receiving host and that TCP will forward and deliver data promptly (see Chapter 8). By default, Windows 2000 TCP/IP completes a recv call when one of the following conditions is met:

- Data arrives with the PSH bit set.
- The user recv buffer is full.
- 0.5 seconds have elapsed since any data arrived.

If a client application runs on a computer with a TCP/IP implementation that doesn't set the push bit on send operations, delays may result. Although it's best to correct this on the client, a configuration parameter, *IgnorePushBitOnReceives*, was introduced in Windows NT4 and is supported in Windows 2000. This parameter is contained in the system file afd.sys. It forces the receiving host to treat all arriving packets as if the push bit were set.

Winsock Functions

The Winsock2 specification encompasses all the Berkeley-style socket routines that were included in Winsock1.1. These are listed in Table 18.3. More details, including syntax and parameters, are available in the Reference section of the platform SDK documentation.

Microsoft-Specific Extensions

The Winsock specifications provide a number of extensions to the standard set of Berkeley routines, which allow message- or function-based asynchronous access to network events and enable overlapped I/O. Not all of these extensions were introduced in Winsock2, but they are all supported. Although use of these extended routines isn't mandatory (except for WSAStartup and WSACleanup), it is strongly recommended. Table 18.4 lists the Microsoft-specific extensions to Winsock1.1.

New Features in Winsock2

Winsock2 architecture follows the Windows Open System Architecture (WOSA) model, which provides access to multiple transport protocols. This architecture defines a standard Service Provider Interface (SPI) between the Application Programming Interface (API), with its functions exported from the Winsock2 DLL

Table 18.3   Winsock1.1 socket routines used in Winsock2.

Routine	Description
accept	Acknowledges an incoming connection and associates it with an immediately created socket. The original socket is returned to the listening state.
bind	Assigns a local name to an unnamed socket.
Closesocket	Removes a socket from the per-process object reference table. Blocks only if SO_LINGER is set with a nonzero time-out on a blocking socket.
connect	Initiates a connection on the specified socket.
Getpeername	Retrieves the name of the peer connected to the specified socket.
Getsockname	Retrieves the local address to which the specified socket is bound.
Getsockopt	Retrieves options associated with the specified socket.
htonl*	Converts a 32-bit quantity from host-byte order to network-byte order.
htons*	Converts a 16-bit quantity from host-byte order to network-byte order.
inet_addr*	Converts a character string representing a number in the Internet standard notation to an Internet address value.
inet_ntoa*	Converts an Internet address value to a dot-separated ASCII string; i.e., "a.b.c.d".
ioctlsocket	Provides control for sockets.
listen	Listens for incoming connections on a specified socket.
ntohl*	Converts a 32-bit quantity from network-byte order to host-byte order.
ntohs*	Converts a 16-bit quantity from network-byte order to host-byte order.
recv	Receives data from a connected socket.
recvfrom	Receives data from either a connected or an unconnected socket.
select	Performs synchronous input/output (I/O) multiplexing.
send	Sends data to a connected socket.
sendto	Sends data to either a connected or an unconnected socket.
setsockopt	Stores options associated with the specified socket.
Shutdown	Shuts down part of a full-duplex connection.
socket	Creates an endpoint for communication and returns a socket descriptor.

NOTE: *The routines marked with an asterisk (*) are retained for backward compatibility with Winsock1.1 and should be used only for sockets created with the AF_INET address family.*

Table 18.4   Microsoft-specific extensions to Winsock1.1.

Routine	Description
WSAAccept	An extended version of accept that allows for conditional acceptance.
WSAAsyncGetHostByAddr* WSAAsyncGetHostByName* WSAAsyncGetProtoByName* WSAAsyncGetProtoByNumber* WSAAsyncGetServByName* WSAAsyncGetServByPort*	Functions that provide asynchronous versions of the standard Berkeley getXbyY functions. For example, WSAAsyncGetHostByName provides an asynchronous, message-based implementation of the Berkeley gethostbyname function.
WSAAsyncSelect*	Performs an asynchronous version of select.
WSACancelAsyncRequest*	Cancels an outstanding instance of a WSAAsyncGetXByY function.
WSACleanup	Signs off from the underlying Windows Sockets DLL.
WSACloseEvent	Destroys an event object.
WSAConnect	An extended version of connect that allows for the exchange of connect data and Quality of Service (QoS) specifications.
WSACreateEvent	Creates an event object.
WSADuplicateSocket	Creates a virtual socket, which allows an underlying socket to be shared.
WSAEnumNetworkEvents	Discovers occurrences of network events.
WSAEnumProtocols	Retrieves information about each available protocol.
WSAEventSelect	Associates network events with an event object.
WSAGetLastError*	Obtains details of the last Winsock error.
WSAGetOverlappedResult	Gets completion status of overlapped operations.
WSAGetQOSByName	Supplies QoS parameters based on a well-known service name.
WSAHtonl	Extended version of htonl.
WSAHtons	Extended version of htons.
WSAIoctl	Overlapped-capable version of IOCTL.
WSAJoinLeaf	Adds a multipoint leaf to a multipoint session.
WSANtohl	Extended version of ntohl.
WSANtohs	Extended version of ntohs.
WSAProviderConfigChange	Receives notifications of service providers being installed or removed.
WSARecv	An extended version of recv that accommodates scatter/gather I/O and overlapped sockets and provides the flags parameter as IN OUT.

(continued)

Table 18.4   *Microsoft-specific extensions to Winsock1.1* (continued).

Routine	Description
WSARecvFrom	An extended version of recvfrom that accommodates scatter/gather I/O and overlapped sockets and provides the flags parameter as IN OUT.
WSAResetEvent	Resets an event object.
WSASend	An extended version of send that accommodates scatter/gather I/O and overlapped sockets.
WSASendTo	An extended version of sendto that accommodates scatter/gather I/O and overlapped sockets.
WSASetEvent	Sets an event object.
WSASetLastError*	Sets the error to be returned by a subsequent WSAGetLastError.
WSASocket	An extended version of socket that takes a WSAPROTOCOL_INFO structure as input and allows overlapped sockets to be created.
WSAStartup*	Initializes the underlying Winsock DLL.
WSAWaitForMultipleEvents	Blocks on multiple event objects.

NOTE: *The routines marked with an asterisk (*) were originally Winsock1.1 functions.*

WS2_32.dll and from the protocol stacks. As a result, Winsock2 support isn't limited to TCP/IP protocol stacks as it is with Winsock1.1. Figure 18.2 illustrates the Winsock2 architecture. This is a general illustration that's not specific to any particular transport provider or to any particular operating system.

When only TCP/IP was supported, applications needed to define only two socket types. Connectionless protocols used SOCK_DGRAM sockets, and connection-oriented protocols used SOCK_STREAM sockets. In Winsock2, these are just two of the many socket types, and developers can no longer rely on socket type to describe all the essential attributes of a transport protocol. Protocol-specific attributes are defined in *helper* DLLs, described later in this chapter.

Winsock2 extends Winsock1.1 functionality in a number of areas. These are summarized in Table 18.5.

Overlapped I/O

Overlapped I/O follows the model established in Win32. Winsock2 requires that all transport providers support this capability. Both send and receive operations can be overlapped. Receive functions can be invoked several times to post receive buffers in preparation for incoming data; send functions can be invoked several times to queue multiple buffers to send. Overlapped I/O can be

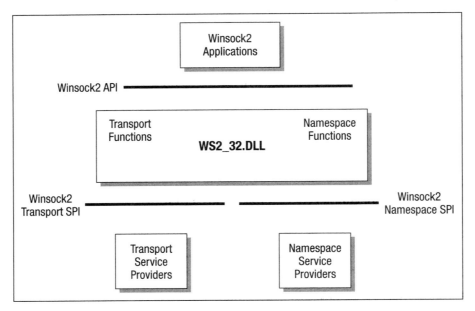

Figure 18.2   Winsock2 architecture.

Table 18.5   New Winsock2 features.

Feature	Description
Access to protocols other than TCP/IP	Allows simultaneous access to a number of installed transport protocols.
Overlapped I/O with scatter/gather	Incorporates the overlapped paradigm for socket I/O and scatter/gather capabilities.
Protocol-independent name resolution facilities	Includes a standardized set of functions for querying and working with many types of name resolution domains, such as DNS, the Service Advertising Protocol (SAP), and X.500.
Protocol-independent multicast multipoint	Discovers what multipoint or multicast capabilities a transport and provides and uses these facilities in a generic manner.
QoS	Establishes conventions that applications use to negotiate required service levels for such parameters as bandwidth and latency (see Chapter 9).
Other extensions	Incorporates shared sockets and conditional acceptance, exchange of user data at connection setup/teardown time, and protocol-specific extension mechanisms.

performed only on sockets created through the WSASocket function with the WSA_FLAG_OVERLAPPED flag set or on sockets created through the socket function. Winsock2 functions are described later in this chapter.

Although an application can rely on a series of overlapped send buffers being sent in the order supplied, the corresponding completion indications might occur in a different order. On the receiving side, buffers can be filled in the order in which they're supplied, but the completion indications might occur in a different order.

NOTE: *In the first Wsock32.dll (the 32-bit version of Winsock1.1), the socket function created sockets with the overlapped attribute set by default. To ensure backward compatibility with legacy Wsock32.dll implementations, this is also the case for Winsock2. To be more compatible with the rest of the Win32 API, however, sockets that are created with WSASocket don't have the overlapped attribute set by default. This attribute is applied if the WSA_FLAG_OVERLAPPED bit is set.*

Scatter/Gather

Scatter/gather (or vectored) I/O is implemented by functions such as WSASend, WSASendTo, WSARecv, and WSARecvFrom, which can take an array of application buffers as input parameters. This is useful where portions the message that's being transmitted consist of one or more fixed-length header components in addition to the message body. If scatter/gather is implemented, header components don't need to be concatenated by the application into a single contiguous buffer prior to sending. On receipt, the header components are automatically split off into separate buffers, leaving the message body unaffected, or *pure*.

Shared Sockets

The WSADuplicateSocket function enables socket sharing across processes. A source process calls this function to obtain a WSAPROTOCOL_INFO structure for a target process identifier. It uses an IPC mechanism to pass the contents of this structure to a target process. The target process then uses the WSAPROTOCOL_INFO structure in a call to WSPSocket. The socket descriptor returned by this function is an additional socket descriptor to an underlying socket, and the underlying socket is therefore *shared*; that is, it's referenced by more than one descriptor. Sockets can be shared among threads in a given process without using the WSADuplicateSocket function, because a socket descriptor is valid in all threads of a process.

The two (or more) descriptors that reference a shared socket can be used independently for I/O operations. However, Winsock2 doesn't implement access control, so the processes must coordinate any operations on a shared socket.

**18. Network
Application Interfaces**

IP Multicasting

Winsock2 provides support for IP multicasting (see Chapter 6) only on AF_INET sockets of types SOCK_DGRAM and SOCK_RAW.

Connection Setup and Teardown

The accept routine acknowledges an incoming connection and associates it with an immediately created socket. Winsock2 introduces the WSAAccept routine, an extended version of accept that allows for *conditional acceptance.*

Provided that the service provider supports the feature, an application can obtain caller information, such as identifier and QoS, before deciding whether to accept an incoming connection request. This is done with a callback to an application-supplied condition function. User-to-user data specified by parameters in the WSAConnect function and the condition function of WSAAccept can be transferred to a peer during connection establishment.

It's also possible to exchange user data between the endpoints at connection teardown time. The end that initiates the teardown calls the WSASendDisconnect function to indicate that no more data will be sent and to initiate the connection teardown sequence. For some protocols, part of teardown is the delivery of disconnect data from the teardown initiator. After receiving notice that the remote end has initiated teardown (typically by the FD_CLOSE indication), the WSARecvDisconnect function can be called to receive the disconnect data.

Function Extensions

Unlike what happens in Winsock1.1, each individual stack vendor doesn't supply its own version of the Winsock2 DLL (Ws2_32.dll). As a result, stack vendors can't implement extended functionality by adding entry points to the DLL. Instead, Winsock2 uses the WSAIoctl function to enable service providers to offer provider-specific functionality extensions.

To invoke an extension function, the application requests a pointer to the desired function. This is done through the WSAIoctl function, using the SIO_GET_EXTENSION_FUNCTION_POINTER command code. The input buffer to the WSAIoctl function contains an identifier for the indicated extension function; the output buffer contains the function pointer itself. The application can then invoke the extension function directly without using the DLL.

Service provider vendors allocate Globally Unique Identifiers (GUIDs) to identify extension functions. Vendors who create such functions should publish full details about them. This makes it possible for extension functions to be offered by more than one service provider vendor. An application can obtain the function pointer and use the function without needing to know which service provider implements the function.

The Winsock2 Identifier Clearinghouse

Winsock1.1 supports a single address family (AF_INET) comprising a small number of well-known socket types and protocol identifiers. Winsock2 retains this address family for compatibility reasons, but also supports new transport protocols with new media types. Therefore, several new address family, socket type, and protocol values are introduced in Winsock2.

The Winsock2 identifier clearinghouse allows protocol stack vendors to obtain unique identifiers for new address families, socket types, and protocols. File Transfer Protocol (FTP) and World Wide Web (WWW or Web) servers supply current identifier/value mappings and request the allocation of new ones. The URL for the Winsock2 identifier clearinghouse is **www.stardust.com/winsock**.

Backward Compatibility

Winsock2 is backward compatible with Winsock1.1 at both the source and the binary levels. Current Winsock1.1-compliant applications operate in a Winsock2 implementation without modification of any kind, provided that at least one TCP/IP service provider is installed.

Source code compatibility is provided by ensuring that most Winsock1.1 functions are recognized in Winsock2. Winsock1.1 source code can be moved to the Winsock2 system by including the new header file, Winsock2.h, and linking with the appropriate Winsock2 libraries. This, however, should be seen as only the first step. The additional functionality that's provided by Winsock2 can be used to improve your applications, and it's recommended that you modify your programs, where appropriate, to use the new Winsock2 features.

NOTE: *Winsock1.1 applications that use blocking hooks must be modified, because blocking hooks aren't supported in Winsock2.*

For existing Winsock1.1 applications to work unchanged at a binary level, TCP/IP-based transport and name resolution service providers need to be present in the Winsock2 system. To enable this functionality, Winsock2 provides additional Winsock1.1-compatible DLLs (Winsock.dll and Wsock32.dll). These are known as *shim* components. Figure 18.3 illustrates the Winsock2 compatibility structure.

The Winsock2 installation guidelines state that there should be no negative impact to existing Winsock-based applications on an end-user system when additional Winsock2 components are introduced.

I/O Control Operation Codes

The Winsock2 socket I/O Control (IOCTL) operation codes (opcodes) are listed in Table 18.6. Protocol-specific IOCTL opcodes can be found in the Protocol-specific Annex that's downloaded with the platform SDK.

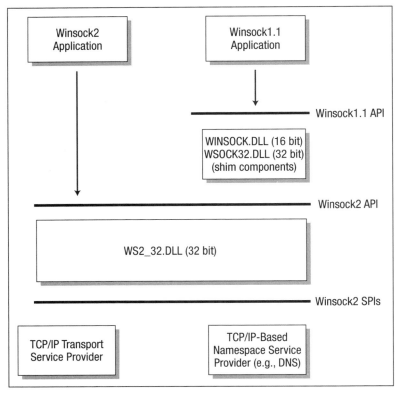

Figure 18.3   The Winsock2 compatibility structure.

Table 18.6   Winsock2 socket IOCTL opcodes.

Opcode	Action
SIO_ASSOCIATE_HANDLE	Associate the socket with the specified handle of a companion interface.
SIO_ENABLE_CIRCULAR_QUEUEING	Enable circular queuing.
SIO_FIND_ROUTE	Request that the route to the specified address be discovered.
SIO_FLUSH	Discard the current contents of the sending queue.
SIO_GET_BROADCAST_ADDRESS	Retrieve the protocol-specific broadcast address to be used in sendto or WSASendTo.
SIO_GET_QOS	Retrieve the current flow specification(s) for the socket.
SIO_GET_GROUP_QOS	Reserved.
SIO_MULTIPOINT_LOOPBACK	Control whether data sent in a multipoint session will also be received by the same socket on the local host.
SIO_MULTICAST_SCOPE	Specify the scope over which multicast transmissions will occur.

(continued)

Table 18.6   *Winsock2 socket IOCTL opcodes* (continued).

Opcode	Action
SIO_SET_QOS	Establish new flow specification(s) for the socket.
SIO_SET_GROUP_QOS	Reserved.
SIO_TRANSLATE_HANDLE	Obtain a corresponding handle for a socket that's valid in the context of a companion interface.
SIO_ROUTING_INTERFACE_QUERY	Obtain the address of the local interface that should be used to send to the specified address.
SIO_ROUTING_INTERFACE_CHANGE	Request notification of changes in information reported through SIO_ROUTING_INTERFACE_QUERY for the specified address.
SIO_ADDRESS_LIST_QUERY	Obtain the list of addresses to which the application can bind.
SIO_ADDRESS_LIST_CHANGE	Request notification of changes in information reported through SIO_ADDRESS_LIST_QUERY.

Winsock2 Functions

The new Winsock2 data transport and name registration and resolution functions are listed in Tables 18.7 and 18.8, respectively. There's some overlap between these functions and those listed in Table 18.4, because Microsoft-specific extensions to Winsock1.1 have been implemented as core functions in Winsock2.

Table 18.7   *Winsock2 data transport functions.*

Function	Description
WSAAccept	An extended version of accept that allows for conditional acceptance.
WSACloseEvent	Destroys an event object.
WSAConnect	An extended version of connect that allows for exchange of connect data and QoS specification.
WSACreateEvent	Creates an event object.
WSADuplicateSocket	Creates a new socket descriptor for a shared socket.
WSAEnumNetworkEvents	Discovers occurrences of network events.
WSAEnumProtocols	Retrieves information about each available protocol.
WSAEventSelect	Associates network events with an event object.
WSAGetOverlappedResult	Gets completion status of an overlapped operation.
WSAGetQOSByName	Supplies QoS parameters based on a well-known service name.
WSAHtonl	Extended version of htonl.
WSAHtons	Extended version of htons.
WSAIoctl	Overlapped-capable version of ioctlsocket.

(continued)

***Table 18.7   Winsock2 data transport functions** (continued).*

Function	Description
WSAJoinLeaf	Joins a leaf node to a multipoint session.
WSANtohl	Extended version of ntohl.
WSANtohs	Extended version of ntohs.
WSAProviderConfigChange	Receives notifications of service providers being installed or removed.
WSARecv	An extended version of recv that accommodates scatter/gather I/O and overlapped sockets and provides the flags parameter as IN OUT.
WSARecvDisconnect	Terminates reception on a socket and retrieves the disconnect data if the socket is connection-oriented.
WSARecvFrom	An extended version of recvfrom that accommodates scatter/gather I/O and overlapped sockets and provides the flags parameter as IN OUT.
WSAResetEvent	Resets an event object.
WSASend	An extended version of send that accommodates scatter/gather I/O and overlapped sockets.
WSASendDisconnect	Initiates termination of a socket connection and, optionally, sends disconnect data.
WSASendTo	An extended version of sendto that accommodates scatter/gather I/O and overlapped sockets.
WSASetEvent	Sets an event object.
WSASocket	An extended version of socket that takes a WSAPROTOCOL_INFO structure as input and allows overlapped sockets to be created.
WSAWaitForMultipleEvents	Blocks on multiple event objects.

Table 18.8   Winsock2 name registration and resolution functions.

Function	Description
WSAAddressToString	Converts an address structure to a human-readable numeric string.
WSAEnumNameSpaceProviders	Retrieves the list of available name registration and resolution service providers.
WSAGetServiceClassInfo	Retrieves all the class-specific information pertaining to a service class.
WSAGetServiceClassNameByClassId	Returns the name of the service associated with a given type.
WSAInstallServiceClass	Creates a new service class type and stores its class-specific information.

(continued)

Table 18.8   Winsock2 name registration and resolution functions (continued).

Function	Description
WSALookupServiceBegin	Initiates a client query to retrieve name information as constrained by a WSAQUERYSET data structure.
WSALookupServiceEnd	Finishes a client query started by WSALookupServiceBegin and frees resources associated with the query.
WSALookupServiceNext	Retrieves the next unit of name information from a client query initiated by WSALookupServiceBegin.
WSARemoveServiceClass	Removes a service class type permanently.
WSASetService	Registers, or removes from the Registry, a service instance within one or more namespaces.
WSAStringToAddress	Converts a human-readable numeric string to a socket address structure suitable for passing to Winsock2 routines.

The documentation accompanying the platform DDK gives comprehensive instructions on how to use the functions listed in this chapter. This documentation includes sections on programming considerations, event handling, error codes, and detailed function syntax and parameters. Possibly the best place to start is with the sample programs. If you understand and can successfully modify sample code, you're well on your way to writing applications.

Winsock Helper DLLs

WSH DLLs are user-mode components that are provided by transport driver writers to enable the Winsock2 interface to be used with their transports. Windows 2000 implements a DLL (msafd.dll) that's a sockets service provider. When a transport driver is installed in the system, it installs a transport-specific WSH DLL. Network setup automatically configures msafd.dll to be the service provider for that WSH DLL. Figure 18.4 illustrates this architecture for the TCP/IP WSH DLL (wshtcpip.dll). A similar architecture is used for other transports.

When an application makes a call to a Winsock2 function, msafd.dll resolves the call and accesses the appropriate WSH DLL for assistance. Some Winsock2 functions don't require this assistance—for example, once a socket has been established, sending or receiving data doesn't need a WSH DLL. In cases such as these, msafd.dll can communicate directly with the transport by calling Win32 functions.

Where function calls rely on transport-specific features, or where the implementation can vary from transport to transport, the transport-specific WSH DLL will be used to resolve these ambiguities. For example, WSAJoinLeaf adds a socket to an established multipoint session. Each transport implements the addition of new

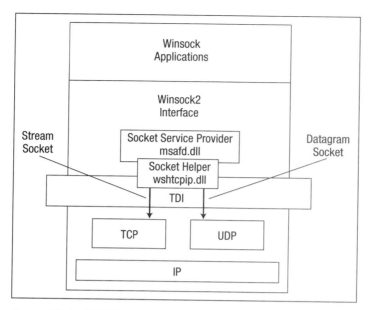

Figure 18.4   WSH DLL architecture.

connections to a multipoint session differently. Consequently, msafd.dll calls the appropriate WSH DLL to support the sockets interface according to the transport-specific implementation.

When an application is establishing a socket, it specifies an address family, a socket type, and a protocol. These arguments must uniquely identify a transport driver to support the socket. Winsock2 searches for a match between these arguments and the configuration information stored in the Registry for WSH DLLs. If it finds a match, Winsock2 calls down through msafd.dll to the WSH*Xxx* functions exported by the WSH DLL. Otherwise, the application's call to socket fails.

If a match is found, Winsock2 calls LoadLibrary on the WSH DLL and then calls GetProcAddress to retrieve the entry point for each exported WSH*Xxx* function. These WSH*Xxx* functions are called as necessary to query for protocols supported by the helper DLL, to translate addresses, and to process WSH-supported options when getsockopt and setsockopt calls occur. Socket addresses specified by applications (SOCKADDR structures) are automatically converted to TDI-defined addresses used by underlying transport drivers.

WSH Functions

Every WSH DLL exports a set of WSH*Xxx* functions. Each transport implements these functions in a corresponding WSH DLL, depending on the features supported by the transport. Winsock2 treats all WSH DLLs as trusted code, and a bug in a WSH*Xxx* function manifests itself as one or more bugs in the Winsock2 interface.

Table 18.9 summarizes the functions that are exported by WSH DLL.

To support the new Winsock2 extensions for leaf/root sockets, socket groups, and logical representation of sockets, the optional functions listed in Table 18.10 are implemented.

WSH functions are included in the Windows 2000 DDK, which was described in Chapter 2 and again in Chapter 17. The build function and the breakpoint routines supplied in the DDK can be used to advantage in software development. If you intend writing interface routines between transport drivers and Winsock2 applications, then refer to these chapters and to the detailed documentation that's downloaded with the DDK.

Table 18.9   WSH functions.

Function	Description
WHSEnumProtocols	Returns a list of protocols (Winsock PROTOCOL_INFO structures) that the WSH DLL supports.
WSHGetSockAddrType	Parses a socket address.
WSHGetSocketInformation	Called whenever getsockopt is passed an option that Winsock doesn't explicitly support.
WSHGetWildCardSockAddr	Called when Winsock needs to perform an automatic socket bind.
WSHGetWinsockMapping	Returns information about the address family, socket type, and protocol parameter triples supported by the WSH DLL.
WSHNotify	Called to notify the helper DLL of a state transition.
WSHOpenSocket	Called when a socket is opened.
WSHSetSocketInformation	Called whenever an option that Winsock doesn't explicitly support is passed to setsockopt.

Table 18.10   Optional WSH functions.

Function	Description
WSHAddressToString	Returns a logical string representation of a socket address that can be used for display purposes.
WSHGetBroadcastSockaddr	Obtains a valid broadcast address for a socket.
WSHGetProviderGuid	Returns the GUID that identifies the protocols supported by a helper DLL.

(continued)

Table 18.10   Optional WSH functions (continued).

Function	Description
WSHGetWSAProtocolInfo	Returns a pointer to protocol information for the protocol(s) supported by a helper DLL. This function is used only during setup.
WSHIoctl	Obtains information or performs actions based on a unique control code.
WSHJoinLeaf	Performs any protocol-specific actions that must be taken to add a socket to a multipoint session.
WSHOpenSocket2	Performs the protocol-specific actions for creating a new socket. If this function is exported, it replaces the WSHOpenSocket function.
WSHStringToAddress	Converts a logical string representation of a socket address to a SOCKADDR structure.

Immediate Solutions

Installing the Microsoft Platform SDK

The Microsoft platform SDK facilitates application development for the Windows 2000, Windows NT4, and Windows $9x$ operating systems; the Microsoft BackOffice family of products; and Microsoft Internet Explorer versions $3.x$ and later. It also provides limited support for Win64 development. Its key objectives are to simplify the installation of your development environment, introduce the latest developments, and provide information about existing technologies.

A full installation of the SDK requires the following:

- Windows 2000, Windows NT4, Windows 98, or Windows 95. If possible, install the SDK on a Windows 2000 machine.

- Microsoft Internet Explorer 4.02 or later (or an equivalent non-Microsoft browser).

- A C/C++ compiler, such as Microsoft Visual C++ 5, Service Pack 3 or later (preferably later), to build C/C++ samples.

- Microsoft Visual Basic to build VB samples.

- Approximately 920MB of hard-disk space (523.1MB of files are downloaded, but they need a bit more space when installed). Significantly more space is needed when installing to a FAT partition. A "typical" (in effect a minimum) install will download 12.2MB of files, not including the download program itself. This, however, doesn't give you any documentation, tools, sample files, or source files.

- Compiling the entire set of SDK samples requires approximately 2GB of additional disk space.

To install the platform SDK, proceed as follows:

1. Log on to your development machine as an administrator.

2. If you have the platform SDK CD-ROM provided by the Microsoft Developers Network (MSDN), insert it. The CD-ROM should autoboot, and you can go directly to Step 7 of this procedure. Otherwise, connect to the Internet, start your browser, and go to Step 3.

3. Access **www.microsoft.com/msdownload/platformsdk/ setuplauncher.htm** (if this URL doesn't work, then go to **www.microsoft.com** and follow the "download" links).

4. Adjust the size of your browser's Internet cache, as specified in Table 18.11. If necessary, refer to your browser's help files for instructions on how to do this.

5. If your machine is running Windows NT4, Windows 98, or Windows 95, you need to update Windows Installer to version 1.1. You can ignore this step on a Windows 2000 machine. Click the link on the installation Web page, then download and run InstMsi.exe. The file is 1.46MB in size. After you've updated Windows Installer, you need to reboot your machine and repeat Steps 1 through 3 of this procedure.

6. Click the link to access the platform SDK setup file, then download and run psdk-86.exe. The file is 848KB in size.

7. The MS Platform Setup Wizard starts. Click Next.

8. Accept the license agreement. Click Next.

9. Supply user information. Click Next.

10. Select the installation type. If you want to install documentation, tools, and sample and source code, then choose Custom. Click Next.

11. Specify an installation location or accept the default. Click Next.

12. If you selected custom installation, the Custom Installation Tips screen appears. Click Next.

13. Specify your installation requirements, as illustrated in Figure 18.5. Clicking the Disk Space button lets you check that you have sufficient disk space available. When you've specified everything you want to download, click Next.

14. Click Next (again).

15. If you're downloading the full SDK from the Internet, wait until half a gigabyte of files downloads. Unless your connection is a lot faster than mine, this will take a long time.

16. Click Finish.

Table 18.11   Recommended browser cache settings.

Operating System	Recommended Cache Size
Windows 2000	204MB
Windows NT4	204MB
Windows 98 Second Edition	204MB
Windows 98	400MB
Windows 95	204MB

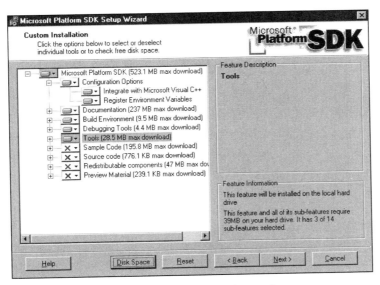

Figure 18.5   Specifying installation requirements.

Using the Platform SDK Tools

If you install the full platform SDK, you have access to two sets of tools: the platform SDK tools for application programming development, and a separate set of debugging tools. All the procedures in this set assume that you're logged on to your development machine with sufficient permissions to use the tools. The procedures also assume a Windows 2000 development system. Some of the tools have less functionality on Windows 9x and NT4 systems.

Using WinDiff

WinDiff can compare files and directories. This is useful if (for example) you're debugging file transfer routines. This procedure assumes that you want to compare directories. To use the WinDiff tool, proceed as follows:

1. Access Start|Programs|Platform SDK|Tools and select WinDiff.

2. In the File pull-down menu, choose the operation you want to perform; in this case, Compare Directories.

3. Supply the paths to the directories that you want to compare. You can also specify whether or not to include subdirectories. Click OK.

4. You should obtain a screen similar to Figure 18.6. Open files will be highlighted and can't be compared. The tool will, however, compare the file creation times.

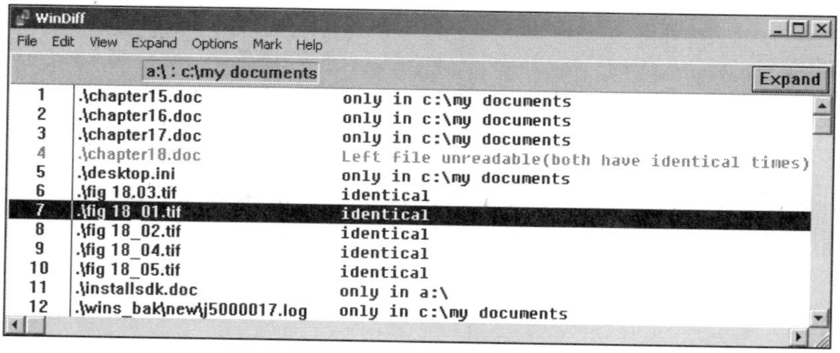

Figure 18.6   Comparing directories.

5. If you want to edit any file, select it and click the Edit pull-down menu. You can choose to edit the file in the directory listed on the left or on the right of the directory box, or a composite of both files.

6. For information about other WinDiff operations, refer to the Help pull-down menu.

Using Spy

Spy can tell you when particular messages are being sent and received by system components. You can specify individual messages, message types, and the message *window*, which is the system component or process that's generating the messages. To use Spy, proceed as follows:

1. Access Start|Programs|Platform SDK|Tools and select Spy.

2. On the Spy pull-down menu, click Select Window.

3. Specify the window that you want to use, or check All Windows. Click OK.

4. On the Options pull-down menu, select Output. You can direct your output to a screen window, to a file, or to a communication port. Click OK.

5. On the Options pull-down menu, select Messages. You can select individual messages or message groups. If you select some but not all messages in a group, the checkbox will be checked but grayed. Figure 18.7 shows the Messages dialog box.

6. Click OK.

7. Click Start! When you've captured the required messages, click Stop!

Using the Running Object Table Viewer

A Running Object Table (ROT) is a globally accessible look-up table on each host computer that keeps track of objects that can be identified by an identifier, or *moniker*, and that are currently running on the host. The most common type of

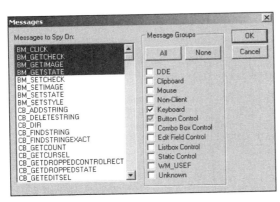

Figure 18.7   The Messages dialog box.

moniker provider is a compound-document link source that includes server applications that support linking to their documents and container applications that support linking to embedded objects within their documents.

To view an ROT, proceed as follows:

1. Access Start|Programs|Platform SDK|Tools and select ROT Viewer.

2. Click Update! to update the display. Figure 18.8 shows a ROT Viewer information screen.

Using Process Walker

Process Walker lets you access information about a process that's currently running. The process should either be written with breakpoints or else be one that waits for user input. To use Process Walker, proceed as follows:

1. Access Start|Programs|Platform SDK|Tools and select PWalk.

2. On the Process pull-down menu, select Load Process.

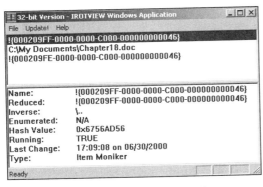

Figure 18.8   A ROT viewer information screen.

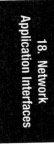

3. Browse to the process, select it, then click Open.

4. The process should stop at a breakpoint or a user input point. If the process is in a continuous loop, you can suspend or resume it from the process menu. Figure 18.9 shows process details.

5. Use the Sort menu to sort the information by Address, Protection, Size, State, or Base Address.

6. Use the View menu to view statistics and memory contents.

Using Process Viewer

Process Viewer lets you examine and modify process and thread characteristics. To use Process Viewer, proceed as follows:

1. Access Start|Programs|Platform SDK|Tools and select PView.

2. Select a process and a thread that are of interest.

3. Examine process and thread characteristics, such as thread start addresses, priorities, and CPU and memory usage.

4. Click Memory Detail. You should get a Memory Details information box similar to Figure 18.10. Click OK to close the box.

5. You can, optionally, amend the process status or kill the process. Potentially, this could halt the entire system, so make sure that you've saved edited files before using these Process Viewer features.

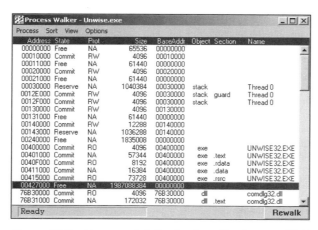

Figure 18.9   Process details displayed by Process Walker.

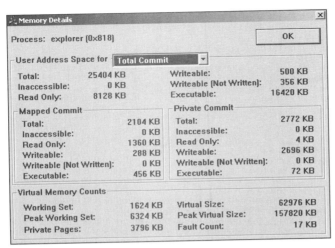

Figure 18.10   The Memory Details information box.

Using the PStat Tool

The PStat command-line tool gives you access to more than process statistics. The tool opens a Command Console and lists statistics, but the Command Console window also allows access to the folder that stores the executable files for many other platform SDK tools. To use the PStat tool, proceed as follows:

1. Access Start|Programs|Platform SDK|Tools and select PView.

2. A list of statistics appears. Scroll the screen to read this.

3. Enter **dir *.exe**. This lists all the executable command-line utilities that are provided.

4. You can access any command-line utility by entering its file name (without the .EXE extension). This procedure usually accesses information about the utility's function and syntax. Refer also to the procedure "Obtaining Details of All Platform SDK Tools" later in this chapter.

Using the OLE/COM Object Viewer

This tool lets you view and manipulate Component Object Model (COM) objects that can be linked to or embedded in applications. To use the OLE/COM Viewer, proceed as follows:

1. Access Start|Programs|Platform SDK|Tools and select OLE – Com Viewer.

2. Select an object, as shown in Figure 18.11, and access its Registry, Implementation, Activation, Launch Permissions, and Access Permissions tabs. You can also create instances and set instance flags, and view and modify system configuration information. The tool gives you access to the Registry editor. Use this feature carefully.

18. Network Application Interfaces

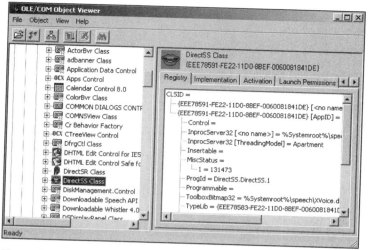

Figure 18.11   The OLE/COM Object Viewer.

Creating Dialog Boxes, Images, and Help Files

The platform SDK provides tools to create pop-up dialog boxes, compiled help files, resource scripts, images, and icons. To access these tools, proceed as follows:

1. Access Start|Programs|Platform SDK|Tools.

2. Select the appropriate tool as follows:

   - To create pop-up dialog boxes, select Dialog Editor. This lets you build a dialog on screen and insert tools that you select from the editor's toolbox, manage a group of dialog boxes for an application, and insert dialog boxes into application *resource scripts*. You can create custom controls and specify styles for all your dialog box elements.

   - To create and compile help files, select Help Compiler. This starts the Microsoft Help Workshop tool, which lets you create help (HLP) files, edit project and content files, and test and report on help files. You can combine topic (RTF) files with bitmaps and other elements to create compiled files that can be read by the Microsoft Windows Help program.

   - To create images, click Image Editor. This lets you create cursors, bitmaps, and icons for insertion into a resource script file.

3. To obtain more details, access the help files for the tool you select.

Installing and Using HTML Help Workshop

If you're writing applications that are accessed by browsers (possibly over the Internet), you need to install HTML (Hypertext Markup Language) Help

Workshop. This tool is used to create and manage help structures that are accessed (for example) by the Help Viewer in Internet Explorer. Installing HTML Help Workshop also installs HTML Help Image Editor.

To install and use HTML Help Workshop and HTML Help Image Editor, proceed as follows:

1. Access Start|Programs|Platform SDK|Tools and select HTML Help Workshop Setup.
2. Click Accept to accept the license agreement.
3. Click Next to start installation.
4. Specify an installation directory or accept the default. Click Next.
5. Choose the setup type. Click Next.
6. If you chose a custom setup, specify the components that you want to install. Click Next.
7. Select the program icon group or accept the default. Click Next.
8. Type your name. Click Next.
9. The Tool is installed. Click OK to close the information box.
10. Access Start|Programs|HTML Help Workshop and select either HTML Help Workshop or HTML Help Image Editor.
11. Refer to the in-context help files for guidance on using the tools.

Using Heap Walker

Heap Walker lets you examine the global heap (the system memory that the operating system uses) and local heaps used by active applications and DLLs. This is useful for analyzing the effects your application has when it allocates memory from the global heap or when it creates user interface or graphics objects.

To use Heap Walker, proceed as follows:

1. Access Start|Programs|Platform SDK|Tools and select Heap Walker.
2. The main heap is displayed by default. Use the Object pull-down menu to view other available heaps and show the memory contents for any heap object.
3. Use the Sort pull-down menu to arrange the heap information.
4. Use the Walk pull-down menu to walk through the heap.

Using Dependency Walker

Dependency Walker is used when you have interdependent modules that are linked either at compile/link time (for example, static dependencies) or at run time (for

18. Network Application Interfaces

example, dynamic dependencies). Dependency Walker lets you walk through a module and its dependent modules. The tool can (for example) let you discover:

- The minimum set of files required to run a particular application
- Why a module is loaded with an application
- What functions a particular module exposes
- The complete path of all the modules being loaded for a particular application
- The base addresses of all modules that are loaded for an application

Dependency Walker can be used as a debugging tool when you get error messages that tell you a DLL can't be found, a procedure entry point can't be located, an application failed to initialize properly, or a program is too big to fit in memory. To use Dependency Walker, proceed as follows:

1. Access Start|Programs|Platform SDK|Tools and select Depends.
2. Select Open from the File pull-down menu.
3. From the View pull-down menu, you can configure the search order, highlight matching modules, define the file extensions that are of interest, configure an external viewer, and start profiling the module. Profile Walker can simulate the ShellExecute function when starting your application or inject a small DLL into the application being profiled to obtain details that can be gathered only from within the application itself.

Figure 18.12 shows the Dependency Walker tool. For more details, refer to the tool's extensive help files.

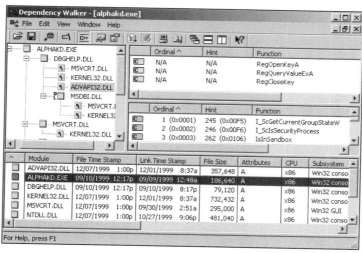

Figure 18.12   Dependency Walker.

Using DDESpy

The Dynamic Data Exchange (DDE) protocol provides a method of transferring data between applications that use shared memory. Applications can use the DDE protocol for one-time data transfers and for continuous exchanges in which applications send updates as new data become available. DDESpy monitors DDE operations. To use DDESpy, proceed as follows:

1. Access Start|Programs|Platform SDK|Tools and select DDESpy.

2. Use the Output menu to select whether output is to be sent to a file, a debug terminal, or the DDESpy window. If you choose to send to a file, you must specify the output file name. You can use the Mark command to add text to the display as a marker.

3. Use the Monitor menu to indicate the information that DDESpy displays. One or more of the following can be specified:

   - String handle data
   - Sent DDE messages
   - Posted DDE messages
   - Callbacks
   - Errors
   - Filters

TIP: You can use the Filters option to choose the types of DDE messages and callbacks to monitor.

4. Use the Track menu to specify which activity is tracked. DDESpy creates a separate window for the display of information, and you can sort the displayed information in the tracking window. This is useful if you're searching for a particular event or handle.

Using the Debug Monitor

The Debug Monitor runs in its own Command Console window and displays messages that your application sends by using the OutputDebugString function. To access the Debug Monitor, proceed as follows:

1. Access Start|Programs|Platform SDK|Tools and select DbMon.

Viewing Clipboard Content Information

The Data Object viewer displays details of objects currently in the clipboard or drag-and-drop objects. To view this information, proceed as follows:

1. Access Start|Programs|Platform SDK|Tools and select Data Object Viewer.

18. Network Application Interfaces

2. In the Clipboard pull-down menu, select View Clipboard Data Object.

3. Use the Data Object pull-down menu to show the object descriptor and obtain the values of the associated flags.

Using the Windows Debugger

The platform SDK provides the same Windows Debugger tool that is downloaded with the Windows 2000 DDK. This tool is accessed through the Start|Programs| Debugging Tools menu. It can be configured by using the Debug Wizard. The Windows Debugger tool is described in Chapter 2 and again in Chapter 17.

Related solution:	See page:
Debugging Drivers	621

Obtaining Details of All Platform SDK Tools

Space considerations make it impracticable to describe all of the many tools provided with the platform DDK. The above procedures describe the use of the more significant tools—that is, those that are accessed through the Start menu. To obtain a list and descriptions of all the tools installed with the platform SDK, proceed as follows:

1. Access Start|Programs|Platform SDK and select Platform SDK Documentation.

2. In the Search tab, type **Tools**. Click List Topics.

3. Select Platform SDK Tools. This is typically about number 3 on the topics list.

4. Click Display.

5. Scroll down the list to find the tool whose details you want to find. Click the hypertext link to get details.

Using the Windows 2000 Driver Development Kit

The set of procedures for downloading and using the Windows 2000 DDK was described in Chapters 2 and 17. Refer to the related solutions table on the next page for details.

Configuring a WSH DLL

Standardized configuration must be set up in the Registry for any additional WSH DLL that you introduce in an interface routine. The Registry is edited using regedt32.exe, which is located in the %Systemroot%\System32 folder.

WARNING! Before editing the Registry, make sure that all your important files are backed up. Save the Registry key before you edit it.

To configure a WSH DLL, check that the Registry has the entries described below. You may not have to set these up manually (see the tip following the procedure), but if the subkeys aren't set up as described you need to edit them.

Under the subkey:

```
HKEY_LOCAL_MACHINE\
        STSTEM\
            CurrentControlSet\
                Services\
                    Winsock\
                        Parameters
```

You require a value entry of type REG_MULTI_SZ that specifies a list of protocols (or transport drivers), each of which has a corresponding WSH DLL. The names stored in this list match the key names for the corresponding transport drivers under the subkey:

```
HKEY_LOCAL_MACHINE\
        SYSTEM\
            CurrentControlSet\
                Services\
```

Under the subkey:

```
HKEY_LOCAL_MACHINE\
       SYSTEM\
            CurrentControlSet\
                 Services\
                         TransportDriverName\
                              Parameters\
                                   Winsock
```

you require the following value entries:

- *Mapping*—a REG_BINARY value that describes the address family, socket type, and protocol parameter triples supported by the WSH DLL. The format for this binary data is the WINSOCK_MAPPING structure, as defined in the wsahelp.h file that's downloaded with the Windows 2000 DDK.

- *HelperDllName*—A REG_EXPAND_SZ value that specifies the path to the WSH DLL.

- *MinSockaddrLength*—A REG_DWORD value that specifies the smallest valid SOCKADDR size, in bytes, for the WSH DLL.

- *MaxSockaddrLength*—A REG_DWORD value that specifies the largest valid SOCKADDR size, in bytes, for the WSH DLL.

TIP: Windows 2000 setup utilities provide functions that perform most of the necessary tasks to set up WSH DDL Registry information for a transport driver. These routines are AddWinsockInfo and RemoveWinsockInfo in the setup file utility.inf, which can be found in the system directory. A transport driver's installation script can call AddWinsockInfo, passing in the key name under Services of the transport driver, the full path name of the transport-specific WSH DLL, and the minimum and maximum SOCKADDR lengths. AddWinsockInfo then stores the standardized information in the Registry. For an example of a transport's call to this setup function, refer to oemnxptc.inf (the installation script for TCP/IP), which is also located in the system directory.

Chapter 19

Network Management and Troubleshooting

In Depth

This chapter describes the wide variety of tools available in Windows 2000 for network management and troubleshooting. It covers Simple Network Management Protocol, Event Viewer, the Performance Logs and Alerts Tool, System Monitor, Network Monitor, and the various command-line tools.

Before starting to troubleshoot a problem, however, you have to find out exactly what it is. You need to take a commonsense approach, remembering that the least reliable part of any system is located between the mouse and the seat. There are a number of questions you should ask:

- Did it ever work?
- What's still working?
- What has stopped working?
- How are the things that do and don't work related?
- What's it doing now that it didn't do before?
- What's it not doing now that it did do before?
- What was changed just before the problem occurred?

Then, there are two questions to ask yourself:

- Have I solved this problem before and documented the solution?
- Has the problem been solved by someone else and documented in TechNet?

This leads to the other important thing you need to do, and I can't emphasize this enough: *document the problem and the solution.* A job isn't complete unless it's documented. It's not easy for the harassed system support person, network engineer, or consultant to find the time to do the documentation. Find the time. It pays handsomely in the long run.

Simple Network Management Protocol

Windows 2000 implements Simple Network Management Protocol (SNMP) versions 1 and 2C. SNMP is widely used in TCP/IP networks and also in Internetwork Packet Exchange (IPX) networks. RFC 1157 defines how communication occurs between SNMP-capable devices and which types of messages are allowed.

Although SNMP primarily provides a network management service, it can detect device errors and other network problems. It also provides a primitive form of security through the use of *traps* and *communities*.

SNMP manages such network hosts as computers, routers, bridges, switches, and hubs from a central computer that runs network management software. It uses a distributed architecture of management systems and agents to perform the following management services:

- *Remote device configuration*—The management system can send configuration information to each networked host. This function is possible, but atypical.

- *Network performance monitoring*—Processing speed and network throughput can be tracked, and information about the success of data transmissions collected.

- *Detection of network problems*—Alarms can be configured on network devices. When an alarm is triggered, the device forwards an event message to the management system. Common types of alarms include device shutdown and restart, link failure on a router, and inappropriate access.

- *Network usage auditing*—Overall network usage can be monitored to identify user or group access, as can usage types for network devices and services.

SNMP Management System

The SNMP management system, also called *management console*, sends update requests to an SNMP agent. The requests are for such information as the amount of hard disk space available or the number of active sessions. The management system can also send information that initiates changes to an agent's configuration, but this is rare because access to an SNMP agent is typically read-only.

SNMP Agent

The SNMP agent allows remote, centralized management of computers that run:

- Windows 2000 Server
- Windows 2000 Professional
- Windows 2000 Windows Internet Name Service (WINS)
- Windows 2000 Dynamic Host Configuration Protocol (DHCP)
- Internet Information Service version 5 (IIS5)
- Local Area Network (LAN) Manager

To access information that's provided by the SNMP agent, you need at least one SNMP management system application on the host that acts as the management system. The Windows 2000 SNMP service supports but doesn't currently include SNMP management software.

TIP: For more information about SNMP management software and applications, see the Windows 2000 Resource Kit. Details are available at **http://windows.microsoft.com/windows2000/reskit**.

The Windows 2000 SNMP Service, which is agent software, responds to information requests from one or more management systems. The SNMP Service can be configured to determine which statistics are tracked and which management systems are authorized to request information.

Typically, agents don't originate messages other than *trap* messages. A trap is an alarm-triggering event on an agent, such as a system reboot or an illegal access attempt. Management hosts and agents belong to an SNMP *community*, which is a collection of hosts that are grouped together for administrative purposes. Only management systems and agents within the same community can communicate with each other. An attempted access by a management system from outside the community will result in a trap message.

SNMP agent services are listed in Table 19.1.

You can also configure agent properties, such as a contact name (normally a network administrator) and the location of the contact.

Management Information Bases

The information that the management system requests is contained in a Management Information Base (MIB). A MIB contains various types of information about a network host. If, for example, the host were a computer the MIB could hold the version of network software running on that computer and the available hard drive space.

Table 19.1 SNMP agent services.

Service	Description
Physical	Enabled if the host manages physical devices such as hard disks.
Applications	Enabled if the host uses applications that send data using the TCP/IP protocol suite. This service should always be enabled.
Datalink and subnetwork	Enabled if the host manages a bridge.
Internet	Enabled if the host is an IP gateway (router).
End-to-end	Enabled for IP hosts. This service should always be enabled.

The Internet Management Information Base II (MIB II), defined in RFC 1213, is a set of manageable objects representing various types of information about TCP/IP components in a network, such as the network interfaces list, routing table, and TCP connections table. Windows 2000 SNMP supports the following MIBs:

- Host Resources MIB (RFC 1514)
- LAN Manager MIB II
- DHCP MIB
- WINS MIB
- IIS MIB

Third parties can develop their own MIBs for use with the Windows 2000 SNMP service. Such MIBs must adhere to the Structure for Management Information (SMI) defined in RFC 1902, which describes the object syntax for specifying how MIB data is referenced and stored.

TIP: *For detailed information about MIB objects, refer to the Windows 2000 Resource Kit.*

Router MIBs

A Windows 2000 router that's an SNMP agent supports the following MIBs:

- Internet MIB II (see above)
- IP Forwarding Table MIB (RFC 1354)
- Microsoft Routing Internet Protocol version 2 (RIPv2) for IP MIB
- Wellfleet-Series7-MIB for Open Shortest Path First (OSPF)
- Microsoft BOOTP for IP MIB

Remote Access Service Server

A Remote Access Service (RAS) server that participates in the SNMP service as an SNMP agent supports the Internet MIB II.

Multicasting MIBs

Multicasting uses the Internet Group Management Protocol (IGMP—see Chapter 6). Objects in the IGMP MIB are documented in the Internet draft **draft-ietf-idmr-igmp-mib-0x.txt**; objects in the IP Multicast Routing MIB are documented in **draft-ietf-idmr-multicast-routmib-0x.txt**, where (in both cases) x is the current version number. Refer to the Internet Engineering Task Force (IETF) site at **www.ietf.org**.

SNMP Messages

Both agents and management systems use SNMP messages to inspect and communicate host information. SNMP messages are sent using User Datagram Protocol (UDP). Internet Protocol (IP) is used to route the messages between the management system and host. When SNMP management programs send requests to a network device, the agent software on that device receives the requests and retrieves information from MIBs. The agent then sends the requested information back to the initiating SNMP management program. SNMP messages are described in Table 19.2.

SNMP Operation

As illustrated in Figure 19.1, SNMP works as follows:

1. The management system (Server 1) sends an SNMP datagram to an agent (Host A), using the agent's host name or IP address.

2. The agent receives the datagram and verifies the community name to which the management system belongs. If it's a valid community name, the agent retrieves the requested data. If the community name is incorrect, the agent sends an authentication failure trap to its trap destination (Host B).

3. The agent returns the datagram to the management system with the requested information.

Table 19.2   SNMP messages.

Message	Description
Get	Sent by an SNMP management system to request information about a single MIB entry on an SNMP agent.
Set	If an SNMP management system is permitted write access to an agent (unusual), this message is used to assign an updated MIB value to the agent.
Trap	An unsolicited message sent by an SNMP agent to an SNMP management system when the agent detects that a certain type of event (such as an illegal access attempt) has occurred locally on the managed host. An SNMP management console that receives a trap message is known as a *trap destination*.
Get-next	Sent by an SNMP management system to browse the entire tree of management objects. The Get-next message is used to obtain tabular information, such as the contents of an IP route table.
Getbulk	Requests that the data transferred by the agent be as large as possible within given restraints of message size. The maximum message size should not be larger than the Path Maximum Transmission Unit (PMTU—see Chapter 8), or fragmentation can occur.

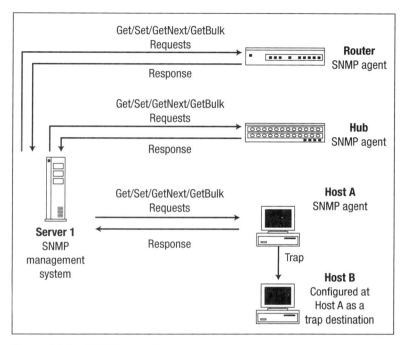

Figure 19.1   SNMP operation.

NOTE: *In Figure 19.1, the hub and router illustrated take no part in the operation as described. They're included as a reminder that network computers aren't the only hosts that can use an SNMP system.*

SNMP Communities

Groups of SNMP hosts (agents and management systems) are assigned to communities for security checking or for administrative purposes. Communities are identified by assigned community names. A host can belong to several communities at the same time, but an agent doesn't accept requests from management systems outside its list of assigned community names.

A community name is the equivalent of a shared password for groups of network hosts and should be selected and managed as you would manage any password. Physical proximity usually determines which hosts belong to the same community, although the best practice is to define communities by functional organization. Figure 19.2 illustrates SNMP communities.

NOTE: *There's no relationship between community names and domain or workgroup names. If no community is defined for an SNMP host, it's a member of the community* public *by default.*

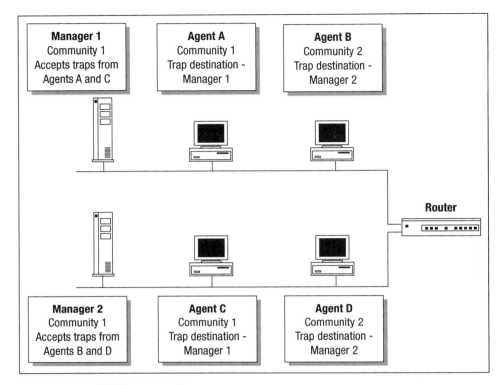

Figure 19.2   SNMP communities.

SNMP Security Properties

SNMP provides security through the use of community names and authentication traps. The following options are configured to define SNMP security properties:

- *Accepted community names*—The SNMP service requires at least one default community name. The common community name *public* is universally accepted in all SNMP implementations. You can add additional community names. If an SNMP request is received from a community that isn't on the list, it will generate an authentication trap.

- *Rights*—Permission levels can be defined to determine how the SNMP agent processes requests from a selected community.

- *Accept SNMP packets from any host*—If this option is selected (the default), no SNMP packets are rejected on the basis of the name or address of the source host, provided that host is a member of an accepted community.

- *Accept SNMP packets from these hosts*—If this option is selected, only SNMP packets received from the hosts in the list are accepted. Otherwise, the SNMP message is rejected and an authentication trap sent. This selection provides greater security than the use of community names alone, because a community may contain many hosts.

- *Send authentication trap*—When an SNMP agent receives a request that doesn't contain the correct community name, or isn't sent from a member of an acceptable host list, it sends an authentication trap message to one or more trap destinations. This option is checked by default.

Event Viewer

Event Viewer is often the first port of call during troubleshooting. Most of us have seen the dreaded message "One or more services failed to start, see Event Viewer for details". You can access Event Viewer and the event logs to gather information about hardware, software, and system problems. The EventLog service starts automatically when you start Windows 2000.

There is another, less obvious form of troubleshooting for which you use the Event Viewer tool. If someone is trying to log on using another person's account (possibly yours) or if users aren't able to access resources that they should be able to (or can access resources that they shouldn't be able to), then you may not have a system failure, but you surely have trouble. Event Viewer is also used to monitor Windows 2000 security events, as defined by the domain's audit policies.

Event Viewer records events in three types of log:

- *System log*—Contains events logged by Windows 2000 system components. For example, the failure of a driver to load during startup is recorded in the system log. Windows 2000 predetermines the event types logged by system components. All users can view the system log.

- *Security log*—Contains events specified by the computer's audit policy. These events could include valid and/or invalid logon attempts (usually the latter), in addition to events related to resource use—such as creating, opening, or deleting files, folders, or printers. By default, only administrators can set up audit policy and manage the security log. For information on enabling and implementing audit policy, refer to the Immediate Solutions section of this chapter.

- *Application log*—Contains events logged by programs (for example, file errors). Program developers decide which events to monitor. All users can view the application log.

NOTE: *All Event Viewers contain the system, security, and application logs. Some contain additional logs. For example, Event Viewers on domain controllers (DCs) will contain directory service and file replication service logs. Event Viewers on Domain Name System (DNS) servers will contain DNS server logs. These logs are treated in the same way as the system log.*

Interpreting an Event

You can obtain details about an event on any of the event logs by double-clicking that event (see the Immediate Solutions section later in this chapter). The information takes the form of an event header followed by an event type. Identities (IDs) are sometimes determined by whether or not *impersonation* is taking place. Impersonation occurs when one process takes on the security attributes of another. The event error, information, and warning types are used in the system and application logs. The success and failure audit types are used in the security logs. Event types are associated with icons; for example, a padlock for a failure audit.

Tables 19.3 and 19.4 give details of the event header and type information.

Table 19.3   Event header information.

Information	Meaning
Date	The date on which the event occurred.
Time	The local time at which the event occurred.
User	The account name of the user on whose behalf the event occurred. This is the client ID if the event was caused by a server process, or the primary ID if impersonation isn't taking place. A security log entry may contain both primary and impersonation IDs.
Computer	The name of the computer where the event occurred—usually the computer on which the EventLog service is running.
Event ID	A number corresponding to the particular event type.
Source	The software that logged the event. This can be either a program name or a system component, such as a driver name.
Type	A classification of the event severity—Error, Information, or Warning in the system and application logs and Success Audit or Failure Audit in the security log.
Category	A classification of the event by the event source (such as logon and logoff, object access, or privilege use).

Table 19.4   Event type.

Type	Description
Error	A significant problem, such as loss of data or loss of functionality—for example, a service fails to load during startup.
Warning	An event that isn't immediately significant, but may indicate a possible future problem—for example, disk space is low.
Information	The successful operation of an application, driver, or service—for example, a network driver loads successfully.
Success Audit	A security access attempt that succeeds—for example, a user successfully opens an audited file.
Failure Audit	A security access attempt that fails—for example, a failed logon attempt.

Some events generate a data field that contains binary data (displayed in hexadecimal format and its ASCII equivalent). The designer of the source program that recorded the event can interpret the meaning of this data.

Figure 19.3 shows the event details for a WINS error event in the system log.

Finding Specific Events

When you're viewing a large log, possibly built up over a period of time, you can use the find and filter facilities to locate events of interest. For example, you might be experiencing some difficulty with DNS service and want to find all warning or error events related to that service. Maybe you suspect that someone is trying to log in using an account that isn't his or her own. In this case, you can search for all logon failures in the security log.

You can use the Find command (see Immediate Solutions) to find a specified event or events. It's often more convenient, however, to filter the log so that it displays a subset of events with specific characteristics. Filtering has no effect on log contents, but merely changes the view. All events are logged continuously, not just the ones specified by the filter. You can filter events using one or more of the following criteria:

- *View events from*—Events that occur at or after a specific date and time.
- *View events to*—Events that occur up to and including a specific date and time.
- *Event type*—Information, warning, error, success audit, failure audit.
- *Source*—See Table 19.3.

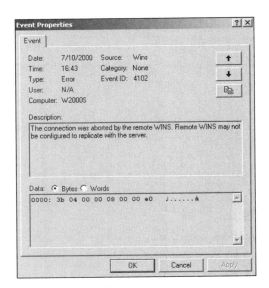

Figure 19.3   A WINS error event.

- *Category*—See Table 19.3.
- *User*—Matches a user account name.
- *Computer*—Matches a computer name.
- *Event ID*—See Table 19.3.

The Find command also uses the above criteria, except for "view events from" and "view events to".

Archiving Event Logs

By default, the maximum size of an event log is 512KB, and events aren't over-written until they're at least seven days old. It's therefore possible for a log to get full. If this happens, logging stops. Although you can set a log to overwrite events as needed, this isn't a complete solution because it can result in the loss of valuable information. In particular, security information shouldn't be overwritten unless it has been saved for later reference.

TIP: *You can set auditing policies in the Registry that cause the system to halt when the security log is full. In the subkey HKEY_LOCAL_MACHINE\SYSTEM\CurrentControlSet\Control\Lsa, set the parameter* CrashOnAuditFail *to 1.*

The answer is to archive the logs regularly. Once a log is archived, you can allow events to be overwritten, or you can clear the log manually. Archived logs allow you to track trends and possibly to solve potential problems before they become serious. If you solved a problem previously and it recurs, comparing current logs with archived logs and referring to a documented solution can save you a lot of time and effort. Archiving has no effect on the log contents. If you want to clear the log, you need to do this manually after you've archived it.

An event log can be archived in one of three file formats:

- Log-file format (EVT)—Lets you view the archived log again in Event Viewer.
- Text-file format (TXT)—Lets you access the information by using a text editor or a word processor.
- Comma-delimited text-file format (CSV)—Lets you access the information by using spreadsheet or database software.

> **WARNING!** *If you archive the log in text or in comma-delimited file format, the binary data isn't saved.*

Monitoring Security Events

By default, no audit policy is defined and no events are recorded in the security log. To enable security event logging, an administrator has to define and implement an audit policy. In some cases, this requires only one operation. If you define an audit policy that records logon failures, then logon failures will be recorded. If, on the other hand, you define an audit policy that records both successful and unsuccessful object access, you have to implement that policy by specifying which files, folders, and printers are to be monitored. You also need to specify the groups and/or individuals for which you want to set up this monitoring.

Using Group Policy sets up audit policy. File and object access monitoring is implemented by first setting up the general Group Policy, then using Windows Explorer to specify the objects and users to be monitored.

Too much information is as bad as too little. Security auditing should be useful, but manageable. You're unlikely to record logon successes, but almost certainly want to record logon failures. You won't record access to every file and printer, but you should record both successful and unsuccessful attempts to access confidential information. If you're the only person that manages the user database, you probably won't record account management events. If, on the other hand, this task is delegated to Account Operators, you may decide that it's wise to keep a record of their activities.

As with many administrative tasks, defining and implementing security auditing is relatively easy. Finding the time to study the security log on a regular basis is much more difficult. If you intend to implement an audit policy, your first task is to schedule and reserve a time slot to check the security log.

NOTE: *You can audit file and folder access on NTFS volumes only.*

The Performance Logs and Alerts Tool

Two Windows 2000 tools—Performance Logs and Alerts, and System Monitor—implement the functionality previously provided by Windows NT4 Performance Monitor. Performance Logs and Alerts supports detailed monitoring of the utilization of operating system resources and logs performance data from local or remote computers. You can view logged counter data using System Monitor or export the data to spreadsheet programs or to databases for analysis and report generation. The Performance Logs and Alerts tool offers the following capabilities:

- It collects data in a comma-separated or tab-separated format for easy import to spreadsheet programs. A binary log-file format is also provided for circular logging—that is, the process of continuously logging data to a single file, overwriting previous data with new data as necessary. Binary logs are also used for logging (for example) threads or processes that may begin after the log starts collecting data.

- It enables counter data to be viewed during collection as well as after collection has stopped.

- Data collection occurs regardless of whether or not any user is logged on to the computer that's being monitored.

- It lets you define start and stop times, file names, file sizes, and other parameters for automatic log generation.

- Multiple logging sessions can be managed from a single console window.

- Alerts enable a message to be sent, a program run, or a log started when a selected counter's value exceeds or falls below a specified setting.

Performance Logs and Alerts lets you define performance objects, performance counters, and object instances and set sampling intervals for monitoring data about hardware resources and system services. It also offers the following options for recording performance data:

- Logging can be started or stopped manually; it can also be started or stopped automatically, based on a user-defined schedule.

- Additional settings can be configured for automatic logging, such as automatic file renaming and parameters for stopping and starting a log based on the elapsed time or the file size.

- Trace logs can be implemented that record data when certain activities, such as a disk Input Output (I/O) operation or a page fault, occur. When the event happens, the provider sends the data to the Performance Logs and Alerts service. This differs from the operation of counter logs, which return data to the system when the update interval has elapsed, rather than waiting for a specific event.

- A program can be defined that runs when a log is stopped.

NOTE: *The Performance Logs and Alerts service must be stopped when exporting log data to Microsoft Excel, because Microsoft Excel requires exclusive access to the log file. This isn't, however, the case for most data analysis programs. Usually, you can work with data from a log file while the service is collecting data in that file.*

System Monitor

Performance Logs and Alerts lets you create counter and trace logs and set alert conditions. System Monitor is an ActiveX control that lets you view these logs, as line graphs, histograms, or reports. The tool lets you capture and display real-time data and generate reports.

System Monitor can measure the performance of your own computer or other computers on a network, include monitored data in reports generated by Microsoft Office applications (such as Word), create HTML pages from performance views, and create reusable monitoring configurations that can be installed on other computers.

Configuring Monitoring

You configure monitoring by deciding what objects you want to monitor, what computers you want to monitor them on, and at what time intervals logging should occur. The Performance Logs and Alerts tool and the System Monitor tool both use the same objects. The former creates logs and alerts, the latter views the results and accesses real-time data.

Performance Objects

A range of performance objects are built into the operating system (OS), typically corresponding to major hardware components, such as memory, processors, and so on. Services (such as WINS) or server programs (such as SQL Server) provide additional performance objects. Each performance object is associated with a set of counters that provide information about specific aspects of the system or service. The default objects used most frequently to monitor system components are:

- Cache
- Memory
- Objects
- Paging File
- Physical Disk
- Process
- Processor
- Server
- System
- Thread

Table 19.5 lists some of the Windows 2000 services and features that provide performance objects in addition to those listed above.

I haven't expanded every acronym or explained what every object in Table 19.5 represents. Most of the terms can be found in the Glossary, but the best method of obtaining details about performance objects and their associated counters is to click Explain in the Add Counters dialog box when adding counters to Performance Logs and Alerts or System Monitor. The procedure to do this is described in the Immediate Solutions section of this chapter.

Depending on how the counter is defined, its value may be either of the following:

- The most recent measurement of an aspect of resource utilization. Counters defined in this way are called instantaneous counters. An example is Process\Thread Count, which shows the number of threads for a particular process the last time this was measured.

Table 19.5   *Performance objects provided by Windows 2000 features and services.*

Feature or Service	Performance Objects
Browser, Workstation, and Server Services	Browser, Redirector, and Server objects.
Connection Point Services	PBServer Monitor object.
Directory Service	NTDS object.
Indexing Service	Indexing Service, Indexing Service Filter, and HTTP Indexing Service objects.
NetBEUI	NetBEUI and NetBEUI resource objects.
Print server activity	Print queue object.
Quality of Service (QoS) Admission Control	ACS/RSVP Service and Interface objects.
TCP/IP	ICMP, IP, NBT, TCP, and UDP objects.
WINS	WINS object.

- The average of the last two measurements over the period between samples. An example is Memory\Pages/sec—a rate per second based on the average number of memory pages written to virtual memory during the last two samples.

NOTE: *Other counter types can be defined as described in the Platform Software Development Kit (SDK). Downloading the Platform SDK and its accompanying documentation is described in Chapter 18.*

Instances

Some performance objects can have multiple *instances*. For example, there are several instances of the Process object, one for each process, and a computer with multiple CPUs will have multiple instances of the Processor object. If an object has multiple instances, you can add counters to track statistics for each instance or for all instances at once.

NOTE: *The combination of computer name, object, counter, instance, and instance index is known as the* counter path. *Counter path is typically written as follows:* Computer_name\Object_name(Instance_name#Index_Number)\Counter_name

Configuring Logs and Graphs

You can use graphs for short-term, real-time monitoring of a local or remote computer. Choose the update interval depending on the type of activity you're interested in. Logs are useful for record keeping and extended monitoring. Logged data can be exported for report generation and presented as graphs or histograms by using System Monitor. Logging is the most practical way to monitor multiple computers.

Start by logging activity over 15-minute intervals for routine monitoring. If you're monitoring activity of a specific process at a specific time, set a frequent update interval. If, however, you're monitoring a problem that manifests itself slowly (such as a memory leak) use a longer interval.

Setting the update interval to a frequent rate (low value) can cause the system to generate a large amount of data. This can be difficult to work with and can increase the overhead of running Performance Logs and Alerts. Monitoring a large number of objects and counters can also generate large amounts of data and consume disk space. You need to strike a balance between the number of objects that you monitor and the sampling frequency, so that you keep log file size within manageable limits.

Choosing What to Monitor

Start by monitoring activity of components in the following order:

1. Memory
2. Processors
3. Disks
4. Network

Table 19.6 shows the (minimum) recommended counters for server monitoring. When examining specific resources, include additional counters for the performance object of interest.

Table 19.6   Recommended counters.

Component	What's Monitored	Counters
Memory	Usage	Memory\Available Bytes, Memory\Cache Bytes.
Memory	Bottlenecks or leaks	Memory\Pages/sec, Memory\Page Reads/sec, Memory\Transition Faults/sec, Memory\Pool Paged Bytes, Memory\Pool Nonpaged Bytes.
Processor	Usage	Processor\% Processor Time (all instances).
Processor	Bottlenecks	System\Processor Queue Length (all instances), Processor\Interrupts/sec, System\Context switches/sec.
Disk	Usage	Physical Disk\Disk Reads/sec, Physical Disk\Disk Writes/sec, LogicalDisk\% Free Space.
Disk	Bottlenecks	Physical Disk\Avg. Disk Queue Length (all instances).
Network	Usage	Network Segment\% Net Utilization.
Network (TCP/IP)	Throughput	Network Interface\Bytes total/sec, Network Interface\Packets/sec, Server\Bytes Total/sec, Server\Bytes Transmitted/sec, Server\Bytes Received/sec.

> **TIP:**   *Although they're not memory object counters, the following are also useful for memory analysis: Paging File\%
> Usage object (all instances), Cache\Data Map Hits %, Server\Pool Paged Bytes, and Server\Pool Nonpaged Bytes.*

Logical Disk Counters

The OS doesn't collect logical disk counter data by default. To obtain counter data for logical drives,
you need to enter **diskperf -yv** at the command prompt. By default, the operating system uses the
diskperf -yd command to obtain physical drive data.

Interpret the % Disk Time counter carefully, because this counter may not accurately reflect utilization
on multiple-disk systems. If you have multiple disk drives—possibly in a Redundant Array of
Independent Drives (RAID) configuration—use the % Idle Time counter as well.

RAID is often considered to be an acronym for Redundant Array of Inexpensive Drives (or Disks).
However, Microsoft's documentation uses "Independent Drives". I believe this makes more sense.
"Inexpensive" is a relative term and is difficult to define.

> **NOTE:**   *You must install the Network Monitor driver for Network Monitor in order to use the Network Segment\%
> Net Utilization counter.*

Monitoring Remote Computers

You can implement performance logging on a central computer, drawing data
continuously from other computers. Alternatively, you can configure each computer to collect data pertaining to its own counters. You would then run a batch
program at regular intervals to transfer the data to the central computer for analysis
and archiving.

If you choose the first of these options, known as *centralized data collection*, you
can collect data from multiple systems into a single log file. This, however, causes
additional network traffic and may be restricted by the available memory on the
central computer. When you're adding counters to a log, you can specify a remote
computer in the Add Counters dialog box. See the Immediate Solutions section of
this chapter for details.

If you choose the second option, known as *distributed data collection*, this doesn't
create the memory and network traffic problems associated with centralized collection. However, it does delay data availability. Distributed data collection is
implemented using the Computer Management tool.

To monitor remote systems from your computer, you must start the Performance
Logs and Alerts Service using an account that has permission to access the remote computers that you want to monitor. By default, the service is started under
the local computer's system account, which generally has permission to access

services and resources only on the local computer. Using Services in the Computer Management tool lets you update the properties of the Performance Logs and Alerts service and change the account under which it runs.

Network Monitor

Network Monitor, described in Chapter 3, is used to monitor network traffic. The standard version of Network Monitor supplied with Windows 2000 Server enables you to monitor all traffic to and from the server on which it's running. A full version of Network Monitor, supplied with Microsoft System Management Server (SMS), enables you to monitor all network traffic on your server's subnet.

In order to do this, the full version of Network Monitor disables the hardware filters on your server's Network Interface Card (NIC), so that the server processes every frame on the network. This is known as putting the NIC into *promiscuous mode*, which results in the server's suffering a significant performance hit. The full version of Network Monitor is a very powerful tool, but it should be used sparingly. It is, however, used in troubleshooting, where monitoring only traffic to and from a server may not be adequate.

Where faults are intermittent, such as problems caused by duplicate IP addresses when both of the offending machines are seldom on the network at the same time, Network Monitor may solve the problem where tools, such as Arp, cannot. Even a fairly short network capture contains a lot of information. If you use Network Monitor for debugging, you need to be familiar with capture and display filters and with capture triggers. These are explained in Chapter 3, and I've added references to the appropriate sections in the Immediate Solutions section of this chapter.

Command-Line Tools

Graphical User Interfaces (GUIs), such as Event Viewer and Performance Monitor, provide powerful and effective monitoring and fault finding facilities. When it comes to determining the exact fault and fixing it, however, many professionals rely on the command-line tools. These may look difficult, with their many switches and text-based output, but the switches give you detailed control, and the output can often give more detail, and more accurate information, than can any graphics display.

Ipconfig

I've used the Ipconfig tool, particularly the **ipconfig /all** command, to fix more faults than all of the other tools put together. This tool shows you the IP address, subnet mask, default gateway, and Media Access Control (MAC) address for every interface in your computer. It tells you what NIC drivers you have installed and where your computer is obtaining WINS, DNS, and DHCP information (if relevant).

```
Command Prompt                                    _ □ X
C:\>ipconfig /all

Windows 2000 IP Configuration

        Host Name . . . . . . . . . . . : w2000s
        Primary DNS Suffix  . . . . . . : coriolis.com
        Node Type . . . . . . . . . . . : Hybrid
        IP Routing Enabled. . . . . . . : Yes
        WINS Proxy Enabled. . . . . . . : No
        DNS Suffix Search List. . . . . : coriolis.com

Ethernet adapter Local Area Connection:

        Connection-specific DNS Suffix  . :
        Description . . . . . . . . . . : Intel(R) PRO/100+

        Physical Address. . . . . . . . : 00-D0-B7-48-1D-2E
        DHCP Enabled. . . . . . . . . . : No
        IP Address. . . . . . . . . . . : 195.162.230.173
        Subnet Mask . . . . . . . . . . : 255.255.255.0
        Default Gateway . . . . . . . . : 195.162.231.1
        DNS Servers . . . . . . . . . . : 195.162.230.1
                                          195.162.231.1
        Primary WINS Server . . . . . . : 195.162.230.1
```

Figure 19.4   Using the Ipconfig tool.

Figure 19.4 shows the output of an **ipconfig /all** command for a statically configured computer. Inspection of the results should tell you that either the default gateway is incorrect or (less likely) the default subnet mask should be modified (for example, to 255.255.254.0) to permit supernetting (see Chapter 5).

Ipconfig is also used to release and renew IP addresses when testing DHCP. Table 19.7 lists the Ipconfig switches.

Ping

The Ping tool is used to verify IP-level connectivity. The **ping** command sends an Internet Control Message Protocol (ICMP) echo request to a target name or IP address. Typically, the IP address of the target host is pinged first. If the host responds, it's then pinged by name to test name resolution.

Table 19.7   The Ipconfig switches.

Switch	Function
/all	Produces a detailed configuration report for all interfaces.
/flushdns	Removes all entries from the DNS name cache.
/registerdns	Refreshes all DHCP leases and reregisters DNS names.
/displaydns	Displays the contents of the DNS resolver cache.
/release *adapter*	Releases the IP address for a specified interface.
/renew *adapter*	Renews the IP address for a specified interface.
/showclassid *adapter*	Displays all the DHCP class IDs allowed for the adapter specified.
/setclassid *adapter classID_to_set*	Changes the DHCP class ID for the adapter specified.

If you can't reach the target host, you can test IP connectivity by successive **ping** commands. Pinging the loopback address, 127.0.0.1, verifies that TCP/IP is installed and configured on the local host. If this ping fails, the IP stack isn't responding, possibly because the TCP drivers are corrupted, the NIC is faulty, or another service is interfering with IP.

Pinging the IP address of the local computer verifies that it was added to the network correctly. Pinging the IP address of the default gateway verifies that this gateway is functioning and that you can communicate with a local host.

TIP: *The **ipconfig /all** command pings both the loopback address and the IP address of the local host. If **ipconfig /all** returns the expected configuration information, you don't need to carry out these tests.*

Ping can also be used to determine the PMTU between two computers (see Chapter 8). In combination with the Arp tool, Ping can be used to determine the MAC address of a computer on the same subnet. Ping lets you specify the size of packets to use, how many packets to send, whether to record the route used, what Time-to-Live (TTL) value to use, and whether to set the Don't Fragment (DF) flag. Table 19.8 lists the Ping switches.

> **WARNING!**   **If Internet Protocol Security (IPSec) is implemented, Ping will fail until a Security Association (SA) has been agreed between the hosts. See Chapter 7 for details.**

Table 19.8   Ping switches.

Switch	Function
-t	Pings the specified host until stopped.
-a	Resolves addresses to host names.
-n *count*	Sets the number of Echo Requests to send.
-l *size*	Sends packets of a specified size.
-f	Sets the DF flag in outgoing packets.
-i *TTL*	Specifies a TTL for outgoing packets.
-v *TOS*	Specifies type of service (see Chapter 9).
-r *count*	Records the route for the specified number of hops.
-s *count*	Sets a timestamp for the specified number of hops.
-j *host-list*	Specifies a loose source route along the host-list.
-k *host-list*	Specifies a strict source route along the host-list.
-w	Sets a wait period (in milliseconds) for a response.

Tracert

Tracert is a route-tracing tool that uses the IP TTL field and ICMP error messages to determine the route from one host to another through a network. It works by incrementing the TTL value by one for each ICMP Echo Request that it sends, then waiting for an ICMP Time Exceeded message. The TTL starts with an initial value of one; after each trace, the TTL is incremented by one. Thus, a packet sent out by Tracert travels one hop further on each successive trip. Tracert switches are listed in Table 19.9.

> **NOTE:**   Some routers, known as black hole routers, silently drop packets with expired TTLs. These routers don't appear in the Tracert display. Refer to Chapter 8 for details of how to detect black hole routers.

> **TIP:**   Use of the **-d** switch speeds up Tracert operation considerably.

PathPing

The PathPing tool combines the functionality of the Ping and Tracert tools and, also, provides additional information. PathPing sends packets to each router on the way to a final destination over a period of time. As a result, the tool can calculate the packet loss at any given router or link, and you can pinpoint which routers or links might be causing network problems. Table 19.10 lists the PathPing switches.

Although PathPing is a powerful and useful tool, the results it returns should be treated with caution. Routers are designed to route packets quickly, with very little processing. This is known as *fast track* routing. A router doesn't fast-track a PathPing packet, but instead processes it using ICMP Echo Requests and Echo Replies to test route connectivity. Thus, packets can be lost through congestion that would otherwise have been fast-tracked through the router without loss. Always compare the PathPing statistics with actual packet-loss data.

Nevertheless, if PathPing identifies a router as being a problem, it probably is.

Table 19.9   Tracert switches.

Switch	Function
-d	Prevents the resolution of router interface addresses to host names.
-h *maximum_hops*	Specifies a maximum number of hops to reach destination.
-j *host_list*	Specifies loose source routing along the host-list.
-w *timeout*	Indicates how many milliseconds to wait for each reply.

Table 19.10   PathPing switches.

Switch	Function
-n	Specifies that addresses aren't resolved to host names.
-h *max_hops*	Specifies the maximum number of hops used to search for a target.
-g *destination address router IP addresses or NetBIOS names*	Specifies a loose source route along the host-list.
-p *milliseconds*	Specifies the number of milliseconds to wait between pings.
-q *number_queries*	Specifies the number of queries per hop.
-R	Checks to see if each router in the path supports the Resource Reservation Protocol (RSVP—see Chapter 9). The **-R** switch is used to test for QoS connectivity.
-T	Attaches a layer 2 priority to the packets and sends it to each of the network devices in the path. The **-T** switch is used to test for QoS connectivity.
-w *milliseconds*	Waits the specified number of milliseconds for each reply.

Arp

The Arp tool is used to view the Address Resolution Protocol (ARP) cache, which holds IP address/MAC address pairs for any hosts whose IP addresses have recently been resolved (see Chapter 3). If two hosts on the same subnet can't ping each other successfully, use the **arp -a** command on each computer to see if they have the correct MAC addresses listed for each other.

If another host with a duplicate IP address exists on the network, the ARP cache may have the MAC address for the other computer placed in it. Problems related to duplicate MAC addresses can often be solved using Arp, although sometimes (if both computers are seldom on the network at the same time) the problem is intermittent and Network Monitor is required. You can determine another computer's MAC address remotely by first pinging it, then using the **arp -a** command. Table 19.11 lists the Arp switches.

Table 19.11   Arp switches.

Switch	Function
-a	Displays all the current ARP entries for all interfaces.
-d	Removes the listed entry from the ARP cache.
-g	Displays all the current ARP entries for all interfaces (same as **-a**).
-s *ip_address mac_address*	Adds a static entry to the ARP cache.
-N *interface_address*	Lists all ARP entries for the specified interface.

Route

Route is used to view and modify the IP route table. **Route print** displays a list of current routes that the host knows about, with the current active default gateway shown at the end of the list. **Route add** and **route delete** add and remove routes, respectively. Added routes can be made persistent by using the **-p** switch. Nonpersistent routes are removed when the computer reboots or the interface is deactivated (for example, when a computer with media sense enabled is removed from the network).

Two hosts can exchange IP datagrams if they have a route to each other or if they use a default gateway that knows about a route between them. Route tables can be set up manually, but routers normally exchange information using protocols, such as Routing Information Protocol (RIP) or OSPF (see Chapter 4). Table 19.12 lists the Route switches.

NOTE: Symbolic names for the destination are obtained from the networks file. Symbolic names for the gateway are obtained from the hosts file. Both files (if they exist) are located in the %Systemroot%\Systems32\Drivers\Etc folder.

Table 19.12   Route switches.

Switch	Function
-f	Clears the route table of all gateway entries.
-p	Specifies that a route is added to both the routing table and the Registry, so that the route is automatically added to the routing table each time TCP/IP is initialized.
print *destination*	Displays the route table. If *destination* is included, only the routes to that destination are displayed.
add *destination* **mask** *netmask* *gateway* **metric** *metric* **if** *interface*	Adds a route for the specified destination using the forwarding IP address of the gateway. The metric and if options are optional.
delete *destination*	Deletes a route for the specified destination.
change *destination* **mask** *netmask gateway* **metric** *metric* **if** *interface*	Modifies an existing route.
mask *netmask*	Specifies that the next parameter is the network mask. If a network mask isn't specified, it defaults to 255.255.255.255.
metric *metric*	Specifies the cost to reach the destination. Routes with lower metrics are chosen before routes with higher metrics.
if *interface*	Specifies the interface over which the destination is available.

Netstat

Netstat displays protocol statistics, current TCP/IP connections, and listening ports. The tool can be used to display the contents of the IP route table and any persistent routes. You can view all protocol statistics or statistics for a specific protocol only. You can view connections for a specified protocol. The tool also displays interface (Ethernet) statistics.

The Netstat output lists discards and errors. Discards are packets received that contained errors or couldn't be processed. Errors indicate damaged packets. Both discards and errors should be at or near zero. Errors in the Sent column indicate overloading of the local network or a bad physical connection. Errors and discards in the Receive column indicate an overloaded local network, an overloaded local host, or a physical network problem.

Table 19.13 lists the Netstat switches.

TIP: *Using the **-n** switch significantly speeds up Netstat operation.*

Nbtstat

Nbtstat is used to troubleshoot NetBIOS name-resolution problems. The tool lets you remove and correct preloaded NetBIOS name cache entries. It can display, purge, and reload the name cache (without rebooting); display the names that have been registered locally on the system by NetBIOS applications, such as the server and redirector; and display a count of all NetBIOS names that were resolved by broadcast and by querying a WINS server.

Table 19.13   Netstat switches.

Switch	Function
-a	Displays all connections and listening ports.
-r	Displays the contents of the route table.
-n	Specifies that Netstat doesn't convert addresses and port numbers to names.
-s	Displays per-protocol statistics for IP, ICMP, TCP, and UDP.
-p *protocol*	Displays connection information for the specified protocol. The protocol can be TCP, UDP, or IP. If used with the **-s** option, this switch shows statistics for the specified protocol. In this case, the protocol can be TCP, UDP, IP, or ICMP.
-e	Displays network statistics.
interval	Displays a new set of statistics each interval (in seconds). If you don't specify an interval, Netstat shows the statistics once.

You can carry out a NetBIOS adapter status command on a computer specified either by name or IP address. This returns the local NetBIOS name table for the computer and the MAC address of its adapter card. The tool can be used to list the current NetBIOS sessions and their status, including statistics. The list can contain either the names or the IP addresses of remote computers. Table 19.14 lists the Nbtstat switches.

WARNING!   Nbtstat switches are case sensitive.

Nslookup

Nslookup is used to troubleshoot DNS problems. When you start the tool (by entering **nslookup** with no arguments), it shows the host name and IP address of the DNS server that's configured for the local system, then displays a command prompt for further queries. Type a question mark to display all available commands. Close the program by entering **exit**.

You can find a host's IP address by entering the host name. By default, Nslookup uses the DNS server configured for the computer on which it is running, but you can use an alternative DNS server if you want to. When you enter a host name, Nslookup appends the domain suffix of the computer to the host name (for example, w2000s.coriolis.com) before querying DNS. If the name isn't found, the domain suffix is *devolved* by one level (for example, to coriolis.com) and the query

Table 19.14   Nbtstat switches.

Switch	Function
-a *name*	Returns the NetBIOS name table and MAC address for the computer specified by *name*.
-A *ip_address*	Returns the NetBIOS name table and MAC address for the computer specified by *ip_address*.
-c	Lists the contents of the NetBIOS name cache.
number	Specifies a display interval in seconds.
-n	Displays the names registered locally by NetBIOS applications, such as the server and redirector.
-r	Displays a count of all names resolved by broadcast or by a WINS server.
-R	Purges the name cache and reloads all #PRE entries from the lmhosts file.
-RR	Releases and reregisters all names with the name server.
-s	Displays the NetBIOS sessions table, converting destination IP addresses to computer NetBIOS names.
-S	Displays the NetBIOS sessions table with destination IP addresses.

is repeated. If a Fully Qualified Domain Name (FQDN) is typed in with a trailing dot (see Chapter 14), then the DNS server is queried only for that name and no devolution is performed. If you want to discover the IP address of a host that isn't in your domain, you must use an FQDN.

Nslookup has a debug mode that's set by entering **set debug** or (for more detail) **set d2**. In this mode, the tool lists the steps that it takes to complete its commands.

The Nslookup switches are listed in Table 19.15. Optional parameters are shown in brackets. Table 19.16 lists the options that can be specified by the set switch.

Hostname

Hostname is used without arguments and simply returns the local computer's host name. It's seldom used on its own as a debugging tool, but can be useful, for example, in batch files.

Table 19.15   Nslookup switches.

Switch	Function
nslookup	Launches the Nslookup tool.
set debug	Launches debug mode from within Nslookup.
set d2	Launches verbose debug mode from within Nslookup.
host *name*	Returns the IP address for the specified host.
name	Displays information about the host/domain *name* using the default server.
name1 name2	As above, but uses *name2* as the server.
help or ?	Displays information about common commands.
set *option*	Sets an option (for example, **set d2**). The Nslookup options are listed in Table 19.6.
server *name*	Sets the default server to *name*, using the current default server.
lserver *name*	Sets the default server to *name*, using the initial server.
finger [*user***]**	Fingers the optional *user* at the current default host.
root	Sets current default server to the root.
ls [*opt***]** *domain* **[>***file***]**	Lists addresses in *domain* with optional output to *file*. The *opt* variable can be **-a** (canonical names and aliases), **-d** (all records), or **-t** (type).
view *file*	Sorts the output file generated by the **ls** switch (see above) and displays it page by page.
exit	Exits Nslookup and returns to the command prompt.

Table 19.16   Nslookup options specified by the set switch.

Option	Description
all	Displays options, current server, and host.
[no]debug	Displays debugging information.
[no]d2	Displays verbose debugging information.
[no]defname	Appends the domain name to each query.
[no]recurse	Asks for a recursive answer to a query (see Chapter 14).
[no]search	Uses the domain search list.
[no]vc	Always uses a virtual circuit.
domain=*name*	Sets the default domain name to *name*.
srchlist=*n1[n1/n2/...]*	Sets the domain to *n1* and the search list to *n1*, *n2*, and so on.
root =*name*	Sets the root server to *name*.
retry=*x*	Sets the number of retries to *x*.
timeout=*x*	Sets the initial timeout interval to *x* seconds.
type=*type*	Sets the query type (for example, A, ANY, CNAME, MX, NS, PTR, SOA, SRV—see Chapter 14).
querytype=*type*	Identical to **type**.
class=*query_class*	Sets the query class (for example IN, ANY).
[no]msxfr	Uses fast zone transfer.
ixfrver=*x*	Specifies the current version to use in an Incremental Zone Transfer (IXFR) request (see Chapter 14).

Netdiag

Netdiag is a powerful diagnostic tool that isolates networking and connectivity problems. It can run a wide range of tests and is straightforward to use, requiring no parameters or switches (other than the optional **/fix** switch) to be specified. The tool diagnoses network problems by checking all aspects of a host computer's network configuration and connections. It can examine TCP/IP, IPX, and NetWare configurations; it can repair simple DNS problems.

Netdiag isn't installed in Windows 2000 by default. It can be installed from the Support\Tools folder on the Windows 2000 CD-ROM. For information about installing and using the Windows 2000 Support Tools and Support Tools Help, see the file sreadme.doc in the same CD-ROM folder. Once the tools are installed, refer to the Windows 2000 Support Tools help files for detailed information.

Netdiag performs its tests by examining Dynamic Link Library (DLL) files, output from other tools, and the Registry to find potential problems. It checks to see which network services or functions are enabled, then runs the network configuration tests described (briefly) in Table 19.17 in the order listed.

Table 19.17   Netdiag tests.

Test	Description
NDIS	Lists the network adapter configuration details. If this test shows an unresponsive network adapter, the remaining tests are aborted.
IPConfig	Tests that TCP/IP is installed and configured, pings the DHCP and WINS servers, and checks that the default gateway is on the same subnet as the IP address.
Member	Confirms primary domain details, checks that the NetLogon service is started, adds the primary domain to the domain list, and queries the primary domain security identifier (SID).
NetBTTransports	Lists NetBT transports managed by the redirector. Prints error information if no NetBT transports are found.
APIPA	Checks if any interface is using Automatic Private IP Addressing (APIPA).
IPLoopBk	Pings the IP loopback address 127.0.0.1.
DefGw	Pings all the default gateways for each interface.
NbtNm	Checks that the workstation service name <00> is equal to the computer name. It also checks that the messenger service name <03> and server service name <20> are present on all interfaces and that none of these names are in conflict.
WINS	Sends NetBT name queries to all configured WINS servers.
Winsock	Uses the Windows Sockets WSAEnumProtocols () function (see Chapter 18) to retrieve available transport protocols.
DNS	Checks whether the DNS cache service is running and whether the local computer is correctly registered on the configured DNS servers. If the computer is a DC, this test checks to see whether all the DNS entries in Netlogon.dns are registered on the DNS server. If the entries are incorrect and the **/fix** option is on, the tool attempts to re-register the DC record on a DNS server.
Browser	Checks whether the workstation service is running. Retrieves the transport lists from the redirector and from the browser. Checks whether the NetBT transports are in the list generated by the NetBTTransports test. Checks whether the browser is bound to all the NetBT transports. Checks whether the computer can send mailslot messages.
DsGetDc	First finds a generic DC from Directory Services (DS), finds the primary domain controller, then finds a Windows 2000 DC. If the tested domain is the primary domain, the test checks whether the domain Global Unique Identifier (GUID) stored in Local Security Authority (LSA) is the same as the domain GUID stored in the DC. If the **/fix** option is on, DsGetDc tries to fix the GUID in LSA. If this test finds a fault that it can't fix, it returns a fatal error.
DcList	Gets a list of domain controllers in the domain from the DS on a DC. If there's no DC information for the domain, the test tries to get a DC from DS. It gets the DC list from the target DC, checks the status of each DC, and adds all the DCs into the DC list of the tested domain.

(continued)

19. Network Management and Troubleshooting

Table 19.17   Netdiag tests (continued).

Test	Description
Trust	Tests trust relationships to the primary domain.
Kerberos	Connects to LSA and looks up the Kerberos package. Gets the ticket cache of the Kerberos package and checks that the Kerberos package has a ticket for the primary domain and the local computer.
LDAP	Tests that the Lightweight Directory Access Protocol (LDAP) is running on all the active DCs found in the domain.
Route	Displays the static and persistent entries in the routing table, including destination address, subnet mask, gateway address, interface, and metric.
NetStat	Displays protocol statistics and current TCP/IP network connections.
Bindings	Lists all bindings, whether the binding is currently enabled, and the owner of the binding.
WAN	Displays the settings and status of currently active remote access connections.
Modem	Retrieves all available line devices. Displays the configuration of each line device.
NetWare	Determines whether NetWare is using the directory tree or bindery logon process, determines the default context if NetWare is using the directory tree logon process, and finds the server to which the host attaches itself at startup.
IPX	Examines the network's IPX configuration, including Frame Type, Network ID, Router MTU, and whether packet burst or source routing are enabled.
IPSec	Tests whether IP security is enabled and displays a list of active IPSec policies.

TIP: *Details of additional diagnostic tools in the Windows 2000 resource kit can be found at **http://windows. microsoft.com/windows2000/reskit***.

Registry Editor

Finally, and with some trepidation, I'll describe the most powerful, useful, and dangerous tool that you have available. If you know your way around the Registry, know *exactly* what you're doing, and have backed up everything of value, then Registry editing lets you discover and repair faults very quickly indeed. The facility of editing the Registry on remote machines lets you repair a computer when its keyboard, mouse, and/or screen are out of operation.

The regedt32.exe program is located in the %Systemroot%\System32 folder. When you've started the tool, access the Options pull-down menu and enable Read Only Mode. Registry editor is typically used in this mode, and you can obtain a great deal of information quickly and easily by reading the values in the Registry subkeys. You'll find a lot of what you're looking for in the subkey:

```
HKEY_LOCAL_MACHINE\
        SYSTEM\
            CurrentControlSet\
                Services\
```

Figure 19.5 shows a remote Registry edit on a machine with a nonoperational keyboard. The start value for the keyboard driver is 0; it should be 0x1. You can check this by looking at the Registry on a fully operational computer. Taking the Registry Editor out of read-only mode, double-clicking the parameter, and specifying the correct value solves the problem.

There isn't space here for an in-depth look at the Windows 2000 Registry. If you want to learn more about it, refer to a book such as *Windows 2000 Registry Little Black Book* by Nathan Wallace, published by The Coriolis Group,© 2000, ISBN 1-57610-348-X.

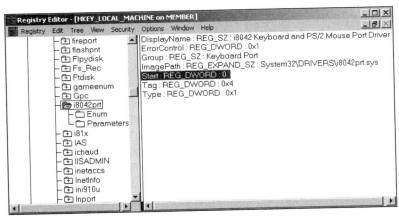

Figure 19.5   Using the Registry Editor.

Immediate Solutions

Installing SNMP

SNMP must be installed on any host that participates in the SNMP service. It starts automatically after installation. To install SNMP, proceed as follows:

1. Log on to the host as an administrator.

2. Access Start|Settings|Control Panel and double-click Add/Remove Programs.

3. Click Add/Remove Windows Components.

4. Select Management and Monitoring Tools (but don't clear the checkbox), then click Details.

5. Check the Simple Network Management Protocol checkbox, then click OK.

6. If prompted, insert the Windows 2000 Server CD-ROM or type the path to the distribution files, then click Continue.

7. Click Finish. Close the Add/Remove Programs dialog box.

8. Close the Control Panel.

Configuring SNMP

If you change existing SNMP settings, your changes take effect immediately. If, however, you're configuring SNMP for the first time, you must restart SNMP for your settings to take effect. You can configure SNMP agent properties, traps, and security settings using this set of procedures.

Configuring an SNMP Agent

To configure a host as an SNMP agent, proceed as follows:

1. Log on to the host as an administrator.

2. Access Start|Programs|Administrative Tools and select Computer Management.

3. Expand Computer Management (Local)|Services and Applications and click Services.

4. In the details pane, select SNMP Service.

5. On the Action pull-down menu, select Properties.

6. Select the Agent tab.

7. Type the name of the person who administers the computer in the Contact box.

8. Type the computer's system location in the Location box.

9. In the Service tab, check the appropriate checkboxes. Refer to Table 19.1 in the In Depth section of this chapter for details, or right-click any dialog box and click What's This?

10. Click OK.

11. Close the Computer Management console.

NOTE: *To configure hosts (such as hubs) that aren't network computers as SNMP agents, refer to the manufacturer's documentation.*

Configuring Traps

To configure a trap, you need to specify the community name and the host to which trap messages are sent. Because community names are treated in the same way as passwords, they're case-sensitive. To configure traps, proceed as follows:

1. Log on to the host as an administrator.

2. Access Start|Programs|Administrative Tools and select Computer Management.

3. Expand Computer Management (Local)|Services and Applications and click Services.

4. In the details pane, select SNMP Service.

5. On the Action pull-down menu, select Properties.

6. Select the Traps tab.

7. In the Community name box, type the case-sensitive community name to which trap messages should be sent. Click Add to list.

8. In the Trap destinations section, click Add.

9. In the Host name, IP or IPX address box, type information to identify the trap host. Click Add.

10. Repeat Steps 7 through 9 until you've added all the communities and trap destinations that you require.

11. Click OK.

12. Close the Computer Management console.

Configuring Security

SNMP security properties were described in the In Depth section of this chapter. Security can be implemented by using communities and by restricting access to specified hosts. To configure SNMP security properties, proceed as follows:

1. Log on to the host as an administrator.

2. Access Start|Programs|Administrative Tools and select Computer Management.

3. Expand Computer Management (Local)|Services and Applications and click Services.

4. In the details pane, select SNMP Service.

5. On the Action pull-down menu, select Properties.

6. On the Security tab, check Send authentication trap if you want a trap message sent whenever authentication fails. This should be checked by default.

7. Under Accepted community names, click Add.

8. In the SNMP Service Configuration dialog box, right-click the Community rights drop-down box and click What's This? You should get a permission list similar to that shown in Figure 19.6.

9. Select a permission level that the host will use to process SNMP requests from the selected community. Typically, Read Only is selected.

10. In the Community Name box, specify a case-sensitive community name, then click Add.

11. Repeat Steps 7 through 10 if you want to add additional communities to the Accepted community names list.

12. Specify the conditions under which this computer will accept SNMP packets from a host:

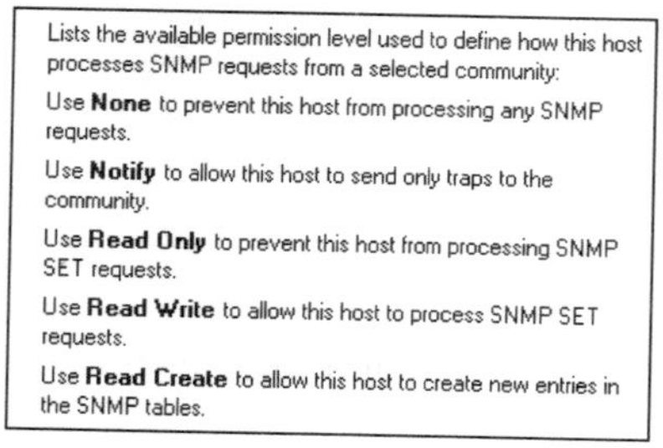

> Lists the available permission level used to define how this host processes SNMP requests from a selected community:
>
> Use **None** to prevent this host from processing any SNMP requests.
>
> Use **Notify** to allow this host to send only traps to the community.
>
> Use **Read Only** to prevent this host from processing SNMP SET requests.
>
> Use **Read Write** to allow this host to process SNMP SET requests.
>
> Use **Read Create** to allow this host to create new entries in the SNMP tables.

Figure 19.6   SNMP Service permissions.

- To accept SNMP requests from any host in the specified community, regardless of identity, click Accept SNMP packets from any host.
- To limit acceptance of SNMP packets, click Accept SNMP packets from these hosts, click Add; type the appropriate host name, IP address, or IPX address; then click Add again.

13. Repeat Step 12 if you want to add more than one host to the Accept SNMP packets from these hosts list. Figure 19.7 illustrates typical SNMP security settings.

14. Click OK.

15. Close the Computer Management console.

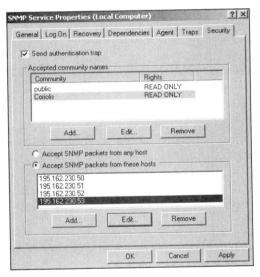

Figure 19.7   Setting SNMP security properties.

Starting or Stopping the SNMP Service

To start or stop the SNMP service, proceed as follows:

1. Log on to the host as an administrator.

2. Access Start|Programs|Administrative Tools and select Computer Management.

3. Expand Computer Management (Local)|Services and Applications and click Services.

4. In the details pane, select SNMP Service.

5. On the Action pull-down menu, select Start, Stop, Pause, Resume, or Restart, as appropriate. Restart stops the service, then starts it again.

TIP: *You can also start and stop the SNMP service from the Command Console by entering* **net start snmp** *and* **net stop snmp**, *as appropriate.*

Defining and Implementing an Audit Policy

Domain-level audit policy is defined on a DC. If you're implementing object auditing, you need to do this on the computer where the object is located. However, domain level policy has to be set up first to enable you to do this.

Defining an Audit Policy

This procedure defines an audit policy that monitors failed logon attempts and allows auditing of both successful and unsuccessful object access. Logon attempts are audited at domain level. Object access auditing is enabled at local machine level. To enable this to be set up, the Default Domain Controllers Group Policy Object (GPO) must be set to "Not Defined" for object access auditing. Otherwise, domain policy will override local policy.

This is a typical audit policy. If you want to set up a different policy, amend the procedure as appropriate. To define an audit policy, proceed as follows:

1. Log on to a DC as an administrator.
2. Access Start|Programs|Administrative Tools and select Active Directory Users and Computers.
3. Expand the domain icon, right-click Domain Controllers, and select Properties.
4. On the Group Policy tab, select Default Domain Controllers Policy and click Edit.
5. Expand Computer Configuration|Windows Settings|Security Settings|Local Policies and select Audit Policy. The configurable audit policies appear in the details pane, as shown in Figure 19.8.
6. Double-click Audit logon events.
7. Ensure that the Define these policy settings checkbox is checked (it should be by default). Check the Failure checkbox. Click OK.

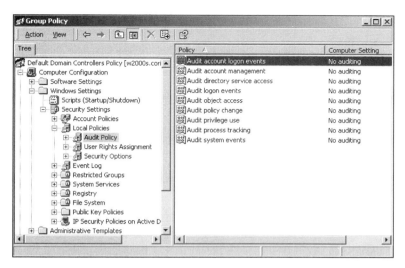

Figure 19.8   Audit Policies.

8. Repeat Steps 6 and 7 for Audit account logon events.

9. Double-click Audit object access. Uncheck the Define these policy settings checkbox. Click OK.

10. Close the Group Policy console.

11. Click OK to close the Domain Controllers Properties box.

12. Close the Active Directory Users and Computers console.

Implementing an Object Access Audit Policy

You define an audit policy that lets you monitor object access on the computer where the object is located. You then need to specify which objects are to be monitored and for which users and groups monitoring should be set up. Normally, only resources that are accessed over the network are monitored (although you can monitor access to a file or folder that can only be accessed locally, if you want to do so). You can audit files and folders only if they're on an NTFS partition.

To implement object access auditing, proceed as follows:

1. Log on as an administrator to the computer where the object is located. If you're auditing access to a printer, for example, log on to the print server.

2. Access Start|Run and enter **mmc**.

3. On the Console menu, click Add/Remove Snap-in. Click Add.

4. In the Snap-in list box, select Group Policy. Click Add.

5. In the Select Group Policy Object dialog box, ensure that Local Computer is selected. Click Finish.

6. Click Close. Click OK.

7. Expand Local Computer Policy|Computer Configuration|Windows Settings|Security Settings|Local Policies and click Audit Policy.

8. Double-click Audit object access in the details pane.

9. Check both the Success checkbox and the Failure checkbox. Click OK.

10. Close the Group Policy console.

11. Access Start|Tools|Accessories and select Windows Explorer.

12. Expand the directory tree and right-click the object that you want to audit. Click Properties.

13. On the Security tab, click Advanced.

14. In the Access Control Settings dialog box, select the Auditing tab.

15. Click Add. Select a user or group whose accesses you want to audit. Typically, the Everyone group is selected.

16. Specify the access events that you want to audit, as shown (for example) in Figure 19.9.

17. If you want to limit audit properties to the contents of a container only (in the case of a folder), check the appropriate checkbox.

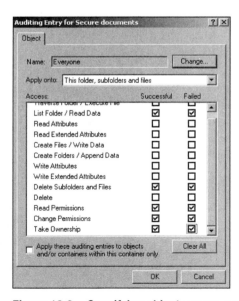

Figure 19.9   Specifying object access auditing.

18. Click OK. If you want to add more groups with different auditing configurations, use the Add button as before (see Step 15).

19. You may decide not to allow inheritable policies from a parent object to propagate to this object. You can also reset auditing properties on child objects and propagate the inheritable auditing policies that you have specified to these child objects. Check or uncheck the appropriate checkboxes, as required.

20. Click OK. Click OK (again) to close the Properties dialog box.

21. Close Windows Explorer.

Using Event Viewer

The use of the Event Viewer tool is straightforward. Discovering why there's an error recorded in a log and what you can do to fix the problem may be rather more complex. To view, search, filter, archive, and clear event logs, proceed as follows:

1. Access Start|Programs|Administrative Tools and select Event Viewer.

2. Select the log that you want to view.

3. Right-click the selected log and click Refresh. This ensures that you're viewing the latest information.

4. In the details pane, double-click an event of interest. You can use the up and down arrows to scroll through the list of events without closing the Event Properties dialog box.

5. Click OK to close the Event Properties dialog box.

6. To find a specific event, right-click the selected log, click View, then select Find.

7. Specify one or more search criteria, as shown in Figure 19.10.

8. Click Find Next. Double-click the located events to view their properties. Click Restore Defaults in the Find dialog box and close the box.

9. To filter the selected log, right-click it, click View, and select Filter. This opens the Filter tab of the Log Properties box. The criteria that can be specified in this tab are the same as those in the Find dialog box (see Figure 19.10), with the addition of From and To boxes. Click OK to view the filtered log.

10. To restore the original log view, access the Log Properties Filter tab, click Restore Defaults, then click OK.

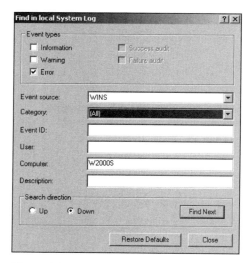

Figure 19.10   Specifying search criteria.

11. To change log size and overwrite criteria, right-click the selected log and click Properties. Specify the required maximum log size and the action to take if this size is reached. In this dialog box you can also clear the log and specify that a low-speed connection is used. The Using a low-speed connection checkbox is checked if you're looking at a log on a remote computer over a slow Wide Area Network (WAN) link. Click OK to close the Log Properties box.

12. To save the log file in binary (EVT) format, right-click the selected log and select Save Log File As. Specify a path and file name.

13. To save the selected log as a text file, right-click it and select Export List. Specify the path and filename, and whether the file is tab-delimited (TXT) or comma-delimited (CSV). You can also specify whether or not to use the Unicode character set.

14. If you want to customize the way you view the log, it's good practice to create a new log view, rename it, and customize the new view. Right-clicking the selected log accesses the New Log View command. When you've created a new view, select it, right-click it, click View, then use the Choose Columns, Filter, and Customize commands to set the view to your specifications.

15. To view the event logs on another computer, click Event Viewer in the left pane. On the Action pull-down menu, select Connect to another computer. Specify the path to the other computer or use the Browse button.

Recovering from a Full-Security-Log System Halt

Under the heading "Archiving Event Logs" in the In Depth section of this chapter, we saw that Windows 2000 can be stopped on a computer if the security log reaches its maximum size. This prevents security events from being overwritten. If Windows 2000 is stopped in this way, you have to archive and clear the security log, then delete and replace the Registry key. The procedure to do this is as follows:

1. Restart the computer and log on as an administrator.

2. Archive the security log, as described in the previous procedure, then delete all events in the log.

3. Open Registry Editor (regedt32.exe in %Systemroot%\system32) and locate the key:

```
HKEY_LOCAL_MACHINE\
        SYSTEM\
            CurrentControlSet\
                Control\
                        Lsa
```

4. Delete and replace the *CrashOnAuditFail* parameter, using data type REG_DWORD and a value of 1.

5. Close Registry Editor and restart the computer.

WARNING! *Incorrect Registry editing may severely damage your system.*

Enabling Network Segment Counters

If you want to enable network segment counters, such as Network Segment\% Net Utilization, you need to install the Network Monitor driver (unless you've already installed Network Monitor, in which case the driver is installed). To install the Network Monitor driver, proceed as follows:

1. Log on as an administrator to the host that you want to monitor.

2. Access Start|Settings and select Control Panel.

3. Double-click Network and Dial-up Connections.

4. Right-click Local Area Connection and select Properties.

5. Click Install.

6. In the Select Network Component Type dialog box, select Protocol and click Add.

7. In the Select Network Protocol dialog box, check Network Monitor Driver, then click OK.

8. If prompted for additional files, insert your Windows 2000 CD-ROM or type a path to the network location of the files.

9. Click Close.

10. Close Network and Dial-up Connections.

11. Close the Control Panel.

Changing Account Properties for the Performance Logs and Alerts Service

If you want to implement centralized data collection (see the In Depth section of this chapter), you need to change the properties of the Performance Logs and Alerts Service so that it logs on using an account that has permission to access the remote computers. The procedure to do this is as follows:

1. Log on to the centralized collection host as a domain administrator.

2. Access Start|Programs|Administrative Tools and select Computer Management.

3. Expand Computer Management (Local)|Services and Applications and click Services.

4. In the details pane, select Performance Logs and Alerts.

5. On the Action pull-down menu, select Properties.

6. Select This account.

7. Browse to an account that can access other machines; for example, an administrator account on a domain controller (you'll probably use your own account). Click OK.

8. Supply and confirm a password. Click OK.

9. Click OK (again) to close the message box.

10. Close the Computer Management console.

Creating and Viewing a Counter Log

Performance Logs and Alerts is used to create a counter log. System Monitor is used to read the log data.

Creating a Counter Log

To create a counter log, proceed as follows:

1. Log on as a domain administrator. This will enable you to access remote computers if you need to do so.

2. Access Start|Programs|Administrative Tools and select Performance.

3. Expand Performance Logs and Alerts and select Counter Logs. Existing logs are listed in the details pane. A green icon indicates that a log is running; a red icon indicates that a log is stopped.

4. Right-click Counter Logs and select New Log Settings.

5. Type the name of the log, then click OK.

6. On the General tab, click Add.

7. Select the counters that you want to log, clicking Add for each counter. The Select Counters dialog box has a number of controls:

   • You can either use local computer counters or select counters from another computer. If you choose the latter option, either type the computer name or IP address in the Select counters from computer drop-down box, or choose the computer from the drop-down list.

   • Select the performance object from the Performance object drop-down box.

   • If the performance object has more than one instance, select an instance from the list or click All instances.

   • Select a counter from the list or click All counters.

   • Click Explain to find out what the selected counter measures. Figure 19.11 shows the Select Counters and Explain Text dialog boxes.

TIP: *If you move the Select Counters dialog box window down the screen, you can see the counters being added to the log.*

---

8. When you've added all the counters that you want to monitor, click Close.

9. On the General tab, specify the sample interval.

10. Access the Log Files tab. You can specify the file location, change the file name, specify whether a numeric or date identifier will be added to the file name, change the log file type, and limit the log size.

11. Select the Schedule tab. If you get a message informing you that the folder to hold the log files doesn't exist, click Yes to create it now.

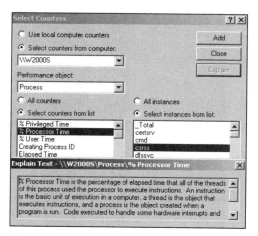

Figure 19.11   Adding a counter and finding out what it does.

12. By default, a log starts as soon as it's created and is stopped manually. You can schedule start and stop times or choose to make both start and stop manual. You can also choose to start a new log or to execute a command when logging stops. To do this, you have to set the log to stop after a specified period of time.

13. Click OK. If you set the log to start immediately, it will show as a green icon on the Performance console details pane. If you chose manual start, you can right-click the log to start it.

14. Close the Performance Console.

Viewing a Counter Log

To view a counter log, proceed as follows:

1. Log on as a domain administrator. If you're using centralized data collection, log on to the computer that's collecting the data.

2. Access Start|Programs|Administrative Tools and select Performance.

3. Optionally, you can expand Performance Logs and Alerts, select Counter Logs, and stop the log that you want to view. You don't have to stop a log to view it if you don't want to.

4. Select System Monitor and click the View Log File Data control.

5. Locate the log file. By default, it's in a folder called PerfLogs. Select the log file and click Open.

6. Click the Add control. You can add some or all of the counters that have been captured in the log file.

7. If you've been using centralized data collection, access the Select counters from this computer drop-down box and select a computer.

8. For every computer, select the counters and instances that you want to view. Click Add to add each counter or each instance of a counter.

TIP: *If you can add only local computer counters, although you specified remote computer counters when setting up the log file, refer to "Changing Account Properties for the Performance Logs and Alerts Service" earlier in this chapter.*

9. Click Close.

10. Right-click anywhere on the System Monitor display area and select Properties.

11. The General tab lets you change the appearance of your display. If you're unsure about the function of any of the controls, right-click the control and click What's This?

12. On the Source tab, use the View Range slidebar control to set the view range for the log file.

13. The Data tab lets you add and remove counters and set colors and line styles.

14. The Graph tab lets you specify a graph scale, grid type, general title, and vertical axis title.

15. The Colors and Fonts tabs let you set background colors and text fonts.

16. Click OK when you've finished configuring System Monitor properties.

17. Use the View Histogram, View Chart, and View Report tools to view the data.

Defining Alerts

An alert can log an entry in the application event log, start a performance data log, or run a program. Alerts are generated when a counter value either rises above or falls below a preset limit. To define an alert, proceed as follows:

1. Log on as a domain administrator. This will enable you to access remote computers if you need to do so.

2. Access Start|Programs|Administrative Tools and select Performance.

3. Expand Performance Logs and Alerts and select Alerts. Existing alerts are listed in the details pane. A green icon indicates that an alert is running; a red icon indicates that an alert is stopped.

4. Right-click Alerts and select New Alert Settings.

5. Type the name of the Alert, then click OK.

6. Add one or more counters, as described in the procedure "Creating a Counter Log" earlier in this chapter. Click Close when you've finished.

7. On the General tab, highlight each of the added counters in turn and specify an alert condition (Under or Over) and a limit. You can also specify a sample rate on this tab.

8. On the Action tab, specify what you want to happen if an alert is triggered.

9. On the Schedule tab, specify start and stop criteria.

10. Click OK.

11. Close the Performance Console.

Monitoring Real-Time Performance Data

System Monitor lets you monitor data in real time. This can be useful if you're looking for a brief event that happens fairly often. You can set your update frequency as high as once per second (the default). To monitor real-time data, proceed as follows:

1. Log on as a domain administrator. If you're using centralized data collection, log on to the computer that's collecting the data.

2. Access Start|Programs|Administrative Tools and select Performance.

3. Select System Monitor and click the View Current Activity control.

4. Click the Add control. Add counters as described in the procedure "Creating a Counter Log" earlier in this chapter. Click Close.

5. Optionally, right-click anywhere on the System Monitor display and select Properties. You can configure display properties as described in the procedure "Viewing a Counter Log" earlier in this chapter.

Installing and Using Network Monitor

The procedures for installing Network Monitor, capturing data, and setting up filters and triggers are described in Chapter 3. See the cross-reference table below. If you want to install the SMS version of Network Monitor, refer to the SMS documentation.

19. Network Management and Troubleshooting

Using the Command-Line Tools

Do not attempt to memorize the syntax and switches in the command-line tools. Don't rely on information taken from a book (not even this one). The procedure for using a command-line tool is as follows:

1. Log on to the appropriate computer as an administrator.

2. Access Start|Programs|Accessories and select Command Prompt.

3. With most tools, you can enter the name of the tool, followed by **/?** or by no arguments at all (for example, **ping /?**, **tracert**). Nslookup requires that you start the tool, then enter **?** or **help**.

4. Use the syntax and switches as described on the screen, for example:

- **ping -n 10 -s 3 -w 1000 www.coriolis.com**.
- **tracert -d -h 40 -w 500 www.coriolis.com**.
- **pathping -n -h 40 -p 1000 -w 500 -T www.coriolis.com**.
- **nbtstat -c -n 10**.
- **ipconfig /displaydns**.
- **arp -s 195.162.230.50 00-D0-B7-4C-23-86**.
- **route add 195.162.231.200 mask 255.255.255.255 195.162.230.1 metric 2 if 2**.
- **netstat -n -s -p icmp 10**.
- **nslookup**, followed by **ls -d coriolis.com**.

Refer to the In Depth section of this chapter for a list of the command-line tools. Test them all out and familiarize yourself with them, hopefully before you have to use them for real.

Chapter 20

Internet Protocol Version 6

In Depth

Chapter 5 looked at Internet Protocol version 4 (IPv4) namespace and the reasons why what seemed like an inexhaustible resource in the early 1980s is now nearing total depletion. Some relief has been provided with the growing use of Network Address Translators (NATs) to map multiple private addresses (typically in the 10.0.0.0/8 address range) to a smaller number of public IP addresses. However, NATs don't support standards-based network layer security, and there can be problems when connecting two organizations that both use the same subset of the private address space.

The number of Internet routes continues to expand. Typically, more than 70,000 routes are held in the route table of an Internet backbone router. Internet-connected devices and appliances also use IPv4 address space, and these are rapidly gaining in popularity. The IPv4 address space will be totally depleted soon. It could have happened by the time you read this. To address this problem, the Internet Engineering Task Force (IETF) developed a suite of protocols and standards known originally as IP-Next Generation (IPng), but now called IP version 6 (IPv6). The IPv6 portion of the Internet is known as the *6bone*.

Issues Addressed by IPv6

IPv6 mainly addresses the issue of IPv4 address space depletion and provides a resource that's truly (so it's claimed) inexhaustible. The protocol suite, however, also addresses other known IPv4 issues. The issues identified and the IPv6 solutions are described below.

IPv6 Address Space

IPv6 has a 128-bit address space (compared to 32 bits for IPv4). In theory, this gives a total of 2^{128} (340,282,266,920,938,463,463,374,607,431,768,211,464) addresses—a number too large to comprehend. To give you idea of its scale, it represents $6.5*2^{23}$ addresses for every square meter of the earth's surface. In practice, the IPv6 address space allows for multiple levels of subnetting and address allocation between the Internet backbone and individual subnets within an organization.

Configuration

Typically, IPv4 is configured either manually or by using Dynamic Host Configuration Protocol (DHCP). The IETF identified a need for simpler and more automatic configuration of addresses and other settings.

As a result, IPv6 supports both stateful and stateless address configuration. Stateful configuration uses DHCP version 6 (DHCPv6). If stateless address configuration is used, hosts on a link automatically configure themselves with IPv6 addresses for the link (called *link-local addresses*) and (optionally) with addresses that are derived from prefixes advertised by local routers.

Header Size and Extension Headers

IPv4 and IPv6 headers aren't compatible, and a host or router must use both IPv4 and IPv6 implementations in order to recognize and process both header formats. It was, therefore, a design aim to keep the size of the IPv6 header within a reasonable limit. Both nonessential fields and option fields are moved to extension headers placed after the IPv6 header. As a result, the IPv6 header is only twice as large as the IPv4 header, and the size of IPv6 extension headers is constrained only by the size of the IPv6 packet.

Routing Table Size

The IPv6 global addresses that are used on the 6bone are designed to create an efficient, hierarchical, and summarizable routing infrastructure that's based on the common occurrence of multiple levels of Internet Service Providers (ISPs). On the 6bone, backbone routers have greatly reduced routing tables that correspond to the routing infrastructure of Top-Level Aggregators.

NOTE: *Refer to the descriptions of Variable Length Subnet Masks (VLSM) and Classless Interdomain Routing (CIDR) in Chapter 5 to understand what's meant by summarizable routing.*

Network-Level Security

Private communication over the Internet requires encryption to protect data from being viewed or modified in transit. Internet Protocol Security (IPSec) provides this facility, but its use is optional in IPv4. IPv6 makes IPSec mandatory. This provides a standards-based solution for network security needs and improves interoperability between different IPv6 implementations.

Real-Time Data Delivery

Quality of Service (QoS) exists in IPv4 (see Chapter 9), and bandwidth can be guaranteed for real-time traffic (such as video and audio transmissions) over a network. However, IPv4 real-time traffic support relies on the Type of Service (ToS) field and the identification of the payload, typically using a User Datagram Protocol (UDP) or Transmission Control Protocol (TCP) port.

The IPv4 ToS field has limited functionality, and payload identification using a TCP and UDP port isn't possible when an IPv4 packet payload is encrypted. Payload identification is included in the Flow Label field of the IPv6 header, so payload encryption doesn't affect QoS operation.

Reduction of Broadcast Traffic

IPv4 relies on Address Resolution Protocol (ARP) broadcasts to resolve IP addresses to the Media Access Control (MAC) addresses of the Network Interface Cards (NICs). Broadcasts increase network traffic and are inefficient because every host processes them.

The Neighbor Discovery (ND) protocol for IPv6 uses a series of Internet Control Message Protocol for IPv6 (ICMPv6) messages that manage the interaction of nodes on the same link (neighboring nodes). ND replaces ARP broadcasts, ICMPv4 Router Discovery, and ICMPv4 Redirect messages with efficient multicast and unicast ND messages.

IPv6 Addressing

The most obvious feature of IPv6 is its 128-bit address space that (in theory) can define approximately 3.4×10^{38} possible addresses. The IPv6 addressing architecture (described in RFC 2373) divides IPv6 address space based on the value of high order bits. These fixed value high order bits are known as a Format Prefix (FP).

Table 20.1 shows the current allocation of the IPv6 address space by FPs.

Currently, the unicast addresses that can be used with IPv6 nodes consist of aggregatable global unicast addresses, link-local unicast addresses, and site-local unicast addresses. All of these together represent only 15 percent of the IPv6 address space.

Address Syntax

The IPv6 128-bit address is divided at 16-bit boundaries, and each 16-bit block is converted to a 4-digit hexadecimal number. Colons are used as separators. This representation is called *colon-hexadecimal*.

Thus, the following is an IPv6 aggregatable global unicast address:

```
21CD:0053:0000:0000:03AD:003F:AF37:8D62
```

Table 20.1   IPv6 address space allocation.

Allocation	FP
Reserved	0000 0000
Unassigned	0000 0001
Reserved for Network Service Access Point (NSAP) allocation	0000 001
Reserved for Internetwork Packet Exchange (IPX) allocation	0000 010
Unassigned	0000 011
Unassigned	0000 1
Unassigned	0001
Aggregatable global unicast addresses	001
Unassigned	010
Unassigned	011
Unassigned	1001
Unassigned	101
Unassigned	110
Unassigned	1110
Unassigned	1111 0
Unassigned	1111 10
Unassigned	1111 110
Unassigned	1111 1110 0
Link-local unicast addresses	1111 1110 10
Site-local unicast addresses	1111 1110 11
Multicast addresses	1111 1111

IPv6 representation can be further simplified by removing the leading zeros within each 16-bit block. However, each block must have at least a single digit. With leading zero suppression, the address representation becomes:

```
21CD:53:0:0:3AD:3F:AF37:8D62
```

A contiguous sequence of 16-bit blocks set to 0 in the colon-hexadecimal format can be compressed to "::". Thus, the previous example address could be written:

```
21CD:53::3AD:3F:AF37:8D62
```

Some types of addresses contain long sequences of zeros and thus provide good examples of the use of this notation. For example, the multicast address FF05:0:0:0:0:0:0:2 can be compressed to FF05::2.

Prefixes

The prefix is that part of the address that indicates either the bits that have fixed values or the network identifier bits. IPv6 prefixes are expressed in the same way as CIDR IPv4 notation, or *slash* notation (see Chapter 5). For example, 21CD:53::/64 is the subnet on which the address 21CD:53::23AD:3F:AF37:8D62 is located. In this case, the first 64 bits of the address are the network prefix. An IPv6 subnet prefix (or subnet ID) is assigned to a single link. Multiple subnet IDs can be assigned to the same link. This technique is called *multinetting*.

> **NOTE:**   *Only prefix length notation is supported in IPv6. There's no direct equivalent of IPv4 subnet mask representation (such as 255.255.255.0).*

Address Types

There are three types of IPv6 addresses: unicast, multicast, and anycast.

- *Unicast*—Identifies a single interface within the scope of the unicast address type. Packets addressed to a unicast address are delivered to a single interface. RFC 2373 allows multiple interfaces to use the same address, provided that these interfaces appear as a single interface to the IPv6 implementation on the host. This accommodates load-balancing systems.

- *Multicast*—Identifies multiple interfaces. Packets addressed to a multicast address are delivered to all interfaces that are identified by the address.

- *Anycast*—Identifies multiple interfaces. Packets addressed to an anycast address are delivered to the *nearest* interface that's identified by the address. The nearest interface is the closest in terms of routing distance. An anycast address is used for one-to-one-of-many communication, with delivery to a single interface.

> **NOTE:**   *IPv6 addresses identify interfaces rather than nodes. A node is identified by any unicast address that's assigned to one of its interfaces.*

Unicast Addresses

IPv6 supports the following types of unicast addresses:

- Aggregatable global
- Link-local
- Site-local
- Special
- NSAP and IPX

Aggregatable Global Unicast Addresses

Aggregatable global unicast addresses are the IPv6 equivalent of IPv4 public addresses. They're globally routable and reachable on the 6bone. These addresses can be *aggregated* to produce an efficient routing infrastructure. The *scope* of an aggregatable global unicast address (that is, the region over which it's unique) is the entire 6bone.

Figure 20.1 illustrates the aggregatable global unicast address structure. The various fields are as follows:

- *FP*—See Table 20.1.
- *Top Level Aggregator Identity (TLA ID)*—Indicates the TLA for the address. This identifies the highest level in the routing hierarchy. TLAs are administered by the Internet Assigned Numbers Authority (IANA) and allocated to local Internet registries. These, in turn, allocate individual TLAs to large, long-haul ISPs. *Default-free routers* (routers in the highest level of the 6bone routing hierarchy) don't have default routes; they have routes that correspond to the allocated TLAs.
- *Reserved bits (Res)*—These 8 bits are reserved for future use when the size of either the TLA ID or the NLA ID needs to be increased.
- *Next Level Aggregator Identity (NLA ID)*—Used to identify a specific customer site. This field enables an ISP to create multiple levels of addressing hierarchy within a network, both to organize addressing and routing for downstream ISPs and to identify sites.
- *Site Level Aggregator Identity (SLA ID)*—Used by an individual organization to identify subnets within its site.
- *Interface ID*—Indicates the interface on a specific subnet.

The fields within the aggregatable global unicast address create a three-level structure:

- The FP, TLA ID, reserved bits, and NLA ID form the *public topology*.
- The SLA ID forms the *site topology*.
- The interface ID (as its name suggests) identifies the *interface*.

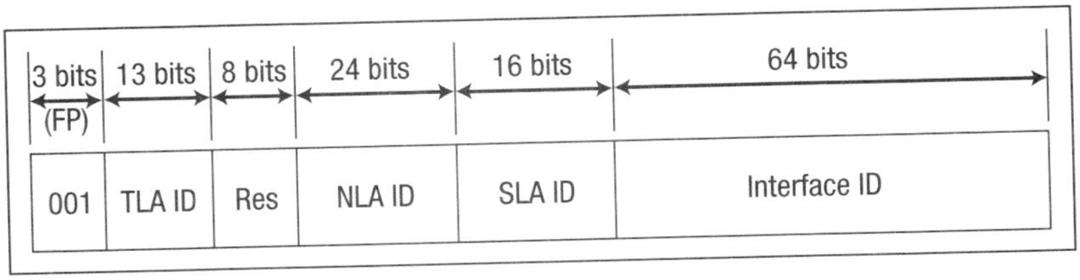

Figure 20.1   The aggregatable global unicast address structure.

> **NOTE:**   For more information on aggregatable global unicast addresses, see RFC 2374.

Link-Local Addresses

Link-local addresses are identified by an FP of 1111 1110 10 (see Table 20.1). Nodes use them when communicating with neighboring nodes on the same link. Link-local addresses are equivalent to IPv4 addresses that are autoconfigured by using the 169.254.0.0/16 prefix. The scope of a link-local address is the local link. A link-local address is required for Neighbor Discovery processes and is always automatically configured, even if no other unicast address is present.

Figure 20.2 shows the structure of the link-local address.

Link-local addresses always begin with FE80. The remainder of the network identifier is all zeros, and there's always a 64-bit interface identifier. Thus, the prefix for link-local addresses is FE80::/64. An IPv6 router never forwards link-local traffic beyond the link.

Site-Local Addresses

Site-local IPv6 addresses are equivalent to the IPv4 private address space (10.0.0.0/8, 172.16.0.0/12, and 192.168.0.0/16). Private intranets that don't have a direct, routed connection to the 6bone can use site-local addresses without conflicting with aggregatable global unicast addresses. The scope of a site-local address is the site (or organization internetwork). Site-local addresses aren't automatically configured and must be assigned either through stateless or stateful address configuration processes.

Figure 20.3 illustrates the structure of the site-local address.

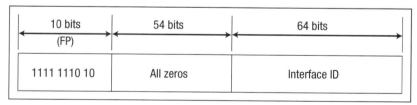

Figure 20.2   The link-local address structure.

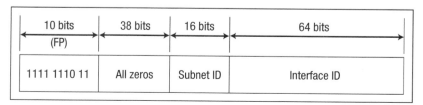

Figure 20.3   Site-local address structure.

The first 48 bits of site-local addresses always begin with FEC0, followed by 32 zeros. Following the 48 fixed bits is a 16-bit subnet identifier that you can use to create subnets within your organization. The 64-bit Interface ID field identifies a specific interface on a subnet.

TIP: *The aggregatable global unicast address and site-local address share the same structure after the first 48 bits. In aggregatable global unicast addresses, the SLA ID identifies the subnet within an organization; for site-local addresses, the Subnet ID performs the same function. You can therefore create a subnetted routing infrastructure that's used for both site-local and aggregatable global unicast addresses.*

Special Addresses

Two special IPv6 addresses are implemented as follows:

- *Unspecified address*—The unspecified address 0:0:0:0:0:0:0:0 (or ::) is used to indicate the absence of an address and is equivalent to the IPv4 unspecified address 0.0.0.0. It's typically used as a source address for packets attempting to verify whether a tentative address is unique. It's never assigned to an interface or used as a destination address.

- *Loopback address*—The loopback address 0:0:0:0:0:0:0:1 (or ::1) is used to identify a loopback interface and is equivalent to the IPv4 loopback address 127.0.0.1.

Compatibility Addresses

The two following types of compatibility addresses are defined to aid migration from IPv4 to IPv6 and the coexistence of both types of hosts:

- *IPv4-compatible address*—The IPv4-compatible address 0:0:0:0:0:0:w.x.y.z (or ::w.x.y.z) is used by *dual-stack* nodes that are communicating with IPv6 over an IPv4 infrastructure. The last four octets (w.x.y.z) represent the dotted decimal representation of an IPv4 address. Dual-stack nodes are nodes with both IPv4 and IPv6 protocols. When the IPv4-compatible address is used as an IPv6 destination, the IPv6 traffic is automatically encapsulated with an IPv4 header and sent to the destination using the IPv4 infrastructure.

- *IPv4-mapped address*—The IPv4-mapped address 0:0:0:0:0:FFFF:w.x.y.z (or ::FFFF:w.x.y.z) is used to represent an IPv4-only node to an IPv6 node. The IPv4-mapped address is never used as the source or destination address of an IPv6 packet.

NSAP and IPX Addresses

NSAP and IPX IPv6 address types are defined to provide ways of mapping NSAP and IPX addresses to IPv6 addresses:

- *NSAP addresses*—Use the FP 0000001 and map the last 121 bits of the IPv6 address to an NSAP address. For more information on NSAP address mappings, see RFC 1888.

- *IPX addresses*—Use the FP 0000010 and map the last 121 bits of the IPv6 address to an IPX address. At the time of writing, the mapping of an IPX address to an IPv6 address hasn't been defined.

Multicast Addresses

Multicast addresses can't be used as source addresses or as intermediate destinations in a routing header. IPv6 multicast addresses have an FP of 11111111 (they always start with "FF"). Subsequent fields specify flags, scope, and group ID, as shown in Figure 20.4.

The functions of the multicast address fields are as follows:

- *Flags*—Holds the flag settings. Currently the only flag defined is the Transient (T) flag that uses the low-order field bit. If this flag is set to 0, it indicates that the multicast address is permanently assigned (or *well known*) and has been allocated by IANA. If the flag is set to 1, it indicates that the multicast address is transient.

- *Scope*—Indicates the scope of the IPv6 internetwork for which the multicast traffic is intended. Routers use the multicast scope, together with information provided by multicast routing protocols, to determine whether multicast traffic can be forwarded. For example, traffic with the multicast address FF02::2 has a link-local scope (scope value 2). An IPv6 router never forwards this traffic beyond the local link. Table 20.2 lists the scope field values.

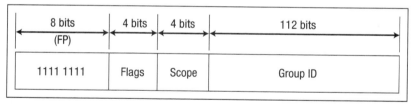

Figure 20.4   Multicast address structure.

Table 20.2   Scope field values.

Value	Scope
0	Reserved
1	Node-local scope
2	Link-local scope
5	Site-local scope
8	Organization-local scope
E	Global scope
F	Reserved

- *Group ID*—Identifies the multicast group and is unique within the scope. Permanently assigned group IDs are independent of the scope. Transient group IDs are relevant only to a specific scope. Multicast addresses from FF01:: through FF0F:: are reserved, well-known addresses.

The following addresses are defined to identify all nodes for the node-local and link-local scopes:

- *FF01::1*—Node-local scope all-nodes multicast address
- *FF02::1*—Link-local scope all-nodes multicast address

The following addresses are defined to identify all routers for the node-local, link-local, and site-local scopes:

- *FF01::2*—Node-local scope all-routers multicast address
- *FF02::2*—Link-local scope all-routers multicast address
- *FF05::2*—Site-local scope all-routers multicast address

In theory, you can have 2^{112} group IDs. In practice, however, because of the way that IPv6 multicast addresses are mapped to Ethernet multicast MAC addresses, RFC 2373 recommends assigning the group ID from the low-order 32 bits of the IPv6 multicast address and setting the remaining original group ID bits to zero. In this way, each group ID maps to a unique Ethernet multicast MAC address. Figure 20.5 illustrates the modified IPv6 multicast address.

Solicited-Node Multicast Address

The solicited-node multicast address facilitates the querying of network nodes during address resolution. IPv6 uses the Neighbor Discovery message to resolve a link-local IPv6 address to a node MAC address. Rather than use the local-link scope all-nodes multicast address (which would be processed by all nodes on the local link) as the Neighbor Solicitation message destination, IPv6 uses the solicited-node multicast address. This address comprises the prefix FF02::1:FF00:0/104 and the last 24 bits of the IPv6 address that's being resolved.

For example, if a node has the link-local address FE80::6B:28C:16D2:C97, the corresponding solicited-node address is FF02::1:16D2:C97.

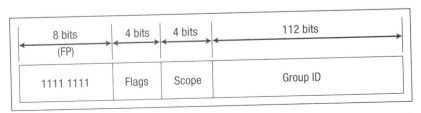

Figure 20.5   The IPv6 multicast address modified for MAC address mapping.

The result of using the solicited-node multicast address is that address resolution uses a mechanism that isn't processed by (or doesn't *disturb*) all network nodes. Because of the relationship between the MAC address, the interface ID, and the solicited-node address, the solicited-node address acts as a pseudo-unicast address for efficient address resolution.

Anycast Addresses

An anycast address is assigned to multiple interfaces, and packets sent to an anycast address are forwarded by the routing infrastructure to the nearest of these interfaces. The routing infrastructure must be aware of the interfaces that are assigned anycast addresses and their distance in terms of routing metrics. Currently, anycast addresses are used only as destination addresses and are assigned only to routers. Anycast addresses are assigned from the unicast address space, and the scope of an anycast address is the scope of the unicast address type from which the anycast address is assigned.

The Subnet-Router anycast address is predefined. It's created from the subnet prefix for a given interface. To construct the Subnet-Router anycast address, the bits in the subnet prefix retain their current values and the remaining bits are set to zero. Figure 20.6 illustrates the Subnet-Router anycast address.

All router interfaces attached to a subnet are assigned the Subnet-Router anycast address for that subnet. The Subnet-Router anycast address is used for communication with one of multiple routers that are attached to a remote subnet.

Host Addresses

A typical IPv6 host is multihomed because it has at least two addresses with which it can receive packets—a link-local address for local link traffic and a routable site-local or aggregatable address. A host is assigned the following unicast addresses:

- A link-local address for each interface
- Unicast addresses for each interface (for example, a site-local address and one or more aggregatable global unicast addresses)
- A loopback address (::1)

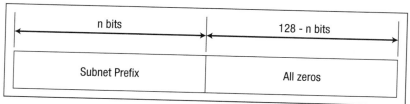

Figure 20.6   The Subnet-Router anycast address.

In addition, each host listens for traffic on the following multicast addresses:

- The node-local scope all-nodes multicast address (FF01::1)
- The link-local scope all-nodes multicast address (FF02::1)
- The solicited-node address for each unicast address
- The multicast addresses of joined groups

Router Addresses

An IPv6 router is assigned the following unicast addresses:

- A link-local address for each interface
- Unicast addresses for each interface (for example, a site-local address and one or more aggregatable global unicast addresses)
- A Subnet-Router anycast address
- Additional anycast addresses (optional)
- A loopback address (::1)

Additionally, each router listens for traffic on the following multicast addresses:

- The node-local scope all-nodes multicast address (FF01::1)
- The node-local scope all-routers multicast address (FF01::2)
- The link-local scope all-nodes multicast address (FF02::1)
- The link-local scope all-routers multicast address (FF02::1)
- The site-local scope all-routers multicast address (FF05::2)
- The solicited-node address for each unicast address
- The multicast addresses of joined groups

Interface Identifiers

Addresses that have 64-bit interface IDs—that is, addresses that have prefixes 001 through 111—derive their interface ID values from the 64-bit EUI-64 address, as defined by the Institute of Electrical and Electronics Engineers (IEEE). EUI-64 addresses are either assigned to network adapter cards or derived from IEEE 802 addresses (known as MAC addresses).

NOTE: *This derivation of IPv6 interface identifiers is based on RFC 2373. An alternative derivation of the IPv6 interface ID that changes over time is discussed in the Internet draft "Privacy Extensions for Stateless Address Autoconfiguration in IPv6." Refer to the IETF site at **www.ietf.org**.*

IEEE 802 Addresses

The 48-bit IEEE 802 (MAC) address consists of a 24-bit company ID (also called the manufacturer ID) that's uniquely assigned to each network adapter manufacturer by the IEEE and a 24-bit extension ID (also called the board ID).

The second least significant bit in the first octet of the company ID is called the Universal/Local (U/L) bit. This is used to indicate whether the address is universally or locally administered. If the U/L bit is set to 0, the address is as defined by the IEEE and the board manufacturer. If the U/L bit is set to 1, the network administrator has overridden the manufactured address and specified a different address. In the latter case, the address must be unique on the network. In the former case, the address is globally unique, or *universally administered.*

The other bit of interest is the lowest order bit in the first octet. This is called the Individual/Group (I/G) bit and indicates whether the address is unicast (the bit is set to zero) or multicast (the bit is set to one).

The great majority of network adapter addresses are universally administered unicast MAC addresses with both the U/L and I/G bits set to zero.

IEEE EUI-64 Addresses

The IEEE EUI-64 address has a 24-bit company ID and a 40-bit extension ID. It uses the U/L and I/G bits in the same way as the IEEE 802 address.

To create an EUI-64 address from an IEEE 802 address, the 16-bits value FFFE is inserted into the IEEE 802 address between the company ID and the extension ID.

For example, let's suppose the IEEE 802 address is:

```
00-00-E8-5A-E3-B0
```

Inserting the additional 16 bits as specified gives:

```
00-00-E8-FF-FE-5A-E3-B0
```

Converting this to colon hexadecimal gives an EUI-64 address of:

```
0000:E8FF:FE5A:E3B0
```

Converting EUI-64 to Interface ID

The conversion of the EUI-64 address to create an IPv6 address interface ID is straightforward. We invert the U/L bit. If the bit is zero (which it usually is), we convert it to one, and vice versa. In the example given, the first octet is:

```
00000000
```

Inverting the U/L bit gives:

```
00000010
```

Thus, the IPv6 address interface ID derived from the MAC address 00-00-E8-5A-E3-B0 is:

```
200:E8FF:FE5A:E3B0
```

The significant fact is that the interface ID in these IPv6 addresses that require this field is calculated from the hardware address (IEEE 802 or IEU-64) of the network adapter card.

Mapping Multicast Addresses to Ethernet Addresses

When IPv6 multicast packets are transmitted on an Ethernet link, the corresponding destination MAC address is 33-33-aa-aa-aa-aa, where aa-aa-aa-aa represents the last 32 bits of the IPv6 multicast address.

To receive IPv6 multicast packets efficiently on an Ethernet link, network adapters can store additional interesting MAC addresses in a table on the network adapter. If an Ethernet frame with an interesting MAC address is received, it's passed to the upper layers for additional processing. For every multicast address that the host listens to, there's a corresponding entry in the table of interesting MAC addresses.

For example, a host with the Ethernet MAC address 00-00-E8-5A-E3-B0 (link-local address of FE80::200:E8FF:FE5A:E3BO) registers the following multicast MAC addresses with the Ethernet adapter:

- The address of 33-33-00-00-00-01, which corresponds to the link-local scope all-nodes multicast address of FF02::1.
- The address 33-33-FF-5A-E3-B0, which corresponds to the solicited-node address of FF02::1:FF5A:E3B0. The solicited-node address is the prefix FF02::1:FF00:0/104 combined with the last 24 bits of the unicast IPv6 address.

Additional multicast addresses on which the host is listening are added and removed as needed from the table of interesting addresses on the Ethernet network adapter.

IPv6 Packet Structure

An IPv6 packet consists of a 40-byte (or octet) header followed by a variable-length payload. The payload is further divided into an extension headers section and an upper-layer Protocol Data Unit (PDU). The header, together with the extension headers, implements the functionality of the IPv4 header (see Chapter 4).

There can be one extension header, more than one, or (typically) none. Extension headers are of varying lengths and can expand to accommodate all the extension data needed for IPv6 communication. Figure 20.7 illustrates the IPv6 packet structure.

A Next Header field in the IPv6 header indicates the first extension header. Within each extension header, another Next Header field indicates the next extension header. The last extension header indicates the upper layer protocol (such as TCP, UDP, or ICMPv6) that's contained within the upper layer PDU. The upper layer PDU typically consists of an upper layer protocol header and its payload (for example, an ICMPv6 message, a UDP message, or a TCP segment).

The IPv6 packet payload (extension headers and upper layer PDU) is normally up to 65,535 bytes long. Payloads greater than 65,535 bytes can be sent using the Jumbo Payload option in the Hop-by-Hop Options extension header (see below under IPv6 Extension Headers).

IPv6 Header

The IPv6 header, defined in RFC 2460, consists of eight fields:

- *Version*—This 4-bit field is used to indicate the IP version and is set to a value of 6.

- *Traffic Class*—This 8-bit field indicates the class (or priority) of the IPv6 packet and performs a function similar to the IPv4 ToS field.

- *Flow Label*—This 20-bit field indicates that the packet belongs to a specific sequence of packets between a source and destination and requires special handling by intermediate IPv6 routers. The Flow Label is used for nondefault QoS connections, such as those used by real-time (audio and video) data. By default, this field is set to a value of 0.

- *Payload Length*—This 16-bit field indicates the length of the IP payload. For payload lengths greater than 65,535 bytes, the Payload Length field is set to 0 and the Jumbo Payload option is specified.

- *Next Header*—This 8-bit field indicates either the first extension header (if present) or the protocol in the upper layer PDU (such as TCP, UDP, or

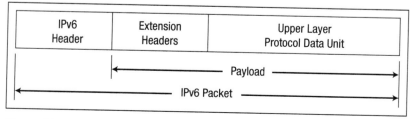

Figure 20.7   The IPv6 packet structure.

ICMPv6). If the field is used to indicate an upper-layer protocol, it holds the same values that are used in the IPv4 Protocol field. Table 20.3 lists the (decimal) values in the Next Header field and the types of header or upper layer protocol that each represents. The same values are used in the extension headers section of the IPv6 packet.

- *Hop Limit*—This 8-bit field indicates the maximum number of links over which an IPv6 packet can travel before being discarded. The Hop Limit field is similar to the IPv4 Time-to-Live (TTL) field. Whenthe Hop Limit equals 0, the packet is discarded and an ICMPv6 Time Expired message is sent to the source address.
- *Source Address*—This 128-bit field stores the IPv6 address of the originating host.
- *Destination Address*—This 128-bit field stores the IPv6 address of the current destination host. In most cases, the Destination Address field is set to the final destination address. If, however, a routing extension header is present, the Destination Address may be set to the next router interface in the source route list.

IPv6 Extension Headers

In IPv6, delivery and forwarding options are moved to extension headers. The only extension header that needs to be processed at each intermediate router is the Hop-by-Hop Options extension header. Extension headers are processed in the order in which they are present. Because the only extension header that's

Table 20.3   Next Header field values.

Value	Header or Protocol
0	Hop-by-Hop Options header
6	TCP
17	UDP
41	Encapsulated IPv6 header
43	Routing header
44	Fragmentation header
46	Resource Reservation Protocol (RSVP)
50	Encapsulating Security Payload
51	Authentication header
58	ICMPv6
59	No Next header
60	Destination Options header

processed by every node on a path is Hop-by-Hop Options, it must be first. RFC 2460 recommends that extension headers be placed in the IPv6 header in the following order:

1. Hop-by-Hop Options
2. Destination Options (for intermediate destinations when the Routing header is present)
3. Routing
4. Fragment
5. Authentication
6. ESP
7. Destination Options (for the final destination)

Typically, no extension headers are present in an IPv6 packet. If either the intermediate routers or the destination requires special handling, the sending host adds one or more extension headers. Each extension must start and end at a 64-bit (8-byte) boundary. Extension headers of variable size contain a Header Extension Length field and must use padding as needed to ensure that their size is a multiple of 8 bytes.

Hop-by-Hop Options Header

The Hop-by-Hop Options header is used to specify delivery parameters at each hop on the path to the destination. It contains the following fields:

- *Next Header*—This 8-bit field contains the value of the next header, as listed in Table 20.3.

- *Header Extension Length*—This 8-bit field contains a value equal to the number of 8-byte blocks in the Hop-by-Hop Options extension header, not including the first 8 bytes. Padding options are used to ensure 8-byte boundaries.

- *Options*—This variable length field contains the Hop-by-Hop options. An option either describes a specific characteristic of the packet delivery or provides padding. The option type both identifies the option and determines the way it is handled by the processing node. The option length identifies its length. The option value is the data associated with the option. This method of storing data in a header field is known as Type-Length-Value (TLV). RFCs 2460, 2675, and 2711 define the options listed in Table 20.4.

Destination Options Header

The Destination Options header is used to specify packet delivery parameters for either intermediate destinations or the final destination. The Next Header and Header Extension Length fields in the Destination Options header are defined in the same way as in the Hop-by-Hop Options header. Options specified in the Destination Options header can perform two functions:

Table 20.4   Hop-by-Hop Options.

Option	Type	Description
Pad1	0	Inserts a single byte of padding.
PadN	1	Inserts 2 or more bytes of padding.
Jumbo Payload	194	Indicates a payload size greater than 65,535 bytes.
Router Alert	5	Indicates to the router that the contents of the packet require additional processing. The Router Alert option is used for Multicast Listener Discovery and RSVP.

NOTE: *Payload sizes of up to 4,294,967,295 bytes can be indicated with the Jumbo Payload option by using a 32-bit Jumbo Payload Length field. An IPv6 packet with a payload size greater than 65,535 bytes is called a jumbogram.*

- If a Routing header is present, delivery or processing options are specified for each intermediate destination.
- Delivery or processing options are specified for the final destination.

Routing Header

IPv6 source nodes use the Routing extension header to specify a list of intermediate destinations through which the packet travels to on its way to its final destination. Currently only Routing Type 0 is defined (RFC 2460). A Routing Type 0 header contains the following fields:

- *Next Header*—Same as in the Hop-by-Hop header.
- *Header Extension Length*—Same as in the Hop-by-Hop header.
- *Routing Type*—This 8-bit field is currently set to 0.
- *Segments Left*—This 8-bit field holds a pointer that indicates the next intermediate destination.
- *Reserved*—This 32-bit field is reserved for future use.
- *Routing type-specific data*—A list of intermediate destination addresses. When the IPv6 packet reaches an intermediate destination, the address of the next intermediate destination (based on the value in the Segments Left field) becomes the Destination Address in the IPv6 header.

Fragment Header

The Fragment header is used for fragmentation and reassembly. This header contains the following fields:

- *Next Header*—Same as in the Hop-by-Hop header.
- *Reserved*—This 8-bit field is reserved for future use.
- *Fragment Offset*—This 130-bit field indicates the position of the fragment relative to the original IP payload.

- *Reserved*—This 2-bit field is reserved for future use.
- *More Fragments Flag*—This 1-bit (flag) field indicates whether more fragments follow the current fragment.
- *Identification*—This 32-bit field identifies this specific IP packet. If the IP packet is fragmented, all of the fragments retain the Identification field value so that the destination node can group the fragments for reassembly.

Because the use of the Fragment Offset field is defined for 8-byte fragment blocks, the Fragment header can't be used for IPv6 jumbograms. In IPv6, only source nodes can fragment payloads. If the payload submitted by the upper-layer protocol is larger than the link or path Maximum Transmission Unit (MTU), IPv6 fragments the payload at the source and uses the Fragment extension header to provide reassembly information.

When an IPv6 packet is fragmented, it's initially divided into unfragmentable and fragmentable parts as follows:

- Each intermediate node must process the unfragmentable part between the fragmenting node and the destination. This part consists of the IPv6 header, the Hop-by-Hop Options header, the Destination Options header for intermediate destinations, and the Routing header.
- The fragmentable part must be processed only at the final destination node. This part consists of the Authentication Header (AH), the Encapsulating Security Payload (ESP) header, the Destination Options header for the final destination, and the upper layer PDU.

When IPv6 fragment packets are formed, each packet consists of the unfragmentable part, a fragment header, and a portion of the fragmentable part.

Authentication Header

The AH contains information that's used to authenticate the node that sent the packet (data authentication), verify that the data wasn't modified in transit (data integrity), and ensure that captured packets can't be retransmitted and accepted as valid data (anti-replay protection). The AH is described in RFC 2402 and is part of the Security Architecture for the Internet Protocol defined in RFC 2401. It contains the following fields:

- *Next Header*—Same as in the Hop-by-Hop header.
- *Payload Length*—Specifies the payload length in 8-byte blocks.
- *Reserved*—This 8-bit field is reserved for future use.
- *Security Parameters Index*—This 32-bit field identifies a specific IPSec Security Association (SA).

- *Sequence Number*—This 32-bit field holds a sequence number that provides anti-replay protection.

- *Authentication Data*—This 32-bit field contains an Integrity Check Value (ICV) that provides data authentication and integrity.

The AH doesn't, by itself, encrypt the data to provide data confidentiality. To provide this function, the AH is used in conjunction with the ESP header (see RFC 2402).

ESP Header and Trailer

Whereas the AH provides data authentication and integrity services for the entire IPv6 packet, the ESP header and trailer provide these services for the encapsulated payload. The ESP header contains Security Parameters Index and Sequence Number fields similar to those in the AH. The ESP trailer, which follows the payload data, contains the following fields:

- *Padding*—This variable-length field ensures that the trailer terminates at the appropriate boundary.

- *Padding Length*—This 8-bit field specifies the number of padding bytes used.

- *Next Header*—Same as in the Hop-by-Hop header.

- *Authentication Data*—This 32-bit field contains the ICV.

ICMPv6

IPv6 uses ICMPv6 (documented in RFC 2463) to report delivery errors or forwarding errors and to provide a simple echo service for troubleshooting. ICMPv6 also provides a framework for the following:

- *Neighbor Discovery (ND)*—A series of five ICMPv6 messages that manage node-to-node communication on a link

- *Multicast Listener Discovery (MLD)*—A series of three ICMP messages that manage subnet multicast membership

ICMPv6 Header

The ICMPv6 header contains the following fields:

- *Type*—This 8-bit field indicates the ICMPv6 message type. The high order bit is set to 0 in error messages and to 1 in informational messages.

- *Code*—This 8-bit field distinguishes between multiple messages of a given message type. If there's only one message for a given type, the Code field is set to 0.

- *Checksum*—This 16-bit field stores the ICMP message checksum.

- *Message body*—This variable length field contains message-specific data.

Error Messages

ICMPv6 error messages report errors in the forwarding or delivery of IPv6 packets, either by the destination node or by an intermediate router. They include Destination Unreachable, Packet Too Big, Time Exceeded, and Parameter Problem.

Destination Unreachable

A router or a destination host sends a Destination Unreachable message when a packet can't be forwarded to its destination. The Type field is set to 1 and the Code field to a value from 0 through 4. Following the Checksum field, the Message body starts with a 32-bit Unused field. The remainder of the Message body contains a portion of the discarded packet.

The number of bytes of the discarded packet that are contained in the Destination Unreachable message varies, depending on whether there are IPv6 extension headers present. In any case, the size of the complete IPv6 packet that contains the Destination Unreachable message can't exceed 1280 bytes.

Table 20.5 lists the Code field values field for the various Destination Unreachable messages.

Packet Too Big

A Packet Too Big message is sent when the packet can't be forwarded because the MTU of the forwarding link is smaller than the IPv6 packet size. The Type field is set to 2 and the Code field to 0. Following the Checksum field, the Message body contains a 32-bit MTU field that stores the MTU for the link on which the packet was being forwarded. The remainder of the Message body contains a portion of the discarded packet, as described above for the Destination Unreachable message.

Table 20.5   Code field values for Destination Unreachable messages.

Value	Description
0	No route that matches the destination can be found in the routing table.
1	Communication with the destination is prohibited by administrative policy. Typically, this is sent when the packet is discarded by a firewall.
2	The address is beyond the scope of the source address.
3	The destination address is unreachable. Typically, this is sent because the destination's link-layer address can't be resolved.
4	The destination port is unreachable. Typically, this is sent when an IPv6 packet containing a UDP message arrives at a destination, but there are no applications listening on the destination UDP port.

Time Exceeded

A Time Exceeded message is sent by a router when the Hop Limit field in the IPv6 header is zero. The Type field is set to 3 and the Code field to either 0 or 1. The Code field is followed by a Checksum field and then by a Message body that contains a 32-bit Unused field and a portion of the discarded packet. The Message body for the Time Exceeded message is the same as the Message body for the Destination Unreachable message.

A Code field value of 0 indicates that the Hop Limit field in the IPv6 header is 0. This, in turn, indicates either that the Hop Limit of outgoing packets isn't large enough to reach the destination or that a routing loop exists. A Code field value of 1 indicates that the fragmentation reassembly time of the destination host is exceeded.

Parameter Problem

A router or a destination host sends a Parameter Problem message when an error that prevents further processing is encountered in either the IPv6 header or in an extension header. The Type field is set to 4 and the Code field to a value from 0 through 2. Following the Checksum field, the Message body contains the 32-bit Pointer field, which indicates the byte offset in the offending IPv6 packet where the error was encountered. This, in turn, is followed by a portion of the discarded packet, as described earlier for the Destination Unreachable message.

Table 20.6 lists the Code field values for the various Parameter Problem messages.

Informational Messages

The ICMPv6 informational messages Echo Request and Echo Reply, defined in RFC 2463, provide diagnostic capabilities to aid troubleshooting.

Echo Request

An Echo Request message is sent to a destination to solicit an Echo Reply message. This facility provides a simple diagnostic aid when troubleshooting reachability and routing problems. The Echo Request message Type field is set to 128 and the Code field to 0. Following the Checksum, the Message body contains 16-bit Identifier and Sequence Number fields. The values in these fields are set by

Table 20.6   Code field values for Parameter Problem messages.

Value	Description
0	An error was encountered in a field within the IPv6 header or an extension header.
1	An unrecognized Next Header field value was encountered.
2	An unrecognized IPv6 option was encountered.

the sending host and are used to match an incoming Echo Reply message with its corresponding Echo Request. The variable-length Data field that follows the Sequence Number field contains zero or more bytes of data. The sending host also sets this field.

Echo Reply

An Echo Reply message is sent in response to an Echo Request message. The Echo Reply message Type field is set to 129 and the Code field to 0. Following the Checksum, the Message body contains 16-bit Identifier and Sequence Number fields and a variable length Data field. These fields contain the same values as those in the Echo Request message that prompted the Echo Reply.

Path MTU Discovery

A sending node uses the receipt of ICMP Packet Too Big messages to discover the path MTU. The process is as follows:

1. The sending node initially assumes that the path MTU is the link MTU of the interface on which the traffic is being forwarded and sends IPv6 datagrams of the assumed path MTU size.

2. If a router on the path is unable to forward the packet, it discards it and sends an ICMP Packet Too Big message back to the sending node. The ICMP Packet Too Big message contains the link MTU of the link on which the forwarding failed.

3. The sending node sets the path MTU for packets being sent to the destination to the value of the MTU field in the ICMPv6 Packet Too Big message.

This process is repeated as many times as necessary. The path MTU is determined when either no additional ICMPv6 Packet Too Big messages are received or an acknowledgment is received from the destination.

Neighbor Discovery

Neighbor Discovery (ND) is implemented by a set of messages and processes that determine relationships between neighboring nodes. Hosts use it to discover neighboring routers, addresses, address prefixes, and other configuration parameters. Nodes use it to determine whether a neighbor is reachable, to resolve the link-layer address of a neighboring node to which an IPv6 packet is being forwarded, and to determine when the link-layer address of a neighboring node has changed. Routers use it to advertise their presence, to send host configuration parameters and on-link prefixes, and to inform hosts of a better next-hop address to forward packets for a specific destination.

Table 20.7 lists the ND processes that are documented in RFC 2461.

Table 20.7   **IPv6 ND Processes.**

Process	Description
Router discovery	The process by which a host discovers the local routers on an attached link.
Prefix discovery	The process by which hosts discover the network prefixes for local link destinations.
Parameter discovery	The process by which hosts discover additional operating parameters, including the link MTU and the default hop limit for outgoing packets.
Address autoconfiguration	The process for configuring IP addresses for interfaces in either the presence or absence of a stateful address configuration server, such as DHCPv6.
Address resolution	The process by which nodes resolve a neighbor's IPv6 address to its link-layer address.
Next-hop determination	The process by which a node determines the IPv6 address of the neighbor to which a packet is being forwarded, based on the destination address. The forwarding or next-hop address is either the destination address or the address of an on-link default router.
Neighbor unreachability detection	The process by which a node determines that the IPv6 layer of a neighbor is no longer receiving packets.
Duplicate address detection	The process by which a node determines that an address considered for use isn't already in use by a neighboring node.
Redirect function	The process of informing a host of a better first-hop IPv6 address to reach a destination.

Neighbor Discovery Messages

All of the IPv6 ND functions are performed through the following messages:

- Router Solicitation
- Router Advertisement
- Neighbor Solicitation
- Neighbor Advertisement
- Redirect

NOTE: *To ensure that ND messages received originated from a node on the local link, all ND messages are sent with a hop limit of 255. A received ND message is silently discarded if its IPv6 header Hop Limit field isn't set to 255. This provides protection against ND-based network attacks launched from off-link nodes.*

Router Solicitation Message

The multicast Router Solicitation message is sent by IPv6 hosts to discover IPv6 routers that are present on the link. A host sends this message to prompt routers to respond immediately, rather than waiting for a periodic Router Advertisement message. The Type field in this message is set to 133, and the Code field is set to 0. Following the Checksum, the message contains the following fields:

- *Reserved*—This 32-bit field is reserved for future use and is set to 0.

- *Options*—This variable-length field contains the Source Link-Layer Address option. ND options are described in the next part of this section.

Router Advertisement Message

IPv6 routers send a Router Advertisement message either periodically or in response to a Router Solicitation message. The message contains the information required by hosts to determine the link prefixes, the link MTU, whether or not to use address autoconfiguration, and the durations for which addresses created through address autoconfiguration are both valid and preferred.

The Type and Code fields are set to 134 and 0 respectively. Following the Checksum, the message contains the following fields:

- *Cur Hop Limit*—This 8-bit field indicates the default value of the Hop Count field in the IPv6 header for packets sent by hosts that receive the Router Advertisement message.

- *Managed Address Configuration flag*—When set to 1, this flag indicates that hosts receiving the Router Advertisement message must use a stateful address configuration protocol to obtain addresses, in addition to the addresses derived from stateless address autoconfiguration.

- *Other Stateful Configuration flag*—When set to 1, this flag indicates that hosts receiving the Router Advertisement message must use a stateful address configuration protocol to obtain nonaddress configuration information.

- *Reserved*—This 6-bit field is reserved for future use and is set to 0.

- *Router Lifetime*—This 16-bit field indicates the lifetime (in seconds) of the router as the default. A Router Lifetime of 0 indicates that the router can't be considered a default router.

- *Reachable Time*—This 32-bit field indicates the amount of time (in milliseconds) that a node can consider a neighboring node reachable after receiving a reachability confirmation. A Reachable Time value of 0 indicates that the router doesn't specify the Reachable Time.

- *Retrans Timer*—This 32-bit field indicates the amount of time (in milliseconds) between retransmissions of Neighbor Solicitation messages. Retrans Timer is used during Neighbor Unreachability Detection. A Retrans

Timer value of 0 indicates that the router doesn't specify the time between retransmissions.

- *Options*—This variable length field contains the Source Link-Layer Address option, the MTU option, and the Prefix Information option.

Neighbor Solicitation Message

The Neighbor Solicitation message is sent by IPv6 hosts to discover the link-layer address of an on-link IPv6 node. Typically, Neighbor Solicitation messages are multicast for address resolution and unicast when the reachability of a neighboring node is being verified. The Type and Code fields are set to 135 and 0, respectively. Following the Checksum, the message contains the following fields:

- *Reserved*—This 32-bit field is reserved for future use and is set to 0.

- *Target Address*—This 128-bit field indicates the target's IPv6 address.

- *Options*—This variable-length field contains the Source Link-Layer Address option. The Source Link-Layer Address option isn't included during duplicate address detection, in which the source address is the unspecified address (::).

Neighbor Advertisement Message

An IPv6 node sends a Neighbor Advertisement message in response to a Neighbor Solicitation message. A node also sends unsolicited Neighbor Advertisement messages to inform neighboring nodes of changes in link-layer addresses.

The Neighbor Advertisement message contains information that enables nodes to determine the message type (solicited or unsolicited), the link-layer address of the sender, and the sender's role on the network. The Type and Code fields are set to 136 and 0, respectively. Following the Checksum, the message contains the following fields:

- *Router flag*—This flag is set to 1 when the sender is a router and to 0 when the sender is not. The Router flag is used by Neighbor Unreachability Detection.

- *Solicited flag*—When set to 1, this flag indicates that the Neighbor Advertisement message was sent in response to a Neighbor Solicitation message. The Solicited flag is set to 0 for both multicast Neighbor Advertisements and unsolicited unicast Neighbor Advertisements.

- *Override flag*—When set to 1, this flag indicates that the link-layer address in the included target link-layer address option should override the link-layer address in the existing neighbor cache entry. If the Override flag is set to 0, the enclosed link-layer address updates a neighbor cache entry only if the link-layer address isn't known.

- *Reserved*—This 29-bit field is reserved for future use and is set to 0.

- *Target Address*—This 128-bit field indicates the address being advertised. For solicited Neighbor Advertisement messages, the target address is contained in the Target Address field in the corresponding Neighbor Solicitation message. For unsolicited Neighbor Advertisement messages, the target address is the address whose link-layer address has changed.

- *Options*—This variable-length field contains the Target Link-Layer Address option.

Redirect Message

The Redirect message is sent by an IPv6 router to inform an originating host about a better first-hop address for a specific destination. Redirect messages are sent by routers for unicast traffic only and are processed by originating hosts. The Type and Code fields are set to 137 and 0, respectively. Following the Checksum, the message contains the following fields:

- *Reserved*—This 32-bit field is reserved for future use and is set to 0.

- *Target Address*—This 128-bit field indicates the better next-hop address for packets addressed to the node in the Destination Address field. For off-link traffic, the Target Address field is set to the local-link address of a local router; for on-link traffic, the field is set to the Destination Address field in the Redirect message.

- *Destination Address*—This 128-bit field contains the destination address of the packet that caused the router to send the Redirect message. On receipt at the originating host, the Target Address and Destination Address fields are used to update forwarding information for the destination.

- *Options*—This variable-length field contains the Target Link-Layer Address option (when known by the router) and the Redirected Header option.

Neighbor Discovery Options

ND options provide additional information, typically indicating MAC addresses, on-link network prefixes, on-link MTU information, and redirection data. These options are formatted using TLV. The 8-bit Type field indicates the type of ND option, as listed in Table 20.8. The 8-bit Length field indicates the length of the entire option. The variable-length Value field contains the data for the option.

Source/Target Link-Layer Address Options

The Source Link-Layer Address option indicates the link-layer address of the ND message sender. This option is included in the Neighbor Solicitation, Router Solicitation, and Router Advertisement messages.

Table 20.8   IPv6 ND option types.

Type	Option
1	Source Link-Layer Address
2	Target Link-Layer Address
3	Prefix Information
4	Redirected Header
5	MTU

The Target Link-Layer Address option indicates the link-layer address of the neighboring node to which IPv6 packets should be directed. This option is included in the Neighbor Advertisement and Redirect messages.

In addition to Type and Length fields, both options specify a variable length Link-Layer Address field that contains the link-layer address of the source or target. RFC 2464 gives details of how the link-layer address is formatted.

Prefix Information Option

The Prefix Information option is sent in Router Advertisement messages to indicate both address prefixes and address autoconfiguration information. Multiple Prefix Information options can be included in a Router Advertisement message, indicating multiple address prefixes. The Type field is set to 3, and the Length field for this option is always set to 4. The Value section of the option contains the following fields:

- *Prefix Length*—This 8-bit field indicates the number of leading bits in the Prefix field (discussed later in this list) that comprise the address prefix. It holds a value from 0 through 128.

- *On-link flag*—When set to 1, this flag indicates that the addresses implied by the included prefix are available on the link on which this Router Advertisement message was received.

- *Autonomous flag*—When set to 1, this flag indicates that the included prefix is used to create an autonomous (or stateless) address configuration.

- *Reserved 1*—This 6-bit field is reserved for future use and is set to 0.

- *Valid Lifetime*—This 32-bit field indicates the number of seconds that an address, which is based on the included prefix and uses stateless address configuration, remains valid. The Valid Lifetime field also indicates the number of seconds that the included prefix is valid for on-link determination. For an infinite valid lifetime, this field is set to 0xFFFFFFFF.

- *Preferred Lifetime*—This 32-bit field indicates the number of seconds that an address, based on the included prefix and using stateless address configuration, remains in a preferred state. Stateless autoconfiguration addresses that are still valid are either in a preferred or deprecated state. In the preferred state, the address can be used for unrestricted communication. In the deprecated state, the use of the address isn't recommended for new communications, although existing communications using a deprecated address can continue.

- *Reserved 2*—This 32-bit field is reserved for future use and is set to 0.

- *Prefix*—This 128-bit field indicates the prefix for the IPv6 address that's derived through stateless autoconfiguration. The combination of the Prefix Length field and the Prefix field unambiguously describes the prefix, which, when combined with the interface identifier for the node, creates an IPv6 address.

Redirected Header Option

The Redirected Header option is sent in Redirect messages to specify the IPv6 packet that caused the router to send the Redirect message. It can contain all or part of the redirected packet. In addition to the Type field (set to 4) and the Length field, this option contains the following fields:

- *Reserved*—This 48-bit field is reserved for future use and is set to 0.

- *Portion of redirected packet*—Contains as much as possible of the packet that caused the Redirect message to be sent, within the constraint of a maximum Redirect Message size of 1280 bytes.

MTU Option

The MTU option is sent in Router Advertisement messages to indicate the link MTU. This option is used when the MTU for a link isn't well known or needs to be set because of a translational bridging configuration. The MTU option overrides the MTU reported by the interface hardware.

In bridged or Layer 2 switched environments, it is possible to have different link-layer technologies with different link-layer MTUs on the same network segment—for example, Fiber Distributed Data Interface (FDDI) and Ethernet. The MTU option is used to indicate the highest MTU supported by all link-layer technologies on the network segment.

In addition to the Type and Length fields (set to 5 and 1, respectively), this option contains the following fields:

- *Reserved*—This 16-bit field is reserved for future use and is set to 0.

- *MTU*—This 32-bit field indicates the MTU that should be used by the host for the link on which the Router Advertisement was received. The value in this field is ignored if it's larger than the link MTU.

Neighbor Discovery Processes

The ND protocol provides message exchanges for the following processes:

- Address resolution (including duplicate address detection)
- Router discovery (including prefix and parameter discovery)
- Neighbor unreachability detection
- Redirect function

Address Resolution

The address resolution process for IPv6 nodes consists of an exchange of Neighbor Solicitation and Neighbor Advertisement messages to resolve the link-layer address of the on-link next-hop address for a given destination.

The sending host sends a multicast Neighbor Solicitation message on the appropriate interface. The multicast address of this message is the solicited-node multicast address that's derived from the target IP address. The message also includes the link-layer address of the sending host in the Source Link-Layer Address option.

When the target host receives the Neighbor Solicitation message, it updates its own neighbor cache based on the source address of that message and the link-layer address in the Source Link-Layer Address option. The target node then sends a unicast Neighbor Advertisement message to the sender of the Neighbor Solicitation message. The Neighbor Advertisement message includes the Target Link-Layer Address option.

When it receives the Neighbor Advertisement message from the target, the sending host updates its neighbor cache with an entry for the target based on the information in the Target Link-Layer Address option. At this point, unicast IPv6 traffic between the sending host and the Neighbor Solicitation message target can be sent.

Duplicate Address Detection

IPv6 nodes use the Neighbor Solicitation and Neighbor Advertisement messages to detect duplicate addresses on the local link. A host that wants to use an IPv6 link-local address sends a solicited-node multicast Neighbor Solicitation message to that address. If another host on the local link (the defending host) is already using that address, it responds with a multicast Neighbor Advertisement message with both Source and Target Address fields set to the duplicate address.

Upon receipt of this message, the node disables the use of the duplicate IP address on the interface. If the node doesn't receive a Neighbor Advertisement that defends the use of the IPv6 address, it initializes the address on the interface.

Router Discovery

Router discovery is the process through which nodes attempt to discover routers on the local link. Router discovery processes differ, depending on whether the host is active on the link or is initializing on the link.

IPv6 routers periodically send Router Advertisement messages on the local link advertising their existence as routers. They also provide configuration parameters, such as default hop limit, MTU, and prefixes. Active IPv6 hosts on the local link receive the Router Advertisement messages and use the contents to maintain the default router list, the prefix list, and other configuration parameters.

A host that's initializing on the link sends a Router Solicitation message to the link-local scope all-routers multicast address (FF02::2). Upon receipt of a Router Solicitation message, all routers on the local link send a unicast Router Advertisement message to the node that sent the Router Solicitation message. The node receives these messages and uses their contents to build the default router and prefix lists and set other configuration parameters.

In addition to identifying a default router, the IPv6 router discovery process also configures the following:

- The default setting for the Hop Limit field in the IPv6 header
- Whether (or not) the node should use a stateful address protocol to obtain addresses and other configuration parameters
- The timer values used in reachability detection and the retransmission of Neighbor Solicitation messages
- The list of network prefixes defined for the link
- The local link MTU

Neighbor Unreachability Detection

Reachability is defined as the ability to send an IPv6 packet to a neighboring node and have that packet successfully received and processed by the neighbor. The definition of reachability doesn't require that the packet be successfully delivered to a remote node across a router—only that it reaches the neighboring router.

To determine whether a neighbor is reachable, IPv6 can use either upper-layer protocols that indicate communication progress or Neighbor Solicitation and Neighbor Advertisement messages.

In the case of TCP traffic, communication progress is indicated when new data (or acknowledgment segments for sent data) is received. For UDP traffic, this progress indication may not be present. In this case, the node sends unicastNeighbor Solicitation messages to the next-hop neighbor to monitor its ongoing reachability.

The receipt of a solicited Neighbor Advertisement is considered proof of reachability. Unsolicited Neighbor Advertisement or Router Advertisement messages aren't considered proof of reachability, because neighbor unreachability detection detects *symmetric reachability*. That is, packets must be able to travel to and from the desired neighboring node. For an unsolicited Neighbor Advertisement or Router Advertisement message, only the path from the node sending the message is confirmed. This is called *asymmetric reachability*.

IPv6 has a Router Lifetime field in the Router Advertisement message, which indicates the length of time that the router can be considered a default router. If, however, the current default router becomes unavailable, the condition is detected through neighbor unreachability detection and a new router is chosen immediately from the default router list. If a host receives a Neighbor Advertisement from a router where the Router flag is set to 0, the host removes that router from the default router list and, if necessary, chooses another router.

Redirect Function

Routers use the redirect function to inform originating hosts of a better first-hop neighbor to which traffic should be forwarded for a specific destination. Redirect is used in two instances:

- Another router on the local link is closer (in terms of route metric) to the destination.
- The destination is a neighbor.

The IPv6 redirect process is as follows:

1. The originating host forwards a unicast packet to its default router.
2. The router processes the packet and notes that the address of the originating host is a neighbor and that the addresses of both the originating host and the next-hop are on the same link.
3. The router forwards the packet to the appropriate next-hop address.
4. The router sends the originating host a Redirect message. The Target Address field of the Redirect message contains the next-hop address of the node to which the originating host should send packets addressed to the destination.
5. Upon receipt of the Redirect message, the originating host updates the destination address entry in its destination cache. If the Target Link-Layer Address option is included in the Redirect message, its contents are used to create or update the corresponding neighbor cache entry.

Host Sending Algorithm

An IPv6 host uses the following algorithm when sending a packet to an arbitrary destination:

1. Check the destination cache for an entry matching the destination address.

2. If an entry matching the destination address is found in the destination cache, obtain the next-hop address in the destination cache entry. Go to Step 4.

3. If no entry matching the destination address is found in the destination cache, determine whether the destination address matches a prefix in the prefix list.

   • If the destination address matches a prefix in the prefix list, the next-hop address is set to the destination address. Go to Step 4.

   • If the destination address doesn't match a prefix in the prefix list, the next-hop address is set to the address of the current default router. Go to Step 4.

   • If there's no default router (and there are no routers in the default router list), the next-hop address is set to the destination address. Go to Step 4.

4. Check the neighbor cache for an entry matching the next-hop address.

   • If an entry matching the next-hop address is found in the neighbor cache, obtain the link-layer address. Go to Step 5.

   • If no entry matching the next-hop address is found in the neighbor cache, use address resolution to obtain the link-layer address for the next-hop address. Go to Step 5.

5. Send the packet using the link-layer address of the neighbor cache entry.

Multicast Listener Discovery

Multicast Listener Discovery (MLD), documented in RFC 2710, is a set of ICMPv6 messages that are exchanged by routers and nodes and enable routers to discover the set of multicast addresses for which there are listening nodes for each attached interface.

An MLD message packet consists of an IPv6 header, a Hop-by-Hop Options extension header, and the MLD message. The Hop-by-Hop Options extension header contains the IPv6 Router Alert Option documented in RFC 2711. This is used to ensure that routers process MLD messages even if they're sent to multicast addresses on which the routers aren't listening.

The MLD Messages are Multicast Listener Query, Multicast Listener Report, and Multicast Listener Done.

Multicast Listener Query

A router uses Multicast Listener Query to query a link for multicast listeners. The General Query is used to query for multicast listeners of all multicast addresses. The Multicast-Address-Specific Query is used to query for multicast listeners of a specific multicast address.

In the MLD Multicast Listener Query message, the Type field is set to 130 and the Code field is set to 0. The 16-bit Maximum Response Delay and Reserved fields follow the Checksum field. The Maximum Response Delay is the maximum amount of time in milliseconds within which a multicast group member must report its membership using a MLD Multicast Listener Report message. The Reserved field is unused.

In the General Query, the 128-bit Multicast Address field is set to the unspecified address (::). In the Multicast-Address-Specific Query, the Multicast Address field is set to the specific multicast address that's being queried.

Multicast Listener Report

A multicast listener uses Multicast Listener Report either to report interest in receiving multicast traffic for a specific multicast address or to respond to a Multicast Listener Query.

In the MLD Multicast Listener Report message, the Type field is set to 131 and the Code field is set to 0. The Maximum Response Delay field isn't used and is set to 0. The Multicast Address field is set to the specific multicast address that is being reported.

Multicast Listener Done

A multicast listener uses Multicast Listener Done to report that it's no longer interested in receiving multicast traffic for a specific multicast address. In the MLD Multicast Listener Done message, the Type field is set to 132 and the Code field is set to 0. The Maximum Response Delay field isn't used and is set to 0. The Multicast Address field is set to the specific multicast address for which the sending node is no longer interested in receiving multicast traffic.

Address Autoconfiguration

IPv6 can configure itself automatically, even without the use of a stateful configuration protocol. By default, an IPv6 host can configure a link-local address for each interface. By using router discovery, a host can also determine the addresses of routers, other configuration parameters, additional addresses, and on-link prefixes. The Router Advertisement message includes an indication of whether a stateful address configuration protocol should be used.

Address autoconfiguration (described in RFC 2462) can be performed only on multicast-capable interfaces.

Autoconfigured Address States

Autoconfigured addresses are in one or more of the following states:

- *Tentative*—The address is in the process of being verified as unique. Verification is done through duplicate address detection. A node can't receive unicast traffic sent to a tentative address. It can, however, receive and process multicast Neighbor Advertisement messages sent in response to the Neighbor Solicitation message that has been sent during duplicate address detection.

- *Preferred*—An address whose uniqueness has been verified. A node can send and receive unicast traffic to and from a preferred address. The Preferred Lifetime field in the Prefix Information option of a Router Advertisement message determines the period of time that an address can remain in the preferred state.

- *Deprecated*—An address that's still valid, but whose use is discouraged for new communication. Existing communication sessions can use a deprecated address. A node can send and receive unicast traffic to and from a deprecated address.

- *Valid*—An address from which unicast traffic can be sent and received. The valid state includes both the preferred and deprecated states. The Valid Lifetime field in the Prefix Information option of a Router Advertisement message determines the amount of time that an address remains in the valid state. The valid lifetime must be greater than or equal to the preferred lifetime.

- *Invalid*—An address to or from which a node can no longer send or receive unicast traffic. An address enters the invalid state after its valid lifetime expires.

NOTE: *Apart from the autoconfiguration of link-local addresses, address autoconfiguration is specified only for hosts. Routers obtain address and configuration parameters through other means, such as manual configuration.*

Autoconfiguration Types

There are three types of autoconfiguration:

- *Stateless*—Configuration is based on the receipt of Router Advertisement messages with the Managed Address Configuration and Other Stateful Configuration flags both set to 0 and with one or more Prefix Information options.

- *Stateful*—Configuration is based on the use of a stateful address configuration protocol. A host uses stateful address configuration when it receives

Router Advertisement messages with no prefix options and with either the Managed Address Configuration flag or the Other Stateful Configuration flag set to 1. A host will also use a stateful address configuration protocol when there are no routers present on the local link.

- *Both*—Configuration is based on receipt of Router Advertisement messages with Prefix Information options and with either the Managed Address Configuration or the Other Stateful Configuration flag set to 1.

For all types of autoconfiguration, a link-local address is always configured.

The Autoconfiguration Process

The address autoconfiguration process for an IPv6 node is as follows:

1. A tentative link-local address is derived based on the link-local prefix of FE80::/64 and the 64-bit interface identifier.

2. A Neighbor Solicitation message is sent with the Target Address field set to the tentative link-local address. This uses duplicate address detection to verify the uniqueness of the tentative link-local address.

3. If no Neighbor Advertisement message is received, the tentative link-local address is assumed to be unique and valid. The link-local address is initialized for the interface. The corresponding solicited-node multicast link-layer address is registered with the network adapter.

NOTE: *If a Neighbor Advertisement message is received in response to the Neighbor Solicitation message, this indicates that another node on the local link is using the tentative link-local address. In this case, address autoconfiguration stops and manual configuration must be performed on the node.*

For an IPv6 host, the address autoconfiguration continues as follows:

1. The host sends a Router Solicitation message.

2. If no Router Advertisement messages are received, the host uses a stateful address configuration protocol to obtain addresses and other configuration parameters.

3. If a Router Advertisement message is received, the Hop Limit, Reachable Time, Retrans Timer, and MTU (if the MTU option is present) are set.

4. For each Prefix Information option present:
   - If the On-Link flag is set to 1, the prefix is added to the prefix list.
   - If the Autonomous flag is set to 1, the prefix and the 64-bit interface identifier are used to derive a tentative address.

5. Duplicate address detection is used to verify the tentative address's uniqueness.

- If the tentative address is in use, the use of the address isn't initialized for the interface.

- If the tentative address isn't in use, the address is initialized. This includes setting the valid and preferred lifetimes, based on the Valid Lifetime and Preferred Lifetime fields in the Prefix Information option. It also includes registering the corresponding solicited-node multicast link-layer address with the network adapter.

6. If the Managed Address Configuration flag in the Router Advertisement message is set to 1, a stateful address configuration protocol is used to obtain additional addresses.

7. If the Other Stateful Configuration flag in the Router Advertisement message is set to 1, a stateful address configuration protocol is used to obtain additional configuration parameters.

IPv6 and the Domain Name System

RFC 1886 describes Domain Name System (DNS) enhancements for IPv6. These consist of the AAAA (called "quad A") host address resource record and the IP6.INT domain for reverse queries. The AAAA record has a Type value of 28 and requires a host name and a 128-bit IPv6 address. The procedure for creating an AAAA record manually is described in the Immediate Solutions section of this chapter.

The IP6.INT domain has been created for IPv6 reverse queries, also called pointer (PTR) queries, that determine a host name based on the IP address. To create the namespace for reverse queries, each hexadecimal digit in the 32-digit IPv6 address is listed in inverse order.

For example, the address:

```
FE80::2D0:B7FF:FE4C:2386
```

is expanded to:

```
FE80:0000:0000:0000:02D0:B7FF:FE4C:2386
```

The resulting reverse lookup entry is thus:

```
6.8.3.2.C.4.E.F.F.F.7.B.0.D.2.0.0.0.0.0.0.0.0.0.0.0.0.0.0.8.E.F.IP6.INT
```

RFC 1886 doesn't provide an easy method of propagating changes to AAAA records. This issue is addressed using the new "A6" resource record that's described in the Internet Draft "DNS Extensions to Support IPv6 Address Aggregation and Renumbering." Refer to **www.ietf.org**.

Immediate Solutions

Downloading and Installing Microsoft IPv6

Currently, Microsoft provides a technology preview version of IPv6 for use by developers. This is the recommended IPv6 implementation on Windows 2000. The technology preview version won't run on any other version of Windows. The Microsoft Research IPv6 implementation, available at **www.research.microsoft. com/msripv6/**, can be downloaded and installed on both Windows 2000 and Windows NT4 operating systems. Currently, there are no plans to support Windows 95, 98, or CE.

Downloading IPv6

To download the technology preview version of IPv6, proceed as follows:

1. Log on as an administrator to the computer you want to use as a distribution server for the IPv6 files.

2. Create a folder called (for example) IPv6Kit. This procedure uses this folder as both a download and a distribution folder. If you want to split these functions, create two folders.

3. Share the folder that you're using as a distribution folder. The minimum permission for this procedure is Administrators/Read, but you can choose to give the Administrators group full control. Don't forget to remove the Everyone group.

4. Access **www.msdn.microsoft.com/downloads/sdks/platform/tpipv6.asp**. If this doesn't work (URLs can change), search the Microsoft Software Developers Network (MSDN) site for IPv6.

5. Click Download the Microsoft IPv6 Technology Preview.

6. Read the end-user license agreement. Currently, this software is a preview. Ensure that you understand the limitations and restrictions on its use.

7. Click I Agree.

8. If you get a security alert, click Yes to clear it.

9. If you get an Internet redirection alert, click Yes to clear it.

10. Select Save this program to disk, then click OK.

11. Specify a download directory (for example, C:\Ipv6Kit), then click Save.

12. Open Windows Explorer and double-click the downloaded self-extracting EXE file. This is named tpipv6-*xxxxxx*, where *xxxxxx* specifies a release date.

13. Specify your distribution folder (for example, C:\Ipv6Kit), then click Unzip.

14. Click OK. Click Close.

Installing IPv6

When IPv6 installation files have been downloaded and unzipped to a folder, the protocol can be installed on a connection. Typically, it will be installed on a Local Area Connection that's used to access the Internet. To install IPv6, proceed as follows:

1. Log on as an administrator to the computer on which you want to install IPv6. If the installation files are in a shared directory, this computer must be on a subnet that can access the share.

2. Access Start|Settings|Network and Dial-up Connections and select Local Area Connection.

3. Click Properties.

4. Click Install.

5. Select Protocol, then click Add.

6. If you get a Select Device warning message telling you that drivers can't be found, click OK to close the message box. Otherwise, click Have Disk.

7. Specify the location of the IPv6 installation files either by typing the path or by using the Browse button.

8. Click OK.

9. Select Microsoft IPv6 Protocol (it will probably be the only protocol on the list), then click OK.

10. Click Close to close the Local Area Connection Properties box.

11. Click Close (again) to close the Local Area Connection Status box.

Using the IPv6 Command-Line Tools

The ipv6 command-line tool has a number of subcommands, each with its own set of arguments and options. Figure 20.8 shows a list of these subcommands. The 6to4cfg command-line tool automatically discovers a host's globally routable IPv4 address and creates a 6to4 prefix, thereby implementing IPv6 to IPv4

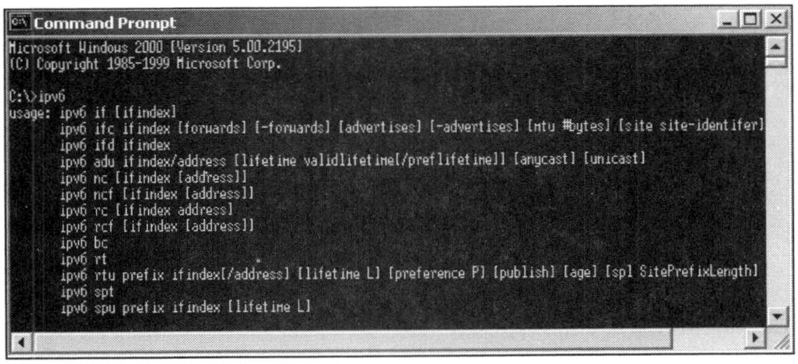

Figure 20.8   The ipv6 tool subcommands.

configuration. The ping6 tool is similar to ping in IPv4, except that you need to specify a source address if you're pinging a link-local destination. The ipsec6 tool configures IPSec policies and security associations.

All of these tools run from the Command Console (access Start|Programs| Accessories and select Command Prompt).

Checking a Connection between Two Link-Local Hosts

This procedure (and all subsequent procedures in this section) assumes that you've logged in as an administrator and accessed the Command Console. For this particular procedure, you need to be logged on to two hosts, which we'll call Host A and Host B, that are on the same subnet. To test connectivity, proceed as follows:

1. On Host A, enter **ipv6 if**. Note the preferred address for the Local Area Connection. Figure 20.9 shows a typical output.

2. Repeat the same procedure on Host B.

3. Use the **ping6** command to ping Host A's preferred address from Host B.

4. Use the **ping6** command to ping Host B's preferred address from Host A (optional). Figure 20.10 shows a successful **ping6** command.

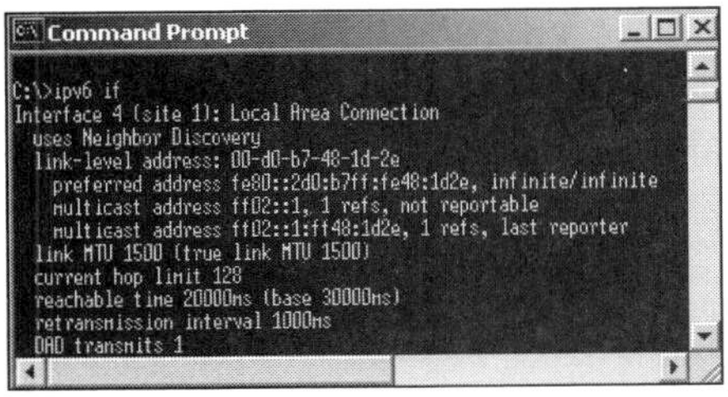

Figure 20.9   Displaying an interface configuration.

Figure 20.10 Testing connectivity.

Setting Interface Attributes

An interface can be *forwarding*, in which case it forwards received packets that aren't assigned to it. It can also be *advertising*, in which case it sends router advertisements. The interface MTU can be set to a value between the minimum IPv6 MTU (1280 bytes) and the link's maximum (or true) MTU, as reported by **ipv6 if**. To set interface attributes, proceed as follows:

1. Enter **ipv6 if**. Note the Local Area Connections interface number (typically 4) and its true MTU (typically 1500 bytes). The remainder of this procedure assumes these typical values.

2. Set the interface attributes as follows:

   • To specify the interface as forwarding, enter **ipv6 ifc 4 forwards**.

   • To specify the interface as nonforwarding, enter **ipv6 ifc 4 -forwards**.

   • To specify the interface as advertising, enter **ipv6 ifc 4 advertises**.

   • To specify the interface as nonadvertising, enter **ipv6 ifc 4 -advertises**.

   • To specify an MTU, enter (for example) **ipv6 ifc 4 mtu 1400**.

TIP: *You can abbreviate "forwards" to "forw" and "advertises" to "adv".*

Displaying and Amending Cache and Table Information

You can use the ipv6 tool to list the contents of various caches and tables as follows:

1. Enter **ipv6 if**. Note the interface number of any interface you want to specify.

2. Display and amend the information as follows:

   • To display the contents of a neighbor cache, enter **ipv6 nb**. You can follow this command with an interface number, so that the cache is displayed only for that interface. If you specify an interface, you can also specify an IPv6 address. In this case, only entries pertinent to that address are displayed.

- To flush all neighbor caches, enter **ipv6 ncf**. As above, you can specify an interface number and an IPv4 address.

TIP: *Only neighbor cache entries without references are purged. The route cache entries hold references to neighbor cache entries, so if you're flushing both caches, flush the route cache first.*

- To display the contents of the route cache, type **ipv6 rc**. If an interface number and a destination address are specified, the command displays the route cache entry for reaching that destination via that interface. Otherwise, all route cache entries are displayed.

- To flush the route cache, enter **ipv6 rcf**. As before, you can either flush all entries or specify an interface number and destination to flush a specific entry.

- To display the contents of the binding cache, which holds bindings between home addresses and care-of addresses for Mobile IPv6, enter **ipv6 bc**.

- To add a unicast or anycast address to an interface, enter **ipv6 adu** *interface_number/address* **lifetime** *valid/preferred* **[anycast]** **[unicast]**. If anycast isn't specified, unicast is assumed. A typical entry is **ipv6 4/fe80::2d0:b7ff:fe48:1d2e lifetime 100000/50000**. Lifetimes are in seconds. Specifying a valid lifetime of zero removes an address.

- To display the contents of the site prefix table, enter **ipv6 spt**. Site prefixes are normally configured from router advertisements.

- To add or update a prefix manually, enter **ipv6 spu** *prefix* *interface_number* **[lifetime** *lifetime*]. If the lifetime isn't specified, then it's infinite. A zero lifetime deletes the prefix.

- To display the contents of the routing table, enter **ipv6 rt**.

- To add a route to a routing table, enter **ipv6 rtu** *prefix* *interface_number* **[/***next_hop***]** **[lifetime** *lifetime*] **[preference** *preference*] **[publish]** **[age]** **[spl** *site_prefix_length*]. The default lifetime is infinite, and the default preference is zero. By default, a published route won't age and an unpublished route will. To delete a route, specify a zero lifetime.

- To delete an interface, enter **ipv6 ifd** *interface_number*. You can't delete the loopback and tunnel pseudo interfaces.

Implementing IPv6 to IPv4 Configuration

The 6to4cfg tool automates IPv6 to IPv4 configuration. The tool discovers a host's globally routable IPv4 address and creates a 6to4 prefix. To implement IPv6 to IPv4 configuration, enter **6to4cfg [-r] [-s] [-u] [-R** *relay***] [-b] [-S** *address***]** **[***filename***]**. The switches work as follows:

- To specify the host as a 6to4 gateway router on its local network and to enable routing on all interfaces and assigned subnet prefixes, use the **-r** switch.

- To enable site-local addressing, use the **-s** switch. This switch takes effect only if the **-r** switch is also used.

- To reverse any configuration changes that you've implemented, use the **-u** switch. For example, **6to4cfg -r -u** reverses the effect of the **6to4cfg -r** command.

- To specify the name or IPv4 address of a 6to4 relay router, use the **-R** switch followed by the appropriate name or address. The default name is 6to4.ipv6.microsoft.com.

- To ensure that the 6to4cfg tool picks the best relay address rather than the first, use the **-b** switch.

- To specify the local IPv4 address for the 6to4 prefix, use the **-S** switch.

- To write the configuration script to a file, specify the *filename* parameter. If this isn't specified, the **6to4cfg** command configures the computer immediately. Specifying **con** displays the configuration script on the screen.

Configuring IPSec Policies and Security Associations

The ipsec6 tool is used to configure IPv6 policies and Security Associations (SAs). Figure 20.11 shows the ipsec6 subcommands and options. The **ipsec6 c** command creates the file *filename*.spd for security policies and the file *filename*.sad for SAs. Use these files as templates. They can be edited using a text editor (such as Notepad) and used in the other subcommands.

TIP: *For more information on using the IPv6 command-line tools, access* **http://msdn.microsoft.com/downloads/ sdks/platform/tpipv6/start.asp**.

Figure 20.11   The ipsec6 subcommands and options.

Adding an IPv6 Address Record in DNS

To add an IPv6 AAAA host record to the DNS database manually, proceed as follows:

1. Log on as administrator to either a primary or an Active Directory integrated DNS server.
2. Access Start|Programs|Administrative Tools and select DNS.
3. Expand the server name icon and select the appropriate forward lookup zone.
4. On the action pull-down menu, select New Other Records.
5. In the Resource Record Type dialog box, select IPv6 Host, then click Create Record.
6. Create the AAAA record as per the example illustrated in Figure 20.12. Click OK.
7. Click Done to close the Resource Record Type dialog box.
8. Close the DNS console.

Related solution:	Found on page:
Adding Additional Resource Records	488

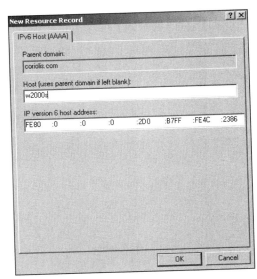

Figure 20.12   Creating an IPv6 AAAA record.

Appendix A
TCP/IP Configuration Parameters

Windows 2000 TCP/IP obtains its configuration data from the Registry. This information is written to the Registry by the setup program and the Dynamic Host Configuration Protocol (DHCP) client service (if enabled). This appendix defines all of the Registry parameters used to configure the protocol driver, *tcpip.sys*, which implements the standard TCP/IP network protocols.

In most cases, optimal default values for configurable aspects of the protocols are encoded into the drivers, although some installations may, exceptionally, require changes to default values. To handle these exceptions, optional Registry parameters can be created that modify the default behavior of the protocol drivers.

WARNING! The Windows 2000 TCP/IP implementation is mostly self-tuning. Adjusting Registry parameters may affect system performance adversely.

TCP/IP Parameters

All TCP/IP parameters are Registry values located under the Registry key:

```
HKEY_LOCAL_MACHINE
        \SYSTEM
             \CurrentControlSet
                    \Services
                          \Tcpip
                                \Parameters
```

These parameters are classified according to how they're configured, except for the Asynchronous Transfer Mode Address Resolution Protocol (ATM ARP) client parameters, which are listed separately. Values specific to an adapter are listed under the subkey for that adapter. The classification of parameters in this appendix is as follows:

- Parameters configured using the Registry Editor
- Parameters configurable from the user interface
- Parameters configured using the **route** command
- Nonconfigurable parameters
- ATM ARP client parameters

If any of these parameters are changed using the Registry Editor, a reboot of the system is normally required for the change to take effect. A reboot usually isn't required if values are changed using the Network Connections interface.

Parameters Configurable Using the Registry Editor

Some of these parameters are placed in the Registry by default during the installation of TCP/IP components; others are optional parameters that are created to modify the default behavior of the protocol drivers. These parameters are modified and created using the Registry Editor (*regedt32.exe*).

AllowUserRawAccess

Key: Tcpip\Parameters

Value Type: REG_DWORD—Boolean

Valid Range: 0, 1 (False, True)

Default: 0 (False)

Description: This parameter controls access to raw sockets. If it's set to True, nonadministrative users have access to raw sockets. By default, only administrators have this access right.

TIP: For more information on raw sockets, see the Windows Sockets (Winsock) specifications, available from **ftp://
ftp.microsoft.com/bussys/winsock/winsock2**.

ArpAlwaysSourceRoute

Key: Tcpip\Parameters

Value Type: REG_DWORD—Boolean

Valid Range: 0, 1, or not present (False, True, or not present)

Default: Not present

Description: By default, the stack first transmits ARP queries without source routing, and then retries with source routing enabled if no reply is received. If you set this parameter to False, all IP broadcasts will be sent without source routing;

if you set it to True, it forces TCP/IP to transmit all ARP queries with source routing enabled on Token Ring networks.

ArpCacheLife

Key: Tcpip\Parameters

Value Type: REG_DWORD—number of seconds

Valid Range: 0 to 0xFFFFFFFF

Default: Not present. If the *ArpCacheLife* parameter isn't specified, the defaults for ARP cache time-outs are a two-minute time-out on unused entries and a ten-minute time-out on used entries.

Description: Used with the *ArpCacheMinReferencedLife* parameter to control the Time to Live (TTL) of dynamic cache entries.

ArpCacheMinReferencedLife

Key: Tcpip\Parameters

Value Type: REG_DWORD—number of seconds

Valid Range: 0 to 0xFFFFFFFF

Default: 600 seconds (10 minutes)

Description: Controls the minimum time until a referenced ARP cache entry expires. This parameter is used in combination with the *ArpCacheLife* parameter, as follows:

- If *ArpCacheLife* is greater than or equal to *ArpCacheMinReferencedLife*, then both referenced and unreferenced dynamic ARP cache entries expire in *ArpCacheLife* seconds.
- If *ArpCacheLife* is less than *ArpCacheMinReferencedLife*, then unreferenced entries expire in *ArpCacheLife* seconds, and referenced entries expire in *ArpCacheMinReferencedLife* seconds.

Entries in the ARP cache are referenced each time an outbound packet is sent to the IP address in the entry.

ArpRetryCount

Key: Tcpip\Parameters

Value Type: REG_DWORD—number

Valid Range: 1 to 3

Default: 3

Description: This parameter controls the number of times that the computer sends a gratuitous Address Resolution Protocol (ARP) request for its own IP address(es) while initializing. Gratuitous ARP requests are sent to ensure that the IP address is not already in use elsewhere on the network. The parameter controls the number of ARP requests sent—not the number of retries.

ArpTRSingleRoute

Key: Tcpip\Parameters

Value Type: REG_DWORD—Boolean

Valid Range: 0, 1 (False, True)

Default: 0 (False)

Description: If True, this parameter causes ARP broadcasts that are source-routed (Token Ring) to be sent as single-route broadcasts, rather than as all-routes broadcasts.

ArpUseEtherSNAP

Key: Tcpip\Parameters

Value Type: REG_DWORD—Boolean

Valid Range: 0, 1 (False, True)

Default: 0 (False)

Description: If True, this parameter forces TCP/IP to transmit Ethernet packets using 802.3 Subnetwork Access Protocol (SNAP) encoding. By default, the stack transmits packets in Digital Intel Xerox (DIX) Ethernet format. It always receives both formats.

DatabasePath

Key: Tcpip\Parameters

Value Type: REG_EXPAND_SZ—character string

Valid Range: A valid Windows 2000 file path

Default: *%SystemRoot%*\system32\drivers\etc

Description: Specifies the path to the standard Internet database files (hosts, lmhosts, network, protocols, services). This parameter is used by the Winsock interface.

DefaultTOSValue

Key: Tcpip\Parameters

Value Type: REG_DWORD—number

Valid Range: 0 to 255

Default: 0

Description: Specifies the default Type of Service (TOS) value set in the header of outgoing IP packets. This setting may be overridden by a program that uses option *IP_TOS(IPPROTO_IP level)*, provided that *DisableUserTosSetting* is not set. Enabling Quality of Service (QoS) policy on the network will also override it.

TIP: *Refer to RFC 791 for a definition of TOS values.*

DefaultTTL

Key: Tcpip\Parameters

Value Type: REG_DWORD—number of seconds/hops

Valid Range: 1 to 0xFF (1 to 255 decimal)

Default: 128

Description: Specifies the default TTL value set in the header of outgoing IP packets. The TTL determines the maximum amount of time that an IP packet may live on the network without reaching its destination. It is effectively a limit on the number of routers that an IP packet may pass through before being discarded. The value is a counter that's decremented by one every second and by one (or more than one) every time the packet passes through a router. Thus, a packet that goes through multiple routers will live on the network for significantly less than 128 seconds.

DisableDHCPMediaSense

Key: Tcpip\Parameters

Value Type: REG_DWORD—Boolean

Valid Range: 0, 1 (False, True)

Default: 0 (False)

Description: This parameter can be used to control DHCP media sense behavior. By default, media sense events trigger the DHCP client to take an action, such as attempting to obtain a lease. If this parameter is set to True, the DHCP client will ignore media sense events from the interface.

DisableIPSourceRouting

Key: Tcpip\Parameters

Value Type: REG_DWORD—Boolean

Valid Range: 0, 1 (False, True)

Default: 1 (True)

Description: IP source routing is a mechanism that allows the sender to determine the IP route that a datagram should take through a network. Tools such as **tracert** use it. Windows 2000 disables IP source routing by default.

DisableMediaSenseEventLog

Key: Tcpip\Parameters

Value Type: REG_DWORD—Boolean

Valid Range: 0, 1 (False, True)

Default: 0 (False)

Description: Used to disable logging of DHCP media sense events. By default, media sense events, such as connection to and disconnection from the network, are logged in the event log for troubleshooting purposes.

DisableTaskOffload

Key: Tcpip\Parameters

Value Type: REG_DWORD—Boolean

Valid Range: 0, 1 (False, True)

Default: 0 (False)

Description: Instructs the TCP/IP stack to disable the offloading of tasks to the network card. This parameter is typically set to True for troubleshooting and test purposes. Task offload is enabled by default.

DisableUserTOSSetting

Key: Tcpip\Parameters

Value Type: REG_DWORD—Boolean

Valid Range: 0, 1 (False, True)

Default: 1 (True)

Description: Used to allow programs to manipulate the TOS bits in the header of outgoing IP packets. Individual applications are not normally permitted to manipulate TOS bits, because this can defeat system policy mechanisms, such as QoS policies. The parameter, therefore, defaults to True. Refer also to *DefaultTOSValue*.

DontAddDefaultGateway

Key: Tcpip\Parameters \Interfaces*interface*

Value Type: REG_DWORD—Boolean

Valid Range: 0, 1 (False, True)

Default: 0 (False)

Description: When Point-to-Point Tunneling Protocol (PPTP) is installed, a default route is set for each Local Area Network (LAN) adapter. You can disable the default route on an interface adapter by setting this parameter to True.

> **WARNING!** If you set DontAddDefaultGateway to True, you may need to configure static routes for hosts that are reached using a router other than the default gateway.

EnableAddrMaskReply

Key: Tcpip\Parameters

Value Type: REG_DWORD—Boolean

Valid Range: 0, 1 (False, True)

Default: 0 (False)

Description: Controls whether the computer responds to an Internet Control Message Protocol (ICMP) address mask request.

EnableBcastArpReply

Key: Tcpip\Parameters

Value Type: REG_DWORD—Boolean

Valid Range: 0, 1 (False, True)

Default: 1 (True)

Description: Controls whether the computer responds to an ARP request when the source Ethernet address in the ARP is not unicast (if, for example, it's multicast or broadcast).

WARNING!   **Network Load Balancing Service (NLBS) won't work properly if EnableBcastArpReply is set to False.**

EnableDeadGWDetect

Key: Tcpip\Parameters

Value Type: REG_DWORD—Boolean

Valid Range: 0, 1 (False, True)

Default: 1 (True)

Description: By default, TCP performs dead-gateway detection and may ask IP to change to a backup gateway if connections to the current default gateway are experiencing difficulties.

EnableFastRouteLookup

Key: Tcpip\Parameters

Value Type: REG_DWORD—Boolean

Valid Range: 0, 1 (False, True)

Default: 0 (False)

Description: Fast route lookup can speed up route lookups at the expense of nonpaged pool memory. This parameter is created by the Routing and Remote Access Service (RRAS).

EnableMulticastForwarding

Key: Tcpip\Parameters

Value Type: REG_DWORD—Boolean

Valid Range: 0, 1 (False, True)

Default: 0 (False)

Description: Used by the routing service to control whether IP multicasts are forwarded. This parameter is created by the RRAS.

EnablePMTUBHDetect

Key: Tcpip\Parameters

Value Type: REG_DWORD—Boolean

Valid Range: 0, 1 (False, True)

Default: 0 (False)

Description: Enables TCP to detect *black hole* routers while doing Path Maximum Transmission Unit (PMTU) discovery. A black hole router is one that doesn't return ICMP destination unreachable messages when it needs to fragment an IP datagram that has the don't fragment bit set. TCP depends on receiving these messages to perform PMTU discovery and tries to send segments without the don't fragment bit set if several retransmissions of a segment go unacknowledged and if the *EnablePMTUBHDetect* parameter is set to True. Enabling black hole detection increases the maximum number of retransmissions that are performed for a given segment.

EnablePMTUDiscovery

Key: Tcpip\Parameters

Value Type: REG_DWORD—Boolean

Valid Range: 0, 1 (False, True)

Default: 1 (True)

Description: Instructs TCP to discover the MTU over the path to a remote host. By discovering the path MTU and limiting TCP segments to this size, TCP can eliminate fragmentation at routers along the path that connect networks with different MTUs. Setting this parameter to False causes an MTU of 576 bytes to be used for all connections to hosts that aren't on the local subnet.

FFPControlFlags

Key: Tcpip\Parameters

Value Type: REG_DWORD—Boolean

Valid Range: 0, 1 (False, True)

Default: 1 (True)

Description: Enables (or disables) Fast Forwarding Path (FFP). FFP-capable network adapters can receive routing information from the stack and forward subsequent packets in hardware, without passing them up to the stack. If **FFPControlFlags** is set to False, TCP/IP instructs all FFP-capable adapters not to do any fast forwarding on this computer. This parameter is created by the RRAS.

FFPFastForwardingCacheSize

Key: Tcpip\Parameters

Value Type: REG_DWORD—number of bytes

Valid Range: 0 to 0xFFFFFFFF

Default: 100,000 bytes

Description: Defines the maximum amount of memory that a driver that supports fast forwarding and uses system memory for its cache can allocate for its fast-forwarding cache. If the device has its own memory for fast-forwarding cache, this parameter is ignored.

ForwardBroadcasts

Key: Tcpip\Parameters

Value Type: REG_DWORD—Boolean

Valid Range: 0, 1 (False, True)

Default: 0 (False)

Description: Currently the forwarding of broadcasts is not supported, and this parameter is ignored.

ForwardBufferMemory

Key: Tcpip\Parameters

Value Type: REG_DWORD—number of bytes

Valid Range: The network MTU minus a (reasonable) value smaller than 0xFFFFFFFF

Default: 74240 (enough for 50 1,480-byte packets, rounded to a multiple of 256)

Description: Determines how much memory IP initially allocates to store packet data in the router packet queue. When this buffer space is filled, the system attempts to allocate more memory. Packet queue data buffers are 256 bytes in length, and the value of this parameter should, therefore, be a multiple of 256. If the IP routing function isn't enabled, this parameter is ignored, and no buffers are allocated. *MaxForwardBufferMemory* controls the maximum amount of memory that can be allocated for this function.

GlobalMaxTcpWindowSize

Key: Tcpip\Parameters

Value Type: REG_DWORD—number of bytes

Valid Range: 0 to 0x3FFFFFFF (1073741823 decimal)

Default: Not present

TIP: *GlobalMaxTcpWindowSize can be set to values greater than 64K only when connecting to other systems that support RFC 1323 Window scaling. Also, Window scaling must be enabled using the Tcp1323Opts parameter.*

Description: Used to set a global limit for the TCP window size on a system-wide basis. (The *TcpWindowSize* parameter can be used to set the receive window on a per-interface basis.)

IPAutoconfigurationAddress

Key: Tcpip\Parameters\Interfaces*interface*

Value Type: REG_SZ—string

Valid Range: A valid IP address

Default: None

Description: Where the DHCP client stores the IP address chosen by autoconfiguration.

> **WARNING!** **This value should not be altered.**

IPAutoconfigurationEnabled

Key: Tcpip\Parameters, Tcpip\Parameters\Interfaces*interface*

Value Type: REG_DWORD—Boolean

Valid Range: 0, 1 (False, True)

Default: 1 (True)

Description: Enables or disables IP autoconfiguration. This parameter can be set globally or per interface. If a per-interface value is present, it overrides the global value for the interface.

IPAutoconfigurationMask

Key: Tcpip\Parameters, Tcpip\Parameters\Interfaces*interface*

Value Type: REG_SZ—string

Valid Range: A valid IP subnet mask

Default: 255.255.0.0

Description: Controls the subnet mask assigned to the client by autoconfiguration. This parameter can be set globally or per interface. If a per-interface value is present, it overrides the global value for the interface.

IPAutoconfigurationSeed

Key: Tcpip\Parameters, Tcpip\Parameters\Interfaces*interface*

Value Type: REG_DWORD—number

Valid Range: 0 to 0xFFFF

Default: 0

Description: Used internally by the DHCP client. This parameter should not be modified.

IPAutoconfigurationSubnet

Key: Tcpip\Parameters, Tcpip\Parameters\Interfaces*interface*

Value Type: REG_SZ—string

Valid Range: A valid IP subnet

Default: 169.254.0.0

Description: This parameter controls the subnet address used by autoconfiguration to pick an IP address for the client. This parameter can be set globally or per interface. If a per-interface value is present, it overrides the global value for the interface.

IGMPLevel

Key: Tcpip\Parameters

Value Type: REG_DWORD—number

Valid Range: 0 to 2

Default: 2

Description: This parameter determines to what extent the system supports IP multicasting. At level 0, the system provides no multicast support. At level 1, the system can send IP multicast packets but cannot receive them. At level 2, the system can send IP multicast packets and participate fully in Internet Group Management Protocol (IGMP) operations to receive multicast packets.

IPEnableRouter

Key: Tcpip\Parameters

Value Type: REG_DWORD—Boolean

Valid Range: 0, 1 (False, True)

Default: 0 (False)

Description: Setting this parameter to True causes the system to route IP packets between the networks to which it is connected.

IPEnableRouterBackup

Key: Tcpip\Parameters

Value Type: REG_DWORD—Boolean

Valid Range: 0, 1 (False, True)

Default: 0 (False)

Description: Setup writes the previous value of *IPEnableRouter* to this key. It should not be altered manually.

KeepAliveInterval

Key: Tcpip\Parameters

Value Type: REG_DWORD—time in milliseconds

Valid Range: 1 to 0xFFFFFFFF

Default: 1,000 (one second)

Description: Determines the interval between keep-alive retransmissions until a response is received. Once a response is received, the delay until the next keep-alive transmission is controlled by the value of *KeepAliveTime*. The connection is aborted after the number of retransmissions specified by *TcpMaxDataRetransmissions* have gone unanswered.

KeepAliveTime

Key: Tcpip\Parameters

Value Type: REG_DWORD—time in milliseconds

Valid Range: 1 to 0xFFFFFFFF

Default: 7,200,000 (two hours)

Description: Controls how often TCP attempts to verify that an idle connection is still intact by sending a keep-alive packet. If the remote system is still reachable and functioning, it acknowledges the keep-alive transmission.

TIP: *An application may enable this feature on a connection. Keep-alive packets are not sent by default.*

MaxForwardBufferMemory

Key: Tcpip\Parameters

Value Type: REG_DWORD—number

Valid Range: Size of network MTU to 0xFFFFFFFF

Default: 2097152 decimal (2MB)

Description: This parameter limits the total amount of memory that IP can allocate to store packet data in the router packet queue. This value must be greater than or equal to the value of the *ForwardBufferMemory* parameter. Refer also to *ForwardBufferMemory*.

MaxForwardPending

Key: Tcpip\Parameters\Interfaces*interface*

Value Type: REG_DWORD—number

Valid Range: 1 to 0xFFFFFFFF

Default: 0x1388 (5,000 decimal)

Description: Limits the number of packets that the IP forwarding engine submits for transmission to a specific network interface at any time. Additional packets are queued in IP until outstanding transmissions on the interface are complete. The default value is sufficient for most network adapters, which transmit packets very quickly. If, however, a single RAS interface multiplexes many slow serial lines, then configuring a larger value for *MaxForwardPending* may improve performance.

MaxFreeTcbs

Key: Tcpip\Parameters

Value Type: REG_DWORD—number

Valid Range: 0 to 0xFFFFFFFF

Default: 2,000 (Server), 1,000 (Workstation). The defaults are smaller in computers that have less than 63MB of RAM (unusual for Windows 2000).

Description: Controls the available number of cached (preallocated) Transport Control Blocks (TCBs). A TCB is a data structure that's maintained for each TCP connection.

MaxFreeTWTcbs

Key: Tcpip\Parameters

Value Type: REG_DWORD—number

Valid Range: 1 to 0xFFFFFFFF

Default: 1,000

Description: Controls the number of TCBs in the TIME_WAIT state that are allowed on the TIME_WAIT state list. Once this number is exceeded, the oldest TCB will be scavenged from the list. In order to maintain connections in the time-wait state for at least 60 seconds, this value should be greater than or equal to the number of graceful connection closures per second multiplied by 60. In most cases, the default value is adequate.

MaxHashTableSize

Key: Tcpip\Parameters

Value Type: REG_DWORD—number (must be a power of two)

Valid Range: 0x40 to 0x10000 (64 to 65536 decimal)

Default: 512 (decimal)

Description: Controls how quickly the system finds a TCP control block. The parameter value should be increased if the value of *MaxFreeTcbs* is increased from its default.

TIP: If the value of **MaxHashTableSize** isn't a power of two, the system configures the hash table to the next power of two value. For example, a setting of 1,000 is rounded up to 1,024.

MaxNormLookupMemory

Key: Tcpip\Parameters

Value Type: REG_DWORD—number

Valid Range: 0 to 0xFFFFFFFF (0xFFFFFFFF means no limit on memory)

Default: 5,000,000 bytes or 40,000 routes (Server), 150,000 bytes or 1,000 routes (Workstation). The Server default is smaller in computers that have less than 63MB of RAM (unusual for Windows 2000).

Description: Controls the maximum amount of memory that the system allocates for the route table data and the routes themselves. It's designed to prevent memory exhaustion on a computer that has a large number of routes.

MaxNumForwardPackets

Key: Tcpip\Parameters

Value Type: REG_DWORD—number

Valid Range: 1 to 0xFFFFFFFF

Default: 0xFFFFFFFF

Description: Limits the total number of IP packet headers that can be allocated for the router packet queue. This value must be greater than or equal to the value of *NumForwardPackets*. (Refer to the description of *NumForwardPackets*.)

MaxUserPort

Key: Tcpip\Parameters

Value Type: REG_DWORD—maximum port number

Valid Range: 5,000 to 65,534 (decimal)

Default: 0x1388 (5,000 decimal)

Description: Controls the maximum port number used when an application requests any available user port from the system. Normally, short-lived ports are allocated in the range 1,024 to 5,000. Setting this parameter to a value less or greater than the valid range causes either the minimum or maximum valid value (respectively) to be used.

MTU

Key: Tcpip\Parameters\Interfaces*interface*

Value Type: REG_DWORD—number

Valid Range: 68 to the MTU of the underlying network

Default: 0xFFFFFFFF

Description: Overrides the default MTU for a network interface. The size includes the transport header. Values larger than the MTU for the underlying network cause the transport to use the network default MTU. Values smaller than 68 cause the transport to use an MTU of 68.

> **WARNING!   By default, TCP/IP uses PMTU detection and queries the NIC driver to find out what local MTU is supported. Altering the MTU parameter is normally unnecessary and may result in reduced performance.**

NumForwardPackets

Key: Tcpip\Parameters

Value Type: REG_DWORD—number

Valid Range: 1 to a (reasonable) value smaller than 0xFFFFFFFF

Default: 0x32 (50 decimal)

Description: Determines the number of IP packet headers allocated for the router packet queue. When all headers are in use, the system attempts to allocate more, up to the value of *MaxNumForwardPackets*. The value of *NumForwardPackets* should be greater than or equal to the *ForwardBufferMemory* value divided by the maximum IP data size of the networks that are connected to the router. It should be less than or equal to the *ForwardBufferMemory* value divided by 256. The optimal number of forward packets for a given *ForwardBufferMemory* size depends on the type of traffic that's carried on the network and is somewhere in between these two values. If routing is disabled, this parameter is ignored, and no headers are allocated.

NumTcbTablePartitions

Key: Tcpip\Parameters

Value Type: REG_DWORD—number

Valid Range: 1 to 0xFFFF

Default: 4

Description: Controls the number of TCB table partitions. The TCB table can be portioned to improve scalability on multiprocessor systems by reducing contention on the TCB table. A suggested maximum value is two times the number of CPUs.

> **WARNING!**   *This value should not be modified without careful performance study.*

PerformRouterDiscovery

Key: Tcpip\Parameters\Interfaces*interface*

Value Type: REG_DWORD—Boolean

Valid Range: 0 to 2

Default: 2 (DHCP-controlled, but off by default)

Description: This parameter controls whether Windows 2000 attempts to perform router discovery on a per-interface basis. Refer also to *SolicitationAddress-Bcast*.

TIP: *Router discovery is defined in RFC 1256.*

PerformRouterDiscoveryBackup

Key: Tcpip\Parameters\Interfaces*interface*

Value Type: REG_DWORD—Boolean

Valid Range: 0, 1 (False, True)

Default: None

Description: Used internally to keep a backup copy of the *PerformRouterDiscovery* value. This parameter should not be modified.

PPTPTcpMaxDataRetransmissions

Key: Tcpip\Parameters

Value Type: REG_DWORD—number

Valid Range: 0 to 0xFF

Default: 5

Description: Controls the number of times that a PPTP packet is retransmitted if it is not acknowledged. This parameter enables the retransmission of PPTP traffic to be configured separately from regular TCP traffic.

SackOpts

Key: Tcpip\Parameters

Value Type: REG_DWORD—Boolean

Valid Range: 0, 1 (False, True)

Default: 1 (True)

Description: Controls whether or not Selective Acknowledgment (SACK) support is enabled.

TIP: *SACK is specified in RFC 2018.*

SolicitationAddressBcast

Key: Tcpip\Parameters\Interfaces*interface*

Value Type: REG_DWORD—Boolean

Valid Range: 0, 1 (False, True)

Default: 0 (False)

Description: Configures Windows 2000 to send router discovery messages as broadcasts rather than multicasts. By default, if router discovery is enabled, router discovery solicitations are sent to the all-routers multicast group (224.0.0.2). Refer also to *PerformRouterDiscovery*.

SynAttackProtect

Key: Tcpip\Parameters

Value Type: REG_DWORD—Boolean

Valid Range: 0, 1 (False, True)

Default: 0 (False)

Description: Specifies whether TCP should adjust the retransmission of SYN-ACKS so that connection responses time out more quickly if it appears that there's a SYN-ATTACK in progress. The determination of the time-out period is based on the *TcpMaxPortsExhausted* parameter.

Tcp13230pts

Key: Tcpip\Parameters

Value Type: REG_DWORD—number (flags)

Valid Range: 0 to 3

Default: 0 (RFC 1323 options disabled)

Description: This parameter controls RFC 1323 Timestamps and Window-scaling options. Timestamps and Window scaling are enabled by default, but can be manipulated with flag bits. Bit zero controls Window scaling, and bit one controls Timestamps. The result of each of the possible values of this parameter is shown in Table A.1.

TcpDelAckTicks

Key: Tcpip\Parameters\Interfaces*interface*

Value Type: REG_DWORD—number

Valid Range: 0 to 6

Default: 2 (200 milliseconds)

Table A.1 **The *Tcp13230pts* parameter.**

Value	Effect
0	Disables RFC 1323 options
1	Only Window scale enabled
2	Only Timestamps enabled
3	Both options enabled

Description: Specifies the number of 100-millisecond intervals used for the de-layed-ACK timer on a per-interface basis. Setting this parameter value to 0 disables delayed acknowledgments, which causes the computer to acknowledge immediately every packet it receives.

WARNING!   Do not change this value without first studying the environment carefully.

TcpInitialRTT

Key: Tcpip\Parameters\Interfaces*interface*

Value Type: REG_DWORD—number

Valid Range: 0 to 0xFFFF

Default: 3 seconds

Description: Controls the initial time-out used for a TCP connection request and initial data retransmission on a per-interface basis. Tune this parameter cautiously, because exponential backoff is used. Setting a value larger than 3 seconds results in much longer time-outs to nonexistent addresses.

TcpMaxConnectResponseRetransmissions

Key: Tcpip\Parameters

Value Type: REG_DWORD—number

Valid Range: 0 to 255

Default: 2

Description: Controls the number of times that a SYN-ACK is retransmitted in response to a connection request if the SYN is not acknowledged. If this value is greater than or equal to 2, the stack employs SYN-ATTACK protection internally. If it's less than 2, the stack doesn't read the Registry values for SYN-ATTACK protection. Refer also to *SynAttackProtect, TCPMaxPortsExhausted, TCPMaxHalfOpen,* and *TCPMaxHalfOpenRetried.*

TcpMaxConnectRetransmissions

Key: Tcpip\Parameters

Value Type: REG_DWORD—number

Valid Range: 0 to 255 (decimal)

Default: 3

Description: Determines the number of times that TCP retransmits a connect request (SYN) before aborting the attempt. During a connect attempt, the retransmission time-out is doubled with each successive retransmission. The initial time-out is controlled by the *TcpInitialRTT* Registry value.

TcpMaxDataRetransmissions

Key: Tcpip\Parameters

Value Type: REG_DWORD—number

Valid Range: 0 to 0xFFFFFFFF

Default: 5

Description: Controls the number of times that TCP retransmits an individual data segment (other than connection request segments) before aborting the connection. The retransmission time-out is doubled with each successive retransmission on a connection and is reset when responses resume. The Retransmission Timeout (RTO) value is adjusted dynamically, using the historical measured round-trip time, or Smoothed Round-Trip Time, (SRTT) on each connection. *TcpInitialRTT* controls the initial RTO on a new connection.

TcpMaxDupAcks

Key: Tcpip\Parameters

Value Type: REG_DWORD—number

Valid Range: 1 to 3

Default: 2

Description: This parameter determines the number of duplicate ACKs that must be received for the same sent data sequence number before fast retransmit is triggered.

TcpMaxHalfOpen

Key: Tcpip\Parameters

Value Type: REG_DWORD—number

Valid Range: 100 to 0xFFFF

Default: 100 (Server), 500 (Workstation)

Description: Controls the number of connections in the SYN-RCVD state allowed before SYN-ATTACK protection begins to operate. Refer also to *SynAttackProtect*.

TcpMaxHalfOpenRetried

Key: Tcpip\Parameters

Value Type: REG_DWORD—number

Valid Range: 80 to 0xFFFF

Default: 80 (Server), 400 (Workstation)

Description: Controls the number of connections in the SYN-RCVD state for which there has been at least one retransmission of the SYN sent before SYN-ATTACK protection begins to operate. Refer also to *SynAttackProtect*.

TcpMaxPortsExhausted

Key: Tcpip\Parameters

Value Type: REG_DWORD—number

Valid Range: 0 to 0xFFFF

Default: 5

Description: Controls the point at which SYN-ATTACK protection starts to operate. SYN-ATTACK protection starts to operate when a number of connect requests equal to the *TcpMaxPortsExhausted* value have been refused by the system.

TcpNumConnections

Key: Tcpip\Parameters

Value Type: REG_DWORD—number

Valid Range: 0 to 0xFFFFFE

Default: 0xFFFFFE

Description: Specifies the maximum number of connections that TCP can have open simultaneously.

TcpTimedWaitDelay

Key: Tcpip\Parameters

Value Type: REG_DWORD—time in seconds

Valid Range: 30 to 300 (decimal)

Default: 0xF0 (240 decimal)

Description: Determines the length of time that a connection stays in the TIME_WAIT state while being closed. While a connection is in the TIME_WAIT state, the socket pair can't be reused. The TIME_WAIT state is also known as the 2MSL state, because the value should be twice the maximum segment lifetime on the network.

TIP: *See RFC 793 for more information about the TIME_WAIT state.*

TcpUseRFC1122UrgentPointer

Key: Tcpip\Parameters

Value Type: REG_DWORD—Boolean

Valid Range: 0, 1 (False, True)

Default: 0 (False)

Description: Determines whether TCP uses the RFC 1122 specification for urgent data or whether it employs the mode used by Berkeley Software Distribution (BSD)-derived systems. The two mechanisms interpret the urgent pointer in the TCP header and the length of the urgent data differently and are not interoperable. The default of False specifies BSD mode.

TcpWindowSize

Key: Tcpip\Parameters, Tcpip\Parameters\Interface*interface*

Value Type: REG_DWORD—number of bytes

Valid Range: 0 to 0x3FFFFFFF (1073741823 decimal)

Default: The algorithm for calculating the default value for this parameter is complex. The default is the smallest of the following values:

- 0xFFFF
- *GlobalMaxTcpWindowSize*
- The larger of four times the maximum TCP data size on the network or 16,384, rounded up to an even multiple of the network TCP data size

The default is (typically) 17,520 for Ethernet, but this value may shrink slightly if a connection is established to another computer that supports extended TCP header options, such as SACK and timestamps, because these options increase the TCP header beyond the usual 20 bytes.

Description: Determines the maximum TCP receive-window size offered. The receive-window specifies the number of bytes that a sender can transmit without receiving an acknowledgment. In general, larger receive-windows improve performance over high-delay, high-bandwidth networks. For greatest efficiency, the receive-window should be an even multiple of the TCP Maximum Segment Size

(MSS). A value set for a specific interface overrides the system-wide value on that interface. Refer also to *GobalMaxTcpWindowSize*.

TIP: *TcpWindowSize values greater than 64K can be achieved only when connecting to other systems that support RFC 1323 window scaling.*

TrFunctionalMcastAddress
Key: Tcpip\Parameters

Value Type: REG_DWORD—Boolean

Valid Range: 0, 1 (False, True)

Default: 1 (True)

Description: Determines whether IP multicasts are sent using the token ring multicast address described in RFC 1469 (the default) or using the subnet broadcast address.

TypeOfInterface
Key: Tcpip\Parameters\Interfaces*interface*

Value Type: REG_DWORD—number

Valid Range: 0 to 3

Default: 0 (allow multicast and unicast)

Description: This parameter determines whether the interface is enabled for unicast, multicast, or both traffic types and whether those traffic types can be forwarded. The effect of each parameter setting is described in Table A.2.

NOTE: *Because this parameter affects forwarding and routes, it may be possible for a local application to send multicasts out over an interface, even when multicast traffic is disabled. This occurs if there are no other interfaces in the computer that are enabled for multicast and a default route exists.*

Table A.2   TypeOfInterface values.

Value	Effect
0	Both unicast and multicast traffic are allowed
1	Unicast traffic is disabled
2	Multicast traffic is disabled
3	Both unicast and multicast traffic are disabled

UseZeroBroadcast

Key: Tcpip\Parameters\Interfaces*interface*

Value Type: REG_DWORD—Boolean

Valid Range: 0, 1 (False, True)

Default: 0 (False)

Description: Determines the broadcast address. If this parameter is set to True, IP will use zeros broadcasts (0.0.0.0) instead of ones broadcasts (255.255.255.255). Most systems use ones broadcasts, but some use zeros broadcasts.

WARNING! Systems that use different broadcast addresses should not be used on the same network.

Parameters Configurable from the User Interface

The following parameters are created and modified automatically as a result of information supplied by the user. There is (or should be) no need to configure them directly in the Registry.

DefaultGateway

Key: Tcpip\Parameters\Interfaces*interface*

Value Type: REG_MULTI_SZ—list of dotted decimal IP addresses

Valid Range: Any set of valid IP addresses

Default: None

Description: Specifies the gateways used to route packets that are destined for a remote subnet and for which a more specific route doesn't exist. If this parameter has a valid value, it overrides *DhcpDefaultGateway*.

Domain

Key: Tcpip\Parameters\Interfaces*interface*

Value Type: REG_SZ—Character string

Valid Range: Any valid DNS domain name

Default: None

Description: Specifies the DNS domain name of the interface. If it exists, this parameter overrides the *DhcpDomain* parameter, which is specified by the DHCP client.

EnableDhcp

Key: Tcpip\Parameters\Interfaces*interface*

Value Type: REG_DWORD—Boolean

Valid Range: 0, 1 (False, True)

Default: 0 (False)

Description: If this parameter is set to True, the DHCP client service attempts to use DHCP to configure the first IP interface on the adapter.

EnableSecurityFilters

Key: Tcpip\Parameters

Value Type: REG_DWORD—Boolean

Valid Range: 0, 1 (False, True)

Default: 0 (False)

Description: Determines whether IP Security (IPSec) filters are enabled. These filters are disabled by default. Refer also to *TcpAllowedPorts*, *UdpAllowedPorts*, and *RawIPAllowedPorts*.

Hostname

Key: Tcpip\Parameters

Value Type: REG_SZ—character string

Valid Range: Any valid DNS host name

Default: The computer name

Description: Specifies the DNS host name of the system, which is returned by the **hostname** command.

IPAddress

Key: Tcpip\Parameters\Interfaces*interface*

Value Type: REG_MULTI_SZ—list of dotted-decimal IP addresses

Valid Range: Any set of valid IP addresses

Default: None

Description: Specifies the addresses of the IP interfaces to be bound to the adapter. If the first address in the list is 0.0.0.0, the primary interface on the adapter is configured from DHCP. There must be a valid subnet mask value in the *SubnetMask* parameter for each IP address that's specified in this parameter.

NameServer

Key: Tcpip\Parameters\Interfaces*interface*

Value Type: REG_SZ—a space-delimited list of dotted decimal IP addresses

Valid Range: Any set of valid IP address

Default: None

Description: Specifies the DNS name servers that WinSock queries to resolve names.

PPTPFiltering

Key: Tcpip\Parameters\Interfaces*interface*

Value Type: REG_DWORD—Boolean

Valid Range: 0, 1 (False, True)

Default: 0 (False)

Description: Controls how PPTP filtering is enabled on a per-adapter basis. If the value of this parameter is set to True, the adapter accepts only PPTP connections.

RawIpAllowedProtocols

Key: Tcpip\Parameters\Interfaces*interface*

Value Type: REG_MULTI_SZ—list of IP protocol numbers

Valid Range: Any set of valid IP protocol numbers

Default: None

Description: Specifies the list of IP protocol numbers for which incoming datagrams are accepted on an IP interface when security filtering is enabled. The parameter controls the acceptance of IP datagrams by the raw IP transport, which is used to provide raw sockets. It does not control IP datagrams that are passed to other transports, such as TCP. An empty list indicates that no values are acceptable. A single value of zero indicates that all values are acceptable. If this parameter is missing from an interface, then (again) all values are acceptable.

SearchList

Key: Tcpip\Parameters

Value Type: REG_SZ—space-delimited list of DNS domain-name suffixes

Valid Range: Any set of valid DNS domain-name suffixes

Default: None

Description: Specifies a list of domain-name suffixes to append to a name that's to be resolved through DNS, if resolution of the unadorned name fails. By default, only the value of the *Domain* parameter is appended. The *SearchList* parameter is used by the Winsock interface. Refer also to *AllowUnqualifiedQuery*.

SubnetMask

Key: Tcpip\Parameters\Interfaces*interface*

Value Type: REG_MULTI_SZ—list of dotted decimal IP addresses

Valid Range: Any set of valid IP addresses.

Default: None

Description: Specifies the subnet masks to be used with the IP interfaces bound to the adapter. If the first mask in the list is 0.0.0.0, the primary interface on the adapter is configured using DHCP. There must be a valid subnet mask value in this parameter for each IP address specified in the *IPAddress* parameter.

TcpAllowedPorts

Key: Tcpip\Parameters\Interfaces*interface*

Value Type: REG_MULTI_SZ—list of TCP port numbers

Valid Range: Any set of valid TCP port numbers

Default: None

Description: Specifies the list of TCP port numbers for which incoming SYNs are accepted on an IP interface when security filtering is enabled. An empty list indicates that no values are acceptable. A single value of zero indicates that all values are acceptable. If this parameter is missing from an interface, then (again) all values are acceptable.

UdpAllowedPorts

Key: Tcpip\Parameters\Interfaces*interface*

Value Type: REG_MULTI_SZ—list of UDP port numbers

Valid Range: Any set of valid UDP port numbers

Default: None

Description: This parameter specifies the list of UDP port numbers for which incoming datagrams are accepted on an IP interface when security filtering is enabled. An empty list indicates that no values are acceptable. A single value of zero indicates that all values are acceptable. If this parameter is missing from an interface, then (again) all values are acceptable.

Parameters Configurable Using the Route Command

The **route** command can store persistent IP routes as values under the Tcpip\Parameters\PersistentRoutes Registry key. Each route is stored in the value name string as a comma-delimited list of the form:

```
destination,subnet mask,gateway,metric
```

The value type is REG_SZ. Addition and deletion of these values is accomplished using the **route** command. There is (or should be) no need to configure them directly.

Noncofigurable Parameters

The following parameters are created and used internally by TCP/IP components and should never be modified using the Registry editor. They are listed here for reference only.

DhcpDefaultGateway

Key: Tcpip\Parameters\Interfaces*interface*

Value Type: REG_MULTI_SZ—list of dotted decimal IP addresses

Valid Range: Any set of valid IP addresses

Default: None

Description: Specifies the list of default gateways to be used to route packets that are not destined for a local subnet and for which a more specific route does not exist. This parameter is created by the DHCP client service (if enabled) and is overridden by a valid *DefaultGateway* parameter value.

DhcpIPAddress

Key: Tcpip\Parameters\Interfaces*interface*

Value Type: REG_SZ—dotted decimal IP address

Valid Range: Any valid IP address

Default: None

Description: Specifies the DHCP-configured IP address for the interface. If the **IPAddress** parameter contains a first value other than 0.0.0.0, that value overrides this parameter.

DhcpDomain

Key: Tcpip\Parameters\Interfaces*interface*

Value Type: REG_SZ—character string

Valid Range: Any valid DNS domain name

Default: None (provided by DHCP server)

Description: Specifies the DNS domain name of the interface. If the *Domain* parameter exists, it overrides the *DhcpDomain* value.

DhcpNameServer

Key: Tcpip\Parameters

Value Type: REG_SZ—a space-delimited list of dotted decimal IP addresses

Valid Range: Any set of valid IP address

Default: None

Description: Specifies the DNS name servers queried by Winsock to resolve names. This parameter is created by the DHCP client service (if enabled) and is overridden by a valid *NameServer* parameter value.

DhcpServer

Key: Tcpip\Parameters\Interfaces*interface*

Value Type: REG_SZ—dotted decimal IP address

Valid Range: Any valid IP address

Default: None

Description: Specifies the IP address of the DHCP server that granted the lease on the IP address in the *DhcpIPAddress* parameter.

DhcpSubnetMask

Key: Tcpip\Parameters\Interfaces*interface*

Value Type: REG_SZ—dotted decimal IP subnet mask

Valid Range: Any subnet mask that is valid for the configured IP address

Default: None

Description: Specifies the DHCP-configured subnet mask for the address specified in the *DhcpIPAddress* parameter.

DhcpSubnetMaskOpt

Key: Tcpip\Parameters\Interfaces*interface*

Value Type: REG_SZ—Dotted decimal IP subnet mask

Valid Range: Any subnet mask that's valid for the configured IP address

Default: None

Description: Builds the *DhcpSubnetMask* parameter, which is used by the stack.

Lease

Key: Tcpip\Parameters\Interfaces*interface*

Value Type: REG_DWORD—time in seconds

Valid Range: 1 to 0xFFFFFFFF

Default: None

Description: Used by the DHCP client service to store the time, in seconds, for which the lease on the IP address for the adapter is valid.

LeaseObtainedTime

Key: Tcpip\Parameters\Interfaces*interface*

Value Type: REG_DWORD—time in seconds

Valid Range: 1 to 0xFFFFFFFF

Default: None

Description: Contains the absolute time (in seconds, since midnight of January 1, 1970) at which the lease on the IP address for the adapter was obtained.

LeaseTerminatesTime

Key: Tcpip\Parameters\Interfaces*interface*

Value Type: REG_DWORD—time in seconds

Valid Range: 1 to 0xFFFFFFFF

Default: None

Description: Contains the absolute time (in seconds, since midnight of January 1, 1970) at which the lease on the IP address for the adapter expires.

LLInterface

Key: Tcpip\Parameters\Adapters*interface*

Value Type: REG_SZ—Windows 2000 device name

Valid Range: A legal Windows 2000 device name

Default: Empty string

Description: Directs IP to bind to a different link-layer protocol than the built-in ARP module. The value is the name of the Windows 2000 device to which IP should bind.

NTEContextList

Key: Tcpip\Parameters\Interfaces*interface*

Value Type: REG_MULTI_SZ—number

Valid Range: 0 to 0xFFFF

Default: None

Description: Identifies the context of the IP address associated with an interface.

T1

Key: Tcpip\Parameters\Interfaces*interface*

Value Type: REG_DWORD—time in seconds

Valid Range: 1 to 0xFFFFFFFF

Default: None

Description: Contains the absolute time (in seconds, since midnight of January 1, 1970) at which the DHCP service first tries to renew the lease on the IP address for the adapter by contacting the server that granted the lease.

T2

Key: Tcpip\Parameters\Interfaces*interface*

Value Type: REG_DWORD—time in seconds

Valid Range: 1 to 0xFFFFFFFF

Default: None

Description: Contains the absolute time (in seconds, since midnight of January 1, 1970) at which the DHCP service tries to renew the lease on the IP address for the adapter by broadcasting a renewal request. This should happen only if the service is unable to renew the lease with the original server.

ATM ARP Client Parameters

The ATM ARP client parameters are located, with the TCP/IP parameters for each interface, under the AtmArpC subkey.

SapSelector
Key: Tcpip\Parameters\Interfaces*interface*\AtmArpC

Value Type: REG_DWORD—number

Valid Range: 1 to 255

Default: 1

Description: Specifies the selector byte value used by the ATMARP client as the twentieth byte of its ATM address. The resulting address is used to register with the ATMARP server and the Multicast Address Resolution Server (MARS).

AddressResolutionTimeout
Key: Tcpip\Parameters\Interfaces*interface*\AtmArpC

Value Type: REG_DWORD—time in seconds

Valid Range: 1 to 60

Default: 3

Description: Specifies how long the ATMARP client waits for a response after sending an ARP request for a unicast IP address (or a MARS request for a multicast/broadcast IP address). If this timer elapses, the ATMARP client retransmits the request. The maximum number of retransmissions is specified as *MaxResolutionAttempts* minus one.

ARPEntryAgingTimeout
Key: Tcpip\Parameters\Interfaces*interface*\AtmArpC

Value Type: REG_DWORD—time in seconds

Valid Range: 90 to 1800

Default: 900 seconds (15 minutes)

Description: Specifies how long the ATMARP client retains address resolution information for a unicast IP address before it's invalidated.

InARPWaitTimeout
Key: Tcpip\Parameters\Interfaces*interface*\AtmArpC

Value Type: REG_DWORD—time in seconds

Valid Range: 1 to 60

Default: 5

Description: Specifies how long the ATMARP client waits for a response after sending an Inverse Address Resolution Protocol (InARP) request to revalidate a unicast IP address to ATM address mapping.

MaxResolutionAttempts
Key: Tcpip\Parameters\Interfaces*interface*\AtmArpC

Value Type: REG_DWORD—number

Valid Range: 1 to 255

Default: 4

Description: Specifies the maximum number of attempts made by the ATMARP client to resolve a unicast, multicast, or broadcast IP address to an ATM address (or addresses).

MinWaitAfterNak
Key: Tcpip\Parameters\Interfaces*interface*\AtmArpC

Value Type: REG_DWORD—time in seconds

Valid Range: 1 to 60

Default: 10

Description: Specifies how long the ATMARP client waits after receiving a failure (ARP NAK) response from the ARP server or MARS.

ServerConnectInterval
Key: Tcpip\Parameters\Interfaces*interface*\AtmArpC

Value Type: REG_DWORD—time in seconds

Valid Range: 1 to 30

Default: 5

Description: Specifies how long the ATMARP client waits after a failed attempt to connect to the ARP server before retrying the connection.

ServerRefreshTimeout
Key: Tcpip\Parameters\Interfaces*interface*\AtmArpC

Value Type: REG_DWORD—time in seconds

Valid Range: 90 to 1,800

Default: 900 seconds (15 minutes)

Description: Specifies the interval at which the ATMARP client sends an ARP request with its own IP/ATM address information to refresh the ATMARP server's cache.

ServerRegistrationTimeout

Key: Tcpip\Parameters\Interfaces*interface*\AtmArpC

Value Type: REG_DWORD—time in seconds

Valid Range: 1 to 60

Default: 3

Description: Specifies how long the ATMARP client waits for an ARP response in reply to an ARP request that it sent to register its own IP/ATM information with the ATMARP server.

DefaultVcAgingTimeout

Key: Tcpip\Parameters\Interfaces*interface*\AtmArpC

Value Type: REG_DWORD—time in seconds

Valid Range: 10 to 1,800

Default: 60

Description: Specifies the inactivity time-out for all virtual connections initiated by the ATMARP client (this does not apply to permanent virtual connections). Inactivity is defined as a condition of no data activity in either direction.

MARSConnectInterval

Key: Tcpip\Parameters\Interfaces*interface*\AtmArpC

Value Type: REG_DWORD—time in seconds

Valid Range: 1 to 30

Default: 5

Description: Specifies how long the ATMARP client waits after a failed attempt to connect to the MARS before retrying the connection.

MARSRegistrationTimeout

Key: Tcpip\Parameters\Interfaces*interface*\AtmArpC

Value Type: REG_DWORD—time in seconds

Valid Range: 1 to 60

Default: 3

Description: Specifies how long the ATMARP client waits for an MARS join packet in reply to a MARS join packet that it sent to register its ATM address with the MARS.

JoinTimeout

Key: Tcpip\Parameters\Interfaces*interface*\AtmArpC

Value Type: REG_DWORD—time in seconds

Valid Range: 5 to 60

Default: 10

Description: Specifies how long the ATMARP client waits for a MARS join packet in reply to a MARS join packet it sent to initiate membership to an IP multicast group (or the IP broadcast address).

LeaveTimeout

Key: Tcpip\Parameters\Interfaces*interface*\AtmArpC

Value Type: REG_DWORD—time in seconds

Valid Range: 5 to 60

Default: 10

Description: Specifies how long the ATMARP client waits for a MARS leave packet in reply to a MARS leave packet that it sent to terminate membership from an IP multicast group (or the IP broadcast address).

MaxJoinLeaveAttempts

Key: Tcpip\Parameters\Interfaces*interface*\AtmArpC

Value Type: REG_DWORD—number

Valid Range: 1 to 10

Default: 5

Description: Specifies the maximum number of attempts made by the ATMARP client to join or leave an IP multicast (or broadcast) group.

MaxDelayBetweenMULTIs

Key: Tcpip\Parameters\Interfaces*interface*\AtmArpC

Value Type: REG_DWORD—time in seconds

Valid Range: 2 to 60

Default: 5

Description: Specifies the maximum delay expected by the ATMARP client between successive MARS multi packets corresponding to a single MARS request.

ARPServerList
Key: Tcpip\Parameters\Interfaces*interface*\AtmArpC

Value Type: REG_MULTI_SZ

Valid Range: A list of strings containing ATM addresses.

Default: 47000790001020000000000000000A03E00000200

Description: This is the list of ARP Servers with which the ARP client may register. The ARP client attempts to register using each address, in sequence, until successful.

MARSServerList
Key: Tcpip\Parameters\Interfaces*interface*\AtmArpC

Value Type: REG_MULTI_SZ—list of strings

Valid Range: A list of strings containing ATM addresses.

Default: 47000790001020000000000000000A03E00000200

Description: This is the list of MARS Servers with which the ARP client may register. The ARP client attempts to register using each address, in sequence, until successful.

MTU
Key: Tcpip\Parameters\Interfaces*interface*\AtmArpC

Value Type: REG_DWORD—number of bytes

Valid Range: 9,180 to 65,527

Default: 9,180

Description: Specifies the maximum transmission unit reported to the IP layer for the interface.

Appendix B

NetBIOS over TCP/IP Configuration Parameters

All of the NetBIOS over TCP/IP (NetBT) parameters are Registry values. If the system is configured using Dynamic Host Configuration Protocol (DHCP), a change in parameters takes effect if you issue the command **ipconfig /renew** from a command prompt. Otherwise, you must reboot the system for a change in any of these parameters to take effect.

NetBT Parameters

NetBT parameters are located under one of two subkeys:

```
HKEY_LOCAL_MACHINE
        \SYSTEM
            \CurrentControlSet
                    \Services
                            \NetBT
                                    \Parameters


HKEY_LOCAL_MACHINE
        \SYSTEM
            \CurrentControlSet
                    \Services
                            \NetBT
                                \Parameters
                                        \Interfaces
                                            \interface
```

In the second case, *interface* refers to the subkey for a network interface to which NetBT is bound and takes a value that's specific to the interface.

These parameters are classified according to how they're configured. The classification of parameters in this appendix is as follows:

- Parameters configurable using the Registry editor
- Parameters configurable using the connections user interface
- Nonconfigurable parameters

Parameters Configurable Using the Registry Editor

The parameters in this section are installed with default values during the installation of the TCP/IP components. They can be modified using the Registry editor (*regedt32.exe*). Some of the parameters are visible in the Registry by default. Others are optional and are created to modify the default behavior of the NetBT driver.

BacklogIncrement

Key: Netbt\Parameters

Value Type: REG_DWORD—number

Valid Range: 3 to 0x14 (1 to 20 decimal)

Default: 3

Description: Specifies the number of free connection blocks to be specified by the system if fewer than two of these blocks exist when a connection attempt is made to the NetBIOS TCP port (139). One connection block is required for each NetBT connection, and each connection block consumes 78 bytes of memory. A limit on the total number of connection blocks allowed can be set using the *MaxConnBackLog* parameter. The *BackLogIncrement* parameter was added to address Internet SYN-ATTACK issues.

BcastNameQueryCount

Key: Netbt\Parameters

Value Type: REG_DWORD—number

Valid Range: 1 to 0xFFFF

Default: 3

Description: This value determines the number of times NetBT broadcasts a query for a specific name without receiving a response.

BcastQueryTimeout

Key: Netbt\Parameters

Value Type: REG_DWORD—time in milliseconds

Valid Range: 100 to 0xFFFFFFFF

Default: 0x2EE (750 decimal)

Description: Determines the time interval between successive broadcast name queries for the same name.

BroadcastAddress

Key: Netbt\Parameters

Value Type: REG_DWORD—4-byte hexadecimal IP address

Valid Range: 0 to 0xFFFFFFFF

Default: The ones-broadcast address for each network.

Description: Forces NetBT to use a specific address for all broadcast name related packets. By default, NetBT uses the ones-broadcast address appropriate for each net. For example, for a network of 155.162.0.0 with a subnet mask of 255.255.0.0, the subnet broadcast address is 155.162.255.255. This parameter would be set if, for example, the network uses the zeros-broadcast address (set using the *UseZeroBroadcast* TCP/IP parameter). The appropriate subnet broadcast address would then be 155.162.0.0 in the example above. *BroadcastAddress* would thus be set to 0x9BA20000. This parameter is global and is used on all subnets to which NetBT is bound.

CachePerAdapterEnabled

Key: Netbt\Parameters

Value Type: REG_DWORD—Boolean

Valid Range: 0, 1 (False, True)

Default: 1 (True)

Description: Determines whether or not NetBIOS remote name caching is done on a per-adapter basis.

CacheTimeout

Key: Netbt\Parameters

Value Type: REG_DWORD—time in milliseconds

Valid Range: 0xEA60 to 0xFFFFFFFF

Default: 0x927C0 (600,000 milliseconds, or 10 minutes)

Description: Determines the time for which names are cached in the remote name table.

ConnectOnRequestedInterfaceOnly

Key: Netbt\Parameters

Value Type: REG_DWORD—Boolean

Valid Range: 0, 1 (False, True)

Default: 0 (False)

Description: Limits NetBT connections solely to computers that are reachable via the local host's own adapter. When the redirector on a multihomed computer calls another host, it places calls on all NetBT transports (protocol/adapter combinations) to which it is bound. Each transport attempts to reach the target name independently. Setting this parameter limits each transport to connecting to local hosts only, thus preventing crossover traffic.

DNSServerPort

Key: Netbt\Parameters

Value Type: REG_DWORD—UDP port number

Valid Range: 0 to 0xFFFF

Default: 0x35 (decimal 53)

Description: Determines the destination port number to which NetBT will send name service-related packets, such as name queries and name registrations. The Microsoft WINS Server listens on the specified port.

EnableDns

Key: Netbt\Parameters

Value Type: REG_DWORD—Boolean

Valid Range: 0, 1 (False, True)

Default: 1 (True)

Description: Enables DNS for NetBT name resolution. If this parameter is set to True (the default), NetBT queries DNS for names that can't be resolved by WINS, broadcast, or the lmhosts file.

EnableProxyRegCheck

Key: Netbt\Parameters

Value Type: REG_DWORD—Boolean

Valid Range: 0, 1 (False, True)

Default: 0 (False)

Description: Controls whether the proxy name server sends a negative response to a broadcast name registration if the name is already registered with WINS or is in the proxy's local name cache with a different IP address. If this parameter is set to True, this feature prevents a system from changing its IP address as long as WINS has a mapping for the name. For this reason, it's disabled by default.

InitialRefreshT.O.

Key: Netbt\Parameters

Value Type: REG_DWORD—time in milliseconds

Valid Range: 960,000 to 0xFFFFFFF

Default: 960,000 (16 minutes)

Description: Specifies the initial refresh time-out used by NetBT during name registration. NetBT tries to contact the WINS servers at one-eighth of this time interval when it is first registering names. A successful registration response contains the new refresh interval to be used.

LmhostsTimeout

Key: Netbt\Parameters

Value Type: REG_DWORD—time in milliseconds

Valid Range: 1,000 to 0xFFFFFFFF

Default: 6,000 (6 seconds)

Description: Specifies the time-out value for lmhosts and DNS name queries submitted by NetBT.

MaxConnBackLog

Key: Netbt\Parameters

Value Type: REG_DWORD—number

Valid Range: 2 to 0x940 (2 to 40,000 decimal)

Default: 1,000

Description: Determines the maximum number of connection blocks that NetBT allocates. Refer also to *BackLogIncrement*.

MaxPreloadEntries

Key: Netbt\Parameters

Value Type: REG_DWORD—number

Valid Range: 0x3E8 to 0x7D0 (1,000 to 2,000 decimal)

Default: 1,000 decimal

Description: Determines the maximum number of entries that are preloaded from the lmhosts file. Entries to be preloaded into cache are flagged in the lmhosts file using the #PRE tag.

MaxDgramBuffering
Key: Netbt\Parameters

Value Type: REG_DWORD—number of bytes

Valid Range: 0x20000 to 0xFFFFFFFF

Default: 0x20000 (128K)

Description: Specifies the maximum amount of memory that NetBT allocates dynamically for all outstanding datagram transmissions. Once this limit is reached, further transmissions fail because of insufficient resources.

NameServerPort
Key: Netbt\Parameters

Value Type: REG_DWORD—UDP port number

Valid Range: 0 to 0xFFFF

Default: 0x89

Description: Determines the destination port number to which NetBT sends name service-related packets, such as name queries and name registrations. The Microsoft WINS Server listens on port 0x89 (138 decimal). NetBIOS name servers from other vendors can listen on different ports.

NameSrvQueryCount
Key: Netbt\Parameters

Value Type: REG_DWORD—number

Valid Range: 0 to 0xFFFF

Default: 3

Description: Determines the number of times that NetBT sends a query to a WINS server for a specified name without receiving a response.

NameSrvQueryTimeout
Key: Netbt\Parameters

Value Type: REG_DWORD—time in milliseconds

Valid Range: 100 to 0xFFFFFFFF

Default: 1,500 (1.5 seconds)

Description: Determines the time interval between successive name queries to WINS for a specified name.

NodeType

Key: Netbt\Parameters

Value Type: REG_DWORD—Number

Valid Range: 1, 2, 4, 8 (b-node, p-node, m-node, h-node)

Default: 1 or 8, depending on the WINS server configuration

Description: This parameter determines the methods that NetBT uses to register and resolve names. Table B.1 describes the effect of each setting. Resolution through lmhosts and/or DNS (if enabled) follows these methods. If this parameter is present, it overrides the *DhcpNodeType* parameter. If neither parameter is present, the system defaults to b-node if there are no WINS servers configured for the client, or to h-node if there is at least one WINS server configured.

NoNameReleaseOnDemand

Key: Netbt\Parameters

Value Type: REG_DWORD—Boolean

Valid Range: 0, 1 (False, True)

Default: 0 (False)

Description: Determines whether the computer releases its NetBIOS name when it receives a name-release request from the network. This parameter enables the administrator to protect the machine against malicious name-release attacks.

RandomAdapter

Key: Netbt\Parameters

Value Type: REG_DWORD—Boolean

Table B.1 **NetBT name resolution nodes.**

Node	Resolution Method
b-node	Broadcasts
p-node	Uses point-to-point name queries to a name server (such as WINS)
m-node	Broadcasts first, then queries the name server
h-node	Queries the name server first, then broadcasts

Valid Range: 0, 1 (False, True)

Default: 0 (False)

Description: Determines whether NetBT will randomly choose the IP address to put in a name-query response from all of its bound interfaces. This parameter applies to a multihomed host only. Usually, the response contains the address of the interface that the query arrived on. This feature is used for load balancing by a server that has two interfaces on the same network.

RefreshOpCode

Key: Netbt\Parameters

Value Type: REG_DWORD—Number

Valid Range: 8, 9

Default: 8

Description: Forces NetBT to use a specific operation code in name-refresh packets. The default of 8 is used by Microsoft implementations and by most others. Some implementations, such as those by Ungermann-Bass, use the value 9. In order to interoperate, two implementations must use the same operation code.

ScopeId

Key: Netbt\Parameters

Value Type: REG_SZ—Character string

Valid Range: An asterisk (*) or any valid DNS domain name that consists of two dot-separated parts (such as **coriolis.com**)

Default: None

Description: Specifies the NetBIOS name scope for the node. If this parameter contains a valid value, it overrides the DHCP parameter of the same name. A blank value (empty string) is ignored. Setting this parameter to the value "*" indicates a null scope and overrides the DHCP parameter.

WARNING!   This value must not begin with a period.

SessionKeepAlive

Key: Netbt\Parameters

Value Type: REG_DWORD—time in milliseconds

Valid Range: 60,000 (decimal) to 0xFFFFFFFF

Default: 3,600,000 (1 hour)

Description: Determines the time interval between keep-alive transmissions on a session. Setting the value to 0xFFFFFFFF disables keep-alives.

SingleResponse
Key: Netbt\Parameters

Value Type: REG_DWORD—Boolean

Valid Range: 0, 1 (False, True)

Default: 0 (False)

Description: Specifies whether NetBT supplies the IP address from only one of its bound interfaces in name-query responses. By default, the addresses of all bound interfaces are included. This parameter applies to a multihomed host only.

Size/Small/Medium/Large
Key: Netbt\Parameters

Value Type: REG_DWORD

Valid Range: 1, 2, 3 (Small, Medium, Large)

Default: 1 (Small)

Description: Determines the size of the name tables that are used to store local and remote names. If the system is acting as a proxy name server, the value is automatically set to 3 (Large) to increase the size of the name cache hash table. In general, however, a setting of 1 (Small) is adequate. Hash table buckets are sized as shown in Table B.2.

SMBDeviceEnabled
Key: Netbt\Parameters

Value Type: REG_DWORD—Boolean

Valid Range: 0, 1 (False, True)

Default: 1 (True)

Table B.2   Hash table bucket sizes.

Setting	Size
Small	16
Medium	128
Large	256

Description: Used to disable the Service Message Block (SMB) device for trouble-shooting purposes. The SMB device is a Windows 2000 network transport that's enabled by default and (optionally) permits the administrator to disable NetBIOS completely.

TryAllNameServers

Key: Netbt\Parameters

Value Type: REG_DWORD—Boolean

Valid Range: 0, 1 (False, True)

Default: 0 (False)

Description: Specifies whether the client continues to query additional name servers, from the list of configured servers, when a NetBIOS session setup request to one of the IP addresses fails. If this parameter is enabled, attempts are made to query all the WINS servers in the list and connect to all the IP addresses supplied before failing the request.

TryAllIPAddrs

Key: Netbt\Parameters

Value Type: REG_DWORD—Boolean

Valid Range: 0, 1 (False, True)

Default: 1 (True)

Description: Determines the order in which a client attempts to connect to IP addresses returned by a WINS server. When WINS returns a list of addresses in response to a name query, they are sorted into a preference order based on whether any of them are on the client's subnet. If this parameter is True (the default), the client pings each address in the list and attempts to connect to the first one that answers the ping. Otherwise, it tries to connect to the first IP address in the sorted list and fails if that connection attempt fails.

UseDnsOnlyForNameResolutions

Key: Netbt\Parameters

Value Type: REG_DWORD—Boolean

Valid Range: 0, 1 (False, True)

Default: 0 (False)

Description: Used to disable all NetBIOS name queries. NetBIOS name registrations and refreshes are still used, and NetBIOS sessions are allowed. The

NetbiosOptions parameter can be used to disable NetBIOS on an interface completely.

WinsDownTimeout

Key: Netbt\Parameters

Value Type: REG_DWORD—time in milliseconds

Valid Range: 1,000 to 0xFFFFFFFF

Default: 15,000 (15 seconds)

Description: Determines the time that NetBT waits before trying to use WINS again after it fails to contact any WINS server. This feature enables computers (such as laptops) that are temporarily disconnected from the network to proceed through boot processing, without waiting to time-out each WINS name registration (or query) individually.

Parameters Configurable from the Connections User Interface

The parameters in this section are set as a result of user-supplied information. There should be no need to configure them directly in the Registry.

EnableLmhosts

Key: Netbt\Parameters

Value Type: REG_DWORD—Boolean

Valid Range: 0, 1 (False, True)

Default: 1 (True)

Description: Determines whether NetBT searches the lmhosts file (if it exists) for names that can't be resolved by WINS or broadcast. By default, there is no lmhosts file database directory, so no action is taken, even though the parameter value is True.

EnableProxy

Key: Netbt\Parameters

Value Type: REG_DWORD—Boolean

Valid Range: 0, 1 (False, True)

Default: 0 (False)

Description: Specifies whether the system acts as a proxy name server for the networks to which NetBT is bound. A proxy name server answers broadcast queries for names that it has resolved through WINS; it allows a network of b-node implementations to connect to servers on other subnets that are registered with WINS.

NameServerList

Key: Netbt\Parameters\Interfaces*interface*

Value Type: REG_MULTI_SZ—a space-separated list of dotted decimal IP addresses

Valid Range: Any list of valid WINS server IP addresses

Default: Blank (no address)

Description: Specifies the IP addresses of the list of WINS servers that are configured for the computer. If this parameter contains a valid value, it overrides the DHCP parameter of the same name.

TIP: *This parameter replaces the Windows NT4 parameters NameServer and NameServerBackup.*

NetbiosOptions

Key: Netbt\Parameters\Interfaces*interface*

Value Type: REG_DWORD—number

Valid Range: 1, 2

Default: 1

Description: Controls whether NetBIOS is enabled on a per-interface basis. When enabled, the value is 1; when disabled, the value is 2. If this parameter doesn't exist, then the *DHCPNetbiosOptions* parameter is used. Otherwise, *DHCPNetbiosOptions* is ignored.

Nonconfigurable Parameters

The parameters in this section are created and used internally by the NetBT components and should never be modified using the Registry editor. They are listed here for reference only.

DHCPNameServerList

Key: Netbt\Parameters\Interfaces*interface*

Value Type: REG_MULTI_SZ—a space-separated list of dotted decimal IP addresses

Valid Range: Any list of valid WINS server IP addresses

Default: Blank (no address)

Description: Specifies the IP addresses of the list of WINS servers, as provided by the DHCP service. Refer also to *NameServerList*, which overrides this parameter if it's present.

TIP: *This parameter replaces the Windows NT4 parameters DHCPNameServer and DHCPNameServerBackup.*

DHCPNetbiosOptions
Key: Netbt\Parameters\Interfaces*interface*

Value Type: REG_DWORD—number

Valid Range: 1, 2

Default: 1

Description: Written by the DHCP client service. Refer to the *NetbiosOptions* parameter for a description.

DhcpNodeType
Key: Netbt\Parameters

Value Type: REG_DWORD—number

Valid Range: 1, 2, 4, 8

Default: 1

Description: Specifies the NetBT node type. It is written by the DHCP client service, if enabled. A valid NodeType value overrides this parameter. Refer to **NodeType** and Table B.1 for a description of NetBT node types.

DhcpScopeId
Key: Netbt\Parameters

Value Type: REG_SZ—character string

Valid Range: A dot-separated name string (for example, coriolis.com)

Default: None

Description: Specifies the NetBIOS name scope for the node. This parameter is written by the DHCP client service, if enabled. Refer to *ScopeId* for more information.

WARNING! **This value must not begin with a period.**

NbProvider
Key: Netbt\Parameters

Value Type: REG_SZ—character string

Valid Range: _tcp

Default: _tcp

Description: Used internally by the Remote Procedure Call (RPC) component. The default value should not be changed.

TransportBindName
Key: Netbt\Parameters

Value Type: REG_SZ—character string

Valid Range: Not applicable

Default: \Device\

Description: Used internally during product development. The default value should not be changed.

Appendix C

Winsock and DNS Registry Parameters

Some of the Registry parameters that control the operation of Windows Sockets (Winsock) and the Domain Name System (DNS) are inserted into the Registry on setup. If you want to use parameters that are not visible in the Registry after setup, you can insert them manually using the Registry editor. You need do this only if you want to change the default values. If a parameter isn't inserted into the Registry automatically, then its default value is assumed.

Winsock and DNS Parameters

The parameters in this appendix fall into four classifications:

- AFD registry parameters
- Dynamic Domain Name System (DDNS) registration parameters
- DNS caching resolver service registry parameters
- Name resolution parameters

AFD Registry Parameters

Winsock parameters control the operation and default settings for the *afd.sys* kernel-mode driver. For backward compatibility, some of these parameters can take one of three defaults (for example 4/8/24). The default calculation is based on the amount of memory detected in the system.

- The first value is the default for smaller computers (less than 19MB).
- The second value is the default for medium computers (up to 32MB for Windows 2000 Professional and up to 64MB for Windows 2000 Server).
- The third value is the default for large computers (greater than 32MB for Professional and greater than 64MB for Server).

In practice, the third default is the one calculated. Windows 2000 Professional is rarely installed on machines that have 32MB RAM or less, nor is Windows 2000

Server commonly installed on machines that have 64MB or less. These values are well below Microsoft's recommendations.

Winsock parameters are located under the subkey:

```
HKEY_LOCAL_MACHINE
        \SYSTEM
              \CurrentControlSet
                      \Services
                             \Afd
                                       \Parameters
```

DefaultReceiveWindow

Value Type: REG_DWORD—number

Default: 4096/8192/8192

Description: Specifies the number of receive bytes that AFD buffers on a connection before it imposes flow control. For some applications, increasing the value of this parameter gives slightly better performance at the expense of increased resource utilization. Applications can modify this value on a per-socket basis.

DefaultSendWindow

Value Type: REG_DWORD

Default: 4096/8192/8192

Description: Specifies the number of send bytes that AFD buffers on a connection before it imposes flow control.

DisableAddressSharing

Value Type: REG_DWORD—Boolean

Valid Range: 0 (False), 1 (True)

Default: 0 (False)

Description: Enables or disables address sharing between processes. Setting this value to True ensures that, if a process opens a socket, no other process can steal data from it.

DisableRawSecurity

Value Type: REG_DWORD—Boolean

Valid Range: 0 (False), 1 (True)

Default: 0 (False)

Description: Enables or disables the check for administrative privileges when attempting to open a raw socket. This parameter isn't used for Windows 2000 TCP/IP, which manages its own security for raw sockets. Refer to the TCP/IP **AllowUserRawAccess** registry parameter, described in Appendix A.

DynamicBacklogGrowthDelta
Value Type: REG_DWORD—number

Valid Range: 0 to 0xFFFFFFFF

Default: 0

Description: Controls the number of free connections that are created when additional connections are necessary. Take care when altering this value, because a large value could lead to excessive free-connection allocations. The suggested value for a system under heavy attack is 0xA.

TIP: *Although this parameter still exists, the TCP stack has been hardened against SYN-ATTACK in Windows 2000, and it shouldn't be necessary to use this feature.*

EnableDynamicBacklog
Value Type: REG_DWORD—Boolean

Valid Range: 0, 1 (False, True)

Default: 0 (False)

Description: Enables or disables dynamic backlog globally. Setting the value to True enables the Windows 2000 dynamic backlog feature.

FastCopyReceiveThreshold
Value Type: REG_DWORD—number

Default: 1,024

Description: Defines the threshold at which buffer locking and mapping occurs. When an application posts a receive packet that has a buffer that's smaller than the current packet being buffered by Winsock, AFD has two options. It can make an additional copy of the packet and then copy data to the application buffers directly (which is a two-stage copy because application buffers cannot be accessed directly under the lock), or it can lock and map application buffers and copy data once.

> **WARNING!**   The default for this parameter was established by testing and is considered to be the best overall value for performance. Don't change it unless you have a good reason for doing so.

FastSendDatagramThreshold

Value Type: REG_DWORD—number

Default: 1,024

Description: Determines the threshold below which datagrams are sent using fast Input/Output (I/O). Fast I/O is implemented by copying data and bypassing the I/O subsystem, instead of mapping memory and going through the I/O subsystem. This is advantageous for small amounts of data. This value was established by testing, and changing it is not generally recommended.

IgnorePushBitOnReceives

Value Type: REG_DWORD—Boolean

Valid Range: 0, 1 (False, True)

Default: 0 (False)

Description: Causes AFD to treat all incoming packets as if the push bit were set. This should be done only as a work-around when client TCP/IP implementations aren't pushing data properly. The default value is, therefore, False.

IrpStackSize

Value Type: REG_DWORD—number

Valid Range: 1 to 255

Default: 4

Description: Specifies the number of I/O Request Packet (IRP) stack locations that are used for AFD by default. Changing this value is not recommended.

LargeBufferSize

Value Type: REG_DWORD—number

Default: PAGE_SIZE (4,096 bytes on I386, 8,192 bytes on Alpha)

Description: Specifies the size of large buffers used by AFD. Smaller values use less memory; larger values can improve performance.

LargeBufferListDepth

Value Type: REG_DWORD—number

Default: 0/2/10

Description: Specifies the depth of the large buffer look-aside list.

MaxActiveTransmitFileCount

Value Type: REG_DWORD—number

Valid Range: 0 to 0xFFFF (Server), 2 (Professional)

Default: 0 (Server), 2 (Professional)

Description: Allows configuration of the maximum number of concurrent TransmitFile requests outstanding. A setting of zero means that this number is unlimited, except by system resources. This parameter isn't configurable for Windows 2000 Professional.

MaxFastTransmit

Value Type: REG_DWORD—number

Valid Range: 0 to 0xFFFFFFFF

Default: 64K

Description: Controls the maximum amount of data that's transferred in a TransmitFile request using fast I/O. Changing this value is not generally recommended.

MaxFastCopyTransmit

Value Type: REG_DWORD—number

Valid Range: 0 to 0xFFFFFFFF

Default: 128

Description: Controls the maximum size of data that uses copy instead of cached memory on the *fast-path* (that is, using fast I/O). Changing this value is not generally recommended.

MediumBufferSize

Value Type: REG_DWORD—number

Default: 1,504

Description: Specifies the size of medium buffers used by AFD.

MediumBufferListDepth

Value Type: REG_DWORD—number

Default: 4/8/24

Description: The depth of the medium buffer look-aside list.

MinimumDynamicBacklog

Value Type: REG_DWORD—number

Valid Range: 0 to 0xFFFFFFFF

Default: 0

Description: Controls the minimum number of free connections that are allowed on a listening endpoint. If the number of free connections drops below this value, a thread is queued to create additional free connections. Too large a value can lead to a performance reduction; the suggested value for a system under heavy SYN-ATTACK is 20.

TIP: Although this parameter still exists, the TCP stack has been hardened against SYN-ATTACK in Windows 2000, and it shouldn't be necessary to use this feature.

MaximumDynamicBacklog

Value Type: REG_DWORD—number

Valid Range: 0 to 0xFFFFFFFF

Default: 0

Description: Controls the maximum number of *quasi-free* connections allowed on a listening endpoint. Quasi-free connections include the number of free connections plus those connections in a half-connected (SYN_RECEIVED) state. No attempt is made to create additional free connections if doing so would exceed this value. This value should not exceed 5,000 for each 32MB of RAM.

OverheadChargeGranularity

Value Type: REG_DWORD—number

Valid Range: A power of two

Default: One page

Description: Determines in what increments overhead is charged. The default is one page, and the intention is to charge and contain attack-type applications that try to exhaust system memory.

PriorityBoost

Value Type: REG_DWORD—number

Valid Range: 0 to 16

Default: 2

Description: Defines the priority boost that AFD gives to a thread when I/O operations for that thread are complete. If a multithreaded application experiences thread starvation, the problem can be remedied by reducing this value.

SmallBufferListDepth

Value Type: REG_DWORD—number

Default: 8/16/32

Description: Specifies the depth of the small buffer look-aside list.

SmallBufferSize

Value Type: REG_DWORD—number of bytes

Default: 128

Description: Specifies the size of small buffers used by AFD.

StandardAddressLength

Value Type: REG_DWORD—number of bytes

Default: 22

Description: Specifies the length of typical Transport Driver Interface (TDI) addresses. If you use an alternate transport protocol that uses very long addresses, increasing this value results in a slight performance improvement.

TransmitIoLength

Value Type: REG_DWORD—number

Default: PAGE_SIZE/PAGE_SIZE*2/65536 (for Server)

Description: Specifies the default size for I/O reads and sends that are performed by **TransmitFile()**. For Windows 2000 Professional, the default I/O size is one page.

TransmitWorker

Value Type: REG_DWORD—number

Valid Range: 0x10, 0x20

Default: 0x10

Description: Controls how AFD uses system threads. Setting this value to 0x10 causes AFD to use system threads to perform I/O operations that are initiated by a *TransmitFile* request that contains more than two *SendPacketLength*'s worth of data. Setting it to 0x20 causes AFD to execute everything in the context of the same thread; this setting can improve performance by reducing the number of context switches in long *TransmitFile* requests.

Dynamic DNS (DDNS) Registration Parameters

These parameters control the behavior of the DDNS registration client. They are
located under one of two subkeys:

```
HKEY_LOCAL_MACHINE
        \SYSTEM
                \CurrentControlSet
                        \Services
                                \Tcpip
                                        \Parameters
```

```
HKEY_LOCAL_MACHINE
        \SYSTEM
                \CurrentControlSet
                        \Services
                                \Tcpip
                                        \Parameters
                                                \Interfaces
                                                        \interface
```

In the second case, *interface* takes a value that's specific to the interface.

DefaultRegistrationTTL

Key: Tcpip\Parameters

Value Type: REG_DWORD—seconds

Default: 0x384 (900 decimal, or 15 minutes)

Valid Range: 0 to 0xFFFFFFFF

Description: Specifies the Time to Live (TTL) value sent with DDNS registrations.

EnableAdapterDomainNameRegistration

Key: Tcpip\Parameters\Interfaces*interface*

Value Type: REG_DWORD—Boolean

Valid Range: 0 (False), 1 (True)

Default: 0 (False)

Description: Enables or disables DNS dynamic update registration of a specific
adapter's domain name information. When this value is True and *DisableDynamic-
Update* is False, the given adapter's address(es) are registered under the adapter's
domain name and under the system's primary domain name.

DisableDynamicUpdate

Key: Tcpip\Parameters, Tcpip\Parameters\Interfaces*interface*

Value Type: REG_DWORD—Boolean

Valid Range: 0 (False), 1 (True)

Default: 0 (False)

Description: Used to disable DNS dynamic update registration. This parameter is both a per-interface parameter and a global parameter, depending on where the registry key is located. If the value at the Tcpip\Parameters level is set to True, then dynamic update is disabled for the entire system. If the value at the Tcpip\Parameters level is set to False, then dynamic update can be disabled on a per-adapter basis.

DisableReplaceAddressesInConflicts

Key: Tcpip\Parameters

Value Type: REG_DWORD—Boolean

Valid Range: 0 (False), 1 (True)

Default: 0 (False)

Description: Turns off the "last writer wins" address registration conflict rule.

DisableReverseAddressRegistrations

Key: Tcpip\Parameters\Interfaces*interface*

Value Type: REG_DWORD—Boolean

Valid Range: 0 (False), 1 (True)

Default: 0 (False)

Description: Used to enable or disable DNS dynamic update reverse address (PTR) record registration. If the DHCP server that configures the computer is a Windows 2000 Server, it is capable of registering the PTR record with the DNS dynamic update protocol. However, if the DHCP server isn't capable of performing DNS dynamic update PTR registrations and if you don't want to register PTR records with the DNS dynamic update protocol, you can set this parameter to True.

UpdateSecurityLevel

Key: Tcpip\Parameters

Value Type: REG_DWORD—flags

Valid Range: 0, 0x00000010, 0x00000020, 0x00000100

Default: 0

Description: Controls the security that's used for DNS dynamic updates. It defaults to zero, which is to try nonsecure updates and, if refused, to send secure dynamic updates. Valid values are listed in Table C.1.

Table C.1   DNS update security settings.

Setting	Result
0x00000000	Nonsecure updates
0x00000010	Security OFF
0x00000020	Security ON
0x00000100	Secure ONLY ON

DNS Caching Resolver Service Registry Parameters

The Windows 2000 DNS caching resolver service caches DNR answers, so that the DNS server isn't queried repeatedly for the same information. The service can be stopped using the Service Control Manager MMC snap-in. Registry parameters for this service are located under the Registry key:

```
HKEY_LOCAL_MACHINE
    \SYSTEM
            \CurrentControlSet
                    \Services
                            \Dnscache
                                    \Parameters
```

AdapterTimeoutCacheTime
Value Type: REG_DWORD—seconds

Valid Range: 0–0xFFFFFFFF

Default: 300 (5 minutes)

Description: Specifies the time that a particular adapter on a multihomed machine is disabled when a DNS query attempt fails (times out) for all of that adapter's DNS servers. If, for example, a PC has two adapters and the DNS servers on one of the networks are unreachable, then the adapter is marked as unusable for the specified period of time.

CacheHashTableSize

Value Type: REG_DWORD—number

Valid Range: Any prime number greater than zero

Default: 0xD3 (211 decimal)

Description: Specifies the maximum number of rows in the hash table used by the DNS caching resolver service. It shouldn't be necessary to change this parameter value.

CacheHashTableBucketSize

Value Type: REG_DWORD—number

Valid Range: 0 to 0x32 (50 decimal)

Default: 0xA (10 decimal)

Description: Specifies the maximum number of columns in the hash table used by the DNS caching resolver service. It shouldn't be necessary to change this parameter value.

DefaultRegistrationRefreshInterval

Value Type: REG_DWORD—time in seconds

Valid Range: 0 to 0xFFFFFFFF

Default: 0x15180 (86,400 decimal, or 24 hours)

Description: Specifies the DDNS registration refresh interval.

MaxCacheEntryTtlLimit

Value Type: REG_DWORD—time in seconds

Valid Range: 0 to 0xFFFFFFFF

Default: 0x15180 (86,400 decimal)

Description: Specifies the maximum cache entry TTL. This parameter setting overrides any larger value that's set on a specific record. To prevent stale records, the value should be set to 24 hours (the default) or less.

MaxSOACacheEntryTtlLimit

Value Type: REG_DWORD—time in seconds

Valid Range: 0 to 0xFFFFFFFF

Default: 120 (2 minutes)

Description: Specifies the maximum time for which the resolver cache caches any Start of Authority (SOA) records. This parameter setting overrides any larger TTL value for a specific SOA record that's returned from a DNS query.

NegativeCacheTime

Value Type: REG_DWORD—time in seconds

Valid Range: 0 to 0xFFFFFFFF

Default: 0x12C (300 decimal, or 5 minutes)

Description: Controls the cache time for negative records. This value should not be set to more than one day.

NegativeSOACacheTime

Value Type: REG_DWORD—time in seconds

Valid Range: 0 to 0xFFFFFFFF

Default: 0x78 (120 decimal, or 2 minutes)

Description: Specifies the cache time for negative SOA records. DNS registrations that fail are retried at 5- and 10-minute intervals. If this value is set to five minutes or more, retries are answered negatively from cache, although the server could be available. For this reason, a setting of less than five minutes is recommended.

NetFailureErrorPopupLimit

Value Type: REG_DWORD—Boolean

Valid Range: 0 (False), 1 (True)

Default: 0 (False)

Description: Enables a user interface pop-up to indicate that the DNS resolver was unable to query (reach) the configured DNS servers for a repeated number of query attempts.

NetFailureCacheTime

Value Type: REG_DWORD—time in seconds

Valid Range: 0 to 0xFFFFFFFF

Default: 0x1E (30 decimal)

Description: Specifies the general network failure cache time. After it has been detected that a time-out error is occurring for queries against all known DNS servers, the resolver will not issue queries for the period of time specified by this parameter. This avoids delays when the network doesn't respond. It's recommended that this value should be less than five minutes.

Name Resolution Parameters

Parameters used by the Domain Name Resolver (DNR) service are located under the Registry key:

```
HKEY_LOCAL_MACHINE
    \SYSTEM
            \CurrentControlSet
                    \Services
                            \Tcpip
                                \Parameters
```

AllowUnqualifiedQuery

Value Type: REG_DWORD—Boolean

Valid Range: 0 (False), 1 (True)

Default: 0 (False)

Description: Specifies whether or not the DNR queries the DNS server(s) with the host name, followed only by a dot (an unqualified query). For example, if your computer is in yourdomain.com and you ping a computer called target, DNS by default is queried for target.mydomain.com only. When this parameter is set to True, target. is also queried.

DisjointNameSpace

Value Type: REG_DWORD—Boolean

Valid Range: 0 (False), 1 (True)

Default: 1 (True)

Description: Instructs the DNR to treat each interface as a disjoint name space. On a multihomed computer, a query to the DNS server(s) that is configured for one interface may result in a name error. If this parameter is True (the default), the resolver will try the query against possible DNS servers that are configured for other interfaces before it returns results.

PrioritizeRecordData

Value Type: REG_DWORD—Boolean

Valid Range: 0 (False), 1 (True)

Default: 1 (True)

Description: Specifies whether or not the DNR sorts the addresses that are returned in response to a query for a multihomed host. By default, the DNR sorts addresses that are on the same subnet as one of the interfaces in the querying computer and places them at the top of the list. This gives preference to a common-subnet IP address.

QueryIpMatching
Value Type: REG_DWORD—Boolean

Valid Range: 0 (False), 1 (True)

Default: 0 (False)

Description: Specifies whether or not the IP address of the DNS server that's queried is matched to the IP address of the server that sent the DNS response. This ensures that the resolver isn't being fooled by a random query response from a computer other than the intended DNS server.

UseDomainNameDevolution
Value Type: REG_DWORD—Boolean

Valid Range: 0 (False), 1 (True)

Default: 1 (True)

Description: Enables or disables domain name *devolution* for unqualified DNS queries. Devolution is the process of attempting to locate a host in the DNS by first appending the domain suffix of the client to the host name, then querying for the full string. If that query fails, one label at a time is removed, and the query is resubmitted.

Appendix D

The Network Shell Utility

The Network Shell utility is a command-line, scripting interface for configuring and monitoring Windows 2000. The **netsh** command enables you to run this utility and display or modify computer configuration. It also provides a scripting feature that you can use to run a list of commands in batch mode and can be run on a remote computer specified by its name or Internet Protocol (IP) address.

This appendix doesn't cover all the features of the Network Shell utility, which can be expanded using helper DLL files to perform a wide range of functions. The purpose of the appendix is to list and describe the **netsh** commands that can be used to configure TCP/IP settings and services—such as demand-dial interface, IP routing, and Remote Access Service (RAS) commands. The global Network Shell commands are listed, but are not discussed in detail. Information on the Network Shell online, offline and script modes, and the helper DLLs can be found in the Windows 2000 product documentation.

TIP: *You can abbreviate Network Shell commands to the shortest unambiguous string. For example, **netsh sh ip int** is equivalent to **netsh show ip interface**.*

Global Commands

The **netsh** commands may be used in a context—for example, routing commands, RAS commands, and so on. Also, global commands may be used to configure the Network Shell environment. Table D.1 lists the **netsh** global commands. When you type the command at the command-line prompt, precede each of the table entries with **netsh**. Alternatively, enter **netsh** with no arguments, then enter the command at the netsh> prompt. To display the syntax of a command, follow it with a question mark (for example, **netsh add helper ?**).

Table D.1   The Network Shell global commands.

Command	Description
..	Moves up one context level.
? or **help**	Displays command-line Help.
show version	Displays the current version of Windows and the Network Shell utility.
show netdlls	Displays the current version of installed Network Shell helper DLLs.
add helper	Adds a Network Shell helper DLL.
delete helper	Removes a Network Shell helper DLL.
show helper	Displays the installed Network Shell helper DLLs.
cmd	Creates a Windows 2000 command window.
online	Sets the current mode to online.
offline	Sets the current mode to offline.
set mode	Sets the current mode to online or offline.
show mode	Displays the current mode.
flush	Discards any changes in offline mode.
commit	Commits changes made in offline mode.
set audit-logging	Turns on or off the logging facility.
show audit-logging	Displays current audit logging settings.
set loglevel	Sets the level of logging information.
show loglevel	Displays the level of logging information.
set machine	Specifies the computer on which the **netsh** commands are executed.
show machine	Displays the computer on which the **netsh** commands are executed.
exec	Executes a script file containing **netsh** commands.
quit or **bye** or **exit**	Exits the Network Shell utility.
add alias	Adds an alias for an existing command.
delete alias	Deletes an alias for an existing command.
show alias	Displays all defined aliases.
dump	Writes configuration to a text file and creates a script.
popd	Pops a context from the stack (script mode only).
pushd	Pushes the current context on the stack (script mode only).

IP Routing Commands

Network Shell commands can be used to configure and display general IP routing settings and settings specific to the Routing Internet Protocol (RIP) and Open Shortest Path First (OSPF) protocol. They are also used to configure routing for the Internet Group Management Protocol (IGMP), the Dynamic Host Configuration Protocol (DHCP), the Domain Name Service (DNS), and the Network Address Translation (NAT) service. Tables D.2 through D.8 list the **netsh** IP routing commands.

Where there are multiple commands for a particular function, they're indicated by separating the individual commands with a slash (/). For example, the command **routing ip nat set/show global** represents the two separate commands: **routing ip nat set global** and **routing ip nat show global**.

When you type the command at the command-line prompt, precede each of the table entries with **netsh**, or else enter the commands at the netsh> prompt. To display the syntax of a command, follow it with a question mark (for example, **netsh routing ip add filter ?**).

Table D.2   General IP setting configuration commands.

Command	Description
routing ip add/delete/set/show interface	Adds, deletes, configures, or displays general IP routing settings on a specified interface.
routing ip add/delete/set/show filter	Adds, deletes, configures, or displays IP packet filters on a specified interface.
routing ip add/delete/show boundary	Adds, deletes, or displays multicast boundary settings on a specified interface.
routing ip add/set ipiptunnel	Adds or configures an IP-in-IP interface.
routing ip add/delete/set/show rtmroute	Adds, deletes, configures, or displays a nonpersistent Route Table Manager route.
routing ip add/delete/set/show persistentroute	Adds, deletes, configures, or displays persistent routes.
routing ip add/delete/set/show preferenceforprotocol	Adds, deletes, configures, or displays the preference level for a routing protocol.
routing ip add/delete/set/show scope	Adds, deletes, configures, or displays a multicast scope.

(continued)

Table D.2   General IP setting configuration commands (continued).

Command	Description
routing ip set/show loglevel	Configures or displays the global IP logging level.
routing ip show helper	Displays all Network Shell utility subcontexts of IP.
routing ip show protocol	Displays all running IP routing protocols.
routing ip show mfe	Displays multicast forwarding entries.
routing ip show mfestats	Displays multicast forwarding entry statistics.
routing ip show boundarystats	Displays IP multicast boundaries.
routing ip show rtmdestinations	Displays destinations in the Route Table Manager routing table.
routing ip show rtmroutes	Displays routes in the Route Table Manager routing table.

Table D.3   RIP IP routing configuration commands.

Command	Description
routing ip rip set/show global	Configures or displays global RIP-for-IP settings.
routing ip rip add/delete/set/show interface	Adds, deletes, configures, or displays RIP-for-IP settings on a specified interface.
routing ip rip add/delete peerfilter	Adds or removes a RIP peer filter.
routing ip rip add/delete acceptfilter	Adds or removes a RIP route filter to the list of routes being accepted.
routing ip rip add/delete announcefilter	Adds or removes a RIP route filter to the list of routes being announced.
routing ip rip add/delete/show neighbor	Adds or removes a RIP neighbor, or displays RIP peer statistics.
routing ip rip set/show flags	Configures or displays RIP-related flag settings on a specified interface.
routing ip rip show globalstats	Displays global RIP statisics.
routing ip rip show ifbinding	Displays IP address bindings for interfaces.
routing ip rip show ifstats	Displays RIP statistics for each interface.

Table D.4   OSPF IP routing configuration commands.

Command	Description
routing ip ospf set/show global	Configures or displays global OSPF settings.
routing ip ospf add/delete/set/show interface	Adds, removes, configures, or displays OSPF settings on a specified interface.
routing ip ospf add/delete/set/show area	Adds, removes, configures, or displays an OSPF area.
routing ip ospf add/delete/show range	Adds, removes, or displays a range for a specified OSPF area.
routing ip ospf add/delete/set/show virtif	Adds, removes, configures, or displays an OSPF virtual interface.
routing ip ospf add/delete/show neighbor	Adds, removes, or displays an OSPF neighbor.
routing ip ospf add/delete/set/show protofilter	Adds, removes, configures, or displays routing information sources for OSPF external routes.
routing ip ospf add/delete/set/show routefilter	Adds, removes, configures, or displays route filtering for OSPF external routes.
routing ip ospf show areastats	Displays OSPF area statistics.
routing ip ospf show lsdb	Displays the OSPF link state database.
routing ip ospf show virtifstats	Displays OSPF virtual link statistics.

Table D.5   GMP IP routing configuration commands.

Command	Description
routing ip igmp set/show global	Configures or displays IGMP global settings.
routing ip igmp add/delete/set/show interface	Adds, deletes, configures, or displays IGMP on the specified interface.
routing ip igmp add/delete staticgroup	Adds or deletes a static multicast group for the specified interface.
routing ip igmp show grouptable	Displays the IGMP host groups table.
routing ip igmp show ifstats	Displays the IGMP statistics for each interface.
routing ip igmp show iftable	Displays the IGMP host groups for each interface.
routing ip igmp show proxygrouptable	Displays the IGMP group table for the IGMP proxy interface.
routing ip igmp show rasgrouptable	Displays the group table for a RAS client interface.

Appendix D The
Network Shell Utility

Table D.6   DHCP IP routing configuration commands.

Command	Description
routing ip autodhcp set/show global	Configures or displays global DHCP allocator parameters.
routing ip autodhcp set/show interface	Configures or displays DHCP allocator settings for a specified interface.
routing ip autodhcp add/delete exclusion	Adds or deletes an exclusion from the DHCP allocator range of addresses.
routing ip relay set global	Configures DHCP Relay Agent global settings.
routing ip relay add/delete/set interface	Adds, removes, or configures DHCP Relay Agent settings on a specified interface.
routing ip relay add/delete dhcpserver	Adds or removes a DHCP server IP address to or from the list of DHCP server addresses.
routing ip relay show ifbinding	Displays IP address bindings for Relay Agent interfaces.
routing ip relay show ifconfig	Displays DHCP Relay Agent configuration for each interface.
routing ip relay show ifstats	Displays DHCP statistics for each interface.

Table D.7   DNS IP routing configuration commands.

Command	Description
routing ip dnsproxy set/show global	Configures or displays global DNS proxy parameters.
routing ip dnsproxy set/show interface	Configures or displays DNS proxy parameters for a specified interface.

Table D.8   NAT IP routing configuration commands.

Command	Description
routing ip nat set/show global	Configures or displays global NAT settings.
routing ip nat add/delete/set/show interface	Adds, deletes, configures, or displays NAT settings for a specified interface.
routing ip nat add/delete addressrange	Adds or deletes an address range to the NAT interface public address pool.
routing ip nat add/delete addressmapping	Adds or deletes a NAT address mapping.
routing ip nat add/delete portmapping	Adds or deletes a NAT port mapping.

Demand-Dial Interface Commands

Network Shell commands can be used to configure and display demand-dial interface settings on a computer running Windows 2000 Server and the Routing and Remote Access Service (RRAS). Table D.9 lists the **netsh** interface commands.

Where there are multiple commands for a particular function, they're indicated by separating the individual commands with a slash (/). For example, the command **interface set/show interface** represents the two separate commands **interface set interface** and **interface show interface**.

When you type the command at the command-line prompt, precede each of the table entries with **netsh**, or else enter the command at the netsh> prompt. To display the syntax of a command, follow it with a question mark (for example, **netsh interface set interface ?**).

Table D.9   Demand-dial interface configuration commands.

Command	Description
interface set/show interface	Enables, disables, connects, disconnects, and displays the configuration of demand-dial interfaces.
interface set/show credentials	Configures or displays the username, password, and domain name on a demand-dial interface.

RAS Commands

Network Shell commands can be used to configure and display RAS settings. Table D.10 lists the **netsh** RAS commands.

Where there are multiple commands for a particular function, they're indicated by separating the individual commands with a slash (/). For example, the command **ras set/show authmode** represents the two separate commands **ras set authmode** and **ras show authmode**.

When you type the command at the command-line prompt, precede each of the table entries with **netsh**, or else enter the command at the netsh> prompt. To display the syntax of a command, follow it with a question mark (for example, **netsh ras add authtype ?**).

Table \D.10   *RAS commands.*

Command	Description
ras add/delete/show registeredserver	Adds or removes the specified RAS server from the RAS and IAS Servers security group in Active Directory, or displays whether the computer is a RAS server in a specified domain. For a change to take effect, you need to restart the computer.
ras show activeservers	Displays current remote access servers running Windows 2000 on the network.
ras set/show authmode	Configures or displays whether and when dial-in connections are authenticated.
ras add/delete/show authtype	Adds, deletes, or displays the types of authentiation that the RAS server will use.
ras add/delete/show client	Adds, deletes, or displays currently connected remote access clients.
ras add/delete/show link	Adds to, deletes from, or displays the list of configuration of software compression and Link Control Protocol (LCP) extensions.
ras add/delete/show multilink	Adds to, deletes from, or displays the list of multilink and Bandwidth Allocation Protocol (BAP) settings.
ras set/show tracing	Configures or displays tracing settings.
ras set/show user	Configures or displays remote access settings for user accounts.
ras ip set access	Configures whether IP traffic from remote access clients is forwarded to the networks to which the remote access server is connected.
ras ip set addrassign	Configures the method by which the remote access server assigns IP addresses to incoming connections.
ras ip set addrreq	Configures whether remote access clients or demand-dial routers can request their own IP addresses.
ras ip show config	Displays IP remote access configuration.
ras ip set negotiation	Configures whether IP is negotiated for remote access connections.
ras ip delete pool	Deletes the static IP address pool.
ras ip add/delete range	Adds or removes a range of addresses to or from the static IP address pool.

(continued)

Table D.10 RAS commands (continued).

Command	Description
ras aaaa add/delete/set/show acctserver	Adds, deletes, configures, or displays Remote Authentication Dial-in User Service (RADIUS) accounting servers.
ras aaaa set/show authentication	Configures or displays the authentication provider.
ras aaaa add/delete/set/show authserver	Adds, deletes, configures, or displays RADIUS authentication servers.

DHCP Commands

In addition to the Network Shell commands for DHCP IP routing configuration that are listed in Table D.6, the utility provides a set of commands for use in administering DHCP servers. These commands can be used as an alternative to console-based management.

First-Level DHCP Commands

Table D.11 lists commands that can be used at the DHCP Network Shell prompt (dhcp>). To access this prompt, enter **netsh** without any arguments at the command prompt, then enter **dhcp** without any arguments at the netsh> prompt. You can also enter these commands directly from the command prompt by preceding them with **netsh dhcp**—for example, **netsh dhcp show server**.

> **TIP:** To redirect output of the **dump** command to a text file, use the standard MS-DOS redirection operator (>). For example, **dump > config.txt** dumps the configuration of the currently selected DHCP server to the config.txt file. You can also do this from the command prompt by entering **netsh dhcp dump > config.txt**. To obtain more information about a file, follow it with a question mark (for example, **dump ?**).

Table D.11 First-level DHCP commands.

Command	Description
list	Lists all available DHCP commands.
dump	Dumps DHCP server configuration to command output or a text file.
add server	Adds a DHCP server to the DHCP console.
delete server	Deletes a DHCP server from the DHCP console.
show server	Displays all DHCP servers currently added under the DHCP console.
server [\\servername | address]	Shifts the current DHCP command-line context to the server specified by either its name or IP address.

DHCP Server Commands

Table D.12 lists commands that can be used at the DHCP Server Network Shell prompt (dhcp server>). To access this prompt, enter **server** without any arguments at the dhcp> prompt. You can also enter these commands directly from the command prompt by preceding them with **netsh dhcp server** (for example, **netsh dhcp server delete optionvalue 18**).

Table D.12   DHCP server commands.

Command	Description
add class	Adds a class to the current DHCP server.
add mscope	Adds a multicast scope to the current DHCP server.
add optiondef	Adds a new option type definition to the current DHCP server.
add scope	Adds a new scope to the current DHCP server.
delete class	Deletes a class from the current DHCP server.
delete mscope	Deletes a multicast scope from the current DHCP server.
delete optiondef	Deletes a new option type definition from the current DHCP server.
delete optionvalue	Deletes a new option type definition from the current DHCP server.
delete scope	Deletes a new scope from the current DHCP server.
delete superscope	Deletes a new superscope from the current DHCP server.
initiate auth	Initiates or retries authorization of the current DHCP server in Active Directory.
scope [scope_ip_address]	Switches the command context to DHCP scope where the scope is specified by its IP network address.
mscope [mscope_name]	Switches the command context to DHCP multicast scope where the multicast scope is specified by name.
set auditlog	Sets the audit log path parameters for the current DHCP server.
set backupinterval	Sets the backup interval of the current DHCP server.
set backupdatabasepath	Sets the database backup path to be used by the current DHCP server.
set databasecleanupinterval	Sets the database cleanup interval of the current DHCP server.
set databaseloggingflag	Sets/resets the database logging flag for the current DHCP server.
set databasename	Sets the name of the DHCP server database file for the current DHCP server.
set databasepath	Sets the path of the DHCP server database file for the current DHCP server.

(continued)

Table D.12   DHCP server commands (**continued**).

Command	Description
set databaserestoreflag	Sets/resets the database restore flag for the current DHCP server.
set databaserestoreflag	Sets/resets the database restore flag for the current DHCP server.
set detectconflictretry	Sets the number of conflict detection attempts made by the current DHCP server.
set dnsconfig	Sets the DNS dynamic update configuration for the current DHCP server.
set optionvalue	Sets a server option value, which will be applied for all scopes defined at the current server.
set server	Sets the current server in the Server mode.
set userclass	Sets the userclass name for use in subsequent command operations.
set vendorclass	Sets the vendor class name for use in subsequent command operations.
show all	Displays all information for the current DHCP server.
show auditlog	Displays audit log path parameters for the current DHCP server.
show bindings	Displays bindings information for the current DHCP server.
show class	Displays all class information for the current DHCP server.
show detectconflictretry	Displays the number of conflict detection settings for the current DHCP server.
show dnsconfig	Displays the DNS dynamic update configuration for the current DHCP server.
show mibinfo	Displays Management Information Base (MIB) information for the current DHCP server.
show mscope	Displays all information about multicast scopes for the current DHCP server.
show optiondef	Displays all defined and available options for the current DHCP server.
show optionvalue	Displays all available option values currently set for the specified DHCP server.
show scope	Displays scope information for the current DHCP server.
show server	Displays information about the current DHCP server.
show dbproperties	Displays server database configuration information for the current DHCP server.
show serverstatus	Displays status information for the current DHCP server.
show userclass	Displays the current user class setting at the specified DHCP server.
show vendorclass	Displays the current vendor class setting at the specified DHCP server.
show version	Displays current version information for the specified DHCP server.

DHCP Scope Commands

Table D.13 lists commands that can be used at the DHCP Server Network Shell prompt (dhcp server scope>). To access this prompt, enter a scope, identified by IP address, at the dhcp server> prompt (for example, **scope 195.162.230.10**). You can also enter these commands directly from the command prompt (for example, **netsh dhcp server scope 195.162.230.10 initiate reconcile**). However, at this level of complexity it's usually preferable to go via the context tree.

Table D.13   DHCP scope commands.

Command	Description
add excluderange	Adds a range of excluded addresses to the current scope.
add iprange	Adds a range of IP addresses to the current scope.
add reservedip	Reserves an IP address for use by a specified MAC address in the current scope.
delete excluderange	Deletes an exclusion range of previously excluded IP addresses in the current scope.
delete iprange	Deletes a range of IP addresses from the current scope.
delete optionvalue	Removes or clears an assigned scope option value from the current scope.
delete reservedip	Deletes a reservation for an IP address in the current scope.
delete reservedoptionvalue	Removes an option value assigned for a reserved client in the current scope.
initiate reconcile	Checks and reconciles the current scope.
set comment	Sets the comment for the current scope.
set name	Sets the name of the current scope.
set optionvalue	Sets an option value for the current scope.
set reservedoptionvalue	Sets the value of an option (for example the router option 003) that's allocated a reserved IP address in comments for the current scope.
set scope	Sets the scope to be used in subsequent operations.
set state	Sets/resets the state of the current scope to either an active or an inactive state.
set superscope	Sets the superscope to be used in subsequent operations.
show clients	Displays all available version 4 clients for the current scope.
show clientsv5	Displays all available version 5 clients for the current scope.
show excluderange	Displays all currently excluded ranges of IP addresses for the current scope.

(continued)

Table D.13   DHCP scope commands **(continued).**

Command	Description
show iprange	Displays all available address ranges for the current scope.
show optionvalue	Displays all option values that are set for the current scope.
show reservedip	Displays all currently reserved IP addresses for the current scope.
show reservedoptionvalue	Displays all currently set option values for a reserved client IP address in the current scope.
show scope	Displays information for the current scope.
show state	Displays the state (active or inactive) of the current scope.

DHCP Multicast Scope Commands

Table D.14 lists commands that can be used at the DHCP Server Network Shell prompt (dhcp server mscope>). To access this prompt, enter a multicast scope, identified by scope name, at the dhcp server> prompt.

Table D.14   DHCP multicast scope commands.

Command	Description
add excluderange	Adds a range of excluded addresses to the current multicast scope.
add iprange	Adds a range of IP addresses to the current multicast scope.
delete excluderange	Deletes an exclusion range of previously excluded IP addresses in the current multicast scope.
delete iprange	Deletes a range of IP addresses from the current multicast scope.
initiate reconcile	Checks and reconciles the current multicast scope.
set comment	Sets the comment for the current multicast scope.
set lease	Sets the lease duration for multicast scope IP addresses.
set mscope	Sets the multicast scope to be used in subsequent operations.
set name	Sets the name of the current multicast scope.
set state	Sets or resets the state of the current multicast scope.
set ttl	Sets the Time-to-Live (TTL) value for the current multicast scope.
show clients	Displays all available clients for the current multicast scope.
show excluderange	Displays all currently excluded ranges of IP addresses for the current multicast scope.
show iprange	Displays all available IP address ranges for the current multicast scope.
show lease	Displays the current lease duration settings for the multicast scope.

(continued)

Table D.14   DHCP multicast scope commands (continued).

Command	Description
show mibinfo	Displays Management Information Base (MIB) information for the current multicast scope.
show mscope	Displays information for the current multicast scope.
show state	Displays the state of the current multicast scope.
show ttl	Displays the TTL value for the current multicast scope.

WINS Commands

Network Shell commands can be used to configure and display WINS settings. These commands can be used as an alternative to console-based management.

First-Level WINS Commands

Table D.15 lists commands that can be used at the WINS Network Shell prompt (wins>). To access this prompt, enter **netsh** without any arguments at the command prompt, then enter **wins** without any arguments at the netsh> prompt. You can also enter these commands directly from the command prompt by preceding them with **netsh wins** (for example, **netsh wins dump**).

WINS Server Commands

Table D.16 lists commands that can be used at the WINS Network Shell server prompt (wins server>). To access this prompt, enter **server** at the command prompt. If you don't provide an argument to identify the server, the default WINS server will be used. You can also enter these commands directly from the command prompt by preceding them with **netsh wins server** (for example, **netsh wins server check database**).

Table D.15   First-level WINS commands.

Command	Description
list	Lists all available WINS commands.
dump	Dumps WINS server configuration to command output.

Table D.16   WINS server commands.

Command	Description
add name	Registers a name to the server.
add partner	Adds a replication partner to the server.
add pngserver	Adds a list of Persona Non Grata (PNG) servers for the current server.

(continued)

Table D.16 **WINS server commands** (continued).

Command	Description
check database	Checks the consistency of the database.
check name	Checks a list of name records against a set of WINS servers.
check version	Checks the consistency of the version number.
delete name	Deletes a registered name from the server database.
delete partner	Deletes a replication partner from the list of replication partners.
delete records	Deletes or tombstones all or a set of records from the server.
delete owners	Deletes a list of owners and their records.
delete pngserver	Deletes all or selected PNG servers from the list.
init backup	Initiates backup of the WINS database.
init import	Initiates import from an lmhosts file.
init pull	Initiates and sends a pull trigger to another WINS server.
init pullrange	Initiates and pulls a range of records from another WINS server.
init push	Initiates and sends a push trigger to another WINS server.
init replicate	Initiates replication of the database with replication partners.
init restore	Initiates restoring of the database from a file.
init scavenge	Initiates scavenging of the WINS database for the server.
init search	Initiates search on the WINS database for the server.
reset statistics	Resets the server statistics.
set autopartnerconfig	Sets the automatic replication partner configuration information for the server.
set backuppath	Sets the backup parameters for the server.
set burstparam	Sets the burst handling parameters for the server.
set logparam	Sets the database and event logging options.
set migrateflag	Sets the migration flag for the server.
set namerecord	Sets renewal, verification and extinction intervals, and extinction timeout for the server.
set periodicdbchecking	Sets periodic database checking parameters for the server.
set pullpartnerconfig	Sets the configuration parameters for the specified pull partner.
set pushpartnerconfig	Sets the configuration parameters for the specified push partner.
set pullparam	Sets the default pull parameters for the server.
set pushparam	Sets the default push parameters for the server.
set replicateflag	Sets the replication flag for the server.

(continued)

Appendix D The
Network Shell Utility

Table D.16   **WINS server commands** (continued).

Command	Description
set startversion	Sets the start version ID for the database.
show browser	Displays all active domain master browser [1Bh] records.
show database	Displays the database and records for the specified server.
show info	Displays configuration information.
show name	Displays detailed information for a particular record in the server.
show partner	Displays pull or push (or both) partners for the server.
show partnerproperties	Displays default partner configuration.
show pullpartnerconfig	Displays configuration information for a pull partner.
show pushpartnerconfig	Displays configuration information for a push partner.
show reccount	Displays number of records owned by a specific server.
show recbyversion	Displays, by version, the records owned by a specific server.
show server	Displays the currently selected server.
show statistics	Displays the statistics for the WINS server.
show version	Displays the current version counter value for the WINS server.
show versionmap	Displays the owner ID to Maximum Version Number (MVN) mappings.

Glossary

6bone—The Internet Protocol version 6 (IPv6) portion of the Internet.

802.1p—A Layer 2 (Data-link layer) Quality of Service mechanism that defines how devices such as Ethernet switches should prioritize traffic.

Acknowledgment (ACK)—A signal used in Transmission Control Protocol (TCP) operation.

Active Control List (ACL)—A list of entries in an Active Directory object's security descriptor that grant or deny specific access rights to individuals or groups.

Active Directory—The Windows 2000 hierarchical directory that stores domain security policy and account information.

Active Directory Service Interfaces (ADSI)—A Component Object Model (COM)-based directory service model that allows ADSI-compliant client applications to access a wide variety of directory protocols, including Active Directory and Lightweight Directory Access Protocol (LDAP), while using a single, standard set of interfaces.

Active Server Pages (ASP)—A server-side scripting environment that's used to create and run dynamic, interactive Web server applications.

Address Resolution Protocol (ARP)—Resolves Internet Protocol version 4 (IPv4) addresses to Media Access Control (MAC) addresses.

Adjacency—A logical relationship between neighboring Open Shortest Path First (OSPF) routers that's used to synchronize the link state database.

Advanced Research Projects Agency (ARPA)—This agency was created in 1968 and was funded to develop a high-speed, packet-switching communications network.

All Local Packet Filter—Prevents Network Monitor from monopolizing the Central Processing Unit (CPU).

American National Standards Institute (ANSI)—A group that defines standards for the information processing industry.

American Standard Code for Information Interchange (ASCII)—A code developed by the American National Standards Institute (ANSI) that encodes characters in 7-bit units. These units are normally padded with an eighth bit that can represent parity.

Answering router—The destination router in a Routing and Remote Access Service (RRAS) connection. If a Virtual Private Network (VPN) is used, the answering router is a tunnel endpoint.

Anycast—A message that's sent to a specific group of hosts, all of which share the same anycast address, but is processed only by the host that's closest to the sender in terms of route metric.

Application(s) Programming Interface (API)—Software designed to make computer functions available to an application (for example, Windows Sockets).

Area Border Routers (ABRs)—Connect the Open Shortest Path First (OSPF) backbone area to other areas.

Arp—A utility that's used to view and modify the Address Resolution Protocol (ARP) cache.

ARPAnet—The predecessor of the Word Wide Web.

Asymmetric cryptography—A cryptographic process in which two different keys are needed, one to encrypt, the other to decrypt. Together, the keys make up a private key/public key pair.

Asymmetric Digital Subscriber Line (ADSL)—A subscriber line with a high bandwidth in one direction and a lower bandwidth in the other. ADSLs can be used to advantage by (for example) remote access clients who download significantly more information than they upload.

Asynchronous Transfer Mode (ATM)—A cell-based data transfer technique that offers fast-packet technology; real-time, demand-led switching; and efficient use of network resources.

Audit policy—A policy set by an administrator that determines which events are written to Event Viewer's security log. Typically, a policy can be defined that records unsuccessful logon attempts and successful and unsuccessful access to sensitive files.

Authentication—Verification of a connection attempt's credentials.

Glossary

Authentication Header (AH)—A packet header that contains information that's used to authenticate the node that sent the packet (data authentication), verify that the data wasn't modified in transit (data integrity), and ensure that captured packets can't be retransmitted and accepted as valid data (anti-replay protection).

Authentication Service (AS) Exchange—A Kerberos subprotocol used when the Key Distribution Center (KDC) gives the client a logon session key and a Ticket Granting Ticket (TGT).

Authenticator—A piece of information encrypted using a secret key and containing a timestamp field.

Authorization—Verification that an authenticated connection attempt is allowed.

Automatic Private IP Addressing (APIPA)—An automatic IP address allocation system that's used if no other address allocation method is available. APIPA allocates addresses from 169.254.0.1 through 169.254.255.254. The subnet mask is set to 255.255.0.0. It's designed for networks that consist of a single network segment and aren't connected to the Internet.

Autonomous System (AS)—The Open Shortest Path First (OSPF) routers in an organization define an AS. By default, only OSPF routes that correspond to directly connected network segments are propagated within the AS.

Autonomous System Boundary Routers (ASBRs)—An ASBR advertises external routes within the Open Shortest Path First Autonomous System (OSPF AS).

Auto-static routes—Static routes that are automatically added to the route table for a router after routes are requested across a demand-dial connection by using version 2 of the Routing Internet Protocol (RIPv2).

Bandwidth Allocation Control Protocol (BACP)—A control and messaging protocol associated with Bandwidth Allocation Protocol (BAP).

Bandwidth Allocation Protocol (BAP)—Manages links dynamically over a Remote Access Service (RAS) multilink connection, adding and removing links as required by the level of network traffic.

Berkeley Internet Name Domain (BIND)—A Domain Name System (DNS). BIND version 8.1.2 is compatible with Windows 2000, but the Windows 2000 DNS is recommended because it can be integrated with Active Directory.

Berkley Software Distribution (BSD)—BSD Unix, released in September 1983, was the first software release to include TCP/IP protocols in its generic operating system.

Binding order—The order in which a Network Interface Card (NIC) driver or a service attempts to use the protocols to which it's bound.

Glossary

841

Bindings—Associations between protocols and Network Interface Card (NIC) drivers and, also, between protocols and services. Bindings can be enabled or disabled, and the binding order can be changed.

Biometrics—The use of a physical characteristic, such as a fingerprint or retina scan, to verify a user's identity. Used as an alternative to personal identity number (PIN) entry during smart card logon.

Black hole router—A router that silently drops IP datagrams that can't be fragmented.

BOOTP Relay Agent—A host or (more commonly) a BOOTP-enabled router that permits Dynamic Host Configuration Protocol (DHCP) to configure hosts on remote subnets.

Bootstrap Protocol (BOOTP)—Enables the dynamic assignment of IP addresses. BOOTP was designed principally for the configuration of diskless workstations and is a predecessor of Dynamic Host Configuration Protocol (DHCP).

Broadcast Media Extension—An extension to the Network Driver Interface Specification version 5 (NDIS5) that supports high-speed unidirectional broadcast media, such as Direct TV, PrimeStar, or Intercast.

Broadcast Personal Computer (PC)—Broadcast PC enables a computer to import and process multimedia streams from a variety of sources, including cable, direct broadcast satellite (DBS), and digital video disk (DVD).

Browser service—Identifies resources on a network and maintains a resource list so that browse clients can access these resources.

Calling router—The source router in a Routing and Remote Access Service (RRAS) connection. If a Virtual Private Network (VPN) is used, the calling router is a tunnel endpoint.

Certificate—A digitally signed statement dealing with a particular subject public key. Its issuer (holding another pair of private and public keys) signs the certificate. A certificate is also known as a *digital identity*.

Certificate Authority (CA)—An entity or service that issues certificates and acts as a guarantor of the binding between the subject public key and the subject identity information contained in the certificates that it issues.

Certificate chain—A certificate chain leads from one entity, and that entity's public key, through a series of Certificate Authorities (CAs), terminating in a certificate issued by someone that a second entity implicitly trusts. Such a certificate is called a *trusted root certificate*.

Certificate mapping—An association between a certificate and a user account.

Certificate Revocation List (CRL)—A list of revoked certificates against which a certificate-supported authentication request is checked. A cancelled or expired certificate must be placed on the CRL for its revocation to be effective.

Certificate Server—Microsoft Certificate Server provides customizable services for issuing and managing certificates for applications using public key cryptography. This enables a Windows 2000 domain to issue certificates internally and be its own Certificate Authority (CA).

Challenge Handshake Authentication Protocol (CHAP)—An encrypted authentication mechanism that avoids transmission of the actual password on the connection.

Character Generator (CHARGEN)—A TCP/IP Simple protocol service that sends the set of 95 printable ASCII characters. CHARGEN is used as a tool for testing or troubleshooting line printers.

Classless Interdomain Routing (CIDR)—Removes the concept of class from Internet Protocol (IP) address assignment and management. Instead of predefined classes (A, B, and C), CIDR allocations are defined by a starting address and a range.

Client/Server (CS) Exchange—A Kerberos subprotocol used when the client presents the session ticket for admission to a service.

Clustering—Allows multiple servers to be connected through clustering software so they appear as one computer. Clustering is available in Windows 2000 Advanced Server and increases fault tolerance, because another server can pick up the request load if one server stops working.

Convert—A utility that converts from the File Allocation Table (FAT) disk filing system to the New Technology Filing System (NTFS).

Cryptographic Application Programming Interface (CryptoAPI)—A standard interface to the cryptographic functionality supplied by Cryptographic Service Providers (CSPs). CryptoAPI includes a set of certificate management services that support X.509 version 3 standard certificates and provide persistent storage, enumeration services, and decoding support.

Cryptographic Service Provider (CSP)—An entity that provides cryptography services. CSPs may be software-based or may take advantage of cryptographic hardware devices.

Cryptography—The use of cryptographic algorithms that mathematically combine plaintext data and an encryption key to generate encrypted data (ciphertext). A decryption key is then used to derive the plaintext data from the ciphertext.

Glossary

Cyclic Redundancy Check (CRC)—A value that's calculated for a block of data and added to a frame that contains that data. On receipt of the frame, a remote host recalculates the CRC and checks that the transmitted CRC matches this calculation. This helps ensure data integrity.

Data Encryption Standard (DES)—A standard for encrypting data. 3DES uses three 128-bit keys. DES uses a single 56-bit key.

Data Encryption Standard-Cipher Block Chaining (DES-CBC)—A secret key algorithm used for confidentiality. A random number is generated and used with a secret key to encrypt data.

Daytime—A TCP/IP Simple protocol service that returns messages containing the day of the week, month, day, year, current time (in *hh:mm:ss* format), and time-zone information.

Dcpromo—A Run command that promotes a Windows 2000 server to a domain controller.

Dead gateway detection—Allows Transmission Control Protocol to detect a failure of the default gateway and to adjust the IP routing table so that another gateway is used.

Defense Advanced Research Projects Agency (DARPA)—This agency replaced ARPA in 1972.

Delegated Authentication—A proxy mechanism that allows a service to impersonate its client when connecting to other services.

DHCP scope—A range of IP addresses that can be assigned by Dynamic Host Configuration Protocol on a specific network.

Dial-up—A service that enables remote access through telephone lines, using either Point-to-Point Protocol (PPP) or Serial Line Internet Protocol (SLIP).

Differentiated Services (DiffServ)—A Layer 3 (Network layer) Quality of Service mechanism; it defines 6 bits in the IP header that determine how an IP packet is prioritized.

Diffie-Hellman (DH) Technique—A public key cryptography algorithm that allows two communicating entities to agree on a shared key. DH starts with two entities exchanging public information. Each entity then combines the other's public information with its own secret information to generate a shared-secret value.

Digital identity (Digital ID)—See *Certificate*.

Glossary

Digital signature—A digital signature ensures that data has been sent by the entity that purports to have sent it. It's based on a mathematical transform that combines the sender's private key with the data to be signed.

Discard—A TCP/IP Simple protocol service that discards all messages received on a port without response or acknowledgment. Discard is used to implement a null port for receiving and routing TCP/IP test messages during network setup and configuration.

Distance Vector Multicast Routing Protocol (DVMRP)—A multicast routing protocol used by a multicast router to propagate multicast group listening information to other multicast-capable routers.

Distributed File System (Dfs)—Unites files on different computers into a single namespace.

Domain Controller (DC)—A Windows 2000 Server that stores user and computer accounts, access control lists, and Active Directory information. There can be one or more DCs within a domain, all of which replicate this information with each other.

Domain Name System (DNS)—The locator service used on the Internet and in most private intranets. DNS is the most widely used directory service in the world.

Don't Fragment (DF)—A flag that indicates that an IP packet can't be fragmented.

Driver Development Kit (DDK)—A set of routines, functions, sample code, debugging tools, and documentation that can be downloaded to assist in writing miniport and transport drivers. For example, the Windows 2000 DDK can be downloaded from the Microsoft Developers Network download site.

Dynamic BOOTP—An extension of the Bootstrap Protocol (BOOTP) that enables a Dynamic Host Configuration Protocol (DHCP) server to configure BOOTP clients.

Dynamic Domain Name System (DDNS)—The Windows 2000 implementation of DNS that maintains a dynamic database of domain names and corresponding Internet Protocol (IP) addresses.

Dynamic Host Configuration Protocol (DHCP)—A protocol that dynamically assigns IP addresses and other configuration parameters.

Echo—A TCP/IP Simple protocol service that echoes data from any messages it receives on a server port. Echo is used as a network debugging and monitoring tool.

Glossary

Encapsulated Security Payload (ESP)—A header and trailer that provide data authentication and integrity services for an encapsulated payload.

Enterprise root Certificate Authority (CA)—This CA forms the root of a Windows 2000-based corporate CA hierarchy. It issues certificates to users and computers within a corporation.

Enterprise subordinate Certificate Authority (CA)—This CA issues certificates within a corporation, but isn't the most trusted CA in that corporation, because it is subordinate to another CA in the hierarchy.

EUI-64 address—A 64-bit hardware address defined by the Institute of Electrical and Electronic Engineers (IEEE). EUI-64 addresses are either assigned to Network Interface Cards (NICs) or derived from 48-bit Media Access Control (MAC) addresses.

Event Viewer—A debugging and information-gathering tool that maintains logs that gather information about hardware, software, and system problems and about audit events specified by the audit policy.

Extensible Authentication Protocol (EAP)—A protocol used for user authentication.

Extensible Authentication Protocol Transport Layer Security (EAP-TLS)—A strong authentication method based on public key certificates.

Extensible Markup Language (XML)—Provides semantic rules that describe the complex structure of data or documents in the same way that Hypertext Markup Language (HTML) describes the format of a Web document.

External Data Representation (XDR) functions—Functions that are used by (for example) Remote Procedure Calls (RPCs) to ensure that data is represented on the network in a standard fashion and is readable at both ends.

Fast forward path—Another term for fast packet forwarding.

Fast packet forwarding—Occurs when either multiport or single-port network adapters, such as 802.3, FastEthernet, or Fiber Distributed Data Interface (FDDI), are used with Windows 2000 routing code to forward packets from one port to another on the same or a similar adapter card without passing the packet to the host processor.

Fiber Distributed Data Interface (FDDI)—An optical fiber-based token-passing ring Local Area Network (LAN) technology with dual, counter-rotating rings.

File Allocation Table (FAT)—A disk filing system provided for compatibility with Windows 9*x*, Windows 3.*x*, and MS-DOS operating systems. Windows 2000 supports both FAT16 and FAT32.

Glossary

File Transfer Protocol (FTP)—An applications-level protocol that runs over Transmission Control Protocol (TCP) and is used to transfer files from one computer to another over a network.

Finger—A connectivity utility that's used to obtain information about a user currently logged on to a remote host.

Firewire—See *IEEE 1394*.

Flow control—Internet Control Message Protocol (ICMP) controls data flow by using source quench messages. If a host sends datagrams to a target at a rate that's saturating the routers or links between them, it receives source quench message asking it to slow down.

Forest—Two or more domain trees connected through trust relationships between the root domains.

Fortezza—A U.S. government security standard that satisfies the Defense Message System security architecture requirements. Fortezza offers a cryptographic mechanism that provides message confidentiality, integrity, authentication, nonrepudiation, and access control to messages, components, and systems.

Forwarded Ticket—A Kerberos Ticket Granting Ticket (TGT) with the FORWARDABLE flag set. If a client wants to delegate the task of obtaining tickets for back-end servers to a front-end server, it asks the Key Distribution Center (KDC) for a forwarded TGT.

Ftp—A connectivity utility that uses File Transfer Protocol (FTP) to copy files from and to a remote computer.

Fully Qualified Domain Name (FQDN)—A dot-delimited host name that uniquely identifies a host within the total domain namespace; for example, **www.microsoft.com**.

Generic Quality-of-Service (GQoS)—An extension to the Windows Sockets Application Programming Interface. GQoS provides applications with a method of reserving network bandwidth between client and server.

Graphical Identification and Authentication (GINA)—A dynamic link library (DLL) that's responsible for collecting logon data from the user, packaging it in a data structure, and sending it to the Local Security Authority (LSA) for verification.

Graphical User Interface (GUI)—A screen display with which a user interacts during a computer session. GUIs make use of Windows, Icons, Menus, and Pointers (WIMP) in such systems as Microsoft Windows.

Glossary

Group Policy—Settings contained in a Group Policy Object (GPO), which can then be applied to Active Directory objects, such as sites, domains, or Organizational Units (OUs).

Group Policy Editor—A tool provided by the Group Policy Microsoft Management Console (MMC) snap-in to edit Group Policy Objects (GPOs).

Group Policy Object (GPO)—An Active Directory object that contains group policies; for example, security policy. GPO settings can be applied to sites, domains, or Organizational Units (OUs).

Hash Message Authentication Code (HMAC)—A secret key algorithm that uses a keyed hash function to produce a digital signature, which can be verified by the receiver. If the message changes in transit, the hash value is different and the IP packet is rejected.

Host group—A number of hosts identified by a single IP destination address.

Host header names—Used with a single Internet Protocol address to enable an Internet Information Service (IIS) server to host multiple Web sites.

Hostname—A utility that returns a computer's host name.

Hosts file—A static file that can be used for host name resolution.

HTTP compression—Enhances the transmission of pages between the Web server and compression-enabled clients and is particularly useful where bandwidth is limited.

HTTP Header—Enables a Web server to return values to a client browser in the header of the Hypertext Markup Language (HTML) page.

HTTP Keep-Alives—Allow a client to maintain an open connection with a Web server rather than reopening the connection with each new request.

Hypertext Markup Language (HTML)—A set of semantic rules that describe the format of a Web document.

Hypertext Transport Protocol (HTTP)—The de facto standard for transferring World Wide Web documents over networks. The current version is HTTP1.1.

IEEE 1394—The Institute of Electrical and Electronic Engineers Firewire standard for peripheral devices.

IEEE 802 address—See *Media Access Control (MAC) address*.

Industry Standard Architecture (ISA)—An 8/16-bit bus architecture that's standard on Intel X86 computers.

Information (INF) file—A text file that contains all the necessary information about devices and files to be installed. Plug and Play (PnP) uses INF files for dynamic device configuration.

Infrared Data Association (IrDA)—A group of device manufacturers that publishes a standard for transmitting data via infrared light waves.

Institute of Electrical and Electronics Engineers (IEEE)—A professional organization, one of whose remits is to develop and publish standards (such as IEEE 802.3). The IEEE also allocates the first 24 bits of Media Access Control (MAC) addresses to Network Interface Card (NIC) manufacturers.

Integrated Services Digital Network (ISDN)—A worldwide digital communications network that evolved from existing telephone lines.

Integrated Services over Asynchronous Transfer Medium (ISATM)—A Quality of Service (QoS) mechanism that automatically maps Generic QoS (GQoS) requests to ATM QoS on Internet Protocol over ATM networks.

Integrated Services over Low Bit Rate (ISSLOW)—A Quality of Service (QoS) mechanism that improves latency for prioritized traffic on slow Wide Area Network (WAN) links.

Interior Gateway Protocol (IGP)—Any protocol that's used to propagate network reachability and routing information within an autonomous system. For example, Routing Internet Protocol (RIP) is an IGP.

Intermediate Certificate Authority—See *Subordinate Certificate Authority*.

International Standards Organization Open Systems Interconnection (ISO OSI) seven-layer model—A conceptual model that uses a seven-layer architecture to standardize levels of service and types of interaction for hosts exchanging information over a network.

Internet Assigned Numbers Authority (IANA)—The organization that assigns and manages Internet Protocol (IP) addresses.

Internet Authentication Service (IAS)—A Remote Authentication Dial-in User Service (RADIUS) server that a Routing and Remote Access (RRAS) server can use as its authentication and/or accounting provider.

Internet Control Message Protocol (ICMP)—A protocol that provides maintenance and routing facilities for the Internet Protocol (IP).

Internet Engineering Task Force (IETF)—A standards-setting body responsible for defining (for example) the Public Key Infrastructure X.509 (PKIX) draft standards.

Glossary

Internet Group Management Protocol (IGMP)—A protocol that provides support for Internet Protocol version 4 (IPv4) multicasting.

Internet Protocol (IP)—An unreliable, connectionless, routable, low-level protocol that controls packet sorting and delivery over both intranets and the Internet. Windows 2000 supports both IP version 4 (IPv4) and IP version 6 (IPv6).

Internet Protocol–next generation (Ipng)—Internet Protocol version 6 (IPv6).

Internet Protocol (IP) address—A 32-bit (IPv4) or 128-bit (IPv6) binary number that's used to uniquely identify a host and its network.

Internet Protocol (IP) Authentication Header (AH)—Provides integrity, authentication, and anti-replay by using an algorithm to compute a keyed message hash (Hash Message Authentication Code) for each IP packet.

Internet Protocol Encapsulating Security Protocol (IESP)—Provides confidentiality, using the Data Encryption Standard-Cipher Block Chaining (DES-CBC) algorithm.

Internet Protocol Security (IPSec)—A Network layer (Layer 3) protocol, invisible to the user, that uses industry-standard encryption algorithms and a comprehensive security management approach to provide security for all TCP/IP communications on both sides of an organization's firewall.

Internet Protocol version 6 (IPv6)—A version of IP that uses 128 bits, or 16 octets, to define addresses.

Internet Router Discovery Protocol (IRDP)—Provides a method of discovering and configuring default gateways. IRDP is implemented as part of Internet Control Message Protocol (ICMP).

Internet Security Association and Key Management Protocol (ISAKMP)—ISAKMP defines a common framework to support the establishment of Security Associations.

Internet Service Provider (ISP)—A third-party organization that provides connections to the World Wide Web.

Internetwork Diameter—The diameter of an internetwork is a measure of its size in terms of hops or other metrics.

Internetwork Packet Exchange (IPX)—A protocol used (principally) by Novell networks. IPX performs similar functions to Internet Protocol (IP).

IP helper—An Application Programming Interface (API) that prevents Internet Protocol (IP) datagrams from being dropped when a User Datagram Protocol

(UDP)-based application sends multiple datagrams to a single destination address without any pauses between them.

Ipconfig—A utility that determines a host's MAC address, IP address, subnet mask, default gateway address, WINS server address, and so on. Ipconfig can be used to release and renew a dynamically allocated IP configuration.

IPSec Tunnel Mode—Encrypts IP payloads, encapsulates them in an IP header, and sends them across an IP network, such as the Internet.

ISAPI filter—A program that responds to events during the processing of a Hypertext Transfer Protocol (HTTP) request. ISAPI is an acronym for Internet Server Application Programming Interface.

Issuing Certificate Authority—See *Subordinate Certificate Authority*.

Kerberos—A three-headed dog that guards the gates of the Underworld. The Kerberos authentication protocol uses a shared secret between two principals, which is distributed by a trusted third party or Key Distribution Center.

Kerberos 5—A shared secret, industry standard Internet security protocol. The default Windows 2000 primary authentication protocol.

Kerberos trust—A two-way, transitive trust that's created automatically when a domain is added to a domain tree.

Key Distribution Center (KDC)—A trusted intermediary in a shared secret protocol (such as Kerberos 5) that issues secret keys (or *key pads*).

Key pad—A secret key known to two, and only two, entities.

Large TCP Windows—An optional TCP feature that recalculates and scales the TCP Window size dynamically and can improve TCP/IP performance when large amounts of data are in transit.

Layer 2 Tunneling Protocol (L2TP)—Encrypts IP, IPX, or NetBEUI traffic, then sends it over any medium that supports point-to-point datagram delivery, such as IP, X.25, Frame Relay, or Asynchronous Transfer Mode (ATM).

Lightweight Directory Access Protocol (LDAP)—A protocol that requires the operating system to enforce access control.

Line Printer Daemon (LPD)—The Unix print redirector. If LPD is installed on a Windows 2000 print server, that server can accept print jobs from a Unix host.

Line Printer Queue (LPQ)—The Unix service for managing print queues.

Line Printer Remote (LPR)—The Unix print service.

Link state database—A map of an internetwork that's maintained by Open Shortest Path First (OSPF) routers and updated after any change to the network topology.

Lmhosts file—A static file that can be used for remote NetBIOS name resolution.

Local Area Network (LAN)—A communications system that links computers and other devices into a network, usually via a wiring-based cable scheme. Computers on a LAN are on the same Logical IP Subnet (LIS), although a LAN may have gateways to other networks, including the Internet.

Local Security Authority (LSA)—A service that checks a user's logon credentials.

Locator—A service that translates a domain name (for example, **www.mycompany. com**) into an Internet Protocol (IP) address.

Logical IP Subnet (LIS)—A LIS is defined by a set of Internet Protocol (IP) addresses and a subnet mask. All devices on a LIS can communicate with each other without passing messages through a router.

Logon session key—A session key that's valid only until the Ticket Granting Ticket (TGT) expires or the user logs off.

Long Fat Network (LFN)—A network where the Transmission Control Protocol (TCP) buffer space is too small for efficient transmission, but can't be increased because it's at the maximum window size that the protocol allows. LFN (in this case) is pronounced "elephant."

Long File Name (LFN)—A file name that exceeds the 8.3 length restriction imposed by some operating systems. LFN (in this case) is pronounced "ell eff en."

Lpq—A utility that queries the print job list (or print queue) of a Line Printer Daemon (LPD) print server.

Lpr—A utility that uses Line Printer Remote (LPR) to sends print jobs to remote Unix printers managed by Line Printer Daemon (LPD) print server software.

Magic Packet—A specific frame that's sent to a node or station on the network. When the network controller receives a magic packet frame, it will alert the system to wake up.

Mailslot—A second-class, unreliable mechanism for sending a message from one computer to another over User Datagram Protocol (UDP), where both computers are identified by their NetBIOS names.

Management Information Base (MIB)—Contains various types of information about a network host. Simple Network Management Protocol (SNMP) agents send the information held in MIBs to SNMP management systems.

Maximum Segment Size (MSS)—A value held in a Transmission Control Protocol (TCP) field that indicates the maximum segment size for a link. Historically, the MSS for a host has been the Maximum Transmission Unit (MTU) at the link layer minus 40 bytes for the IP and TCP headers. However, Windows 2000 support for additional TCP options has increased the typical TCP+IP header to 52 or more bytes. The MSS is used in Path Maximum Transmission Unit (PMTU) discovery.

Maximum Transmission Unit (MTU)—The size of the largest data packet that can be sent over a single link without fragmentation.

Media Access Control (MAC) address—A 48-bit address used by network hardware devices, such as Network Interface Cards (NICs). MAC addresses are sometimes termed IEEE 802 addresses.

Media sense support—Enables the Network Interface Card (NIC) to notify media connect and media disconnect events to the protocol stack.

Message Digest Algorithms (MD2, MD4, and MD5)—Hash functions used for digital signature applications where a large message has to be compressed in a secure manner before being signed with a private key.

Message Digest Function 95 (MD5)—A hash function that produces a 128-bit value.

Messaging Application Programming Interface (MAPI)—The Windows Open Services Architecture (WOSA) Messaging API.

Metabase—A hierarchical structure for storing Internet Information Service (IIS) configuration settings. It provides easier administration and requires less disk space than the Registry.

Microsoft Challenge Handshake Authentication Protocol (MSCHAP)—An encrypted authentication mechanism that avoids transmission of the actual password on the connection. MSCHAP is very similar to CHAP, except that it provides an additional level of security because it allows the server to store hashed rather than clear-text passwords. MSCHAP v2 is similar to MSCHAP, but runs only on Windows 2000 machines.

Microsoft Developers Network (MSDN&trade)—Provides tools and information to assist software development.

Glossary

Microsoft Graphical Identification and Authentication (MSGINA)—See *Graphical Identification and Authentication (GINA)*.

Microsoft Management Console (MMC)—Provides a universal Graphical User Interface (GUI) for administering Windows 2000. Individual tools for specific purposes run under the MMC framework and are known as MMC snap-ins.

Microsoft Point-to-Point Encryption (MPPE)—An encryption method based on the Rivest-Shamir-Adleman (RSA) RC4 algorithm.

Microsoft RAS protocol—Used by Windows NT3.1, Windows for Workgroups, MS-DOS, and LAN Manager Remote Access Service clients.

MILnet—A U.S. Department of Defense TCP/IP network developed in parallel with ARPAnet. Under normal circumstances, MILnet is part of the Internet.

Miniport Call Manager (MCM)—Controls a Network Interface Card (NIC) that has on-board connection-oriented protocol-signaling capabilities.

Multicast—A message that's sent to a specific group of hosts, all of which share the same multicast address.

Multicast Address Dynamic Client Allocation Protocol (MADCAP)—A protocol that supports multicast scopes and defines how MADCAP servers can provide Internet Protocol (IP) addresses dynamically to MADCAP clients.

Multicast backbone (Mbone)—The multicast-capable portion of the Internet.

Multicast Heartbeat—A regular multicast notification to a specified group address that's used to verify that IP multicast connectivity is available on a network.

Multicast Server (MCS)—Manages the shared or group use of multicast Internet Protocol (IP) addresses and streams data traffic to members that share the use of the specified group address.

Multihomed—A computer that's configured with more than one Internet Protocol (IP) address is multihomed.

Multiple adapter model—A model used when dynamically routing nonbroadcast technology (for example, Frame Relay) networks. Each Frame Relay virtual circuit appears as a point-to-point link with its own network identity, and all endpoints are assigned IP addresses.

Multipurpose Internet Mail Extensions (MIME) mappings—Specify the file types that a Web server returns to client browsers.

Glossary

Mutual Authentication—A feature of the Kerberos 5 protocol that ensures that parties at both ends of a network connection know that the party on the other end is who it claims to be.

Nagle algorithm—An algorithm used by Transmission Control Protocol (TCP) to reduce the number of very small segments sent, especially on slow remote links.

Named pipe—A connection used to transfer data between separate processes, usually on separate computers.

Nbtstat—A utility that returns NetBIOS over TCP/IP information, such as the names that applications registered locally on the system.

Neighbor Discovery (ND) protocol—A series of Internet Control Message Protocol for Internet Protocol version 6 (ICMPv6) messages that manage the interaction of nodes on the same link.

NetBIOS Name Service (NBNS)—A service that resolves NetBIOS names to IP addresses. Microsoft Windows uses the Windows Internet Name Service (WINS) as an NBNS.

NetBIOS over TCP/IP (NetBT)—Implements the NetBIOS programming interface over the TCP/IP protocol, thus extending the reach of NetBIOS client and server programs to Wide Area Networks (WANs) and providing interoperability between Windows 2000 and such operating systems as Windows NT4 and Windows $9x$.

Netdiag—A diagnostic tool that isolates networking and connectivity problems by checking all aspects of a host computer's network configuration and connections. Netdiag is part of the Windows 2000 Resource Kit.

Netstat—A utility that displays protocol statistics and current TCP/IP connections.

Network Address Translation (NAT)—A service that's used to protect a corporate intranet by converting internal intranet IP addresses to legal Internet IP addresses at a firewall or other NAT device. In Windows 2000, NAT is integrated with the operating system and doesn't require a separate server.

Network Basic Input/Output System (NetBIOS)—Defines a software interface and a naming convention. NetBIOS names consist of 15 characters that define the name and a 16th character that defines the name type.

Network Basic Input/Output System Enhanced User Interface (NetBEUI)—A broadcast-based nonroutable protocol used by Local Area Networks (LANs).

Glossary

Network Control Protocol (NCP)—A first-generation protocol used by ARPAnet in the 1970s.

Network Device Interface Specification (NDIS)—A document developed by Microsoft and 3Com. Windows device driver interfaces written to this specification enable a single Network Interface Card (NIC) to bind to multiple network protocols across the NDIS interface. Windows 2000 supports NDIS version 5 (NDIS5).

Network Dynamic Data Exchange (NetDDE)—A facility that uses NetBIOS Application Programming Interfaces to communicate with underlying network components and thus maintains a link between client and server applications.

Network Filing System (NFS)—A set of standards published by Sun Microsystems. NFS is designed to utilize the TCP/IP stack, although it uses User Datagram Protocol (UDP) rather than Transport Control Protocol (TCP) as its transport protocol. (See *Open Network Computing.*)

Network Interface Card (NIC)—Hardware that translates binary data to electrical signals, and vice versa. A NIC puts signals on to and pulls signals from a network.

Network load balancing clusters—Provide scalability and availability with clusters of up to 32 servers.

Network Monitor—A tool that's used to monitor network traffic. The standard version of Network Monitor supplied with Windows 2000 Server enables you to monitor all traffic to and from the server on which it's running. A full version of Network Monitor, supplied with Microsoft System Management Server (SMS), enables you to monitor all network traffic on your server's subnet.

Network News Transfer Protocol (NNTP)—Used for the distribution, browsing, retrieval, and posting of news articles using a reliable, stream-based transmission protocol such as Transmission Control Protocol (TCP).

Network Operating System (NOS)—An operating system that supports internetworking; for example, Microsoft Windows 2000.

Network shell (netsh)—A utility that provides a wide range of commands that enable Windows 2000 configuration from the Command Console or through batch files.

New Technology Filing System (NTFS)—A disk filing system that allows local file security, auditing, and NTFS file compression. NTFS is the recommended Windows 2000 disk filing system.

Non-Broadcast Multiple Access (NBMA) model—A model used when dynamically routing nonbroadcast technology (for example, Frame Relay) networks. The Frame Relay service provider's network, or Frame Relay cloud, is treated as an Internet Protocol (IP) network, and its endpoints are assigned IP addresses. This is also known as the single adapter model.

Nslookup—A utility that's used for troubleshooting Domain Name System (DNS) problems, such as host name resolution.

NT LAN Manager (NTLM)—A security protocol that's used in mixed environments and supported by Windows 2000 for compatibility with downstream operating systems, such as Windows NT4.

NWLink—Microsoft's 32-bit implementation of Internetwork Packet Exchange/Sequenced Packet Exchange (IPX/SPX). NWLink is used for communication with Novell NetWare hosts.

Oakley—A key determination protocol that uses the Diffie-Hellman (DH) key exchange algorithm. Oakley supports Perfect Forward Secrecy (PFS).

Offload-IPSec—A feature that enables a Network Interface Card (NIC) to perform Internet Protocol Security (IPSec) encryption processing.

Offload-TCP—A feature that enables a Network Interface Card (NIC) to perform Transmission Control Protocol (TCP) checksum calculations.

OnNow specification—Defines four device power states from D0 (fully on) through D3 (fully off).

Open Network Computing (ONC)—A set of standards published by Sun Microsystems. The ONC standards are better known as the Network Filing System (NFS).

Open Shortest Path First (OSPF)—A protocol that dynamically discovers routes and builds routing tables. OSPF is used in large, complex internetworks.

Organizational Unit (OU)—An Active Directory component that can contain users, groups, and computers.

Out-of-band signaling—Transmits an additional signal alongside the information signal to monitor and control the transmission. It uses a separate channel of the local area network (LAN) and allows network management devices to access LAN devices even when the LAN itself isn't functioning.

Packet Scheduler—A system component involved in Quality of Service (QoS) and Resource Reservation Protocol (RSVP).

Glossary

Password Authentication Protocol (PAP)—A clear-text authentication scheme that returns the user name and password in clear text (unencrypted).

Path Maximum Transmission Unit (PMTU)—The size of the largest data packet that can be sent over a path, or series of links, without fragmentation.

PathPing—A utility that traces the route a packet takes to a destination and displays information on packet losses for each router in the path.

Payload—The data to be transferred across a network.

Peer Web Services—A facility that's provided with Windows 2000 Professional to implement Web-publishing services similar to those offered by the Internet Information Service, but for 10 simultaneous connections or fewer.

Per hop behaviors (PHBs)—Traffic priority classes. Differentiated Services (DiffServ) traffic can be prioritized into 64 PHBs.

Perfect Forward Secrecy (PFS)—PFS ensures that if a single key is compromised, access is permitted only to data protected by that single key.

Performance Logs and Alerts—A debugging and data collection tool that supports detailed monitoring of the utilization of operating system resources and logs performance data from local or remote computers.

Peripheral Channel Interconnect (PCI)—A bus architecture standard.

Peripheral router—A router attached to multiple networks, only one of which has a neighboring router.

Permanent Virtual Circuit (PVC)—A fixed virtual circuit between two users. No call setup or clearing procedures are required.

Personal Computer Memory Card International Association (PCMCIA)—An organization that defines standards for PC hardware.

Personal Identity Number (PIN)—A four-digit number used to confirm the identity of a smart card user.

Ping—A utility that verifies IP-level reachability. The **ping** command can be used to send an Internet Control Message Protocol (ICMP) echo request to a target name or IP address. Ping was originally an acronym for Packet Internet Groper, but is now a computer term in its own right.

Plug and Play (PnP)—A facility that enables dynamic recognition of installed hardware and streamlined hardware configuration.

Point-to-Point Protocol (PPP)—A set of industry-standard framing and authentication protocols that enable Remote Access Service (RAS) clients to access remote networks through any server that complies with the PPP standard.

Point-to-Point Tunneling Protocol (PPTP)—Encrypts IP, IPX, or NetBEUI traffic, encapsulates it in an IP header, and sends it across an IP network, such as the Internet.

Post Office Protocol version 3 (POP3)—Permits a client with limited resources to access a maildrop on a server dynamically and (typically) to retrieve mail that the server is holding for it. The protocol requires few resources and has limited functionality.

Procedures for Internet/Enterprise Renumbering (PIER) group—An Internet Engineering Task Force (IETF) working group that's looking at issues such as address ownership versus address leasing. The PIER group is also charged with the task of developing a renumbering strategy.

Promiscuous mode—When a Network Interface Card (NIC) is put into promiscuous mode, this inhibits the initial hardware filtering so that every frame the host detects on the network is indicated. This enables a network sniffer, such as Network Monitor, to capture all the traffic on a subnet.

Protocol—A set of rules by which one network entity communicates with another.

Proxy Ticket—Enables one application to impersonate another, even when it's calling a third application. See also *Delegated Authentication*.

Public Key Cryptography—Cryptography using asymmetric encryption and decryption keys. An encryption key converts plaintext into ciphertext. A decryption key (related but not identical to the encryption key) turns the ciphertext back into plaintext. Thus, every user has a pair of keys, consisting of a public key and a private key.

Public Key Cryptography for Initial Authentication in Kerberos (PKINIT)—A protocol that integrates public key-based authentication with the Windows 2000 Kerberos access-control system.

Public Key Cryptography Standards (PKCS)—A set of industry standards based on Rivest-Shamir-Adleman (RSA) public key ciphers. PKCS#10 defines certificate-request messages. PKCS#7 defines responses containing the resulting certificate or certificate chain. A PKCS#12 message contains a private/public key pair that's encrypted using a password.

Glossary

Public Key Infrastructure (PKI)—The Windows 2000 PKI provides an integrated set of services and administrative tools for creating, deploying, and managing public key-based applications using public key cryptography.

Public Key Infrastructure X.509 (PKIX)—A set of draft standards drawn up by the Internet Engineering Task Force (IETF).

QoS Admission Control Service (QoS ACS)—Gives network administrators control over which hosts on a network get which levels of Quality of Service.

Quality of Service (QoS)—A set of service requirements that a network must meet to assure an adequate service level for data transmission. Implementing QoS enables real-time programs to make efficient use of network bandwidth.

Quote of the Day (QUOTE)—A TCP/IP Simple protocol service that returns a quotation as one or more lines of text in a message.

Rcp—A connectivity utility that uses Remote Copy Protocol (RCP) to copy files from one computer to another. The main function of this utility is to copy files between Windows 2000 and Unix computers.

Read Only Memory (ROM)—A memory device that holds data that can't be changed programmatically and aren't deleted on power-down.

Real Time Control Protocol—Provides services to Real-Time Transport Protocol (RTP). The primary function of RTCP is to provide information about the quality of data distribution to an application.

Realm—The Kerberos equivalent of a Windows 2000 domain.

Real-Time Streaming Protocol (RTSP)—Streams multimedia data in one-to-many applications over unicast and multicast and supports interoperability between clients and servers from different vendors.

Real-Time Transport Protocol (RTP)—Provides end-to-end delivery services to support applications that transmit real-time data.

Redirector—A Local Area Network (LAN) device driver that translates operating system requests into network events and transmits them (sometimes through an interface) to the appropriate protocol stack.

Referral Ticket—A Ticket Granting Ticket (TGT) encrypted with the interdomain key that the Key Distribution Center (KDC) in one domain shares with the KDC in another. Referral tickets are used during cross-domain authentication.

Registry—A computer's configuration database.

Registry Editor—A tool typically used in read-only mode to get information from the Registry. It can be used to configure and debug a local or a remote computer. It should be used with care.

Reliable Restart—An Internet Information Service version 5 (IISv5) feature that implements a one-step restart process. There's no need to reboot, nor is it necessary to start separate services manually.

Remote Access Service (RAS)—Enables remote clients to log on to a network using validated accounts and to use network resources as if they were logged on to a host on that network. Windows 2000 RAS is part of the integrated Routing and Remote Access Service (RRAS).

Remote Authentication Dial-in User Service (RADIUS)—A service used to manage remote user authentication and authorization. Typically, RADIUS is used in a large network with a number of Virtual Private Network (VPN) servers.

Remote Copy Protocol (RCP)—A protocol used to copy files from one computer to another. The Rcp connectivity utility uses RCP to copy files between Windows 2000 and Unix computers.

Remote Procedure Call (RPC)—The mechanism by which an application on a client calls a function on a server.

Renewable Kerberos Ticket—A Kerberos ticket in which the RENEWABLE flag is set. This enables session keys to be refreshed periodically without issuing a completely new ticket.

Replay Attack—An attempt by a malignant third party to impersonate one of the parties sharing a secret key by capturing and replaying an authenticator.

Request for Comments (RFC)—RFC documents define and describe Internet protocols and related services.

Resource Records—Domain Name System (DNS) records. Examples are the Start of Authority (SOA) record, the Name Server (NS) record, the host address (A) record, and the Pointer (PTR) record that's typically used for reverse lookup.

Resource Reservation Protocol (RSVP)—A Layer 3 signaling protocol used to reserve bandwidth for individual flows on a network.

Rexec—A connectivity utility that runs a process on a remote computer.

RIP Listener—A Routing Internet Protocol version 1 (RIPv1) silent component provided by Windows 2000 Professional.

Rivest-Sharmir-Adelman (RSA)—An organization that develops and defines hash algorithms, public key ciphers, and other cryptography standards.

Glossary

Rogue DHCP Server Detection—A Windows 2000 enhancement that prevents unauthorized, or rogue, Dynamic Host Configuration Protocol (DHCP) servers from creating address assignment conflicts.

Root domain—The first (or top) domain in a domain tree.

Route—A utility that's used to view or modify the route table.

Route metric—The cost of a route through an internetwork. Route metric measures hop count, or the number of routers that a packet passes through to get to a destination. Some hops that involve slow links can be allocated a metric greater than one.

Router discovery—A method of enabling hosts to discover routers on their subnet dynamically and to detect default gateways.

Routing and Remote Access Service (RRAS)—A service that implements remote access, through either telephone lines or Virtual Private Networks.

Routing Internet Protocol (RIP)—A protocol that dynamically discovers routes and builds routing tables. Windows 2000 supports RIP versions 1 and 2.

Rsh (Remote shell)—A connectivity utility that runs commands on a remote Unix host.

Scavenging—The deletion of stale records in a database.

Script—A batch (BAT), command (CMD), or executable (EXE) file that runs when a computer starts up or shuts down, or whenever a user logs on or off at any type of workstation on the network.

Secedit—A command-line tool for configuring and analyzing local computer settings based on a set of security templates.

Secret Key Cryptography—Communication partners share a cryptographic key and use knowledge of this key to verify one another's identity. See also *Symmetric Key*.

Secure Attention Sequence (SAS)—In Windows 2000 (and NT4), this is Ctrl+Alt+Delete. Inserting a smart card also generates an SAS.

Secure Channel (SChannel)—A CryptoAPI-based service that supports network authentication and encryption using the industry-standard Transport Layer Security (TLS) and Secure Sockets Layer (SSL) protocols.

Secure Hash Algorithm (SHA) 1—A hash function that produces a 160-bit value.

Glossary

Secure HTTP (HTTPS)—Uses the Secure Sockets Layer version 3 (SSL3) and Transport Layer Security (TLS) protocols over Hypertext Transport Protocol to implement a secure method of transferring Web documents over a network.

Secure Sockets Layer version 3 (SSL3)—A security protocol used to encrypt Internet browser traffic and implement secure Internet sites. See also *Transport Layer Security (TLS)*.

Secure Sockets Layer version 3/Transport Layer Security (SSL3/TLS)—See *Transport Layer Security (TLS)*.

Security Association (SA)—Defines the common security services, mechanisms, and keys used to protect a communication from source to destination.

Security Group Filtering—The Active Control List (ACL) Editor can be used to filter the effect of policies within a Group Policy Object (GPO), depending on the security group membership of a user or computer account.

Security host—An authentication device that verifies whether a user at a remote Access Service (RAS) client is authorized to connect to a Routing and Remote Access (RRAS) server. The security host sits between the client and the server and provides an extra layer of security by requiring a hardware key to provide authentication.

Security Parameters Index (SPI)—A unique identifier used to distinguish between multiple security associations (SAs) that exist at the receiving computer.

Security Support Provider (SSP)—A component of the Kerberos protocol that enables the Local Security Authority in one domain to communicate directly with the Key Distribution Center (KDC) in another.

Security Support Provider Interface (SSPI)—The Win32 interface between transport level applications and network security service providers. SSPI Application Programming Interfaces (APIs) integrate authentication, message integrity, and privacy into distributed applications.

Selective Acknowledgment (SACK)—Conveys extended acknowledgment information from the receiver to the sender over an established TCP connection.

Sequenced Packet Exchange (SPX)—A protocol used (principally) by Novell networks. SPX performs similar functions to Transmission Control Protocol (TCP).

Serial Line Internet Protocol (SLIP)—A Remote Access Service (RAS) protocol that's typically used by Unix RAS servers. Windows 2000, NT4, and NT3.5 RAS clients support SLIP and can connect to a RAS server using the SLIP standard. A Windows 2000 RRAS server doesn't support SLIP clients.

Glossary

Server clusters—Provide availability through the failover clustering of two connected servers.

Server Message Block (SMB)—A distributed system that enables access to another computer's files and peripherals over a network as if they were local.

Session key—A unique, short-term secret key for two parties to use when they authenticate each other for a single communication session. See also *Logon session key*.

Session ticket—A data structure in which the server copy of a session key is embedded, along with information about the client. The entire structure is then encrypted with the key that the Key Distribution Center (KDC) shares with the server. The client uses the ticket when it contacts the server.

Shiva Password Authentication Protocol (SPAP)—An authentication mechanism used in a mixed environment to support clients using Shiva LAN Rover software.

Shortest Path First (SPF)—An algorithm used by the Open Shortest Path First (OSPF) protocol to generate route tables.

Silent RIP—A silent Routing Internet Protocol (RIP) host processes received RIP announcements, but doesn't broadcast RIP advertisements. The RIP announcements are used to build the routing table for the host.

Silly Window Syndrome (SWS)—A problem that occurs when a receiver advances the right Transmission Control Protocol (TCP) window edge whenever it has any new buffer space available to receive data, and when the sender uses any incremental window (no matter how small) to send more data. This can result in tiny data segments being sent consistently, even though both sender and receiver have a large total buffer space for the connection.

Simple Mail Transport Protocol (SMTP)—A protocol designed to transfer email reliably and efficiently. It's independent of the transmission protocol used and requires only a reliable ordered data stream channel.

Simple Network Management Protocol (SNMP)—A protocol that enables the configuration management of hubs, bridges, routers, switches, and remote computers.

Single adapter model—See *Non-Broadcast Multiple Access (NBMA) model*.

Slow convergence problem—A problem that occurs when using Routing Internet Protocol version 1 (RIPv1). When the network topology changes or when a router goes down, it may take several minutes before the RIP routers reconfigure themselves to the new topology.

Glossary

Slow Start algorithm—An algorithm used by Transmission Control Protocol (TCP) to prevent congestion when a connection is first established.

Small Computer System Interface (SCSI)—A standard, high-speed, parallel interface (typically) used for connecting computers to peripheral devices such as hard disks.

Smart card—A small plastic card, similar to an Automatic Teller Machine (ATM) card, that holds a user's logon credentials.

SNMP Agent—Responds to requests from a Simple Network Management Protocol management system and sends information updates. An SNMP agent can also send a trap message if an unexpected event occurs.

SNMP community—For administration and security purposes, Simple Network Management Protocol (SNMP) agents and management systems are grouped into communities. If an SNMP agent receives a request for information from a management system that's outside its community, it will send a trap message.

SNMP Management System—Sends update requests to a Simple Network Management Protocol agent. The requests are for such information as the amount of hard disk space available or the number of active sessions.

Socket—An endpoint for network communication. A socket is created by specifying the IP address of its host, the type of service (connection-oriented or connectionless), and the port number being used.

Software Development Kit (SDK)—A set of routines, functions, sample code, debugging tools, and documentation that can be downloaded to assist in developing software, such as application routines. For example, the Windows Platform SDK can be downloaded from the Microsoft Developers Network download site.

Source quench message—See *Flow control*.

Standalone root Certificate Authority (CA)—The root of a CA trust hierarchy. A standalone CA can issue certificates outside a corporation's enterprise network.

Standalone subordinate Certificate Authority (CA)—Operates as a solitary certificate server, or exists in a CA trust hierarchy. Typically, a Standalone root CA issues certificates only to other CAs, whereas a Standalone subordinate CA issues certificates to users.

Streaming—A transmission methodology that breaks data into packets that are sized to reflect the available bandwidth between the client and server.

Glossary

Stub—An Open Shortest Path First (OSPF) area can be configured as a stub when there's only one exit point from the area (or when the choice of exit point need not be made on a per-external-destination basis).

Subnet Bandwidth Management (SBM)—A service provided by the Windows 2000 Quality of Service (QoS) implementation for controlling bandwidth on a subnet.

Subnet mask—Identifies what part of an Internet Protocol (IP) address defines the network and what part defines the host.

Subnetting—Dividing a single subnet into several smaller subnets.

Subordinate Certificate Authority (CA)—A CA in a certificate chain, other than the root CA. Subordinate CAs are often referred to as *intermediate* or *issuing* CAs.

Supernetting—Combining several subnets to create a single, large subnet.

Superscope—A number of Dynamic Host Configuration Protocol (DHCP) scopes grouped together into a single administrative entity.

Switched Virtual Connection (SVC)—A temporary virtual circuit between two users that's torn down when communication is completed.

Symmetric key—A single key that's capable of both encryption and decryption. Symmetric keys are used in secret key cryptography.

System Monitor—A tool that can be used to view the data collected by the Performance Logs and Alerts tool and to view resource usage in real time.

TCP fast retransmit—An algorithm that causes immediate retransmission of a missing TCP data segment.

TCP Quiet Time—On power-up, or when recovering from a crash in which sequence numbering information was lost, the Transmission Control Protocol keeps quiet (that is, it doesn't assign any sequence numbers) for an interval equal to the Maximum Segment Lifetime (MSL) of two minutes.

TCP receive window size—The amount of received data (in bytes) that can be buffered at one time on a Transmission Control Protocol connection. This is the amount of data that the transmitting host sends before waiting for an acknowledgment.

Telnet utility—A connectivity utility that uses the Telnet protocol to provide terminal emulation services to a TCP/IP host running Telnet server software.

Glossary

Telnet—A protocol that provides a bidirectional, 8-bit, byte-oriented communications facility and gives a standard method of interfacing terminal devices with terminal-oriented processes. Telnet is typically (but not exclusively) used for terminal emulation.

Tftp—A connectivity utility that uses trivial file transport protocol (TFTP) to send information to and get information from a remote host.

Ticket Granting Ticket (TGT)—A special type of session ticket that a Key Distribution Center (KDC) grants to itself and uses when communicating with the client.

Ticket-Granting Service (TGS) Exchange—A Kerberos subprotocol used when the Key Distribution Center (KDC) distributes a service session key and a session ticket for the service.

Timestamp—A feature that's used in challenge/response dialogs to assist in setting up secure channels and authenticating users. Timestamps are valuable in countering replay attacks. The Transmission Control Protocol (TCP) uses timestamps to measure Round Trip Time (RTT) and adjust retransmission time-outs.

Time-to-Live (TTL)—The value in a packet's TTL field determines how many hops a packet travels through an internetwork before it's discarded. Although the TTL is stated in seconds, it's effectively a hop-count because a hop, or passage through a router, takes much less than one second. Each router decrements a packet's TTL by at least one.

Total Cost of Ownership (TCO)—The concept that the cost of a system isn't merely the cost of the hardware and software, but includes configuration time, maintenance time, familiarization time, and so on. Microsoft's stated aim in Windows 2000 design is to reduce the TCO as much as possible.

Tracert—A utility that determines the route from one host to another through a network.

Transitive trust—In a transitive trust, if domain A trusts domain B and domain B trusts domain C, then domain A trusts domain C.

Transmission Control Protocol (TCP)—A protocol that provides a reliable, connection-based, byte-stream service to applications.

Transmission Control Protocol/Internet Protocol (TCP/IP)—A routable protocol suite that provides (almost) universal connectivity. TCP/IP is the protocol suite of the Internet.

Glossary

Transport Control Block (TCB)—A data structure that's maintained for each Transmission Control Protocol (TCP) connection.

Transport Driver Interface (TDI)—An abstraction layer that forms a buffer between transport providers (or protocol stacks) and high-level application interfaces.

Transport Layer Security (TLS)—A protocol based on Secure Sockets Layer version 3 (SSL3/TLS) that supports client authentication by mapping user credentials in the form of public key certificates to existing Windows accounts.

Tree—A multiple domain structure in which every domain trusts all other domains in the tree.

Trivial File Transfer Protocol (TFTP)—A standard protocol for file transfer with minimal capability and minimal overhead. TFTP runs over User Datagram Protocol (UDP) and is connectionless and unreliable. It's mainly used for transferring small files.

Trusted root certificate—A certificate issued by a Certificate Authority (CA) that a user implicitly trusts.

Tunneling—A method of transferring data for one network over a second, intermediate network. Tunneling protocol encapsulates frames or packets in an additional header, which provides routing information so that the encapsulated payload can traverse the intermediate network.

Type of Service (ToS)—The ToS bits in an Internet Protocol version 4 header can determine the Quality of Service (QoS) level applied to a packet. See also *Differentiated Services (DiffServ)*.

Unicast—A message that's sent to a specific host identified by a unique computer name or address.

Uniform Resource Locators (URLs)—Provides hypertext links between documents on the World Wide Web. URLs specify the server to access, the access method, and the location.

Uninterruptable Power Supply (UPS)—A device that maintains power on a system in the event of a power failure. The function of a UPS is to allow a system to shut down gracefully, and it can be configured to trigger shut-down programs in the event of a power outage.

Universal Serial Bus (USB)—A standard interface for computer peripherals (for example, digital cameras).

Universal Time (UT)—A standard time that's the same as Greenwich Mean Time (GMT).

User Datagram Protocol (UDP)—A connectionless, unreliable transport protocol. UDP is widely used for the transmission of (for example) email traffic or real-time (video and audio) data.

Variable Length Subnet Masks (VLSMs)—Allow more than one subnet mask to be assigned to a network, so that the extended network prefixes of different network segments have different lengths.

Virtual Connection (VC)—On a local system, a VC is an endpoint (or association) between a client, call manager, or Miniport Call Manager (MCM) and a miniport that can host a single call. On a network, a VC refers to a connection between two communicating endpoints.

Virtual directory—A directory on a Web site that appears to client browsers as though it were a subfolder of the Web site's home directory. It can, however, be located elsewhere on the directory tree, on another volume, on another computer in the Web server's domain, or on a remote host.

Virtual link—A logical point-to-point connection to an Area Border Router (ABR) that's physically connected to the backbone from an ABR that isn't.

Virtual Private Network (VPN) Server—A Routing and Remote Access Service (RRAS) server enabled for VPN connections.

Virtual Private Network (VPN)—Enables a user to tunnel through the Internet or another public network, while maintaining the same level of security that would be provided by a private network.

Wake-on-LAN power management—A power management system in which all participating network components must agree to a power-down request. The computer can be awakened from a lower power state by the detection of a change in the network (such as a cable reconnection) or the receipt of a network wakeup frame or magic packet.

WebDAV—An extension of the Hypertext Transport Protocol version 1.1 (HTTP 1.1) standard that's used to expose storage media, such as file systems, over an HTTP connection.

Wide Area Network (WAN)—A network implemented by WAN technologies, such as analog and digital telephone lines, Integrated Services Digital Network (ISDN), Asynchronous Transfer Mode (ATM), and so on. WANs typically contain several subnets linked by routers.

Glossary

Windows Internet Name System (WINS)—A service that maintains a dynamic database of computer NetBIOS names and their equivalent IP addresses. WINS is the Microsoft Windows NetBIOS Name Service (NBNS).

Windows Management Instrumentation (WMI)—Provides Web-Based Enterprise Management (WBEM)-compatible control of Network Driver Interface Specification (NDIS) miniports and their associated adapters.

Windows NT LAN Manager (NTLM)—A primary security protocol used by Windows NT4 and previous versions of Windows NT. NTLM will continue to be supported for backward compatibility.

Windows Scripting Host (WSH)—The Microsoft interface for running object-oriented scripts.

Windows Sockets (Winsock)—An application programming interface that provides access to the protocol stack for supported applications. Windows 2000 supports Winsock version 2 (Winsock2).

WINS proxy—A Windows Internet Name Service (WINS) client that's configured to act on behalf of other hosts that can't use WINS directly.

X.509v3 Public Key Certificates—Credentials used by Active Directory for granting access to resources for subjects (such as users) that don't have Kerberos credentials.

Xerox Networking System (XNS)—A protocol stack developed by Xerox for Ethernet Local Area Networks (LANs).

Index

FTP, 2, 290–293
  anonymous access, 292
  block mode, 291
  compressed mode, 291
  Data Transfer Process, 290
  file structures, 291
  packet structure, 292
  Protocol Interpreter, 290
  stream mode, 291
  TCP error detection, 292
  transmission modes, 291–293
FTP clients, transferring files to and from, 322–323
ftp command, 16, 290, 311–315
  file transfer with, 320–323
FTP Restart protocol, 378
FTP servers
  authenticating, 367–368
  port numbers, 290
FTP sites
  creating, 320–321
  default sites, automatic creation of, 378
  Properties dialog box, 380–381
Fully Qualified Domain Names. *See* FQDNs.

G

Gateways, 113
  dead, detection of, 240–241, 254
  default. *See* Default gateways.
  HTTP use, 297
  IPSec settings for, 211–212
  remote address resolution in, 83–85
  in routing tables, 112
  source quench messages from, 182
Generic QoS. *See* GqoS.
Generic Quality-of-Service API. *See* GQoS API.
Generic Security Service API. *See* GSS-API.
Generic Security Systems. *See* GSS.
GET HTTP method, 297–298
gethostbyaddr function, 633
GINA DLL, 346
Global heap, examining, 657
Global scoping, 129
Globally Unique Identifiers. *See* GUIDs.
GlobalMaxTcpWindowSize parameter, 237
GQoS, 265
GQoS API, 9
Graphical Identification and Authentication. *See* GINA DLL.
Graphs, for monitoring, 678–679
Group NetBIOS names, 493–494, 579, 627–628
Group Policy, 675
GSS, 449
GSS-API, 466

Guaranteed service, 269–270
GUIDs
  for extension functions, 640
  registering with WMI, 52

H

H-node clients, 495
Hall, Martin, 631
Handles, to credentials, 347, 357, 360
Handshake, three-way, 230–231
Hard disks, turning off, 63
Hardware
  automatic and dynamic recognition of, 11, 49. *See also* PnP.
  MAC addresses of, 81
Hardware configuration
  Plug and Play capabilities for, 11
  streamlined, 49
Hash Message Authentication Code. *See* HMAC.
Hashing, 367
Hashs, 367
HEAD HTTP method, 298
Header Checksum, 108–109
Heap Walker, 657
Heaps, examining, 657
Hellman, Martin, 205
Hello interval, 121
  configuring, 144, 146
Help files, creating, 656
Helper DLLs, 637
Hexadecimal notation, 6
Hibernation, configuring, 64
HMAC, 205
Home directory
  for FTP sites, 381
  for Web sites, 380
Hop counts, 108
Host (A) records, adding to zones, 486–487
Host groups
  addresses of, 17
  definition of, 13
Host header names, 374
Host headers, 15, 375–376
Host identities, 157
  in Class A networks, 153
Host Information (HINFO) RR, 454
Host membership query message, 194
Host membership report message, 194
Host names, 15
  aliases for, 453
Host route, 110–111
Host RR, 452
Hostname, 689

Interprocess Communication Environment.
  See IPCE.
Interprocess Communication (IPC), sockets
  paradigm as, 632
Intranets
    address conversion to Internet addresses, 7
    Integrated Windows Authentication for, 368
    private addresses for, 154
    site-local unicast addresses on, 718–719
IOCTL opcodes, of Winsock2, 641–643
IOCTL requests, 590–592
IP, 12
    advanced settings for, 24–25
    datagrams. *See* Datagrams.
    functions of, 107
    routing, 110–114
IP address detection, 126–127
IP addresses, 152–154
    for APIPA, 29
    classes of, 152–153
    classful allocation of, 152–154
    classless allocation of, 163–164
    conflicts among, 435–436
    dotted decimal notation for, 152
    duplicate, detection of, 17–18, 741
    dynamic assignment of, 409. *See also* DHCP.
    efficient use of, 160
    filtering Network Monitor display by, 99–100
    host header names with, 375–376
    leases on. *See* Leases.
    monitoring usage of, 417–418
    for multicasting, 129, 190–191
    multiple, binding to single NIC, 375
    multiple, for each NIC, 127
    network prefix, 155
    octets of, 152
    for private networks, 166
    for RAS clients, 531
    remote client requests for, 541
    reservations for. *See* Reservations.
    reserved range, 11
    resolution of, 80–85. *See also* ARP.
    return of unused addresses, 163–164, 167
    static IP pool, 38
    subnet masks, 154–155
    for subnets, 158–159
IP/ATM, broadcasting and multicasting on, 131
IP Authentication Header. *See* AH.
IP Encapsulating Security Protocol. *See* ESP.
IP filter lists, 214
IP filtering, 381
IP header, 108–109
IP Helper API, 8–9, 87
IP Multicast Routing MIB, 667

IP-Next Generation (IPng), 712. *See also* IPv6.
IP over ATM (IP/ATM), 18, 130–131
IP routing. *See* Routing.
IP Time-to-Live field. *See* TTL.
IP-to-ATM address resolution, 148
IP traffic, across remote connections, 541
IP Traffic Security, 214
IPCE, 301
Ipconfig, 16, 30, 681–682
ipconfig/registerdns command, 489
IP6.INT domain, 748
IPSec, 7–8, 18, 204, 370
    attribute specification, 212–215
    configuring, for domain, 219–220
    configuring, for single computers, 215–219
    default security method, 222
    filtering property settings, 27
    IPv6 policies configuration, 754
    IPv6 use of, 713
    operation of, 211–212
    for OUs, 223–224
    policy-setting rules, 224
    router settings for, 211–212
    Security Associations configuration, 754
    security policies, 212–215
    security protocols, 206
    standards supported by, 204–206
    testing, 216, 218–220
    unassigning, 219
IPSec encryption, NIC implementation of, 55
IPSec packets
    capturing, 221
    monitoring, 208–210
IPSec SAs, 208
ipsec6 tool, 751, 754
IPSec Tunnel Mode, 548
IPv4, 5, 152–154
    address space exhaustion, 167–168, 712
    versus IPv6, 712–714
    as Windows 2000 default configuration, 12
IPv4-compatible address, 719
IPv4-mapped address, 719
IPv6, 5–6, 167–168, 712
    address autoconfiguration capabilities, 745–748
    address configuration, 713
    address space, 712, 714
    broadcasts, minimal use of, 714
    command-line tools, 750–754
    DNS enhancements for, 748
    downloading, 749–750
    header format, 713
    host sending algorithm, 744
    ICMPv6 messages use, 731–734
    installing, 750

Poison-reverse processing, 139
Policy control, 266
POP3, 304–306
    commands, 305–306
    states, 305
POP3 servers, 304–306
Port numbers
    filtering traffic by, 214
    for outbound calls, 243
    for passing DHCP broadcasts, 414
    site identification with, 375
    for TCP programs, 229
    UDP, 259
Ports, 229
    inactive, 185
    for L2TP and PPTP, 571
    recycling, 243
    restricting traffic on, 27
    sockets on, 229
POST HTTP method, 298
Post Office Protocol. *See* POP3.
Power-down requests, 6–7, 48
Power management, 6–7, 46–49
    configuring, 63–64
    no network activity–based, 48
Power-state changes, 582
    notification of, 584
Power states, 47
Power-up, TCP quiet time during, 231
PPP, 8, 14
    authentication protocols, 533–534
    frames, 8
    RAS support for, 532
PPP negotiation, 532
PPTP, 8, 14, 548–549
    adding port for, 571
    versus L2TP, 550
    with MPPE, 555–556
Preauthentication data, 342
    for smart card logons, 348
Preshared key authentication, 213, 217
Print servers, sending jobs to, 14, 328–331
Print Services for Unix, 328–331
PrioritizeRecordData parameter, 244, 472
Private IP addresses, 11
Private key/public key pair, 347–348
Private networks
    address allocation for, 166
    multicast IP address specification on, 129
Procedures for Internet/Enterprise Renumbering (PIER), 167
Process accounting, 383, 400
Process Limits, 377
Process throttling, 377
Process Viewer, 654

Process Walker, 653–654
Processes
    accessing information about, 653–654
    modifying, 654
    viewing, 654
Propagation delay, 246
Protocol drivers, 42
Protocol Interpreter. *See* PI.
Protocol stack, media sense support, 44
Protocol statistics, viewing, 16, 687
ProtocolBindAdapter function, 580
ProtocolPnPEvent function, 581
Protocols
    filtering traffic by, 214
    and NICs or services, bindings between, 61–62
ProtocolUnbindAdapter function, 586
Proxies, 298
Proxy servers
    Digest Authentication across, 367
    IPSec settings for, 211–212
Proxy tickets, 334–335, 355
PSH bit, 234, 634
PStat Tool, 655
Public Key Certificates, 213
Public key cryptography, 300–301
    IIS support of, 366
    for smart card logons, 347–348
Public key/private key pair, 370
Public Web sites, 372
Publishing directory, creating, 404–405
Pull replication partners, 500, 523–524
Push bit, 634
Push replication partners, 500–501, 523–524
PUT HTTP method, 298
PVCs, 57

Q

QoS, 265–266
    aggregate mechanisms, 265
    for connectionless datagram transmission, 577
    for IPv6, 713–714
    NDIS5 support for, 56–57
    negotiation of, 56–57
    Packet Scheduler. *See* Packet Scheduler.
    per-flow mechanisms, 265
    traffic control mechanisms, 268–269
QoS Admission Control, 258, 270–272
    accounting services, 285–286
    Any Authenticated User enterprise policy, 272–274
    configuring, 279–288
    features of, 270
    functionality of, 271–272

RRAS, 38, 110, 530
  administering from Command Console, 572
  dial-up connections on, 559–561
  enabling, 559–562
  for VPN servers, 561–562
RRAS servers, 530
  BAP response messages, 534
  configuring, 562–564
  dial-in properties enforcement, 539
  dial-up, 546–547
  static address pool specification on, 38–39
  static IP pool for RAS clients, 531
  as VPN servers, 547
RRAS snap-in, 133–134
RRs, 449, 451–454
  adding to zones, 486–489
  aging, 467–469
  non-RFC-compliant, 476
  ownership of, 467, 481
  refreshing, 470
  reregistration of, 465
  scavenging, 467–470
  secure dynamic updates for, 466
  security of, 467
  stale, 467
  TTL values, 461
RSA home page, 236
RSA Laboratories, 334
RSHD, 318
rsh utility, 17, 318
RST flag, 230, 234
RSVP, 9–10, 261, 265–267
  refresh messages for, 267
  with RTSP, 265
RSVP logs, 275–277, 283–285
RSVP messages, 267–268
RSVP QoS control request messages, 266
RSVP reservation requests, 266–267
RTCP, 261, 263–264
  packet types, 264
RTO, 19, 241
RTP, 261–263
  header components, 262–263
RTSP, 261, 264–265
RTT, 19, 188, 228
Running Object Table Viewer, 652–653

S

SACK, 5, 227, 246
  disabling, 253
  TCP support for, 238–239
SACK-Permitted option, 238
SackOpts parameter, 239

SAs, 205–208
  configuration of, 754
  lifetimes of, 208
  multiple, 206
  soft, 208
SASL, 305
Satellite communication, microwave wireless transmission, 44
SBM, 265
Scale factor for windows, 237–238
Scatter/gather I/O, 639
Scavenging, 467–470
ScavengingPeriod parameter, 469
Scopes, 421
  configuring, 31–34, 431–433, 439–440
  creating, 431–433
  DHCP, 421
  DNS server information for, 32, 34
  exclusion ranges, 32–33, 421, 424, 432, 435
  interscope consistency, 409, 434
  multicast. *See* Multicast scopes.
  planning, 423–424
  reconciling, 434
  setting range and subnet mask, 32–33
  statistics on, 418
  superscopes, 422, 424–425, 436–437
Script Source Access, 399
Scripting languages, SSPI API access through, 357
Scriptless ASP, 389
Searching through files, 386
Secret-key cryptography, 336–338
  key distribution center for, 338–342
Secret keys, 346–347
Secure HTTP, 300–301
Secure Server policy, 212
Secure Sockets Layer version3/Transport Layer Security. *See* SSL3/TLS.
Secure Web sites, 372
Security, 365. *See also* IPSec.
  for OSPF, 126
  port numbers for, 375
  for remote communications, 538–544
  for RIP, 119–120
  SNMP capabilities, 670–671
  for static routes, 116
  for Web sites, 380
Security Accounts Manager (SAM) database, 347
Security Associations. *See* SAs.
Security contexts, 357, 361
Security events, monitoring, 671, 674–675
Security hosts, 542–543
Security log, 371, 671
  archiving and deleting, 703
  full-log halts, 674, 703

5555555

555

55555

5

DLLs for, 645–648
extensions, provider-specific, 640
identifier clearinghouse, 641
IP multicasting support, 640
name registration and resolution functions, 644–645
open system architecture of, 634. 637, 638
overlapped I/O, 637, 639
scatter/gather I/O, 639
socket IOCTL opcodes, 641–643
socket sharing capabilities, 639
Winsock1.1 socket routines in, 634–635
Winsock interface, 631–634
Winsock2 interface, 626
Wireless media, 44
WMI, 51–52
disable-collection requests, 52
disable-event requests, 52
WMI clients, 52
Workgroup servers, 417
WSH DLLs, 645–648
configuring, 661–662
WSH*Xxx* functions, 646–648

X

X.25
OSPF over, 125
RIP over, 119
Xerox Networking System (XNS) protocol stack, 2–3
XML, 390

Z

Zone files
manual reconfiguration of, 6
primary and secondary, 455–456
replicating, 456–458
Zone transfers, 456–458
full-zone, 457–458
incremental, 458, 470–472
latency, reducing, 463
manual initiation of, 485
Zones, 451, 454–455
ACLs for, 466
adding, 479
adding domains to, 485–486
adding records to, 486–489
delegating responsibility across, 455, 484–485
Directory Service (DS)-integrated, 462
modifying properties of, 482–484
Properties dialog box, 482
root domain, 454
scavenging parameters based on, 468–469
secondary DNS servers for, 478–479
secure dynamic updates in, 466
updating, 464
ZwCreateFile, 582–583

Windows® 2000 Titles from Coriolis

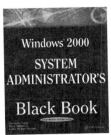

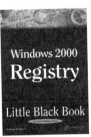

What's on the CD-ROM

The Windows 2000 TCP/IP companion CD-ROM contains elements specifically selected to enhance the usefulness of this book, including:

- The Network Monitor capture files arc.cap and arc1.cap. These demonstrate the structure of Address Resolution Protocol (ARP) packets used in Internet Control Message Protocol (ICMP) messages during a **ping** command.
- The Network Monitor capture file ftp.cap. This contains network traffic captured during a File Transfer Protocol operation and illustrates the structure of a Transmission Control Protocol (TCP) packet.
- The Network Monitor capture file http.cap. This contains network traffic captured during a Web page access.
- The Network Monitor capture files dhcp.cap and dhcp1.cap. These contain network traffic captured during a Dynamic Host Configuration Protocol (DHCP) lease establishment and renewal operations.
- The Network Monitor capture file ipsec.cap. This contains network traffic captured during a **ping** command where the packet payload is encrypted by Internet Protocol Security (IPSec).
- The Network Monitor capture file logon.cap. This contains network traffic captured during a user logon.
- Text files containing all of the Request for Comments (RFC) documents referenced in this book. These files are provided by kind permission of the Internet Engineering Task Force (IETF). This valuable resource means that you can access an RFC document immediately at any time, without needing to be connected to the Internet.
- The HTML file index_rfc.htm. This lets you access any of the RFC files on your CD-ROM quickly and easily by using your Web browser.

System Requirements

Software

- To view the Network Monitor files you'll need the Network Monitor tool that's installed with Microsoft Windows NT4 or 2000 Server. However, the Immediate Solutions contained in this book require Windows 2000 Server.

Hardware

- An Intel (or equivalent) Pentium 133MHz processor is the minimum platform required. A faster processor is recommended.
- 128 MB of RAM is the minimum requirement for Windows 2000 Server.
- No additional disk storage space is required as all necessary files can be downloaded directly from the CD-ROM.